De Gruyter Handbook of SME Entrepreneurship

De Gruyter Handbooks in Business, Economics and Finance

De Gruyter Handbook of Personal Finance
Edited by: John E. Grable and Swarn Chatterjee

De Gruyter Handbook of Entrepreneurial Finance
Edited by: David Lingelbach

De Gruyter Handbook of Organizational Conflict Management
Edited by: LaVena Wilkin and Yashwant Pathak

De Gruyter Handbook of Sustainable Development and Finance
Edited by: Timothy Cadman and Tapan Sarker

De Gruyter Handbook of Responsible Project Management
Edited by: Beverly L. Pasian and Nigel Williams

De Gruyter Handbook of Business Families
Edited by: Michael Carney and Marleen Dieleman

De Gruyter Handbook of Sustainable Entrepreneurship Research
Edited by: Gjalt de Jong, Niels Faber, Emma Folmer, Tom Long, Berfu Ünal

For more information, scan QR code below or visit https://www.degruyter.com/serial/dghbef-b/html

De Gruyter Handbook of SME Entrepreneurship

Edited by
Marina Dabić and Sascha Kraus

DE GRUYTER

ISBN 978-3-11-221388-9
e-ISBN (PDF) 978-3-11-074765-2
e-ISBN (EPUB) 978-3-11-074772-0
ISSN 2748-016X
e-ISSN 2748-0178

Library of Congress Control Number: 2023939560

Bibliographic information published by the Deutsche Nationalbibliothek
The Deutsche Nationalbibliothek lists this publication in the Deutsche Nationalbibliografie;
detailed bibliographic data are available on the internet at http://dnb.dnb.de.

© 2025 Walter de Gruyter GmbH, Berlin/Boston
This volume is text- and page-identical with the hardback published in 2023.
Typesetting: Integra Software Services Pvt. Ltd.
Printing and binding: CPI books GmbH, Leck

www.degruyter.com

Contents

Part 3: **Processes and Performance of SMEs**

Part 4: **Entrepreneurial Capital, Gender, and SMEs**

Part 5: **SMEs and their Stakeholders: The Role of Customers, Investors, Employees, Suppliers, Communities, Governments, Trade Associations, etc.**

About the Editors

Marina Dabić is Full Professor of Entrepreneurship and International Business at the University of Zagreb, Faculty of Economics and Business, Zagreb, Croatia, University of Dubrovnik, Dubrovnik Croatia, and University of Ljubljana School of Economics and Business, Ljubljana, Slovenia. She prepared a background report for OECD/EC HEinnovate for Croatia. Her papers have appeared n a wide variety of international journals, including the *Journal of International Business Studies*, the *Journal of World Business*, the *Journal of Business Research*, *Tecnnovation*, *Technological Forecasting and Social Change*, *Small Business Economics*, the *Small Business Management Journal*, the *International Journal of Human Resource Management*, *IEEE - Transactions on Engineering Management*, *Organizational Dynamics*, and many others. Prof. Dabić is Associate Editor of *Technological Forecasting and Social Change*, Department Editor for *IEEE - Transactions on Engineering Management*, and Editor-in-Chief for *Technology in Society*. She was also a Member of the IEEE-TEMS Board of Governors.

Sascha Kraus is Full Professor of Management at the Free University of Bozen-Bolzano, Italy. He holds a doctorate in Social and Economic Sciences from Klagenfurt University, Austria, a Ph.D. in Industrial Engineering and Management from Helsinki University of Technology and a Habilitation (Venia Docendi) from Lappeenranta University of Technology, both in Finland. Previously, he held Full Professor positions at Utrecht University, The Netherlands, the University of Liechtenstein, École Supérieure du Commerce Extérieur Paris, France, and at Durham University, United Kingdom. He also held Visiting Professor positions at Copenhagen Business School, Denmark and at the University of St.Gallen, Switzerland, and was EECPCL Participating Professor at Harvard University. His main research areas are strategy, internationalization, entrepreneurship, and innovation. He is the author of more than 100 academic articles, his research being published in journals such as: *Global Strategy Journal*, *International Journal of Management Reviews*, *Journal of Business Research*, *Journal of Product Innovation Management*, *Journal of World Business*, and *Long Range Planning*. He is Editor-in-Chief of the journal *Review of Managerial Science*, Editor of *Small Business Economics*, and Associate Editor of the *Journal of Small Business Management* and the *Journal of Innovation and Knowledge*.

https://doi.org/10.1515/9783110747652-203

List of Contributors

Lise Aaboen is Professor of technology-based entrepreneurship at Department of Industrial Economics and Technology Management, Norwegian University of Science and Technology, Norway Her research interests include incubators, new technology-based firms, entrepreneurship education and early customer relationships. She is co-editor of *International Journal of Entrepreneurial Behavior & Research* and has published in a range of journals, including *Technovation, Industrial Marketing Management, Journal of Purchasing and Supply Management*, and *Entrepreneurship Education & Pedagogy*.

Sunday Abayomi Adebisi holds dual professorship in the Department of Business Administration, University of Lagos (UNILAG), Nigeria. He is the first occupier-professor of the Dr. Mike Adenuga (Jnr) Professorial Chair of Entrepreneurial Studies and also a professor of Entrepreneurship Hub and Strategic Management. He also serves as the Director of the Entrepreneurship and Skills Development Centre, UNILAG. He won the hosting right of the African Research Universities Alliance (ARUA) Centre of Excellence for Unemployment and Skills Development (ARUA, CoE-USD) to make UNILAG a leader and hub in Africa for research in sustainable entrepreneurship. He is also the Director of the Centre of Excellence (ARUA, CoE-USD). His research interests include entrepreneurship hub management, innovation, start-up enablement, sustainable strategic management, and comparative strategy as well as international entrepreneurship. He has led several innovative projects and research at the local and global stage, and has authored more than 50 journal articles.

Manuel Bäuml is a global advisor in supply chains, transportation, and logistics at Amazon Web Services based in Singapore. He was previously Head of Transformation at Luxasia and a Senior Project Manager with McKinsey & Company. He obtained his Ph.D. in Management from the University of St.Gallen, Switzerland.

John H. Batchelor, Dr., is an associate professor of management at the University of West Florida. He currently teaches undergraduate and MBA classes related to management, human resources, and entrepreneurship. His research interests include entrepreneurship, meta-analysis, experiential learning, and emotions. Dr. Batchelor's work has appeared in almost 30 peer-reviewed journal articles which include top journals such as the *Journal of Organizational Behavior, Organizational Dynamics*, and *Intelligence*. He also serves as the chair of the UWF Business Administration Department and is a former president and fellow of the Small Business Institute.

Tatiana Beliaeva, D.Sc. (Econ. & Bus. Adm.) from LUT University (Finland), Candidate of Economic Sciences from St. Petersburg University (Russia), is Senior Entrepreneurship Researcher at Skopai, a Deep Tech and AI start-up, in partnership with KEDGE Business School (France). Previously, she worked as a postdoctoral researcher at Université Paris-Sud/Université Paris-Saclay. Her primary research interests are in the areas of entrepreneurship, strategic orientations, big data and AI in management and entrepreneurship, and small business research. Her research has been published in journals such as *Entrepreneurship Theory and Practice, Global Strategy Journal, Technological Forecasting and Social Change, Business Strategy and the Environment*, and *Journal of Business Research*. ORCID: https://orcid.org/0000-0003-0527-2745

Ramchandra Bhusal, Dr., is Lecturer in Finance and Accounting at Queen Margaret University, Edinburgh. Ramchandra has been working in academia for over seven years. His core areas of research include entrepreneurial finance and access to finance for small businesses, particularly owned by a marginalized group of entrepreneurs. He is currently working on a number of projects that examine demand-side issues in small business financing. Ramchandra is an Associate Fellow of Advance HE. He is available for collaboration in interdisciplinary research. ORCID: 0000-0002-5684-5112

https://doi.org/10.1515/9783110747652-204

Dieter Bögenhold is a (full) professor in the Faculty of Management and Economics at the University of Klagenfurt, Austria, and Head of the Department of Sociology and the doctoral program "Entrepreneurship and Economic Development." He completed his Ph.D. and Habilitation at the Faculty of Sociology, Bielefeld University, Germany, with academic works on self-employment and decentral production. His previous appointments were in Germany, Sweden, Italy, and Finland. His research areas include inequalities and global studies, consumption and lifestyles, interdisciplinary studies, political economy and sociology of economics, and history of economic thought. Dieter serves currently on the board of the European Academy of Management (EURAM), and the board of the VHB Committee Science Theory and Business Ethics. His most recent books are *Consumption and Life-styles* (Palgrave Publishers, 2018, with Farah Naz*), Unheard Voices: Women, Work and Political Economy of Global Production* (Palgrave Publishers, 2019, 2021, with Farah Naz), and *Neglected Links in Economics and Society: Inequality, Organization, Work and Economic Methodology* (Palgrave, 2021). ORCID: 0000-0003-2893-3534

Britta Boyd, Dr., has been senior researcher at the Witten/Herdecke University since November 2020. She is also an adjunct professor at the Beijing Institute of Technology. From 2007 to 2020 she researched and taught at the Syddansk Universitet in the subjects of international marketing, business marketing, corporate social responsibility, and entrepreneurship.

Alexander Brem is Endowed Chaired Professor and Institute Head at the University of Stuttgart, Germany. In addition, he is Honorary Professor at the University of Southern Denmark. His research focus is on technological innovation and entrepreneurship.

Wee Ching Pok, Ph.D., has been a Senior Lecturer in Finance at Flinders since May 2013. Prior to joining Flinders University, she served in a public university in Malaysia. Her research interests include financial derivatives (risk management, volatility, and prediction), stock and bond markets (volatility and determinants of bond yield spread), financial reporting (sustainability and risk reporting), corporate finance (debt and dividend policies, mergers and acquisitions, risk management strategies), and corporate governance. ORCID: 0000-0002-4792-8792

Susanna Chui is currently Assistant Professor at the School of Business of the Hang Seng University of Hong Kong. She teaches leadership, social entrepreneurship, sustainability, mentoring internship, and management modules. She is also the Associate Director of MSc in the Entrepreneurship Management programme. Susanna's research interests include leadership and identity, social entrepreneurship, and social impact measurement. While pursuing her academic research, her research experience also extends to examining social impact measurement, CSR, stakeholder management and human resources issues in organizational contexts. The current collaborative research project she is steering is the workplace happiness index which is a collaboration with the Chief Happiness Officer (CHO) Association founders in Hong Kong. This research project aims at informing small and medium-sized enterprises and the business sector at large on organizational culture that promotes employee wellbeing beyond COVID-19. She completed her Ph.D. in Leadership in 2018 from Durham University Business School, UK. She has published in peer-reviewed academic journals and presented her work at international conferences. She is an Associate Editor of the *Journal of Social Entrepreneurship* and a peer reviewer for several leading management and interdisciplinary journals. ORCID: 0000-0002-1112-8865

Marina Dabić is Full Professor of Entrepreneurship and International Business at University of Zagreb, Faculty of Economics and Business, Croatia. She prepared a background report for OECD/EC HEinnovate for Croatia. Her papers have appeared in a wide variety of international journals, including the *Journal of International Business Studies*, the *Journal of World Business*, the *Journal of Business Research, Technological Forecasting and Social Change, Small Business Economics*, the *Small Business Management Journal*, the *International Journal of Human Resource Management, IEEE- Transactions on Engineering Management, Organizational Dynamics*, and many others. Prof. Dabić is Associate Editor of *Technological Forecasting and*

Social Change, Department Editor for *IEEE – Transactions on Engineering Management*, and Associate Editor for *Technology in Society*. She is also Member of the IEEE-TEMS Board of governors. ORCID https://orcid.org/0000-0001-8374-9719

Léo-Paul Dana is a professor at Dalhousie University. He is also a member of the Entrepreneurship and Innovation Chair, which is part of LabEx Entreprendre at the Universite de Montpellier. A graduate of McGill University and HEC-Montreal, he has served as Marie Curie Fellow at Princeton University and Visiting Professor at INSEAD. He has published extensively in a variety of journals, including *Entrepreneurship: Theory and Practice, International Business Review, International Small Business Journal, Journal of Business Research, Journal of Small Business Management, Journal of World Business, Small Business Economics*, and *Technological Forecasting and Social Change*. ORCID: 0000-0002-0806-1911

Justin L. Davis, Dr., is Professor of Strategic Management and Entrepreneurship at the University of West Florida (UWF) in Pensacola, Florida. Dr. Davis received his Ph.D. in Organizational Strategy and Entrepreneurship from the University of Texas at Arlington, his MBA from Texas Tech University, and his bachelor's degree from Dallas Baptist University. His research focuses in the areas of entrepreneurship and market efficiency, including entrepreneur confidence, early-stage venture start-ups, identification of non-traditional trading market inefficiencies, and sports gambling markets and has been published in over two dozen outlets. Dr. Davis has provided consulting services for dozens of small businesses and start-ups. In addition, his teaching has been primarily focused in the areas of business strategy and entrepreneurship.

Ziad El-Awad holds a Ph.D. in Business Administration from Lund University and works as a research fellow at the Sten K. Johnson Centre for Entrepreneurship. His research investigates how new ventures develop routinized behaviors through entrepreneurial learning to ensure their successful development and growth. More specifically, El-Awad's work unpacks entrepreneurial learning at multiple levels, exploring how individual streams of experience transpose into the venture and the key role of the new venture team for bridging between individual and venture levels of learning. El-Awad's research also focuses on entrepreneurial ecosystems, bringing exciting knowledge of the role and impact of entrepreneurship graduates in such systems. The research explores why and how entrepreneurship graduates engage in enterprising and innovative activities in and around the university and identifies policy and economic implications of such activities on the dynamic development of entrepreneurial ecosystems. El-Awad's work is featured in top ranked journals including *Research Policy, Entrepreneurship Regional Development, International Journal of Entrepreneurial Behavior and Research* (IJEBR), and the *Learning Organization*, to name a few. ORCID: 0000-0002-2589-6507

Hary Febriansyah, Ph.D., is Assistant Professor and Director of the Center of Knowledge for Business Competitiveness (CK4BC) at the School of Business and Management, Bandung Institute of Technology (ITB), Indonesia. He completed his doctoral degree from Innsbruck University, School of Management, Austria. Since 2006, he has been working with ITB in two primary fields of expertise: strategic human capital management and change management for the workplace and higher education. He works collaboratively with the Indonesian government, international agencies and universities, state-owned enterprises, private companies, and social communities. Hary has published articles in international journals and book chapters, with his recent chapters including: "How Is It Different from Conventional Learning? The Growing Trend of Corporate Universities in Indonesia," in P. Ordoñez de Pablos, X. Zhang, & K. Chui (Eds.), *Innovative Management and Business Practices in Asia* (2019, IGI-Global Publishers); and "The Entrepreneurial Role of Indonesian Universities in the Economic Development of Rural Communities: In Search of Empowerment," in *Research Handbook on Entrepreneurship in Emerging Economies: A Contextualized Approach* (Edward Elgar Publishing, 2020). ORCID: 0000-0002-6578-7735

Filippo Ferrari is Adjunct Professor at the Department of Management of Bologna University, Italy. His field of research is grounded in the overlapping area of organizational behavior and design and work and organizational psychology. He investigates how socio-psychological factors (motivational and cognitive processes, emotional dynamics) affect organizational features and performance. ORCID: 0000-0002-7509-2320

Jörg Freiling, Dr., is Full Professor and Head of the LEMEX Chair in Small Business and Entrepreneurship at University of Bremen, Faculty of Business Studies and Economics. His major research fields are transnational entrepreneurship, immigrant entrepreneurship, refugee entrepreneurship, entrepreneurial ecosystems, entrepreneurial support systems (incubators, accelerators, etc.), and entrepreneurship theory. Jörg Freiling is involved in many editorial boards and review boards of international journals and has been published in international journals including *Journal of Management Studies*, *Organization Studies*, *Entrepreneurship & Regional Development*, and *International Small Business Journal*.

Nazha Gali is currently an Assistant Professor of Strategy and Entrepreneurship at Odette School of Business, University of Windsor, and a Research Faculty at the Institute for Research on Innovation & Science (IRIS), University of Michigan, Ann Arbor. She completed her PhD in 2018 in Management, Entrepreneurship from Durham University Business School, UK and was awarded the Outstanding Thesis Award. She has worked in diverse research projects in entrepreneurship, social entrepreneurship, corporate social responsibility, leadership, gender, and team science. She is an expert in mixed research methods and econometric and secondary data analysis. She has published in top peer-reviewed academic journals such as *Entrepreneurship Theory and Practice, British Journal of Management, Technological Forecasting and Social Change, Corporate Governance, and Journal of Management and Organization* and presented her work at international and national conferences. She is a peer reviewer for several leading entrepreneurship, management, and interdisciplinary journals. She is an Associate Member of the Academy of Management and a Member of the Impact Scholar Community. ORCID: 0000-0002-0525-0629

Olusoji James George is currently Professor of International Business and Strategy at the Department of Business Administration, University of Lagos, Nigeria. He has worked in various multinational companies in Nigeria and South Africa since 1980 and moved to the United Kingdom in 2005 for his two doctoral degrees which were awarded by the Brunel University, West London, UK and the University of Bradford, UK. He is the author of two renowned management books entitled *Impact of Culture on the Transfer of Management Practices in Former British Colonies* and *Culture, the 'Rejected Jewel' in the Transfer of Management Practices in Former British Colonies: Case of Cadbury*. He also co-authored *Thoughts on CSR and Corporate Social Irresponsibility* and has over 50 academic and practitioner journal articles to his name.

Agnès Guerraz, Ph.D. in applied mathematics, started her career as a researcher at Orange Labs. She then joined Xerox Research Center Europe where she became head of innovation for Xerox Global Services. She decided after this experience to get involved in French public research centers and universities such as INRIA where she was Deputy Director of Innovation and Technology Transfer and the University of Grenoble Alpes as Director of the Department of Partnerships and Innovation. She came back to the private sector as founder and former director of Thuasne Lab and finished her career at Skopai, a start-up she co-founded and developed in partnership with reputable public and private partners in AI. Agnès obtained her Ph.D. in applied mathematics in 2002 from the University of Grenoble. Her research focused on artificial intelligence. She co-authored the analysis methodology of innovative companies at the heart of Skopai.

Mouhoub Hani is a lecturer at Paris 8 Vincennes Saint-Denis University. His research is conducted in the field of strategic management and he is particularly interested in inter-organizational relationships in complex global network structures. As an extension of his doctoral work, he has published articles on reticular coopetition and on dynamic interactions between coopetitors. He has mainly published articles on global network coopetition in international journals like the *Journal of Business & Industrial Marketing*.

He is now interested in the roles and profiles of entrepreneurs and pivotal actors within and between platforms and ecosystems.

Reija A. Häkkinen, M.Sc., works in University of Jyväskylä as a career specialist in the field of entrepreneurship education. Her research interests are on how organizations may benefit from emergent entrepreneurial behavior of organizational members in their renewal process. Her research may be of interest especially for organizations and decision makers who want to enhance the well-being and strength-based cooperation between their employees and other stakeholders. ORCID: 0000-0002-6441-5542

Elsebeth Holmen is a professor in the Department of Industrial Economics and Technology Management, at the Norwegian University of Science and Technology, Trondheim, Norway. Her research interests are in the areas of strategy, public procurement, inter-organizational relationships, and networks. She has published papers in journals such as *Journal of Business Research, Industrial Marketing Management, Journal of Business and Industrial Marketing*, and *Journal of Purchasing and Supply Management*.

Tin Horvatinovic, Ph.D., is a teaching and research assistant at the Department for Managerial Economics, Faculty of Economics and Business, University of Zagreb, Zagreb, Croatia, where he teaches entrepreneurship. He finished his Ph.D. in 2021 with the following topic: the impact of causal and effectual approaches to entrepreneurship on business performance of small and medium enterprises in the Republic of Croatia. He also attended LSE Summer School, Cambridge Summer Institute, and the Applied Econometrics workshop. His research interests include entrepreneurial finance, entrepreneurial intentions and entrepreneurial logic. He is the author of several articles published in refereed international journals. His paper "Climbing Up the Regional Intellectual Capital Tree: An EU Entrepreneurial Ecosystem Analysis" won the "Mijo Mirkovic" award for the best paper in the field of economics in 2021. ORCID: 0000-0001-7447-9913

Mathew (Mat) Hughes is Schulze Distinguished Professor and Professor of Innovation and Entrepreneurship at the University of Leicester School of Business, UK. Mat is an expert on the strategy and management of entrepreneurship and innovation. He has published in leading journals including *Strategic Entrepreneurship Journal, Entrepreneurship Theory and Practice, British Journal of Management, Journal of Product Innovation Management, and Journal of Family Business Strategy*. Mat is Associate Editor of the Journal of Business Research and Journal of Family Business Strategy, and Senior Editor of FamilyBusiness.org.

Sanel Jakupović is the Rector of the Pan-European University "APEIRON" Banja Luka, Bosnia and Herzegovina (2021–2025), a full professor and has a Ph.D. in economics. At his home university, he was promoted to an assistant professor in 2009, an associate professor in 2014, and in 2020 to a full professor of economics. In the past 11 years, Professor Jakupović has performed significant duties at the University "APEIRON": he was Vice Dean of the Faculty of Business Economics (2011–2013), Dean of the Faculty of Business Economics (2013–2021), Director of the Scientific Research Institute (2016–2021), and Vice-Rector for Scientific Work and International Cooperation of the University (2019–2021). ORCID: 0000-0001-5940-6126

Jacques de Jongh is a lecturer in the School of Economics in the Faculty of Economics and Management Sciences, North-West University. He is currently pursuing his Ph.D. in Economics and has several international publications and conference proceedings. ORCID: 0000-0001-8672-0292

Juha Kansikas, Ph.D., works as University Lecturer of Entrepreneurship at the Jyväskylä University School of Business and Economics, University of Jyväskylä, Finland. Kansikas has post doc qualifications (Docent) in Business (Entrepreneurship) and in Education Sciences (Entrepreneurship education). Kansikas is currently co-leading an Academy of Finland research project on business elite and executive education. In addition to this, in fall 2021 he was a special researcher for the University of Jyväskylä Council of Education on studying academic entrepreneurship education. His research interests are business elites, entrepreneurship, entrepreneurship education, and family entrepreneurship. ORCID: 0000-0001-9820-5503

Katrin Kizilkan is a doctoral candidate at the University of Lueneburg, Germany, Department of Entrepreneurship and Startup Management. She focuses on the entrepreneurial finance landscape, the symbiosis of new financial intermediation traditional sources, and the use of new digital communication platforms. She investigates the communication behavior of the starter on social media to draw conclusions about which user behavior is promising and can thus point the way forward for other starters. In addition, she is an entrepreneurial self-starter with the ambition to combine practice and science. ORCID: 000-003-1381-8541

Lena Leifeld, B.A., B.A. After an internship at the Family Business Center of MCI | The Entrepreneurial School, Lena has been employed there as a project assistant since March 2019. She completed her bachelor's degree in Sociology at the University of Innsbruck and in Business Administration at MCI. In the Family Business Center she has already been able to contribute to various projects alongside her master's studies in Organization Studies as well as Sociology at the University of Innsbruck. Currently she is writing her master's thesis on branding strategies of family businesses at the Institute for Organization and Learning.

Thierry Levy is a lecturer at Paris 8 Vincennes Saint-Denis University. He conducts his research in the field of strategic management and more particularly in entrepreneurship. He has published on the entrepreneurship of singular publics or those considered as such (women; immigrants; eco-entrepreneurs) and on their support. He is now interested in collective entrepreneurial dynamics (in the context of networks, platforms or simple teams).

Vincent Mangematin is Dean and Academic Director of KEDGE Business School in France. As a scholar, he is Professor of Strategic Management and Management of Innovation. His research stands at the intersection of strategic management and innovation. He focuses on emergent phenomena and on the transformative influence of digital technologies in the society. In recent years, he has been focusing on business models as an approach to renew strategy. He is recognized as a stimulating scholar on topics related to innovation and emergence. He is Associate Editor at *Technology Forecasting and Social Change*. ORCID: 0000-0001-9949-4116

Magdalena Marczewska, Ph.D., is Assistant Professor at the Faculty of Management, University of Warsaw. She specializes in innovation and technology management, as well as project management, with the focus on environmental technologies. She is a participant of research projects commissioned by the Polish Ministry of Environment, European Commission, the World Intellectual Property Organization, the Polish Patent Office, and the National Science Centre. Elsewhere, she is also a participant of numerous international research and education programs, such as at the University of Kentucky, London School of Economics and Political Science, University of Padova, Vienna University of Economics and Business, Harvard Business School, University of Ferrara and Lund University. ORCID: 0000-0003-4301-2741

William C. McDowell, Dr., is the Paul R. Gowens Endowed Professor of Entrepreneurship and the Department Chair of Management in the McCoy College of Business at Texas State University. He received his Ph.D. in Management from the University of North Texas. His research focuses on small business and entrepreneurship, and he has testified as an expert witness before the U.S. House of Representatives. His research focuses primarily on entrepreneurship and small business. He has authored over 70 articles in his field and serves as the Editor-in-Chief of the *Journal of Small Business Strategy* and Associate Editor of the *Journal of Business Research* and the *International Entrepreneurship and Management Journal*.

Natanya Meyer is Associate Professor in the Department of Business Management in the College of Business and Economics, University of Johannesburg. She is part of the DHET-NRF SARChI

Entrepreneurship Education Chair. Her research focuses on entrepreneurial and economic-related topics as well as tourism studies. She is an editor, editorial board, and scientific committee member, as well as reviewer for several national and international journals. ORCID: 0000-0003-3296-7374

Mihaela Mikic, Ph.D., is Associate Professor at the Department for Managerial Economics Faculty of Economics and Business, University of Zagreb, Zagreb, Croatia, where she teaches entrepreneurship, business planning, fundamentals of entrepreneurship, and small business management. Her research interests include: entrepreneurship, social entrepreneurship, women entrepreneurship, internationalization, small business management, and small business financing. She is the author of several articles published in refereed international journals and three books. Additionally, she serves as a reviewer and editorial board member for a number of journals. Her paper "Climbing Up the Regional Intellectual Capital Tree: An EU Entrepreneurial Ecosystem Analysis" won the "Mijo Mirkovi" award for the best paper in the field of economics in 2021. ORCID: 0000-0003-3966-2530

Valerie Nickel, BSc, BSc, MSc, is part of the Family Business Center at MCI | The Entrepreneurial School since 2018. She is researching and teaching in the field of family businesses with a special focus on gender dynamics, identity work, and narratives in family firms. She graduated from the University of Innsbruck with bachelor's degrees in "Management and Economics" as well as "Health and Competitive Sports" and with a master's degree in Applied Economics. In 2019, she started her dissertation exploring the interplay of contemporary roles, social structures, and identity work which is supported by the EQUA Stiftung Munich with a fellowship. She was part of the doctoral colloquium Gender and Gender Relations in Transitions in 2020.

W. Timothy O'Keefe, Dr., is Dean Emeritus at the University of West Florida after serving nearly 25 years as professor of accounting while taking on administrative positions such as Dean, Interim Dean, Associate Dean, and MBA Director. Dr. O'Keefe's research encompasses international business, financial reporting standards, managerial accounting, and small business development. His work has been published in a wide variety of professional journals, including *Accounting Horizons, American Journal of Small Business, Business Horizons, Financial Executive, Tax Executive, Management Accounting, Government Accountant's Journal*, and *CPA Journal*. O'Keefe received a bachelor's degree in business administration from Stetson University, and master's and doctorate degrees in business administration from Florida State University. He is a Certified Public Accountant in the state of Florida.

Adeniyi Damilola Olarewaju is a teacher of International Business at Tecnologico De Monterrey, Mexico. He earned a doctorate degree (Ph.D.) in Management from University of Lagos (UNILAG) with specialization in internationalization of indigenous Nigerian firms. He was the first recipient of the Postgraduate Trust Fund in UNILAG for outstanding academic performance in 2017. Additionally, in 2017, one of his cases emerged as the winning case for the 2016 EFMD Case Writing Awards Competition in the African Business Cases Category. His research interests include institutional environments in developing and emerging economies, internationalization of indigenous firms, and sustainable entrepreneurship. He has a diploma from Harvard Business School (HBS) in the Certificate of Readiness Program (CORe) and is a 2020 Paul R. Lawrence Fellow. He has published and presented many peer-reviewed articles at international conferences and is passionate about imparting knowledge. ORCID: 0000-0001-5156-8634

Zulaicha Parastuty is a lecturer in the Faculty of Management and Economics at the University of Klagenfurt, Austria and in the Department of International Management at the Johannes Kepler University Linz, Austria. She holds a doctoral degree in social science and economics from the University of Klagenfurt, Austria and a master's degree from the Delft University of Technology, the Netherlands. Her research topics are entrepreneurship, innovation management, strategy management and organizational behavior. She has published in several reputable outlets such as *European Management Journal, Review Managerial Science* and presented her research globally. Having an educational background in engineering, management, and economics, her research approach is interdisciplinary. She is currently taking on a role at the Infineon Technologies, Austria in the field of innovation, funding and cooperation. ORCID: 0000-0001-6703-983X

Ann-Charlott Pedersen is a professor in the Department of Industrial Economics and Technology Management at the Norwegian University of Science and Technology, Trondheim, Norway. Her research interests are in the area of inter-organizational relationships and networks. She has published papers in the areas of supply networks, purchasing and supply management, strategizing in networks, and resource development in journals such as *Journal of Business Research*, *Industrial Marketing Management*, *Journal of Business and Industrial Marketing*, and *Journal of Purchasing and Supply Management*.

Jasna Poček is a postdoctoral researcher at Free University Bozen-Bolzano and Research Fellow at Lund University (LU), Sweden. She is affiliated with the Sten K Johnson Center for Entrepreneurship, LU and the Center for Innovation Policy Research (CIRCLE), LU. Previously Jasna worked alongside the United Nations Labour Agency on market reforms and inclusive entrepreneurship ecosystems that promote decent work across the globe. Currently her research interests gravitate around policy implications of management research (entrepreneurship and innovation), including the role of institutional theory for understanding of framework conditions that drive innovation and entrepreneurship forward. She has published in international peer reviewed journals such as *International Journal of Entrepreneurial Behaviour and Research*, *European Planning Studies*, *International Review of Entrepreneurship*, and *Global Jourist*. In 2022, as part of an interdisciplinary team of researchers, she was awarded a prestigious Swedish Central Bank "Riksbanken" award, to study the impact of Covid-19 policy responses on the cross border EU regions. ORCID: 0000-0002-6362-2320

Alicia Rodríguez is Associate Professor of Entrepreneurship and Family Business at Carlos III University of Madrid (Spain), where she is the Co-Director of the MSc. in Entrepreneurship and New Venture. She studies firms' internationalization and innovation strategies, with a special interest in SMEs and in offshoring of knowledge intensive activities; she has particular expertise in governance modes of innovation – insourcing, outsourcing and alliances. Her research has been published in leading journals such as *Strategic Management Journal*, *Journal of International Business Studies*, *Long Range Planning*, *Technovation*, *Industry and Innovation*, among others. ORCID: 0000-0003-2813-9066

Aidin Salamzadeh is an assistant professor at the University of Tehran. His interests are start-ups, new venture creation, and entrepreneurship. Aidin serves as an associate editor at *Revista de Gestão*, *Innovation and Management Review* (Emerald), *Entrepreneurial Business and Economics Review*, *Journal of Women's Entrepreneurship and Education* as well as an editorial advisory in *The Bottom Line* (Emerald). Besides, he is a reviewer in numerous distinguished international journals. Aidin is a member of the European SPES Forum (Belgium), the Asian Academy of Management (Malaysia), Ondokuz Mayis University (Turkey), and the Institute of Economic Sciences (Serbia). He is the co-founder of the Innovation and Entrepreneurship Research Lab (London). ORCID: 0000-0001-6808-1327

Reinhard Schulte holds a chair for Start-Up Management at Leuphana University of Lüneburg, Germany, and is Head of the Centre for Entrepreneurship in Theory and Application at Leuphana. Current research interests include new venture development, start-up counselling, and new venture finance. His recent publications have focused on new venture growth and on the investment behavior of young companies. ORCID: 0000-0003-0731-7134

Nina Schumacher is a doctoral researcher and the Chair of Start-up Management at Leuphana University, Lüneburg, Germany, specializing in digital entrepreneurship. Her research interests include success factors of digital entrepreneurship at the macro-, meso-, and micro-level, investigating topics such as the relevance of entrepreneurship ecosystems for start-up success, the entrepreneurial personality, and the relevance of business model components from a venture capital investor's perspective. Her work has been published in handbooks and journals such as the *Handbook on Digital Business Ecosystems* and *International Journal of Business and Management*. ORCID: 0000-0003-0837-5061

Boyka Simeonova is Associate Professor of Innovation, at the University of Leicester School of Business, UK. Boyka is an expert on the management of knowledge and innovation. She has published in leading journals including the International Journal of Entrepreneurial Behavior and Research, Information Systems Journal, and Journal of Information Technology.

Jadranka Švarc, Ph.D., is a senior researcher at the Institute of Social Sciences Ivo Pilar, Zagreb, Croatia. She is an expert in science and innovation policy in transition countries, with more than 10 years' worth of practical experience in innovation policy in Croatia. She received her doctorate in sociology of science from the Faculty of Philosophy, University of Zagreb. Between 2006 and 2012, she lectured in innovation policy at the University of Applied Sciences, Baltazar, Zapresic. She was engaged in a large number of national and international projects, including the analyses of the Croatian RTI policy under the ERAWATCH and RIO projects. She publishes extensively in the area of science, innovation, and technology studies with an emphasis on the Croatian science and innovation systems.

Agus Syarip Hidayat, Ph.D., is a senior researcher at the Economic Research Centre, National Research and Innovation Agency (BRIN) Indonesia. His research interest includes industrial policy, Small-Medium Enterprises (SMEs), trade, and regional economic integration. He is also a passionate academic and experienced consultant at various international agencies. ORCID: 0000-0002-4863-6193

Silke Tegtmeier is Associate Professor of Entrepreneurship at the University of Southern Denmark. She is immediate Past President of the European Council for Small Business and Entrepreneurship. Her research focus is on cognitive perspectives of the individual in entrepreneurship.

Allan Villegas-Mateos, Dr., is Research Associate at HEC Paris in Qatar. He holds a Ph.D. in Business Administration with a major in entrepreneurship from the EGADE Business School in Mexico. He also graduated from the bachelor program in Business Creation and Development from the same institute. Dr. Allan is the author of the book *Qatar's Entrepreneurial Ecosystem – Edition 2021: Empowering the Transformation* and has published in peer-reviewed journals including the *Journal of Entrepreneurship in Emerging Economies* and the *International Journal of Entrepreneurship*. He is a recognized research member of the National Council of Science and Technology and lifetime member of the business honor society Beta Gamma Sigma. ORCID: 0000-0002-7431-5326

Thierry Volery is Professor of Entrepreneurship at the Zurich University of Applied Sciences (ZHAW) and Visiting Professor at the University of St.Gallen. His teaching and research interests include the start-up process, entrepreneurship behavior, entrepreneurial leadership, entrepreneurship education, and innovation management. He obtained his Ph.D. in Management from the University of Fribourg, Switzerland.

Maximilian Wagenknecht is a doctoral candidate at the Department of Entrepreneurship and Startup Management at the Leuphana University of Lueneburg, Germany. His research focuses on the conceptual and practical analysis of lean start-ups in conjunction with adapted risk strategies and holistic risk management. In addition to his research activities, he also teaches business administration and entrepreneurship and is a jury member at a start-up competition in northern Germany. ORCID: 0000-0003-1877-1316

Kevin Walther is a Ph.D. candidate at the Department of Business Studies at Uppsala University. He is a member of the Management and IT Research school and a graduate of the Nordic Research School of International Business (Nord-IB). Before his Ph.D. studies, he worked in the cloud computing and digital payment industry. He holds a bachelor's degree in Economics and Business Administration from the

University of Zurich and a master's degree in International Business from Uppsala University. His current research interests includes internationalization in a digital context, business model innovation, the digital economy, and the video games industry. His published research investigates the digital transformation of the video games industry toward a cloud gaming environment. ORCID 0000-0002-4201-932X

Marzenna Anna Weresa, Ph.D., is a full professor of Economics at the World Economy Research Institute, SGH Warsaw School of Economics. She holds a Ph.D. degree in Economics (1995) and habilitation (D.Sc.) in Economics (2002) from the Warsaw School of Economics. In 1999–2000, she worked as a research fellow at the University College London. Her research and academic teaching focus on issues relating to innovation, technology transfer, FDI, and competitiveness. She has authored and co-authored over 100 books and scientific articles. She has carried out numerous research projects as a scientific coordinator, member of a steering committee, principal researcher or a member of scientific team executed and financed under international scientific schemes, such as the EU Framework Programme for Research and Innovation "Horizon 2020," NATO Science Program, Bloomberg Initiative Grants, and COST Actions. She has been involved with many advisory projects for enterprises and governmental organizations in the field of internationalization strategies, R&D, and innovation. Since 2012 she has worked as an expert of the European Commission providing advice on policies for research and innovation working in the following expert groups: "Innovation for Growth – I4G," RISE, "Economic and Societal Impact of Research and innovation (ESIR),"and "MLE – The evaluation of business R&D grant schemes." ORCID: 0000-0003-3112-3460

Duane Windsor, Ph.D. from Harvard University, BA from Rice University, is the Lynette S. Autrey Professor of Management in Rice University's Jesse H. Jones Graduate School of Business. His research and teaching emphasize corporate social responsibility and stakeholder theory. He served as editor-in-chief of the academic journal *Business & Society* (2007–2014), sponsored by the International Association for Business and Society (IABS). He served as an associate editor for Sage Publication's multi-volume *Encyclopedia of Business Ethics and Society* (first and second editions), edited by Robert W. Kolb. His research articles and other works have appeared in such journals as *Academy of Management Journal*, *Academy of Management Review*, *Asia Pacific Business Review*, *Business & Society*, *Business Ethics Quarterly*, *Cornell International Law Journal*, *Critical Sociology*, *Journal of Business Ethics*, *Journal of Business Research*, *Journal of Management Studies*, *Philosophy of Management*, and *Public Administration Review*. He has published several books. ORCID 0000-0003-0406-1030

Anita Zehrer, Prof. Dr., is currently Head of the Family Business Center as well as Head of Research (Management & Society) at the MCI | The Entrepreneurial School. She graduated from Innsbruck University with a Ph.D. in Social Sciences and became professor in 2015. She acted as Deputy Head of the MCI Tourism Department as well as Deputy Head of the Academic Council. She was Adjunct Professor at the University of Notre Dame in Sydney, Australia (2012–2016), and the University of Canberra, Australia (2013–2016). From 2009 to 2018 she served as Vice-President of the German Association for Tourism Research DGT, from 2014 to 2017 she was Member of the Tourism Advisory Board of the Federal Ministry of Foreign Affairs and Energy, Germany, and from 2016 to 2017 she was tourism expert at the Committee of Regions at the European Union. Her research interests are diverse and include entrepreneurship and family business management. She has broad competence in interdisciplinary research and business.

Junyu Zhou has a Ph.D. in Innovation and Strategic Management from Loughborough University. Her Ph.D. topic focuses on multi-hierarchical-level individual ambidexterity and performance. Junyu received her M.Sc. from the University of Glasgow and her bachelor's degree from Shandong University. Junyu's research interests include ambidextrous innovation, entrepreneurship, leadership behavior, empowerment, knowledge sharing, coordination mechanisms. She has published conference papers and has attended the Journal of Product and Innovation Management conference. Additionally, she has teaching experience on entrepreneurship, innovation, and strategic management.

Marina Dabić and Sascha Kraus

An Introduction to a Theory of SME Entrepreneurship

Background and Motivation

Small- and medium-sized enterprises (SMEs) are considered the engines of worldwide economies and the main sources of job creation (Wiklund et al., 2019). In most OECD economies, SMEs account for more than 90 percent of all companies and for 50 percent of overall employment (OECD, 2017). In 2021, there were approximately 22.6 million SMEs in the European Union, with the vast majority of these being micro-sized firms which employ less than ten people. A further 1.3 million enterprises were small firms, made up of between 10 and 49 employees, and just over 200,000 were medium-sized firms with 50 to 249 employees (Statista.com, 2021). Similar figures apply in the USA, where SMEs contribute to almost 50 percent of all economic activities (Highfill et al., 2020).

The majority of textbooks used to pass on knowledge in universities and business schools around the world were developed in the last decades of the previous century. These are largely based on results from research conducted on large companies. However, researchers have repeatedly asserted that the management of SMEs differs from the management of large companies. For example, already around 40 years ago, Welsh and White (1981) noted that "a small business is not a little big business" (p. 20). In other words, SME management (and the management of their sub-group young SMEs, i.e., start-ups) cannot simply be regarded as a downsized version of large business management. Consequently, the instruments and tools of one cannot be transferred 1:1 to the other, but must first be adapted to their applicability in the other context. Management techniques should therefore always consist of a flexible and easily adaptable set of tools supporting entrepreneurs in making optimal decisions (Fink & Kraus, 2009). In light of the paramount importance of SMEs in emerging, developing, and developed economies worldwide, it has become even more essential to investigate the underlying mechanisms and practices of management in SMEs and start-ups (Sen et al., 2022).

While the pure management side of these enterprises has already been discussed in detail over the last two decades, this handbook concentrates more on the entrepreneurship side of matters, i.e., on the growth- and innovation-orientation of SMEs. However, if we assume that management and entrepreneurship are in fact overlapping skills whose respective application depends on the specific situation, and that

Marina Dabić, University of Zagreb, Faculty of Economics and Business, Croatia; University of Dubrovnik, Dubrovnik, Croatia; University of Ljubljana School of Economics & Business, Slovenia
Sascha Kraus, Free University of Bozen-Bolzano, Faculty of Economics & Management, Italy

https://doi.org/10.1515/9783110747652-001

SME management differs from that of large companies, we must also assume that SME entrepreneurial behavior differs from that of large companies. On the one hand, it is time for a dedicated theory of "SME Entrepreneurship" to emerge, namely with regards to questions pertaining to the extent to which entrepreneurial thinking and behavior in SMEs can be differentiated from that of start-ups and large companies (i.e., corporate entrepreneurship). On the other hand, we should consider what kind of different entrepreneurship manifestations exist overall within a widely heterogeneous group of SMEs. This is where the *De Gruyter Handbook of SME Entrepreneurship* comes in.

Entrepreneurship has thus far been defined through two main streams: one stream – the dominant one – explained and explored entrepreneurship through traits of entrepreneurship (e.g., innovativeness, development, creativity, and novelty), while the other one emphasized entrepreneurial results and outcomes (e.g., value creation) (Sharma and Chrisman, 1999; Ferreira et al., 2019). Entrepreneurship research has become established in institutional theory (Bruton et al., 2010), which highlights institutions as key clusters governing social, economic, and political structures (Dabić et al., 2021). Entrepreneurial ecosystems play an important role in driving innovation, which has been recognized as a competitive advantage for any SME (Kang et al., 2021). Institutional theory encourages enterprises to create formal and informal rules that influence companies' cultures and help entrepreneurs to manage their businesses. Additionally, the knowledge-based view and resource-based view have been used to detect the ways in which SMEs are managing their resources, capabilities, and knowledge; how good are they are at absorbing newly acquired knowledge from outside of their enterprise; and how their dynamic capabilities influence SMEs in terms of their ability to create value. The paradox of innovation raises questions with regards to whether it is better for an enterprise to either protect or share their knowledge and technologies when it comes to ensuring a positive effect on their performance (Bassett-Jones, 2005). Innovation theory can help us to answer this question.

Entrepreneurial thinking and action, combined with prerequisite adaptability and innovative capacity, the identification of worldwide opportunities, and the ability to think not just "outside-of-the-box" but rather "without boxes," serve as the key to survival, success, and future viability for SMEs. In ambiguous business conditions and rapidly changing environments, there are no standard procedures and rules. As such, previous patterns of entrepreneurial behavior cannot be universally applied (Eggers et al., 2014). Because of this, it has become vital for researchers to conceptualize original business models (Bouwman et al., 2019; Cosenz and Bivona, 2021; Hock-Doepgen et al., 2021) and develop fresh decision-making techniques and methods for SMEs that are in line with the new business requirements of the modern world. The investigation verified the differences in the intensity of innovation, risk appetite, and proactivity as crucial elements of the companies' diversity in both the private and public sector. The success and survival of SMEs strongly depends on the effectiveness of individual decision-making processes. This highlights the firm's need to establish proper entrepreneurial decision-making processes to maintain its competitive advantage in a continuously changing environment (Brouthers et al., 1998; Covin et al., 2020).

The business world has transformed immensely in recent decades. Consequently, entrepreneurs now work in an increasingly fast-paced, highly competitive, and internationalized environment. As a result, they must reevaluate the objectives of their enterprise, and their stakeholders must be more flexible. As a result of such dynamic growth, start-ups and unicorn companies are constantly re-examining and reconsidering their markets, reorganizing their relations, and adjusting their business models. Thus, the degree to which the entrepreneurial ecosystem is established has a special role to play (Cunningham et al., 2019).

SMEs are confronting new barriers in terms of digitalization costs and are dealing with new trends pertaining to Industry 4.0 technologies and digital transformation (Ross et al., 2015; Franco et al., 2021; Kraus et al., 2022; Chatterjee et al., 2022). SMEs should use new technology to their advantage and explore, for example, how big data analytics can help them to improve their customer service (Wang & Wang, 2020). Innovative business models represent one of the most important capabilities for SME success and growth (Bouncken et al., 2020). Therefore, "digital entrepreneurship" is currently an increasingly emerging research topic, which is also of concrete practical interest with regard to the digital transformation of SMEs (Švarc & Dabić 2021; Garzella et al., 2021; Kraus et al., 2019).

Cutting-edge technologies and globalization have encouraged SMEs to expand their businesses into the global market (Dabić et al., 2020). In line with this, the internationalization process of SMEs must be examined (Morais & Ferreira, 2020; Schulz et al., 2009). In our new digital era, exploring the influence of human resource management (Heneman et al., 2000) in SMEs has become more important than ever. The organizational culture enables SMEs to shape their identity, consequently encouraging digitalization and sustainability (Isensee et al., 2020). Knowledge sharing can upgrade customer relationships, trust, and organizational learning in SMEs, ultimately improving performance (Anand et al., 2021). For SMEs to survive, it is crucial that they collaborate and exchange knowledge and technology with different stakeholders (Silva et al., 2019; Spithoven et al., 2013; Van de Vrande et al., 2009).

The overlaps in terms of theoretical approaches reveal that there are opportunities for researchers to contribute to the SME entrepreneurship field in terms of theory development, the analysis of different levels of analysis, the examination of processes within SMEs, or the assessment of stakeholder relationships. This handbook addresses a wide range of these issues and strives to provide a comprehensive overview of the topics related to SMEs with regards to entrepreneurship and innovation. As such, it includes chapters on topics, theories, and practices on diverse facets of "SME Entrepreneurship." These chapters further expand the broad subject area of "SME Entrepreneurship," revealing it to be an exciting, relevant, and timely field of research and distinguishing it from pure "SME Management" and the "Corporate Entrepreneurship" of large established companies.

We are therefore very pleased that, within a comparatively short period of time, we have been able to attract such a respectable group of established academics and young, up-and-coming researchers from the fields of entrepreneurship, SME management, family firm research, innovation management, and other related areas to contribute their latest research results and shed more light on the field of "SME Entrepreneurship." This handbook is made up of a total of 29 chapters, with contributions from 59 authors from 25 different countries (Australia, Austria, Bosnia and Herzegovina, Canada, Croatia, Denmark, Finland, France, Germany, Hong Kong, Indonesia, Iran, Italy, Mexico, New Zealand, Nigeria, Norway, Poland, Qatar, South Africa, Spain, Sweden, Switzerland, the United States of America, and the United Kingdom).

Structure of the Book

Part 1: Novel Theories of Entrepreneurship in SMEs

Part 1 consists of five chapters

Jörg Freiling's chapter, entitled "SME Entrepreneurship and Entrepreneurship Theory: A Systematic Literature Analysis in the Light of Entrepreneurial Functions," addresses the theory of entrepreneurial functions. These functions evolved in the eighteenth century, but this chapter aims to specify what entrepreneurs need to do now. Debates that were once primarily economic are now more orientated towards business and management. This shift calls for a condensed overview of this field of research. The author's response is a systematic literature review, framed by the research question "What do we know about the core entrepreneurial functions of SMEs in light of entrepreneurship theory, and what is the impact of these functions?" The emphasis here is on the implications of entrepreneurship theory in SME management. The study reveals that the business stream deviates from the economics stream by virtue of its more empirical work and its more comprehensive set of functions, which are made up of different schools of thought.

Justin L. Davis, John H. Batchelor, W. Timothy O'Keefe, and William McDowell, in their chapter entitled "Formal but Illegitimate? Examining the Mongrel Economy," examine the economies in which SMEs operate (i.e., formal, informal, renegade, and mongrel). Each of these economies offers substantial benefits when aligned properly with the characteristics of specific SMEs. Current literature lacks proper conceptualization of "mongrel" economies, which are legal entities that are considered illegitimate by the majority (or vocal majority) of society. The mongrel economy is developed using existing theories on economic boundaries, such as Webb et al. (2009). This chapter highlights the market penetration benefits of the mongrel economy for upstart SMEs with little social or financial capital that possess legitimacy within subgroups of society. The authors provide an explanation of how some SMEs can use the reputation of their founder(s) in a subset of society as start-ups, and then pivot into the larger formal economy once they enter the growth cycle.

Adeniyi Damilola Olarewaju, Sunday Abayomi Adebisi, and Olusoji James George are authors of the chapter entitled "SME internationalization and Strategy Tripod Perspective – Evidence from an emerging economy," which contributes to the development of novel theories on entrepreneurship in SMEs. The authors investigated the international performance of SMEs using the strategy tripod perspective. The originality of this chapter lies in its combination of institutional theory, the resource-based view, and the industry-based view, which are used to explain SMEs' internationalization in an emerging African country. The results of this study are based on 134 SMEs from Nigeria and the findings indicate that, although government effectiveness does not directly influence SME's international performance, market orientation and competitive intensity positively effect internationalization.

"Internationalization of Small-sized Game Development Firms – A Born Global Theory Perspective," by Kevin Walther, analyzes the extent to which the born global theory of internationalization serves to help us to understand the internationalization of small-sized, entrepreneurial game development firms. Founder, organizational, and macro-environmental factors are elements for interview founders of small-sized game development firms using digital platforms to distribute their games. The findings show that firms that develop their own games are being pushed to internationalize immediately because of the heavily globalized and digitalized nature of the industry. Despite the digital nature of this industry, not all types of firms are born global firms, as some SME firms serve as subcontractors to larger development teams. This chapter provides a three-stage framework which differentiates small-sized game developers and delivers insights into entrepreneurship in the digital context of the video games industry.

In his chapter titled "Entrepreneurial Investment Cycle – A Large Scale Longitudinal Study," Reinhard Schulte looks at the investment patterns of young companies. Using a large data set, this study is the first to show how newly founded companies build up and develop capital stock over time. Based on an investment time series of more than 4,000 young German companies, the study models typical development patterns in the initial years after founding. The data demonstrates not only typical times and levels of investment, but also the length of investment waves. What is particularly interesting is that, in addition to the expected investment peak immediately upon market entry, a second maximum is reached a few years later. There are about nine years between these two peaks. The initial new venture investment cycle is therefore bimodal. On this basis, the entrepreneurial investment cycle can be differentiated into four distinctly featured stages.

Part 2: SMEs from the Perspective of Different Levels of Analysis (Macro, Meso, and Micro)

Part 2 consists of 10 chapters

The chapter entitled "Antecedents of individual ambidexterity at three hierarchical levels: A literature review," by Junyu Zhou, Boyka Simeonova, and Mathew Hughes, reviews what we know about the existing antecedents of individual ambidexterity. Individual ambidexterity – the capacity of individuals to balance exploration-focused and exploitation-focused tasks – is very important for SMEs, because failing to explore new opportunities effectively while failing to generate revenue and refine their products and services jeopardizes the viability of a business. The authors outline the nomological network of individual ambidexterity and extend it by discussing new and additional antecedents crucial to the context of SME entrepreneurship. Organizational and individual antecedents, along with individual ambidexterity, are unpacked using hierarchical heterogeneity theory and are classified into three hierarchical levels: senior management, middle management, and frontline employees. This chapter (i) contributes to the conceptual map of individual ambidexterity; (ii) develops a nomological network of multi-hierarchical-level individual ambidexterity, with its existing, new, and additional organizational and individual antecedents; and (iii) outlines potential implications through its systematic review of the literature on SME entrepreneurship.

The chapter by Ziad El Awad and Jasna Poček, entitled "Life science companies' engagement with their university-based entrepreneurship ecosystem: a multi-layered approach," offers insights into the relational and engagement logics of small life science companies in university-based entrepreneurship ecosystems. The current literature focuses primarily on macro level understandings of ecosystem engagements and interconnections, considering the role played by support system organizations. This chapter assumes a unique approach and contributes to theory by portraying engagement from an actor-centered, small company's perspective. The chapter examines multiple case studies of inductive analysis, based on interviews with life science companies situated around Lund University's entrepreneurship ecosystem. In their analysis, the authors highlight three distinctive layers of engagement logics for small companies within the ecosystem: network, relations, and governance. Furthermore, the authors underline the importance of interdependencies between these three engagement logics in facilitating better access to resources from the ecosystem.

In their chapter titled, "Linking Young SME entrepreneurial Activity and Economic Development," Natanya Meyer and Jacques de Jongh analyze the relationships between entrepreneurial activity and economic development, along with their contributions to economic growth and development in the Visegrád group. Entrepreneurial activity has had a profound impact on shaping economic growth and development. The authors make use of an in-depth descriptive analysis, and secondary time-series

rely affects SME performance, and that the effect is stronger when the firm's capalities are considered. This study contributes to the collaborative advantage theory / reformulating the constructs that fit for SMEs in order to strengthen inter-firm ust building and synchronize the firms' responses to changes in their external factors. This study also provides new insights by incorporating relational capital as a on-price factor in motivating firms to share wider access to resources.

The chapter entitled "Sustainable Collaborative Business Models for Energy Efficient Solutions – An Exploratory Analysis of Danish and German SMEs" was written by Britta Boyd, Alexander Brem, and Silke Tegtmeier. The authors focus on the developing dynamics of innovation and productivity, as challenges that are continuously changing and are repeatedly remedied through the constant development of new technologies and business models. Boyd, Brem, and Tegtmeier investigate the similarities and differences – in terms of dependencies between networks, energy efficiency, and success – between SMEs in energy intensive industries that are situated in a specific geographical border region. The results reveal that the outcomes of a project depend on collaboration between other companies operating within the region. Based on these findings, open and collaborative business models are endorsed. New collaborative business models are expected to involve circular economy, resource efficiency, or energy storage. These findings confirm that collaboration across geographical boundaries can help SMEs to solve problems. Future research should focus on further developing collaborative, sustainable business models in order to facilitate energy efficient solutions.

Part 3: Processes and Performance of SMEs

Part 3 of the handbook is made up of eight chapters

In the chapter entitled "The Digital Transformation of SMEs," Magdalena Marczewska and Marzenna Anna Weresa present a framework for managing the digital transformation of SMEs and link the objectives, resources, impact, and outcomes of digital transformation. Input and output success metrics are also identified. The theoretical background of this chapter pertains to achieving competitive advantages through analysis of structural change and its impact. The chapter proclaims that dynamic capabilities for the digital transformation of SMEs are triggered by external factors, such as changing consumer behaviors and disruptive digital competitors. Internal factors enabling digital transformation include a well-designed digital strategy, implementation of technological mix management, and the re-shaping of operational setups and company culture. The chapter also provides new insights on the outcomes of SME digitalization, revealing that it can bring about innovation, working condition improvements, increased efficiency, and changes in environmental footprint. To achieve these outcomes, the digital transformation needs to be supported by organizational agility, executives' high involvement, and employee training. Moreover, the authors provide suggestions for SME managers on how to monitor the progress of their companies' digital journey, offering examples of key performance indicators.

Jadranka Švarc and Marina Dabić, in their chapter "Are the 'Guys who Play Games' Shaping our Economic Future? The Croatian Economy's Potential for Digital Transformation," discuss the situation in Croatia. Following the sale of game development company "Nanobit" to the Swedish Stillfront Group in 2020 for one billion HRK ($148 million), one of the headlines in the public media read "Croatia is hit by a technological fever." Given that Croatia is one of the least developed EU member states, with many of its companies operating in low- and medium-tech sectors, the purpose of this research is to explore whether digital transformation can contribute towards recovering such a low-tech service-based economy, or if this speculation is purely media hype. The research is explorative, and it includes an analysis of structural factors (the potential of the ICT sector), institutional factors (socio-economic environment), and the relationship between them. The findings suggest that Croatia has promising prospects in terms of its digital transformation. Digital transformation can also facilitate a potentially obstructive institutional environment, rooted in crony capitalism and state paternalism, as a result of the distinct character of the business models brought about by frontier digital technologies.

In the chapter "Should Entrepreneurs Effectuate? A Conceptual Examination on the Effects of Effectuation on Firm Performance," Tin Horvatinović, Mihaela Mikić, and Sanel Jakupović scrutinize the state of the art empirical research that tries to clarify the role that effectual approaches to entrepreneurship play in explaining differing levels of business performance. This line of research has recently gained momentum in high-quality journals, both in terms of the number of publications on this topic and increasing numbers of article citations. These studies detected that effectuation had a positive impact on business performance. To establish the hypothesis development framework used for justifying such results, high standards were applied. The literature seemed to reveal a consensus on what was the most appropriate measure of effectuation. Despite these positive factors, scholars need to exercise prudence when recommending that entrepreneurs employ effectuation, given the use of lacking statistical procedures and conflicting findings on the sole effect that effectuation principles have on business performance.

The chapter "How do SMEs Perform in Developing Countries? The Case of Indonesia," by Hary Febriansyah, Zulaicha Parastuty, and Dieter Bögenhold, explores how SMEs manage their businesses in Indonesia, how they recognize the importance of resources inside their organization, and how they manage changes. The article discusses the growth factors for SMEs in a developing country through the lens of internal and external factors. The research is based upon a qualitative approach, investigating four Indonesian SMEs using a multi-case analysis. The data is gathered through in-depth interviews and cross-case analysis. Four dimensions emerge as critical pillars for understanding the factors that influence SME performance and growth. The study looks at how owners manage their visions and the daily operations of their business, with the most critical dimension being strategy and the environment. Several implications are outlined for policymakers and business practices.

Léo-Paul Dana and Aidin Salamzadeh, in the chapter entitled "The Role of Culture and Entrepreneurial Opportunities in SME Entrepreneurship: A Systematic Literature Review," shed light on various aspects of the connections between culture, entrepreneurial opportunities, and SME entrepreneurship. A systematic literature review on the aforementioned topic is conducted, and insights are provided on the impact that culture and entrepreneurial opportunities in SME entrepreneurship have on literature development. The authors categorized the literature into two groups: (i) those that explicitly mentioned a relationship between culture and SME entrepreneurship; and (ii) those that implicitly mentioned it. They also identify the state of the art knowledge in this field and highlight the key trends and research streams. Their analysis is shaped by Shane and Venkataraman's (2001) approach towards the individual-opportunity nexus and Lundström and Stevenson's (2005) framework concerning the differences between SME and entrepreneurship policies. This chapter concludes with some remarks and directions for future research.

Tatiana Beliaeva, Vincent Mangematin, and Agnès Guerraz, in the chapter titled "Emerging Artificial Intelligence Methods for Predicting SME growth: Opportunities and Challenges," examine how emerging methods that are based on massive amounts of data may contribute to firm growth predictions. The current literature on firm growth calls for the performance improvement of firm growth models. Artificial intelligence (AI) and machine learning have made it possible for us to process large amounts of real-time data and make accurate predictions about future events. By reviewing the literature on SME growth and on AI-driven research in entrepreneurship and management, this chapter synthesizes the existing knowledge base on SME growth, compares AI-based methods with traditional methods, and proposes avenues for future research. This chapter highlights the opportunities enabled by AI, such as its enhanced ability to predict by means of a data-driven approach. The challenges are related to the theoretical explanations behind these predictions. Furthermore, the review provides implications for researchers willing to leverage AI methods in their growth studies, and practitioners looking to support their decision-making.

Part 4: Entrepreneurial Capital, Gender, and SMEs

Part 4 of the handbook contains four chapters

In the chapter entitled "Entrepreneurial Teams and Collective Dynamics: Toward an Eco(systemic) Perspective," Thierry Levy and Mouhoub Hani propose a literature review of entrepreneurial teams' emergence. The available literature is currently facing development setbacks in terms of collective efficacy and dynamics. This chapter provides an explanation and offers new insights on the aforementioned issue, thus contributing to widening this theoretical gap. Due to the lack of explanations of team clashes, they develop a systemic model of entrepreneurial team building and development. This systemic modelling of team dynamics could also be applied to collective small firms' engagement in networks, platforms, and even ecosystems. The authors also suggest that this system is relevant for use when analyzing collective dynamics, such as digital platforms and social networks. They posit that team success requires the articulation of four dimensions: (1) *Affectio Societatis*; (2) synergy; (3) commitment; and (4) shared vision. The authors propose platforms and ecosystems as an extension of the entrepreneurial team, and they outline some implications for further research in entrepreneurship scholarship.

Ramchandra Bhusal, in his chapter entitled "The Impact of Entrepreneurial Capital on Preferences for External Financing: An Empirical Study of Ethnic Minority Business Owners in the UK," examines the impact of social, cultural, and human capital on preferences for external financing among ethnic minority business owners in the UK. The findings show that entrepreneurial capital (a pool of social, cultural, and human capital) has an impact on ethnic entrepreneurs' finance-seeking behaviors. More specifically, entrepreneurs who choose to embrace extended social networks prefer bank financing, and ethnic entrepreneurs who embrace multiculturalism and have a propensity for acculturation prefer alternative sources of financing. Similarly, business owners with postgraduate qualifications have a positive preference for alternative financing. Higher levels of education have a positive impact on shaping preferences for asset financing. This empirical study provides insights into the relationship that exists between the holding of non-financial capital and preferences for external sources of financial capital.

The chapter "Internalizing Gender Equality: Narratives of Family Business Entrepreneurs" examines growing entrepreneurial identities affected by gender structures in family firms. Given that family-owned and family-led companies provide a context wherein more female entrepreneurs are able to establish themselves at the top of a business, the chapter aims to shed light on influencing factors as well as supportive dynamics. The authors, Valerie Nickel, Anita Zehrer, and Lena Leifeld, apply the lens of identity work, with a special focus on its primary form – identity talk. Thus, the qualitative approach obtains in-depth knowledge gained from narratives of family business entrepreneurs' dyads from Germany and Austria. The stories told reveal predominant frames that revolve around self-positioning and interactions with the firms' environments.

Nina Schumacher, in her chapter on "Success Factors of Digital Start-ups. A Qualitative Analysis of Entrepreneurial Personality from the Perspective of German Venture Investors," outlines the success characteristics of digital start-ups from the perspective of German venture investors. The chapter explains the general impact of personality characteristics, the importance of taking into account information and assessments provided by third parties, and the significance of intrinsic motivations and entrepreneurial energy in the investment decision process of venture capital investors. The study follows an exploratory three-dimensional research approach that adopts a micro-perspective approach to entrepreneurial personality, a meso-perspective on the business model, and a macro-perspective on the entrepreneurial context, thus operating in a very young research field. Furthermore, the experts' assessment of success characteristics offers a valuable perspective that has not gained sufficient attention in literature to date. Finally, based on a qualitative content analysis, the author provides empirical added value for researchers and practitioners with regards to focal points in German venture capital investors' implicit or explicit valuation models.

Part 5: SMEs and Their Stakeholders: The Role of Customers, Investors, Employees, Suppliers, Communities, Governments, Trade Associations etc

Part 5 is made up of four chapters

Duane Windsor, in the chapter entitled "The Multiple Responsibilities of SMEs and Entrepreneurs," examines how SME owners and entrepreneurs can integrate multiple responsibilities into new understandings of business. There are five key responsibilities: economic, environmental sustainability, ethical, social or community, and stakeholder. The procedure adopted holds economic responsibility (including profitability) constant in order to examine other responsibilities. The author contrasts this proposed understanding of SMEs and entrepreneurship with the conventional agency theory of publicly traded corporations, which emphasizes profitability. A crucial difference here is that SMEs and new ventures can be privately owned, rather than publicly traded. Owners or entrepreneurs integrate their personal values with external conditions in an attempt to reach a viable solution. The proposed concept should help to improve the welfare and sustainability of the key participants, including society and the natural environment, as well as firms and their stakeholders. When forming ventures, owners and entrepreneurs can embed this conception from the outset.

In the chapter "Exploring Early Customer Portfolios of Start-ups: Capturing Patterns of Relationship Development States," Lise Aaboen, Elsebeth Holmen, and Anne-Charlotte Pedersen explore patterns of relationship development states in early start-ups' customer portfolios. By analyzing interviews from 20 start-ups, using a framework that combines literature on customer portfolios and relationship development states, four patterns in the portfolios of customer relationship development states are identified: Paradise lost, Pearls on a string, Picture perfect, and Persuasion. Based on these four patterns, the authors concluded that the start-ups' customer relationship state portfolio can be characterized by whether the start-up is pursuing a narrow or broader customer relationship portfolio strategy, and whether it mostly utilizes its value offering potential for enticement or engineering in its relationship portfolio.

Nazha Gali and Susanna L.M. Chui, in their chapter on "The Role of Research Universities in Catalyzing Value Creation," focus on the role of education in catalyzing value creation and the positive impact of research universities' publicly funded research projects. The research question "How could universities and science provide tools that have a positive impact on the economy, including SMEs?" is addressed. Firstly, previous research that has been conducted on the impact of universities on the economy, SMEs, and their communities is presented. Subsequently, the data curation efforts led by the Institute for Research on Innovation and Science (IRIS), which is a consortium of US research universities using big administrative data, is used to explain and provide evidence on the impact of higher education universities on the economy, SMEs, the career pathways of students, and on national prosperity. Finally, the engagement of business school students in the examination of entrepreneurial ethics in a research university in Hong Kong is examined. The outcomes of the research serve to inform the business sectors of the values that shape responsible management for important customer stakeholder groups.

Reija Hakkinen and Juha Kansikas, in their chapter "Entrepreneurial Culture Creation through Employee Effectuation," attempt to improve our understanding of how entrepreneurial endeavors, aimed towards high performance and good customer service, are initiated by employees. In tourism services, the value creation for the consumer lies not only in the transaction-focused transfer of financial capital, services, and products, but also in the socially constructed interactions between tourism employees and customers. The challenge lies in the fact that consumers have versatile expectations, which create demand for unique value-creation in each transaction. Employees often need to respond to customer expectations without prior detailed planning. Thus, the authors in this chapter investigate the theoretical enablement and preventative idea-generation behavior and actions in customer service through the lens of effectuation logics. Focus groups were conducted in an attempt to empirically understand the perspectives and reasoning of the participants. The purpose was to analyze the research data at two levels: among the groups and between the groups. The results increase employee effectuation understanding, suggesting that a positive managerial attitude alone is not enough to foster and support entrepreneurial and service-related behaviors amongst employees. More concrete HR support and the acknowledgement of employee skills and capabilities are needed in order for the organization to benefit from entrepreneurial and service-related behaviors.

Concluding Remarks

With this *Handbook of SME Entrepreneurship*, we have tried to bring together some of the key research activities on this important field in order to generate a contemporary body of knowledge that provides a focused view of a range of topics, all of which will hopefully be able to serve as fertile ground for future research in the field.

In finalizing this work, we have recognized additional research gaps within the field and discussed further emerging topics, thus opening up the possibility for these considerations to be investigated in further subsequent research. With this in mind, we would like to welcome you to the network. We invite you to share your feedback and opinions with us – electronically as well as in real life at conferences or workshops.

This publication effort would not have been possible without the people participating directly or indirectly in the compilation of this book (authors, reviewers, our excellent contacts at *De Gruyter*, researchers, academics, and managers). These individuals have all added value and have come together to deliver chapters that analyze the actualities that support the future growth of SMEs. Their work allows us to prepare entrepreneurs, managers, and students for the events they face now and increasingly in the future when they work in SMEs, such as prospects, success and failure, enthusiasm, cognitions, strengths and courageousness, resilience, triumph stories, and the discovery of new knowledge, skills, ventures, insights, and inspirations that will help them to demonstrate their most critical real-life visions in the business world.

References

Anand, A., Muskat, B., Creed, A., Zutshi, A., & Csepregi, A. (2021). Knowledge sharing, knowledge transfer and SMEs: Evolution, antecedents, outcomes and directions. *Personnel Review*, in press, DOI: https://doi.org/10.1108/PR-05-2020-0372.

Bassett-Jones, N. (2005). The paradox of diversity management, creativity and innovation. *Creativity and Innovation Management*, *14*(2), 169–175.

Bouncken, R.B., Kraus, S., & Martínez-Pérez, J.F. (2020). Entrepreneurship of an institutional field: The emergence of coworking spaces for digital business models. *International Entrepreneurship and Management Journal*, *16*(4), 1465–1481.

Bouwman, H., Nikou, S., & de Reuver, M. (2019). Digitalization, business models, and SMEs: How do business model innovation practices improve performance of digitalizing SMEs? *Telecommunications Policy*, *43*(9), 101828.

Brouthers, K.D., Andriessen, F., & Nicolaes, I. (1998). Driving blind: Strategic decision-making in small companies. *Long Range Planning*, *31*(1), 130–138.

Bruton, G.D., Ahlstrom, D., & Li, H.-L. (2010). Institutional theory and entrepreneurship: Where are we now and where do we need to move in the future? *Entrepreneurship Theory and Practice*, *34*(3), 421–440.

Chatterjee, S., Chaudhuri, R., Vrontis, D., & Thrassou, A. (2022). SME entrepreneurship and digitalization–the potentialities and moderating role of demographic factors. *Technological Forecasting and Social Change*, *179*, 121648.

Cosenz, F., & Bivona, E. (2021). Fostering growth patterns of SMEs through business model innovation. A tailored dynamic business modelling approach. *Journal of Business Research*, *130*, 653–669.

Covin, J.G., Rigtering, J., Hughes, M., Kraus, S., Cheng, C.-F., & Bouncken, R. (2020). Individual and team entrepreneurial orientation: Scale development and configurations for success. *Journal of Business Research*, *112*, 1–12.

Cunningham, J.A., Menter, M., & Wirsching, K. (2019). Entrepreneurial ecosystem governance: A principal investigator-centered governance framework. *Small Business Economics*, *52*(2), 545–562.

Dabić, M., Maley, J., Dana, L.P., Novak, I., Pellegrini, M.M., & Caputo, A. (2020). Pathways of SME internationalization: A bibliometric and systematic review. *Small Business Economics*, *55*(3), 705–725.

Dabić, M., Vlačić, B., Kiessling, T., Caputo, A., & Pellegrini, M. (2021): Serial entrepreneurs: A review of literature and guidance for future research. *Journal of Small Business Management*, in press, DOI: 10.1080/00472778.2021.1969657.

Eggers, F., Kraus, S., & Covin, J. (2014). Traveling into unexplored territory: Pioneering innovativeness and the role of networking, customers, and turbulent environments. *Industrial Marketing Management*, *43*(8), 1385–1393.

Ferreira, J.J., Fernandes, C.I., & Kraus, S. (2019). Entrepreneurship research: Mapping intellectual structures and research trends. *Review of Managerial Science*, *13*(1), 181–205.

Fink, M., & Kraus, S. (2009). *The management of small and medium enterprises*. Routledge.

Franco, M., Godinho, L., & Rodrigues, M. (2021). Exploring the influence of digital entrepreneurship on SME digitalization and management. *Small Enterprise Research*, *28*(3), 269–292.

Garzella, S., Fiorentino, R., Caputo, A., & Lardo, A. (2021). Business model innovation in SMEs: The role of boundaries in the digital era. *Technology Analysis & Strategic Management*, *33*(1), 31–43.

Heneman, R.L., Tansky, J.W., & Camp, S.M. (2000). Human resource management practices in small and medium-sized enterprises: Unanswered questions and future research perspectives. *Entrepreneurship Theory and Practice*, *25*(1), 11–26.

Highfill, T., Cao, R., Schwinn, R., Prisinzano, R., & Leung, D. (2020). *Measuring the small business economy*. US Department of Commerce, Bureau of Economic Analysis.

Hock-Doepgen, M., Clauss, T., Kraus, S., & Cheng, C.F. (2021). Knowledge management capabilities and organizational risk-taking for business model innovation in SMEs. *Journal of Business Research*, *130*, 683–697.

Isensee, C., Teuteberg, F., Griese, K.M., & Topi, C. (2020). The relationship between organizational culture, sustainability, and digitalization in SMEs: A systematic review. *Journal of Cleaner Production*, 122944.

Kang, Q., Li, H., Cheng, Y., & Kraus, S. (2021). Entrepreneurial ecosystems: Analysing the status quo. *Knowledge Management Research & Practice*, *19*(1), 8–20.

Kraus, S., Durst, S., Ferreira, J.J., Veiga, P., Kailer, N., & Weinmann, A. (2022). Digital transformation in business and management research: An overview of the current status quo. *International Journal of Information Management*, *63*, 102466.

Kraus, S., Palmer, C., Kailer, N., Kallinger, F.L., & Spitzer, J. (2019). Digital entrepreneurship: A research agenda on new business models for the twenty-first century. *International Journal of Entrepreneurial Behavior & Research*, *25*(2), 353–375.

Morais, F., & Ferreira, J.J. (2020). SME internationalisation process: Key issues and contributions, existing gaps and the future research agenda. *European Management Journal*, *38*(1), 62–77.

OECD. (2017). *Enhancing the contributions of SMEs in a global and digitalised economy*. OECD.

Ross, P.K., Blumenstein, M.J.T.A., & Management, S. (2015). Cloud computing as a facilitator of SME Entrepreneurship. *Technology Analysis & Strategic Management*, *27*(1), 87–101.

Schulz, A., Borghoff, T., & Kraus, S. (2009). International entrepreneurship: towards a theory of SME internationalization. *International Journal of Business and Economics*, *9*(1), 1–12.

Sen, S., Savitskie, K., Mahto, R.V., Kumar, S., & Khanin, D. (2022). Strategic flexibility in small firms. *Journal of Strategic Marketing*, in press, DOI: https://doi.org/10.1080/0965254X.2022.2036223

Sharma, P., & Chrisman, J.J. (1999). Toward a reconciliation of the definitional issues in the field of corporate entrepreneurship. *Entrepreneurship Theory and Practice*, *23(3)*, 11–28.

Silva, A.R.D., Ferreira, F.A., Carayannis, E.G., & Ferreira, J.J. (2019). Measuring SMEs' propensity for open innovation using cognitive mapping and MCDA. *IEEE- Transactions on Engineering Management*, *68*(2), 396–407.

Spithoven, A., Vanhaverbeke, W., & Roijakkers, N. (2013). Open innovation practices in SMEs and large enterprises. *Small Business Economics*, *41*(3), 537–562.

Statista.com. (2021). Number of small and medium-sized enterprises (SMEs) in the European Union (EU27) from 2008 to 2021, by size. https://www.statista.com/statistics/878412/number-of-smes-in-europe-by-size/

Švarc, J., & Dabić, M. (2021). Transformative innovation policy or how to escape peripheral policy paradox in European research peripheral countries. *Technology in Society, 67*. https://doi.org/10.1016/j.techsoc.2021.101705.

Van de Vrande, V., De Jong, J.P., Vanhaverbeke, W., & De Rochemont, M. (2009). Open innovation in SMEs: Trends, motives and management challenges. *Technovation, 29*(6–7), 423–437.

Wang, S., & Wang, H. (2020). Big data for small and medium-sized enterprises (SME): A knowledge management model. *Journal of Knowledge Management, 24*(4), 881–897.

Welsh, J.A., & White, J.F. (1981). Small business ratio analysis: A cautionary note to consultants. *Journal of Small Business Management, 20.*

Wiklund, J., Nikolaev, B., Shir, N., Foo, M.D., & Bradley, S. (2019). Entrepreneurship and well-being: Past, present, and future. *Journal of Business Venturing, 34*(4), 579–588.

Part 1: **Novel Theories of Entrepreneurship in SMEs**

Jörg Freiling

1 SME Entrepreneurship and Entrepreneurship Theory: A Systematic Literature Analysis in the Light of Entrepreneurial Functions

Abstract: Research on entrepreneurial functions (here referred to as entrepreneurship theory) has a long tradition in economics. Business studies started researching on entrepreneurial functions much more recently. In particular, in the last two decades a number of publications have dealt with entrepreneurial functions. What is currently lacking is a condensed overview of this field of research. This chapter responds to this gap and conducts a systematic literature review on the implications of entrepreneurship theory to SME management. Based on the research question "What do we know about the core entrepreneurial functions of SMEs in the light of entrepreneurship theory and about the impact when performing these functions?" the study analyzes 28 publications on the core of the topic. The study finds that the business stream deviates from the economics stream, presents more empirical research, adds more functions related to current environmental challenges, and helps mitigate the often bemoaned "realization gap" of economic entrepreneurship theory. Contributions are a structured overview of the entire research, an identification of schools and approaches within this field, and proposals for future research.

Keywords: entrepreneurship theory, entrepreneurial functions, SME entrepreneurship, schools of thought, innovation, arbitrage, risk-taking, risk management, coordination

Introduction

What do entrepreneurs do? And what is to be done in terms of entrepreneurial action for the sake of goal achievement in a small business context? Looking at the very nature of these questions, their fundamental character for entrepreneurship studies is evident. It may be hard to precisely specify the beginning of entrepreneurship research (Marchesnay, 2008). However, there is much evidence that it traces back to the eighteenth century seminal work of Cantillon (1725/1755) and some meaningful and impactful follow-up contributions in the early twentieth century (e.g., Schumpeter, 1911/1934; Knight, 1921; Kirzner, 1973; Casson, 2003) that address the mentioned questions in the light of the so-called "entrepreneurial functions." This debate accelerated vital discourses in later deca-

Jörg Freiling, Faculty of Business Studies and Economics, University of Bremen

https://doi.org/10.1515/9783110747652-002

des that center around the above-mentioned questions – with the only exception that little has been done so far to translate the findings to the reality of SME management. Nevertheless, in the last two decades more and more attempts have been made to move from conceptual and theoretical considerations to analyzing entrepreneurial functions in real-life contexts like quantitative studies on entrepreneurial drivers of profitable growth (Freiling & Lütke Schelhowe, 2014) or qualitative studies on entrepreneurial roots of hubristic behavior (Sundermeier et al., 2020). This shift is meaningful insofar as it changed the understanding of the content of entrepreneurial functions from mono-topical conceptualizations to multi-topical ones (Freiling, 2009). The according publications reveal an evident explanatory power of core constructs of SME management though entrepreneurial functions. However, as the current scholarly status is highly fragmented with interesting, yet rather contextual findings (e.g., Chiles et al., 2010; Lounsbury et al., 2019; Sundermeier et al., 2020), scholars in comparable situations call for a systematic literature to identify and condense the previous findings and to draw conclusions based on this (Dabić et al., 2020). Kraus et al. (2020, p. 1028) state "(. . .) within a certain research field, authors with diverse backgrounds see constructs, theories and so on with their own eyes, which results in a scattered field. SLRs can help to overcome this issue by synthesizing the field (. . .)." This applies to research on entrepreneurial functions as well, and the focus of this systematic literature analysis of contributions on entrepreneurial functions is, thus, on the business, not economics level.

Despite the fundamental relevance of the questions to entrepreneurship studies, it is, of course, a simplification to call the emerging theory of entrepreneurial functions "entrepreneurship theory" (Boutillier & Uzunidis, 2014; Sautet, 2017). However, given the long tradition and the basic nature for the field, this simplification seems to be acceptable, not ignoring also that other fields of entrepreneurial studies raise similar claims and use the same term for labeling their research streams (e.g., Mishra & Zachary, 2015, for the theory of entrepreneurial value creation, and Guzmán Cuevas, 1994, for a general overview).

Basically, the term "entrepreneurial functions" has a somewhat "mechanistic" sound and has to fight against the perceived "dust" on very old contributions to the field that go far beyond the roots of management studies. Consequently, at the very beginning the debate on entrepreneurial functions rests predominantly on economic research and found an implicit grounding in entrepreneurship studies with a business background only in most recent decades (Schneider, 2011). The mechanistic picture of "functions," however, is to some extent irritating. It suggests that an entrepreneur simply has to perform certain functions to provide a certain output or outcome. However, to perform certain entrepreneurial functions in (small business) reality may have several implications that deserve much more attention than paid in research on entrepreneurial function so far. Many thoughtful debates and publications, particularly but not solely belonging to the research tradition of the New Austrian School (e.g., Mises, 1949; Kirzner, 1973), lead to a rich body of conceptual knowledge – but with an often bemoaned "realization gap" (Boettke, 1994; Foss; 1994; Loasby, 2002). This realization gap implies breaking the abstract conceptualizations and considerations down to real life in business – and to follow Gartner's (1989) claim of not looking at what the entrepreneur is, but to look at what (s)he does.

In the last decades, however, the striking evidence of lacking empirical work and the missing applications in the field of small business research animated scholars to turn the research direction and to close the gap. For about two decades, research on entrepreneurial functions in an SME management has been conducted. This gives rise to the impression that a systematic literature review (SLR) could be beneficial to condense the findings and to address issues for future research along the following research question: what do we know about the core entrepreneurial functions of SMEs in the light of entrepreneurship theory and about the impact when performing these functions? For the sake of clarity, this SLR only relates to entrepreneurial functions in SME studies and equals, for simplification reasons, theorizing on entrepreneurial functions with entrepreneurship theory. The chapter does not intend to consider the huge body of publications on entrepreneurial functions in general. The reason for this is the enormous heterogeneity and the simple fact that the emphasis of these publications is on economics rather than (small) business studies. It could be a task on its own to conduct an SLR on contributions from economics and would be beyond the scope of this volume. An SLR on entrepreneurial functions research in the realm of SME management, however, is beneficial for the following reasons (Paul et al., 2021): (i) providing a first state of the art of research in this particular field; (ii) provoking new research by raising issues for follow-up initiatives; and (iii) avoiding replicative research due to lacking transparency.

To socialize and orientate the reader, it is useful to clarify the basic terms against the background of the relevant research tradition. With the above-mentioned understanding of entrepreneurship theory as theory of entrepreneurial functions, the question arises of what entrepreneurial functions are, who performs these functions, and what is meant in terms of impact according to the research question. While most of the publications seem to circumvent a clear definition by pointing to content issues like risk bearing, organizing, and innovation (Keilbach, 2009), others try to condense the very nature. In this vein, entrepreneurial functions are those tasks to be performed and those roles to be played by entrepreneurially acting people (not only the entrepreneurs themselves) that keep and, thus, impact the competitiveness of the company (Schoppe et al., 1995; Schneider, 2011). Accordingly and different from economic publications, the impact focus of this SLR is on the company level. Foss and Klein (2012) stress that entrepreneurial functions focus on activities and behaviors of entrepreneurs and adopt a process perspective. One can argue whether the theory of entrepreneurial functions belongs to the novel theories of entrepreneurship in SMEs, as this section of this edited volume suggests. In terms of tradition and origin, it is hard to regard this kind of entrepreneurship theory as novel. However, the more this theory moved towards business and management studies, the more this theory changed its face towards practical applications in business. Notably, this change of application was accompanied by a remarkable turn in understanding what the relevant entrepreneurial functions are when it comes to entrepreneurial action in real life. Particularly in the case of SME management, the turn in nature is evident and the character novel to SME business studies. There are good reasons to consider the theory of entrepreneurial functions among the novel theories of SME management. Moreover, in view of many alternate conceptions of entrepreneurial functions in the realm of (small business) management, there is a strong need to condense the current state of research through SLR which is, to date, not available in this field.

So doing, prior research suggests considering the following issues. First, while entrepreneurship research identifies at least three schools of thought in the realm of entrepreneurial functions – namely the American (Chicago), German, and Austrian School (Hébert & Link, 1988) –, publications are predominantly in English but to some extent also in German (Schneider, 2011), French (Boutillier & Uzunidis, 2014), and Spanish (Huerta de Soto, 1994). While the content of the Spanish publications is available in comparable English publications of the respective authors, the same holds for most of the publications in German as well. One exception is one group of authors forming an interesting stream in entrepreneurial functions research that is only in available in German (Schneider, 2011). The same holds for some French publications. To consider these contributions, German and French publications were considered. Second, there is a certain tradition in research on entrepreneurial functions not only to publish in journals but via books or edited volumes as well. Again, in most cases only journal publications may represent the state in literature but with more exceptions than in other fields of research. A SLR should take this into account and deliver a structured landscape of (small) business-related publications of different languages, identify new ways of illuminating this research field by particularly inductive empirical research, and locate up-and-coming developments of enriching the very nature of entrepreneurial functions in the light of recent business challenges.

Systematic Literature Review: Procedure and Review Protocol

According to Littell et al. (2008, pp. 1–2), systematic literature reviews belong to "(. . .) research that bears on a particular question, using organized, transparent, and replicable procedures at each step in the process." An SLR helps to identify, evaluate, and summarize the state-of-the-art of a specific theme in the literature (Paul et al., 2021).

The main steps of an SLR are: (i) planning the review including the specification of the need and the development of a review protocol; (ii) identifying, evaluating, and selecting the publications; (iii) extracting and synthesizing the findings; and (iv) disseminating the review findings (Tranfield et al., 2003; Kraus et al., 2020). In this vein, having specified the need above, the next step is outlining the review protocol of this SLR (Kraus et al., 2020; Paul et al., 2021). A review protocol lists the parameters for the search and makes decisions along the search strings, the databases, inclusion and exclusion criteria, or quality criteria (Kraus et al., 2020). The review protocol design follows the most recent proposal by Paul et al. (2021) with three main stages and related sub-stages as follows: (i) assembling (including identification and acquisition); (ii) arranging (including organization and purification); and (iii) assessing (including evaluation and reporting).

Assembling: Identification

The identification of relevant literature rests on the relevant domain (SME management) and theory (entrepreneurship theory in terms of entrepreneurial functions), the above-stated research question, the source type, and the source quality. Given the nature of the research question, this chapter adopts a theory-based search among the established ways of conducting a systematic literature analysis (Palmatier et al., 2018; Paul et al., 2021). A theory-based review analyzes the development of a specified theory in a certain domain (Gilal, 2019; Paul & Rosado-Serrano, 2019, Dabić et al., 2020). To sharpen the focus and to consider the most recent turn in research on entrepreneurial functions, this theory-based review addresses only the business-related publications on entrepreneurial functions and emphasizes SME management issues as the center point of most recent research. In terms of source type and quality, this SLR favors journal publications but needs to consider most of the other kinds of academic publications as well (books, book chapters, dissertations – but excluding working papers, proceedings, reviews, and editorials). The reason for this is that, besides the considerable spread and heterogeneity of publications, the long history of research on entrepreneurial functions animated many scholars to publish not only in (refereed) journals but in the outlets included above as well. While this convention has vanished in the last couple of years, the earlier years are still influenced by this practice and require corresponding selection decisions.

Assembling: Acquisition

The acquisition of literature considers the search mechanism, the search period, and the search keywords. Literature lists several search mechanisms that differ in the scope of indexing and availability – and, thus, the quality and quantity of listed publications. While some scholars favor inclusive search mechanisms like Google Scholar (e.g., Paul et al., 2021), others are more skeptical in terms of reproducibility and quality (Kraus et al., 2020). Given the standard databases for search runs, there are differences regarding the options of the search mechanism to filter literature. It is, thus, useful to select the search mechanism along the targets of the search. As this study targets a certain discipline and domain, different kinds of outlets and publications in different languages, the search mechanism should support this. Scopus appeared to be the best fit in this sense and was chosen, accordingly. The first iteration yielded 776 results in terms of publications. Following the advice not to rely only on one mechanism and to check for completeness, Google Scholar was considered for this check (Kraus et al., 2020; Paul et al., 2021). Additionally, the review of all relevant publications identified included a review of the references to check whether relevant publications appear that the databases did not provide via the chosen search procedure. The search period allows for refining the search for core publications. Research on entrepreneurial functions was in the centuries before the recent one, almost exclusively of the economic kind. Only a few authors with business roots published before 2000 (e.g., Tiessen, 1997) with most of them continuing to publish in the new century (e.g., Schneider, 2011). Against this background, a search of publications in the last two decades with the main search mechanism will suffice, particularly given the additional Google Scholar cross-check mentioned above and an additional references check of the reviewed publications. In line with recommendations from literature, the search period is 2001–2021 (Paul et al., 2021). In terms of the search keywords, the focus should be narrow to avoid listing too many publications without relevance. The chosen keywords are: "entrepreneur* functions" and "entrepreneurship theory" – with its translations into the other relevant languages.

Arranging: Organization

This step relates to the codes and the code book to record the publications of the search (Paul et al., 2021). Depending on the target and style of this SLR, the review rests on the following codes: publication outlet, type of research, language, approach of entrepreneurial functions, affiliation to a specific branch or cluster of entrepreneurial functions research, ambition, implications, and current impact measured by the number of citations.

Arranging: Purification

Informed by the coding, this position allows taking the decision of filtering the publications at hand. While matching the research question stands at the fore of this process, there is also a need to sort out duplicates and predatory titles (Paul et al., 2021). The process of removing publications typically starts with the analysis of the titles, followed by the keywords, abstracts, and the main content. In this case, all titles, keywords, and abstracts were reviewed before an exclusion took place to avoid sorting out relevant publications that look topically irrelevant at first glance. The exclusion of publications rests on the following criteria: other domains than (small) business research (to exclude particularly the numerous publications from economics with other explananda, i.e. phenomena to be explained); different understandings of entrepreneurial functions than the established one mentioned above; no connection to entrepreneurship theory in the sense of this study; no evident reference to entrepreneurial functions; irrelevance to SME management; and, of course, literatures without a sound academic background. In most cases of the publication sift, the focus on economic facets of entrepreneurial functions led to the exclusion. Also the understanding of entrepreneurship theory deviated considerably so that several publications did not address entrepreneurial functions in the way stated above.

Assessing: Evaluation

The evaluation sub-step makes decisions on the analysis method and the agenda proposal method (Paul et al., 2021). The analysis method should consider the content in the light of the research question and the type of SLR. As a theory-based search, it is of pivotal interest to understand the conceptualization of entrepreneurial functions, the way the conceptualization took place, and how far entrepreneurial functions relate to performance of small businesses. Moreover, structures and developments of this research stream are relevant to responding to the research question within this first SLR of this kind on the topic. This already relates to the model of proposing an agenda. Recurring on current practice, the search should contribute to developing a research agenda in terms of open content related questions, application of methods to specify findings, epistemological procedures to advance research, and ontological issues to contribute to a more comprehensive picture.

Assessing: Reporting

Paul et al. (2021) claim that SLRs should cater to different groups of readers and adapt to these groups accordingly. This review targets two groups, namely scholars interested in SME management and those in organization and management theory. For the latter group, the results should show the distinct profile of the business stream of entrepreneurship theory and its internal structures. Particularly clusters or schools of thoughts would be useful to recognize the development, the position, and the "white spaces" of this theory. As for SME management, it is important to locate what the debate on entrepreneurial functions delivers to leadership in small businesses that goes beyond other approaches.

On this note, the next section reviews the 28 included publications. The number of finally relevant publications is, to date, not very big and many of the 776 English, 20 German, and eight French publications do not relate to the core of the topic. However, the accompanying Google Scholar search increased the number and reveals a number where an initial SLR makes sense.

Synthesis and Interpretation

The first part of the research question targets the core entrepreneurial functions of SMEs in the light of entrepreneurship theory. What this SLR delivers in this regard is, at first, a finding that goes beyond typical conceptualizations well-known from the long tradition of entrepreneurial functions in economics. While economic research – with the often bemoaned "realization gap" – stresses the relevance of single entrepreneurial functions like bearing risks, innovation or arbitrage (Cantillon, 1725/1755; Knight, 1921; Schumpeter, 1911/1934; Kirzner, 1973), the (small) business stream deviates from this view. Developed in much later times, the environment changed considerably and seems to challenge companies differently and considerably. The so-called "VUCA" setting (volatility, uncertainty, complexity, and ambiguity in making decisions) is only one visible manifestation (Bennet & Lemoine, 2014). One response to these challenges is the performance of a set of entrepreneurial functions, formerly developed in economics. While there are still publications stressing the performance of only one function (Hulbert et al., 2015), most of the concepts are more fine-grained and deal with a bigger number of entrepreneurial functions (Mezias & Kuperman, 2001; Sundermeier et al., 2020). It is a first insight that we can differentiate between mono-functional, bi-functional, and multi-functional concepts. One explanation for the turn to a multitude of functions relates to empirical publications that confront concepts with reality more intensively, identify new spheres of entrepreneurial activity, and, thus, can help with closing the realization gap.

Another finding in this regard is that in case of multi-functional concepts the publications sometime refer to the respective entrepreneurial functions equally and without any priorities (Dejardin et al., 2015; Gerbaulet, 2016). Other publications, however, structure the entrepreneurial functions on a topical (Freiling & Lütke Schelhowe, 2014) or hierarchical basis (Schneider, 2011).

Table 1.1 provides an overview of all searched publications that also considers these two different ways to develop conceptions of entrepreneurial functions for SME management. The appendix also displays the publications outlets (21 journal articles with eight in A-ranked journals, four books, three book chapters), the type of research (conceptual, qualitative or quantitative empirical) of the publications, and the impact in terms of citations (Google Scholar, August 31, 2021).

While the mentioned items of Table 1.1 represent the "anatomy" of the publications, the next step is to dive deeper to understand the formed structures in small business research on entrepreneurial functions and content. This allows for providing a specified response to the first part of the research question. In this regard, prior economic research imprinted the structures of business research on entrepreneurial functions to some extent. Anyway, an independent profile is already evident in many publications. Strong historical imprints relate to some concepts of the mono-functional (Hulbert et al., 2015) or bi-functional approaches (Uzunides et al., 2014). Nevertheless, some approaches of this kind also went completely new ways and opened up content that is

Table 1.1: Anatomy of the publications.

Name and Year	Outlet	Type of research	Kind of Entrepreneurial Function approach	Citations
Amuda, 2020	Acad of Strat Mngm J	conceptual	multi-functional list (explorative kind)	0
Boutillier & Uzunidis, 2014	REMI	conceptual	mono-functional tradition	12
Chiles et al., 2007	OSS	conceptual	ambidextrous multi-functional system	424
Chiles et al., 2010	OSS	conceptual	ambidextrous multi-functional system	175
Dejardin et al., 2015	Book Chapter	qualitative	multi-functional list	1
Estevao & Freiling, 2009	ZfM	conceptual	ambidextrous multi-functional system	2
Fontela et al., 2006	foresight	conceptual	multi-functional list (explorative kind)	78
Foss & Klein, 2012	Book	conceptual	mono-functional tradition	606
Foss et al., 2007	OSS	conceptual	mono-functional tradition	259
Freiling, 2005	Book chapter	conceptual	ambidextrous multi-functional system	6
Freiling, 2008	JEE	conceptual	ambidextrous multi-functional system	56
Freiling, 2009	IJTIP	conceptual	ambidextrous multi-functional system	18
Freiling, 2020	Book chapter	conceptual	ambidextrous multi-functional system	0
Freiling & Luetke Schelhowe, 2014	JEMI	quantitative	ambidextrous multi-functional system	45
Freiling & Pöschl, 2020	JSBE	qualitative	ambidextrous multi-functional system	0
Freiling & Wessels, 2010	Wirtschaftspolitische Blätter	conceptual	ambidextrous multi-functional system	3
Gerbaulet, 2016	Book	conceptual	multi-functional list	15
Hulbert et al., 2015	J of Strat Mktg	qualitative	mono-functional	31
Keyhani, 2019	SEJ	conceptual	ambidextrous multi-functional system	9

Table 1.1 (continued)

Name and Year	Outlet	Type of research	Kind of Entrepreneurial Function approach	Citations
Lounsbury et al., 2019	JMS	conceptual	mono-functional	37
Mezias & Kuperman, 2001	JBV	conceptual	multi-functional list	170
Peng et al., 2014	JWB	conceptual	multi-functional list (explorative kind)	44
Poeschl & Freiling, 2020	JOCM	qualitative	ambidextrous multi-functional system	2
Reckenfelderbäumer, 2001	Book (Habil. Thesis)	conceptual	hierarchical multi-functional system	17
Schneider, 2011	Book	conceptual	hierarchical multi-functional system	39
Sundermeier et al., 2020	JMS	qualitative	ambidextrous multi-functional system	7
Tiessen, 1997	JBV	conceptual	bi-functional set	651
Uzunidis et al., 2014	J of Innovation and Eship	conceptual	bi-functional set	44

Source: own compilation (for journal abbreviations cf. the references).

new to the debates on entrepreneurial functions. Particularly, Lounsbury et al. (2019) departed from former content by pointing to recent needs of symbolic management and communication as a way to gain legitimacy in societies and markets. Consequently, and inspired by cultural entrepreneurship, Lounsbury et al. (2019) launched entrepreneurial storytelling among the entrepreneurial functions. In a similar vein, Gerbaulet (2016) added to the set of four established entrepreneurial functions – namely, innovation, risk-taking, arbitrage, and coordination – reputation building as a fifth function and as a value-driven core driver of performance.

Besides developing the debate on entrepreneurial functions by bringing new functions to the table that respond to recent business developments, the possibly most pervasive trend is to form a set of more or less interrelated functions. While scholars like Gerbaulet (2016), Mezias and Kuperman (2001), Dejardin et al. (2015) or Fontela et al. (2006) listed functions one by one, there are other approaches trying to systemize entrepreneurial functions within a frame. One logic of developing such systems is about organizing a set of functions that all rest on the same logical level and differ in terms of context relevance. In particular, those publications favoring the ambidexterity concept of March (1991) to develop an according set of entrepreneurial functions go this way (Freiling, 2008; Freiling & Lütke Schelhowe, 2014; Poeschl &

Freiling, 2020; Sundermeier et al., 2020). These ambidextrous multi-functional approaches consist of explorative functions (innovation and risk management) and exploitative functions (internal coordination and arbitrage). They stand vis-à-vis the hierarchical multi-functional approaches that prioritize certain functions for some reasons. A prominent example is Schneider's (2011) approach that seeks to constitute an entrepreneurial theory of the firm. In so doing, the constitutive function is about taking the income risks of other people by founding a multi-person company, the survivability of which depends on two accompanying functions, namely arbitrage on markets and implementing change through breaking resistance internally.

Mono-functional approaches on the one side and multi-functional approaches without order and with hierarchical order on the other side form a triangle-like space for schools of entrepreneurship theory dealing with entrepreneurial functions from a (small) business angle. Figure 1.1 illustrates this space with two dimensions, namely (i) number of entrepreneurial functions of the approach and (ii) the question of ordering these functions. The positioning space is a triangle for the simple reason that ordering functions can only become an issue if we depart from mono-functional approaches.

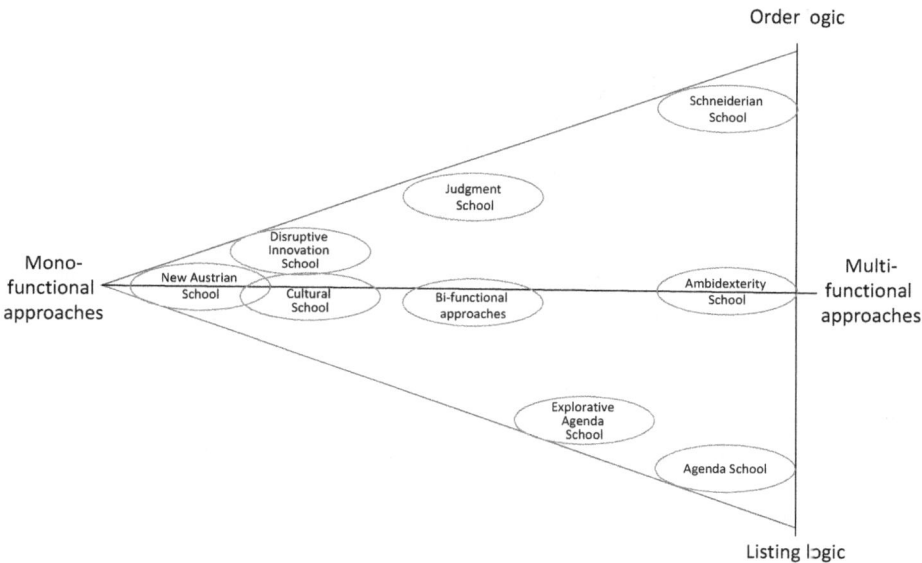

Figure 1.1: Schools of thought in small business entrepreneurship theory.
Source: own illustration.

Table 1.1 and Figure 1.1 reveal how the space within the triangle can be filled. A review of the publications helped in revealing their nature in terms of research ambition, relevant entrepreneurial functions, their implications, and the findings. Table 1.1 materializes the results of the review by assigning the publications to certain schools of thought. Insofar as the according column in Table 1.1 on the kind of the entrepreneurial function(s) approach lists the assignments, Figure 1.1 can build on condensing and mapping the state of the art in entrepreneurship theory.

A first cluster in Figure 1.1 are those schools that favor a certain function for evident reasons. Those approaches comprise the tradition of the Modern Austrian Economics (and related focus on opportunity recognition and arbitrage) like Hulbert et al. (2015), the disruptive innovation school inspired by Schumpeter (Boutillier & Uzunidis, 2014), and the cultural school – with the latter bringing with entrepreneurial storytelling a completely new function to the table (Lounsbury et al., 2019). The schools of this cluster share the embeddedness of SMEs in markets and environments and the need to cope with this. However, the ways to do this mentioned above differ from school to school.

A different cluster is formed by those schools who see a strong need to perform a certain function and are aware of other functions on a more or less subordinate level. The judgment school refers to Knight (1921) and departs from the opportunity debate of the Kirznerian kind (Kirzner, 1973). In this view, entrepreneurial judgment under uncertainty stands in the foreground and implies taking decisions on owning, controlling, and combining heterogeneous assets on a more or less subsequent level (Foss & Klein, 2012; Foss et al., 2007). The role of uncertainty is decisive as entrepreneurial judgment involves capital ownership at stake. Another school like this is the metafunctional school which is similar and more explicit in favoring an overarching function like innovation as an umbrella for subordinate functions. To date, the metafunctional school, established in economics (Braun, 2016), did not make it to (small) business applications and is thus not explicitly placed in the space of Figure 1.1.

Three schools form another cluster in Figure 1.1. The common denominator is the principle to deal with more than one function without an ambition to structure the functions in any way. These schools list certain functions, sometimes small in number (bi-functional approaches), sometimes bigger (lists or agendas of entrepreneurial functions). Bi-functional approaches still deal with a rather limited set of functions (Tiessen, 1997; Uzunidis et al., 2014). The recent applications in SME management all focus on innovation but differ in terms of the tandem function (risk-bearing of Uzunidis et al., 2014; resource leveraging in the case of Tiessen, 1997) which is – like innovation – explorative in case of Uzunidis et al. (2014) and exploitative in case of Tiessen (1997). Among those schools favoring a list of functions, the explorative branch (explorative agenda school) centers around innovation and opportunities (e.g., Amuda, 2020). Fontela et al. (2006) name motivation, ambition, innovation, cooperation, and proactiveness as entrepreneurial functions. In so doing, their work is close to research on entrepreneurial orientation (Lumpkin & Dess, 1996) as a different, yet related branch of entrepreneurship research. For SME management this explorative orientation is useful as particularly established and traditional small businesses are often highly committed to exploiting the core business and neglecting new business exploration. The agenda school circumvents the explorative orientation by listing functions that cover a wider range. Mostly, protagonists of this school point to a diverse set of functions, all standing one by one. Gerbaulet (2016), as one representative, finds himself in the tradition of Barreto (1989) and lists innovation, risk-taking, arbitrage, and coordination, adding reputation building to the catalog. The list may be rather comprehensive but raises the question of how to combine and align entrepreneurial functions to cope with the challenges of SMEs.

The last cluster according to Figure 1.1 comprises multi-functional schools that are structured or prioritized. The Schneiderian School follows the publications of Schneider (2011) and his entrepreneurial theory of the firm. While the logic of his approach follows explananda of a theory of the firm, he focuses on survivability in competition which is highly suitable for SME management in international competition. Schneider presents an evolutionary approach and considers the dynamics of competition by emphasizing the need to cope with uncertainty and to implement change. The ambidexterity school (Chiles et al., 2007; Freiling, 2008; Chiles et al., 2010) shares these needs as well and advocates a more managerial understanding of the interplay of the explorative (innovation and risk management) and exploitative functions (internal coordination and arbitrage) to allow SMEs to make explorative or exploitative turns whenever required from a leadership angle. The ambidexterity is an issue that is already implicitly considered by Tiessen (1997) but elaborated in more detail by concepts of the main protagonists (Freiling & Lütke Schelhowe, 2014; Sundermeier et al., 2020). Moreover, the ambidexterity school differentiates – as well as the Schneiderian school – between entrepreneurial functions to be operated internally or externally from a company's viewpoint and calls for alignment of all functions (Sundermeier et al., 2020).

Having responded to the first part of the research question, the list according to Table 1.1 and the "map" according to Figure 1.1 allow an overview of the state of this theory and list both "traditional" entrepreneurial functions (innovation, risk-taking, arbitrage, and coordination), as a legacy of economic contributions to entrepreneurship theory, and more recent functions. Notably, the entrepreneurial functions introduced more recently refer to more invisible issues of leadership and SME management in the light of dealing with intangibles. Entrepreneurial storytelling and reputation management build on established structures of the business branch of entrepreneurship theory, as these functions provide legitimacy in societies and markets and help bridging between exploration and exploitation on the one hand and external and internal issues on the other (Gerbaulet, 2016; Lounsbury et al., 2019). Entrepreneurship theory comes across with a rather comprehensive and nuanced response to the first part of the research question.

As for the second part of the research question on the impact of performing entrepreneurial functions, entrepreneurship theory is not so well developed – neither the economics branch nor the business one. A main difference, however, is the simple fact that (small) business research conducted empirical fieldwork to locate potential impacts. Nevertheless, the body of empirical knowledge is still rather low. From the 28 publications of this search, most of them are conceptual, with five publications resting on qualitative empirical research and one article on quantitative research.

Empirical research is of pivotal relevance to specify the impact of the execution of entrepreneurial functions as conceptual research can primarily speculate or argue. While sound reasoning should not be under-estimated, a confrontation with real life is of the utmost importance to create feedback and to find out whether, how far, and in which direction performed entrepreneurial functions work. Freiling and Lütke Schelhowe (2014) found that all of the performed entrepreneurial functions, as well as all of them in alignment, have an impact on performance and, on a lower level, on corporate growth. Their conceptualization of entrepreneurial functions allows for explanation of about half of the variance of the performance of the SMEs they researched. Their results give rise to the impression that considering both explorative and exploitative functions are useful to an entire understanding of an entrepreneurial driven SME management.

While performance measures often dominate when it comes to SME management debates, there are many other constructs relevant to SME management in different contexts. When it comes to crises and disruptions in small businesses, the findings of Poeschl and Freiling (2020) relate to business successions in family firms and analyze whether a managerial vacuum in succession occurs and how it can be mitigated or circumvented by entrepreneurial action along the entrepreneurial functions. They stress how delegation, the development of routines, and prioritization of tasks allow family firms to perform entrepreneurial functions even if the predecessor is about to leave the company and the successor is not fully in place. Freiling (2020) found regarding startups shocked by the implications of the Covid-19 pandemic that the researched cases showed reaction patterns that can well be interpreted in terms of the ambidextrous approach to entrepreneurial functions. When environmental conditions undergo drastic changes, startups experiment and iterate by exploitative moves to cope with the new situations. When the exploitative moves do not mitigate the problem, they turn to explorative moves particularly by business model innovations. With low asset commitments due to their early stage of development, startups managed to cope with Covid-19 by entrepreneurial responses in many cases. These findings show that the way entrepreneurial functions are employed and aligned provides responsiveness to small businesses. Sundermeier et al. (2020) employ the ambidextrous approach to reveal that hubristic leadership in startups is not only detrimental in terms of company building and development but allows startups to make moves to address opportunities that would not be available otherwise. Implications like these contribute to SME management as entrepreneurial functions help in specifying leadership behavior and showing how far certain styles and intensities of leadership are beneficial or detrimental.

As a footnote, another stream of entrepreneurship theory looks at the origins of entrepreneurial functions (Uzunidis et al., 2014; Lounsbury et al., 2019). This SLR reveals asymmetry in terms of findings. Much emphasis is put on impacts of entrepreneurial functions on output and outcome measures. The question of what constitutes entrepreneurial functions, however, is almost a white spot. What the available publications reveal is the pivotal yet under-researched role of different capitals like resource capital (e.g., intellectual, social, and human capital) and institutional capital (e.g., legitimacy, norms, rules) (Lounsbury et al., 2019; similarly Uzunidis et al., 2014).

Another reason to conduct (more) empirical research is the chance to specify the constructs. While one can easily talk about arbitrage, coordination, etc., it is valuable to know what kind of activities allow the performing of these functions in reality. To develop and sharpen the constructs is accordingly another core issue of empirical research. Both qualitative and quantitative research allow insights to develop and specify or modify sub-constructs of entrepreneurial functions (Freiling & Lütke Schelhowe, 2014; Poeschl & Freiling, 2020; Sundermeier et al., 2020).

Reflections and Conclusions

Entrepreneurship theory of the business branch analyzed in this study is still in its infancy. There not many publications outside the economic core domain and, for the time being, the development is not very dynamic – although it is evident that the business oriented stream of research on entrepreneurial functions contributes meaningfully to SME management. This calls for explanations.

Basically, research on entrepreneurial functions seems to carry a heavy "load of economic history" that does not seem to be unrelated to bemoaned realization gaps (Boettke, 1994; Foss; 1994; Loasby, 2002). Given this profile, the discussion may look a bit abstract for researchers in management studies so that it is not easy to recognize and tap the theory's potential. Over and above this, this stream of entrepreneurship theory has still a strong imbalance between theory-driven and conceptual work on the one side and empirical fieldwork on the other. Most recent publications with an empirical background give rise to the impression that entrepreneurial functions are a useful means to explain causalities regarding organizational and management phenomena. Nevertheless, it is still too early for optimism in this regard, as much more fine-grained empirical research is necessary for a more educated assessment. In this respect, research could benefit from more fine-grained qualitative research that goes beyond case study research and employs action research and ethnographies for a deeper understanding of backgrounds of entrepreneurial functions, fine-grained conceptualizations, and developments over time. Moreover, quantitative research is needed to test causal relationships on a broader basis to develop findings that could be generalized.

Basically, there is considerable disconnectedness of research streams or schools belonging to this theoretical movement. The limited number of cross-citations among different publications is an indicator for a common ground that may exist but on a small level. This raises the follow-up question of whether departing from the economic roots is beneficial or detrimental for entrepreneurship theory. The above-mentioned turn to more empirical research could be useful to conduct inductive empirical research. Inductive work, e.g. inspired by grounded theory (Charmaz, 2014), would allow building theory from data. To the best of our knowledge, there are virtually no attempts so far to build constructs of entrepreneurial functions inductively. There is much room to develop meaningful conceptualizations. This may go along with the question of the identification of entrepreneurial functions that have not been discussed before or that emerge out of recent developments. The function of entrepreneurial storytelling according to Lounsbury et al. (2019) is one example for such "discoveries" of more recent times. Simultaneously, the publications of Lounsbury et al. (2019) and Gerbaulet (2016) point to phenomena of management studies that are – like values, culture, organizational identities – deeply rooted in companies and could allow new insights. At the same time questions arise over whether new developments in digitalization open the door to the identification of new entrepreneurial functions. This may relate to developments like artificial intelligence that could illuminate entrepreneurial functions differently.

Within the economic branch of entrepreneurial functions a certain "realization gap" that has emerged over time. It is a chance and a challenge of the business branch to mitigate or even fill this gap. There are some indications that more recent publications open up new avenues to close this gap and to move closer to small business reality. One of these developments is the turn from a more "mechanical" understanding of entrepreneurial functions to be fulfilled by entrepreneurially acting people inside SMEs to deeper rooted issues of sense-making in the interplay between SMEs and their social environment. There are two more recent publications that developed obviously independent from one another but share the same roots. While Gerbaulet (2016) pointed to the notion of entrepreneurs as "reputators" (a neologism both in German and English language), Lounsbury et al. (2019) referred to entrepreneurial storytelling at the company/environment interface. It is inevitable that recent contexts call for moves like that, and it is particularly this business-oriented stream of entrepreneurship theory that responded already, although it "(. . .) is marginalized (. . .) in the mainstream entrepreneurship literature" (Lounsbury et al., 2019, p. 1214). There is still much more to learn about to what extent entrepreneurial functions relate to the deep structures of companies and the interaction with the social environment. Against this background, future research finds a wide ground to advance our knowledge.

In ontological regards, the literature focused both on personal and organizational issues of performing entrepreneurial functions. It is evident that the above raised issues imply that on both ontological levels there are still important issues for future research. What is still a blind spot is the relationship with the level of entrepreneurial and innovation ecosystems. It is evident that small businesses, particularly startups, benefit considerably from active participating in entrepreneurial ecosystems. Established small businesses and ventures collaborate with increasing intensity on formats of innovation ecosystems and pool their resources. It is still unclear to what extent participation in ecosystems like that has an impact on performing entrepreneurial functions by small businesses. In the same vein, there is an exchange between small businesses and other institutions of these ecosystems so that ecosystems develop on this basis. This opens the door for analyzing the performance of entreprenɔurial functions in and of ecosystems.

Contribution and Implications

This SLR makes four contributions. First, it connects previously scattered publications in the field within a two-dimensional framework that goes beyond current systematizations in literature (e.g., Freiling, 2008). Second, in doing so, the SLR condenses research activities in three different languages and attempts to integrate important content of the non-English publications (e.g. Schneider, 2011; Boutillier & Uzunidis, 2014) in current research debates. Third, while the emphasis on entrepreneurial functions research is so far predominantly on economic publications (e.g., Mises, 1949; Kirzner, 1973; Huerta de Soto, 1994), this SLR outlines the business dimension and the related potential of the field (e.g., Lounsbury et al., 2019). Fourth, in relation to this the SLR identifies the potential of inductive studies on entrepreneurial functions to shed different light on the research field and to allow progress that builds ɔn the first attempts. This may also contribute to closing the realization gap of research on entrepreneurial functions (Boettke, 1994; Foss; 1994).

Limitations

The search of this study was, owing to the research state, rather inclusive. Most of the publications were considered for the sake of a rather comprehensive overview. This is at the expense of typical quality criteria like excluding all publicatioas beyond peer-reviewed articles. While this limitation seems to be justifiable regarding the early state of research, depending on the maturity level of research follow-up reviews could be more exclusive – and analyze how much this influences the results.

Not unusual for an SLR, the search copes with the challenge of heterogeneity. The heterogeneity in this research field, however, seems to be rather high. Publications differ in the epistemological procedure considerably, employ a variety of different lenses, and address very different empirical backgrounds. "Apples and oranges effects" are, thus, a challenge that reminds readers to handle the findings with care, particularly if contributions from different disciplinary backgrounds address similar topics. According to Fontela et al. (2006), the different "spheres" (financiaː, managerial, psychosocial) illustrate what this may imply.

As many SLRs run the risk of sorting out relevant publications, this ɛpplies for this study as well. Nevertheless, the search in two databases, with one being very inclusive and the additional check of references of reviewed publications, mitigated the problem.

Finally, the findings give rise to the impression that entrepreneurship theory in the realm of entrepreneurial functions could have some potential in terms of opportunities to inspire SME management. This relates to origins of entrepreneurial functions, cognitive and sociological foundations, or impact on performance measures. Entrepreneurship scholars tend to say that it may be a matter of opportunity recognition and opportunity (re-)creation to tap this potential.

References

Amuda, Y.J. (2020). Conceptualization of entrepreneurship education for future workforce in developing countries in the 21st century. *Academy of Strategic Management Journal*, *19*(6), 1–11.

Barreto, H. (1989). *The entrepreneur in microeconomic theory. Disappearance and explanation*. Routledge.

Bennett, N., & Lemoine, J. (2014). What VUCA really means for you. *Harvard Business Review*, *92*(1–2), 27.

Boettke, P. (1994). Alternative paths forward for Austrian economics. In P. Boettke (Ed.), *The Elgar companion to Austrian economics* (pp. 601–615), E. Elgar.

Boutillier, S., & Uzunidis, D. (2014). L'empreinte historique de la théorie de l'entrepreneur. *Revue d'Economie et de Management de l'innovation*, *45*(3), 97–119.

Braun, E. (2016). The enterprise is the actual place for the entrepreneurial function in economic theory, TUC Working Papers in Economics, No. 16. Clausthal Technical University. http://dx.doi.org/10.21268/20161214-170238

Cantillon, R. (1725/1755). *Essai sur la nature du commerce en général*. Institut Coppet.

Casson, M. (2003). *The entrepreneur – an economic theory*, Second ed. Edward Elgar.

Charmaz, K. (2014). *Constructing grounded theory*. Second ed. Sage.

Chiles, T.H., Bluedorn, A.C., & Gupta, V.K. (2007). Beyond creative destruction and entrepreneurial discovery: A radical Austrian approach to entrepreneurship. *Organization Studies*, *28*(4), 467–493.

Chiles, T.H., Tuggle, C.S., McMullen, J.S., Bierman, L., & Greening, D.W. (2010). Dynamic creation: Extending the radical Austrian approach to entrepreneurship. *Organization Studies*, *31*(1): 7–46.

Dabić, M., Vlačić, B., Paul, J., Dana, L.-P., Sahasranamam, S., & Glinka, B. (2020). Immigrant entrepreneurship: A review and research agenda. *Journal of Business Research*, *113*, 25–38. https://doi.org/10.1016/j.jbusres.2020.03.013

Dejardin, M., Nizet, J., & Van Dam, D. (2015). Entrepreneurial functions by organic farmers. In P. Kyrö (Ed.), *Handbook of entrepreneurship and sustainable development research* (pp. 392–401). E. Elgar.

Estevão, M. J., & Freiling, J. (2009). Strategieproliferation durch Kundenintegration? *Zeitschrift für Management*, *4*(3), 235–256.

Fontela, E., Guzmán, J., Pérez, M., & Santos, F.J. (2006). The art of entrepreneurial foresight. *Frontiers*, *8*(6), 3–13.

Foss, N.J. (1994). The theory of the firm: The Austrians as precursors and critics of contemporary theory. *Review of Austrian Economics*, *7*(1), 31–64.

Foss, K., Foss, N.J., & Klein, P.G. (2007). Original and derived judgment: An entrepreneurial theory of economic organization. *Organization Studies*, *28*(12), 1893–1912.

Foss, N.J., & Klein, P.G. (2012). *Organizing entrepreneurial judgment*. Cambridge University Press.

Freiling, J. (2005). Unternehmerfunktionen als Brücke zwischen Marketing und Innovationsmanagement, In J. Amelingmeyer & P.E. Harland (Eds.), *Technologiemanagement & marketing* (pp. 133–154). Gabler.

Freiling, J. (2008). SME management – what can we learn from entrepreneurship theory? *International Journal of Entrepreneurship Education*, *6*(1), 1–19.

Freiling, J. (2009). Uncertainty, innovation, and entrepreneurial functions: Working out an entrepreneurial management approach. *International Journal of Technology Intelligence and Planning, 5*(1), 22–35.

Freiling, J. (2020). Startups und COVID-19 – Entrepreneure am seidenen Faden. In J. Günther & J. Wedemeier (Eds.), *Struktureller Umbruch durch COVID-19* (pp. 27–42). HWWI.

Freiling, J., & Lütke Schelhowe, C. (2014). The impact of entrepreneurial orientation on the performance and speed of internationalization. *Journal of Entrepreneurship, Management and Innovation, 10*(4), 169–199.

Freiling, J., & Poeschl, A. (2020). Family-external business succession: The case of management buy-ins. *Journal of Small Business & Entrepreneurship, 32*. DOI:10.1080/08276331.2020.1771812

Freiling, J., & Wessels, J. (2010). Das Scheitern junger Unternehmen im Spiegel der Entrepreneurship-Theorie. *Wirtschaftspolitische Blätter, 57*(3), 315–332.

Gartner, W.B. (1989). ""Who is an entrepreneur?" is the wrong question." *American Journal of Small Business, 12*(4), 11–32.

Gerbaulet, D. (2016). *Der Unternehmer als Reputator*. Mohr Siebeck.

Gilal, F.F., Zhang, J., Paul, J., & Gilal, N.G. (2019). The role of self-determination theory in marketing science: An integrative review and agenda for research. *European Management Journal, 37*(1), 29–44.

Guzmán Cuevas, J.J. (1994). Toward a taxonomy of entrepreneurial theories. *International Small Business Journal, 12*(4), 77–88.

Hébert, R.F., & Link, A.N. (1988). *The entrepreneur: Mainstream views and radical critiques*. Second ed. Praeger.

Hébert, R.F., & Link, A.N. (2009). *A history of entrepreneurship*. Routledge.

Huerta de Soto, J. (1994). *Socialismo, Cálculo Económico y Función Empresarial*. Unión Editorial.

Hulbert, B., Gilmore, A., & Carson, D. (2015). Opportunity recognition by growing SMEs: A managerial or entrepreneurial function? *Journal of Strategic Marketing, 23*(7), 616–642.

Keilbach, M. (2009). Why entrepreneurship matters for Germany. In Z.J. Acs, D.B. Audretsch, & R.J. Strom (Eds.), *Entrepreneurship, growth, and public policy* (pp. 202–215). Cambridge University Press.

Keyhani, M. (2019). Computational modeling of entrepreneurship grounded in Austrian economics: Insights for strategic entrepreneurship and the opportunity debate. *Strategic Entrepreneurship Journal, 13*(2), 221–240.

Kirzner, I.M. (1973). *Competition and entrepreneurship*. Chicago University Press.

Knight, F. (1921). *Risk, uncertainty and profit*. Houghton Mifflin.

Kraus, S., Breier, M., & Dasí-Rodriguez, S. (2020). The art of crafting a systematic literature review in entrepreneurship research. *International Entrepreneurship and Management Journal, 16*, 1023–1042. https://doi.org/10.1007/s11365-020-00635-4

Littell, J.H., Corcoran, J., & Pillai, V.K. (2008). *Systematic reviews and metaanalysis*. Oxford University Press.

Loasby, B.J. (2002). Content and method: An epistemic perspective on some historical episodes. *European Journal of the History of Economic Thought, 9*(1), 72–95.

Lounsbury, M., Gehman, J., & Glynn, M.A. (2019). Beyond homo entrepreneurus: Judgment and the theory of cultural entrepreneurship. *Journal of Management Studies, 56*(6), 1214–1236.

Lumpkin, G.T., & Dess, G.G. (1996). Clarifying the entrepreneurial orientation construct and linking it to performance. *Academy of Management Review, 21*, 135–172.

March, J.G. (1991). Exploration and exploitation in organizational learning. *Organization Science, 2*(1), 71–87.

Marchesnay, M. (2008). L'entrepreneur: Une histoire française. *Revue française de gestion, 188–189*, 77–95.

Mezias, S.J., & Kuperman, J.C. (2001). The community dynamics of entrepreneurship: The birth of the American film industry, 1895–1929. *Journal of Business Venturing, 16*(3), 209–233.

Mises, L.V. (1949). *Human action – a treatise on economics*. Yale University Press.

Mishra, C., & Zachary, R.K. (2015). The theory of entrepreneurship. *Entrepreneurship Research Journal, 5*(4), 251–268.

Palmatier, R.W., Houston, M.B., & Hulland, J. (2018). Review articles: Purpose, process, and structure. *Journal of the Academy of Marketing Science, 46*(1), 1–5. https://doi.org/10.1007/s11747-017-0563-4

Paul, J., & Criado, A.R. (2020). The art of writing literature review: What do we know and what do we need to know? *International Business Review, 29*(4), 101717. https://doi.org/10.1016/j.ibusrev.2020.101717

Paul, J., Lim, W.M., O'Cass, A, Hao, A.W., & Bresciani S. (2021). Scientific procedures and rationales for systematic literature reviews (SPAR-4-SLR). *International Journal of Consumer Studies, 45*, O1–O16. https://doi.org/10.1111/ijcs.12695

Paul, J., & Rosado-Serrano, A. (2019). Gradual internationalization vs. born-global/international new venture models: A review and research agenda. *International Marketing Review, 36*(6), 830–858. https://doi.org/10.1108/IMR-10-2018-0280

Peng, M.W., Lee, S.-H., & Hong, S.J. (2014). Entrepreneurs as intermediaries. *Journal of World Business, 49*, 21–31.

Poeschl, A., & Freiling, J. (2020). The way toward a new entrepreneurial balance in business succession processes: The case of management buy-ins. *Journal of Organizational Change Management, 33*(1), 157–180.

Reckenfelderbäumer, M. (2001). *Zentrale Dienstleistungsbereiche und Wettbewerbsfähigkeit*. Gabler.

Sautet, F. (2017). Austrian market theory and the entrepreneurial function as opportunity recognition. In C. Léger-Jarniou, & S. Tegtmeier (Eds.), *Research handbook on entrepreneurial opportunities* (pp. 88–112). E. Elgar.

Schneider, D. (2011). *Betriebswirtschaftslehre als Einzelwirtschaftstheorie der Institutionen*. Gabler.

Schoppe, S.G., Wass von Czege, A., Münchow, M.-M., Stein, I., & Zimmer, K. (1995). *Moderne Theorie der Unternehmung*. Oldenbourg.

Schumpeter, J.A. (1911/1934). *Theorie der wirtschaftlichen Entwicklung*. Duncker & Humblot (The theory of economic development. Transaction Books).

Sundermeier, J., Gersch, M., & Freiling, J. (2020). Hubristic start-up founders: The neglected bright and inevitable dark manifestations of hubristic leadership in new venture creation processes. *Journal of Management Studies, 57*(5), 1037–1067.

Tiessen, J.H. (1997). Individualism, collectivism, and entrepreneurship: A framework for international comparative research. *Journal of Business Venturing, 12*(5), 367–384.

Tranfield, D., Denyer, D., & Smart, P. (2003). Towards a methodology for developing evidence-informed management knowledge by means of systematic review. *British Journal of Management, 14*(3), 207–222.

Uzunidis, D., Boutillier, S., & Laperche, B. (2014). The entrepreneur's 'resource potential' and the organic square of entrepreneurship: Definition and application to the French case. *Journal of Innovation and Entrepreneurship, 3*(1), 1–17.

Justin L. Davis, John H. Batchelor, W. Timothy O'Keefe,
and William McDowell

2 Formal but Illegitimate? Examining the Mongrel Economy

Abstract: This chapter extends research examining economies in which SMEs operate. We propose the presence of the mongrel economy (i.e., comprised of legal but illegitimate businesses). We discuss implications of this economy and its similarities and differences from the formal and informal economies proposed by Webb et al. (2009). In this conceptual chapter, we investigate how SMEs are connected to the mongrel economy and how constituent associations can be used as low-cost legitimacy tools (Austin et al. 2006; Murphy et al., 2007). Other forms of economies are discussed to provide clarity on how various economies operate, thus contrasting economies to illustrate their differences. Future directions of research related to the informal and mongrel economies are provided. Additionally, specific opportunities for SMEs in the mongrel economy are presented.

Keywords: informal economy, institutional theory, social capital, legitimacy, SMEs

Introduction

Entrepreneurship is dependent on the ability to identify and exploit opportunities (Jones & Barnir, 2019; Filser et al., 2020). By their nature, the informal, renegade, and mongrel economies provide a setting of enhanced opportunity, lower barriers to entry, and superior financial returns in comparison to the formal economy for some SMEs (see Joshi et al., 2014 for discussion). Regardless of the depth in which a firm or individual participates in these economies, the potential benefits of each economy can be enticing and/or, sometimes, make an opportunity appropriate (or not) for pursuit. Here the decision to choose which economy to enter should be a strategic choice used to position the enterprise in the most favorable economy based on the unique aspects of the individual entity.

Webb et al. (2009) discussed the various economic boundaries that organizations operate within. These included the formal, informal, or renegade economy (see Figure 2.1). This positioning is based on the organizational means (operations) and ends (output) being legal/illegal and legitimate/illegitimate at both the formal and informal institutional levels. Their study focused primarily on the informal economy, including the operations

Justin L. Davis, John H. Batchelor, W. Timothy O'Keefe, University of West Florida, Pensacola, Florida
William McDowell, McCoy College of Business at Texas State University

https://doi.org/10.1515/9783110747652-003

taking place in this economy and how regulation, institutions, and identities play a role in this setting.

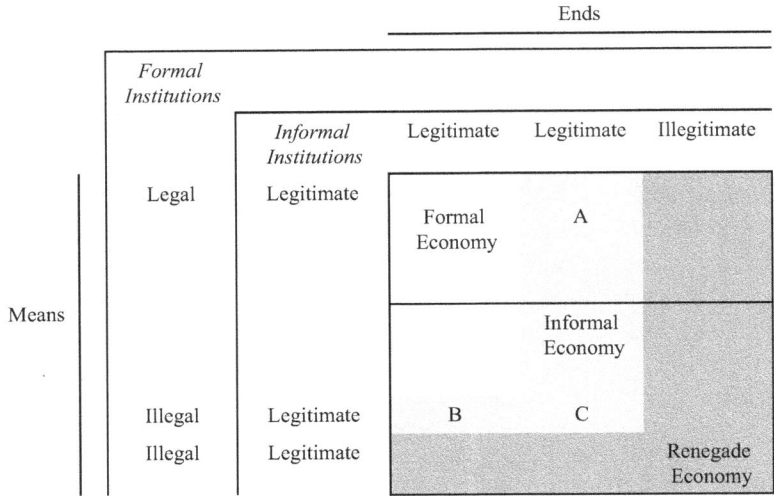

Figure 2.1: Institutional categories of entrepreneurial activities.

The current study builds on the work of Webb and colleagues (2009). A review of literature in the area of informal economies and renegade economies is provided. Then, using an institution's perspective, we provide a discussion of an additional economic positioning in which firms operate legal businesses (both means and ends) at a formal institutional level, but are considered illegitimate (either means and/or ends) at an informal institutional level. In doing this, we introduce the mongrel economy and emphasize the social, regulative, and institutional elements at play in this part of the legal business climate. We further address the social, institutional, and regulative elements at play in the renegade economy and the varying legitimacy of the activities in this economy at an informal institutional level. Further, opportunities specific to SMEs with regard to this economy are explored.

Specific consideration is given to the varying role and importance of the different types of social capital (legitimacy), depending on the economy in which an organization is operating. We make propositions based on the similarities, differences, and crossover between the formal, mongrel, informal, and renegade economies. We conclude with a discussion of the growing need for research on mongrel, informal, and renegade economies. Specific discussion is given on the role of SMEs in such economies. Emphasis is placed on directions for future research and the need to assess institutions at the interplay between the different economies.

Literature Review

In this section we discuss the institutional categories of entrepreneurship activity outlined by Webb et al (2009). Further we add the new categorization of a "mongrel" economy that brings additional clarity to the role of legitimacy as it relates to legal enterprises.

Informal Economy

There is a growing body of research that focuses on the informal economy (Ferreira et al., 2019). Webb et al. (2009) suggest that informal markets emerge as a result of incongruence between formal and informal institutions. Differing views of what is considered to be "legitimate" by formal and informal institutions (or groups) will lead to the emergence of these informal markets. The ability to recognize and exploit these emerging markets can lead to exchange opportunities for entrepreneurs. Informal institutions are, by definition, illegal in some aspect (i.e., means or ends). However, they are also considered legitimate by informal institutions based on the social acceptance of the means and/or ends by a large group in society (Webb et al., 2009). Thus, organizations conducting business in the informal economy operate within the norms, values, and beliefs of at least one large group in a social system, providing legitimacy for the actions regardless of legality.

Formal Economy

The clear demarcation of formal vs. informal/renegade is the legality of all operations – regardless of legitimacy. In their model, legitimacy is a necessary but not sufficient element for an organization to participate in the formal economy. The activity/organization must also be legal as assessed by formal institutions to fall into this formal economy classification. In essence, the definition of formal vs. informal is dependent on issues such as formal tax filings, reporting of required information to governing authorities, and adherence to labor and/or product-level minimum standards.

An embedded assumption in the Webb et al. (2009) model is the co-alignment between legality and legitimacy in the formal economy. This is evident in their assertion that all activities falling into the "Formal Economy" category are assumed to be legitimate by all informal institutions in both "means" and "ends." Thus, the model supports the assertion that all institutions assessed as legal by formal governing regulative institutions are, by default, considered to be legitimate at an informal institutional level, and operate within the bounds of the formal economy. This all-inclusive categorization fails to consider the potential for incongruence between legality and legitimacy. Thus, we propose the mongrel economy as occupying the space of legal, yet illegitimate. This categorization is discussed later in this section.

Renegade Economy

Investigation of the assumption of legality questions the existence of a black and white view of the issue and begs for the consideration of the existence of a continuum. Legality is dictated formally through regulative institutions in a given society. These laws vary by country, making country context an important factor to consider especially for immigrant entrepreneurship (Dabic et al., 2020b). By law, there are certain taxes, regulation, hiring, and other standard requirements for businesses operating in the formal economy. Thus, the line between legality and illegality provides a very clear demarcation between operating in the formal vs. informal economy – if a firm is operating outside the legal expectations imposed by regulation in a society, it is operating outside the formal economy. However, once deemed to be acting in an illegal fashion, one must further distinguish between those firms operating in the informal economy by using either/both legitimate means and legitimate ends. A firm using illegitimate means that results in illegitimate ends is then classified as participating in the renegade (criminal) economy.

Mongrel Economy

The discussion up to this point begs for the analysis of firms that are operating in the formal economy but are potentially viewed as illegitimate. We believe this to be a gap in the literature that has yet to be addressed. Thus, the important question here is, "are all legally operating firms considered to be formal?" That is, does legal mean legitimate? We answer this question by arguing that there is an additional legal category for organizations that are legal but lack (or have yet to achieve) legitimacy. We term such organizations as operating in the "mongrel" economy.

At this point in time, most research in this area has viewed legality synonymously with legitimacy when examining the economic categorical positioning of a firm. However, if legitimacy is defined as "what some large groups in a particular society understand to be . . . *legitimate* – as specified by norms, values, and beliefs," then the assumption of the co-presence of legality and legitimacy in all situations is misplaced (Webb et al., 2009, p. 492). Thus, it is not unreasonable to assume that there are numerous organizations in place in what is considered to be the formal economy that are viewed by large groups (or the majority of society) as being illegitimate. Several examples are useful for discussion of this discrepancy. For instance, in 1973, abortion procedures were legalized. Overnight, the illegal abortion clinics in society went from being forced to operate in the informal economy due to their illegal statu to being able to operate legally in society. However, given the long-standing debate on the ethical and moral views on the practice of abortion procedures, it is safe to say that even after the legalization of abortion clinics, there exists a large group in society who views both the means and ends of this business as illegitimate. For instance, the second largest state in the USA recently passed legislation severely restricting the right to abortion in the state (Planned Parenthood, 2021). From a global perspective, most Central American, South American, and African countries have abortion restrictions if not a ban on abortion altogether, whereas North America and Europe are much less restrictive on access to abortion (World Population Review, 2022). Thus, substantial debate exists on the topic of abortion in the USA and around the globe.

A second example is prostitution. Nevada legalized prostitution in 1971. However, research has shown that prostitution is viewed as socially unacceptable behavior by the vast majority of society (Anderson, 2002). Thus, we again have a legal business operation which is operating in the formal sector of the economy but viewed as illegitimate by a large, even vast majority, of society at large. A third example is the adult film industry. In this case, we have a multi-billion-dollar entertainment industry that is viewed as socially unacceptable by a large group of society. However, regardless of being viewed as illegitimate, the black and white classification system we currently have would place these organizations in the formal economy, along with educational institutions, religious organizations, and other traditionally "pure" organizations.

The issue of legitimacy as discussed above is not necessarily one of an ethical nature, but a question examining the current classification system used for identifying firms operating inside and outside of the formal economy. That is, there are a lot of unknowns when deeming whether firms are legitimate. While the line of demarcation between legality and illegality is very clear, this clarity is offset by the immense gray area surrounding the distinction between legitimate and illegitimate organizations. Thus, we define the mongrel economy as one that is legal (technically) yet illegitimate in the eyes of a large group of the society in which the economy is embedded. To provide clarity, Figure 2.2 offers a two-by-two matrix of the four economies discussed herein and their corresponding legal/legitimacy classifications.

	ILLEGAL	LEGAL
LEGITIMATE	Informal	Formal
ILLEGITIMATE	Renegade	Mongrel

Figure 2.2: Economy category quadrants.

SMEs and new firms face multiple challenges or liabilities. One of the most mentioned of these for SMEs is the liability of newness (Maurer et al., 2022). Establishing legitimacy is one way for firms to overcome this liability (Rutherford et al., 2018). The most relevant way to overcome the liability of newness is to be viewed as legitimate by one's stakeholders (Choi & Shepherd, 2005; Nagy & Lohrke, 2010). It is important to view firm legitimacy as a continuum instead of a dichotomous variable. Although it is a continuum, there is a threshold legitimacy firms must reach to be perceived as legitimate by stakeholders and to remain viable (Rutherford & Buller, 2007; Rutherford et al., 2016).

To overcome the liability of newness and be perceived by stakeholders as legitimate, firms can use reputational signals to substantiate their legitimacy and mitigate negatives such as the liability of newness (O'Toole & Ciochta, 2019). Large firms have more resources to expend on legitimacy efforts than SMEs. As public policy attempts to help firms overcome the liability of newness tend to be ineffective (DeVaughn & Leary, 2018), SMEs are on their own to establish legitimacy. As such, legitimacy cost can be very expensive (Connelly et al., 2011) and lessen profitability (Kirmani & Rao, 2000). Thus, in many cases, such "high quality" signals may not be an option for most SMEs. Thus SMEs must rely on low cost legitimacy symbols such as founder credibility with stakeholders and responsiveness to customers (Zott & Huy, 2007). Specifically, SMEs can use constituent associations and venture identities and goals as low-cost legitimacy techniques (see Murphy et al., 2019; Murphy et al., 2007: Austin et al., 2006).

From a strategic perspective, selecting the appropriate (favorable) environment is key to executing a successful legitimacy strategy (Davis et al., 2008; McDowell et al., 2016; Scott, 1995; Suchman, 1995). Thus we argue that the mongrel economy is an excellent environment for SMEs to execute a low cost legitimacy strategy by appealing to niche or underrepresented aspects of society. The following discussion sheds light on how obtaining legitimacy with stakeholders in economies outside of what is viewed as "legitimate" by society can in some instances be inexpensive and effective.

Temporal Effects on Economic Classification

Shifting Societal Views

While the model in Figure 2.3 provides a theoretical foundation for classifying the different economies in the market, its practical application is subject to changing societal beliefs and legislative decision-making, that is, what is illegitimate today may not be tomorrow. For example, the issue of gay rights has been at the forefront of political discussions since the 1980s. If applying this model to businesses focused on providing a product offering to the homosexual population in the 1970s or 1980s, it is likely that these companies would fall into the "mongrel" or "informal" economies. However, given the continued growth and acceptance of this alternative lifestyle in our society (domestic U.S.), these same organizations, providing the same product offering, would now be placed in either the formal, or sometimes "mongrel" economies – depending on group view. Hence, if a SME used a low cost penetration strategy to appeal to homosexual stakeholders early on, as acceptance grew, so would the firm's legitimacy.

	Formal	Mongrel	Informal	Renegade
Formal Regulation	X	X	–	–
Informal Regulation	X	X	X	X
Ease of access to SC	Very easy	Difficult	Easy	Very difficult
Strength of Social Ties	Weak-Strong	Medium – Very strong	Strong-Very Strong	Very Strong

Figure 2.3: Economic Differences Based on Economy.

Shifting Regulatory Environment

Related to this topic is emergent regulative change and the resulting impact on firm classification in the formal/informal economy. For example, the regulative discussion of the potential legalization of marijuana has been a topic of debate for several years (Caulkins et al., 2014). While the trade of marijuana in the U.S. is believed to be a 92-billion-dollar industry (Long, 2021), this trade is considered part of the informal, or even renegade, economy. When forms of marijuana legalization passed legalizing aspects of this product, it fell into the formal economy – indicating that it is considered both legal and legitimate in some states. In this way, the current model, as proposed by Webb et al. (2009) again synonymizes legality and legitimacy, assuming that formal regulative acceptance is representative of both formal and informal legitimacy. However, an obvious argument would be that regardless of legality, a large group of society would still consider the sale and/or use of marijuana to be illegitimate or unethical at best. With this recognition, there appears to be a gap in the existing model of the formal/informal economies as it currently stands. The mongrel economy classification fills this gap in this situation. Here the firms (specifically SMEs) used appealing to underrepresented subgroups of society as a low-cost targeted legitimacy strategy.

The Economy Distinction of the Mongrel Firm: Black and White or Shades of Gray?

Research on the informal economy has sought to identify the distinguishing characteristics between the formal and informal economies. The most observable distinction is the legal/illegal dichotomy. At its most basic level, this distinction is appropriate at a local, state, and/or national level. However, the transference of such distinction is dependent on the regulative setting of interest and fails to be generalizable across cultural boundaries. To further complicate this categorization debate, we must also consider the presence of the renegade economy and, as presented in the current chapter, the mongrel economy. The renegade economy operates outside of the law, while the mongrel economy operates within the law but is socially questionable by the majority (or vocal majority) of society. This space offers special opportunities to SMEs not available in other economies to help them get over the disadvantages relative to larger firms, such as the liability of newness. Specifically, large firms may be reluctant to enter into a market that is out of the mainstream because it may harm their legitimacy with existing stakeholders, whereas SMEs are not under the same constraints. Thus, the ethically questionable (by some) nature of the mongrel economy can serve as a barrier to entry that benefits SMEs.

SMEs face multiple challenges not faced by larger more established firms. Many of these tie to a lack of structure (Bruderl & Schussler, 1990). SMEs often lack strong ties to suppliers and customers (Freeman et al., 1983). Many of the aforementioned issues are related to what is called the liability of smallness and newness (Stinchcumbe, 1965). In addition to the issues SMEs face due to their size, they also face issues related to obtaining resources because they are small, hence they also suffer from the additional liability of smallness (Gimenez-Fernandez et al., 2020). Thus, taken as a whole, many of the issues SMEs face are due to size and newness (related to legitimacy), and the ensuing lack of access to customers, distribution channels, marketing, and the like.

Herein we argue that the mongrel economy (legal yet illegitimate) is a niche that offers opportunities for SMEs to overcome the liabilities of newness and smallness. As the mongrel economy is legal yet illegitimate, it is not literally underground or a black market, it is simply not in the mainstream and not viewed as legitimate. Although a company may lack legitimacy within society as a whole, it can possess legitimacy with a subset of consumers. One example of such legitimacy is the growth of "free speech" platforms.

In the fall of 2020, when the major social media and streaming platforms began censoring content to appeal to what is considered mainstream, or socially acceptable, it opened the door for other platforms to market themselves as "free speech" platforms. Since that time, new networking and streaming platforms have increased in number and popularity. Here founder credibility (Rutherford et al., 2018) and reputational signals (O'Toole & Ciuchta, 2019) are used in place of more expensive legitimacy signals such as elaborate facilities and high paid executives. These include GAB, Rumble, Odysee, and BitChute. The one thing these companies have in common is their legitimacy as "free speech" or alternative viewpoint platforms to their users. Most of these platforms draw their popularity and success from the legitimacy of their founders. For instance, GABs CEO Andrew Torba is a very vocal Christian, conservative, and describes himself as an "American populist." While these views may not always align with mainstream secular society, they do resonate with a large and growing customer/consumer base. This is just one example of how the mongrel economy operates and the opportunities that exist therein for SMEs. Thus, it is argued that the mongrel economy offers a fruitful playing ground for SMEs to operate and offers special opportunities to overcome the liabilities of newness and smallness they may face in the formal economy without having to resort to the renegade or informal economy, or use expensive (profit reducing) legitimacy signals.

Another fruitful area for SMEs in the mongrel economy is to use it as a springboard into the formal economy by leveraging legitimacy with a portion of society then pivoting to the mainstream. SMEs can act on opportunities that might be considered illegitimate by a broader group of society while applying behaviors (Nagy et al., 2012) and adopting strategies that raise legitimacy (Ueberbacher, 2014; Zimmerman and Zeitz, 2002) across a wider constituency.

For instance, Black Rifle Coffee Company founded in 2014 started off as a niche coffee company targeted toward conservative leaning coffee consumers. The company founders initially marketed the company using their legitimacy as being owned by former members of the US military to appeal to a conservative subset of society. They used their lack of legitimacy with mainstream society as a selling point to their target group of customers to overcome the liabilities of smallness and newness similar in approach to informal entrepreneurship in developing economies (Williams et al., 2017). This launch strategy was successful as their product gained popularity with this target market. During the summer of 2021, the company's CEO Evan Hafer seemed to distance himself from his customer base in an interview with the New York Times (Zenge, 2021). This interview was perceived by many of his customers as a betrayal, as Hafer seemed to espouse moderate values (as compared to his previous right-leaning statements). But, viewed from a strategic point of view, it could be argued that Hafer simply used his legitimacy as a former Green Beret to overcome the shortcomings of being a small, new SME and now that his company is no longer subject to such issues (as it has grown substantially) he is merely trying to pivot to the formal economy by attempting to establish legitimacy with the broader vocal majority of society. While the ethics of such a move (stating misleading personal beliefs to gain market share) might be considered questionable, it is a viable option for SMEs to initially enter a market in the mongrel economy then pivot to the formal economy once the initial benefits of such a penetration strategy are exhausted. Such a path would not be unlike mainstreaming new ventures that launch in the informal economy and migrate over time to the formal (Light, 2004).

Social Capital in the Informal, Renegade, and Mongrel Economies

Informal economies are characterized as illegal yet legitimate. This may seem almost oxymoronic, but upon closer examination the existence of such economies becomes quickly apparent. For example, religious organizations are historically considered legitimate organizations. Further, feeding the poor and providing for the less fortunate is a legitimate cornerstone of most societies. But what happens when these legitimate activities become illegal? For instance, Linnekin (2013) discusses how many local ordinances and laws have made feeding the poor a crime. Thus, overnight, the legitimate practice of churches feeding the poor is now operating in the informal sector.

Cannatelli et al. (2019) discuss how products or services that are viewed by society to be detrimental to society are viewed as illegitimate. Legitimate activities are those that produce positive outcomes (Aldrich & Fiol, 1994; Suchman, 1995). In this context, social capital related to legitimacy is based on producing positive outcomes for society. Feeding the poor and needy is legitimate because of its positive goal boosted by the longstanding social capital churches have built up over time for such endeavors. As an example, the Bread of Life mission in Seattle has been feeding the poor for over 70 years (Linnekin, 2013). By the city of Seattle making such activities illegal, they moved the religious organizations activities into the informal economy rather than the renegade economy (illegal and illegitimate) because of the social capital they hold for their longstanding positive work with the needy. Thus, social capital is a defining point of informal economies and can be leveraged by SMEs to establish legitimacy, as stated in the following proposition:

Proposition 1

As informal economies are, by nature, illegal yet legitimate, social capital is crucial as it is the basis on which legitimacy is based. Therefore, firm social capital (i.e. founder reputation with stakeholders) is a strategic advantage for SMEs in the informal economy.

The renegade economy is characterized as illegal and illegitimate. For SMEs, especially those in mature markets, this is a potential opportunity. This is especially true for SMEs run by people high in the Dark Triad personality traits of psychopathy and Machiavellianism. This special case occurs because they are less constrained by social norms (Kelley et al., 2021) and are more likely to take a bottom-line mentality to unethical practices (see Eissa et al., 2019). Further, some research argues that SMEs employing those high in psychopathy and Machiavellianism excel in creativity and innovation (Kelley et al., 2021). In addition, the excitement of doing something that runs contrary to the law and social norms is appealing to such individuals in its own right. In addition to personality, there is also research that links cognitive factors to entrepreneurial orientation that may come into play. One specific study looked at video gamers (especially those who play "shooting" games) and opportunity recognition (Nieman et al., 2020). Such individuals may also be attracted to this economy because of the excitement associated with such ventures.

In addition to attracting performance driven individuals high in creativity and innovation, renegade economies also offer the prospect of lower tax and compliance costs, relative to formal economies. These lower costs free up additional capital for investment in the firm. For such SMEs, this lower cost can translate into faster growth, especially for newer firms and SMEs, than established larger firms in the formal economy (see Krasniqi, 2007 for discussion). As Rutherford et al. (2018) point out, legitimacy can be expensive. Taken together, the ability to attract highly productive people who may not be accepted in the formal economy (those high in psychopathy and Machiavellianism) and lower cost structure provide certain benefits to SMEs that may not be available in other economies, as stated formally in the following proposition.

Proposition 2

The function of social capital in the renegade economy (illegal and illegitimate) as a regulative force provides efficiencies (i.e., no pay minimums and maximums, potential monopolies, costly legitimacy signals, and no legal institutional barriers) and opportunities for SMEs that are not available in the formal economy.

The mongrel economy is characterized as legal yet illegitimate (by broader society). This is an odd group of characteristics as many assume legality and legitimacy go hand in hand. But this assumption of legality and legitimacy always occurring synonymously, as in the formal economy, is not always valid, and is the key contribution of this conceptual chapter. As discussed earlier, some forms of commerce are completely legal yet not entirely socially acceptable to broader society (or a vocal minority). This is where the mongrel economy operates. This odd grouping of characteristics stands to offer certain benefits for some SMEs.

Generally speaking, the business world in the USA is a secular society (King, 2008). As such, secular beliefs are the mainstream and what is considered socially acceptable. Thus, as society views secularism as the "legitimate" point of view, anything outside of that is considered illegitimate, by broader society. This is an area of opportunity for SMEs who operate outside of the secular environment, such as Christian-based organizations. For the subset of consumers who do not follow secular beliefs, firms run by like-minded individuals are very appealing to this subset of customers who actively seek out such organizations and view them as possessing legitimacy. This can lead to the advantage of being able to sell products at premium prices by appealing to their values (see Ha-Brookshire & Norum, 2011), often using the founder (s) reputation or firm goals as the basis for legitimacy. By appealing to these beliefs, SMEs can connect to the mongrel economy.

To illustrate this point, Pure Flix is a subscription based streaming platform that espouses Christian beliefs and films. It was founded by a devout Christian, David A. R. White. Mr. White is viewed by many in the Christian community as someone who stands up for his beliefs and as a trailblazer in the faith-based film industry. Hence, he is viewed as legitimate by the Christian community but not by the greater secular society. He used his legitimacy with the minority Christian community to compete and thrive outside the norms of society. For example, Netflix currently charges $8.99 for its basic subscription. By comparison, Pure Flix charges $12.99. This is almost a 50% premium, which is rather remarkable considering that the rather small Pure Flix has much less content than Netflix. In essence, customers are paying a premium and attracted to the firm because of the status/legitimacy of the individual at the helm of the organization rather than value for their subscription fees. Recently Pure Flix's streaming service was acquired by Sony Pictures (Faughnder, 2020). Although the specifics of the deal are not public, it is assumed that this was a financial win for the founders of Pure Flix. Thus, by appealing to values that are outside the secular norm of society, such SMEs can foster consumer loyalty and exact premium pricing by leveraging the legitimacy/social capital of the leaders of the SME and the mission and values articulated by the leaders. Legitimacy with one's minority consumer base is vital in such situations (especially for SMEs) as stated in the following proposition:

Proposition 3

As the mongrel economy is legal yet illegitimate, legitimacy with the minority who approves of the economy is vital. Social capital with one's constituents (although outside of the norm of society) is vital to creating legitimacy and thus the success of firms operating in the mongrel economy.

Future Research

Future research should empirically investigate what legitimacy strategies are most effective for SMEs in the mongrel economy. Specifically, future research should look at low-cost strategies focusing on alleviating the liabilities of newness and smallness while increasing profit. Further, legitimate firms are less likely to enter informal or illegitimate economies, thus creating a barrier to entry, positively benefiting SMEs over large organizations in illegitimate and/or informal situations. Finally, more empirical research is needed to look at how SMEs use legitimacy with a minority community (outside the vocal mainstream of society) to initially operate and overcome the liabilities of being a SME before pivoting into the formal economy.

Conclusion

Herein we created and expounded upon a new entrepreneurial institutional category. This is a legal economy that adds complexity to the discussion of what is a "formal" economy. It is argued herein that the "mongrel," or legal and informal economy, is distinct from the formal economy described by Webb et al. (2009). We argue that this economy has specific characteristics that make it attractive to SMEs when the firm has legitimacy with a specific subset of customers outside the norms of greater society.

References

Aldrich, H.E. (1995). Entrepreneurial strategies in new organizational populations. In I. Bull, H. Thomas, & G. Willard (Eds.), *Entrepreneurship: Perspectives on theory building* (pp. 91–108). Elsevier.

Aldrich, E.A., & Fiol, C.M. (1994). Fools rush in? The institutional context of industry creation. *Academy of Management Review, 19*(4), 645–670. https://doi.org/10.5465/amr.1994.9412190214

Anderson, S.A. (2002). Prostitution and sexual autonomy: Making sense of the prohibition of prostitution. *Ethics, 112*(4), 748–480. https://doi.org/10.1086/339672

Austin, J., Stephenson, H., & Wei-Skillern, J. (2006). Social and commercial entrepreneurship: Same, different, or both? *Entrepreneurship Theory and Practice, 30*(1), 1–22.

Beck, T.E., Lengnick-Hall, C.A., Lengnick-Hall, M.L. (2008). Solutions out of context: Examining the transfer of business concepts to non-profit organizations. *Nonprofit Management and Leadership, 19*(2), 153–171.

Bourdieu, P., & Wacquant, L. (1997). *An invitation to reflexive sociology.* University of Chicago Press.

Bruderl, J., & Schussler, R. (1990). Organizational mortality: The liabilities of newness and adolescence. *Administrative Science Quarterly, 35*, 530–547. https://doi.org/10.2307/2393316

Burch, G., Batchelor, J., Reid, R., Fezzey, T., & Kelley, C. (2021). The role of employee personality on information security. *ISACA Journal.* https://www.isaca.org/resources/isaca-journal

Bygrave, W.D., and Hofer, C.W. (1991). Theorizing about entrepreneurship. *Entrepreneurship Theory and Practice, 16*(2), 13–22. https://doi.org/10.1177/104225879201600203

Cannatelli, B.L., Smith, B.R., & Sydow, A. (2019). Entrepreneurship in the controversial economy: Toward a research agenda. *Journal of Business Ethics, 155*, 837–851. https://doi.org/10.1007/s10551-017-3482-x

Caulkins, J.P., Hawken, A., Kilmer, B., & Kleiman, M. (2014). *Marijuana legalization: What everyone needs to know.* Oxford University Press, Incorporated.

Choi, Y.R., & Shepherd, D.A. (2005). Stakeholder perceptions of age and other dimensions of newness. *Journal of Management, 31*, 573–596.

Connelly, B.L., Certo, S.T., Ireland, R.D., & Reutzel, C.R. (2011). Signaling theory: A review and assessment. *Journal of Management, 37*, 39–67.

Dabic, M., Maley, J., Dana, L., Novak, I., Pellegrini, M., & Caputo, A. (2020a). Pathways of SME international: A bibliometric and systematic review. *Small Business Economics, 55*, 705–725. https://doi.org/10.1007/-/s1187-019-00181-6

Dabic, M., Vlacic, B., Paul, J., Dana, L., Sahasranamam, S., & Glinka, B. (2020b). Immigrant entrepreneurship: A review and research agenda. *Journal of Business Research, 113*, 25–38. https://doi.org/10.1016/j.jbusres.2020.03.013

David, R.J., Sine, W.D., & Haveman, H.A. (2013). Seizing opportunity in emerging fields: How institutional entrepreneurs legitimated the professional form of management consulting. *Organization Science, 24*(2), 356–377.

Davis, M.A., Miles, G., & McDowell, W.C. (2008). Environmental scanning as a moderator of strategy–performance relationships: An empirical analysis of physical therapy facilities. *Health Services Management Research, 21*(2), 81–92.

DeVaughn, M. L., & Leary, M. M. (2018). Learn by doing or learn by failing? The paradoxical effect of public policy in averting the liability of newness. *Group & Organization Management, 43*(6), 871–905.

Eissa, G., Wyland, R., Lester, S.W., & Gupta, R. (2019). Winning at all costs: An exploration of bottom-line mentality, Machiavellianism, and organizational citizenship behavior. *Human Resource Management Journal, 29*, 469–489. https://doi.org/10.1111/1748-8583.12241

Ferreira, J.J., Fernandes, C.I., & Kraus, S. (2019). Entrepreneurship research: Mapping intellectual structures and research trends. *Review of Managerial Science, 13*(1), 181–205.

Filser, M., Tiberius, V., Kraus, S., Zeitlhofer, T., Kailer, N., & Müller, A. (2020). Opportunity recognition: Conversational foundations and pathways ahead. *Entrepreneurship Research Journal.* https://doi.org/10.1515/erj-2020-0124

Freeman, J.C., Carroll, G.R., & Hannan, M.T. (1983). The liability of newness: Age dependence in organizational death rates. *American Sociology Review, 48*, 692–710. https://doi.org/10.2307/2094928

Gedajlovic, E., Honig, B., Moore, C.B., Payne, G.T., & Wright, M. (2013). Social capital and entrepreneurship: A schema and research agenda. *Entrepreneurship Theory and Practice, 37*(3), 455–478. https://doi.org/10.1111/etap.12042

Gimenez-Fernandez, E.M., Sandulli, F.D., & Bogers, M. (2020). Unpacking liabilities of newness and smallness in innovative start-ups: Investigating the differences in innovation performance between new and older small firms. *Research Policy, 49*(10), 1–13. https://doi.org/10.1016/j.respol.2020.104049

Faughnder, R. (2020). Seeking Christian viewers, Soby acquires "God's not dead" producers' streaming service. *Los Angeles Times*. https://www.latimes.com/entertainment-arts/business/story/2020-11-12/seeking-christian-viewers-sony-acquires-faith-based-streaming-service

Ha-Brookshire, J.E., & Norum, P.S. (2011). Willingness to pay for socially responsible products: Case of cotton apparel. *Journal of Consumer Marketing, 28*(5), 344–353. https://doi.org/10.1108/07363761111149992

Jones, R.J., & Barnir, A. (2019). Properties of opportunity creation and discovery: Comparing variation in contexts of innovativeness. *Technovation, 79*, 1–10.

Joshi, A., Prichard, W., & Heary, C. (2014). Taxing the informal economy: The current state of knowledge and agendas for future research. *Journal of Development Studies, 50*(10), 1325–1347. https://doi.org/10.1080/00220388.2014.940910

Kelley, J., Arce-Trigatti, A., & Haynes, A. (2021). Beyond the individual: Deploying the sociological imagination as a research method in the neoliberal university. In *The Handbook of Critical Theoretical Research Methods in Education* (pp. 284–302). Routledge.

King, J.E. (2008). Will mainstream management research ever take religion seriously? *Journal of Management Inquiry, 17*(3), 214–224. https://doi.org/10.1177/1056492608314205

Kirmani, A., & Rao, A.R. (2000). No pain, no gain: A critical review of the literature on signaling unobservable product quality. *Journal of Marketing, 64*(2), 66–79.

Kirzner, I.M. (1979). *Perception, opportunity, and profit*. University of Chicago Press.

Krasniqi, B.A. (2007). Barriers to entrepreneurship and SME growth in transition: The case of Kosova. *Journal of Developmental Entrepreneurship, 12*(1), 71–94. https://doi.org/10.1142/S1084946707000563

Light, D.W. (2004). From migrant enclaves to mainstream: reconceptualizing informal economic behavior. *Theory and Society, 33*(6), 705–737. https://doi.org/10.1023/B:RYSO.0000049193.32984.c2

Linnekin, B. (2013). The case against government bans of feeding the homeless. https://reason.com/2013/03/09/bans-on-feeding-homeless-facing-backlash/

Long, A. (2021). Economic impact of marijuana. MJBizDaily. https://mjbizdaily.com/marijuana-industry-expected-to-add-92-billion-to-us-economy-in-2021/

Maurer, J.D., Creek, S.A., Bendickson, J.S., McDowell, W.C., & Mahto, R.V. (2022). The three pillars' impact on entrepreneurial activity and funding: A country-level examination. *Journal of Business Research, 142*, 808–818.

McDowell, W.C., Harris, M.L., & Geho, P.R. (2016). Longevity in small business: The effect of maturity on strategic focus and business performance. *Journal of Business Research, 69*(5), 1904–1908.

Murphy, P.J., Kickul, J., Barbosa, S.D., & Titus, L. (2007). Expert capital and perceived legitimacy: Female-run entrepreneurial venture signaling and performance. *International Journal of Entrepreneurship and Innovation, 8*(2), 127–138.

Murphy, R.J., Pollack, J., Nagy, B., Rutherford, M., & Coombes, S. (2019). Risk tolerance, legitimacy, and perspective: Navigating biases in social enterprise evaluations. *Entrepreneurship Research Journal, 9*(4), 1–19.

Nagy, B., & Lohrke, F. (2010). Chapter 9: Only the Good Die Young? A Review of Liability of Newness and Related New Venture Mortality Research. In *Historical Foundations of Entrepreneurship Research*. Cheltenham, UK: Edward Elgar Publishing. Retrieved May 3, 2023, from https://doi.org/10.4337/9781849806947.00019

Nagy, B.G., Pollack, J.M., Rutherford, M.W., & Lohrke, F.T. (2012). The influence of entrepreneurs' credentials and impression management behaviors on perceptions of new venture legitimacy. *Entrepreneurship Theory and Practice, 36*(5), 941–965. https://doi.org/10.1111/j.1540-6520 2012.00539.x

Nahapiet, J., & Ghoshal, S. (1998). Social capital, intellectual capital, and the organizational advantage. *Academy of Management Review, 23*, 242–266.

Nieman, T., Scott, S., Kraus, S., & Oberreiner, R. (2020). Let the games begin: Finding the nascent entrepreneurial mindset of video gamers. In *Proceedings of the 53rd Hawaii International Conference on System Sciences*, Hawaii, USA, 4375–4744. http://hdl.handle.net/10125/64324

O'Toole, J., & Ciuchta, M.P. (2019). The liability of newer than newness: Aspiring entrepreneurs and legitimacy. *International Journal of Entrepreneurial Behavior and Research, 26*(3), 539–558. http://DOI/10.1108/IJEBR-11-2018-0727

Planned Parenthood. (2021). https://www.plannedparenthoodaction.org/

Portes, A., & Haller, W. (2005). The informal economy. In Neil J. Smelser & Richard Swedberg (Eds.), *The Handbook of Economic Sociology* (pp. 403–425). Russell Sage Foundation and Princeton University Press.

Rutherford, M., & Buller, P. (2007). Searching for the legitimacy threshold. *Journal of Management Inquiry, 16*(1), 78–92.

Rutherford, M.W., Mazzei, M.J., Oswald, S.L., & Jones-Farmer, L. (2018). Does establishing sociopolitical legitimacy overcome liabilities of newness? A longitudinal analysis of top performers. *Group and Organizational Management, 43*(6), 906–935.

Rutherford, M., Tocher, N., Pollack, J., & Coombes, S. (2016). Proposing a financial legitimacy threshold in emerging ventures: A multi-method investigation. *Group and Organization Management, 41*(6), 751–785.

Scott, W.R. (1995). *Institutions and organizations*. Sage.

Siqueira, A.C.O., Webb, J. W., & Bruton, G.D. (2016). Informal entrepreneurship and industry conditions. *Entrepreneurship Theory and Practice, 40*(1), 177–200. https://doi.org/10.1111/etap.12115

Stinchcombe, A.L. (1965). Organizations and social structure. *Handbook of Organizations, 44*, 142–193.

Suchman, M.C. (1995). Managing legitimacy: Strategic and institutional approaches. *Academy of Management Review, 20*, 571–610.

Suchman, M.C., Steward, D.J., & Westfall, C.A. (2001). The legal environment of entrepreneurship: Observations on the legitimization of venture finance in Silicon Valley. In C.B. Schoonhouen & E. Romanell (Eds.), *The entrepreneurship dynamic: Origins of entrepreneurship and the evolution of industries* (pp. 349–383). Stanford University Press.

Thomas, L.D.W., & Ritala, P. (2021, in press). Ecosystem legitimacy emergence: A collective action view. *Journal of Management*. https://doi.org/10.1177/0149206320986617

Tracey, P., & Phillips, N. (2007). The distinctive challenge of educating social entrepreneurs: A postscript and rejoinder to the special issue on entrepreneurship education. *Academy of Management Learning and Education, 6*(2), 264–271.

Ueberbacher, F. (2014). Legitimation of new ventures: A review and research programme. *Journal of Management Studies, 51*(4), 667–698. https://doi.org/10.1111/joms.12077

Webb, J.W., Tihanyi, L., Ireland, R.D., and Sirmon, D.G. (2009). You say illegal, I say legitimate: Entrepreneurship in the informal economy. *Academy of Management Review, 34*(3), 492–510. https://doi.org/10.5465/amr.2009.40632826

Webb, J. W., Khoury, T.A., & Hitt, M.A. (2020). The influence of formal and informal institutional voids on entrepreneurship. *Entrepreneurship Theory and Practice, 44*(3), 504–526. https://doi.org/10.1177/1042258719830310

Williams, C.C., Martinez-Perez, A., & Kedir, A.M. (2017). Informal entrepreneurship in developing economies: The impacts of starting up unregistered on firm performance. *Entrepreneurship Theory and Practice, 41*(5), 773–799. https://doi.org/10.1111/etap.12238

World Population Review (2022). https://worldpopulationreview.com/country-rankings/countries-where-abortion-is-illegal

Zenge, J. (2021). Can the black rifle coffee company become the Starbucks of the right? *New York Times*. nytimes.com.

Zimmerman, M.A., & Zeitz, G.J. (2002). Beyond survival: Achieving new venture growth by building legitimacy. *The Academy of Management Review, 27*(3), 414–431. https://doi.org/10.2307/4134387

Zott, C., & Huy, Q.N. (2007). How entrepreneurs use symbolic management to acquire resources. *Administrative Science Quarterly, 52*, 70–105.

Adeniyi Damilola Olarewaju, Sunday Abayomi Adebisi, and
Olusoji James George

3 SME Internationalization and Strategy Tripod Perspective – Evidence from an Emerging Economy

Abstract: This chapter empirically investigated international performance of small and medium-sized enterprises (SMEs) in an emerging African country using an integrative theoretical approach of institutional theory, resource-based view, and industry-based view. To capture institutional quality, formal and informal institutions were measured through government effectiveness and social network respectively. Also, firm-specific capabilities were assessed through market orientation while industry conditions were measured by competitive intensity. Multi-respondent data was retrieved from 134 SMEs based in Nigeria. Hierarchical moderated regression analysis was employed to test all hypothesized relationships. Results show government effectiveness does not directly influence SMEs' international performance, attesting to the institutional void paradigm. However, social network significantly predicted SMEs' internationalization. Further, it was found that market orientation and competitive intensity have a positive effect on internationalization. Also, both market orientation and competitive intensity positively strengthened the relationship between government effectiveness and internationalization. Additionally, it was found that owners' education affected internationalization, while firm age, firm size, and industry had no significant effect. SMEs with internationalization ambitions in environments with institutional voids should focus on building informal social relationships and developing firm-specific capabilities and should perceive intense competitive rivalry as opportunity for growth. This chapter combined institutional theory, resource-based view, and industry-based view in explaining SMEs' internationalization in the context of an emerging economy.

Keywords: government effectiveness, market orientation, social network, competitive intensity, international performance, institutional void, Nigeria

Adeniyi Damilola Olarewaju, Tecnologico De Monterrey, Mexico
Sunday Abayomi Adebisi, Department of Business Administration, University of Lagos (UNILAG), Nigeria
Olusoji James George, Department of Business Administration, University of Lagos, Nigeria

https://doi.org/10.1515/9783110747652-004

Introduction

More small and medium-sized enterprises (SMEs) are now competing globally (Ahim-bisibwe et al., 2021; Dabić et al., 2020) but their expansion into foreign markets depends on a number of influencing factors (Lahiri et al., 2020). Internationalization of SMEs could be a function of firms' resources and capabilities (He et al., 2016), or influenced by industry structure and conditions (Fernhaber et al., 2007) or dependent on the peculiarity of the institutional environment (Hitt, 2016). However, employing a single strategy approach in understanding firms' internationalization may not provide a complete picture due to associated limitations of each perspective (Gao et al., 2010). Thus, there have been calls for an integrative theoretical approach in explaining the internationalization of SMEs, especially in the context of emerging economies (Gao et al., 2010; Lahiri et al., 2020). This is fundamentally important because SMEs' internationalization could be a function of the interactive combination effects of all three approaches, that is, firm-specific capabilities, industry conditions, and institutional environment, referred to as strategy tripod (Lahiri et al., 2020; Peng et al., 2009).

Further, although there has been an increase in internationalization activities among firms in emerging and transition economies in the last few years (Bahl et al., 2021; Mukherjee et al., 2021), not much is known about the internationalization behavior of firms in emerging African economies (Olarewaju, 2018). In particular, there have been few studies concerning internationalizing firms from emerging economies in Africa even though the region presents unique opportunities for theory-testing (Adomako et al., 2019) and could serve as a laboratory for building alternative paradigms (Barnard et al., 2017). Also, the uniqueness of institutional environment in emerging economies presents a case for further analysis (Zoogah et al., 2015). This is because institutions in emerging economies are quite more significant for international performance compared with those in developed economies as a result of institutional weaknesses due to unpredictability and constant variations (Hitt, 2016).

Consequently, from the perspective of an emerging African economy, this chapter responds to calls for an integrative approach to internationalization of SMEs (Gao et al., 2010; Lahiri et al., 2020). Country- and context-specific studies are especially important in understanding in-depth environmental and institutional peculiarities associated with internationalization of firms (Hitt, 2016). Thus, the strategy tripod perspective (Peng et al., 2009) is relied upon to examine the interactive relationships between formal and informal institutions, industry conditions and firm-specific capabilities in explaining SMEs' internationalization. Government effectiveness (GE) is employed to represent formal institutions due to its visible role in providing legitimacy (He et al., 2016); social network (SN) is a proxy for informal institutions because of the importance of informal relationships in many emerging African economies (Zoogah et al., 2015); market orientation (MO) represents firm-specific capabilities while competitive intensity (CI) is used to reflect industry conditions.

A number of contributions are offered. First, institutional embeddedness of SMEs, as well as associated institutional quality and complexity, does matter. Also the prevailing industry conditions within which SMEs operate and the firm-specific capabilities they are able to build or develop are imperative. To the best of the authors' knowledge, this represents one of the first attempts to understand firms' internationalization in an emerging African country through a strategy tripod prism. Second, in emerging economies with institutional voids, SMEs tend to focus on building capabilities through informal relationships and having a better understanding of customers' needs and preferences. This enables them to compete and grow but, quite importantly, it allows them to seek foreign market expansion. Despite resource constraints and related liabilities in emerging economies, SMEs pursue international expansion objectives by proactively understanding foreign markets, gathering information about customers' preferences, and using research skills to develop marketing solutions to customer needs. Third, international experience and education of managers of SMEs in emerging economies is germane to organizational commitment towards internationalization. The rest of the chapter is therefore structured as follows. The next section focuses on extant literature through strategy tripod perspective and develops the requisite hypotheses. This is subsequently followed by explaining the methodology employed, presenting the findings, and elaborating on the findings through discussions. The chapter concludes with theoretical and practical implications, as well as recommendations for future research.

Theoretical Framework and Hypothesis Development

Strategy Tripod Perspective

The strategy tripod perspective integrates three different theoretical frameworks in explaining organizational strategy and firm performance (Peng et al., 2009; Su et al., 2016). First is the resource-based and dynamic capabilities view, which argues that firms in possession of valuable resource endowments or capabilities are likely to have superior performances (Barney, 1991). Second is the industry-based view, which alludes to the importance of structure and conditions in the industry in which a firm operates. The prevailing industry conditions could constrain or provide incentive for firm performance (Porter, 1980). Third is the institutional theory with emphasis on formal and informal institutional factors which provide legitimacy and rules of the games for firms (North, 1990). While both resource- and industry-based views were quite established as theories explaining organizational strategy, institutions were assumed to be background conditions without any direct influence on strategic actions of organizations due to their largely invisible roles in developed economies (Peng et al., 2009). However, within the framework of emerging economies, institutions are a lot more prevalent and are not just crucial for firm performance, but rather very pertinent for encouraging firms' international business strategies (Hitt, 2016). Thus, it has been canvassed that in analyzing and understanding organizational choices, especially in the context of emerging economies, studies should attempt to incorporate all three theoretical frameworks (Peng et al., 2009; Su et al., 2016). The strategy tripod perspective therefore serves as the framework in this chapter because it guides understanding of SMEs' strategic choices in respect of their international performance, especially from an emerging country viewpoint. It also provides the basis for comprehending the interactive combination effect of all three approaches incorporated within this chapter.

Formal Institutions – Government Effectiveness and Internationalization

Formal institutions help to enforce the duties of a business concern and are made up of legal and statutory rules, laws, and regulations such as constitutions or acts of parliament (North, 1990). A crucial component of a country's formal institutions is GE (Roxas & Chadee, 2013). It refers to the ability of governments to independently and competently formulate and implement policies that guarantee enabling environments for businesses to thrive (Shu et al., 2019). In emerging economies, governments' role is quite visible especially in the area of resource allocation, determining the rules of the game, and establishment of market-supporting institutions that could encourage SMEs to make strategic business choices (He et al., 2016; Shu et al., 2019). Through its actions, governments provide legitimacy and certainty for entrepreneurs and businesses to thrive in their international strategic choices.

Studies have shown that governments' involvement directly and positively influences firms' internationalization efforts (He et al., 2016; Wang et al., 2012). According to Wang et al. (2012), governments exert different institutional pressures on firms and this impacts their willingness and ability to internationalize. Thus, the inherent opportunities and limitations that firms are confronted with in terms of the internationalization strategies to pursue are hinged on GE, policies, and affiliations (He et al., 2016). Based on institutional theory and the argument that institutions provide legitimacy and rules of the games for firms (North, 1990), it is advanced that in an environment with strong GE, there is likely to be little or no ambiguity about how businesses should be conducted (Roxas & Chadee, 2013), thereby making internationalization a lot easier. Hence, it is postulated that GE should positively predict SMEs' internationalization. Thus:

Hypothesis 1: GE is positively related to SMEs' internationalization

Informal Institutions – Social Network and Internationalization

Unlike formal institutions which require codified policies and are usually articulated in written forms, informal institutions are unwritten products of a society's value system and are a function of patterns, beliefs, and customs, which ultimately become norms that guide human and business behavior (Estrin et al., 2013; North, 1990). A major element of informal institutions in many emerging economies is SN (Zoogah et al., 2015). It refers to managers' social ties and informal business relationships with other business actors in the community (Chetty & Holm, 2000; Ibeh & Kasem, 2011). SNs are important for firms' international expansion because they provide information benefits in terms of knowledge of foreign market opportunities, referral trust, and experiential learning (Zhou et al., 2007). They are also important channels for obtaining critical resources and information (Chetty & Holm, 2000). In developing and emerging economies, studies show a positive effect of SNs on internationalization (Ibeh & Kasem, 2011; Ibeh et al., 2012). For instance, in a study of small medium software firms in Syria, Ibeh and Kasem (2011) acknowledged the significance of social and business networks in facilitating initial internationalization, including foreign market selection and firms' internationalization speed. Thus, within the context of an emerging African country such as Nigeria, it is postulated that SNs should have a positive influence on SMEs' internationalization. It is therefore proposed:

Hypothesis 2: SN positively predicts internationalization of SMEs

Capabilities (Resources) – Market Orientation and Internationalization: Predictive and Moderating Effect

Over the last few years, MO has increasingly become a cardinal issue in organizational strategy (Hernández-Linares et al., 2021). In the literature on MO, two dominant schools of thought have emerged (Acosta et al., 2018). The first school argues that MO should be about organizational culture and behavior concerning orientation on customers, competitors, and inter-functional coordination (Narver & Slater, 1990) while the other suggests it should be focused on basic processes involving intelligence generation and dissemination, as well as response design and implementation (Jaworski & Kohli, 1993). Irrespective of philosophical stance, both schools agree that MO is an organizational capability derived from a firm's ability to focus on customer preferences and the continuous improvement in its processes to respond to such preferences (Kumar et al., 2011; Narver & Slater, 1990).Studies on MO of large corporations have highlighted its importance for business profitability, firm performance, and sustained competitive advantage (Jaworski & Kohli, 1993; Kumar et al., 2011). However, compared with big corporations and multinational enterprises, SMEs face the challenge of resource constraints and tend to struggle with strategic capabilities (Dabić et al., 2020;

Fernandes et al., 2020). Further compounding this challenge for SMEs in emerging economies is the absence of market-supporting institutions (Hitt, 2016; Olarewaju, 2018). Regardless of the obstacles, and in line with the resource-based and dynamic capabilities view, SMEs that can develop MO capabilities are not only likely to have better profitability and firm performance (Baker & Sinkula, 2009; Barney, 1991) but could possibly have improved export sales (Acikdilli et al., 2020; Kolbe et al., 2021) and international performance (Fernandes et al., 2020). In their study of Turkish SMEs, Acikdilli et al. (2020) submitted that MO had a direct positive effect on export performance. In respect of the foregoing, it is therefore posited that SMEs' MO should positively predict their internationalization. Consequently:

Hypothesis 3a: MO is positively related to SMEs' internationalization

In environments with strong GE, there will be consistent government policy direction and enforcement of procedures in government transactions (Kaufmann et al., 2009) and such clear rules of the business game could allow firms to increase export sales and boost international performance (He et al., 2016; Wang et al., 2012). However, in emerging economies, formal institutions such as GE tend to be poor or weakly-enforced and this creates institutional voids (Hitt, 2016; Murithi et al., 2019; Peng et al., 2009; Zoogah et al., 2015). As argued by Acosta et al. (2018), MO is a dynamic capability which SMEs can rely upon to generate intelligence on customers and have a better understanding of their preferences. Thus, it is advanced that in emerging countries, managers of SMEs who can develop MO could overcome the presence of institutional voids to achieve their internationalization objectives. Recent studies have attested to the moderating role of MO as it concerns the marketing capabilities or dynamic capabilities and firm performance relationship (Cacciolatti & Lee, 2016; Hernández-Linares et al., 2021). Further, Wu and Nguyen (2019) found that MO can strengthen the predictive effect of dynamic service innovation capability on organizational performance and competitive advantage. MO could therefore have a moderating effect between institutional environment and internationalization. Consequently, it is hypothesized that in environments with institutional voids, SMEs' MO should, on the one hand, have a moderating effect on the direct relationship between GE and internationalization, and on the other hand, strengthen the relationship between SN and internationalization. Hence:

Hypothesis 3b-c: MO moderates the relationship between b) GE and internationalization c) SN and internationalization

Industry – Competitive Intensity and Internationalization: Predictive and Moderating Effect

The degree of competition faced by an organization within an industry is referred to as CI (Fuchs & Köstner, 2016; Jaworski & Kohli, 1993). There is a consensus that firms which operate in environments with little or no competition are likely to be comfortable as market leaders and may not necessarily worry about developing capabilities that could ensure improved organizational performance or international performance (Adomako et al., 2021; Cui et al., 2005; Martin & Javalgi, 2016; Porter, 1980). However, availability of close substitutes from other firms and increased intensity of competition does provide incentives for firms to constantly and continuously develop strategic capabilities in order to stay ahead of the competition (Porter, 1980; Su et al., 2016). Based on the industry-based view and as argued by Porter (1980), environments with intense competition are likely to witness availability of product alternatives, heavy investment in research and development, increased spending on advertisement, and intense price wars. Consequently, SMEs in environments with such intense competitive contexts tend to adapt their strategic efforts accordingly and this leads to improved export and international performance (Adomako et al., 2021; Cadogan et al., 2003; Fuchs & Köstner, 2016). Thus, it is postulated that SMEs confronted with intense domestic competitive rivalry in emerging countries are likely to explore new markets to stay ahead of competitors. It is therefore posited:

Hypothesis 4a: CI positively predicts internationalization of SMEs

Intense competition could be a positive omen for SMEs. A plethora of studies have found that strong domestic competitive rivalry could benefit SMEs, by enabling them to actively seek and explore opportunities in new foreign markets and improve international performance (Adomako et al., 2021; Fuchs & Köstner, 2016; Martin & Javalgi, 2016). The moderating effect of CI on export and international performance therefore appears emphasized (Cadogan et al., 2003; Cui et al., 2005). However, the context of an emerging African country with prevalent institutional voids (Olarewaju, 2018) does provide an alternative premise to test the moderating effect of CI on internationalization of SMEs. In environments with institutional voids, international expansion becomes a lot more difficult for SMEs (Hitt, 2016) but firms tend to adapt to the local market conditions to improve performance (Zoogah et al., 2015). In such environments, firms may be able to overcome these voids by adapting their strategies to the intensity of the prevailing industry conditions to achieve firm internationalization (Adomako et al., 2019). In their treatise on firms in an emerging African country, Adomako et al. (2019) found that CI strengthened the indirect relationship between institutional voids and internationalization of new ventures. Thus, it is hypothesized that in environments with institutional voids, CI should, on the one hand, have a moderating effect on the direct relationship between GE and internationalization, and on the other hand, strengthen the relationship between SN and internationalization. Hence:

Hypothesis 4b-c: CI strengthens the positive effect of b) GE on internationalization c) SN on internationalization

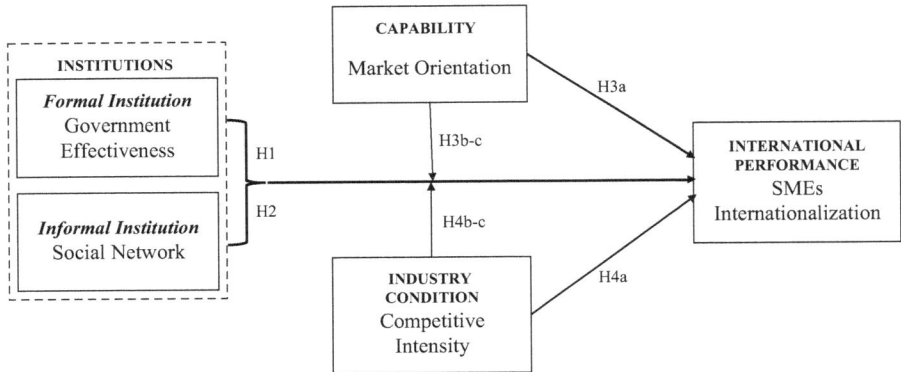

Figure 3.1: Research model.

Methods

Research and Study Context

This chapter examined internationalization of SMEs through the prisms of institutions, resources/capabilities, and industry conditions in the context of Nigeria, which is Africa's fastest growing emerging economy (World Bank, 2021). As at 2019, Nigeria remained Africa's largest country in terms of economic size measured by GDP ($448 billion [current US$]) and a population of 200 million people (World Bank, 2021). The country is defined by an abundance of small and medium-sized enterprises, individual propensity for entrepreneurship especially in the informal economy, resilience of its organizations, several competitive industries, seemingly weak and poorly-enforced formal institutions, and prevalence of informal institutions in many economic strata (Murithi et al., 2019; Olarewaju, 2018; Uzo & Mair, 2014). These factors therefore provide justification for the choice of Nigeria in this chapter and offer an important context to understand SMEs' internationalization from a strategy tripod perspective.

Sampling and Data Collection

In line with previous studies on SME's internationalization (Acikdilli et al., 2020; Fernandes et al., 2020), consideration was given to firms with interest or commitment to exports. Since data gathering can be challenging in emerging African countries (Ibeh & Young, 2001), this chapter focused on SMEs with a reputation of doing legitimate business transactions with other parties. Priority was therefore given to indigenous Nigerian firms who are financial members of organized trade and commerce associations such as Lagos Chamber of Commerce and Industry (LCCI) and Manufacturers Association of Nigeria (MAN). These are the foremost trade associations in Nigeria and have been employed by previous studies (Ibeh & Young, 2001; Olarewaju, 2018).

After an initial screening of the SMEs, 839 firms were invited to participate in the study in June 2019. One hundred and seventy-seven valid responses were received after a three-month period which included reminders through phone calls and emails. The survey specifically targeted the CEO, owner and/or founder because they are deemed strategically conversant with all variables employed in this chapter, including their own internationalization activities. Thus, a screening question on the respondent's position within the firm was included in the questionnaire. Additional screening questions in the survey included commitment to exports and percentage of total sales from exports or international operations. Based on the screening criteria, as well as removal of responses with missing information and data, a total of 134 responses were found to be usable and included in the final sample. The presence of non-response bias was examined through a t-test on key variables between early and late responses. This bias could lead to under- or overestimation of parameters (Podsakoff et al., 2012). Non-response bias was not detected, since examinations revealed there was no significant difference in variables.

Variables and Measures

Dependent Variable

The dependent variable, internationalization, was measured by four items adapted from the study by Zhang et al. (2015) to measure international performance. It was assessed on a seven-point Likert-scale (1 = strongly dissatisfied to 7 = strongly satisfied).

Independent Variables

The independent variables employed in this study are: GE which represented formal institutions, SN as proxy for informal institutions, MO which was used to measure firms' capabilities, and CI which served to assess industry conditions. They were all measured on a seven-point Likert scale (1 = totally disagree to 7 = totally agree). All respective items and their factor loadings may be observed in Table 3.2.

GE was a six-item construct revised from Kaufmann et al. (2009) and Roxas and Chadee (2013). It was designed to capture institutional quality at the country-level as assessed through prevalent government practices. The SN was assessed through a four-item measure adapted from the study by Li et al. (2014). The measure conveyed managers' attitude towards informal relationship building. A three-item construct adapted from Baker and Sinkula (2009) and Yayla et al. (2018) was employed to measure MO. It captured SMEs' capabilities in understanding and continuously improving on customer preferences. Finally, CI was assessed through three items adapted from previous studies (Jaworski & Kohli, 1993; Su et al., 2016). It was designed to evaluate the degree to which SMEs within an industry faced strong competition.

Control Variables

Due to the possibility of confounding effects, certain factors were included as control variables in the study to better explain results from the independent variables. Factors such as firm age, firm size, industry type, and owners' education are considered as influencing firms' internationalization and were included in the study in line with previous studies (Olarewaju, 2018; Zhang et al., 2015). Firm age was measured as the number of years from the firm's founding to 2019 while firm size was the logarithm of the absolute number of employees employed by individual firms. Additionally, ten industries were combined and categorized into four. They were subsequently categorically coded as four dummy variables, since creating so many industry dummies could create degree of freedom constraints (Zhang et al., 2016). Finally, CEO education was categorically measured by a two-step agreement scale asking business owners if they had any form of degrees awarded outside the owner's country (Hsu et al., 2013).

Results and Findings

Variables' Assessment

Although previously validated scales were employed to measure dependent and independent variables in this chapter, further validity and reliability of variables was confirmed through exploratory and confirmatory factor analysis (CFA), using maximum likelihood analysis on AMOS 25 software. The CFA results ($\chi^2_{(87)}$ = 175.64, CFI = 0.92, TLI = 0.89, IFI = 0.93, NFI = 0.86, RMSEA = 0.08) were within acceptable limits (Fornell & Larcker, 1981). Only survey items with factor loadings above 0.70 were retained for the study (Table 3.2), while it was confirmed items loaded properly with other items

Table 3.1: Correlation matrix, descriptives, multicollinearity test (VIF), and square root of AVE (bold diagonal).

	1	2	3	4	5	6	7	8	9	Mean	SD	VIF
1. Internationalization	**0.88**									4.12	1.23	N/A
2. Govt. Effectiveness	0.03	**0.81**								2.82	1.15	1.09
3. Social Network	0.36***	0.09	**0.77**							5.22	0.96	1.38
4. Market Orientation	0.46***	0.17*	0.45***	**0.79**						4.80	1.06	1.57
5. Competitive Intensity	0.39***	0.21**	0.44***	0.50***	**0.81**					4.79	1.10	1.61
6. Firm Age	−0.02	0.02	0.07	−0.01	0.07	1				1.14	0.20	1.26
7. Firm Size	0.04	−0.04	0.05	−0.04	−0.12	0.42***	1			1.60	0.69	1.45
8. Industry	0.05	0.11	0.07	0.11	0.22**	0.05	0.10	1		2.58	0.75	1.09
9. CEO Education	0.28**	0.22**	0.14*	0.30***	0.22**	0.24***	0.36***	0.21**	1	1.57	0.50	1.41

*** p<0.01, ** p<0.05, * p<0.1; SD = Standard deviation; VIF = Variance inflation factor

in their respective latent constructs. A multicollinearity test was conducted through the variance inflation factor (VIF). The VIF values were between 1.09 and 1.61, far less than the recommended threshold of 10.00 (Hair et al., 2018), indicative that multicollinearity violation is not a substantive concern.

Reliability and Validity of Variables

Internal reliability of variables was assessed through their respective Cronbach alpha (α) values. Values ranged between 0.83 and 0.93, all above the acceptable recommendations of 0.70 (Tabachnick and Fidell, 2019). This implied all variables had high item reliability. Further, composite reliability (CR) and average variance extracted (AVE) were employed to assess convergent validity of constructs. Convergent validity and high internal consistency of a latent construct is obtained when CR measures are above 0.70 and AVEs are above 0.50 (Fornell & Larcker, 1981). All variables were above the recommended threshold. Also, the square root of each latent construct's AVE was used to evaluate discriminant validity. According to Hair et al. (2018), discriminant validity is confirmed if the square root of the respective construct's AVE is greater than the respective variable's correlation coefficient values. The bold diagonal values in Table 3.1 represent the obtained values of the square root of AVEs and they are all greater than the respective variable's correlation coefficient values, suggestive of discriminant validity of each variable. Lastly, the principal component extraction method and Varimax rotation was employed to conduct factor analysis (Kaiser-Meyer-Olkin=0.81; Bartlett's test of sphericity {$\chi^2_{(190)}$=1811.45, p<0.01}). Five distinct factors

Table 3.2: Questionnaire items, reliability tests results and factor loadings.

Variables / Items	Factor Loadings
Internationalisation {Cronbach's alpha (α) = 0.93, CR = 0.93, AVE = 0.77}	
Growth in overseas markets (IP1)	0.863
Market shares in overseas markets (IP2)	0.884
Profitability from overseas expansion (IP3)	0.906
Return on investment through overseas sales (IP4)	0.850
Government Effectiveness {Cronbach's alpha (α) = 0.89, CR = 0.92, AVE = 0.65}	
Government in Nigeria does not provide enabling environment for businesses to thrive (GE1)[R]	0.739
The policy direction of government is clear and consistent (GE2)	0.872
Government decisions are effectively implemented in Nigeria (GE3)	0.833
Government encourages businesses to thrive by providing cheap loans (GE4)	0.825
There is availability of information concerning business regulations (GE5)	0.770
Procedures in government transactions are not consistently enforced (GE6)[R]	0.776

Table 3.2 (continued)

Variables / Items	Factor Loadings
Social Network (SN) {Cronbach's alpha (α) = 0.83, CR = 0.86, AVE = 0.60}	
My organization does not enjoy good relationships with suppliers in our industry (SN1)[R]	0.793
Great emphasis is placed on understanding our buyers' needs (SN2)	0.767
Personal relationships with our suppliers and contractors are important to the firm (SN3)	0.758
We constantly invest resources in relationship building with top managers of our suppliers (SN4)	0.785
Market Orientation (MO) {Cronbach's alpha (α) = 0.86, CR = 0.83, AVE = 0.62}	
My company is able to use market research skills to develop effective marketing programs (MO1)	0.814
We are not able to track customer wants and needs effectively (MO2)[R]	0.741
My organization is able to make full use of marketing research information (MO3)	0.806
Competitive Intensity (CI) {Cronbach's alpha (α) = 0.85, CR = 0.85, AVE = 0.65}	
Price competition is a hallmark of our industry (CI1)	0.768
Any action that a company took, others made a swift response (CI2)	0.865
One heard of a new competitive move almost regularly (CI3)	0.784

CR = Composite reliability; AVE = Average variance extracted; [R] = Reverse-coded

with eigenvalues greater than one were extracted and they accounted for 74.93% of the variance in the data.

Common Method Variance

Self-reported surveys could be prone to common method variance because dependent and independent variables were obtained from respondents at the same time (Podsakoff et al., 2012). However, in order to reduce the possibility of this bias, a number of steps were taken. First, respondents were not made aware of the relationship between variables. The complexity associated with the conceptual model especially with moderating effects, made it less likely for respondents to theorize the proposed relationships as highlighted by Zhang et al. (2016). Second, individual survey items of dependent, independent, and moderating variables were separated and randomly distributed throughout the survey. Third, respondents' anonymity and confidentiality of responses was guaranteed. Respondents were encouraged to freely complete the survey without consideration for what they thought could be right or wrong answers. Fourth, to examine the presence of this bias, a principal components factor test of all variables was conducted (Podsakoff et al., 2012) and results showed the common method bias is not a threat as no single factor accounted for more than 50% of variances (% of variance = 31.80%).

Results of Hypotheses and Findings

The hypothesized relationships were tested using a hierarchical moderated regression analysis. The control variables were entered into the regression equation in model 1, with all four predictor variables separately in models 2 to 4 but combined in model 5, and interaction variables separately in models 6 to 7 while model 8 is the full model. The gradual and significant increment in R^2 (0.08 to 0.32) and adjusted R^2 (0.06 to 0.25) from model 1 through to 8 provides justification for inclusion of all variables in the model. Further, the significance of all results in models 1 to 7 remained the same in the combined model.

There was no support for H1, in respect of the hypothesis that GE is positively related to SMEs' internationalization (β = 0.06, p>.10). However, there was support for H2, which hypothesized that SN positively predicts internationalization of SMEs (β = 0.42, p<.01). In respect of H3a, support was found for the postulation that MO is positively related to SMEs' internationalization (β = 0.42, p<.01). Additionally, MO was found to moderate the relationship between GE and internationalization (β=0.14, p<.10), which provided support for H3b. Nonetheless, no support was found for H3c, which posited that MO moderates the relationship between SN and internationalization (β = 0.07, p>.10). Furthermore, support was found for H4a and 4b on the respective hypotheses that CI positively predicts internationalization of SMEs (β = 0.42, p<.01) and does strengthen the positive effect of GE on internationalization (β=0.17, p<.10). However, no support was found for H4c, which advanced that CI moderates the relationship between SN and internationalization (β = 0.02, p>.10). It is emphasized that neither MO nor CI strengthened the relationship between SN and internationalization. A plausible explanation is that SN significantly predicts internationalization by itself and therefore renders any other interaction effect with it insignificant. Finally, all control variables did not have any significant effect on SMEs' internationalization except owners with international education (β=0.76, p<.01), which remained significant through each model.

Table 3.3: Results of hierarchical moderated regression analysis.

Variables/ Dependent Variable: Internationalization	Model 1	Model 2	Model 3	Model 4	Model 5	Model 6	Model 7	Model 8
Control Variables								
Firm Age	−0.46	−0.53	−0.37	−0.72	−0.57	−0.87	−0.58	−0.87
	(0.57)	(0.54)	(0.53)	(0.54)	(0.52)	(0.53)	(0.52)	(0.54)
Industry	0.02	0.04	0.06	0.14	0.11	0.13	0.09	0.12
	(0.14)	(0.13)	(0.13)	(0.13)	(0.13)	(0.13)	(0.13)	(0.13)

Table 3.3 (continued)

Variables/ Dependent Variable: Internationalization	Model 1	Model 2	Model 3	Model 4	Model 5	Model 6	Model 7	Model 8
Firm Size (Employees)	−0.06	−0.07	0.05	0.12	0.09	0.13	0.09	0.13
	(0.17)	(0.16)	(0.16)	(0.17)	(0.16)	(0.16)	(0.16)	(0.16)
CEO Education	0.76***	0.69***	0.41*	0.52**	0.42*	0.45**	0.42*	0.44**
	(0.23)	(0.22)	(0.22)	(0.22)	(0.22)	(0.22)	(0.22)	(0.22)
Main Effects								
Govt Effectiveness [GE] (Formal Institutions) {H1}		0.06			0.10	0.12	0.11	0.13
		(0.09)			(0.08)	(0.08)	(0.08)	(0.09)
Social Network [SN] (Informal Institutions) {H2}		0.42***			0.18	0.22**	0.21*	0.24*
		(0.10)			(0.11)	(0.11)	(0.12)	(0.12)
Market Orientation [MO] (Capability/ Resource) {H3a}			0.47***		0.30***	0.29***	0.3***	0.30***
			(0.10)		(0.11)	(0.11)	(0.11)	(0.11)
Competitive Intensity [CI] (Industry) {H4a}				0.42***	0.23**	0.21*	0.25**	0.21*
				(0.09)	(0.11)	(0.11)	(0.11)	(0.11)
Interaction Effects								
MO*GE (Moderating Effect of MO on GE & Int) {H3b}						0.14*		0.14*
						(0.08)		(0.08)
MO*SN (Moderating Effect of MO on SN & Int) {H3c}						0.07		0.01
						(0.10)		(0.11)
CI*GE (Moderating Effect of CI on GE & Int) {H4b}							0.17*	0.17*
							(0.09)	(0.09)
CI*SN (Moderating Effect of CI on SN & Int) {H4c}							0.02	0.01
							(0.09)	(0.09)
Constant	5.99***	3.98***	2.99***	3.90***	2.35**	2.74**	2.02*	2.59**
	(0.89)	(1.04)	(1.01)	(0.95)	(1.06)	(1.07)	(1.19)	(1.21)
Observations	134	134	134	134	134	134	134	134
R2	0.08	0.19	0.23	0.21	0.30	0.32	0.30	0.32
Adjusted R2	0.06	0.15	0.20	0.18	0.25	0.27	0.24	0.25
F-Stat	2.97**	5.05***	7.76***	6.74***	6.57***	5.80***	5.26***	4.76***

***$p<0.01$, ** $p<0.05$,* $p<0.1$; standard errors in parentheses

Discussion

An important part of the formal institutional environment in emerging economies is governments' interventions (Olarewaju, 2018). The formal institutional environment represented by GE in this study had no significant relationship with SMEs' internationalization and thus, as presently constituted, it does not significantly influence internationalization in Nigeria. This finding attests to the argument that in emerging economies formal institutions are usually missing, poor or weakly-enforced (Hitt, 2016; Peng et al., 2009). In their study of institutions and organizational effectiveness in Africa, Zoogah et al. (2015) submitted that the relevance of formal institutions on organizational behavior may be limited because the formal economy makes up a small proportion of the entire economy. Governments play a crucial role in emerging economies, particularly as this concerns resource allocation and providing frameworks for the establishment of market-supporting institutions that could encourage SMEs to make strategic business choices such as internationalization (He et al., 2016; Wang et al., 2012). However, as found in this study, rather than act as facilitators of efficient business operations and international performance of SMEs, governments appear to be a constraint. Murithi et al. (2019) had argued that governments in emerging African countries do not create a conducive economic and socio-political environment for businesses to thrive. Additionally, business environments in Africa are hampered by weak governance institutions and regulatory inefficiency (Murithi et al., 2019). This creates unnecessary institutional pressures and hurdles for SMEs, imposes additional financial costs, impedes full market participation, and constrains their ability to internationalize their activities.

Generally, the consensus among scholars is that in the absence of strong formal institutions in emerging economies, there is an overwhelming reliance on informal institutions (Hitt, 2016; Peng et al., 2009; Zoogah et al., 2015). This means informal institutions could substitute, complement or compensate for the absence of formal institutions (Zoogah et al., 2015). The findings of this study support this position as it was found that SMEs tend to rely on informal institutions such as SN to pursue their internationalization objectives, since the environment is seemingly characterized by inconsistent government policy directions concerning business regulations and procedures. In their multi-country analysis, Estrin et al. (2013) showed that institutional deficiencies significantly impeded entrepreneurs' growth aspirations, however, the study observed that belonging to local SN does reduce the negative impact of institutional voids on entrepreneurial ambitions (Estrin et al., 2013). Similarly, Chetty and Holm (2000) acknowledged that by focusing on obtaining knowledge through informal network-building with other business actors, managers of SMEs can overcome institutional and internal barriers to internationalization. Thus, when managers of SMEs actively allocate and commit resources to building informal relationships with other business managers, they are making investments in knowledge, intellectual resources, and relational capital (Ibeh & Kasem, 2011; Zhang et al., 2016). This increases the potential internationalization value that managers may benefit through information and knowledge-sharing.

Additionally, the fundamental importance of MO as an organizational resource capable of influencing SMEs' strategic choices in regards to international expansion is highlighted through the findings of this study. The argument that MO is a crucial asset for SMEs concerning export sales and international performance (Fernandes et al., 2020; Kolbe et al., 2021) finds support from this research. Traditionally, SMEs face resource constraints and certain liabilities associated with size in the quest for international expansion (Ahimbisibwe et al., 2021; Dabić et al., 2020), however, these challenges could be overcome if SMEs choose to focus on proactively understanding foreign markets, gathering information about customers' preferences, and using research skills to develop marketing solutions to customer needs. Particularly, findings show that in the context of an emerging economy with formal institutional voids, SMEs could rely on MO to strengthen the predictive effect of weak institutional environment on their international performance. Thus, SMEs confronted with institutional voids could seek to develop firm-specific capabilities and internalize competences related to understanding customers and the market.

In regards to CI, findings showed that intense rivalry and competition within an industry is productively healthy for international expansion. As the study found, competitive industries do provide the stimulus for SMEs to stay engaged and develop competences for foreign markets in order to either keep up with competitors or stay ahead of them. In many cases, SMEs facing intense domestic competition are compelled to adapt, build, and develop strategic capabilities that would enable them explore business opportunities outside their immediate environment. Also, this study found that in environments with institutional obstacles, SMEs are able to overcome these voids by adapting their strategies to the intensity of the prevailing industry conditions to achieve firm internationalization. This further provides support for the position that in emerging economies with institutional voids, CI can push SMEs towards international performance (Adomako et al., 2019).

Lastly, CEO characteristics and demographics could be a factor in international performance (Hsu et al., 2013; Ramón-Llorens et al., 2017), and findings of a positive relationship between CEO education and internationalization in this study is an indication that owners of SMEs with international education are likely to be more committed to internationalization than those without international education. International experience through education in a foreign country provides a CEO with knowledge about procedural requirements of doing business in international markets and increases information processing abilities about foreign market operations (Hsu et al., 2013; Ramón-Llorens et al., 2017). Thus, in the context of an emerging African country, a valuable resource that could assist SMEs in overcoming institutional voids in their desire for foreign business performance is the international education of owners.

Conclusion

A major thrust of this chapter was to comprehend the internationalization of SMEs from a strategy tripod perspective, within the framework of an emerging economy. Apart from incorporating both formal and informal institutional environments into the model, consideration was also given to the predictive influence of a firm's resources and capabilities, and industry conditions, represented by both MO and CI respectively. Formal institutions, as presently constituted, are not facilitators or enablers of international performance of SMEs. This is testament to the presence of institutional voids in many emerging economies, which present SMEs in such environments with numerous challenges. However, in the absence of strong formal institutions, SMEs are able to rely on social relationships, MO, and competitive rivalry within their industries to thrive in foreign markets.

Theoretical and Managerial Implication

In explaining SMEs' internationalization, this chapter employed the strategy tripod perspective as recommended in previous studies (Lahiri et al., 2020; Su et al., 2016) by integrating a resource-based view (Barney, 1991), an industry-based view (Porter, 1980) and institutional theory (North, 1990). The inclusion of all three approaches in this chapter is justified through the findings, which showed the presence of formal institutional voids but predictive influence of informal institutions, firm-specific capabilities, and industry conditions on SMEs' internationalization. Thus, while one or two theoretical approaches may have proven sufficient, however, a combination of all three perspectives allowed for a more thorough and in-depth understanding of SMEs' strategic choice in respect of internationalization, especially from the standpoint of an emerging African economy.

Further, SMEs face the challenge of resource constraints and tend to struggle with the liability of smallness (Ahimbisibwe et al., 2021; Dabić et al., 2020). Managers of SMEs in emerging countries therefore need to concentrate on building informal social relationships and developing MO capabilities. The effect is twofold. Firstly, SMEs are able to survive, compete, perform, and grow in environments with prevalent institutional voids. Secondly, in spite of institutional voids, SMEs are able to pursue their internationalization ambitions based on their ability to obtain critical information about foreign market opportunities from their SN and their capacity to continuously develop capabilities concerning customers' preferences and needs.

Research Limitations and Recommendations for Future Research

This chapter has a few limitations which could serve as avenues for further research. The first is that emphasis was on understanding context-specific predictors of SMEs' internationalization in one country. Although this permitted in-depth examination of variables influencing international performance, however, findings may not be generalized to other countries or regions. Future research could consider two or more countries in other emerging and/or developing economies. Also, a comparative study between developed and emerging economies along the strategy tripod perspective, for instance, provides future research avenues. The second limitation is that the results may have been influenced by the choice of selected institutional variables to represent formal and informal institutional environment, as well as the choice of firm-specific capabilities and industry conditions. Future research may consider other forms of independent predictors to test this chapter's assumptions and propositions in predicting SMEs' internationalization.

References

Acikdilli, G., Mintu-Wimsatt, A., Kara, A., & Spillan, J. (2020). Export market orientation, marketing capabilities and export performance of SMEs in an emerging market: A resource–based approach. *Journal of Marketing Theory and Practice*, 1–16.

Acosta, A., Crespo, Á., & Agudo, J. (2018). Effect of market orientation, network capability and entrepreneurial orientation on international performance of small and medium enterprises (SMEs). *International Business Review*, *27*(6), 1128–1140.

Adomako, S., Amankwah-Amoah, J., Dankwah, G., Danso, A., & Donbesuur, F. (2019). Institutional voids, international learning effort and internationalization of emerging market new ventures *Journal of International Management*, *25*(4), 100666.

Adomako, S., Frimpong, K., Amankwah-Amoah, J., Donbesuur, F., & Opoku, R. (2021). Strategic decision speed and international performance: The roles of competitive intensity, resource flexibility and structures. *Management International Review*, *61*(1), 27–55.

Ahimbisibwe, G., Ntayi, J., Ngoma, M., Bakunda, G., Munene, J., & Esemu, T. (2021). Entrepreneurial mindset: Examining the contribution of deliberative and implemental mindsets to SME internationalization. *Journal of Small Business Strategy*, *31*(3), 47–58.

Bahl, M., Lahiri, S., & Mukherjee, D. (2021). Managing internationalization and innovation tradeoffs in entrepreneurial firms: Evidence from transition economies. *Journal of World Business*, *56*(1), 101150.

Baker, W., & Sinkula, J. (2009). The complementary effects of market orientation and entrepreneurial orientation on profitability in small businesses. *Journal of Small Business Management*, *47*(4), 443–464.

Barnard, H., Cuervo-Cazurra, A., & Manning, S. (2017). Africa business research as a laboratory for theory-building: Extreme conditions, new phenomena, and alternative paradigms of social relationships. *Management and Organization Review*, *13*(3), 467–495.

Barney, J. (1991). Firm resources and sustained competitive advantage. *Journal of Management*, *17*(1), 99–120.

Cacciolatti, L., & Lee, S. (2016). Revisiting the relationship between marketing capabilities and firm performance: The moderating role of market orientation, marketing strategy and organisational power. *Journal of Business Research, 69*(12), 5597–5610.

Cadogan, J., Cui, C., & Li, E. (2003). Export market-oriented behavior and export performance: The moderating roles of competitive intensity and technological turbulence. *International Marketing Review, 20*(5), 493–513.

Chetty, S., & Holm, D. (2000). Internationalisation of small to medium-sized manufacturing firms: A network approach. *International Business Review, 9*(1), 77–93.

Cui, A., Griffith, D., & Cavusgil, S. (2005). The influence of competitive intensity and market dynamism on knowledge management capabilities of multinational corporation subsidiaries. *Journal of International Marketing, 13*(3), 32–53.

Dabić, M., Maley, J., Dana, L., Novak, I., Pellegrini, M., & Caputo, A. (2020). Pathways of SME internationalization: A bibliometric and systematic review. *Small Business Economics, 55*(3), 705–725.

Estrin, S., Korosteleva, J., & Mickiewicz, T. (2013). Which institutions encourage entrepreneurial growth aspirations? *Journal of Business Venturing, 28*(4), 564–580.

Fernandes, C., Ferreira, J., Lobo, C., & Raposo, M. (2020). The impact of market orientation on the internationalisation of SMEs. *Review of International Business and Strategy, 30*(1), 123–143.

Fernhaber, S., McDougall, P., & Oviatt, B. (2007). Exploring the role of industry structure in new venture internationalization. *Entrepreneurship Theory and Practice, 31*(4), 517–542.

Fornell, C., & Larcker, D. (1981). Evaluating structural equation models with unobservable variables measurement error. *Journal of Marketing Research, 18*(1), 39–50.

Fuchs, M., & Köstner, M. (2016). Antecedents and consequences of firm's export marketing strategy: An empirical study of Austrian SMEs (a contingency perspective). *Management Research Review, 39*(3), 329–355.

Gao, G., Murray, J., Kotabe, M., & Lu, J. (2010). A "strategy tripod" perspective on export behaviors: Evidence from domestic and foreign firms based in an emerging economy. *Journal of International Business Studies, 41*(6), 377–396.

Hair, J., Babin, B., Anderson, R., & Black, W. (2018). *Multivariate data analysis (8th ed.)*. Cengage publishers.

He, X., Chakrabarty, S., & Eden, L. (2016). The global emergence of Chinese MNCs: A resource–based view of ownership and performance. *Asian Business & Management, 15*(1), 1–31.

Hernández-Linares, R., Kellermanns, F., & López–Fernández, M. (2021). Dynamic capabilities and SME performance: The moderating effect of market orientation. *Journal of Small Business Management, 59*(1), 162–195.

Hitt, M. (2016). International strategy and institutional environments. *Cross Cultural & Strategic Management, 23*(2), 206–215.

Hsu, W., Chen, H., & Cheng, C. (2013). Internationalization and firm performance of SMEs: The moderating effects of CEO attributes. *Journal of World Business, 48*(1), 1–12.

Ibeh, K., & Kasem, L. (2011). The network perspective and the internationalization of small medium software firms from Syria. *Industrial Marketing Management, 40*(3), 358–367.

Ibeh, K., & Young, S. (2001). Exporting as an entrepreneurial act: An empirical study of Nigerian firms. *European Journal of Marketing, 35*(5/6), 566–586.

Ibeh, K., Wilson, J., & Chizema, A. (2012). The internationalization of African firms 1995–2011: Review and implications. *Thunderbird International Business Review, 54*(4), 411–427.

Jaworski, B., & Kohli, A. (1993). Market orientation: Antecedents and consequences. *The Journal of Marketing, 57*(3), 53–70.

Kaufmann, D., Kraay, A., & Mastruzzi, M. (2009). *Governance matters VIII: Aggregate and individual governance indicators, 1996–2008*. World Bank policy research working paper, (4978).

Kolbe, D., Frasquet, M., & Calderon, H. (2021). The role of market orientation and innovation capability in export performance of small-and medium-sized enterprises: Latin American perspective. *Multinational Business Review*. https://doi.org/10.1108/MBR-10-2020-0202

Kumar, V., Jones, E., Venkatesan, R., & Leone, R. (2011). Is market orientation a source of sustainable competitive advantage or simply the cost of competing? *Journal of Marketing, 75*(1), 16–30.

Lahiri, S., Mukherjee, D., & Peng, M. (2020). Behind the internationalization of family SMEs: A strategy tripod synthesis. *Global Strategy Journal, 10*(4), 813–838.

Li, Y., Chen, H., Liu, Y., & Peng, M. (2014). Managerial ties, organizational learning, and opportunity capture: A social capital perspective. *Asia Pacific Journal of Management, 31* (1), 271–291.

Martin, S., & Javalgi, R. (2016). Entrepreneurial orientation, marketing capabilities and performance: The moderating role of competitive intensity on Latin American International new ventures. *Journal of Business Research, 69*(6), 2040–2051.

Mukherjee, D., Makarius, E., & Stevens, C. (2021). A reputation transfer perspective on the internationalization of emerging market firms. *Journal of Business Research, 123*, 568–579.

Murithi, W., Vershinina, N., & Rodgers, P. (2019). Where less is more: Institutional voids and business families in Sub-Saharan Africa. *International Journal of Entrepreneurial Behavior & Research, 26*(1), 158–174.

Narver, J., & Slater, S. (1990). The effect of a market orientation on business profitability. *Journal of Marketing, 54*(4), 20–35.

North, D. (1990). *Institutions, institutional change and economic performance*. Cambridge University Press.

Olarewaju, A.D. (2018). *Institutional environment, sustainable entrepreneurship and the strategic internationalisation of indigenous Nigerian firms* (unpublished Ph.D. thesis). University of Lagos.

Peng, M., Sun, S., Pinkham, B., & Chen, H. (2009). The institution-based view as a third leg for a strategy tripod. *Academy of Management Perspectives, 23*(3), 63–81.

Podsakoff, P., MacKenzie, S., & Podsakoff, N. (2012). Sources of method bias in social science research and recommendations on how to control it. *Annual Review of Psychology, 63*(1), 539–569.

Porter, M. (1980). *Competitive strategy: Techniques for analyzing industries and competitors*. Free Press.

Ramón-Llorens, M., García–Meca, E., & Duréndez, A. (2017). Influence of CEO characteristics in family firm internationalization. *International Business Review, 26*(4), 786–799.

Roxas, B., & Chadee, D. (2013). Effects of formal institutions on the performance of the tourism sector in the Philippines: The mediating role of entrepreneurial orientation. *Tourism Management, 37*, 1–12.

Shu, C., De Clercq, D., Zhou, Y., & Liu, C. (2019). Government institutional support, entrepreneurial orientation, strategic renewal and firm performance in transitional China. *International Journal of Entrepreneurial Behavior & Research, 25*(3), 433–456.

Su, Z., Peng, M., & Xie, E. (2016). A strategy tripod perspective on knowledge creation capability. *British Journal of Management, 27*(1), 58–76.

Tabachnick, B., & Fidell, L. (2019). *Using multivariate statistics* (7th ed.). Pearson Education.

Uzo, U., & Mair, J. (2014). Source and patterns of organizational defiance of formal institutions: Insights from Nollywood, the Nigerian movie industry. *Strategic Entrepreneurship Journal, 8*(1), 56–74.

Wang, C., Hong, J., Kafouros, M., & Wright, M. (2012). Exploring the role of government involvement in outward FDI from emerging economies. *Journal of International Business Studies, 43*(7), 655–676.

Wu, W., & Nguyen, P. (2019). The antecedents of dynamic service innovation capabilities: The moderating roles of market dynamism and market orientation. *International Journal of Innovation Management, 23*(07), 1950066.

World Bank. (2021). *World development indicators database*. The World Bank Group. https://databank.worldbank.org

Yayla, S., Yeniyurt, S., Uslay, C., & Cavusgil, E. (2018). The role of market orientation, relational capital, and internationalization speed in foreign market exit and re–entry decisions under turbulent conditions. *International Business Review, 27*(6), 1105–1115.

Zhang, X., Ma, X., Wang, Y., Li, X., & Huo, D. (2016). What drives the internationalization of Chinese SMEs? The joint effects of international entrepreneurship characteristics, network ties, and firm ownership. *International Business Review, 25*(2), 522–534.

Zhang, X., Zhong, W., & Makino, S. (2015). Customer involvement and service firm internationalization performance: An integrative framework. *Journal of International Business Studies, 46*(3), 355–380.

Zhou, L., Wu, W., & Luo, X. (2007). Internationalization and the performance of born-global SMEs: The mediating role of social networks. *Journal of International Business Studies, 38*(4), 673–690.

Zoogah, D., Peng, M., & Woldu, H. (2015). Institutions, resources, and organizational effectiveness in Africa. *Academy of Management Perspectives, 29*(1), 7–31.

Kevin Walther

4 Internationalization of Small-sized Game Development Firms – A Born Global Theory Perspective

Abstract: This chapter aims to analyze the extent to which the born global approach to internationalization can be used to understand the internationalization of small-sized game development firms. The interview data were analyzed by the operationalization of concepts based on the three categories of founder, organizational, and macro-environmental drivers to internationalize. The findings show that the firms can be aligned with the different stages of their business development. This paper concludes that the first of these three stages, the subcontractors, are not born global, even though game developers must develop games with global market potential. However, firms that develop their own game are pushed to internationalize immediately by the heavily globalized and digitalized nature of the industry.

Keywords: internationalization process, born global theory, small-sized firms, entrepreneurship, video games industry

Introduction

Small and Medium Enterprises (SMEs) account for the majority of businesses worldwide. The World Bank estimates that 90% of businesses are SMEs, and they account for 50% of employment worldwide (The World Bank, 2021). Thus, SMEs mark the backbone of a national economic system but also of entire industries – as is the case in the video games industry. Take Sweden, for example, where video games have become the country's largest cultural export, thanks to blockbuster hits such as Minecraft or Valheim (both developed by SMEs). Data from the Swedish Games Industry Association show that 95% of the Swedish gaming firms are small-sized firms – meaning that they have less than 50 employees and/or turnovers of less than €10 million (medium-sized firms make up another 3% of the industry) (Dataspelsbranschen, 2020). Despite the large share and number of SME game development firms in Sweden, the large gaming firms still account for most of the Swedish industry's revenue (83% of the total revenue in 2019) (Dataspelsbranschen, 2020). However, a particularity of the video games industry, in comparison to other industries, is that the global market is not only the realm of large companies. Digital platforms have also facili-

Kevin Walther, Department of Urban Studies at Malmö University

https://doi.org/10.1515/9783110747652-005

tated the internationalization of SME game development firms, and developers can release their products with a few clicks of a mouse simultaneously all over the world.

This phenomenon of small firms being able to compete in a global marketplace almost from inception and thus internationalizing with the click of a mouse is the focus of this book chapter. This study draws on the renowned research model of born global firms by Madsen and Servais (1997) and applies this model in the context of an industry that seems to have reduced the barriers of internationalization to a minimum – and where small-sized firms can compete on a global market thanks to globally accessible digital marketplaces. Five interviews of a qualitative nature were used to collect data from founders of small-sized game development firms from different countries to understand the drivers behind the internationalization of their companies. The data revealed a concept for a basic categorization of small-sized game development firms. This concept can be seen as a taxonomy when it comes to analyzing small-sized game development firms and is further elaborated on in the discussion section. The chapter starts with a theoretical section on Madsen and Servais' (1997) born global framework, followed by a short method section. Furthermore, the findings are discussed considering the born global framework, and the chapter concludes with a discussion.

Born Global Model

Definition of Born Globals

A literature review on SME internationalization conducted by Dabić et al. (2020) identifies six main theoretical streams. These are the Uppsala model, born global literature, network theory, transaction cost theory, entrepreneurial theory, and the resource-based view. The born global theory argues that many firms do not follow an incremental stage approach (as suggested by the Uppsala model). Moreover, a born global firm starts its international activities soon after the founding of the firm (Knight & Cavusgil, 2004; Madsen & Servais, 1997; Oviatt & McDougall, 1994; Rialp et al., 2005). Some studies even apply a sharp definition of the phenomenon. A common definition is earning more than 25% in foreign revenues within three years of their establishment (Andersson & Wictor, 2003).

Madsen and Servais (1997) propose three aspects to investigate the rapid internationalization of such born globals (see Figure 4.1) – founder, organization, and environment. Founder factors are related to the background and characteristics of the founder, such as previous international experience, personal ambitions, and motivations to internationalize. Organizational factors are the competencies, routines, and governance structures of the firm that might affect internationalization. Environmen-

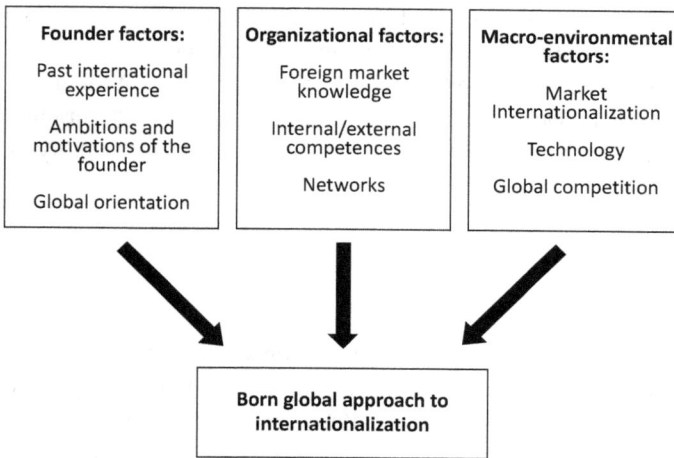

Figure 4.1: Research model for born globals in reference to Madsen and Servais (1997).

tal factors are the macro-environmental trends of higher levels of technology, market internationalization, and specialization (Madsen & Servais, 1997).

Founder-related Factors

The inadequacy of early international business theories in addressing entrepreneurial firms such as born globals led to a growing interest in integrating international business and entrepreneurship research fields. One of the consequences of this merger was an increased focus on the role of the entrepreneur or group of entrepreneurs in defining the speed of the internationalization of the firm (McDougall & Oviatt, 2000). After all, the entrepreneurs represent the foundation upon which the firm is built, so it is reasonable to assume that they will influence the firm's internationalization. The starting point of the process of international entrepreneurship is a business opportunity that presents itself to the individual, who must perceive it and decide on whether to act on it (Mathews & Zander, 2007). The entrepreneur is, therefore, central to the process. Her/his subjective evaluation of the opportunity and its surrounding conditions mediates whether the internationalization will happen and eventually the speed of the process (Oviatt & McDougall, 2005).

There is widespread support in the literature for the claim that a founder with previous international experience positively influences the likelihood of choosing a born global approach (Andersson & Wictor, 2003; Crick & Jones, 2000; Mathews & Zander, 2007). An entrepreneur who has incrementally gathered international experience has both knowledge of foreign markets and networks that can facilitate the internationalization process of a new firm, which, in turn, increases the motivation and ambition to internationalize. Following this argument, Madsen and Servais (1997) propose the strong international experience of the founder(s) as an antecedent of born global firms. Beyond the international experience of an entrepreneur, there is support in the literature for a positive relationship between an entrepreneur with a global mindset/orientation and the internationalization behavior of small firms (Harveston et al., 2000; Kyvik et al., 2013).

Organizational Factors

At the organizational level, the possession of market knowledge can enable firms to internationalize successfully. Market knowledge is considered a key to building an advantage in a foreign location (Oviatt & McDougall, 1994), and it has been suggested that market knowledge specifically acts as a moderator for the speed of internationalization (Oviatt & McDougall, 2005). Having sufficient market knowledge upon founding determines the location and the agile internationalization strategy of born global firms (Autio et al., 2000; Spence & Crick, 2009).

In addition to market knowledge, it is natural to turn to the possession of competencies to explain how firms can achieve rapid internationalization. It is argued by Madsen and Servais (1997) that born globals must have particularly narrow and well-cultivated competencies, which can be exploited to internationalize rapidly. There have been attempts to define what competencies are linked to the born global approach, with varying degrees of detail. Earlier studies already claimed that competencies in relation to the background of the founder, networks, and knowledge enable the success of international entrepreneurs (McDougall et al., 1994). This combination of competencies ensures that the organization is aware of routines to handle the challenges of internationalization, and can indeed be the core from which the company later evolves (Madsen & Servais, 1997; McDougall et al., 1994). Born globals are usually small in size and entrepreneurial at heart, so they often need to supplement internal competencies with external ones whenever that is necessary (Madsen & Servais, 1997). This is reflected in the attention given to capabilities revolving around networking to leverage external competencies in the born global literature (Karra et al., 2008; Knight & Cavusgil, 2004; Weerawardena et al., 2007). The balance between internal and external competencies seems to be a natural part of being a born global firm.

Given the lack of resources usually experienced by born global firms (Gabrielsson & Pelkonen, 2008; Jones et al., 2011; Spence & Crick, 2009), networks are often a way to seek resources and competencies that are required to achieve their business goals, including internationalization (Oviatt & McDougall, 1994). The use of networks for such purposes does not only affect the speed of internationalization but often the choice of foreign location as well, perhaps more so than the psychic distance to the host country (Oviatt & McDougall, 2005). Networks serve therefore as sources of opportunities. Formal as well as informal contacts can be used to facilitate foreign market entry (Coviello & Munro, 1995).

Macro-environmental Factors

To describe a firm's macro-environment in its entirety is a monumental affair, but certain characteristics and conditions of what is called the global business environment are particularly important for the propensity of born global firms (Gabrielsson & Pelkonen, 2008; Madsen & Servais, 1997).

The degree of internationalization of the market, in which the firm is situated, has been suggested to affect the firm's propensity to internationalize rapidly. Theoretical arguments suggest that an internationalized market presents existing international networks and resources that the firm can utilize, thus enabling more rapid internationalization (Madsen & Servais, 1997). Furthermore, a market, and thereby a firm operating in it, is more likely to be more internationalized if the domestic market is relatively small in size in comparison to alternative foreign markets (Madsen & Servais, 1997). An industry that is highly internationalized, perhaps due to its small domestic market size, will encourage the birth of born globals, whereas the born global approach might not be as necessary in industries where serving local markets is a viable strategy (Rasmussan et al., 2001). A major driving factor for born globals, therefore, is the level of internationalization that is present already in the respective industry.

Advancements in technology changed the global business environment and changed the face of global competition. The fact that these global markets exist enables greater specialization, leading to smaller-scale operations with niche target markets, which in the past could not reach large enough markets to survive (Madsen & Servais, 1997). Niche strategies, in turn, enable smaller firms to avoid head-on competition with large MNCs who can target larger portions of the market (Knight et al., 2004). These global customers can be reached by global channels, established international logistics, and improved information technology (Gabrielsson & Pelkonen, 2008). Digital technology, therefore, is an enabling force that makes accelerated internationalization possible, while competition on a global scale encourages firms to chase customers internationally and to prevent loss of market share to competitors (Oviatt & McDougall, 2005). According to Mathews and Zander (2007), engagement with competitors is the last guiding principle in international entrepreneurial dynamics, largely shaping the pathway of resource deployment taken by a firm and, therefore, whether it chooses to approach international markets. Indeed, it can be claimed that the born global phenomenon exists mainly because of the globalized competition and markets that compose the economic system of today (Chetty & Campbell-Hunt, 2004). Moreover, when the product itself can be digitally distributed, as in the case of computer software, the impact of these forces is amplified, and born global theory shows promise in explaining the internationalization of such firms (Gabrielsson & Manek Kirpalani, 2004; Galimberti & Wazlawick, 2015).

Method

In this chapter, semi-structured interviews were conducted with five (co-)founders of small-sized game development firms. The firms were found by looking at games that were newly released on the digital marketplace "Steam" at the time of the data collection. The fact that these firms published (or worked on) games on a digital platform made it likely that they underwent a rapid internationalization. Twenty-eight firms were eventually contacted and eventually five were willing to take part in an interview. The sample includes three firms from Sweden, one from Switzerland, and one from Brazil. The interviews lasted about one hour and were recorded and transcribed. Key questions for the interview guide focused on the educational and work-related background of the founder, international experience before the founding of the firm, using digital platforms to reach a global customer base, working with(out) publishers, the firm's international market experience, entrepreneurship, and general questions on their insights in the video games industry. On the one hand, the interview included open-ended questions which facilitated unexpected answers (Yin, 2013). On the other hand, some questions were framed on data publicly available on the founders' background or their latest games to increase the internal validity. The collected data were recorded and transcribed. To analyze the interview transcripts, a structured content analysis approach was applied (Krippendorff, 2018; Saldana, 2021). This analysis was done in three stages. First, the transcripts underwent open coding which includes describing and conceptualizing the data at a very basic level. This led to first-order categories. Secondly, axial coding was conducted to draw connections between the initial codes and to generate second-order themes. And lastly, selective coding was conducted, where the different categories were aggregated into overarching dimensions (Gioia et al., 2013). The founders' names and the companies were anonymized. A summarized overview of the interviewed companies can be found in Table 4.1.

Findings

Macro-environmental Factors

All founders interviewed for this paper mentioned that having a global mindset was inevitable in this industry. Taking Sweden as an example, this finds support in secondary data. Swedish game firms generate 99% of the industry revenues outside of the domestic market (Dataspelsbranschen, 2020). This highlights that the propensity for rapid internationalization is almost a given, due to the high degree of market internationalization in this industry. This is, of course, given or even accelerated through the digital nature of this industry. Whereas the gaming industry started with

Table 4.1: Overview of the firms and respondents.

Company	Country of origin	Founded	Turnover FY2020	Number of employees	Interviewee role
Alpha Games	Sweden	2010	$0.1 million	1	Owner/ Founder
Beta Games	Sweden	2011	$0.83 million	3	CEO/ Co-founder
Gamma Games	Switzerland	2013	$10.86 million (2019)	10	CEO/ Co-founder
Delta Games	Sweden	2007	$13.27 million	12	CEO/ Co-founder
Epsilon Games	Brazil	2015	$5 million	15	CEO/ Founder

producing software distributed on physical storage devices, the industry moved toward an almost complete digital industry roughly a decade ago. In recent times, more and more digital products are progressing toward a service with a subscription or a microtransactions business model (The Economist, 2019).

In the context of small-sized game development firms, the technological aspects or digital platforms are vital for their existence. This technological aspect, to a large extent, is a prerequisite for those developers to exist since they can directly address large markets, and the digital platforms act as global channels (Gabrielsson & Pelkonen, 2008).

A high degree of internationalization of an industry implies an ideal context for a born global firm (Chetty & Campbell-Hunt, 2004; McDougall & Oviatt, 2000). Other authors even see global competition as the main reason for the existence of the born global phenomenon (Chetty & Campbell-Hunt, 2004). The consumer's country of origin becomes irrelevant to a large extent, which might be partly based on a cultural homogeneity in the video games market. The responses from the founders interviewed for this study show that none of the firms have a profound market assessment of the different regions and especially do not adapt their product, except in terms of language. Such cultural homogeneity across markets is usually another driver for firms to take a born global approach (Oviatt & McDougall, 1994).

It can be said therefore that the macro-environmental factors point any type of firm in the video game industry toward selling outside of the domestic market and therefore internationalizing from inception. This is mostly due to the ease of doing so, thanks to the digital nature of their products and the online distribution, which crosses national borders with a mouse click.

Founder-related Factors

Early research highlighted industries where firms did not establish themselves in the domestic market before they started foreign sales (Bell, 1995). Interestingly, the main reason there was due to the prior experience of the entrepreneur. Madsen and Servais (1997) propose that the experience of the founder determines the geographical location of activities. Mathews and Zander (2007) assume that born global firms are often created by internationally experienced individuals.

However, based on the interviewed founders for this study, this could not be confirmed. None of the interviewees had international experience, either from working abroad (before founding their firms) or from studying abroad. At least in the context of small-sized game development firms, this study sees the international experience as mostly irrelevant.

While literature often explains a global mindset by pointing to past international experience (Kyvik et al., 2013), the lack of international experience did not prevent some of the founders from having an acceptance of the globalized nature of the market in which they acted. The impression from talking to the founders was that the domestic market in every market was indeed too small and making games for the global market was a natural strategy for all the development studios. This global outlook of the world as one large marketplace (Knight & Cavusgil, 2004; Madsen & Servais, 1997) did not seem to be developed from previous exposure to international markets; rather, it seems implicit and commonplace in the industry. In other words, the global nature of the industry is taken for granted.

Two main motivators of entrepreneurs, according to the study by Galloway and Mochrie (2006), are that entrepreneurs "saw an opportunity and acted on it" and that they "wanted to do something that they enjoy." Most of the interviewees mention reasons that fall under these categories when asked why they decided to start their own firm in the video games industry. All of them highlighted their passion for video games and therefore their desire to start their own company either as a long-existing dream or that came up during working in the industry. The identification of a business opportunity is also a motivator, which is also suggested as the spark in the entrepreneurial process (Mathews & Zander, 2007). This spark for founding or developing their own game could be observed in all of the (co-) founders' responses.

Organizational Factors

A general assessment of the potential demand for their games is a preliminary step before development in many cases. However, an important distinction is found in the parameters that are used to define markets. The traditional challenge of overcoming the liability of foreignness through the accumulation of knowledge (Johanson & Vahlne, 1977) is not applicable because the market is not defined in terms of countries but, as some of the interviewees pinpointed, in terms of game genres. This means that instead of serving each country with localized products, the firms look at global trends, such as the popularity of particular games or genres, and develop games accordingly. This seems to be the only sort of market assessment. However, one interviewed founder mentioned that they looked at the regional sales data after their release to analyze in which major region they sold less than expected and provided additional content that would satisfy these players.

This difficulty in understanding the true potential of products could be linked to the complex and creative nature of video games, which makes it difficult to determine the extent of market acceptance (Ström & Ernkvist, 2012). This uncertainty in performance is counterbalanced, for instance, by looking at previous successful games in their target genre.

Additionally, all of the firms could be defined as knowledge-intensive, in the sense that they are largely dependent on products that are developed through the application of extensive knowledge and replicated easily (Oviatt & McDougall, 2005). The games industry is at its core, after all, a software industry which is an industry (according to Oviatt and McDougall (1994)) suitable for rapid internationalization. Software development entails a long production time until a product is finished, but it is much easier to distribute these products due to the mobile nature of knowledge and digital software (Galimberti & Wazlawick, 2015). Also, using the internet as their path to immediate internationalization, these firms do not need to establish themselves physically in any of the countries that they serve (Sinkovics et al., 2013).

The use of partnerships with publishers is also a way to overcome the challenge of funding a project. However, these partnerships are also a way of tapping into the competencies required to publish a game, which are not the same as the ones required for developing it. Thus, the game development firms access complementary resources (e.g., financing) and competencies (e.g., marketing and distribution) provided by publishers to launch their games. The firms tackle resource and competence constraints through hybrid governance structures and partnerships, as described by early research on born globals (Oviatt & McDougall, 1994). According to the interviewees, finding the right cooperative publisher for a game can be a big challenge and, to some extent, determine the success of a project.

The relationship between the developer and the publisher is important and can affect the development process. A common example is that publishers are interested in rushing the release of games. However, it would be wrong to say that publishers affect the speed of internationalization since the necessity to do so immediately is a given anyway in the industry. The role of networks in affecting the internationalization process, for instance, by determining the choice of the foreign market (Oviatt & McDougall, 2005), is undermined by the globalized nature of the target market, which once again eliminates the need for entering local business networks.

Development Paths of Small-sized Game Development Firms in the Gaming Industry

Classification of Firms

A key similarity discovered in the interview data is that all of them have developed, are developing, or want to develop and launch their own game. This revealed an interesting pattern that places all five firms somewhere on the same continuum, which is made up of three distinct stages (although overlapping in one case). The firm's current stage, its potential future strategy, and the past firm development are summarized in the model below (see Figure 4.2).

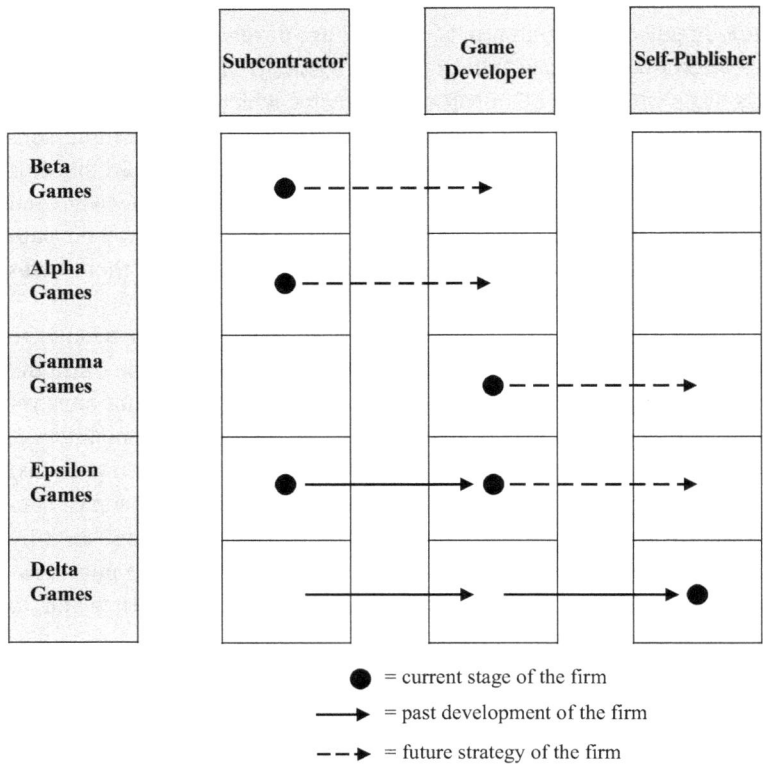

Figure 4.2: Three stages model (own illustration).

Subcontracting seems to be a natural first step to game development in this sample, with four out of five firms having started or being at this stage. Pure subcontractors, such as Alpha Games and Beta Games, are consultants that work on games developed by other firms. Both firms have the intention of developing and launching a game of their own in the future.

The second game developer stage implies that the firm develops a game of their own and aims to or has released it with the support of a publisher. Releasing a game without the support of a publisher stands for the third stage of self-publishers. It is important to note that this third stage is not necessarily the end goal for these firms, nor is it the most optimal stage to be in. It represents simply one of the strategic approaches to being a small firm in this industry.

This proposed model is an interesting finding in itself and elaborating on it, by using the case firms, shows its apparent applicability. In a way, this is an attempt to loosely cluster the firms into three different categories according to the stages. This finding was assessed as a necessary first step to analyze the factors of a born global approach in this context since each stage has particular features and challenges in terms of internationalization. Indeed, a key characteristic of this stages model is that it is a continuum, where a firm might move from one end of subcontracting to the other of self-publishing. However, the model does not suggest that firms can only be in one stage. Firms can cover more than one stage by, for example, having multiple projects running simultaneously (to be described in the example of Epsilon Games).

Subcontractors

Two companies whose founders have been interviewed for this study can be aligned to the first stage, which is subcontractors. In 2017, around 12% of companies in the Swedish gaming industry reported having worked in projects as consultants (Dataspelsbranchen, 2018).

The first example of such a firm that is acting as a subcontractor is Alpha Games. This one-man business provides consulting services in the field of story writing and game mechanics design. The second firm falling in the category of a subcontractor is Beta Games. This company was founded in 2011 and comprises three employees. Beta Games was involved in the development of a large game in the Warhammer universe which is developed and published by Delta Games.

From the perspective of Delta Games, a company that is relying on subcontractors for their projects, the interviewed CEO/co-founder mentioned that his firm sometimes uses subcontractors when they are facing a bottleneck or need help in a certain field of expertise. Additionally, the interviewed CEO/co-founder stated that subcontractors are obliged by contract to deliver in a certain range of quality and by a specific deadline. This makes the whole production to a certain degree more predictable than doing everything in-house.

Asked about their long-term goal, both founders of the subcontracting firms Alpha Games and Beta Games mentioned that they have the ambition and plan to release their own game in the future. The interviewed CEO/co-founder of Beta Games sees subcontracting as a method to obtain the financial basis for their own game in the future. This pattern of business development is also found in the history of Delta Games. The firm started as a subcontractor and has grown into a firm that is developing and publishing its games.

> We had a long-term plan, we started as subcontractors. We were working to learn the trade, then we took on larger subcontracting projects where we had more people involved in the production. Later on, we did work-for-hire for publishers, so we did full games. Then, the natural step, in the end, was to make your own games that are self-funded and self-published, which we are doing right now. (CEO/co-founder, Delta Games)

Furthermore, the CEO/co-founder of Delta Games mentioned that starting as a subcontractor is a common path since it requires a very low financial investment. Also, it is a way to improve the skills that a future development firm must possess.

Game Developers

The interview data revealed two firms that can be categorized into the second stage of game developers. Epsilon and Gamma Games both released games that they developed on their own but launched with the support of a publisher. In this sense, the two firms are similar, but what differentiates them is that they come from another starting point.

The Brazilian firm Epsilon Games is focusing on developing games and services for different clients within the video games industry and consumer product firms. For the latter, they developed interactive content such as websites or apps. Based on one of their founders' passion for video games, they decided to focus their resources on video games, and hence they released their first game in 2016. However, the company still finances itself partially by work-for-hire contract work and therefore acts within both stages of subcontracting and game development.

The second company that acts within the stage of game developers is the Swiss firm Gamma Games. Gamma Games started right away with the development of their own game and were never involved as a subcontractor in any other game development. One main reason for jumping directly into their development was that the founders identified an opportunity in the gaming market due to the lack of new transport simulation games. Besides their passion for gaming, one of the founders was working in a firm that focused on city modeling before starting Gamma Games. With this expertise, he and his co-founder developed a first version of the game in their spare time before they decided to start their firm in 2013 and released their, eventually, highly successful train simulation game together with a publisher in 2014.

Releasing a game through a publisher can be a reasonable way for a game development firm that lacks financial resources and/or knowledge of the whole distribution chain. However, by working with a publisher, they give away a degree of freedom in their development process and often a big cut of their sales profits, as all the founders mentioned.

> Based on their various negotiation experiences with publishers, Gamma Games' CEO/co-founder states that it is important for game developers to have a big focus on the business side because publishers can take advantage of you: Especially when it comes to publishers, you need to be quite strong in negotiations. Usually, publishers want to give you the money in advance, and in return, they make a contract suggestion that they get 80% of the royalties (CEO/co-founder, Gamma Games).

According to the interviewee from Delta Games, releasing a game with a publisher also bears problems and changes the development process fundamentally.

> I'd say the difference is that usually when you have a publisher, you have an external part that puts pressure on delivery. [. . .] Publishers have slots when they must release a game. For example, they book a lot of marketing in advance. Therefore, you are locked in and have to handle everything differently with a publisher. (CEO/co-founder, Delta Games)

Both Gamma Games and Epsilon Games mentioned that for their future projects they are considering releasing their games without a publisher and thus become more independent. Game developers that succeeded in self-publishing fall within the third category.

Self-publishing

The third stage is reached when a firm manages to develop a game and publish it independently, without the support of a publisher. Only one of the five firms in this study's sample has tried their hand at this, but only after having gone through the first two stages.

This company is Delta Games and was founded by four co-founders. Delta Games started as a subcontractor in 2007, working on game development for clients. Then, over the next few years, the firm developed a few titles and worked with publishers to release them. Already in 2011, the firm published its own game. Until 2016, they moved between self-published and publisher-aided releases. Their latest game release sold over one million copies. The idea for the game started by looking at what type of market seemed attractive and how they could stand out in the market, in this case by making a partnership with the well-known intellectual property of Warhammer. Besides the well-known Warhammer brand, Delta Games decided to pick a game genre that is underserved in the market and matched the competencies of the firm.

When it comes to the decision to self-publish, it is justified by two major factors, according to the CEO/co-founder of Delta Games. The first is that they can exercise a greater degree of control over the development process:

> Another major thing that was important for us was to be able to control the release date. We were able to wait until we thought the game was really good and then release it. The agility that we have and also the freedom to develop whatever we want is the upside (CEO/co-founder, Delta Games).

The second and perhaps the most natural justification is that by going at it independently, one can keep a larger part of the revenues by "cutting out the middleman":

> And the thing is that you get a bigger part of the value chain. So, we only paid 30% in distribution fee or something like that. If you have a publisher, they have their cut as well. [..] But if you are comfortable with what you are doing, you can get a bigger cut of the value chain for yourself (CEO/co-founder, Delta Games).

However, as has been displayed in all the cases, funding the development of a game is perhaps the most prominent challenge for the firms in this study. As mentioned, working with a publisher is a way to overcome this challenge. Subcontracting is a method of funding a future project, as in the case of Beta Games. Regarding Delta Games, most of the funding was acquired through the sale of their subsidiary company in 2014. While self-publishing is a strategy that enables greater control over the process and higher potential earnings, it presents the challenge of funding a project and of possessing the competence to do the work that publishers usually do – such as marketing and distribution.

Conclusion

The purpose of this chapter was to analyze whether the born global theory is relevant and applicable in the context of small-sized game development firms. This was conducted by looking at whether antecedent drivers of a born global approach are present in this context.

The data revealed a pattern of small-sized gaming firms being in different stages. The distinction between subcontractors, developers, and self-publishers by the proposed three-stage model is relevant to the question of the born global nature of these firms. The pattern of evolving or showing the desire to evolve from a subcontractor to self-development or publishing self-developed games seems to be the aim of all the interviewed (co-)founders. Interestingly, the case of Gamma Games illustrates an exception, since they skipped the subcontracting stage and started by developing their own game and targeted a global market from inception. All the other companies started as subcontractors, serving their domestic markets and therefore showing little resemblance to a born global approach. As soon as the firm changes its business to make a self-developed game, they target a global market as would a born global. It became evident that internationalization is not a main strategic objective or choice for these firms; rather, it is a requirement for competing in this industry at all.

Thus, the stages model presented in this chapter provides a more nuanced approach of born global small-sized game development firms in the video games industry. A subcontracting firm focuses on a small, specific part of the game development and is integrated into the supply chain of a larger game producer. At least in the sample for this study, this service was provided to domestic firms and thus these subcontracting small-sized firms are not necessarily born global firms. The level of globalization increases when the company moves towards the "game developer" and "subcontractor" stage where the firms target the global market from inception by releasing their product on digital marketplaces.

Consequently, Madsen and Servais' (1997) chosen framework can partially explain the antecedent factors of the rapid internationalization in this context. The macro-environment sets the scene for the apparent requirement of immediate internationalization once a firm develops its own game. Global competition is largely enabled by the digital nature of games and technologies, such as distribution platforms. The chosen organizational factors of foreign market knowledge, competencies, and networks provide interesting and interlinked insights, albeit with limited relation to the internationalization process in the context of small-sized game development firms. The creative nature of the industry complicates the acquisition of market knowledge through formal assessments. The suggested international experience by the born global framework could not be found in this sample. Complementary external competencies and mostly financial support are, in some cases, sought from publishers. Using networks as a tool for internationalization seems limited in the sample, although formal and informal network events are mentioned as bearing some value in finding business partnerships, especially for subcontractors.

However, it becomes evident that existing internationalization frameworks were formulated two or three decades ago when internationalization represented a major barrier, only applicable to firms with a lot of resources. The context of this study, in particular, shows that this is no longer the case, and internationalization in this industry is only a mouse click away due to digital platforms. The video games industry is one example of a few industries that have become sheer digital industries with barely any distribution cost, no economies of scale, and no physical goods crossing a physical border. Mostly, the assumption that internationalization is an incremental and country-by-country approach seems obsolete for digital industries with barely any obstacles toward internationalization. The findings of this chapter are largely in line with more recent literature on born globals that emphasize the relevance of a firm's business model, which is a main factor in a firm's rapid internationalization (Bouncken et al., 2015; Hennart, 2014; Onetti et al., 2012). The different stages of small-sized game development firms, which were identified in this study, are in line with research that promotes investigating firms at an individual level and investigating their business model to gain an understanding of a firm's internationalization process. This study should, therefore, be treated as opening the door for future research in the context of SME firms in the video games industry and business models of SME software firms. More specifically, this article supports the trend in entrepreneurial research that the business models of a firm should be evaluated to understand the internationalization processes of (SME) firms.

References

Andersson, S., & Wictor, I. (2003). Innovative internationalisation in new firms: Born globals–the Swedish case. *Journal of International Entrepreneurship*, *1*(3), 249–275.

Autio, E., Sapienza, H.J., & Almeida, J.G. (2000). Effects of age at entry, knowledge intensity, and imitability on international growth. *The Academy of Management Journal*, *43*(5), 909–924. https://doi.org/10.2307/1556419

Bell, J. (1995). The internationalization of small computer software firms. *European Journal of Marketing*, *29*(8), 60–75. https://doi.org/10.1108/03090569510097556

Bouncken, R.B., Muench, M., & Kraus, S. (2015). Born globals: Investigating the influence of their business models on rapid internationalization. *International Business & Economics Research Journal (IBER)*, *14*(2), 247. https://doi.org/10.19030/iber.v14i2.9109

Chetty, S., & Campbell-Hunt, C. (2004). A strategic approach to internationalization: A traditional versus a 'born-global' approach. *Journal of International Marketing*, *12*(1), 57–81.

Coviello, N.E., & Munro, H.J. (1995). Growing the entrepreneurial firm: Networking for international market development. *European Journal of Marketing*, *29*(7), 49–61. https://doi.org/10.1108/03090569510095008

Crick, D., & Jones, M.V. (2000). Small high-technology firms and international high-technology markets. *Journal of International Marketing*, *8*(2), 63–85.

Dabić, M., Maley, J., Dana, L.-P., Novak, I., Pellegrini, M.M., & Caputo, A. (2020). Pathways of SME internationalization: A bibliometric and systematic review. *Small Business Economics*, *55*(3), 705–725. https://doi.org/10.1007/s11187-019-00181-6

Dataspelsbranchen. (2018). *Swedish game developer index 2018* [Industry Report]. Dataspelsbranchen. http://www.dataspelsbranschen.se/rapporter.aspx

Dataspelsbranchen. (2020). *Spelutvecklarindex 2020*. Dataspelsbranchen. https://dataspelsbranschen.se/spelutvecklarindex

Gabrielsson, M., & Manek Kirpalani, V.H. (2004). Born globals: How to reach new business space rapidly. *International Business Review*, *13*(5), 555–571. https://doi.org/10.1016/j.ibusrev.2004.03.005

Gabrielsson, M., & Pelkonen, T. (2008). Born internationals: Market expansion and business operation mode strategies in the digital media field. *Journal of International Entrepreneurship*, *6*(2), 49–71. https://doi.org/10.1007/s10843-008-0020-z

Galimberti, M.F., & Wazlawick, R.S. (2015). Active internationalization of small and medium-sized software enterprises-cases of French software companies. *Journal of Technology Management & Innovation*, *10*(4), 99–108.

Galloway, L., & Mochrie, R. (2006). Entrepreneurial motivation, orientation and realization in rural economies: A study of rural Scotland. *The International Journal of Entrepreneurship and Innovation*, *7*(3), 173–183.

Gioia, D.A., Corley, K.G., & Hamilton, A.L. (2013). Seeking qualitative rigor in inductive research: Notes on the Gioia methodology. *Organizational Research Methods*, *16*(1), 15–31. https://doi.org/10.1177/1094428112452151

Harveston, P.D., Kedia, B.L., & Davis, P.S. (2000). Internationalization of born global and gradual globalizing firms: The Impact of the manager. *ACR*, *8*(1), 92–97.

Hennart, J. (2014). The accidental internationalists: A theory of born globals. *Entrepreneurship Theory and Practice*, *38*(1), 117–135. https://doi.org/10.1111/etap.12076

Johanson, J., & Vahlne, J.-E. (1977). The internationalization process of the firm – A model of knowledge development and increasing foreign market commitments. *Journal of International Business Studies*, *8*(1).

Jones, M.V., Coviello, N., & Tang, Y.K. (2011). International entrepreneurship research (1989–2009): A domain ontology and thematic analysis. *Journal of Business Venturing*, *26*(6), 632–659. https://doi.org/10.1016/j.jbusvent.2011.04.001

Karra, N., Phillips, N., & Tracey, P. (2008). Building the born global firm. *Long Range Planning* 41(4), 440–458. https://doi.org/10.1016/j.lrp.2008.05.002

Knight, G., & Cavusgil, S.T. (2004). Innovation, organizational capabilities, and the born-global firm. *Journal of International Business Studies*, 35(2), 124–141. https://doi.org/10.1057/palgrave.jibs.8400071

Knight, G., Koed Madsen, T., & Servais, P. (2004). An inquiry into born-global firms in Europe and the USA. *International Marketing Review*, 21(6), 645–665. https://doi.org/10.1108/02651330410568060

Krippendorff, K. (2018). *Content analysis: An introduction to its methodology*. SAGE Publications.

Kyvik, O., Saris, W., Bonet, E., & Felício, J. A. (2013). The internationalization of small firms: The relationship between the global mindset and firms' internationalization behavior. *Journal of International Entrepreneurship*, 11(2), 172–195. https://doi.org/10.1007/s10843-013-0105-1

Madsen, T.K., & Servais, P. (1997). The internationalization of born globals: An evolutionary process? *International Business Review*, 6(6), 561–583. https://doi.org/10.1016/S0969-5931(97)00032-2

Mathews, J.A., & Zander, I. (2007). The international entrepreneurial dynamics of accelerated internationalisation. *Journal of International Business Studies*, 38(3), 387–403.

McDougall, P.P., & Oviatt, B. M. (2000). International entrepreneurship: The intersection of two research paths. *The Academy of Management Journal*, 43(5), 902–906. https://doi.org/10.2307/1556418

McDougall, P.P., Shane, S., & Oviatt, B.M. (1994). Explaining the formation of international new ventures: The limits of theories from international business research. *Journal of Business Venturing*, 9(6), 469–487.

Onetti, A., Zucchella, A., Jones, M.V., & McDougall-Covin, P.P. (2012). Internationalization, innovation and entrepreneurship: Business models for new technology-based firms. *Journal of Management & Governance*, 16(3), 337–368. https://doi.org/10.1007/s10997-010-9154-1

Oviatt, B.M., & McDougall, P.P. (1994). Toward a theory of international new ventures. *Journal of International Business Studies*, 25(1), 45–64.

Oviatt, B.M., & McDougall, P.P. (2005). Defining international entrepreneurship and modeling the speed of internationalization. *Entrepreneurship Theory and Practice*, 29(5), 537–554.

Rasmussan, E.S., Koed Madsen, T., & Evangelista, F. (2001). The founding of the born global company in Denmark and Australia: Sensemaking and networking. *Asia Pacific Journal of Marketing and Logistics*, 13(3), 75–107. https://doi.org/10.1108/13555850110764793

Rialp, A., Rialp, J., Urbano, D., & Vaillant, Y. (2005). The born-global phenomenon: A comparative case study research. *Journal of International Entrepreneurship*, 3(2), 133–171.

Saldana, J. (2021). *The Coding Manual for Qualitative Researchers*. SAGE.

Sinkovics, N., Sinkovics, R.R., & Bryan Jean, R. (2013). The internet as an alternative path to internationalization? *International Marketing Review*, 30(2), 130–155. https://doi.org/10.1108/02651331311314556

Spence, M., & Crick, D. (2009). An exploratory study of Canadian international new venture firms' development in overseas markets. *Qualitative Market Research: An International Journal*, 12(2), 208–233. https://doi.org/10.1108/13522750910948798

Ström, P., & Ernkvist, M. (2012). Internationalisation of the Korean online game industry: Exemplified through the case of NCsoft. *International Journal of Technology and Globalisation*, 6(4), 312–334.

The Economist. (2019). *Mortal Kombat – Google launches its game-streaming platform*. https://www.economist.com/business/2019/11/21/google-launches-its-game-streaming-platform

The World Bank. (2021). *World Bank SME Finance* [Text/HTML]. World Bank. https://www.worldbank.org/en/topic/smefinance

Weerawardena, J., Mort, G.S., Liesch, P.W., & Knight, G. (2007). Conceptualizing accelerated internationalization in the born global firm: A dynamic capabilities perspective. *Journal of World Business*, 42(3), 294–306. https://doi.org/10.1016/j.jwb.2007.04.004

Yin, R.K. (2013). *Case study research: Design and methods* (Fifth edition). SAGE Publications, Inc.

Reinhard Schulte

5 Entrepreneurial Investment Cycle – A Large-scale Longitudinal Study

Abstract: Investment trajectories of new businesses are an often disregarded but vital aspect of new venture development. This study debuts in showing robust evidence of new venture investment time patterns by using investment time series of 4,733 new businesses. Based on a fixed effects nonlinear panel regression approach, the chapter models the trajectory of new venture asset acquisition in the first years after market entry. The results unveil durations and levels of investment patterns. Showing a first investment peak at market entry and a second peak years later, an initial new venture investment cycle is bimodal. Its peak-to-peak duration yields approximately nine years on average. New venture investment can be staggered into three stages, namely an initial, a plateau, and a replacement and expansion stage.[1]

Keywords: new ventures, start-up, investment pattern, investment trajectory, fixed effects model, panel data

Introduction

While investing in new firms always has been a key issue in research on new businesses, the investing of new firms into tangible assets has not drawn much attention. Hordes of scientists put funding topics such as motives, risk perceptions, and investment behavior of investors under the microscope and examine major financers like venture capitalists or banks for their role in new business formation and performance and their investment behavior regarding new and small firms (for example, see Pollinger et al., 2007; Robinson & Cottrell, 2007; Berger & Frame, 2007 for the latter issue).

This study is different because it intends to unveil the investment behavior of new firms when acquiring tangible assets. It explores the use of available funds independently from the sources and structure of funding. Hence, this approach is straightforwardly geared at the recipient side of new venture funding.

The content is original because time series analyses of new venture investments in tangible assets have never been conducted before. This is especially true as this study utilizes a large sample of new enterprises with full-time self-employed business found-

---

[1] An earlier draft of this chapter has been published as a discussion paper at Leuphana University of Lüneburg, Department of Entrepreneurship and Start-up Management.

Reinhard Schulte, Leuphana University of Lüneburg, Germany

https://doi.org/10.1515/9783110747652-006

ers, based on a novel and rich time series dataset of German private firms. This complements the literature, which typically had to be content with cross-sectional data.

The topic is important because the initial investment of a new venture is a precondition for its further development and hence has strategic relevance. Initial investing establishes operational readiness and serves to generate or enhance value. Doing business is not possible without initial investments in most cases. In addition, early development and subsequent establishing of the venture calls for additional investing. Long-term usage and irreversibility of implementation emphasize the strategic importance of new venture investments (NVI), which is especially true for producer goods (Bertola & Caballero, 1994; Gelos & Isgut, 2001; Nilsen & Schiantarelli, 2003). Industry dissimilarities are quite evident within this framework and generate a broad spectrum of NVI levels. This ranges from employee-based services with very modest physical production assets to manufacturing with large machinery needs. That is why we assume that early investments are crucial for the growth and development of new companies.

A highly relevant issue in this context is capital stock, which NVI sets out to adjust (Cooper & Haltiwanger, 2006). Investments change the capital stock across periods. Therefore, investments are intertemporally interdependent. This is why it is not appropriate to analyze NVI only at a particular point in time but in the long-term. So studying NVI imperatively requires time series data. The NVI theorem proposed by Schulte (2018a) sets a theoretical background that is suitable for stating hypotheses to be examined using empirical evidence. The aim of this chapter is therefore twofold: it serves to explore time patterns of NVI behavior empirically and to test NVI time series for the NVI theorem.

Timing, dynamics, and extent of investment at the level of the firm has not always been a viable option for research. For a long time, empirical research on the topic has been impeded by the practical impossibility to access firm level investment data. This is especially true for new venture investment data.

Investment of new businesses can only be studied in an explicitly dynamic setting because of long-term utilization of investment goods and its interdependence with aggregate capital stock. By introducing the conceptual outline of the NVI and the NVI theorem based on the most relevant previous literature, we derive a testable framework for testing the NVI theorem. Advancing our argument, we then explore time series of newly founded businesses for investment trajectories by using a rich and novel dataset of German new enterprises. Utilizing a fixed effects nonlinear panel regression model, we then statistically test for evidence of the theorem. We will provide some empirical evidence suggesting that new venture real investments follow an s-shaped course over time. To emphasize the practical relevance of the phenomenon, different stages of NVI are derived from the data. Finally, we explore implications for future research, policy, and new business counselling.

Literature and Hypotheses

To explain investment into tangible assets by business start-ups, the literature provides some fundamental arguments (Schulte, 2020; Schulte, 2018; Cassar & Friedman, 2009; Forsfält, 1999). Two of them are applicable to new businesses.

First, investment into tangible assets is driven by opportunity. In this sense, investment happens in case of a profitable investment opportunity. For start-ups, an entrepreneurial opportunity offering future added value is a key requirement of starting the venture. Without the prospect of value creation and economic survival, a new company would not invest. Second, real investment is driven by capital markets and interest rates. In this sense, new businesses are influenced by cost of capital in their decision to invest. Rationalized by net present value, enterprises in general can be assumed to invest more with lower lending interest rates (Samuelson & Nordhaus, 2010, 652ff). For potential new entrants, lower interest rates can ease the decision to enter the market by more favorable interest rate conditions and better access to capital. So the opportunity threshold is the main investment driver of new businesses, possibly supported or hindered by cost of capital considerations. Besides, real investment basically is driven by resource availability. Excess liquidity seeking for profitable use needs to be invested. Investment is forced by former profit, but former profit is not an issue of new businesses because of the very lack of internal self-financing in early business development.

Following NVIT, an initial investment peak can be expected as the business starts because implementation of operational readiness requires asset buildup. After this initial peak, investment is supposed to drop in the following years, while capital is in use and gets depleted continually. Later in time, and triggered by capital adjustment and replacement needs, investment rises to a second peak, which is expected to be lower than the first one. The NVIT then proposes a second decline afterwards, altogether forming a bimodal, s-shaped investment time series for start-ups (Schulte, 2016, 2018b). For clearness and unambiguity, we now will call these stages the "first peak stage," which comes soon after market entry, "second peak stage," which marks the later local maximum of investing after some years, and "valley stage," which is located between the two maxima. To simplify notation, we will label stages in chronological order from 1 to 3.

Following the NVIT, we now can conclude that amounts invested in the "first peak stage" (stage 1), which starts at market entry, should be higher than in the "valley stage" (stage 2) following the first peak, and higher than the "second peak stage" (stage 3), which in turn follows the "valley stage." Moreover, "valley stage" investments should be lower than those of the "second peak stage."

Applying this approach, we now can state three respective hypotheses

H1a/b: New venture investment is higher in stage 1 than in stage 2 and in stage 3.

H2: New venture investment is lower in stage 2 than in stage 3.

Please note that we do not make any a priori settings concerning the length of stages at this point. Therefore, data analysis cannot be based on predefined stage durations necessary for methods such as stage-specific comparisons of means. To test within this approach, we rather will perform alternative curve fitting procedures to determine the pattern that fits investment time series of new ventures best and to determine an average peak-to-peak duration.

Data and Methods

Following recommendations of the literature (Schulte, 2018a), this chapter aims to give empirical evidence based on a longitudinal research design by making use of a panel study being capable to show trajectories, duration, and levels of new venture investment. The dataset in use is obtained by employing a unique German panel survey specialized in full-time entrepreneurship and comprising business start-ups as well as business succession and active business participation: The Start-up Panel NRW (SPNRW) is a standardized written survey conducted annually since 2000 by the Centre for Entrepreneurship in Theory and Application using a new business database held by a governmental authority dedicated to the promotion of commerce and trade. The panel is dedicated to long-term monitoring of independent full-time entrepreneurship activities, addressing a quantity of enterprises large enough to produce robust findings on early venture development and covering more than 17,000 business start-ups. Annual response rates range from 35% to 70% (Lambertz & Schulte, 2013, p. 374). The panel, among other data, provides information on firms' annual investment behavior using micro-level time series data from more than 7,000 enterprises. This database is the most detailed and comprehensive source of data on this type of firms in Germany. For this study, we only make use of investment data from newly founded ventures, for a total of 4,733 enterprises, because in cases of successions and participations, businesses are already established and do not have to initially invest.

This chapter analyzes enterprise level time series that have been merged into one set of pooled data. Pooling is necessary here to set an equal reference point in chronological development for all ventures, namely the start of business activity. This pooling provides a beneficial and welcome side effect: influences of different economic business cycles on investment are compensated for by using pooled data, and thus respective biasing effects are filtered out.

The panel investment surveys deliver an unbalanced panel of 4,733 newly founded ventures. To secure a sufficient time series and an adequate development picture of every single enterprise, ventures with only one or two observations were dropped out of the sample. This selection results in 2,381 new ventures with 10,756 observations and thus in 4.52 investment observations per start-up.

This study makes use of the annual investment amounts of ventures providing at least three measured points per unit within the inspected period. Three measured points are necessary for a minimum representation of a supposedly nonlinear development over time (Ployhart & Vandenberg, 2010, p. 97; Chan, 1998). For a single unit, only two measured points would be limited to a linear estimation, and only one would not show development at all.

Investment time series were pooled along the age of the ventures to make them comparable concerning their year of foundation. With this step, possible impacts of different cyclical economic business environments were filtered out. To test investment trajectories over time, data analyses and estimations are thus restricted to investment and age.

The dataset contains companies aged 0–9 years with a size of 4.08 (resp. 5.78) employees on average after two (resp. five) years of business operation. Table 5.1 briefly describes the main features of the sample under inspection. As Table 5.1 shows, the data set is characterized by new individual companies, which are, as typical for start-ups, rather small and still growing. Annual investments cover a range of zero up to several hundred thousand euro, but the major portion remains on a moderate level. The firms analyzed reported annual investments between roughly €14,000 and €32,000 on average. The mean time series starts with the maximum mean amount in the trunk year and drops to its lowest average level in year 7. Thereafter, mean investments increase again up to around €24,000. Net sales per month average €22,750 after two years and €38,150 after five years of business operation. Female business founders are a minority, for as expected founders are mainly male. The sample contains a variety of industries, but is dominated by the manufacturing sector. Sole proprietorships represent about 78% of the sample.

Table 5.1: Sample description.

Variable	n	Mean	StdDev	Median	SE	Min.	Max.
Legal: Ltd. Liability Company[1]	4,731	.125	.331	0	.006	0	1
Legal: Sole Proprietorship[1]	4,731	.781	.414	1	.006	0	1
Gender: Female[1]	4,733	.206	.404	0	.006	0	1
Industry: Manufacturing [1]	3,859	.596	.443	1	.007	0	1
Industry: Services[1]	3,859	.219	.443	0	.007	0	1
Investment trunk year[2] (€'000)	1,266	31.92	.914	25.0	32.51	0	220
Investment year 1 (€'000)	3,300	29.12	.754	19.0	43.33	0	480
Investment year 2 (€'000)	2,636	14.31	.415	7.0	21.32	0	210
Investment year 3 (€'000)	2,013	14.83	.554	6.0	24.84	0	248
Investment year 4 (€'000)	1,665	15.34	.724	5.0	29.55	0	260
Investment year 5 (€'000)	1,221	18.10	1.104	5.0	38.59	0	315
Investment year 6 (€'000)	912	13.86	.889	4.0	26.85	0	202
Investment year 7 (€'000)	663	23.98	1.912	6.0	49.24	0	500
Investment year 8 (€'000)	409	22.94	2.133	9.0	43.13	0	360

Table 5.1 (continued)

Variable	n	Mean	StdDev	Median	SE	Min.	Max.
Investment year 9 (€'000)	135	23.16	3.584	10	41.64	0	250
Net sales per month after 2 years (€'000)	2,521	22.75	.845	12.0	42.45	0	975
Net sales per month after 5 years (€'000)	1,102	38.51	2.76	19.0	91.75	1	1,650
Full time employees after 2 years	2,768	4.08	.097	3.0	5.12	1.0	112.0
Full time employees after 5 years	1,311	5.78	.275	4.0	9.95	1.0	190.0

[1]yes=1, no=0
[2]< 12 months

Cross-tabulation of data can detect that sole proprietorships and service industries are more frequent among smaller enterprises. Smaller enterprises are younger than bigger ones, because most firms are in their early development stage, meaning that they still grow in terms of employment and sales. As already stated, all enterprises are full-time independent ventures. Featuring firms characterized by newness, full time employment, and heterogeneity (concerning industry, legal, sex, and size issues), the sample seems to be appropriate for the given research question.

Because pooled data in use here comprise cases of different age and founding date, and each subsequent year new entrants were to be incorporated into the data set, the sample includes a larger amount of shorter period cases than others. On the other hand, with growing duration of panel surveys, respondents increasingly reject answering repeatedly, which is why case numbers vary over time and decrease with length of period. To control for possibly different investment behavior between drop outs and repetitive respondents, we compared both groups in terms of their pre drop out behavior and in respect to basic business features such as legal form, size, and industry. We didn't find significant differences in this subject.

The features of the data set imply that the sample is not only in line with German foundation activities, but also with other western industrialized countries. To check for possible biases, the data set was compared to secondary data from the Federal Statistical Office and the Federal Sales-Tax Statistics for Germany, concerning legal status, industry, and sales volumes. In the course of this, highly significant correlations (>.99, α<.001) and chi-squares (α<.001) between the data set and the respective reference values became apparent. So this sample appears to give an adequate representation of the population of German start-ups, by sector, size, and legal form.

To approximate investment behavior of new ventures, namely to estimate new venture investment trajectories, linear and cubical curve fitting procedures were employed. Because theory implies a descending investment tendency in general while early business development proceeds, a linear estimation of NVI time series was run at first to check for an overall trend and to set a benchmark for model fit indicators. Testing of the hypotheses proposed was then performed by a cubic curve fitting (Arlinghaus 1994), which allows bimodal trajectories to be estimated and to check for different stages.

A highly relevant issue in modelling NVI trajectories is outlier treatment. Because of the variety of ventures and business models under inspection, NVI necessarily are highly dispersed and spread. Moreover, the lumpiness und intermittentness of investments are in the nature of investment. That is why a wide divergence of investment sums cannot only be ruled out but is acceptable. However, extremely high investments of single units lead to inhomogeneous and strongly spread distributions that moreover tend to bias related estimations.

To cope with this challenge, the literature (Wilcox, 2003; Wilcox & Keselman, 2003) recommends trimming or winsorizing the affected data. We decided to winsorize data because trimming not only excludes cases but cuts off valuable evidence on extreme investment behavior as well. Winsorizing is not connected to the assumption of completely wrong measured points, which have to be omitted, but adopts the view that exaggerated amounts have to be limited to a level adequate for the sample. The potential error of this type of data revision is much lower because extreme declarations do not have to be excluded.

In line with Wilcox and Keselman (2003), winsorizing was set to 0.2 for this study. With this adjustment, dispersion can be reduced to an appropriate level without changing the idiosyncrasy of time series data. Data intervention at the lower end of the distribution is limited to years showing less than 20% of zero investment. Because a vast fraction of zero investment can be expected following initial equipment at market entry, the winsorizing adjustment is limited to a largely noninvasive level.

Curve fittings were based on the fixed effects model computed from the winsorized investment data, based on a centering on individual, unit-specific means (Allison, 2009, pp. 17–18). Fixed effects panel regressions are particularly suitable for investment time series because they allow for consistent estimates despite unobserved heterogeneity of cases by avoiding individual effects of error terms for time invariant third variables (Allison, 2009, pp. 1–2). Non-observable heterogeneity denotes firm-specific effects that cannot be measured because of non-observability. It is associated with features of the individual firms making up the panel that are constant in time. Heterogeneity can be eliminated by centering within individuals because it does not have any temporal variation. The opportunity to control for unobserved heterogeneity is a strong argument for fixed effects modeling here. Utilizing a random effects model would contradict the motive for studying panel data. Time invariant third variables such as industry, gender or legal status especially justify the use of panel data, while random effects modeling is based on the problematic assumption of having no correlated time invariant third variables (Halaby 2004).

Testing was performed using linear and cubic curve panel regressions over years, yielding annual investment, which can be expressed as

$$(y_{it} - y_i) = c + \beta t + e_{it}(linear\ model),$$

and

$$(y_{it} - y_i) = c + \beta_1 t + \beta_2 t^2 + \beta_3 t^3 + e_{it}(cubic\ model),$$

where $(y_{it}\text{-}y_i)$ is the dependent variable, denoted as a difference because of the centering performed for panel regression purposes. c is the estimation constant, representing the intercept of the curve, β_i are regression coefficients that indicate investment slope over time, t is investment years, and e_{it} is the remaining error term of the curve estimation.

To test for robustness of estimations, unit-specific *median* centerings were additionally conducted.

Note that the time variable t is centered deliberately on the date of the business start-up, not on the unit-specific mean point of time, because adequate pooling of data (see above) requires timeline adjustment to make early development behavior comparable for all units.

Results

Modeling the NVI Trajectory

Table 5.2 shows the results of linear and cubic curve fitting. The linear model, implemented as a base benchmark, already delivers highly significant evidence for the presumption of descending investments while early business development proceeds. The results show a positive intercept of approximately €2,500, representing an estimation of mean investment deviation in year 0, and a negative linear slope around -€1,200. Please note that these figures do not represent absolute amounts of investment but unit-specific mean deviations, which are caused by the fixed effects approach utilized here.

However, the base model necessarily blanks out possible nonlinearities in NVI behavior. To test for the nonlinear and presumably bimodal trajectory stated by theory, a cubic curve fitting was performed, showing highly significant results as well and for all variables included (all $\alpha < .001$). With the cubic model, an intercept of approximately €10,000 (year 0) was estimated. Model fit rises by $\Delta R^2 = .2$, from a proper $R^2 = .134$ to a remarkable model fit of $R^2 = .334$.

Both models are highly significant, and both show a highly significant time variable. Cubic modeling considerably increases model fit. Stronger requirements for the number of measured points (>3) do not improve model fit.

Figure 5.1 (see Schulte, 2020) depicts the fixed effects trajectory estimations based on the concurrent models. They are based on single investment data. The tiny circles

Table 5.2: Annual investment observations
(0.2-winsorized, mean-centered).

	linear Model	cubic Model
year	−1.229***	−9.018***
year^2		1.620***
year^3		−.085***
const.	2.574	10.257
N	2,381	2,381
std.err.	7.000	6.139
F	1,666.3***	1,799.3***
R	.366	.578
R^2	.134	.334
adj. R^2	.134	.334

represent single median-centered observations. The abscissa assigns the observations to discrete points in time, for example to the abscissa value "zero" for the investments at foundation or to the abscissa value "2" for those two years after foundation. The ordinate, on the other hand, represents the respective median deviation of each observation. The dotted s-shape represents cubic fitting, while the solid line shows linear fitting.

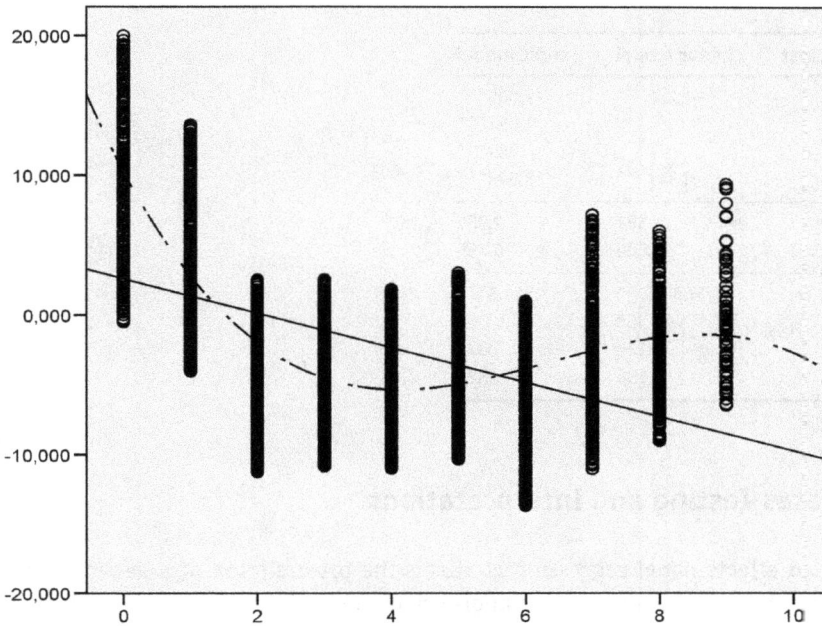

Figure 5.1: Annual investment observations (0.2-winsorized, mean-centered).

Robustness Tests

To test for robustness of the findings, we compared them to alternative specifications and estimations. In case of fixed effects models, the literature recommends replacing the mean with the median to avoid mean-biased centering when doing fixed effects regression (see Wagner, 2011, p. 23). We did so to test the robustness of the results.

Table 5.3 shows the tests for robustness of the regressions performed above to the replacement of individual means by individual medians. The results are quite identical concerning models, variables, and estimation errors. The cubic estimation of the curve trajectory is nearly equal to the base model. Model fit measures (F statistic, R^2) confirm an equally strong validity of estimations. However, the model intercepts are approximately €3,600 higher than those of the two corresponding models, which is an interesting shift caused by median replacement of means. The intercept represents the deviation of the amount invested from a utilized measure of central tendency in year 0. As usual with skewed distributions, in this study, median deviations top mean deviations and thereby cause the difference in intercepts. Unsurprisingly, the difference between mean and median in year 0 (€16,231 to €11,474) yields roughly the same amount as the difference in intercepts between models. Therefore, the models introduced for robustness checks face a parallel shifting of the corresponding curves.

Table 5.3: Robustness test (median-centered panel regressions).

robustness test	linear model	cubic model
year	−1.236***	−9.009***
year^2		1.651***
year^3		−.089***
const.	6.341***	13.893***
N	2,381	2,381
std.err.	7.000	6.195
F	1,687.4***	1,711.5***
R	.368	.568
R^2	.136	.323
adj. R^2	.136	.323

Hypotheses Testing and Interpretations

Linear fixed effects panel regression confirms the presumption of a generally descending NVI behavior. A much more appropriate model fit can be achieved by an s-shaped curve fitting as proposed by the NVI theorem. A bimodal path like that can be described by an (at least) third-degree polynomial, a cubic function. As assumed according to the NVI theorem, coefficients for t and t^3 are negative, while t^2 results are positive. All of them are highly significant.

Therefore, both models and all of their coefficients are highly significant. However, compared to the linear approach, the cubic fitting delivers a much better model fit in terms of standard errors, F-statistics, and especially concerning variance explanation, expressed by R^2. The cubic panel regression yields a surplus of $\Delta R^2=.20$.

The extreme significance of the model underlines the three hypotheses stated at the outset. The variance explanation yielded shows early development as being a highly relevant phenomenon for explanation of NVI behavior. The age variable already explains more than one-third of the trajectory.

The constants computed depict the average initial mean investing difference of a startup. Within the linear model, this intercept averages approximately €2,500 above unit-specific means. Each year, this amount decreases by approximately €1,230. Within the cubic model, the intercept averages approximately €10,300 above unit-specific means, combined with a more intensely negative slope and a second peak, which in total leads to a distinctive s-like shape.

Moreover, the models deliver estimations of the time of peaks and valleys. Given the estimation curve of the s-model, which is

$$(y_{it} - y_i) = 10.257 - 9.018x + 1.620x^2 - 0.085x^3, \; for \; 0 \geq x \geq 9,$$

we can determine the peaks and valley as follows:

first peak: x = 0, valley: x = 4.118, second peak = 8.588

Year 4 marks the valley of the curve, and the second peak is located between years 8 and 9. To ensure significance of differences on the level of annual means, T-testing was additionally performed, comparing pairwise means of relevant years 0, 4, 8, and 9. Table 5.4 shows all differences as being highly significant.

Table 5.4: Mean differences between peaks and valley.

		year 0	year 4	year 8	year 9
T-test (pairwise)	year 0		17.35*** (26.278) n=455	17.99*** (12.114) n=97	./.
	year 4			−2.84*** (−4.989) n=285	−3.64*** (−3.621) n=98

(./. no valid pairs. t-statistics in parentheses. *** α<.001)

However, T-testing calls for normal distribution, which is violated by winsorized data. The results of significance testing may cause false conclusions in this case. Therefore,

Wilcoxon Rank-Sum tests for paired samples were performed to ensure the findings obtained as shown in Table 5.5. This type of nonparametric testing does not require any assumptions of the underlying statistical distribution and, furthermore, carries the advantage of not being subject to outlier burdened mean values.

Table 5.5: Wilcoxon Rank-Sum tests for paired samples of investment in years 0/4/8/9.

		year 0	year 4	year 8	year 9
Z-value (paired years)	year 0		16.780*** n=455	7.398*** n=97	./.
	year 4			−5.051*** n=285	−4.362*** n=98

(./. no valid pairs. *** α<.001)

Wilcoxon Rank-Sum tests confirm all results already obtained by t-statistics. In fact, all three hypotheses can be sustained. As panel regressions verify, initial investments exceed those of stages 2 and 3, while stage 3 investments are higher than those of stage 2, which is confirmed by comparison of means based on a yearly perspective.

Discussion

The linear model verified a decreasing NVI pattern in a first instance of estimation. However, this masks nonlinearities, which have to be presumed following the NVIT. According to this theorem, a bimodal trajectory is more appropriate than a linear one. This pattern can be validated by a more elaborate estimation.

These findings indeed are astonishing considering the fact that the presumed s-shape can be confirmed without further distinctions, such as controlling for industry, size, legal type or other business features. This might be traced to the powerful panel approach, which is especially capable of coping with unobserved heterogeneity much better than cross-sectional approaches of all types. Of course, there are significant differences in the sizes of investments that can be read directly from non-centered NVI distributions. This implies special specifications of the s-curve for subcategories, resulting in different categorical amplitudes, but does not notably change the pattern itself and its longitudinal stretch.

The significant model fit gives strong evidence for the interpretation that time frames and stages do not differ substantially. Thus, strongly divergent estimations for subcategories on the level of a stretch on the time axis of the curve cannot be expected.

Conclusions

This chapter complements the literature presented above by following a completely different approach. It is the first example of a study of new venture investment behavior based on micro-level time series on new ventures.

The model applied fits the data reasonably well using German pooled data. We derived robust predictions of NVI behavior by fitting data to a cubic fixed effects panel regression. Thus, from a technical perspective, the findings are useful. However, why are they relevant, apart from just giving the first evidence of NVI? The relevance is related to more reasons than just exploring a new research area.

First, the study offers new venture theory validation, which has been largely missing so far, within a specific field of research. New venture investment theory has already been discussed in literature. However, its empirical verification and specification has been lacking for a long time. Tackling this rich data set did not only show that new venture investment dynamics are in line with the hypotheses. Going beyond assumptions about patterns of development, the data contribute to specifying the extent of investment, its timing, durations, stages, and amplitudes of trajectories at the level of the firm. Second, it contributes to early business development research, as investment opens up an alternate type of access to new venture progress and organizational buildup. As capital stock is a measure of productive size, NVI, which builds up and adjusts capital stock, most presumably correlates to growth. Linking growth research to NVI may gain a so far unseen knowledge potential. Thus, only with a closer understanding of NVI and by using time series data provided by panel approaches can future research on new business growth be advanced significantly. Third, the study offers initial insights into intertemporal issues of development. Former, current, and future investments are largely interdependent because investment goods are intended for long-term use. Fourth, NVI data allow for linkage to the funding side of the start-up and its respective figures, which might contribute to deeper insights into early stage funding demands and behavior. Altogether, these issues can contribute to a better understanding and more appropriate counseling of start-ups and new ventures.

Limitations of these findings are twofold, namely method specific and panel specific.

Winsorizing centered data, performed here to handle extreme outliers, induces the risk of cutting off important information on particular but nonetheless relevant cases. As already noted above, the impact of winsorizing to a large extent is limited to the upper end of distributions. However, the remaining revision of data may contribute to a cutoff of some heavy investment behavior. Taking into account the possibility of such cases calls for differentiation and possibly classification into subcategories or clusters, respectively. This might be an area for future research.

A more panel-specific limitation is given by the trunk year feature of new venture panel data, resulting from the fact that there is a time span of less than 12 months between the foundation date and the first subsequent panel survey wave in most cases.

Trunk years represent time periods ranging from a few days to nearly a whole year. However, this limitation seems to be tolerable, as most significant amounts are invested at the very beginning of a venture anyway and therefore do not bias investment trajectories over time. Despite a relative underestimation of first observations in the time series, trunk year investments are still higher than those of the first full reported year in the sample, independent from trunk duration and even in cases of very short trunks. Thus, the initial decrease in investments is not biased by trunk years. Obviously, preparation of operational readiness is more important for periodic investment figures than trunk year duration.

Another panel-specific limitation results from decreasing case numbers with longer periods. As shown in the tabulation of descriptives in Table 5.1, the case number of ventures analyzable decreases with venture age. Therefore, the period of observation is limited to less than ten years of early development. Because consolidation periods of new ventures go up to six years on average (Lambertz & Schulte, 2013), this is an appropriate period of time. However, as panel mortality can lead to successor bias, meaning that more successful ventures are more likely to report their investments, later period estimations might be overestimated because of low investing non-respondents. Still, this issue seems to be negligible as investment usually is not considered as a classic performance indicator. Another problem in this respect can be survivor bias, after which only ventures still in business can be surveyed. However, unlike success factor investigations, where viability correlates to success and underachieving enterprises are excluded from observation by market exit, the limitation to surviving ventures is appropriate here because the study targets long-time investment patterns of ventures sustainably active in their market.

The evidence shown drives some implications for policy, management, and particularly for future research.

From an entrepreneur's point of view, the findings are useful for new venture counseling and to locate and relativize their own investment patterns and developments. For entrepreneurs, an understanding of the relation between investment and development is required to control investment-driven growth. Additionally, the findings can serve as a benchmark to assess enterprise-specific behavior. The results obtained can contribute to counseling of new ventures as well.

Implications for theory and future research are even more extensive. First, the findings provide evidence for the presumption that the investigation of NVI is an appropriate and fertile ground for research on early venture development. It seems crucial in this context to mold initial development by chronological sequence to unveil nonlinearities in venture progress over time.

Second, because NVI at best are subject to cross-sectional inspection, the conclusion of a specific temporal pattern of investment suggests further and more detailed longitudinal analyses. The differentiation of subcategories divided by industry, legal form or sex, for example, might be especially promising.

Third, further investigation of NVI time series is supposed to contribute to a better understanding of growth and its patterns on a temporal axis. Better than just static variables could do, time series of growth and investment are much more suitable to reflect dynamics and changes that new businesses have to undergo. Taking the quite obvious assumption that past growth as well as past and current investments contribute to further growth, an integrative look at these four factors makes sense. It also follows that past investments can contribute to an explanation of subsequent investments.

This insight in turn is tangent to a fourth issue. It illustrates and clarifies that the amount of annual investments is not a development indicator comparable to periodic indicators such as sales, as it represents change (of capital stock), not annual performance. It is much more related to workforce and its change over time, which also represents stock size. If there is change like that, the starting position of the subsequent period, and of course all following periods, changes as well. Investment induces long-term effects, and that is why there are temporal interdependencies between investment amounts of subsequent periods. Thus, it is advisable to establish accumulated capital stock for future investigations of investment and links between investment and growth. In turn, the decline of capital stock, caused by depletion and adjustment, also requires explicit future research attention. This might be negligible at the very beginning of the business but applies increasingly with advancing venture age and development. This investment-development connection also questions whether earlier investments impact later ones, and how outcomes of earlier investments affect investments of subsequent periods. In this context, it is important to consider the link between a new firm's financing decisions and its investment decisions (Tsai, 2005). The relationship between NVI, its determinants, and effects must be analyzed in terms of a chronological cause-and-effect logic here.

Finally, besides aiming at a better understanding and explanation of early growth, there are many more issues of interest within the framework of NVI, such as investment and economic viability of the business, investment and change of strategy and structure, or personality features and decision-making behavior of the people investing. A special task for future research is the question of whether investment data can challenge the assumption of liability of newness. One weakness of the respective literature is that it focuses on resources such as employee size, which is used partly as a proxy for financial capital, but does not stand on financial data directly. It is hoped that future research will address, deepen, and answer one or other of these questions.

References

Allison, P.D. (2009). *Fixed effects regression models*. Sage.

Arlinghaus, S. (1994). *Practical handbook of curve fitting*. CRC press.

Berger, A.N., & Frame, W.S. (2007). Small business credit scoring and credit availability. *Journal of Small Business Management*, 45(1), 5–22.

Bertola, G., & Caballero, R. (1994). Irreversibilities and aggregate investment. *Review of Economic Studies*, *61*(2), 223–246.

Cassar, G., & Friedman, H. (2009). Does self-efficacy affect entrepreneurial investment? *Strategic Entrepreneurship Journal*, *3*(3), 241–260. doi:10.1002/sej.73

Chan, D. (1998). The conceptualization and analysis of change over time: An integrative approach incorporating longitudinal mean and covariance structures analysis (LMACS) and multiple indicator latent growth modeling (MLGM). *Organizational Research Methods*, *1*, 421–483.

Cooper, R.W., & Haltiwanger, J.C. (2006). On the nature of capital adjustment costs. *Review of Economic Studies*, *73*(3), 611–633.

Forsfält, T. (1999). *The effects of risk aversion and age on investments in new firms. Timing options and taxation. Essays on the economics of firm creation and tax evasion*. PhD Thesis, University of Stockholm, Sweden.

Gelos, G., & Isgut, A. (2001). Irreversibilities in fixed capital adjustment: Evidence from Mexican and Colombian plants. *Economics Letters*, *74*(1), 85–89.

Halaby, C.N. (2004). Panel models in sociological research: Theory into practice. *Annual Review of Sociology*, *30*, 507–544.

Lambertz, S., & Schulte, R. (2013). Consolidation period in new ventures: How long does it take to establish a start-up? *International Journal of Entrepreneurial Venturing*, *5*(4), 369–390.

Nilsen, O.A., & Schiantarelli, F. (2003). Zeros and lumps in investment: Empirical evidence on irreversibilities and non-convexities. *Review of Economics and Statistics*, *85*(4), 1021–1037.

Ployhart, R.E., & Vandenberg, R.J. (2010). Longitudinal research: The theory, design, and analysis of change. *Journal of Management*, *36*(1), 94–120.

Pollinger, J., Outhwaite, J., & Cordero-Guzmán, H. (2007). The question of sustainability for microfinance institutions. *Journal of Small Business Management*, *45*(1), 23–41.

Robinson, M.J., & Cottrell, T. J. (2007). Investment patterns of informal investors in the Alberta private equity market. *Journal of Small Business Management*, *45*(1), 47–67.

Samuelson, P.A., & Nordhaus, W.D. (2010). *Economics* (19th ed.). McGraw Hill.

Schulte, R. (2016). Investitionen junger Unternehmen. Eine theoretische und empirische Untersuchung der Investitionsmuster deutscher Unternehmensgründungen. *Zeitschrift für KMU & Entrepreneurship*, *64*(3), 185–212. doi: 10.3790/zfke.64.3.185

Schulte, R. (2018a). What do we know about new venture investment time patterns? *Review of Pacific Basin Financial Markets and Policies*, *21*(1). https://doi.org/10.1142/S0219091518500042.

Schulte, R. (2018b). New venture investing trajectories – a large-scale longitudinal study. *Lüneburger Beiträge zur Gründungsforschung*, *13*. https://doi.org/10.2139/ssrn.3458905

Schulte, R. (2020). Entrepreneurial Investing: Das Investitionsverhalten junger Unternehmen. In K. Hölzle, V. Tiberius, & H. Surrey (Eds.), *Perspektiven des Entrepreneuships* (pp. 199–210). Schäffer Poeschel.

Tsai, S.C. (2005). Dynamic models of investment distortions. *Review of Quantitative Finance and Accounting*, *25*(4), 357–381.

Wagner, J. (2011). From estimation results to stylized facts twelve recommendations for empirical research in international activities of heterogeneous firms. *De Economist*, *159*(4), 389–412.

Wilcox, R.R. (2003). *Applying contemporary statistical techniques*. Academic Press.

Wilcox, R.R., & Keselman, H. J. (2003). Modern robust data analysis methods: Measures of central tendency. *Psychological Methods*, *8*, 254–274.

Part 2: **SMEs from the Perspective of Different Levels of Analysis (Macro, Meso, and Micro)**

Junyu Zhou, Boyka Simeonova, and Mathew Hughes

6 Antecedents of Individual Ambidexterity at Three Hierarchical Levels: A Literature Review

Abstract: Scholars in the management area have emphasized individual ambidexterity as it can benefit individual performance and organizational ambidexterity, especially in small and medium-sized enterprises (SMEs) and entrepreneurship. This chapter constructs a nomological network of individual ambidexterity through the lens of hierarchical heterogeneity to introduce three types of individual ambidexterity (i.e., senior managers, middle managers, and frontline employees' ambidexterity) and explains the different antecedents and mechanisms through the paradoxical challenges at these hierarchical levels. This chapter systematically reviews the organizational and individual mechanisms that enable individual ambidexterity at the three hierarchical levels. The nomological network of individual ambidexterity's antecedents describes mechanisms which are organizational context, organizational practices and systems, knowledge resources, leadership, and individual characteristics. The chapter extends the network developed from the literature to recommend additional antecedents of individual ambidexterity. In conclusion, the chapter discusses the implications for SME entrepreneurship.

Keywords: individual ambidexterity, multiple levels, hierarchical heterogeneity, small- and medium-sized enterprises, entrepreneurship, systematic literature review

Introduction

Individual ambidexterity refers to the ability of an individual to complete exploratory and exploitative activities (Mom et al., 2007). While exploration refers to creative behavior and radical innovation on products, services, and processes, exploitation means implementing strategy and incremental innovation, such as completing previous tasks more efficiently (Hughes et al., 2018a; March, 1991; Mom et al., 2007). Individual ambidexterity has emerged in management research as an important individual strategy that can lead to positive individual performance (Good & Michel, 2013; Sok et al., 2018) and is considered the microfoundations of organizational ambidexterity (Rogan & Mors, 2014).

Junyu Zhou, Innovation and Strategic Management, Loughborough University
Boyka Simeonova, Associate Professor of Innovation, Leicester School of Business
Mathew Hughes, Professor of Innovation and Entrepreneurship, University of Leicester School of Business

https://doi.org/10.1515/9783110747652-007

This chapter combines the definition of individual ambidexterity with hierarchical levels in organizations to construct a hierarchical lens of individual ambidexterity (Weber, 1978). At different hierarchical levels (i.e., senior management level, middle management level, and frontline employees' level), individuals have different tasks and requirements, and their access to information and resources also differs. Because of this, the appropriate mechanisms to enable individual ambidexterity at each of the three hierarchical levels may differ. Therefore, it is necessary to review the existing literature to understand which types of antecedents have been found that can facilitate individual ambidexterity at which level and recommend additional antecedents in need of further research. The existing literature has studied disparate factors as the antecedents of individual ambidexterity, but a holistic nomological network from the three different hierarchical levels has not yet been constructed.

The review of the antecedents is organized following the logic that different factors at different levels may influence individual ambidexterity, and this chapter differentiates between organizational-level and individual-level antecedents of individual ambidexterity to provide a comprehensive nomological network of individual ambidexterity. The organizational factors regulate or impact the individuals' activities; however, individual ambidexterity is also an activity of managing the inter-conflict between exploration and exploitation (March & Simon, 1958). Therefore, the mechanisms that enable individual ambidexterity should include organizational- and individual-level factors. This chapter develops a nomological network of individual ambidexterity with its antecedents at organizational and individual levels and their effect on individual ambidexterity at three hierarchical levels: senior management, middle management, and frontline employees.

The chapter then extends the constructed nomological network of individual ambidexterity to include additional antecedents which are important for individual ambidexterity but have not been explored in the literature. This is achieved by considering that individuals need to complete and balance different exploratory and exploitative activities to achieve ambidexterity. At the senior management level, the paradoxical challenges are designing and developing corporate and business strategies where senior managers need to balance cost and risk and consider the organization's objectives (Lubatkin et al., 2006; Rogan & Mors, 2014). At the middle management level, the paradoxical challenges derive from implementing the strategies designed by senior managers and transferring these strategies to the operational tasks for frontline employees (Mustafa et al., 2016), where middle managers need to deal with parallel knowledge and aim to complete their projects creatively and efficiently. At the non-managerial level, frontline employees are distanced from the strategic level and focus on operational tasks. They need to follow the routinized processes to complete work tasks efficiently and exhibit creative working styles to improve their performance largely (Andriopoulos & Lewis, 2009). Therefore, this chapter extends the current understanding of individual ambidexterity and its antecedents and outlines important additional mechanisms to enhance individual ambidexterity at different hierarchical levels.

Notably, most of the current research on individual ambidexterity is in the context of large firms, with limited research and understanding of individual ambidexterity in small- and medium-sized enterprises (SMEs) and the entrepreneurship of SMEs (Hughes, 2018). Entrepreneurship is normally explained as entrepreneurial behavior or orientation in the workplace, consisting of the following dimensions: proactiveness, risk-taking, and innovativeness (Covin et al., 2020; Covin & Slevin, 1989). Ambidexterity is necessary for SME entrepreneurship and performance (Parida et al., 2016). For example, it has been found that entrepreneurship in SMEs is not sufficient for the operation of SMEs, and for SMEs to achieve higher performance, the processes of exploration and exploitation, that is, ambidexterity, is needed (Cenamor et al., 2019; Hughes et al., 2018a; Kohtamäki et al., 2010). In recent years, individual-level entrepreneurship has been prominent (Covin et al., 2020; Kraus et al., 2019; Ritala et al., 2021). The entrepreneurs tend to represent the senior management level, and the individuals at the middle and frontline employees' levels also need to perform entrepreneurship to contribute to the SME's strategy and innovation (Covin et al., 2020; Hughes et al., 2018b; Kraus et al., 2011). However, these individuals experience paradoxical challenges of exploration and exploitation to enhance their entrepreneurship (Volery et al., 2015; Yeganegi et al., 2019). Exploration activities help individuals discover and develop new opportunities for entrepreneurship, and exploitation activities help individuals implement new opportunities to enhance entrepreneurial behavior (Kraus et al., 2019). However, SMEs have limited resources and individuals need to manage the exploration-exploitation challenges to achieve entrepreneurship (Covin et al., 2020; Ritala et al., 2021; Yeganegi et al., 2019).

Compared with large firms, SMEs have limited resources to develop their competitive advantages. Specifically, SMEs tend to have limited tangible and intangible resources, managerial expertise, structural regulations, and endure challenges from their external environments (Chang & Hughes, 2012). These characteristics lead SMEs, particularly entrepreneurial SMEs, to achieve ambidexterity through a contextual approach, i.e., the organization should achieve exploration and exploitation across multiple levels (Gibson & Birkinshaw, 2004; Mu et al., 2020). At the individual level, individual ambidexterity can be seen as the microfoundations of organizational ambidexterity in SMEs (Rogan & Mors, 2014), i.e., individual ambidexterity can enhance the organizational ambidexterity of SMEs (Schnellbächer et al., 2019). Therefore, there is a greater need for organizational members in SMEs to pursue ambidexterity. The scarce resources in SMEs might also restrict individuals' ability to reconcile the conflicts of exploratory and exploitative activities (Gupta et al., 2006), enhancing the paradoxical challenges experienced at individual-level entrepreneurship (Volery et al., 2015). This emphasizes that the appropriate mechanisms need to be utilized to provide more resources, knowledge, and information for individuals in SMEs (Schultz et al., 2013), to reduce the waste of resources, balance the individuals' exploratory and exploitative activities, and to resolve different paradoxical challenges at different hierarchical levels.

This chapter provides recommendations for SMEs and individual-level entrepreneurship on enhancing individual ambidexterity through the different mechanisms outlined in the nomological network of individual ambidexterity developed in this study, contributing to the literature of SME entrepreneurship (Ferreira et al., 2019; Kraus et al., 2021). The nomological network can help individuals experiencing different paradoxical challenges in SMEs to understand various mechanisms, which can be used to enable their ambidextrous behavior. SMEs could use the nomological network developed in this chapter to assess their resources and provisions at different levels, which will help them to evaluate their individual ambidexterity capabilities and to redistribute their limited resources according to the requirements of the different levels (as per the antecedents and mechanisms in the nomological network) to enhance individual ambidexterity, and consequently enhance their organizational ambidexterity and performance.

This chapter's contributions are as follows. The chapter constructs nomological networks of individual ambidexterity through the theory of hierarchical heterogeneity and paradoxical challenges and conducts a systematic review. This nomological network categorizes individual ambidexterity antecedents as organizational and individual level mechanisms and provides these antecedents of individual ambidexterity at three hierarchical levels, as multi-hierarchical-level individual ambidexterity. The chapter extends the literature to include additional unexplored antecedents enhancing individual ambidexterity at the three hierarchical levels. Finally, it concludes with recommendations to SMEs and entrepreneurship in SMEs, contributing to individual ambidexterity and SME entrepreneurship.

Individual Ambidexterity

Definition of Individual Ambidexterity

Individual ambidexterity is important for individual-level entrepreneurship in SMEs, as the achievement of individual-level ambidexterity and entrepreneurship contribute to organizational objectives (Ritala et al., 2021). This emphasizes the need to understand the exploration-exploitation context at the individual level (Covin et al., 2020). While the unified definition of individual ambidexterity is to achieve exploration and exploitation simultaneously at the individual level, the detailed content of individual ambidexterity changes according to the research context, specifically, according to individuals' roles. As organization members are at different hierarchical levels (i.e., senior management level, middle management level, and frontline employee level), their exploration-exploitation challenges differ. According to Mom et al. (2007), managers' exploratory behaviors are "searching for, discovering, creating, and experimenting with new opportunities," and exploitative behaviors are "selecting, implementing, improving and refining existing certainties" (p. 910). At the non-management level, Rosing and Zacher (2017) defined exploration as "experimentation, searching for alternative ways to accomplish a task, and learning from errors" and exploitation as "relying on previous experience, putting things into action, and incrementally improving well-learned actions" (p. 686), which is consistent with Mom et al.'s (2007) definition, except that the focus is transferred from strategies to specific tasks and actions. Therefore, the achievement of individual ambidexterity is different for the different hierarchical levels where ambidextrous behavior increases as seniority increases (Swart et al., 2019). However, the mechanisms contributing to this individual ambidextrous behavior at the different seniority levels are unclear.

Hierarchical Heterogeneity of Individual Ambidexterity

An organization is a coordinated system of individuals with heterogeneous attributes such as goals, information, and behavior (March & Simon, 1958). This heterogeneity occurs across different parts of an organization, and hierarchy is a critical element dividing the organization into different parts (i.e., different hierarchical levels) (Weber, 1978), each containing individuals with heterogeneous attributes. Hierarchical heterogeneity has been called for further research in organizations (Cole & Bruch, 2006; Gibson et al., 2019). As a critical organizational attribute, formalized hierarchical levels (Weber, 1978) (contrasted to the subsystems which view hierarchy through informal relational-based systems; March & Simon, 1958) formulate an authority-based structure in the organization, and create and transfer knowledge and information at different hierarchical levels (Gibson et al., 2019). Therefore, the hierarchical levels can generate organizational heterogeneity that has implications for the work and performance of individuals at those levels (Gibson et al., 2019).

However, scholars emphasize that research on individual ambidexterity at different hierarchical levels is limited (Andriopoulos & Lewis, 2009; Swart et al., 2019). The difference in each level's individual ambidexterity can be observed from their different foci concerning exploration and exploitation activities (Martin et al., 2019; Mom et al., 2007), and different paradoxical challenges or conflicting tensions to be solved by individuals at each level (Adler et al., 1999; Bonesso et al., 2014; Gregory et al., 2015; Simsek et al., 2009).

The hierarchy changes the context around individuals by levels, adjusting the individuals' roles and contributions in completing corporate and business strategies. The lower a level an individual goes, the less empowerment and information they will be exposed to (Gibson et al., 2019), and the fewer expectations they will have in contributing to these strategies. Specifically, senior managers are responsible for designing and developing corporate and business strategies, such as setting the overarching vision and mission. These strategies need to be implemented with the help of middle managers, who are key to translating strategies and the vision of the top management team to lower-level employees (Mustafa et al., 2016). Therefore middle managers have some exposure to strategies but to a lesser extent compared to senior managers. However, at the lowest hierarchical level, frontline employees are distanced from corporate and business strategies, so they are less clear on the strategies and the top management team's goals and vision. They focus more on the targets set in their appraisals and annual performance reviews. Therefore, individuals must complete different working tasks and meet different role specifications by hierarchical levels (Gibson et al., 2019). Hierarchy is an essential element in understanding individuals' ambidextrous behavior.

This chapter constructs a hierarchically-heterogeneous view of individual ambidexterity by explaining the differences of the three hierarchical levels' individual ambidexterity. Based on the formal authority structure in organizations (Weber, 1978), this chapter delineates the hierarchical construction of individual ambidexterity into three levels: senior management, middle management, and non-management (i.e., frontline employees' level). Differences between individual ambidexterity "exist from one hierarchical level to the next" (Gibson et al., 2019, p. 1716). The magnitude and form of individual ambidexterity held by senior managers, middle managers, and frontline employees are inconsistent. Based on this principle, this chapter reviews the antecedents of individual ambidexterity by distinguishing individual ambidexterity's hierarchical levels, discussing the appropriate antecedents to resolve different paradoxical challenges at different hierarchical levels.

Systematic Literature Review Methodology

A search on the Scopus database was conducted using the keywords "ambidexterity" in the context of management "since 2007" because of the empirical paper that studies individual ambidexterity by Mom et al. (2007). To ensure the quality of the papers selected for inclusion, papers in the journal that ranked ABS 3 or above were selected for review. Twenty papers were included as relevant papers. While reviewing and reading the papers, eight additional relevant papers were found and included.

As for the type of firms, two papers are about SMEs' context, 12 papers are about large companies, two papers include SMEs and large firms, while 12 papers did not specify the sample firms' size. It could be seen that there is a lack of individual ambidexterity research in the SME context. As for the hierarchical level of individual ambidexterity, three papers focus on the senior management level, eight papers study the middle management level, 11 papers explore the frontline employee level, and one paper considers multiple levels of individual ambidexterity. In addition, three papers research individual ambidexterity however without any context of hierarchical levels, and one paper mentions managers but does not clarify the specific levels of the samples. Therefore the current research provides a limited understanding of the different mechanisms enhancing individual ambidexterity at different hierarchical levels as a holistic nomological network.

The antecedents of individual ambidexterity are categorized as organizational-level antecedents and individual-level antecedents. Based on the literature review, the organizational-level antecedents (13) are summarized following these themes: organization context (Ajayi et al., 2017; Awojide et al., 2018; Bidmon & Boe-Lillegraven, 2020; Luo et al., 2018); organization practices and systems (Kao & Chen, 2016; Lee & Meyer-Doyler, 2017; Mom et al., 2019; Mom et al., 2009; Panagopoulos et al., 2020; Prieto-Pastor & Martin-Perez, 2015; Zimmermann et al., 2018); and knowledge resources and processes (Hodgkinson et al., 2014; Mom et al., 2007; Rogan & Mors, 2014; Schultz et al., 2013; Torres et al., 2015). The individual-level antecedents (23) are summarized following these themes: leadership behavior (Kauppila & Tempelaar, 2016; Luo et al., 2018; Prieto-Pastor & Martin-Perez, 2015; Salas Vallina et al., 2019; Yu et al., 2020; Zacher et al., 2016; Zacher & Wilden, 2014); and individual characteristics (Bonesso et al., 2014; Enkel et al., 2017; Jasmand et al., 2012; Kauppila & Tempelaar, 2016; Lee & Kim, 2021; Mom et al., 2019; Mom et al., 2015; Shamim et al., 2020; Swart et al., 2019; Tempelaar & Rosenkranz, 2019; Yu et al., 2020; Zhang et al., 2019). Four papers have explored organizational and individual mechanisms to enable individual ambidexterity (Kao & Chen, 2016; Luo et al., 2018; Mom et al., 2019; Prieto-Pastor & Martin-Perez, 2015). The nomological networks based on the review of organizational and individual antecedents of individual ambidexterity at the three hierarchical levels are outlined in Figure 6.1.

These antecedents are explained at the different hierarchical levels in the following sections.

Organizational-Level Antecedents of Individual Ambidexterity

Organizational Context

As theorized by Gibson and Birkinshaw (2004), the elements that formulate a context encouraging ambidexterity include stretch, discipline, social support, and trust. These factors have been examined to positively influence organizational ambidexterity (Gibson & Birkinshaw, 2004). However, there has been no empirical test to measure this context on individual ambidexterity. An empirical study on the role of the organizational culture, which can be considered an element of organizational context, found that middle managers' ambidexterity can be enabled by their organizations' cultural resources (Awojide et al., 2018). Specifically, managers can select manifest-visible cultural values (e.g., improving existing products and process efficiently) to support their exploitative activities and latent-hidden cultural values (e.g., knowledge sharing and change) to promote their exploratory activities. In a study on SMEs, Ajayi et al. (2017) suggested a different organizational context that combines cultural elements, organic

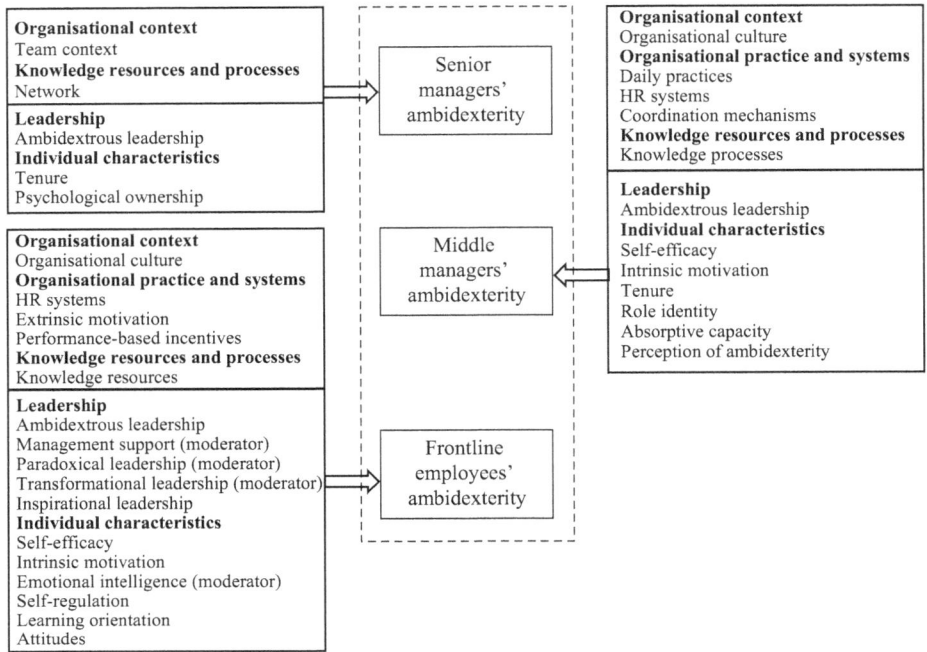

Figure 6.1: Organizational and individual level antecedents of multi-hierarchical-level individual ambidexterity.

structure, knowledge sharing culture, clan culture, and adhocracy culture. These elements can enhance frontline employees' ability to contribute to their organizations' objectives and competitive advantages, so as to then enable their ambidexterity (Ajayi et al., 2017).

Another organizational context antecedent is the team context. For example, team behavioral integration, which is a team characteristic as well as a context of team members, can promote the ambidextrous behavior of team members through team collaboration, efficient and sufficient information and knowledge exchange, and the decision-making process (Hambrick, 1994; Lubatkin et al., 2006). According to Luo et al. (2018), top management teams' behavioral integration can promote senior managers' individual ambidexterity by developing their capabilities to manage complex knowledge, adapt to uncertain environments, and develop complementary skills. This is an example of adapting the context to the group level.

In summary, the literature indicates that different manifestations of organizational culture can influence middle managers and frontline employees' ambidexterity, and team context can enhance senior managers' ambidexterity. However, there have not been any empirical studies on the elements suggested by Gibson and Birkinshaw (2004): stretch, discipline, social support, and trust. Regarding the support element, Bidmon and Boe-Lillegraven (2020) argue that if the work context can provide emotional and cognitive support, such context and support will enhance individuals' exploratory and exploitative capabilities to achieve ambidexterity. However, these have not been studied at a specific level, and since the organizational context could influence the three hierarchical levels' individual ambidexterity (Gibson & Birkinshaw, 2004; Rogan & Mors, 2014), these mechanisms need to be studied at the three hierarchical levels.

Organizational Practices and Systems

As part of the organizational context, organizational practices and systems formulated by organizational members' actions can inspire individuals to participate in the process of perceiving organizational goals and achieving ambidexterity in pursuit of them (Junni et al., 2015). Three types of practices and systems have been studied in the individual ambidexterity area: HR practices and systems, motivation systems, and daily practices and systems.

A high-involvement HR system was introduced as a configuration of six HR practices: recruitment and selection, training, compensation, performance appraisal, job design, and participation (Prieto-Pastor & Martin-Perez, 2015). It can facilitate frontline employees' ambidexterity as it improves employees' abilities, motivations and opportunities, and guides knowledge exchange and employees' behavioral orientation (Prieto-Pastor & Martin-Perez, 2015).

Another HR system, specifically ability-, motivation-, and opportunity-enhancing HR practices, has been studied to influence middle managers' individual ambidexterity and the routines from individual to organizational ambidexterity (Mom et al., 2019). The ability- and motivation-enhancing HR practices can facilitate operational managers' individual ambidexterity, and opportunity-enhancing practices moderate the routines from operational managers' individual ambidexterity to organizational ambidexterity. Furthermore, Panagopoulos et al. (2020) have found that ambidexterity in ability-enhancing practices (i.e., selection and training) ensures that employees have relevant knowledge, skills, and abilities. Ambidexterity in motivation-enhancing practices (i.e., metrics and incentives) and opportunity-enhancing practices (i.e., data and tool use) motivates and enables employees to complete their activities (Panagopoulos et al., 2020). These studies examine the middle managers and frontline employees' ambidexterity and emphasize the role of different HR practices and systems as individual ambidexterity's antecedents.

Another type of organizational practice and system is the motivation system, which influences ambidextrous behavior through individual attitudes, values, and beliefs (Faisal Ahammad et al., 2015; Stokes et al., 2016; Yu et al., 2020). Existing studies of the motivation system as an antecedent of individual ambidexterity include work motivation and incentives. Work motivation is classified into intrinsic motivation and extrinsic motivation (Kao & Chen, 2016). While intrinsic motivation stems from personal attributes, extrinsic motivation results from organization practices and rewards. Kao and Chen (2016) found that intrinsic motivation can facilitate frontline employees' ambidextrous behavior, enhancing their performance. Meanwhile, extrinsic reward (i.e., extrinsic motivation) negatively moderates the relationship between intrinsic motivation and individual ambidexterity as it might inhibit the creative process. Incentive is another motivational factor that helps individuals to manage exploration and exploitation (March, 1991). Lee and Meyer-Doyle (2017) examined performance-based incentives on employees' exploration and exploitation. They found a negative impact of performance-based incentives on employees' exploration. This is because a weakened performance-based incentive enables experiential learning, especially in complex task environments (Lee & Meyer-Doyle, 2017).

Daily practices and systems are another type of organizational practice and system. Zimmermann et al. (2018) explored how middle managers manage ambidextrous requirements with marketing and product development objectives in their daily practices. Their study recommends three configurational practices to enable middle managers to consistently align their initiatives, adapt organizational context, and manage the persistent exploration-exploitation tensions in their daily activities. Configurational practices enable operational managers to understand product exploration and exploitation. Contrasting practices promote the managers' completion of the formal structure with supervision and monitoring systems to achieve market exploration and exploitation. Configurational exposure practices help the managers to combine exploratory and exploitative activities across product and market strategies. Therefore, these three practices work as a system to facilitate middle managers' ambidexterity. However, the influence of the daily practices and systems on senior managers and frontline employees' ambidexterity has not been explored.

In summary, HR practices and systems have been examined at middle managers' and frontline employees' level. According to the literature of HR practices and systems as the antecedents of organizational ambidexterity, more HR practices and systems can help resolve the paradoxical challenges of middle managers and employees, such as a high-performance work system (Chang, 2015; Patel et al., 2013) and an ambidextrous HR system (Garaus et al., 2016). The studies of motivation systems have examined extrinsic motivation and performance-based incentives as antecedents to frontline employees' ambidexterity. According to March (1991), additional types of incentives need further research, for example, empowerment. Additionally, the discussion on practices and systems are limited at the organizational level (i.e., HR practices and systems and motivation systems) and the individual level (i.e., daily practices and systems), and the systems operated at the team level have not been studied, such as transactive memory systems which help knowledge sharing (Simeonova, 2018). Transactive memory systems have been found to influence organizational ambidexterity (Heavey & Simsek, 2014), and research is needed on transactive memory systems' influence on individual ambidexterity.

Knowledge Resources and Processes

Knowledge perspective is an important pillar to constitute the study of ambidexterity (Mom et al., 2007). Developed from the resource-based view, the knowledge-based view supports that organizations' differences are derived from the organization's abilities to develop, organize, and leverage knowledge (Spender, 1996). The organization's ability to develop existing knowledge and create new knowledge facilitates the firm's growth (Kogut & Zander, 1992), indicating the importance of ambidextrous knowledge ability and process.

At the organizational level, researchers have studied the impact of knowledge resources (Revilla et al., 2016), intellectual capital (Kang & Snell, 2009; Lin et al., 2017), knowledge stock (Ramachandran et al., 2019), and knowledge acquisitions on ambidexterity (Xie et al., 2020). The stock and access to these knowledge resources are important to organizations and individuals who need to utilize resources to reconcile their inter-conflict (Gibson & Birkinshaw, 2004; March, 1991).

Knowledge resources are processed horizontally among different functions and vertically at multiple levels, which is important to promote an ambidextrous context in organizations and encourage individual ambidextrous capability and behaviors (Kang & Snell, 2009). Based on the knowledge-based view, knowledge is an important organizational factor that could impact individual behaviors (Mom et al., 2007). Mom et al. (2007) tested the influence of knowledge received from different levels on the middle manager's ambidextrous activities. Knowledge received from higher hierarchical levels enhances the middle managers' exploitative activities, but not their exploratory activities. Knowledge received from lower hierarchical levels enhances the middle manager's exploratory activities, but not their exploitative activities. Furthermore, Torres et al. (2015) found that knowledge received from senior managers benefits middle managers' strategic decision-making capabilities and facilitates their individual ambidexterity and performance. Compared to the nomological network of ambidexterity at the organizational level, additional mechanisms of knowledge resources, such as intellectual capital (Lin et al., 2017) and knowledge acquisitions (Xie et al., 2020), need to be explored for individual ambidexterity.

Network can enhance knowledge-sharing processes. For example, the senior manager's internal and external networks are important levers to balance the tension between exploring new business and exploiting existing business at the individual level (Rogan & Mors, 2014). Rogan and Mors (2014) found that three network characteristics – density, contact heterogeneity, and informality – which influence senior managers' ambidexterity. The manager's external network density influences their ambidexterity through exploration; the internal contact heterogeneity of network ties impacts the manager's ambidexterity through knowledge mobilization; and the informality of network ties helps the mobilization of resources. However, additional mechanisms of knowledge processes have been examined to influence organizational ambidexterity but have not been explored to achieve individual ambidexterity, such as knowledge sharing and exchange (De Clercq et al., 2013) and knowledge integration (Tiwana, 2008). Such processes are power ascribed, and it is important to understand the influence of power and empowerment on individual ambidexterity at the three hierarchical levels (Simeonova, 2018), and the influence of different types of power on individual ambidexterity (Simeonova et al., 2022).

Coordination Mechanisms

Formal coordination mechanisms integrate different activities through existing rules and systems, while informal coordination mechanisms refer to emerging connections that combine different activities across boundaries such as functional boundary or cross-level boundary (Tsai, 2002).

Formal coordination mechanisms include factors such as centralization and formalization (Jansen et al., 2006, 2009). Centralization concerns the role of formal authority hierarchically in an organization's decision-making process (Jansen et al., 2012), while formalization is the extent that rules and procedures govern (Jansen et al., 2006). Centralization has been demonstrated to hinder middle managers' ambidexterity, and formalization not to influence managers' ambidexterity (Mom et al., 2009). This finding is not consistent with a unit-level study which found that the degree of formalization positively influences the units' exploitation by enhancing incremental learning but has no significant effect on exploration (Jansen et al., 2006). Therefore, the impact of formalization on individual ambidexterity might be more complex than it would seem (Mom et al., 2009). Configurations of formal and informal coordination mechanisms that enable individual ambidexterity need research. Another study has demonstrated that control, which can be seen as a manifestation of centralization, hinders individuals' ability to balance exploration and exploitation (Bidmon & Boe-Lillegraven, 2020). This negative effect has been mitigated through the supportive context on individuals' emotion and cognition, indicating a need to understand the interaction between structural and contextual mechanisms (Bidmon & Boe-Lillegraven, 2020). However, hierarchical levels have not been specified, which necessitates research on emotion and cognition support at the three different levels, as these are important mechanisms.

Informal coordination mechanisms include the factors that can integrate information and knowledge such as connectedness, cross-functional interfaces, and social integration (Jansen et al., 2006, 2009; Mom et al., 2009). For example, a manager's participation in cross-functional knowledge processes positively impacts the ambidextrous behavior (Mom et al., 2009). This has been validated by the study of Tempelaar and Rosenkranz (2019) with samples of managers in multinational enterprises, while cross-functional coordination is tested as a moderator between role identity and individual ambidexterity. Connectedness also has a positive relationship with a middle manager's individual ambidexterity, although scholars considered an inverted-U hypothesis (Mom et al., 2009), which needs further explanation. However, social integration as an individual ambidexterity's antecedent needs empirical research. In addition, the combination of formal and informal coordination mechanisms to facilitate ambidexterity needs research as it is argued that formal coordination mechanisms benefit exploitation while informal coordination mechanisms can facilitate exploration (Jansen et al., 2009; Mom et al., 2009).

In summary, the formal and informal coordination mechanisms need further research, particularly at the senior management and frontline employees' levels.

Individual-Level Antecedents of Individual Ambidexterity

The individual-level antecedents can be categorized as leadership behavior and individual characteristics.

Leadership Behavior

Various leadership behaviors reportedly enable followers' individual ambidexterity at the managerial level (Luo et al., 2018) and the non-managerial level (Hunter et al., 2011). At the senior and middle management levels, ambidextrous leadership can facilitate managers' ambidexterity (Luo et al., 2018; Zacher et al., 2016). At the frontline employees' level, the effect of various leadership behaviors has been studied: ambidextrous leadership (Zacher et al., 2016; Zacher & Wilden, 2014), paradoxical leadership (Kauppila & Tempelaar, 2016), management support (Prieto-Pastor & Martin-Perez, 2015), inspirational leadership (Salas Vallina et al., 2019), and transformational leadership (Yu et al., 2020).

For example, Luo et al. (2018) examined ambidextrous leadership as transformational and transactional leadership styles, and found that in a top management team, a CEO's ambidextrous leadership can benefit other senior managers' ambidextrous behavior through team integration. Similarly, paradoxical leadership consists of managerial support with high performance expectations of the manager's followers (Kauppila & Tempelaar, 2016). According to the empirical study of Kauppila and Tempelaar (2016), group managers' paradoxical leadership can help their followers to pursue ambidexterity. It also moderates the relationship between employees' learning orientation and individual ambidexterity, supporting a combination of individual mechanisms to facilitate individual ambidexterity. However, further research is needed to understand the combination of organizational level and individual-level factors on individual ambidexterity at the different hierarchical levels.

In another study, Prieto-Pastor and Martin-Perez (2015) found that supervisors' managerial support of their employees can facilitate employees' ambidextrous behaviors. Supervisors' management support creates a high-involvement context of encouraging organizational contribution and new ideas and improves work efficiency and performance. Therefore, management support contributes to employees' ambidextrous behaviors. Similarly, transformational leadership has been found to positively moderate the effect of individual characteristics (e.g., attitudes and self-efficacy) on individual ambidexterity (Yu et al., 2020). As a dimension of transformational leadership, inspirational leadership can bring enthusiasm and confidence to followers and facilitate the employees' management of the tension between exploration and exploitation (Salas Vallina et al., 2019).

In conclusion, various leadership styles have been studied, including ambidextrous leadership, paradoxical leadership, management support, inspirational leadership, and transformational leadership. However, the majority of these (i.e., management support, paradoxical leadership, and transformational leadership) have been studied as moderators, not as antecedents. However, these are important factors that need research as antecedents to enable individual ambidexterity. Additionally, these factors have been studied at the frontline employee level and not higher levels, however, these are important at higher levels, as leadership could influence the three hierarchical levels and their exploration and exploitation differently (Rosing et al., 2011; Vera & Crossan, 2004). Additional leadership styles, such as transactional leadership (Lin & McDonough, 2011), need research.

Individual Characteristics

Individual characteristics involve factors of personal characteristics, experiences, psychological factors, actions, and capabilities.

Individual ambidexterity is influenced by personal characteristics at the middle management level and frontline employees' level (Bonesso et al., 2014; Jasmand et al., 2012; Raisch et al., 2009). At the middle management level, Jasmand et al. (2012) have found that self-regulation characteristics composed of locomotion orientation and assessment orientation influence individual ambidexterity. Intrinsic motivation is another antecedent of individual ambidexterity as a stable internal characteristic (Kao & Chen, 2016), increasing frontline employees' self-motivation and improving their capability. Additionally, Kao and Chen (2016) found that emotional intelligence moderates the effect of intrinsic motivation on individual ambidexterity. However, as an important factor in the creative process (Kao & Chen, 2016), emotional intelligence needs research as an antecedent of individual ambidexterity at the three hierarchical levels.

Individuals' self-efficacy characteristic describes the extent of individuals viewing their capabilities to complete tasks. It facilitates individual ambidexterity by emphasizing learning capabilities (Kauppila & Tempelaar, 2016), which enhances individual ambidexterity and has been examined at the frontline employee level (Salas Vallina et al., 2019). Mom et al. (2019) have studied self-efficacy as a mediator between ability-enhancing HR practices and operational managers' ambidexterity. Similarly, Yu et al. (2020) found a direct impact from frontline employees' self-efficacy on their ambidexterity.

Tenure is another individual characteristic that has been emphasized as the antecedent of individual ambidexterity. Mom et al. (2015) found that managers' organizational tenure positively influenced their ambidextrous behavior, but their functional tenure is negatively associated with the ambidexterity as it can narrow the manager's knowledge. This view is extended by Bonesso et al. (2014), who found that inter-functional experience positively impacts individual ambidexterity. Specifically, Bonesso et al. (2014) found the middle managers who achieved the consistency between the perception and behavior of ambidexterity have prior work experiences, such as inter-functional, inter-firm, and/or inter-industry experience. These individuals also have emotional and social competencies. Individual ambidexterity also can be impacted by job roles. Andriopoulos and Lewis (2009) explained that the specific actions taken by individuals should be different by levels. Following their suggestions, Swart et al. (2019) examined effects of the level of seniority on individual ambidexterity. Swart et al. (2019) examined five hierarchical levels (administrators, specialists, principal specialists, manager-consultants, and senior managers), and found that senior managers tend to show a higher level of ambidexterity than other groups levels, and that administrators and specialists are less likely to perform exploration activities or behave ambidextrously. Therefore, additional research of antecedents and mechanisms to enhance senior and middle managers' ambidexterity is crucial as these are the most ambidextrous levels.

Individual psychology involves flexible mechanisms to be changed by the environment around the individual. In a study of psychological ownership, senior managers' psychological ownership of the organization and the job interact to motivate individual ambidexterity (Lee & Kim, 2021). Some studies emphasize individual perception as an antecedent of individual ambidexterity, another psychological factor. This factor is derived from role theory (Katz & Kahn, 1966), cognitive theory (Smith & Tushman, 2005), and cognitive dissonance theory (Festinger, 1957), and has been suggested by March (1991) as a motivation of individual behavior. Bonesso et al. (2014) divided individual ambidexterity into two traits: the perception of ambidexterity and the behavior of ambidexterity. The inconsistency between role perception and actual behaviors is a barrier to achieving individual ambidexterity, therefore the individual needs to be able to perceive ambidextrous orientation, and to have the ability to reconcile paradoxical challenges (Gupta et al. 2006; Raisch et al., 2009), and then they can behave ambidextrously. However, Bonesso et al. (2014) did not study the direct relationship between an individual's perception of their ambidexterity and subsequent behavior. Yu et al.'s (2020) empirical study can be viewed as an extension of Bonesso et al.'s (2014) argument. They examined frontline employees' attitude and behavior of ambidexterity and found that attitude enhances ambidextrous behavior directly (Yu et al., 2020). Furthermore, the perception of role identity also can enable individual ambidexterity through the individuals' assessment on information (Tempelaar & Rosenkranz, 2019). Working with different role identities, individuals have the challenge of role transition, that is the transition between different roles, and two continuums are formed based on their perception – role segmentation and role integration – and individuals' perception on role integration can enhance their ambidexterity (Tempelaar & Rosenkranz, 2019).

Various studies have emphasized individual actions, skills, and capabilities to achieve individual ambidexterity. Individual actions were studied to enable individual ambidexterity at five hierarchical levels, involving actions of buffering, gap filling, integrating, role expansion, and tone setting (Swart et al., 2019). It has been found that senior managers perform general and integrated activities such as integration, role expansion, and tone setting to coordinate followers and promote innovation in the organization. The actions of the lower-level employees, such as specialists, are gap filling to complete projects ambidextrously (Swart et al., 2019). According to Zhang et al. (2019), the ability to manage work stress can help individuals manage their performance, and trust-building ability encourages the building of a social support environment. Furthermore, Enkel et al. (2017) found that absorptive capacity is essential for individual ambidexterity. However, except for absorptive capacity at the middle management level, these factors have not been studied at a specific level, and need research at the three hierarchical levels as important individual capabilities enhancing individual ambidexterity.

Additionally, some mechanisms are important at organizational and individual levels and need research to understand their influence on individual ambidexterity at the three hierarchical levels. These mechanisms are trust, transactive memory systems, emotion and cognition support, motivation, knowledge processes, power, and empowerment.

Conclusion and Implications for SMEs

The mechanisms to enable individual ambidexterity can be viewed at three hierarchical levels. Derived from the theories of hierarchical heterogeneity and paradoxical challenges, this chapter has created three nomological networks of individual ambidexterity at three hierarchical levels. Figure 6.1 outlines a nomological network of the existing literature on organizational and individual level antecedents of individual ambidexterity at senior managers, middle managers, and frontline employees' levels. Figure 6.2 outlines a nomological network of the new and additional antecedents of individual ambidexterity, recommended in this chapter, at senior managers, middle managers, and frontline employees' levels. The existing, new, and additional antecedents and mechanisms of individual ambidexterity at senior managers, middle managers, and frontline employees' levels are outlined at Figure 6.3.

In the literature, Swart et al. (2019) have highlighted senior managers as the most ambidextrous level. However, this chapter demonstrated that research on individual ambidexterity at the senior management level is limited and needs expansion and further research. The organizational-level antecedents of senior managers' ambidexterity are team context and network, while the individual-level antecedents are ambidextrous leadership, tenure, and phycological ownership.

Based on the theoretical lenses and the nomological networks developed in this chapter, the following unexplored mechanisms have been outlined as antecedents that need research at the senior management level. Senior managers require an appropriate context to encourage exploratory and exploitative behavior, so the study on organizational context with a configuration of elements needs research (Gibson & Birkinshaw, 2004). As a type of organizational context, the daily practices of senior managers, which can be transformed into exploratory and exploitative activities could also be studied. Different types of knowledge resources and practices can also impact senior managers' decision-making accuracy and efficiency in terms of corporate and business strategies and objectives. Specifically, increasing the amount of knowledge resources (e.g., intellectual capital and knowledge stock) available to senior managers can resolve the paradoxical challenges and help senior managers reconcile conflicts when exploratory and exploitative activities compete for the same resources. Additional important factors which need research are various knowledge processes, such as knowledge sharing and exchange, and knowledge integration. Additional antecedents also include organizational context and culture, trust, motivation, transactive memory systems, coordination mechanisms, power, control, emotion and cognition support. At an individual level additional antecedents of senior managers' individual ambidexterity include leadership styles (e.g., transformational leadership, transactional leadership), various individual characteristics and capabilities.

The antecedents of middle managers' ambidexterity have been the subject of extensive research outlining numerous mechanisms at the organizational and individual levels. At an organizational level, middle managers need an appropriate organizational culture to encourage their actions on exploratory and exploitative actions. For example, some organizational cultures aim to provide emotional and cognitive support to help exploration and exploitation. In the theme of organizational practices and systems, middle managers' behavior can be enhanced by HR practices and systems and daily practices. Regarding coordination mechanisms, middle managers can utilize informal coordination mechanisms to receive more knowledge and information, which can benefit their ambidexterity. Additionally, the ambidextrous leadership of senior managers can facilitate ambidexterity among middle managers. At an individual level, middle managers' personal characteristics (i.e., intrinsic motivation, self-efficacy, and emotional intelligence) and experiences (i.e., tenure) provide them with the motivation and capability to enable their individual ambidexterity. Their psychological factors, actions, and capabilities which can be trained and motivated by the organization are also considered antecedents of ambidextrous behavior.

At the middle management level, the following unexplored mechanisms have been outlined as antecedents which need research. Middle managers require an appropriate organizational context to facilitate their creative behavior, and regulate their routines and their exploitative activities effectively. These processes can be enhanced through organizational practices and systems. For example, a high-involvement HR system can improve the participation of middle managers in the development of corporate and business strategies, and then promote the alignment of middle managers' objectives with organizational objectives. Middle managers also need to understand knowledge resources and processes as outlined at the senior management level. Based on the knowledge-based view, the more knowledge resources obtained by middle managers, the more possibility there is that the middle managers can resolve their paradoxical challenges. The role of leadership at the middle managers' level and its influence on their individual ambidexterity needs considerable extension and research. Unexplored mechanisms include management support, paradoxical leadership, and leadership styles (e.g., transformational, transactional). Additional important antecedents of middle managers' ambidexterity that need research include organizational context, trust, motivation, empowerment, transactive memory systems, coordination mechanisms, power, emotion and cognition support, leadership styles, and various individual characteristics and capabilities.

The research on frontline employees' ambidexterity is skewed towards individual-level antecedents, which means that individual ambidexterity at the lower hierarchical level is self-motivated and organizational and support factors have been omitted. However, these are paramount to support the lower levels and their management of competing exploitation and exploration activities with limited resources, knowledge, information, authority, and support. Therefore, research needs considerable extension to understand the combination on individual and organizational level mechanism to enhance individual ambidexterity at frontline employees' level.

Hierarchical heterogeneity in an organization means that frontline employees receive very limited authority at the operational level. The organizational-level mechanisms that enhance frontline employees' ambidexterity are organizational culture and various HR systems, which can be encouraged or discouraged by motivation systems such as the financial rewarding system. At an individual level, frontline employees' personal characteristics such as their learning orientation, self-regulation, intrinsic motivation, and self-efficacy can improve their ability to balance exploration and exploitation and encourage them to behave ambidextrously.

The unexplored areas of the antecedents of frontline employees can be observed from the factors in this literature review. The work of frontline employees has regulations on their tasks and routines, therefore frontline employees' ambidexterity is considerably managed and influenced by organizational factors. Therefore, additional important organizational-level antecedents of frontline employees' ambidexterity that need research include organizational context, trust, motivation, empowerment, and coordination mechanisms.

The nomological networks of individual ambidexterity developed in this chapter are designed to help individuals in SMEs to understand which type of individual ambidexterity applies to them and how to achieve individual ambidexterity. Compared with large firms, the characteristics of SMEs can be observed from various perspectives such as organizational structure, context, practices and systems, knowledge resources and processes, leadership, and external environments. While large firms tend to have more than three hierarchical levels (Gibson et al., 2019), but SMEs might have less than three. Therefore, organizational members in SMEs tend to have interchangeable roles, with different paradoxical challenges. For example, senior managers participate in implementing business and corporate strategies and middle managers might have the opportunity to contribute to the designing process of corporate strategy (Parida et al., 2016). This also implies that the extent of formal coordination mechanisms tends to be smaller in SMEs and the extent of informal coordination mechanism tends to be larger (Chang & Hughes, 2012; Prajogo & Mcdermott, 2014). Individuals in SMEs can utilize these characteristics to benefit their ambidexterity. Also, individuals' interchangeable roles in SMEs indicate the need to study and understand the influence of organizational and individual-level factors on individual ambidexterity in parallel.

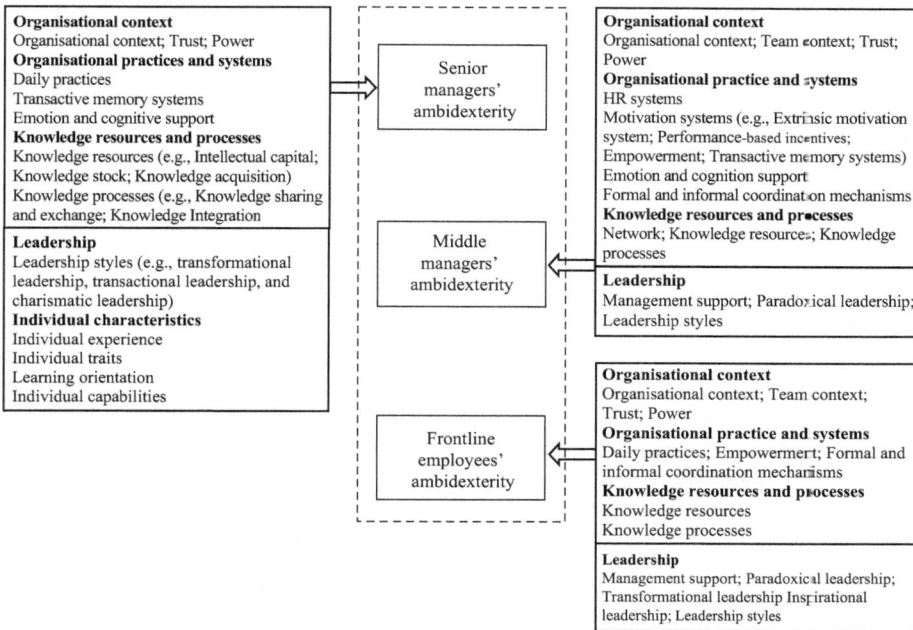

Figure 6.2: New and additional antecedents of multi-hierarchical-level individual ambidexterity.

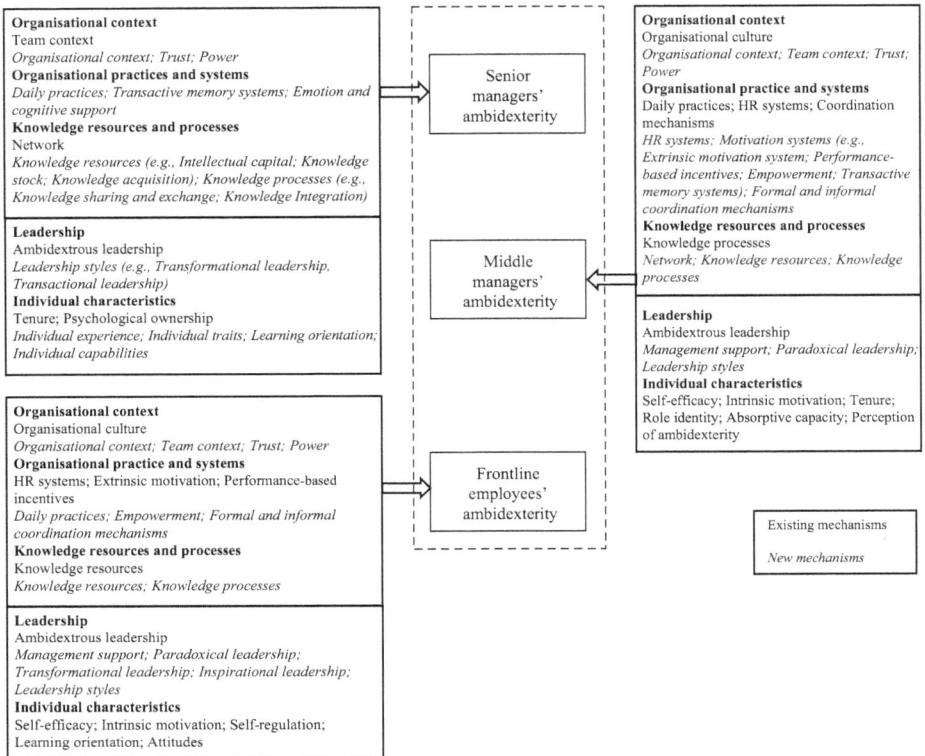

Figure 6.3: Existing, new, and additional antecedents and mechanisms of multi-hierarchical-level individual ambidexterity.

References

Adler, P.S., Goldoftas, B., & Levine, D.I. (1999). Flexibility versus efficiency? A case study of model changeovers in the Toyota production system. *Organization Science, 10*(1), 43–68.

Ajayi, O.M., Odusanya, K., & Morton, S. (2017). Stimulating employee ambidexterity in SMEs. *Management Decision, 55*(4), 662–680.

Andriopoulos, C., & Lewis, M.W. (2009). Exploitation-exploration tensions and organizational ambidexterity: Managing paradoxes of innovation. *Organization Science, 20*(4), 686–717.

Awojide, O., Hodgkinson, I.R., & Ravishankar, M.N. (2018). Managerial ambidexterity and the cultural toolkit in project delivery. *International Journal of Project Management, 36*(8), 1019–1033.

Bidmon, C.M., & Boe-Lillegraven, S. (2020). Now, switch! Individuals' responses to imposed switches between exploration and exploitation. *Long Range Planning, 53*(6), 101928.

Bonesso, S., Gerli, F., & Scapolan, A. (2014). The individual side of ambidexterity: Do individuals' perceptions match actual behaviors in reconciling the exploration and exploitation trade-off? *European Management Journal, 32*(3), 392–405.

Cenamor, J., Parida, V., & Wincent, J. (2019). How entrepreneurial SMEs compete through digital platforms: The roles of digital platform capability, network capability and ambidexterity. *Journal of Business Research, 100,* 196–206.

Chang, Y.Y. (2015). A multilevel examination of high-performance work systems and unit-level organizational ambidexterity. *Human Resource Management Journal, 25*(1), 78–101.

Chang, Y.Y., & Hughes, M. (2012). Drivers of innovation ambidexterity in small- to medium-sized firms. *European Management Journal, 30*(1), 1–17.

Cole, M.S., & Bruch, H. (2006). Organizational identity strength, identification, and commitment and their relationships to turnover intention: Does organizational hierarchy matter? *Journal of Organizational Behavior, 27*(5), 585–605.

Covin, J.G., Rigtering, J.P.C., Hughes, M., Kraus, S., Cheng, C.F., & Bouncken, R.B. (2020). Individual and team entrepreneurial orientation: Scale development and configurations for success. *Journal of Business Research, 112,* 1–12.

Covin, J.G., & Slevin, D.P. (1989). Strategic management of small firms in hostile and benign environments. *Strategic Management Journal, 10*(1), 75–87.

De Clercq, D., Thongpapanl, N., & Dimov, D. (2013). Shedding new light on the relationship between contextual ambidexterity and firm performance: An investigation of internal contingencies. *Technovation, 33*(4–5), 119–132.

Enkel, E., Heil, S., Hengstler, M., & Wirth, H. (2017). Exploratory and exploitative innovation: To what extent do the dimensions of individual level absorptive capacity contribute? *Technovation, 60–61,* 29–38.

Faisal Ahammad, M., Mook Lee, S., Malul, M., & Shoham, A. (2015). Behavioral ambidexterity: The impact of incentive schemes on productivity, motivation, and performance of employees in commercial banks. *Human Resource Management, 54*(S1), S45–S62.

Ferreira, J., Fernandes C., & Kraus, S. (2019). Entrepreneurship research: Mapping intellectual structures and research trends. *Review of Managerial Science, 13*(1), 181–205.

Festinger, L. (1957). *A theory of cognitive dissonance.* Stanford University Press.

Garaus, C., Güttel, W.H., Konlechner, S., Koprax, I., Lackner, H., Link, K., & Müller, B. (2016). Bridging knowledge in ambidextrous HRM systems: Empirical evidence from hidden champions. *International Journal of Human Resource Management, 27*(3), 355–381.

Gibson, C.B., & Birkinshaw, J. (2004). The antecedents, consequences, and mediating role of organizational ambidexterity. *Academy of Management Journal, 47*(2), 209–226.

Gibson, C.B., Birkinshaw, J., Sumpter, D.M., & Ambos, T. (2019). The hierarchical erosion effect: A new perspective on perceptual differences and business performance. *Journal of Management Studies, 56*(8), 1713–1747.

Good, D., & Michel, E.J. (2013). Individual ambidexterity: Exploring and exploiting in dynamic contexts. *Journal of Psychology: Interdisciplinary and Applied, 147*(5), 435–453.

Gregory, R.W., Keil, M., Muntermann, J., & Mähring, M. (2015). Paradoxes and the nature of ambidexterity in IT transformation programs. *Information Systems Research, 26*(1), 57–80.

Gupta, A.K., Smith, K.G., & Shalley, C.E. (2006). The interplay between exploration and exploitation. *Academy of Management Journal, 49*(4), 683–706.

Hambrick, D. (1994). Top management groups: A conceptual integration and reconsideration of the "team" label. *Research in Organizational Behavior, 16,* 171–213.

Heavey, C., & Simsek, Z. (2014). Distributed cognition in top management teams and organizational ambidexterity: The influence of transactive memory systems. *Journal of Management, 43*(3), 919–945.

Hodgkinson, I.R., Ravishankar, M.N., & Aitken-Fischer, M. (2014). A resource-advantage perspective on the orchestration of ambidexterity. *Service Industries Journal, 34*(15), 1234–1252.

Hughes, M. (2018). Organisational ambidexterity and firm performance: Burning research questions for marketing scholars. *Journal of Marketing Management,* 34 (1–2), 178–229.

Hughes, M., Filser, M., Harms, R., Kraus, S., Chang, M.-L., & Cheng, C.-F. (2018a). Family firm configurations for high performance: The role of entrepreneurship and ambidexterity. *British Journal of Management, 29*(4), 595–612.

Hughes, M., Rigtering, J.P.C., Covin, J.G., Bouncken, R.B., & Kraus, S. (2018b). Innovative behavior, trust and perceived workplace performance. *British Journal of Management, 29*(4), 750–768.

Hunter, S.T., Thoroughgood, C.N., Myer, A.T., & Ligon, G.S. (2011). Paradoxes of leading innovative endeavors: Summary, solutions, and future directions. *Psychology of Aesthetics, Creativity, and the Arts, 5*(1), 54–66.

Jansen, J.J.P., Simsek, Z., & Cao, Q. (2012). Ambidexterity and performance in multiunit contexts: Cross-level moderating effects of structural and resource attributes. *Strategic Management Journal, 33,* 1286–1303.

Jansen, J.J.P., Tempelaar, M.P., van den Bosch, F.A.J., & Volberda, H.W. (2009). Structural differentiation and ambidexterity: The mediating role of integration mechanisms. *Organization Science, 20*(4), 787–811.

Jansen, J.J.P., Van Den Bosch, F.A.J., & Volberda, H.W. (2006). Exploratory innovation, exploitative innovation, and performance: Effects of organizational antecedents and environmental moderators. *Management Science, 52*(11), 1661–1674.

Jasmand, C., Blazevic, V., & De Ruyter, K. (2012). Generating sales while providing service: A study of customer service representatives' ambidextrous behavior. *Journal of Marketing, 76*(1), 20–37.

Junni, P., Sarala, R.M., Tarba, S.Y., Liu, Y., & Cooper, C.L. (2015). Guest editors' introduction: The role of human resources and organizational factors in ambidexterity. *Human Resource Management, 54*(S1), S1–S28.

Kang, S.C., & Snell, S.A. (2009). Intellectual capital architectures and ambidextrous learning: A framework for human resource management. *Journal of Management Studies, 46*(1), 65–92.

Kao, Y.L., & Chen, C.F. (2016). Antecedents, consequences and moderators of ambidextrous behaviors among frontline employees. *Management Decision, 54*(8), 1856–1865.

Katz, D., & Kahn, R.L. (1966). *The social psychology of organisation.* Wiley Co.

Kauppila, O.P., & Tempelaar, M.P. (2016). The social-cognitive underpinnings of employees' ambidextrous behavior and the supportive role of group managers' leadership. *Journal of Management Studies, 53*(6), 1019–1044.

Kogut, B., & Zander, U. (1992). Knowledge of the firm, combinative capabilities, and the replication of technology. *Organization Science, 3*(3), 383–397.

Kohtamäki, M., Kautonen, T., & Kraus, S. (2010). Strategic planning and small business performance. *The International Journal of Entrepreneurship and Innovation, 11*(3), 221–229.

Kraus, S., Breier, M., Jones, P., & Hughes, M. (2019). Individual entrepreneurial orientation and intrapreneurship in the public sector. *International Entrepreneurship and Management Journal, 15*(4), 1247–1268.

Kraus, S., Kauranen, I., & Reschke, C.H. (2011). Identification of domains for a new conceptual model of strategic entrepreneurship using the configuration approach. *Management Research Review, 34*(1), 58–74.

Kraus, S., Mahto, R.V., & Walsh, S.T. (2021). The importance of literature reviews in small business and entrepreneurship research. *Journal of Small Business Management,* 1–12.

Lee, K., & Kim, Y. (2021). Ambidexterity for my job or firm? Investigation of the impacts of psychological ownership on exploitation, exploration, and ambidexterity. *European Management Review, 18*(2), 141–156.

Lee, S., & Meyer-Doyle, P. (2017). How performance incentives shape individual exploration and exploitation: Evidence from microdata. *Organization Science, 28*(1), 19–38.

Lin, H.E., & McDonough, E.F. (2011). Investigating the role of leadership and organizational culture in fostering innovation ambidexterity. *IEEE Transactions on Engineering Management, 58*(3), 497–509.

Lin, H.-E., McDonough, E.F., Yang, J., & Wang, C. (2017). Aligning knowledge assets for exploitation, exploration, and ambidexterity: A study of companies in high-tech parks in China *Journal of Product Innovation Management*, *34*(2), 122–140.

Lubatkin, M.H., Simsek, Z., Ling, Y., & Veiga, J.F. (2006). Ambidexterity and performance in small-to medium-sized firms: The pivotal role of top management team behavioral integration. *Journal of Management*, *32*(5), 646–672.

Luo, B., Zheng, S., Ji, H., & Liang, L. (2018). Ambidextrous leadership and TMT-member ambidextrous behavior: The role of TMT behavioral integration and TMT risk propensity. *International Journal of Human Resource Management*, *29*(2), 338–359.

March, J.G. (1991). Exploration and exploitation in organizational learning. *Organization Science*, *2*(1), 71–87.

March, J.G., & Simon, H.A. (1958). *Organizations*. Blackwell.

Martin, A., Keller, A., & Fortwengel, J. (2019). Introducing conflict as the microfoundation of organizational ambidexterity. *Strategic Organization*, *17*(1), 38–61.

Mom, T.J.M., Chang, Y.Y., Cholakova, M., & Jansen, J.J.P. (2019). A multilevel integrated framework of firm HR practices, individual ambidexterity, and organizational ambidexterity. *Journal of Management*, *45*(7), 3009–3034.

Mom, T.J.M., Fourné, S.P.L., & Jansen, J.J.P. (2015). Managers' work experience, ambidexterity, and performance: The contingency role of the work context. *Human Resource Management*, *54*, 133–153.

Mom, T.J.M., Van Den Bosch, F.A.J., & Volberda, H.W. (2007). Investigating managers' exploration and exploitation activities: The influence of top-down, bottom-up, and horizontal knowledge inflows. *Journal of Management Studies*, *44*(6), 910–931.

Mom, T.J.M., Van Den Bosch, F.A.J., & Volberda, H.W. (2009). Understanding variation in managers' ambidexterity: Investigating direct and interaction effects of formal structural and personal coordination mechanisms. *Organization Science*, *20*(4), 812–828.

Mu, T., van Riel, A., & Schouteten, R. (2020). Individual ambidexterity in SMEs: Towards a typology aligning the concept, antecedents and outcomes. *Journal of Small Business Management*, 1–32.

Mustafa, M., Martin, L., & Hughes, M. (2016). Psychological ownership, job satisfaction, and middle manager entrepreneurial behavior. *Journal of Leadership and Organizational Studies*, *23*(3), 272–287.

Panagopoulos, N.G., Rapp, A., & Pimentel, M.A. (2020). Firm actions to develop an ambidextrous sales force. *Journal of Service Research*, *23*(1), 87–104.

Parida, V., Lahti, T., & Wincent, J. (2016). Exploration and exploitation and firm performance variability: A study of ambidexterity in entrepreneurial firms. *International Entrepreneurship and Management Journal*, *12*(4), 1147–1164.

Patel, P.C., Messersmith, J.G., & Lepak, D.P. (2013). Walking the tightrope: An assessment of the relationship between high-performance work systems and organizational ambidexterity. *Academy of Management Journal*, *56*(5), 1420–1422.

Prajogo, D., & Mcdermott, C.M. (2014). Antecedents of service innovation in SMEs: Comparing the effects of external and internal factors. *Journal of Small Business Management*, *52*(3), 521–540.

Prieto-Pastor, I., & Martin-Perez, V. (2015). Does HRM generate ambidextrous employees for ambidextrous learning? The moderating role of management support. *The International Journal of Human Resource Management*, *26*(5), 589–615.

Raisch, S., Birkinshaw, J., Probst, G., & Tushman, M.L. (2009). Organizational ambidexterity: Balancing exploitation and exploration for sustained performance. *Organization Science*, *20*(4), 675–685.

Ramachandran, I., Lengnick-Hall, C.A., & Badrinarayanan, V. (2019). Enabling and leveraging ambidexterity: Influence of strategic orientations and knowledge stock. *Journal of Knowledge Management*, *23*(6), 1136–1156.

Revilla, E., Rodriguez-Prado, B., & Cui, Z. (2016). A Knowledge-based framework of innovation strategy: The differential effect of knowledge sources. *IEEE Transactions on Engineering Management*, *63*(4), 362–376.

Ritala, P., Baiyere, A., Hughes, M., & Kraus, S. (2021). Digital strategy implementation: The role of individual entrepreneurial orientation and relational capital. *Technological Forecasting and Social Change*, *171*, 120961.

Rogan, M., & Mors, M.L. (2014). A network perspective on individual-level ambidexterity in organizations. *Organization Science*, *25*(6), 1860–1877.

Rosing, K., Frese, M., & Bausch, A. (2011). Explaining the heterogeneity of the leadership-innovation relationship: Ambidextrous leadership. *Leadership Quarterly*, *22*(5), 956–974.

Rosing, K., & Zacher, H. (2017). Individual ambidexterity: The duality of exploration and exploitation and its relationship with innovative performance. *European Journal of Work and Organizational Psychology*, *26*(5), 685–708.

Salas Vallina, A., Moreno-Luzon, M.D., & Ferrer-Franco, A. (2019). The individual side of ambidexterity: Do inspirational leaders and organizational learning resolve the exploitation-exploration dilemma? *Employee Relations*, *41*(3), 592–613.

Schnellbächer, B., Heidenreich, S., & Wald, A. (2019). Antecedents and effects of individual ambidexterity – A cross-level investigation of exploration and exploitation activities at the employee level. *European Management Journal*, *37*(4), 442–454.

Schultz, C., Schreyoegg, J., & Von Reitzenstein, C. (2013). The moderating role of internal and external resources on the performance effect of multitasking: Evidence from the R&D performance of surgeons. *Research Policy*, *42*, 1356–1365.

Shamim, S., Zeng, J., Shafi Choksy, U., & Shariq, S.M. (2020). Connecting big data management capabilities with employee ambidexterity in Chinese multinational enterprises through the mediation of big data value creation at the employee level. *International Business Review*, *29*(6), 1–12.

Simeonova, B. (2018). Transactive memory systems and Web 2.0 in knowledge sharing: A conceptual model based on activity theory and critical realism. *Information Systems Journal*, *28*, 592–611.

Simeonova, B., Galliers, R.D., & Karanasios, S. (2022), Power dynamics in organizations and the role of information systems. *Information Systems Journal*, *32*, 233–241.

Simsek, Z., Heavey, C., Veiga, J.F., & Souder, D. (2009). A typology for aligning organizational ambidexterity's conceptualizations, antecedents, and outcomes. *Journal of Management Studies*, *46*(5), 864–894.

Smith, W.K., & Tushman, M.L. (2005). Managing strategic contradictions: A top management model for managing innovation streams. *Organization Science*, *16*(5), 522–536.

Sok, P., Sok, K.M., Danaher, T.S., & Danaher, P.J. (2018). The complementarity of frontline service employee creativity and attention to detail in service delivery. *Journal of Service Research*, *21*(3), 365–378.

Spender, J.-C. (1996). Making knowledge the basis of a dynamic theory of the firm. *Strategic Management Journal*, *17*(S2), 45–62.

Stokes, P., Baker, C., & Lichy, J. (2016). The role of embedded individual values, belief and attitudes and spiritual capital in shaping everyday postsecular organizational culture. *European Management Review*, *13*(1), 37–51.

Swart, J., Turner, N., van Rossenberg, Y., & Kinnie, N. (2019). Who does what in enabling ambidexterity? Individual actions and HRM practices. *International Journal of Human Resource Management*, *30*(4), 508–535.

Tempelaar, M.P., & Rosenkranz, N.A. (2019). Switching hats: The effect of role transition on individual ambidexterity. *Journal of Management*, *45*(4), 1517–1539.

Tiwana, A. (2008). Do bridging ties complement strong ties? An empirical examination of alliance ambidexterity. *Strategic Management Journal*, *29*, 251–272.

Torres, J.P., Drago, C., & Aqueveque, C. (2015). Knowledge inflows effects on middle managers' ambidexterity and performance. *Management Decision*, *53*(10), 2303–2320.

Tsai, W. (2002). Social structure of "coopetition" within a multiunit organization: Coordination, competition, and intraorganizational knowledge sharing. *Organization Science*, *13*(2), 178–190.

Vera, D., & Crossan, M. (2004). Strategic leadership and organizational learning. *Academy of Management Review, 29*(2), 222–240.

Volery, T., Mueller, S., & von Siemens, B. (2015). Entrepreneur ambidexterity: A study of entrepreneur behaviors and competencies in growth-oriented small and medium-sized enterprises. *International Small Business Journal, 33*(2), 109–129.

Weber, M. (1978). *Economy and society: An outline of interpretive sociology.* University of California Press.

Xie, X., Gao, Y., Zang, Z., & Meng, X. (2020). Collaborative ties and ambidextrous innovation: Insights from internal and external knowledge acquisition. *Industry and Innovation, 27*(3), 285–310.

Yeganegi, S., Laplume, A.O., Dass, P., & Greidanus, N.S. (2019). Individual-level ambidexterity and entrepreneurial entry. *Journal of Small Business Management, 57*(4), 1445–1463.

Yu, T., Gudergan, S., & Chen, C.F. (2020). Achieving employee efficiency–flexibility ambidexterity. *International Journal of Human Resource Management, 31*(19), 2459–2494.

Zacher, H., Robinson, A.J., & Rosing, K. (2016). Ambidextrous leadership and employees' self-reported innovative performance: The role of exploration and exploitation behaviors. *Journal of Creative Behavior, 50*(1), 24–46.

Zacher, H., & Wilden, R.G. (2014). A daily diary study on ambidextrous leadership and self-reported employee innovation. *Journal of Occupational and Organizational Psychology, 87*(4), 813–820.

Zhang, Y., Wei, F., & Van Horne, C. (2019). Individual ambidexterity and antecedents in a changing context. *International Journal of Innovation Management, 23*(3).

Zimmermann, A., Raisch, S., & Cardinal, L.B. (2018). Managing persistent tensions on the frontline: A configurational perspective on ambidexterity. *Journal of Management Studies, 55*(5), 739–768.

Ziad El Awad and Jasna Poček

7 Life Science Companies' Engagement with their University-based Entrepreneurship Ecosystem: A Multi-Layered Approach

Abstract: This chapter focuses on life science companies' engagement with their university-based entrepreneurship ecosystem. It analyzes multiple case studies with life science companies based around Lund University in Sweden. Our results demonstrate that life science companies engage with their ecosystem through three interconnected engagement logics: network, relations, and governance. We propose a model that portrays these interconnections as being multi-layered, and theorises their contribution to the interdependencies of the ecosystem.

Keywords: entrepreneurship ecosystem, interconnections, life science

Introduction

Researchers and policymakers alike are increasingly interested in understanding how entrepreneurship ecosystems create the conditions for companies to develop and grow. Most studies in this domain take a top-down approach, demonstrating mechanisms that best support the interactions of entrepreneurs within the ecosystem they inhabit (Wurth et al., 2021). However, recent calls are pushing for an actor-centered approach, seeking to understand the logic behind companies' engagement in their ecosystem. This chapter explores the different engagement logics through which owners develop and grow their ventures, and the interdependence of such logics.

Previous research has acknowledged the importance of engagement and interdependences for understanding the environment in entrepreneurship ecosystems (Isenberg, 2010, 2011). As such, a high degree of engagement and interdependences signals the presence of a governance structure that directs actors' values and ways of behaving (Baumol, 1990). Furthermore, actors often direct these values and behaviors to create coherent spaces (Poček, 2022; Roundy, 2017) that facilitate resource acquisition. However, most studies have taken a macro-level perspective, considering the role of ecosystem support organizations such as universities, technology transfer offices (TTOs) or incubators in facilitating the creation of new ventures. Hence, current research offers little insight into ecosystem engagements and relational aspects from an actor-centered perspective (Roundy, 2017; Wurth et al., 2021; Isenberg, 2016). This

Ziad El Awad, Sten K. Johnson Centre for Entrepreneurship, Lund University, Sweden
Jasna Poček, Center for Innovation Research (CIRCLE), Lund University, Sweden

https://doi.org/10.1515/9783110747652-008

chapter fills this gap by engaging in an inductive study, building on a multiple case study approach, and using interviews with life science company owners located throughout the entrepreneurship ecosystem of Lund University. Lund's entrepreneurship ecosystem is one of the largest in Europe, and is known for supporting leading life science companies such as AstraZeneca, as well as high-tech companies including Sony, Eriksson, Tetra Pak, and Oatly, to name a few.

Our study reveals three layers of engagement logics: network, relational, and governance. It also demonstrates how company owners engage with their entrepreneurship ecosystem, portraying the interconnections and interdependencies between these three engagement logics.

Literature Review

Entrepreneurship Ecosystems

The entrepreneurship ecosystem is a young field of research that is increasingly capturing the attention of researchers (Kang et al., 2019) and national and international policymakers such as OECD and ILO. The "ecosystem" metaphor builds on the legacy of Moore (1993), who coined the term "business ecosystems" and discussed how the functioning of a business is contextually dependent on those players in a system who can provide resources. Later on, management researchers developed the concept of the entrepreneurship ecosystem, a term particularly related to processes that are dependent on the interactions of multiple actors and aimed at helping the innovativeness and growth of companies in a given setting (Acs et al., 2014, 2017; Alvedalen & Boschma, 2017; Audretsch & Belitski, 2016; Auerswald & Dani, 2017; Autio et al., 2018; Bouncken & Kraus, 2021 Isenberg, 2010; Isenberg, 2011; Kang et al., 2019; Mack & Mayer, 2016; Motoyama & Knowlton, 2017; Poček, 2022; Spigel, 2016; Stam, 2015; Spigel & Harrison, 2018).

Isenberg (2010) discusses entrepreneurship ecosystems as "naturally evolved systems," while others see them as systems that evolve through "artificial" processes governed by the state (Cho et al., 2021; Fuerlinger et al., 2015; Meyer et al., 2016). In both cases, these systems provide financing and public support via incubators, accelerators, technology transfer offices, and similar support actors (Acs et al., 2013, 2017; Cantner et al., 2020; Mack & Mayer, 2016; Stam, 2015; Stam & Spigel, 2016). In line with this, scholars also discuss the governance processes of the entrepreneurship ecosystem as being crucial to its performance (Bouncken & Kraus, 2021). Governance of entrepreneurship ecosystems has been analyzed as bottom-up/top-down (Colombo et al., 2019), relational/hierarchical, and as undergoing a transition from hierarchical to relational as the ecosystem matures (Colombo et al., 2019). In this sense, hierarchical governance is imposed by top-down public policies, while the relational approach is nurtured in ecosystems that promote decisions based on dialogue, reeds, and broad consensus among their actors.

While some researchers point out that the ecosystem's boundaries may collide with its governance framework (Cantner et al., 2020; Colombo et al., 2019), others argue that the ecosystem boundary is artificial (Wurth et al., 2021), since entrepreneurs and ecosystem organizations involve interactions with contexts beyond our unit of analysis. Nevertheless, irrespective of its evolution, and although the concept of entrepreneurship ecosystem overlaps with other cluster concepts (Scott et al., 2019), there seems to be a broad consensus among researchers that entrepreneurship ecosystems are environments with evolving geographical boundaries (Cho et al., 2021) whose central figure is the growth-oriented, innovative entrepreneur.

The entrepreneurship ecosystem is portrayed as an environment that is context-dependent (Wurth et al., 2021; Poček, 2020), dynamic and complex (Isenberg, 2010), and aimed at supporting new venture creation processes. In such an environment, the actors of the ecosystem – which do not necessarily have a consolidated action plan for supporting companies (Feldman & Lowe, 2018) – interact in a nonlinear manner (Autio et al., 2014; Isenberg, 2010, 2011) and create interdependences. Literature also discusses the importance of networks in promoting interactions within the ecosystem – and, more specifically, their relational aspects (Scott et al., 2020; Fernandes & Ferreira, 2020). Furthermore, since entrepreneurship is a social activity, entrepreneurs emphasise networking and their need to access resources (Aldrich & Zimmer, 1986).

The evolution and functioning of an entrepreneurship ecosystem depend heavily on the interaction logic it employs (Autio, 2016; Feld, 2012; Roundy, 2017; Bouncken & Kraus, 2021). The interdependencies of an ecosystem have also been linked to its output (Audretsch & Belitski, 2016). The interactions of ecosystem organizations occur at all spatial levels (Wurth et al., 2021; Stam and Spigel, 2017). Each level can have its own complexities, which are related to its organizational, inter-organizational, regional, socio-cultural, political or economic realities (Auerswald & Dari, 2017).

The interaction processes within the ecosystem have been analyzed as submissive to the governance that characterizes the environment (Baumol, 1990; Roundy et al., 2017). If conceptualized through the lens of the institutions of a given environment, governance is relevant for understanding ecosystem organizations' behaviour (Poček, 2020). Traditionally, governance has been related to the entrepreneurship discourse through the scholarly work of Baumol, who elaborated on it as a set of written and unwritten institutions that shape the behavior of entrepreneurs in a given context and point in time. The literature also acknowledges that unwritten institutions such as culture, social norms, and values persist over a long period (North, 1990; Baumol, 1990). Entrepreneurship ecosystem literature discusses unwritten institutions or rules as a set of socially accepted norms, beliefs, and practices that actors must follow if they are to be accepted in their social context (Roundy et al., 2017). Moreover, even if actors operate in the same context, they may not all share similar perceptions of the rules. However, ecosystems in which the actors do share such perceptions are more cohesive than those that lack them (Roundy et al., 2017).

University-based Entrepreneurship Ecosystems

Academic institutions are making growing contributions to the social and economic development of the regions where they are located (e.g., Fetters et al., 2010; Mason & Brown, 2014; Rice et al., 2014; Graham, 2014; Hayter, 2016; Siegel and Wright, 2015). Like any entrepreneurship ecosystem, university-based entrepreneurship ecosystems (UBEEs) are conceptualized through the interconnectivity of their actors and the processes that govern these actors' interactions (Fauzi et al., 2019). Alvedalen and Boschma (2017. n.p.) suggested that, in a UBEE, "the entrepreneur has a central place in the entrepreneurship ecosystem and is the core actor in building and sustaining the ecosystem." The elements of a UBEE function within and around the university and its partner organizations, which may include technology transfer offices (TTOs), incubators, and other actors (Greene et al., 2010). Moreover, to fulfil their "third mission," universities are forming closer links with society by improving procedures for commercializing scientific research, establishing relationships with public and private organizations, and helping to find solutions to societal problems (Brown, 2016; Guerrero et al., 2016).

The evolution of UBEEs through the establishment of venture funds, incubators, and public-private partnerships has also been regarded as a response to criticism of universities' "linear path" to knowledge transfer (Link & Sarala, 2018). Initially, this linear path involved the transmission of knowledge within the university, or between universities, in the form of an invention or a patent, which was then commercialized in a spin-off (Bradley et al., 2013;). To address criticism of this approach (Grimaldi et al., 2011; Hayter, 2016; Hayter and Cahoy, 2018), universities began to integrate other forms of support, such as incubators, programs focused on entrepreneurial action, and establishing proof-of-concept centers (Brown, 2016; Croce et al., 2013).

Moreover, the efficacy of UBEEs has also been discussed as context-embedded, and related to the industrial, organizational, social, and institutional setup of a particular regional setting (Wright et al., 2017; Autio et al., 2014; Mustar et al., 2006). For example, existing studies show that ventures started by graduates within UBEEs are impacted in their development and performance by both the university context and the regional context in which they operate (Bergman et al., 2016; Hayter et al., 2017; Wright et al., 2017). Furthermore, studies suggest that ecosystem efficacy is related to the collective capacity of ecosystem organizations to provide the resources needed for student ventures to succeed (Hayter, 2016) and the development of open relations with actors and organizations beyond the ecosystem (Fuster et al., 2019).

Despite the research to date, UBEEs remain unexplored (Link & Sarala, 2018, particularly in terms of commercial actors' engagement. Therefore, more research is needed to explore the interdependencies and connected dynamics of UBEEs, analyzed from the perspective of company actors themselves (Alvedalen & Boschma, 2017; Wurth et al., 2021). This chapter aims to fill this gap.

Research Design

This study takes an actor-centered approach to understand the logic behind company owners' engagement in their ecosystem. We focus particularly on exploring the engagement of small life science companies, which are less researched than their larger, higher-valued counterparts (Alvedalen, 2021). Indeed, it is precisely these smaller companies that most need our understanding, since they often lack the resources they need to grow (Brännback et al., 2009). Moreover, these companies typically face significant risks and numerous obstacles during their development – which is lengthy, since the average product development time in the life sciences is around 12 years (Alvedalen, 2021). On the other hand, small life science companies are an important driver of economic development, contributing to job creation, industrial renewal, and societal wellbeing (Alvedalen, 2021; Acs & Audretsch, 2005; Schoonhoven & Eisenhardt, 2012; Scholten et al., 2004).

In this chapter, we inductively analyze multiple case studies of nine small life science companies to address our research aims (Eisenhardt, 1989). Our case sampling strategy followed a purposeful logic: companies were selected because they were suitable for fulfilling our research aims (Eisenhardt & Graebner, 2007). We initially identified companies that were operating in a UBEE and were actively commercializing their scientific research. When starting the study, these companies were at a comparable stage in their development, allowing comparability and observation of patterns, which allowed us to replicate results.

In theory development, multiple case studies enable the researcher to "achieve replication logic where each case replicates the other and the emerging theory and, therefore, better explains the underlying relationships between constructs" (Kantur et al., 2013). The replication logic, also discussed by Eisenhardt (1989), makes the multiple-case approach a powerful tool that strengthens methodological rigour.

Data Collection

This chapter builds on 20 interviews with nine company owners in Lund University's Entrepreneurship Ecosystem. Table 7.1 provides details of their companies. The interviews were conducted in person in late 201, with each lasting between 40 and 60 minutes. Interviews followed a semi-structured approach, which allowed us to explore actors' engagement with their entrepreneurship ecosystem. The reason for selecting companies operating in a UBEE is twofold. First, studies have seldom considered studying the engagement patterns of high-growth science companies in their original context, and focusing on a UBEE allows us to do so. Second, science-based companies are high-growth companies that must engage intensively with their ecosystems to fuel their growth. Therefore, they are well suited for exploring engagement in entrepreneurial ecosystems.

Table 7.1: Life science companies interviewed.

Name	Company background
Company 1	Gene editing analysis The owner comes from the university, and the idea came from research at the university.
Company 2	Innovative healthcare products The owner comes from the university, and the idea came from research at the university.
Company 3	Better and smarter food for children The owner is from outside the university, from the regional public sector. The idea came from the personal experience of a company team member.
Company 4	Thyroid hormone devices The owner is from the university. The idea came from a colleague working in another university, currently a company team member.
Company 5	Stroke recovery The owner is from outside the university. They come from the private sector (medical-technical industry).
Company 6	Software development The owner is from outside the university. They come from the private sector (telecommunications research).
Company 7	Electric cars The owner comes from outside the university. They come from the private sector (engineering industry).
Company 8	Telecommunications The owner comes from outside the university, the private sector (telecommunications research), and they partnered with a professor from the university.
Company 9	Software development aiming at helping recovery from implant surgery The owner comes from outside the university. They come from the private sector (telecommunications research).

Context of the Study

The context of this study is the Lund University entrepreneurship ecosystem. The university is situated in southern Sweden, where it helps to provide high-quality jobs and supports the development and growth of high-growth science-based companies. Many support actors are located in the area around the university, where they connect via formal and informal networks. These actors represent technology transfer offices, incubators, science parks, accelerators, cluster organisations, coworking spaces, municipalities, public platforms for innovation, public-private partnerships, VCs, and multinationals such as Tetra Pak, IKEA, Ericsson, Sony, and Axis Communications.

Most companies that have spun off from Lund University are clustered around the Ideon and Medicon Village science parks (both of which belong to the university). Ideon Science Park, which focuses on future transport solutions, smart cities, intelligent materials, and health technology, is one of the oldest and largest science parks in Europe, with around 10,000 people employed in 414 companies. It also has an incubator (Ideon Innovation) and an accelerator (Ideon Open/Beyond). Medicon Village was built on a vacant plot owned by AstraZeneca in Lund. It belongs to the larger cluster of Medicon Valley, which spans the Öresunds or greater Copenhagen region. Medicon Village focuses on life sciences, with particular research interests in cancer, diabetes, the respiratory system, and inflammation. Around 2,200 employees work in its 150 companies. Medicon Village also has an incubator named Smile and an accelerator called Smile Bootcamp.

Data Coding and Analysis

Our aim was to explore the different engagement logics through which owners develop and grow their life science companies, and the interdependences between them. Based on our coded data (see Figure 7.1), we were able to inductively identify three layers of engagement logic: (i) the network logic, (ii) the relational logic and (iii) the governance logic.

We coded our data using NVivo. Our data coding and analysis followed three steps. First, we created first order codes representing the key activities that each company owner reported, giving us a better understanding of their scientific invention and their activities with their ecosystem to initiate, develop, and grow their companies. Based on this initial step, we developed a timeline to understand how events in the venture development process had unfolded.

Second, having gained a sense of the "big picture," we coded how owners explained the relationships between different activities, which helped us categorize activities into second order concepts which together formed the aggregated themes that represent the three engagement logics. For instance, we grouped different activities that manifest the network logic, such as (i) establishing open channels and (ii) build-

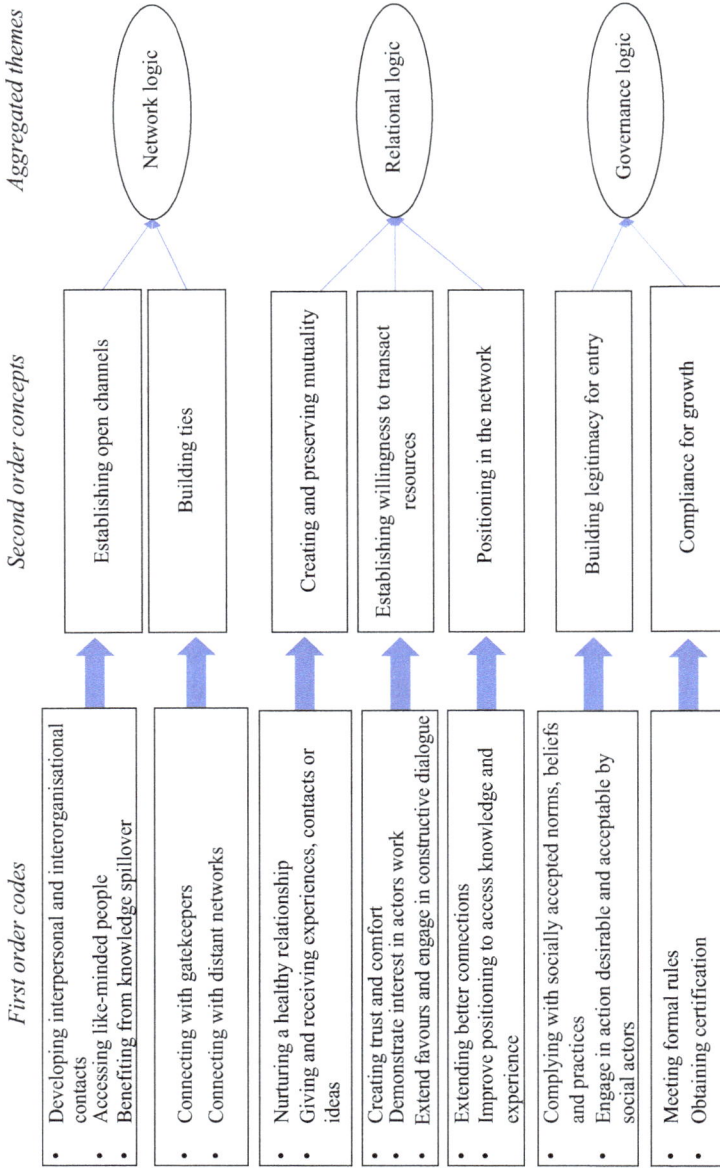

Figure 7.1: Data structure.

ing ties. Other activities that relate to the relational logic were coded as (i) creating and preserving mutuality, (ii) establishing willingness to transact resources, and (iii) positioning in the network, etc.

Third, having established activities under each of these logics, we tabulated the interdependencies between them – for instance, how the network logic interplays with the relational logic, and how governance reinforces relations among actors (see Table 7.2).

Table 7.2: Engagement logics and interdependencies.

Engagement logic	Network logic	Relational logic	Governance logic
Characteristic feature	Exploring ecosystem actors, logics, and ways of working	Resource acquisition	Accepted ways of working, norms, and values
Level	Micro	Meso	Macro
Function in the entrepreneurship ecosystem	Gaining more experience of the ecosystem	Granting access to resources	Reinforcing legitimacy and compliance
Interconnectedness	Strong relational logic improves resource provision among support actors	Improves trust, commitment, and legitimacy between company owners and support actors	High levels of compliance with accepted ways of behaving reinforce relations between ecosystem actors

Results

Our analysis revealed three engagement logics that small life science companies use to engage in the UBEE. First is the network logic, through which actors identify and create pathways to access resources, finance, and knowledge spillovers with other like-minded individuals, firms or supporting institutions. Second, the relational logic is used to create and reinforce relationships with other actors in the network that become conducive to specific resources and scientific knowledge exchange (Carmeli & Azeroual, 2009). The third and final logic, governance, relates to how social entities are organized, directed, and reinforced to behave in ways that are accepted and rewarded by entities within the entrepreneurship ecosystem. We present each of these engagement logics below, before outlining how the various logics interact with and reproduce each other, helping to nurture interconnectivity across the entrepreneurship ecosystem.

The Network Logic

Networking is a cohesive mechanism through which company owners initiate their first encounters with their entrepreneurship ecosystem. Through networking, company owners establish connections with support actors to learn how the ecosystem works and identify the main actors within it. They can also explore opportunities to access resources and finance, and benefit from knowledge spillovers with other like-minded actors or fellow company owners. Networking is, therefore, a fundamental aspect of engagement and a *sine qua non* condition for these companies' birth, development, and growth. We identified two elements that constitute the network logic: (i) establishing open channels and (ii) building ties. We discuss both below.

Establishing Open Channels

Our results show that company owners seek to establish open channels with as many of the networks available to them as they can, in order to allow interpersonal and interorganizational contacts to emerge. Through these contacts, company owners can access and transmit ideas and understand where and how to obtain resources that would otherwise be difficult or impossible to access, or even learn about, elsewhere. For many owners, connecting with like-minded people facilitates learning and opens up the possibility for knowledge spillovers to take place. For example, most company owners we interviewed suggested that being open and humble about sharing knowledge and ideas is the foundation for benefiting from, and contributing to, the network. Two owners commented:

> In order to establish yourself as a valued player in the game [the ecosystem], it is a must that you are open and generous [about sharing your experiences].

> You can always be open to connect with someone who's been there, who's done it before, and you can learn from their experience and get yourself into a position to ask many questions.

Building Ties

Company owners in our study suggested that taking part in networks was a vital first step toward connecting with the ecosystem. However, they also suggested that building ties with key actors was a next step for them to grasp how different components of the ecosystem work, comprehend the logic supporting them, and assess the possibilities for accessing resources. Moreover, building ties with key actors was necessary for creating connections with more distant networks, which may be difficult to access at the outset. Company owners suggested that some of these key actors played the role of gatekeepers, controlling access to industry-specific resources (i.e., domain-specific knowledge and competencies), filtering information and guiding owners to specific resources from distant networks. As such, building ties with gatekeepers is essential in order to access these less-accessible resources: "It's difficult to get into the regional healthcare system for [companies] in general. So here, we tried all kinds of nearby contact with actors in closer networks, and [the healthcare contact] came through some actors in nearby companies who extended these [personal] contacts."

Interestingly, our findings showed that company owners who had to access resources through gatekeepers were those who were foreign to the ecosystem (i.e., had no prior experience operating in it). As such, they had established their networks from scratch, mainly by cultivating proximate networks that did not offer any resources in particular, but were key to getting through to gatekeepers who facilitated the owners' transition to more distant networks. For instance, company owners reported that they found the university – particularly its technology transfer office (TTO) – a good gatekeeping actor that facilitated their initial entry to the entrepreneurship ecosystem. Company owners valued the initial collaborations with academic staff, since they facilitated access to extended financial and knowledge resources in more distant networks. As one company owner explained:

> I started to collaborate with a professor at the university, and when you collaborate with a university employee you can turn to [the TTO] as a company and ask for funds. It's like a filtering process! That's what we did, so . . . he's my co-founder, and we went to the holding company and they invested in us. And then later on others came in, we've got the funding from [government agency for innovation] and EIT Health, and, well, yeah, in different ways it's [an] amazing network that keeps expanding.

On the other hand, company owners who displayed experience and knowledge of the entrepreneurship ecosystem felt that connecting with networks was fairly straightforward. Since they knew where to go and who to contact, they were less dependent on gatekeepers to establish ties with more distant networks.

> Working around here, it was fairly easy for me to identify the resources I needed and start collaborating with a professor at the university.

> When you collaborate with a university employee you can easily build a network with the [TTO], and many other networks that offer the resources you need.

While participating in a network is necessary for acquiring resources and knowledge, company owners in our study noted that the benefits from such networks could only be fully realized if owners could develop and orchestrate symbiotic relationships with gatekeepers: "You need to know people. You need to know a lot of people. It's very relationship-dependent. The more connections you have to the network, and the better they are, the more difference it will make [to your company]."

The Relational Logic

Company owners suggested on several occasions that merely connecting with networks does not always grant access to needed resources. Several owners emphasized the need to upgrade their critical connections with support actors into a solid mutual relationship. Through such a relationship, they could gain the trust and willingness of support actors to grant them access to other networks. This view was important to all company owners, but was particularly prevalent among those with less experience in the ecosystem, who suggested that they needed to put more effort into taking up a strong position in the ecosystem, and being perceived as worthy of support. According to company owners, striving for mutuality in the relationship was necessary to make their initial networks more conducive to resources and knowledge exchange. We identify three crucial elements that constitute the relational logic: (i) creating and preserving mutuality; (ii) willingness to transact resources; and (iii) positioning in the network.

Creating and Preserving Mutuality

Company owners suggested that creating and preserving mutuality is key to nurturing healthy relations. They emphasized that mutuality in a relationship is necessary to signal credibility and the capacity not only to receive from the ecosystem, but also to give back. This giving back can take the form of sharing experiences, contacts or ideas with other members of the ecosystem. As two company owners stated:

> The game is that if somebody gives you something, you need to provide something in return, and this increases the likelihood that you are going to get something more [i.e., resources]. So, if you get that ball rolling, you can get some fantastic returns.

> When you meet an investor, you are judged as a person and whether you are legitimate and worthy of their money, and what they will get in return.

Establishing Willingness to Transact Resources

Company owners in our study also indicated that reaping value from networks depended mainly on the willingness of support actors to transact the resources they possessed. Company owners highlighted that support actors need to trust and feel comfortable extending their resources to others. Equally important is that resource beneficiaries (i.e., company owners, in our case) need to show support actors that they are interested in their work, able to extend favors, and ready to engage in constructive dialogue. As one owner stated: "To establish yourself as a credible, you need to establish yourself as someone who can deliver, [. . .] [someone who is] able to perform, and that comes with experience and getting to know people and having done things for people in the past."

Positioning in the Network

Our results also show that developing relationships is crucial in determining company owners' position in their networks. Those better positioned in the network – i.e., those who manage to extend their connections to other actors in other networks – are better suited to accessing heterogeneous knowledge and experience, which supports their learning and ability to continuously absorb and leverage new information: "It is a valuable context; if you are well positioned in the network, such as being part of a TTO or an incubator, then it lends [you] credibility and lots of access to resources and therefore learning [. . .]."

The Governance Logic

Our analysis revealed the governance logic as of particular concern and importance for small life science companies' engagement with their ecosystem. By "governance logic" we mean compliance with bureaucracy (i.e., formal rules, regulations, and procedures) and accepted ways of doing things, which facilitate companies' access to specific resources and operations within and across the ecosystem. We identify two key elements within the governance logic: (i) building legitimacy for entry and (ii) compliance for growth.

Building Legitimacy for Entry

Complying with bureaucracy was deemed necessary for building legitimacy. This was particularly the case for companies that commercialize scientific knowledge in pharmaceutical, medical or food-related domains. All company owners claimed that it is vital to engage in actions that various social actors perceive as desirable, acceptable, and proper. They also highlighted that in a domain like science, socially accepted norms, beliefs, and practices had to be followed for a company to have its right to exist recognized. As these two owners explained: "When you work towards healthcare, there are many restrictions as well as lots of regulatory work before you are allowed to sell the product. Then, there is procurement and everything that you are allowed to sell. So, it is quite hard to get in there in the beginning."

Compliance for Growth

Company owners discussed compliance with governance as a learning process involving experience and iteration. Once they have repeated the procedure of complying with certifications and other formal rules as requested by the local, regional, national or international authorities, they become knowledgeable about handling similar situations. As two informants mentioned:

> We have to obtain a certification to produce our medical product. It has to be done to obtain some resources needed to sell the medical product to the industry or the healthcare system. So, there is no way to get around it. So, you need to do it.

> For a small company, it is a real challenge. However, we have learned how to do it. We have done three now. It is quite an achievement, I would say, for a small company like us to even submit an application and have it accepted.

Remarkably, small company owners with high growth ambitions had a different take on the challenges related to governance. Those who espoused a strong ambition to grow their ventures beyond Sweden saw bureaucracy in a positive light, suggesting it was a requirement for operating in the life sciences domain more generally. They also suggested that learning to handle local bureaucracy contributed to their experience, which proved beneficial for their work in Europe and internationally. Therefore, ambitious company owners saw regulatory compliance not as a barrier, but as a long-term investment that would facilitate future growth: "This is a global challenge. If you want to make global healthcare products, you need to nail it. On the other hand, if we nail this here, we nail it globally. So, I would not call it a barrier. It's just an investment decision."

Nurturing a Dynamic Multi-layered Interconnection between the Engagement Logics

Our results demonstrate three multilateral logics characterizing and shaping companies' engagement in their entrepreneurship ecosystem. Through these logics, small companies realize various interconnections that help them to commercialize their scientific research, resulting in products and services that benefit society. Whereas in the previous section, we reported findings related to each of the logics, here we discuss the interconnections between them.

Network-relational Logics

As noted earlier, company owners saw the value of building networks in the ecosystem as a first step toward accessing resources. However, our data highlighted that these initial network connections were necessary, but not sufficient, for resource acquisition. Instead, owners utilized a relational logic, whereby they strove to develop strong ties with key support actors and like-minded owners to access and extend resource acquisition. While the critical function of networks is to connect actors in the ecosystem, the provision of resources is largely dependent on a relational logic where elements of mutuality, trust, and positioning become the fabric for company owners to materialize benefits from their network connections, as this quote demonstrates:

> Of course, nothing is easy, so it is not enough to connect through a network, but [you must also] establish relations that allow you to reap value. Having worked around here [in the incubator] for a while, I know people in different companies, and they can talk to their friends if we need someone here for something.

> It is prestigious when you are regarded as a company that secured resources such as funding, and this extends to other networks.

Relational-governance Logics

Our results demonstrate that engagement through a relational logic is necessary for company owners to develop their critical connections with support actors into solid relationships to maintain their image as reliable, established, and trustworthy players. However, we found that complying with a governance logic strongly influenced the benefits company owners derived from their relational logic. On many occasions, company owners argued that it is their responsibility to ensure that their practices and ecosystem activities are deemed acceptable and proper by various actors in the ecosystem. Good governance facilitates high trust among actors, allowing companies to realise benefits and optimize resources through existing relations.

Company owners also observed that governance and building solid relations go hand in hand. Good governance can foster inclusion, participation, integrity, transparency, and accountability, which often enhance actors' positioning in their network and thus grant better access to resources: "The better you comply, the better your position in the network . . . and the [better] relationship you will have with the people you are working with. So this gets you certain allowances that somebody completely new to the ecosystem [could not obtain]."

Discussion and Conclusion

This study was motivated by the increasing interest in understanding entrepreneurship ecosystem engagement and its relational aspects from the actor-centered perspective of life science companies beyond the venture creation phase of development (Isenberg, 2016; Roundy et al., 2017; Wurth et al., 2021). Our analysis and findings lead to three key conclusions. First, company owners' engagement with their ecosystem forms into three logics: network, relational, and governance. Second, company owners' prior experience in the ecosystem can shape the strategy they use to engage with it. Third, engagement in the ecosystem is multi-layered, and these layers are interconnected, creating interdependences in the ecosystem's levels of aggregation (Wurth et al., 2021).

As its primary contribution, this study demonstrates how the owners of small life science companies engage with their entrepreneurship ecosystem and its support structures to reinforce company development and growth. These engagement logics and their interactions are depicted in Figure 7.2.

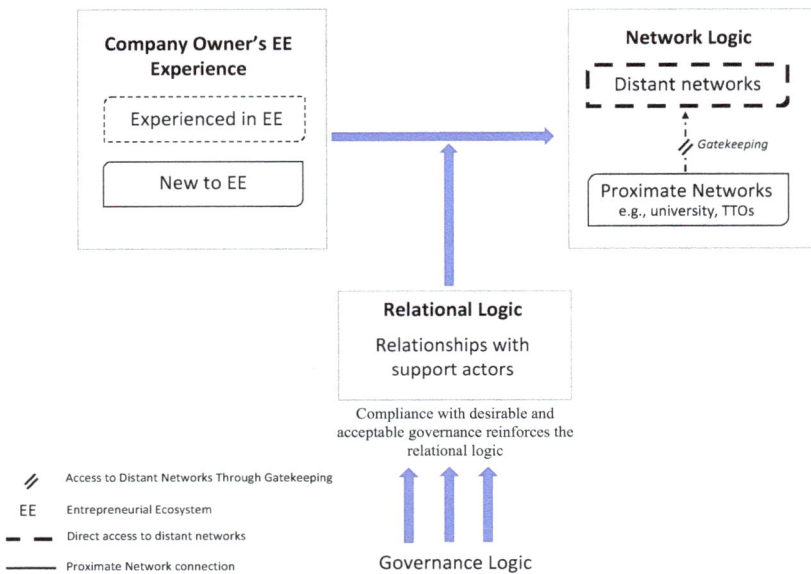

Figure 7.2: Entrepreneurship ecosystem engagement logics and their interconnections.

At the network level of engagement, company owners focus on connecting with key support actors, which helps them reach an initial understanding of the ecosystem and grasp its different components. Moreover, company owners participate in networks to link with key actors who could either facilitate direct access to various tangible (e.g., equipment, machinery, office space) or intangible resources (knowledge, skills, and competencies) or act as gatekeepers who filter access to other more distant networks, where more specific resources are available (Ferreira et al., 2019). Interestingly, company owners' experience in their ecosystem appears to play a role in how they initiate their network connections. For instance, those with no prior experience in the entrepreneurship ecosystem are more likely to begin their engagement with proximate networks. The university or the TTO often represent such networks. Through such networks, company owners get the chance to connect with key support actors to understand the overall infrastructure, how it works, and the logic behind it. However, to access resources within the same network or in more distant networks, company owners need to develop their relational capital with support actors who often act as gatekeepers, filtering and facilitating access to resources. In the case of experienced owners in the ecosystem, such relational capital is more likely to exist, thus facilitating direct access to resources. In this way, the relational logic appears to moderate the relationship between owners' experience in the ecosystem and their access to network resources, since it promotes trust, mutuality, and positioning in the network, which supports access to resources.

On another note, compliance with desirable and acceptable governance appears to reinforce the relational logic, as demonstrated in Figure 7.2. Company owners who can demonstrate high levels of compliance with accepted ways of behaving represented by informal institutions (North, 1990; Autio et al., 2014) are more likely to develop stronger relationships with support actors and other like-minded people and reap benefits as a result. The importance of governance in entrepreneurship has been well highlighted in previous research, which suggests that actions that align with the formal and informal rules of a given context are likely to support entrepreneurial work in that specific context (Isenberg, 2010). Specifically, the company's degrees of institutional integration with an environment can impact the quality of the relationships developed and the resources acquired (Scheidgen, 2021).

In this way, our results show that reaping value from interactions in the ecosystem demands that different layers of engagement logic interact and create interdependences. Moreover, our results detail the engagement logic from an actor-centered perspective, demonstrating the mechanisms through which small life science company owners interact with their ecosystem and, in doing so, gain access to the resources needed for their companies' development and growth.

Finally, resource acquisition is a complex process that is highly embedded in the careful coordination of complex human and social elements of behaviors. Therefore, we put forward trust, mutuality, legitimacy, positioning, and compliance as crucial relational and governance elements needed for actors to benefit from their network connections.

Our study is not free from limitations. Firstly, our interviews focus on only one industry, namely life sciences, within the broad category of science-based companies. Hence, future studies should undertake an analysis to better understand the nuances of ecosystem engagement concerning small companies originating from two or more industries. Secondly, we are aware that our research is carried out in a specific context of a Scandinavian region characterized by low levels of hierarchy in relations and dynamics and a long history of innovation support for high-growth companies. Therefore, the results might be challenging to replicate in somewhat different contexts.

References

Acs, Z.J., & Audretsch, D.B. (2005). *Entrepreneurship, innovation, and technological change* (Vol. 2105). Now Publishers Inc.

Acs, Z. J., Audretsch, D.B., & Lehmann, E.E. (2013). The knowledge spillover theory of entrepreneurship. *Small Business Economics, 41*(4), 757–774.

Acs, Z.J., Autio, E., & Szerb, L. (2014). National systems of entrepreneurship: Measurement issues and policy implications, *Research Policy, 43*(3), 476–494. Doi:10.1016/j.respol.2013.08.016.

Acs, Z.J., Stam, E., Audretsch, D.B., & O'Connor, A. (2017). The lineages of the entrepreneurial ecosystem approach. *Small Business Economics, 49*(1), 1–10.

Aldrich, H.E., & Zimmer, C. (1986). Entrepreneurship through social networks. In D. Sexton & R. Smilor (Eds.), *The art and science of entrepreneurship*. Ballinger Publishing Company.

Alvedalen, J. (2021). *Entrepreneurial ecosystems in life science industry: A study of start-ups, scale ups and resilience of entrepreneurial ecosystems*. Lund University, CIRCLE – Center for Innovation, Research and Competences in the Learning Economy.

Alvedalen, J., & Boschma, R. (2017). A critical review of entrepreneurial ecosystems research: Towards a future research agenda. *European Planning Studies, 25*(6), 887–903.

Audretsch, D.B., & Belitski, M. (2016). Entrepreneurial ecosystems in cities: Establishing the framework conditions. *The Journal of Technology Transfer, 42*(5), 1030–1051.

Auerswald, P.E., & Dani, L. (2017). The adaptive life cycle of entrepreneurial ecosystems: The biotechnology cluster. *Small Business Economics, 49*(1), 97–117.

Autio, E. (2016). Entrepreneurship support in Europe: Trends and challenges for EU policy. Policy Reports. European Commission.

Autio, E., Nambisan, S., Thomas, L.D., & Wright, M. (2018). Digital affordances, spatial affordances, and the genesis of entrepreneurial ecosystems. *Strategic Entrepreneurship Journal, 12*(1): 72–95.

Autio, E., Rannikko, H., Handelberg, J., & Kiuru, P. (2014). Analyses on the Finnish high-growth entrepreneurship ecosystem. *Aalto University publication series BUSINESS + ECONOMY*, 1/2014, 1–85.

Baumol, W.J. (1990). Entrepreneurship: Productive, unproductive, and destructive. *Journal of Political Economy*, 98, 893–921.

Bergmann, H., Hundt, C., & Sternberg, R. (2016). What makes student entrepreneurs? On the relevance (and irrelevance) of the university and the regional context for student start-ups. *Small Business Economics, 47*, 53–76.

Bouncken, R.B., & Kraus, S. (2021). Entrepreneurial ecosystems in an interconnected world: Emergence, governance and digitalization. *Review of Managerial Science, 16*, 1–14.

Bradley, S.R., Hayter, C.S., & Link, A.N. (2013). Models and methods of university technology transfer. *Entrepreneurship Theory and Practice, 9*(6): 571–650.

Brännback, M., Carsrud, A., Renko, M., Östermark, R., Aaltonen, J., & Kiviluoto, N. (2009). Growth and profitability in small privately held biotech firms: Preliminary findings. *New biotechnology, 25*(5), 369–376.

Brown, R. (2016). Mission impossible? Entrepreneurial universities and peripheral regional innovation systems. *Industry and Innovation, 23*(2), 189–205.

Cantner, U., Cunningham, J.A., Lehmann, E.E., & Menter, M. (2020). Entrepreneurial ecosystems: A dynamic lifecycle model. *Small Business Economics*.

Carmeli, A., & Azeroual, B. (2009). How relational capital and knowledge combination capability enhance the performance of work units in a high technology industry. *Strategic Entrepreneurship Journal, 3*(1), 85–103.

Cho, D.S., Paul, R., & Buciuni, G. (2021). Evolutionary entrepreneurial ecosystems: a research pathway. *Small Business Economics*.

Colombo, M.G., Dagnino, G.B., Lehmann, E.E., & Salmador, M. (2019). The governance of entrepreneurial ecosystems. *Small Business Economics*, *52*, 419–428.

Croce, A., Martí, J., & Murtinu, S. (2013). The impact of venture capital on the productivity growth of European entrepreneurial firms: 'Screening' or 'value added' effect? *Journal of Business Venturing*, *28*(4): 489–510.

Eisenhardt, K.M. (1989). Building theory from case study research. *Academy of Management Review, 14*, 532–550.

Eisenhardt, K.M., & Graebner, M.E. (2007). Theory building from cases: opportunities and challenges. *Academy of Management Journal, 50*(1): 25–32.

Fauzi, M.A., Tan, C.N.L., Thurasamy, R., Ojo, A.O. (2019). Evaluating academics' knowledge sharing intentions in Malaysian public universities. Malaysian J. Libr. Inf. Sci. 24, 123–143.

Feld, B. (2012). *Startup communities: Building an entrepreneurial ecosystem in your city.* Wiley.

Feldman, M., and Lowe, N. (2018). Policy and collective action in place. *Cambridge Journal of Regions, Economy and Society, 11*, 335–351.

Fernandes, A.J., & Ferreira, J.M. (2020). Entrepreneurial ecosystems and networks: A literature review and research agenda. *Review of Managerial Science* (in press).

Ferreira, J.J., Fernandes, C.I., & Kraus, S. (2019). Entrepreneurship research: Mapping intellectual structures and research trends. *Review of Managerial Science, 13*(1), 181–205.

Fetters, M.L., Greene, P., Rice, M.P., & Butler, J.S. (2010). *The development of university-based entrepreneurship ecosystems*. Edward Elgar.

Fuerlinger, G., Fandl, U., & Funke, T. (2015). The role of the state in the entrepreneurship ecosystem: Insights from Germany. *Triple Helix, 2*(1), 3.

Fuster, E., Padilla-Meléndez, A., Lockett, N., & del-Águila-Obra, A.R. (2019). The emerging role of university spin-off companies in developing regional entrepreneurial university ecosystems: The case of Andalusia. *Technological Forecasting and Social Change, 141*, 219–231. DOI: 10.1016/j.techfore.2018.10.020

Graham, R. (2014). *Creating university-based entrepreneurial ecosystems: Evidence from emerging world leaders*. Massachusetts Institute of Technology.

Greene, P.G., Rice, M.P., & Fetters, M.L. (2010). University-based entrepreneurship ecosystems: Framing the discussion. In *The development of university-based entrepreneurship ecosystems* Global practices (1–11). Elgar.

Grimaldi, R., M. Kenney, D. S. Siegel and M. Wright (2011). 30 years after Bayh–Dole: reassessing academic entrepreneurship. *Research Policy, 40*, 1045–1057.

Guerrero, M., Urbano, D., Fayolle, A., Klofsten, M., & Mian, S. (2016). Entrepreneurial universities: Emerging models in the new social and economic landscape. *Small Business Economics*, 1–13.

Hayter, C.S. (2016). A trajectory of early-stage spinoff success: The role of knowledge intermediaries within an entrepreneurial university ecosystem. *Small Business Economics, 47*, 633–656.

Hayter, C. S., & Cahoy, D. R. (2018). Toward a strategic view of higher education social responsibilities: A dynamic capabilities approach. Strategic Organization, *16*(1), 12–34. https://doi org/10.1177/1476127016680564

Hayter, C., Lubynsky, R., & Maroulis, S. (2017). Who is the academic entrepreneur? The role of graduate students in the development of university spinoffs, The Journal of Technology Transfer, *42*(6), 1237–1254.

Isenberg, D. (2010). How to start an entrepreneurial revolution. *Harvard Business Review, 88*(6), 40–50.

Isenberg, D. (2011). The entrepreneurship ecosystem strategy as a new paradigm for economic policy: Principles for cultivating entrepreneurship. Institute of International European Affairs.

Isenberg, D. (2016). Scale up – to drive economic growth by catalyzing entrepreneurship ecosystems. https://www.babson.edu/academics/executive-education/babson-insight/entrepreneurship/scale-up-to-drive-growth/

Kang,Q., Li, H., Cheng, Y., & Kraus,S. (2019). Entrepreneurial ecosystems: Analysing the status quo. *Knowledge Management Research and Practice, 19*(1), 8–20.

Kantur, D., & Iseri-Say, A. (2013). Organizational context and firm-level entrepreneurship: a multiple-case analysis. *Journal of Organizational Change Management, 26*(2), 305–325.

Link, A.N., & Sarala, R.M. (2018). Advancing conceptualisation of university entrepreneurial ecosystems: The role of knowledge-intensive entrepreneurial firms. *International Small Business Journal.*

Mack, E., & Mayer, H. (2016). The evolutionary dynamics of entrepreneurial ecosystems. *Urban Studies, 53*(10), 2118–2133.

Mason, C., & Brown, R. (2014). *Entrepreneurial ecosystems and growth oriented entrepreneurship.* OECD.

Meyer, D.F., Meyer, N., & Neethling, J.R. (2016). Perceptions of business owners on service delivery and the creation of an enabling environment. *Administratio Publica, 24*(3), 52–73.

Moore, J.F. (1993). Predators and prey: a new ecology of competition. *Harvard Business Review,* 71, 75–86.

Motoyama, Y., & Knowlton, K. (2017). Examining the connections within the startup ecosystem: A case study of St. Louis. *Entrepreneurship Research Journal, 7*(1), 1–32.

Mustar, P., Renault, M., Colombo, M., Piva, E., Fontes, M., Lockett, A., Wright, M., Clarysse, B., & Moray, N. (2006). Conceptualising the heterogeneity of research-based spin-offs: a multidimensional taxonomy. *Research Policy, 35*(2), 289–308.

North, D.C. (1990). *Institutions, institutional change and economic performance.* Cambridge University Press.

Poček, J. (2020). Which types of institutions influence the development of entrepreneurial ecosystems? A legal systems perspective. *International Review of Entrepreneurship, 18*(3).

Poček, J. (2022). Tendencies towards integration and disintegration of the entrepreneurial ecosystem: An institution-based view of the dynamics. *European Planning Studies.* DOI: 10.1080/09654313.2022.2043831

Rice, M.P., Fetters, M., & Greene, P.G. (2014). University-based entrepreneurship ecosystems: A global study of six educational institutions. *International Journal of Entrepreneurship and Innovation Management, 18* (5–6): 481–501.

Roundy, P. (2017). "Small town" entrepreneurial ecosystems: Implications for developed and emerging economies. *Journal of Entrepreneurship in Emerging Economies, 9*(3), 238–262.

Scheidgen, K. (2021). Degrees of integration: How a fragmented entrepreneurial ecosystem promotes different types of entrepreneurs. *Entrepreneurship and Regional Development.*

Scholten, V., Kemp, R., & Omta, O. (2004). Entrepreneurship for life: The entrepreneurial intention among academics in the life sciences. Paper presented at the European summer university conference.

Schoonhoven, C.B., & Eisenhardt, K.M. (2012). 10 Regions as Industrial Incubators of Technology-based Ventures. *Sources of metropolitan growth,* 210.

Scott, S., Hughes, M., & Kraus, S. (2019). Developing relationships in innovation clusters. *Entrepreneurship and Regional Development, 31*(1–2): 22–45

Scott, S., Hughes, M., & Ribeiro-Soriano, D. (2020). Towards a network-based view of effective entrepreneurial ecosystems. *Review of Managerial Science* (in press).

Siegel, D.S., & Wright, M. (2015). University technology transfer offices, licensing, and start-ups. In A. Link, D. Siegel, & M. Wright (Eds.), *The Chicago handbook of university technology transfer and academic entrepreneurship* (pp. 1–40). The University of Chicago Press.

Spigel, B. (2016). Developing and governing entrepreneurial ecosystems: The structure of entrepreneurial support programs in Edinburgh, Scotland. *International Journal of Innovation and Regional Development, 7*(2): 141–160.

Spigel, B., & Harrison, R. (2018). Toward a process theory of entrepreneurial ecosystems. *Strategic Entrepreneurship Journal, 12*(1): 151–168. https://doi.org/10.1002/sej.1268

Stam, E. (2015). Entrepreneurial ecosystems and regional policy: A sympathetic critique. *European Planning Studies, 23*(9), 1759–1769.

Stam, E., & Spigel, B. (2017). Entrepreneurial ecosystems. In R. Blackburn, D. De Clercq, J. Heinonen, & Z. Wang (Eds.), *The SAGE handbook of small business and entrepreneurship*. SAGE.

Stam, F.C., & Spigel, B. (2016). Entrepreneurial ecosystems. *USE Discussion paper series, 16*(13).

Wright, M., Siegel, D.S., & Mustar, P. (2017). An emerging ecosystem for student start-ups. *The Journal of Technology Transfer, 42*(4), 909–922.

Wurth, B., Stam, E., & Spigel, B. (2021). Toward an entrepreneurial ecosystem research program. *Entrepreneurship Theory and Practice*.

Natanya Meyer and Jacques de Jongh

8 Linking Young SME Entrepreneurial Activity and Economic Development

Abstract: Several studies have pointed out the importance of entrepreneurship and its link to economic growth. However, fewer studies contribute to the link it has toward economic development. Therefore, the chapter aimed to analyze the relationship between entrepreneurial activity and its contribution to economic growth and development in the Visegrád group. A quantitative research design was followed using secondary time series data from 2006 to 2019. A composite index was developed using the employment rate, Human Development Index (HDI), and the percentage of the population above the poverty line to measure economic development. Findings suggest that the variables, entrepreneurial development, economic growth, and economic development, are linked within the Visegrád. Economic and social characteristics amongst these countries seem to influence their performances. Policy stakeholders should ensure the stimulation and development of sound private market sectors primarily structured around responsive micro and macro decision-making.

Keywords: composite index, Czech Republic, entrepreneurship, economic development, economic growth, Hungary, Poland, Slovakia, Visegrád group

Introduction

Entrepreneurial development has been directly linked to economic activity, not just in theory but also in practice. Several studies have pointed out the importance of entrepreneurship and its link to traditional economic growth; however, fewer studies contribute to the link toward economic development and empirical evidence, proving this link is rare (Ambrish, 2014; Meyer & De Jongh, 2018). Studies by Wennekers and Thurik (1999), Herrington and Kew (2013) and Meyer and Meyer (2017) have, however, proven that some relationship between entrepreneurial and economic activity does exist. From a European perspective, these links have proven even more intricate. As pointed out by Chowdhury et al. (2015) and Audretsch et al. (2015), countries and economies administered by common standards, for example under the European Union regulations, are each faced with its own unique modernized and globalized pressures as they bring with them various ways to solve and comprehend these relationships.

Natanya Meyer, Department of Business Management in the College of Business and Economics, University of Johannesburg

Jacques de Jongh, School of Economics in the Faculty of Economics and Management Sciences, North-West University

https://doi.org/10.1515/9783110747652-009

Furthermore, as many of these countries, especially those located in more eastern regions, have commenced with relatively advanced systemic transformations, the impact that the associated innovation and competitiveness from these entrepreneurial activities have had on economic transformations has been vague (Korez-Vide & Tominic, 2016; Rusu & Roman, 2017). Based on the above, the significance of determining and comprehending the extent to which entrepreneurial activity contributes to economic growth and economic development can theoretically assist policymakers in reconsidering current policies surrounding entrepreneurship activity and development, leading to possible economic transformation. In light of this, the chapter's main aim was to compare and analyze the relationship between entrepreneurial activity and its contribution to stimulating economic advancement and alleviating poverty and unemployment in the Visegrád group of countries.

Literature Review

Globally, numerous researchers and policymakers alike have identified entrepreneurs as key contributors to a country's economic success (Toma et al., 2014; Meyer & Meyer, 2017; Pinelli et al., 2021; Kraus et al., 2021). Entrepreneurship can be viewed as a multidimensional phenomenon and defined in the context of psychological, economic, managerial, social, and sociological perspectives (Bula, 2012). Key characteristics of the definition of an entrepreneur include being a risk-taker, spotting opportunities, and acting on them (Bula, 2012; Dvorsky et al., 2018; Oláh et al., 2018; Oláh et al., 2019). Toma et al. (2014) pointed out that entrepreneurship in open and modern economies has become critical for traditional economic growth and socio and economic development. In neo-classical terms, economic growth could be defined as a cumulative increase of output or the build-up of production factors reflecting a numerical measurement of a country's growth and progress (Masoud, 2014). The concept of economic growth is, to a large extent, based on models developed by traditional economists such as Solow (1956), Myrdal (1957), and Rostow (1959). Although GDP and GDP per capita are well-known and used measures to calculate a country's prosperity, one of the main arguments regarding this measurement is that it does not incorporate social aspects such as equality, human development, and social cohesion (OECD, 2005). On the other hand, economic development denotes a multidimensional measuring concept (Todaro & Smith, 2011), providing an all-inclusive overview of a country's progress, specifically regarding social development features (Iyer et al., 2005). That is to say, economic development involves a rounded and comprehensive enhancement of a society's standard of living through the growth of all sectors of the economy, specifically including areas such as education, health, technology, and infrastructure, leading to an overall reduction of poverty and unemployment (Carlson, 1999). Fundamentally, economic development can be described as the balance between economic and social measurements within a country (Huq et al., 2009; Toma et al., 2014).

As mentioned, there is a certain relationship between economic growth, economic development, and entrepreneurship. There has been a proven correlation between per capita GDP and Total Early-stage entrepreneurial Activity (TEA) rates, as mentioned by Herrington and Kew (2013), as well the level of entrepreneurship and economic development (Naudé, 2013; Brown & Thornton, 2013). The following economic background holds importance for its contribution to understanding this link. Attention to supply-side economics and its underlying factors attracted renewed emphasis after the 1980s global stagflation and consequent high unemployment level. During this time, much attention was drawn to the role of entrepreneurship and small businesses (Toma et al., 2014). Many researchers (North & Thomas, 1973; Olsen, 1982; Van de Klundert, 1997, Máté, 2014; Lakner et al., 2018) pointed out that the institutional foundation of an economy is important. However, these research efforts have neglected the role of economic agents (including entrepreneurs) and linked these micro-level institutions to economic outcomes at the macro-level (Wennekers & Thurik, 1999). Many researchers have realized that the bulk of economic growth no longer lies predominantly in contributions by large companies and that small and medium enterprises (SMEs) make a considerable contribution to the GDP (Brock & Evans, 1989; EIM, 1997; Eggers & Kraus, 2011; Toma et al., 2014). Evidence indicates a shift from large precarious firms to smaller, more robust ones has occurred. Since the 1970s, a considerable amount of literature has emerged, making very explicit references to the role and contribution of SMEs in economies (Toma et al., 2014). In 1997 a shift was identified, showing that small business growth exceeded that of large businesses from 1988 to 1997 in Europe (EIM, 1997), while similar trends had previously been identified in the USA (Brock & Evans, 1989). These shifts were due to changes in the world economy, evolution in the types of technology processes, labor supply (lower real wages), increasing education levels, changes in consumer taste, and ease of entry regarding the regulation of business (Wennekers & Thurik, 1999). The realization of these global trends has placed much-needed emphasis on the advancement of the small business sector. Some of the contributing causes of this shift have resulted in increased entrepreneurship development, improved innovation, enhanced industry dynamics, and, most importantly, job creation (Acs, 1992).

Various studies have linked entrepreneurship directly and indirectly to economic growth and development (Wennekers & Thurik, 1999; Herrington & Kew, 2013). In addition, entrepreneurship has been identified as a booster of economic growth for several reasons (Toma et al., 2014). Improved competition is due to an increase in the number of businesses and options to consumers. This in itself can be perceived as economic growth since an increase in the number of businesses eventually leads to a rise in employment levels. Moreover, competition creates a conducive environment leading to the growth of knowledge. These knowledge "spill-overs" can be explained as the effect of information, skills, and experience being transferred to other individuals or businesses. Knowledge spill-over is an important causal instrument for endogenous growth, diversity, and innovation, creating uniqueness and influencing economic growth. Audretsch and Thurik (2000) found empirical evidence supporting some of these statements in a longitudinal study of 23 OECD countries over 20 years (1974–1994). Specifically, this study involved an empirical examination of the quantitative increase of entrepreneurs and the link to employment levels. Results indicated that as the number of entrepreneurs increased, unemployment levels decreased. Similar results were found by Meyer and Meyer (2017). Wennekers and Thurik (1999) also found that entrepreneurship positively affected GDP, improving general employment levels. Additional advantages of entrepreneurship include new product innovation and service development (Toma et al., 2014). However, as with most phenomena, researchers may have differing views. Some studies have neglected to provide empirical evidence that entrepreneurship leads to economic growth, productivity, and employment (Naudé, 2013). There are, furthermore, many underlying factors, such as strict labor laws, low innovation, and a strong trend towards necessity-driven entrepreneurship, which may contribute to the preceding discussion. These, however, do not form part of the scope of this chapter.

Entrepreneurship impacts economic growth and development positively for several reasons. First, the progression of economic development is linked to the outcome of a complex set of activities and discoveries which constitute entrepreneurial actions. Entrepreneurs facilitate the reallocation and distribution of less productive resources to more effective ones (Toma et al., 2014). Second, entrepreneurs are known as key instruments in economic development by directly contributing to employment, innovation, and well-being (Acs & Szerb, 2010). Third, innovative entrepreneurs are essential for developing new products and services that contribute positively to a growing economy (Kressel & Lento, 2012). Lastly, opportunity-driven entrepreneurs have a higher reported level of subjective well-being and job satisfaction, indirectly resulting in them becoming more productive (Naudé et al., 2008; Naudé, 2013). Entrepreneurship development is equally important for economic growth and the general well-being of a country; therefore, a deeper understanding of this topic is crucial.

Research Methodology

A quantitative research design was followed to achieve the chapter's primary objective. A descriptive analysis used time series data ranging from 2006 to 2019. This period was mainly selected based on the availability of the data as the new business density (NBD) variable is only available from 2006. Only data until 2019 was included due to the Covid-19 pandemic that disrupted global economies in 2020 and 2021. Including these data sets in empirical analysis might result in skewed findings due to outlier data points. The main variables under investigation included the annual percentage growth in the gross domestic product (GDP) per capita and the new business density (NBD) rate, which is used as a proxy for young small and medium enterprise (SME) entrepreneurial activity (World Bank, 2019).

Furthermore, the study used a self-constructed composite development index adapted from Meyer et al. (2016) to measure and assess the overall economic development levels. The index consists of three constituent variables: the human development index (HDI), the percentage of the population not at risk of poverty and social exclusion, and the countries' respective employment rates. All variables are equally weighted, with the index score ranging from 0 (low development) to 100 (high development). Finally, to ensure clarity and the analytical soundness of the descriptive analysis, all of the variables under consideration were converted accordingly. Table 8.1 highlights these conversions and their associated interpretations.

Table 8.1: Selected variable identification and interpretation.

Indicator	Variables	Conversion	Interpretation	Database
GDP per capita growth	GDP per capita growth (annual % change)	Measured with a base score of 90	GDP growth rate with a base of 90. A score higher than 90 indicates positive growth, whereas scores lower than 90 indicate negative growth	World Bank
Economic development index	HDI, % of the population not at risk of poverty and social exclusion, employment rate	HDI as percentage; % of the population not at risk of poverty and social exclusion; employment rate. All variables used to construct the index are equally weighted	Index score ranging from 0 to 100. Higher scores indicate higher economic development, and lower scores lower development levels	Eurostat, World Bank, UN.
New Business Density (NBD)	New business registrations per 1000 people aged 15 to 64 years	Measured with a base score of 90	New business density with a base score of 90. A score higher than 90 indicates positive growth	World Bank

Source: authors' compilation.

Based on the variables above, the descriptive analysis focused on all member countries of the Visegrád group. Also known as the V4, the group was formed in 1993 and ultimately represented an alliance of four post-socialist central European countries, namely Poland, Slovakia, Czech Republic, and Hungary (Mogildea, 2017). Its initial objective to integrate central Europe into the larger European community has seen its more modern role at the forefront of driving regional economic cooperation and building stronger international ties within member states. According to Sacio-Szymańska et al. (2016), over the last decade, the prominence of the Visegrád group has increased dramatically in the European Union, with countries accounting for 5.6% of total economic output (GDP) and 9.1% of total exports.

These attributes and the unique intricacies of being governed by common standards yet faced by ever-increasing global and diversified markets prompted the choice of the study area. Furthermore, as these countries embarked on somewhat simultaneous systemic transformations, their inherent differences and unique attributes serve as an interesting framework for analyzing the relationship between entrepreneurial climates and their role in market modernization and socio-economic progress. Given this geographical background, the descriptive inquiry proceeds through a graphical analysis of the trends in the selected variables mentioned in Table 8.1, with Figures 8.1–8.4 depicting each of the V4 members' performance in this regard. Based on these figures, inferences surrounding the countries' entrepreneurial climate and the subsequent relationship with the underlining growth and development performance are made and discussed.

Results and Discussion

Figure 8.1 shows the performance of the Czech Republic for the selected indicators from 2006 to 2019. The figure indicates that the country attributed the highest economic development scores (ECD) (84.47) amongst the Visegrád countries over the selected period. As shown, these have concomitantly been associated with continuously high NBD rates and strong growth performances, especially since 2013. The country has shown remarkably low poverty and social exclusion levels compared to other EU members such as Finland and Demark (Eurostat, 2018). Guasti et al. (2017) attribute these to a strong labor market performance and cohesive redistributive social policy landscape. However, substantial regional differences in this regard do exist.

Notwithstanding the importance of these differences, entrepreneurial activity within the country's borders has contributed notably to underlining economic development levels (Polok et al., 2016). Lukeš (2017) suggests that this has especially revolved around a strong SME sector performance, leading to significant improvements in manufacturing and export industries. Concurrent to these occurrences, various advancements in innovative infrastructural developments and the diversification of economic activity have likewise been observed. Despite the associated advantages that have been linked to the improvement in entrepreneurial activity, the IMF (2016) highlights that various aspects have impeded the potential for the growth of smaller businesses and their subsequent contributions. This includes notable challenges concerning levels of corruption in the business environment, the misuse of public funds needed to support these industries, and various public and private partnership formations that have not been beneficial to the country's more recent growth performance. In addition, amongst the four countries included in the analysis, the Czech Republic also has the highest dependency ratio

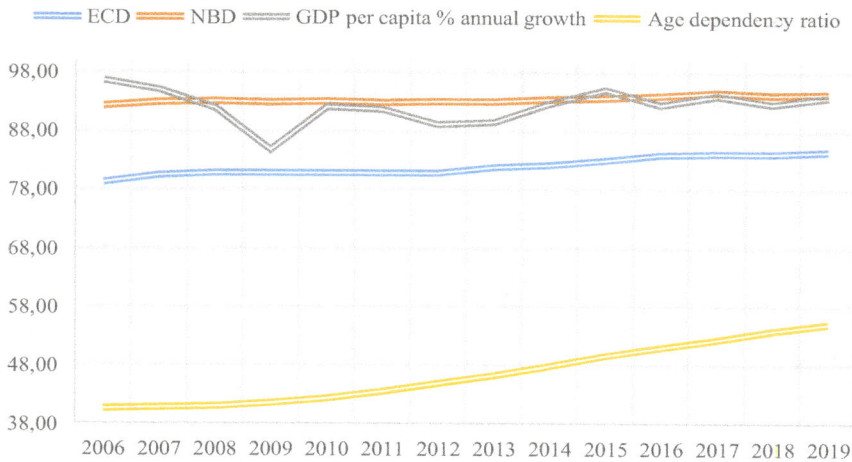

Figure 8.1: Czech Republic's growth trends (2006–2019) regarding ECD, NBD, GDP per capita and dependency ratio.
Source: own compilation from data of World Bank, 2020; Eurostat, 2020; UN, 2020.

(55.1%). Pekarek (2018) states that the country's ageing population has had severe consequences for fiscal stability and lower productivity rates in its workforce, causing concern about social inclusion levels.

Results for Hungary's respective indicators are shown in Figure 8.2. As a transition economy, the Hungarian economy, much like Poland, has experienced significant changes over the last few decades (WEF, 2017). The country has undergone large-scale transitions from a centrally planned system to a pure market system, profoundly impacting the economy's performance (Bozóki, 2008). Results from Figure 8.2 emphasize these impacts, showcasing noticeable declines in economic growth rates and fluctuations in economic development between 2006 and 2013.

From this perspective, underlining economic features of the transition worsened the impact of the financial crises on the economy. Egedy (2012) states that among these drivers were a lack of competitiveness, the domestic market's small size, and structural problems in the labor force. Despite these fluctuations, new business density rates contrastingly showcased increases during 2008 and 2011. The OECD (2016), in relation to these trends, states that entrepreneurial activity was primarily necessity driven, highlighting the value of self-employment as a buffer against economic downturns. Moreover, Szira (2014) attributes the expansion during the period as a key driver for modern economic contributions. From this perspective, the heightened entrepreneurial involvement contributed to more diversified local markets, subcontracting large-scale state-owned enterprises, and spurred competitiveness, especially for export sectors (Dudin et al., 2016). In addition to these positive changes, the country,

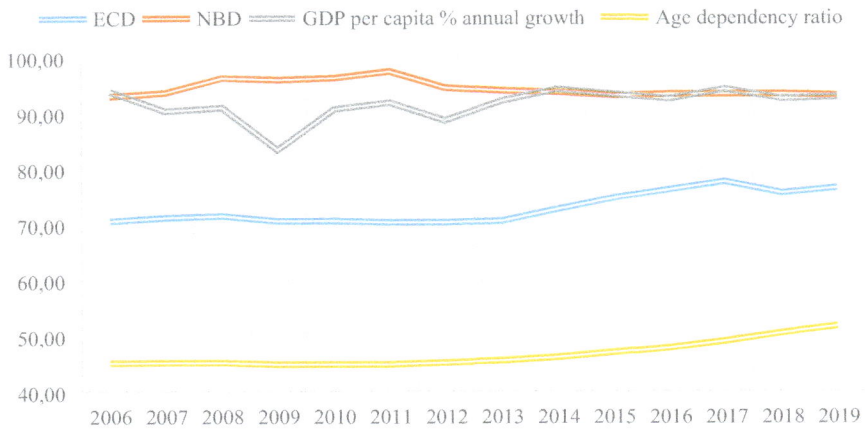

Figure 8.2: Hungarian growth trends (2006–2019) regarding ECD, NBD, GDP per capita and dependency ratio.
Source: own compilation from data of World Bank, 2020; Eurostat, 2020; UN, 2020.

compared to its other Visegrád counterparts, also showcased the lowest growth rate (14.39%) in its dependency figures for the sample period.

As shown in Figure 8.3, Poland has the most stable environment for the respective variables under consideration. Upon reviewing the trends between 2006 and 2019, NBD rates improved slightly from an estimated 90.48 to around 92.99 without any serious deviations. Comparative to other Visegrád members, however, the country illustrates the lowest rates in this regard. Kukuła (2016) attributes these somewhat lower rates to vast regional differences with notably high densities in the more western developed regions instead of the eastern and southern areas with a more agricultural focus. In addition to these trends, economic growth levels showed similar performances. From 2006 to 2019, per capita growth levels averaged around 4%. Given the sluggish growth performance globally, especially after the financial crisis of 2008, the Polish economy has shown a relatively strong performance in this regard. As growth rates between 2008 and 2009 showed noticeable declines, the country was the sole EU member not to pass the contractual point (Orłowski, 2011). According to Paulina (2017), this feature could be ascribed to an inherently strong and stable macroeconomic policy that prioritizes enabling environments for business owners, increased confidence levels of smaller local firms, and the diversification of various export industries.

Apart from the entrepreneurial and growth performances, the country has likewise shown strong performances in developmental and social contexts. As depicted in Figure 8.3, developmental levels in 2006 were estimated below a 70 index score (67.33). During the sample period, index scores showed strong growth of 13.79%, with a developmental score of 76.62 in 2019. Findings from similar studies (Sienkiewicz,

2014), which also noted these strong performances, have attributed this growth to various aspects in which small business development has played a large role in improving Polish labour market outcomes and the improvement in the capacity of the national infrastructural framework. Paulina (2017) further adds to these findings, suggesting that the conducive and inherent entrepreneurial environments contribute to underlining innovation levels and enhanced regional competitiveness for the country. Henceforth from this perspective, strong, stable, and supported economic and entrepreneurial climates seem to prove crucial in improving economic development levels. Considering the age-structure dynamics in the country's development path, next to Slovakia, Poland had the second-lowest dependency ratio in 2019 (49.93%).

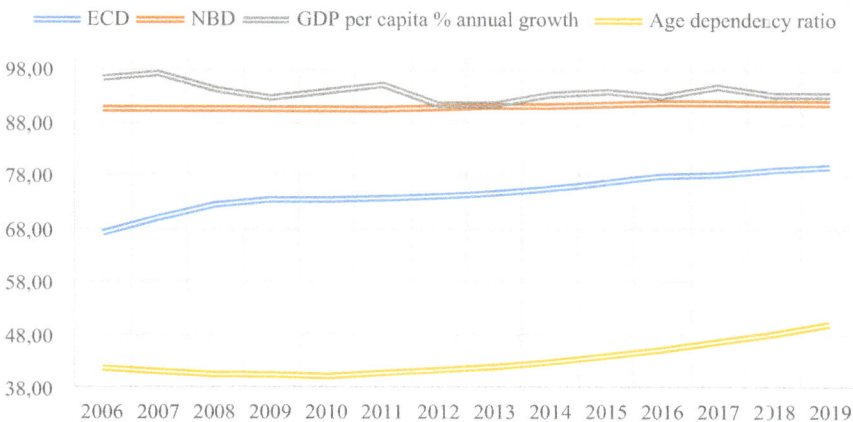

Figure 8.3: Polish growth trends (2006–2019) regarding ECD, NBD, GDP per capita and dependency ratio. Source: own compilation from data of World Bank, 2020; Eurostat, 2020; UN, 2020.

In stark contrast to the stable performance shown by the Polish economy, the Slovakian experience throughout the sample period showcased somewhat more volatile trends. The country's growth performance is specifically reviewed, most notably in Figure 8.4, with significant movement during the financial crisis (2007–2009). Much like the Hungarian experience, activity in the Slovakian economy attributed to a major contraction, moving from a per capita economic growth rate of above 10% in 2007 to –5.55% in the space of two years. Subsequent to these changes, the recovery was rapid. Leading up to 2019, compared to other Visegrád members, the country had the second-highest development scores (79.60) and much similar economic growth rates. From this point of view, most recent performances have been largely ascribed to government support directed towards providing quality business infrastructure, the introduction of various reforms aiming to reduce corporate taxation and red tape together, with a high degree of labour productivity (Biea, 2016). Upon reviewing the age dependency ratio, the country likewise exhibited the lowest estimates compared to the other member countries.

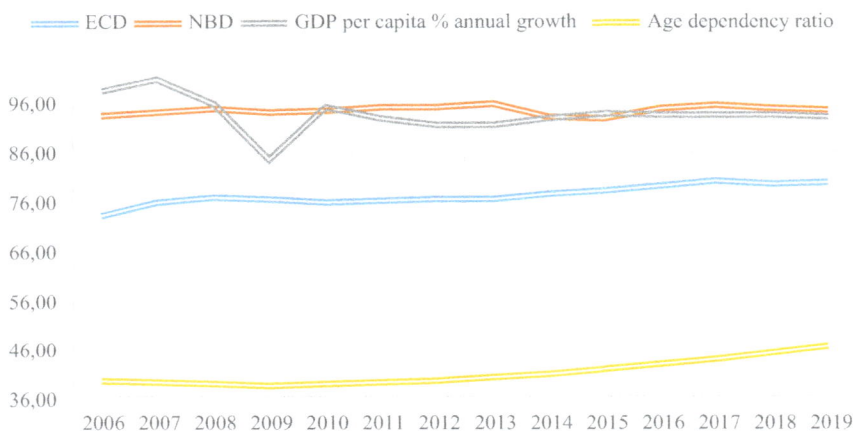

Figure 8.4: Slovakian growth trends (2006–2019) regarding ECD, NBD, GDP per capita and dependency ratio.
Source: own compilation from data of World Bank, 2020; Eurostat, 2020; UN, 2020.

According to Wilson et al. (2016), the link between the Slovakian business environment and positive growth in income levels and various social aspects is shown in several dimensions. These include a large influx of foreign direct investment (FDI) largely based on the more export-orientated scale of small firms in the country (Malega, 2018). While this aspect has largely contributed to the uptick in growth rates, the success of the country's SME sector has significantly improved its social environment. In this regard, more than 60% of the jobs created in the economy originate from these enterprises, concomitantly assisting in poverty alleviation and the reduction of the population at risk of exclusion (Bašová, 2018). Additionally, with the increase of these enterprises, especially in dispersed areas, regional development is largely improved and more so on a microeconomic level (Ján, 2015). This is illustrated in the provision of diversified product ranges, more competitive and efficient production practices, and more equitable access to basic services (Belás et al., 2015). Despite these associated advantages, the potential of the growing entrepreneurial spirit has been impeded by various challenges. This has largely revolved around perceived corruption in the business environment, a significant level of bureaucracy, and concerns surrounding the recent introduction of various taxation laws (Pilkova & Holienka, 2017).

Conclusion

The chapter had the primary objective of analysing the linkages between entrepreneurial activity, economic growth and development levels within the Visegrád group. The chapter's findings disclosed various significant features based on the descriptive analysis. Among the most prominent and common were the underlining advantages associated with conducive entrepreneurial climates. More specifically, this is related to establishing the diversified economic structures and increasing innovation levels inherent to these economies. In addition to these benefits, the findings also revealed that strong and supported business environments acted as resilient buffers to economic shocks, reducing the impact of stringent economic circumstances on social environments. This was likewise showcased in the per capita growth and development trends. These variables seem to showcase a strong interdependency, with performances highly intertwined with these countries' social and economic aspects. Despite their commonalities, however, the unique attributes of each of the countries seem to alter these relationships. These attributes specifically revolved around significant regional, spatial, and economic dissimilarities within each group member. Other distinctive characteristics identified included the misuse of state funds and each member's idiosyncratic trade position. In light of the aforementioned and identified aspects, the chapter's findings extend the underlying knowledge surrounding the intricate nature of entrepreneurship, economic growth, and development. More specifically, it does so in the context of countries that arguably have only recently undertaken significant systemic transformations. In this sense, it furthers the understanding of the required strategies for harnessing innovation and the associated advantages of this process.

Henceforth, based on this, it is recommended that entrepreneurship development within these transitional contexts be proliferated in an attempt to further both social and economic development. Moreover, key stakeholders should create enabling environments by structuring responsive macro and microeconomic policies that seek to support small business development. These policies should eradicate unnecessary red tape, prevent common start-up stumbling blocks, and provide much-needed training programs that promote business confidence. While the findings lend insight into the relationship between entrepreneurial activity and the countries' associated economic and social spheres, it must be acknowledged that the chapter is not without its limitations. Specifically, this refers to the lack of available data that restricted the study to a more descriptive nature. Whilst this did not offer the opportunity to conduct any causal, predictive or confirmatory statistical analyses, it does provide opportunities for further studies to add to the knowledge on the subject. Future studies, subsequently, can adopt various econometric techniques, including panel data analyses, to examine these relationships within the V4 group. Additionally, various comparative based inquiries with similar intercontinental regions can be adopted in order to attain a more definitive understanding of the processes under consideration. Lastly, as the analysis only included data up to 2019, a comparative study before and after 2019 could be conducted in a few years to analyze the impact of the Covid–19 shock.

References

Acs, Z.J. (1992). Small business economics: A global perspective. *Challenges*, *35*, 38–44.

Acs, Z.J., & Szerb, L. (2010). The global entrepreneurship and development index (GEDI). DRUID Conference.

Ambrish, D.R. (2014). Entrepreneurship development: An approach to economic empowerment of women. *International Journal of Multidisciplinary Approach and Studies*, *I*(1), 224–232.

Audretsch, D.B., Belitski, M., & Desai, S. (2015). Entrepreneurship and economic development in cities. *The Annals of Regional Science*, *55*(1), 33–60.

Audretsch, D.B., & Thurik, A.R. (2000). Capitalism and democracy in the 21st century: From the managed to the entrepreneurial economy. *Journal of Evolutionary Economics*, *10*(2000), 17–34.

Bašová, A. (2018). Economic characteristics of SMEs in Slovakia and in Czech Republic, *Social & Economic Revue*, *16*(1), 6–13.

Belás, J., Demjan, V., Habánik, J., Hudáková, M., & Sipko, J. (2015). The business environment of small and medium-sized enterprises in selected regions of the Czech Republic and Slovakia. *E+M Ekonomika a Management*, *18*(1), 95–110.

Biea, N. (2016). Economic growth in Slovakia: Past successes and future challenges. *EU. Economic Brief, No. 008*. Publications Office of the European Union. ISBN 978-92-79-54469-9.

Bozóki, A. (2008). Consolidation or second revolution? The emergence of the new right in Hungary. *Journal of Communist and Transition Politics*, *24*(2), 191–231.

Brock, W.A., & Evans, D.S. (1989). Small business economics. *Small Business Economics*, *1*, 7–20.

Brown, C., & Thornton, M. (2013). How entrepreneurship theory created economics. *The Quarterly Journal of Austrian Economics*, *16*(4), 401–420.

Bula, H.O. (2012). Evolution and theories of entrepreneurship: A critical review on the Kenyan perspective. *International Journal of Business and Commerce*, *1*(11), 81–96.

Carlson, B.A. (1999). Social dimensions of economic development and productivity: Inequality and social performance. An overview. In B.A. Carlson (Ed.), Social dimensions of economic development and productivity: Inequality and social performance (pp. 7–19). United Nations.

Chowdhury, F., Desai, S., Audretsch, D.B., & Belitski, M. (2015). Entrepreneurship, corruption and income inequality. In *The Workshop in Political Theory and Policy Analysis, Bloomington, Indiana, April* (Vol. 1).

Dudin, M.N., Voykova, N.A., Galkina, M.V., & Vernikov, V.A. (2016). Development of Hungary's manufacturing industry in the conditions of European integration. *International Journal of Economics and Financial Issues*, *6*(5), 48–52.

Dvorsky, J., Popp, J., Virglerova, Z., Kovács, S., & Oláh, J. (2018). Assessing the importance of market risk and its sources in the SME of the Visegrad Group and Serbia. *Advances in Decision Sciences*, *22*(A), 1–25.

Egedy, T. (2012). The effects of global economic crisis in Hungary. *Hungarian Geographical Bulletin*, *61*(2), 55–173.

Eggers, F., & Kraus, S. (2011). Growing young SMEs in hard economic times: The impact of entrepreneurial and customer orientations – a qualitative study from Silicon Valley. *Journal of Small Business & Entrepreneurship*, *24*(1), 99–111.

EIM. (1997). The European Observatory for SMEs. 5th Annual report, Zoetermeer.

Eurostat. (2018). People at risk of poverty and social exclusion. http://ec.europa.eu/eurostat/tgm/table.do?
tab=table&init=1&language=en&pcode=t2020_50&plugin=1

Eurostat. (2020). People at risk of poverty and social exclusion. http://ec.europa.eu/eurostat/tgm/table.
do?tab=table&init=1&language=en&pcode=t2020_5&plugin=1

Guasti, P., Mansfeldová, Z., Myant, M., & Bönker, F. (2017). Czech Republic report: Sustainable governance
indicators 2017. Bertelsmann Stiftung.

Herrington, M., & Kew, J. (2013). GEM 2013 South African Report: Twenty years of democracy. University of
Cape Town Centre for Innovation and Entrepreneurship.

Huq, M.M., Clunies-Ross, A., & Forsyth, D. (2009). *Development economics*. McGraw Hill Education.

IMF (International Monetary Fund). (2016). Corruption: Costs and mitigation strategies. IMF. ISBN 978-15-
13-59433-0.

Iyer, S., Kitson, M., & Toh, B. (2005). Social capital, economic growth and regional development. *Regional
Studies, 39*(8), 1015–1040.

Ján, D. (2015). Regional development of small and medium sized enterprises (SMEs) in the Prešov region
with focus on tourism. *Procedia Economics and Finance, 34*(1), 594–599.

Korez-Vide, R., & Tominc, P. (2016). Competitiveness, entrepreneurship and economic growth. In
P. Trąpczyński, L. Puślecki, & M. Jarosinski (Eds.), Competitiveness of CEE Economies and Businesses
(pp. 25–44). Springer International Publishing AG.

Kraus, S., McDowell, W., Ribeiro-Soriano, D.E., & Rodríguez-García, M. (2021). The role of innovation and
knowledge for entrepreneurship and regional development. *Entrepreneurship & Regional Development,
33*(3–4), 175–184.

Kressel, H., & Lento, T.V. (2012). *Entrepreneurship in the global economy: Engine for economic growth*.
Cambridge University Press.

Kukuła, A.J. (2016). The modernisation of the economy of a poorly developed region through the
construction of the knowledge-based economy on the example of the Lublin region in eastern
Poland (2006–2020/30). In A.J. Kukuła (Ed.), *Selected problems of development of Polish regions in the
perspective of 2020*. Wydawnictwo KUL.

Lakner, Z., Kiss, A., Merlet, I., Oláh, J., Máté, D., Grabara, J., & Popp, J. (2018). Building coalitions for a
diversified and sustainable tourism: Two case studies from Hungary. *Sustainability, 10*(4), 1–23.

Lukeš, M. (2017). Entrepreneurship development in the Czech Republic. In A. Sauka & A. Chepurenko
(Eds.), *Entrepreneurship in transition economies: Diversity, trends and perspectives* (pp. 209–224).
Springer.

Malega, P. (2018). Start-ups and their influence on the competitiveness of Slovak Republic. *International
Journal for Advanced Research and Novelty, 4*(9), 1–19.

Masoud, N. (2014). A contribution to the theory of economic growth: Old and new. *Journal of Economics
and International Finance, 6*(3), 47–61.

Máté, D. (2014). Human capital, unions and productivity in a labour-skilled sectoral approach. *Society and
Economy, 36*(3), 369–385.

Meyer, D.F., De Jongh, J.J., & Meyer, N. (2016). The formulation of a composite regional development
index. *International Journal of Business and Management Studies, 8*(1), 100–116.

Meyer, N., & De Jongh, J.J. (2018). The importance of entrepreneurship as a contributing factor to
economic growth and development: The case of selected European countries. *Journal of Economics
and Behavioral Studies, 10*(4), 287–299.

Meyer, N., & Meyer, D.F. (2017). An econometric analysis of entrepreneurial activity, economic growth and
employment: The case of the BRICS countries. *International Journal of Economic Perspectives, 11*(2),
429–441.

Mogildea, M. (2017). The Visegrád group: A regional integration model for advancing the Europeanization
process in central and eastern Europe. Think Visegrád.

Myrdal, G. (1957). *Rich lands and poor*. Harper and Row.

Naudé, W.A. (2013). Entrepreneurship and economic development: Theory, evidence and policy. Discussion paper, IZA DP No. 7507. University of Maastricht.

Naudé, W.A., Gries, T., Wood, E., & Meintjies, A. (2008). Regional determinants of entrepreneurial start-ups in a developing country. *Entrepreneurship and Regional Development, 20*(2), 111–124. DOI: 10.1080/08985620701631498

North, D.C., & Thomas, R.P. (1973). *The rise of the western world: A new economic history*. Cambridge University Press.

OECD (Organisation for Economic Cooperation and Development). (2005). Is GDP a satisfactory measure of growth? http://oecdobserver.org/news/archivestory.php/aid/1518/Is_GDP_a_satisfactory_mea sure_of_growth_.html

OECD (Organisation for Economic Co-operation and Development). (2016). OECD economic surveys. OECD Publishing.

Oláh, J., Kovács, S., Virglerova, Z., Lakner, Z., & Popp, J. (2019). Analysis and comparison of economic and financial risk sources in SMEs of the Visegrad group and Serbia. *Sustainability, 11*(7/1853), 1–19.

Oláh, J., Sadaf, R., Máté, D., & Popp, J. (2018). The influence of the management success factors of logistics service providers on firms' competitiveness. *Polish Journal of Management Studies, 17*(1), 175–193.

Olsen, M. (1982). *The rise and decline of nations: Economic growth, stagflation and social rigidities*. Yale University Press.

Orłowski, W. (2011). Post-accession economic development of Poland. *Eastern Journal of European Studies, 2*(2), 7–20.

Paulina, F. (2017). Development of individual entrepreneurship in Poland under crisis conditions. *Ovidius University Annals, Economic Sciences Series, 17*(1), 484–490.

Pekarek, S. (2018). Population ageing and economic dependency ratio: comparative study of the Czech Republic and Slovakia. *Ecoforum Journal, 7*(1), 69–78.

Pilkova, A., & Holienka, M. (2017). Entrepreneurship development in Slovakia. In A. Sauka & A. Chepurenko (Eds.), *Entrepreneurship in transition economies: Diversity, trends and perspectives* (pp. 225–241). Springer.

Pinelli, M., Lechner, C., Kraus, S., & Liguori, E. (2021). Entrepreneurial value creation: Conceptualising an exchange-based view of entrepreneurship. *Journal of Small Business and Enterprise Development*. DOI: 10.1108/JSBED-04-2021-0155

Polok, D., Michalski, P., Szewczyk, D., Keil, D., Wieczore, S., Kaciakova, P., Incze, Z., Rycerz, J., Nisztuk, T., Dvouletý, O., & Krzemiński, P. (2016). *Future of the Visegrád group*. Lesław Paga Foundation.

Rostow, W.W. (1959). The stages of economic growth. *The Economic History Review, 12*(1), 1–16.

Rusu, V.D., & Roman, A. (2017). Entrepreneurial activity in the EU: An empirical evaluation of its determinants. *Sustainability, 9*(10), 1679–1695.

Sacio-Szymańska, A., Kononiuk, A., Tommei, S., Valenta, O., Hideg, É., Gáspár, J., Markovič, P., Gubová, K., & Boorová, B. (2016). The future of business in Visegrád region. *European Journal of Futures Research, 4*(26), 1–13.

Sienkiewicz, M.W. (2014). Local economic development policy in Poland: Determinants and outcomes. *Zbornik Radova Ekonomskog Fakulteta U Rijeci: Časopis Za Ekonomsku Teoriju I Praksu, 32*(2), 405–427.

Solow, R.M. (1956). A contribution to the theory of economic growth. *The Quarterly Journal of Economics, 70*(1), 65–94.

Szira, Z. (2014). The situation of the SME sector in Hungary. *Management, Enterprise and Benchmarking–In the 21st Century* (1), 107–118.

Todaro, M.P., & Smith, S.C. (2011). *Economic development, 11th ed*. Pearson Education Limited.

Toma, S.G., Grigore, A.M., & Marinescu, P. (2014). Economic development and entrepreneurship. *Procedia, Economics and Finance, 8*, 436–443.

UN (United Nations). (2019). Human development data. http://hdr.undp.org/en/data

Van de Klundert, T.H. (1997). *Groei en institusies: Over de oozaken van economische ontwikkeling*. University Press.

WEF (World Economic Forum). (2017). The inclusive growth and development report. WEF.

Wennekers, S., & Thurik, R. (1999). Linking entrepreneurship and economic growth. *Small Business Economics, 13*, 27–55.

Wilson, N., Ochotnický, P., & Káčer, M. (2016). Creation and destruction in transition economies: The SME sector in Slovakia. *International Small Business Journal, 34*(5), 579–600.

World Bank. (2020). New business density (new registrations per 1000 people ages 15–64). https://data.worldbank.org/indicator/IC.BUS.NDNS.ZS?view=chart

World Bank. (2019). World development indicators. https://databank.worldbank.org/data/source/world-development-indicators

Alicia Rodríguez

9 Governance of Innovation in SMEs: No Place Like Home?

Abstract: Different governance modes of innovation activities can contribute to the competitiveness of firms, but these modes will not necessarily benefit all firms equally. The unique resource endowments and organizational characteristics of SMEs may affect how these firms manage R&D inputs at home and overseas, which will in turn affect the impact of different governance options. This chapter provides an overview of R&D governance modes in SMEs, with a special focus on R&D activities performed overseas. Specifically, R&D activities can be differentiated into those performed internally, those performed in collaboration with other partners, and those outsourced in the home country or abroad – with each mode bringing different implications for the competitiveness of SMEs in terms of innovation. Beyond this, the chapter distinguishes between micro-businesses and larger SMEs, thus making it possible to reveal any potential differences in their governance of innovation activities. To understand the characteristics of these governance modes, this chapter uses a large sample of SMEs in different manufacturing and service sectors from the Spanish Technological Innovation Panel. The findings show that all governance modes of R&D activities – both domestic and international – are related with higher rates of innovation in SMEs. More precisely, a comparison of the different governance modes indicates that domestic collaboration and internal R&D are equally beneficial for innovation in SMEs, followed by captive R&D offshoring and international collaboration strategies, with outsourcing formulae bringing up the rear. Interesting and valuable results emerge for the micro and small firms, results that differ from those for the medium firms and that merit further study by future work.

Keywords: innovation, SME, governance modes, competitiveness, offshore, outsourcing, onshore, internal R&D

Introduction

Small and medium-sized enterprises (SMEs) make up 99 percent of firms in the European Union (EU). These enterprises play a crucial role in the economies of European countries by creating two out of every three jobs in the private sector and contribut-

Acknowledgments: This work is part of the research projects funded by the Government Research Agency of Spanish Ministry of Science and Innovation (PID2019-106874GB-I00/AEI/10.13039/501100011033) and by the European Union NextGenerationEU/ PRTR (MCIN/AEI/10.13039/501100011033; TED2021-130042B-I00).

Alicia Rodríguez, Carlos III University of Madrid, Spain

https://doi.org/10.1515/9783110747652-010

ing more than half the total value-added generated by firms in the EU (European Commission, 2020). Increasing the competitiveness of SMEs, then, is fundamental for the development of any country – and to achieve this, boosting their rates of innovation is vital. Consequently, analyzing what drives innovation in SMEs is a topic of interest for both academia and institutions looking to understand which innovation activities are best suited to these firms and which policies are most effective to bolster their competitiveness (see recent works such as Hervás-Oliver et al., 2021; Muhammad et al., 2022, and the review by Saunila, 2020).

The unique resource endowments, capabilities, and organizational characteristics of SMEs may affect how they manage their R&D inputs at home and overseas (Acs and Audretsch, 1990; Rammer and Schmiele, 2008; Raymond and St-Pierre, 2010; Rodríguez and Nieto, 2016). The objective of this chapter, then, is to advance our knowledge of the different R&D activities performed by SMEs, along with their consequences. Specifically, the chapter analyzes six R&D governance modes in SMEs – distinguishing between micro, small, and medium firms – and examines how they are related to firm competitiveness in terms of innovation performance. Understanding the innovation capacity of SMEs will also be particularly useful for managers looking to improve competitiveness by selecting the best governance mode for innovation activities such as R&D.

Despite the limited resources at their disposal, innovation in SMEs relies on a variety of internal and external sources. Among the latter, collaboration with other firms and research centers has been widely studied as a strategy to improve innovation in SMEs (Hossain & Kauranen, 2016; Torchia & Calabró, 2019; Zahoor & Al-Tabbaa, 2020, among others), one that allows them to bridge the gap that exists with larger firms (Nieto & Santamaría, 2010). Although innovation activities performed in the home country have received more attention, others developed abroad – such as R&D offshoring, outsourcing or collaboration with foreign partners – are also carried out by these firms, as shown in recent works on R&D offshoring (e.g., Baier et al., 2015; Munjal et al., 2019; Rodríguez & Nieto, 2016) and on international R&D collaboration (e.g., Ebersberger & Herstad, 2013; Kapetaniou & Lee, 2019; Van Hemert et al., 2013). For this reason, this chapter provides an overview of six governance modes of R&D activities. Specifically, a distinction is made between R&D activities performed: (i) internally; (ii) in collaboration with partners; or (iii) via contractual agreements (outsourcing), while also identifying if they are developed in the home country or abroad. To do this, a large sample of SMEs from the Spanish *Survey of Technological Innovation Panel* for the period 2008–2016 is used.

The chapter begins with a description of the governance modes of R&D activities and the relation between different R&D strategies and the competitiveness of SMEs. The next sections go on to show the distribution of governance modes depending on the size of the firm and to describe the analysis of the relation between these modes and the competitiveness of SMEs. The chapter closes with a discussion and conclusion section.

Theoretical Background

The decision to perform R&D innovation activities requires a consideration of how to organize them (internally, in collaboration with other firms, or via outsourcing arrangements – commonly referred to as 'make, buy or ally') and where to locate them (in the home country or a foreign country – commonly referred to as domestic or offshore). Figure 9.1 presents a framework detailing the key issues related to each R&D governance mode of innovation activities, along with the major characteristics of SMEs.

The smaller size of SMEs provides them with advantages linked to flexibility and faster response capacity. Their lighter organizational structures also favor the flow of information and promote more agile decision-making processes. In other ways, though, SMEs are at a disadvantage when compared with larger enterprises. SMEs suffer from the small scale and scope of their activities, along with their limited capacities and the difficulties they face to gain access to different types of resources (Cohen & Klepper, 1996; Hewitt-Dundas, 2006).

Despite the constraints of their resource endowments and organizational characteristics, SMEs develop a wide range of internal and external R&D activities (Hervás-Oliver et al., 2021). A priori, no governance mode is better than any other. The best strategy for each firm will depend on its capacity to implement it and overcome the difficulties inherent to its situation, while at the same time maximizing the chosen mode's advantages and minimizing its potential risks. It is crucial, then, to have a clear idea of the pros and cons of each governance mode to be able to weigh the expected benefits against the potential costs (Cuervo-Cazurra et al., 2018; Thakur-Wenz et al., 2020; also see Nieto & Rodríguez, 2022 for a review of international R&D options).

Domestic R&D Governance Modes in SMEs

Academic research into SMEs has typically analyzed innovation activities developed in the home country, with a focus on internal R&D, outsourcing, or collaboration with locally based partners.

Domestic Internal R&D

Onshore internal R&D offers the greatest control over knowledge, which has been shown to be an important factor for innovation (Cuervo-Cazurra et al., 2018). Implementing this option, however, can be particularly challenging for many SMEs due to the high minimum investment required and the elevated fixed costs (Rammer et al., 2009). These are especially difficult obstacles to overcome for small firms commonly facing severe financial constraints (Abraham & Schmukler, 2017; Czarnitzki, 2006).

Small and medium-sized enterprises (SMEs)
✔ Greater flexibility
✔ Lighter organizational structures
✔ Better information flows

- Resource constraints
- Limited capabilities
- Small scale and scope of activities

	Make	**Buy**	**Ally**
Home country	*Internal R&D* • High fixed costs • Minimum investment requirement ✔ Highest control of knowledge	*Outsourcing R&D* • Risk of over-dependence and 'hollowing out' • Risk of information leakage and opportunistic behavior ✔ Benefits via supplier's advantages ✔ Greater flexibility / capacity to adapt	*Domestic R&D collaboration* • Less heterogeneous knowledge • Knowledge-sharing vs. protection dilemma ✔ Easier to negotiate with home-country partners ✔ Easier to share knowledge
Foreign country	*Captive R&D offshoring* • High exposure risk • Capabilities required to set up centers abroad ✔ High control of knowledge ✔ Access to knowledge and personnel with better cost and quality conditions overseas ✔ Tacit knowledge easier to transfer internally	*Offshore R&D outsourcing* • Higher risks and difficulties to control supplier • Incomplete contracts—more difficult to specify contractual conditions • Greater risks in weaker intellectual property rights systems • Challenges to integrate more distant knowledge ✔ Upgraded resources and capabilities ✔ Highest diversity of knowledge	*International R&D collaboration* • Difficulties to share more heterogeneous knowledge—the role of distances between partners • Greater managerial challenges ✔ Access to new knowledge from partners in different innovation system (host country) ✔ Ameliorate the relative resource limitations of SMEs

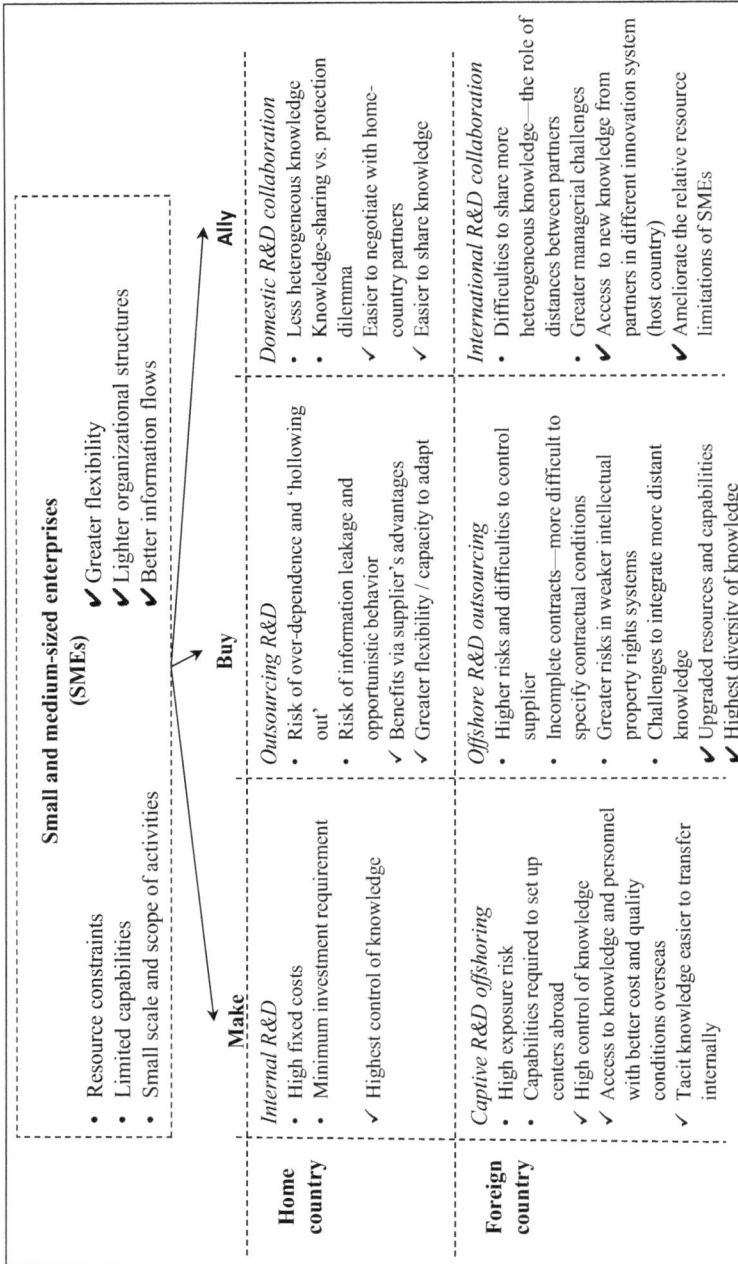

Figure 9.1: Governance modes of innovation activities in SMEs.
Source: author's literature review.

Domestic Outsourcing R&D

In contrast, outsourcing R&D does not require a high resource commitment. And since firms that opt for this approach are able to select the suppliers that offer the best competitive advantages for each case and time, in principle this is an option that SMEs should find easy to implement. This strategy allows firms to concentrate on their core activities and free up resources. Firms also gain flexibility by exploiting the competitive advantages of the supplier to increase their capacity to adapt to market demands. Although outsourcing R&D permits firms to specialize on their core activities, overusing this strategy can reduce their internal capabilities. As Grimpe and Kaiser (2010) argue, "over-outsourcing" poses a serious threat to the innovation performance of firms. The damage firms can suffer as a result of such over-dependence and "hollowing out" can affect their capacity to assimilate and integrate external knowledge (Weigelt, 2009). In line with this, Un and Rodríguez (2018) find that R&D outsourcing has an inverse "U"-shaped relation with product innovation; this research shows that the initial benefits of using outsourced R&D are eventually outweighed by the hollowing out of the firm's ability to innovate. The literature reveals how important it is for firms to be aware of the negative effects of "over-outsourcing" so that they can take the appropriate steps to minimize the risk.

Domestic R&D Collaboration

For its part, technological collaboration with local partners has attracted much attention from scholars, who view it as an attractive way for SMEs to reduce the gap that exists with larger firms and boost their innovation results (Nieto & Santamaría, 2010). Numerous studies find that collaborations and networks are highly relevant for innovation in SMEs (Hervás-Oliver et al., 2021; Lasagni, 2012; Nieto & Santamaría, 2010, among many others), particularly as these firms find it easier to work with local partners with whom they share similar – and therefore easier to integrate – knowledge (Patel et al., 2014). These collaborations enable firms to take advantage of the proximity of the relationship to innovate (Balland et al., 2013: Boschma, 2005; Boschma & Frenken, 2010).

International R&D Governance Modes in SMEs

R&D governance modes developed overseas, such as captive R&D offshoring, offshore R&D outsourcing, and international R&D collaboration have received less attention from scholars. And yet, recent research indicates that these strategies can help SMEs overcome or compensate for their resource constraints by opening the door to knowledge inputs and skilled personnel in better conditions (Baier et al., 2013; Munjal et al.,

2019; Rodríguez & Nieto, 2016). In the last 20 to 30 years, the internationalization of R&D activities has been extensively studied in multinational enterprises (MNEs), but research into this phenomenon in SMEs has been largely neglected. The few existing studies on international R&D activities in SMEs point to the relevance of these strategies for the competitiveness of these firms (Baier et al., 2015; Ebersberger & Herstad, 2013; Khraishi et al., 2020; Munjal et al., 2019; Rodríguez & Nieto, 2016; Van Hemert et al., 2013).

Captive R&D Offshoring

Traditionally, captive offshoring operations were associated with large MNEs (Metters, 2008), who were thought to be the only ones with the resources and experience necessary to establish their own centers successfully in foreign countries. By doing this, firms can internalize the benefits provided by superior resources located abroad while minimizing the risks inherent to cross-border externalization (Kedia & Mukherjee, 2009). On the other side of the coin, offshore outsourcing was viewed as an option for SMEs without the resources and capacity to set up captive operations overseas. Offshore outsourcing of activities is commonly believed to be the most accessible governance mode for smaller firms with limited resource endowments. However, studies such as Baier et al. (2015) and Rodríguez and Nieto (2016) show that SMEs set up offshore captive R&D centers and obtain benefits from them both in terms of innovation and in sales.

Offshore R&D Outsourcing

Offshore R&D outsourcing is characterized by a mixture of benefits and risks associated with outsourcing and offshoring (Thakur-Wernz et al., 2020; Rilla and Squicciarini, 2011). Among the advantages linked with offshore R&D outsourcing, those related to upgrading firms' resource and capability bases are most notable. These include access to more heterogeneous and specialized knowledge and state-of-the-art technologies; other benefits connected to costs, efficiency gains, flexibility, speed to market (timing issues), and even access to new markets provide other examples.

Beyond this, a comparative analysis of the different R&D governance modes reveals that offshore R&D outsourcing offers firms more diverse knowledge, but also the lowest level of control over knowledge (Cuervo-Cazurra et al., 2018). Loss of control and the difficulties to specify contracts (with the resulting existence of numerous incomplete contracts), therefore, are drawbacks that are traditionally linked with offshoring, but which become even more important when dealing with high value-added activities such as R&D. On top of these negatives, firms face the added difficulties of determining if foreign suppliers are complying with their contractual obligations (Ellram et al., 2008). Other risks inherent to offshore R&D outsourcing are related to knowledge sharing with foreign suppliers such as information leakage and opportunistic behavior (Pisano, 1990; Pisano et al., 1988). A further challenge presented by offshore R&D outsourcing revolves around the difficulty of integrating more distant knowledge (Un & Rodríguez, 2018).

International R&D Collaboration

Lastly, international technological collaborations are thought to deliver multiple advantages for SMEs, especially in terms of mitigating their relatively limited resource endowments. Previous studies of international collaborations in SMEs conclude that they increase the innovative capacity of small firms (Ebersberger & Herstad, 2013; Kapetaniou & Lee, 2019; Van Hemert et al., 2013). Although the acquisition of highly diverse and dissimilar knowledge brings benefits, it also increases the complexities and costs of managing the collaborative relationship (Jiang et al., 2010). Many of the major managerial challenges to share and integrate knowledge are similar to those described for offshore R&D outsourcing. Apart from these problems, significant difficulties related to the distance between partners in international collaborations requires careful management for this governance mode to be successful. In comparison to domestic collaboration, international R&D collaboration presents greater managerial challenges because of differences in languages, organizational cultures, and institutional environments. As overcoming these obstacles requires a significant investment of resources to guarantee good communication and control (Narula & Martínez-Noya, 2015), this may cause particular difficulties for many SMEs.

Methodology

Data Collection

To analyze the governance of R&D activities in SMEs, this research uses the *Survey of Technological Innovation Panel*, conducted by the Spanish National Institute of Statistics with the sponsorship of the Spanish Foundation for Science and Technology (FECYT) and the Foundation for Technological Innovation (COTEC). The Technological Innovation Panel (PITEC) offers information on more than 12,000 manufacturing and service firms for various years. The database has been used in previous research on different R&D sourcing strategies (Nieto & Rodríguez, 2011; Rodríguez & Nieto, 2012; Santamaría et al., 2021, among others). Specifically, this study uses a sample of manufacturing and service SMEs for the period 2008–2016 (resulting in more than 64,000 observations). This is an unbalanced panel, thus it includes firms that may not have responded to some of the survey questions in one or more of the years, which causes the number of observations per time period to vary.

Measurement of the Variables

The variables used for the econometric analysis are described below.

Dependent Variable

SME competitiveness is a dichotomous variable that captures the competitiveness of SMEs in terms of the innovation results of the firm. The variable takes the value 1 if the firm has developed a product and/or process innovation; otherwise, it takes the value 0. A product innovation is considered to have been achieved when the firm introduces a product or service into the market that is new or that offers a significant upgrade to its basic features, technical specifications, or other intangible components. For its part, a process innovation is obtained when the firm implements a new or significantly improved production process, distribution method, or support activity for its goods or services.

Independent Variables

(i) Captive R&D Offshoring is a dichotomous variable that takes the value 1 when the firm performs R&D activities in a subsidiary located in a foreign country; otherwise, it takes the value 0.

(ii) International R&D collaboration is a dichotomous variable that takes the value 1 when the firm collaborates on innovation activities with partners based in a foreign country; otherwise, it takes the value 0.

(iii) Offshore R&D outsourcing is a dichotomous variable that takes the value 1 when the firm acquires R&D from other companies, public administrations, universities, or other organizations in a foreign country; otherwise, it takes the value 0.

(iv) Domestic internal R&D is a dichotomous variable that captures if the firm develops R&D activities in its home country. It takes the value 1 when the firm incurs internal R&D expenses; otherwise, it takes the value 0.

(v) Domestic R&D collaboration is a dichotomous variable that takes the value 1 when the firm collaborates on innovation activities with partners based in the home country; otherwise, it takes the value 0.

(vi) Domestic R&D outsourcing is a dichotomous variable that takes the value 1 when the firm acquires external R&D services via contracts or agreements with third parties in the home country.

Control Variables

The analyses include controls for the decision to innovate, firm-specific characteristics, and sector dummies. Specifically, the following control variables are included: (a) firm size is a continuous variable that is constructed with the logarithm of the number of employees; it is used as a proxy for the size of the firm; (b) firm age is a continuous variable that captures the number of years since the firm was founded; it is included as the logarithm of the number of years the firm has been operating; (c) group is a dichotomous variable that indicates if the firm is part of a group of firms; (d) innovation effort measures the innovation effort of firms; it is calculated by dividing the firm's total innovation investments by its total sales; (e) private multinational is a dichotomous variable that indicates if at least 50 percent of the firm's capital is in foreign hands. Lastly, the analyses include dichotomous variables that control for sector in all the models.

Data Analysis

Given the binary nature of the dependent variable, a probit model is specified to analyze the relations of the different R&D governance modes with the innovation results of SMEs. The study uses random effects panel data models. Following previous studies such as by Cuervo-Cazurra et al. (2018) and Nieto and Rodríguez (2011), which examine alternative R&D sources, Wald tests are performed to compare the coefficients of the independent variables in order to evaluate how the different R&D governance modes relate with the probability of innovation in the SMEs.

Results

Preliminary Analyses

An Overview of R&D Governance Modes in SMEs and Innovation Results

Table 9.1 gives an overview of the innovation results of SMEs; it displays the percentages of SMEs that achieve innovations in the sub-samples of firms that perform each of the R&D governance modes and in the sub-sample of firms that does not perform the corresponding governance mode analyzed, along with a comparison of the percentages of the two sub-samples using a t-test of the mean differences for each alternative.

An initial examination of the results indicates that the average percentage of SMEs that innovate is higher in all the sub-samples that perform R&D activities than

Table 9.1: Governance of R&D activities in SMEs and innovation.

Percentages of innovation within SMEs performing the governance mode	Percentages of innovation within SMEs non-performing the governance mode	
Captive R&D Offshoring	No Captive R&D offshoring	Difference[a]
91.2	59.2	31.9***
International collaboration	No International collaboration	Difference[a]
92.4	56.3	36.1***
Offshore R&D outsourcing	No Offshore R&D outsourcing	Difference[a]
87.8	58.6	29.2***
Internal R&D	No Internal R&D	Difference[a]
85.6	37.7	47.9***
Domestic R&D collaboration	No Domestic R&D collaboration	Difference[a]
88.8	49.9	38.9***
Domestic Outsourcing R&D	No Domestic Outsourcing R&D	Difference[a]
86.3	53.8	32.5***

Percentage of observations of firms innovating is 59.4.
[a]One-tailed T-tests on the difference between means (p-values from Student's distribution)
***Denote samples that are significantly different at the 0.001 level

in their respective counterpart sub-samples that do not. The t-test for each of the R&D governance modes analyzed reveals that the difference in the average values of this variable for the respective sub-samples is significant. These results provide support for the idea that SMEs that develop R&D activities are more likely to achieve innovation results (regardless of the governance mode employed).

The next section presents the results of the econometric analyses performed to delve into the relation between the governance modes implemented and the innovation results.

R&D Governance Modes Depending on SME Size: Micro, Small, and Medium

Identifying micro-businesses as a sub-set of SMEs is a valuable exercise because of their owner-manager-entrepreneur centric nature and the constraints they face resulting from underdeveloped capabilities in key business areas. These characteristics set them apart from larger SMEs (Gherhes et al., 2016) and suggest that their innovative behavior may be different. For this reason, Table 9.2 presents the percentages of observations in the sample according to firm size. According to the European Union Recommendation 2003/361/CE, SMEs are defined as firms with fewer than 250 employees; within this group, three sub-categories are identified: micro (with fewer than ten employees); small (with between ten and 49 employees); and medium (with between 50 and 249).

A clear majority of SMEs in the sample – 62 percent – belongs to the small category, followed by medium with 21 percent, and micro with 17 percent.

Table 9.2: Distribution of SMEs in the sample according to their size and R&D governance modes.

	Full sample[a]	Innovation	Home country			Foreign country		
			Domestic Internal R&D	Domestic R&D Collaboration	Domestic R&D Outsourcing	Captive R&D offshoring	International R&D collaboration	Offshore R&D outsourcing
Micro	16.9	36.98	27.2	16.7	8.78	0.04	3.42	1.00
Small	62.1	64.07	48.7	24.7	18.27	0.43	8.34	2.80
Medium	21.0	63.84	49.87	29.14	20.77	1.76	14.18	3.84
SME	100	59.44	45.32	24.30	17.19	0.65	8.74	2.71

Values indicate percentage of observations. (a) Number of observations: 64,425

In Table 9.2, column 1 displays the breakdown of the sample by size (micro, small, medium, along with the totals for all SMEs); column 2 shows the percentages of innovations achieved; and columns 3 to 6 contain the percentages for each of the R&D governance modes adopted.

In terms of innovation results, micro has the lowest percentage of innovations (almost 37 percent of micro-businesses innovate), while the percentages for small and medium both hover around 64 percent.

In terms of the R&D governance mode implemented, the behavior of micro differs from that of small and medium in the home country (internal R&D; collaboration; and outsourcing), while the percentages for the three SME types in foreign countries all vary considerably. It should be noted that internal R&D is the most common governance mode chosen in the home country, followed by collaboration, and with outsourcing proving least popular. In foreign countries, however, external sources gain prominence, with international collaboration modes garnering the highest percentage, followed by offshore R&D outsourcing, and with captive R&D offshoring proving least popular.

Probit Model Results

Table 9.3 displays the results of the analysis of the relation between R&D governance modes and innovation in SMEs (model 1) – in accordance with the European definition (e.g., Rodríguez & Nieto, 2016). In addition, the results for the sub-samples corresponding to micro (model 3), small (model 4), and medium (model 5) are included.

Table 9.3: Results of R&D governance mode and SME innovativeness for all SMEs and the micro, small, and medium sub-samples.

	SME	Micro	Small	Medium
	Model 1	Model 2	Model 3	Model 4
Captive R&D offshoring	0.563***	−0.551	0.280	0.855***
	(0.177)	(1.096)	(0.263)	(0.270)
International collaboration	0.448***	0.508***	0.428***	0.477***
	(0.0511)	(0.145)	(0.0667)	(0.106)
Offshore R&D outsourcing	0.176**	0.0716	0.0898	0.518**
	(0.0810)	(0.246)	(0.0994)	(0.203)
Domestic internal R&D	0.969***	0.715***	0.962***	1.240***
	(0.0262)	(0.0703)	(0.0326)	(0.0648)

Table 9.3 (continued)

	SME	Micro	Small	Medium
	Model 1	Model 2	Model 3	Model 4
Domestic R&D collaboration	1.013***	1.144***	0.958***	1.164***
	(0.0295)	(0.0729)	(0.0375)	(0.0729)
Domestic R&D outsourcing	0.0784**	−0.256***	0.0795**	0.173**
	(0.0324)	(0.0940)	(0.0398)	(0.0790)
Firm size	0.376***	0.419***	0.376***	0.112
	(0.0133)	(0.0422)	(0.0283)	(0.104)
Firm age	−0.515***	−0.834***	−0.523***	−0.132**
	(0.0295)	(0.0729)	(0.0386)	(0.0584)
Group	−0.0791***	0.123	−0.152***	0.0861
	(0.0304)	(0.0820)	(0.0389)	(0.0671)
Innovation effort	0.916***	0.723***	1.332***	2.614***
	(0.111)	(0.178)	(0.170)	(0.548)
Multinational private	0.0184	0.0590	−0.00869	0.114
	(0.0448)	(0.148)	(0.0614)	(0.0768)
Intercept	−0.330**	0.248	−0.0509	−1.150*
	(0.140)	(0.298)	(0.191)	(0.629)
Number of observations	54379	9139	33577	11663
Wald test (χ^2)	6499.8***	988.7***	3488.2***	1445.0***
Log. Likelihood	−24002.3	−4199.7	−15135.2	−4407.3

Standard errors in parentheses. Sector dummies are included in all models.
$^*p < 0.10$, $^{**}p < 0.05$, $^{***}p < 0.01$

In the analyses performed on model 1, the coefficients for the different governance modes (Captive R&D Offshoring; International R&D collaboration; Offshore R&D outsourcing; Domestic internal R&D; Domestic R&D collaboration; and Domestic R&D outsourcing) are all positive and significant. Concerning the micro and small sub-samples, the coefficients of International R&D collaboration, Domestic internal R&D; Domestic R&D collaboration are all positive and significant, but both coefficients of Captive R&D offshoring and Offshore R&D outsourcing are non-significant. In the case of Domestic R&D outsourcing, the coefficient for the micro sub-sample is negative and significant, while the coefficient for the small sub-sample is positive and significant. In contrast, in the medium sub-sample all the coefficients for the independent variables are positive and significant.

Regarding the rest of the variables, the coefficient for firm size is positive and significant in all the models except model 4 (medium sub-sample), in which the coefficient is non-significant. These results indicate that among SMEs larger size is positively related to innovation performance, though this relation is not significant in the medium category. In contrast, the coefficients for the variables of firm age and group are negative and significant. This result shows that younger firms are more likely to achieve innovations – or alternatively, that organizational inertia may act as a barrier to innovation in consolidated firms. And the coefficient for group reveals that SME membership of a business group is not related to enhanced innovation capacity. The coefficients for group in models 2 and 4 (micro and medium, respectively) are not significant. Lastly, in all the models the coefficient for innovation effort is positive and significant, indicating that greater investment in innovation activities is positively related with innovation results and therefore also greater firm competitiveness.

Table 9.4 shows the results of the Wald tests performed on the differences between the coefficients of the R&D governance modes. Determining if the coefficients are statistically different makes it possible to rank the innovation activities. These Wald tests reveal that significant differences exist between the coefficients. The tests comparing alternative R&D governance modes are significant for SME competitiveness (in model 1), with three exceptions: (i) Captive R&D offshoring and International R&D collaboration; (ii) Domestic internal R&D and Domestic R&D collaboration; and (iii) Offshore R&D outsourcing and Domestic R&D outsourcing. The likelihood of the R&D governance modes to achieve innovations can be ranked from higher to lower by examining the size of the coefficients estimated for each option and the results of the Wald tests. As Domestic internal R&D and Domestic R&D collaboration yield the highest coefficients, these two modes are related with greater degrees of SME competitiveness, followed by Captive R&D offshoring and International R&D collaboration, and then outsourcing formats – both Offshore R&D outsourcing and Domestic R&D outsourcing.

Table 9.4: Wald test results for SMEs.

Comparison tests	SME (Model 1)
β Domestic R&D collaboration > β Domestic internal R&D:	$\chi^2 = 1.10$
β Domestic internal R&D > β Captive R&D offshoring:	$\chi^2 = 5.17^{**}$
β Captive R&D offshoring > β International R&D collaboration:	$\chi^2 = 0.39$
β International R&D collaboration > β Offshore R&D outsourcing:	$\chi^2 = 7.48^{***}$
β Offshore R&D outsourcing > β Domestic R&D outsourcing:	$\chi^2 = 1.14$
β Domestic R&D collaboration > β Captive R&D offshoring:	$\chi^2 = 6.33^{**}$
β Domestic R&D collaboration > β International R&D collaboration:	$\chi^2 = 75.70^{***}$
β Domestic R&D collaboration > β Domestic R&D outsourcing:	$\chi^2 = 404.43^{***}$

Table 9.4 (continued)

Comparison tests	SME (Model 1)
β Domestic internal R&D > β Offshore R&D outsourcing:	$\chi^2 = 86.47^{***}$
β Domestic internal R&D > β International R&D collaboration:	$\chi^2 = 80.09^{***}$
β Domestic internal R&D > β Domestic R&D outsourcing:	$\chi^2 = 383.85^{***}$
β Captive R&D offshoring > β Offshore R&D outsourcing:	$\chi^2 = 3.88^{**}$
β International R&D collaboration > β Domestic R&D outsourcing:	$\chi^2 = 37.42^{***}$

Significance levels: ***$p<0.01$, **$p<0.05$, *$p<0.10$.

Tables 9.5–9.7 display the results of the Wald tests performed on the differences between the coefficients of the R&D governance modes for the micro, small, and medium categories, respectively. The R&D governance modes are ranked in terms of their likelihood to achieve innovations by examining the size of the coefficients estimated for each option – from higher to lower – along with the results of the Wald tests.

Table 9.5: Wald test results for micro sub-sample.

Comparison tests (a)	Micro (Model 2)
β Domestic R&D collaboration > β Domestic internal R&D:	$\chi^2 = 15.97^{***}$
β Domestic internal R&D > β International R&D collaboration:	$\chi^2 = 62.66^{***}$
β International R&D collaboration > β Domestic R&D outsourcing:	$\chi^2 = 19.99^{***}$
β Domestic R&D collaboration > β Domestic R&D outsourcing:	$\chi^2 = 12.17^{***}$
β Domestic R&D collaboration > β International R&D collaboration:	$\chi^2 = 13.22^{***}$

Significance levels: ***$p<0.01$, **$p<0.05$, *$p<0.10$.

Table 9.6: Wald test results for small sub-sample.

Comparison tests	Small (Model 3)
β Domestic internal R&D > β Domestic R&D collaboration:	$\chi^2 = 0.01$
β Domestic R&D collaboration > β International R&D collaboration:	$\chi^2 = 40.00^{***}$
β International R&D collaboration > β Domestic R&D outsourcing:	$\chi^2 = 20.09^{***}$
β Domestic internal R&D > β Domestic R&D outsourcing:	$\chi^2 = 245.40^{***}$
β Domestic internal R&D > β International R&D collaboration:	$\chi^2 = 50.07^{***}$
β Domestic R&D collaboration > β Domestic R&D outsourcing:	$\chi^2 = 228.63^{***}$

Significance levels: ***$p<0.01$, **$p<0.05$, *$p<0.10$.

Table 9.7: Wald test results for medium sub-sample.

Comparison tests	Medium (Model 4)
β Domestic internal R&D > β Domestic R&D collaboration:	$\chi^2 = 0.55$
β Domestic R&D collaboration > β Captive R&D offshoring:	$\chi^2 = 1.25$
β Captive R&D offshoring > β Offshore R&D outsourcing:	$\chi^2 = 1.00$
β Offshore R&D outsourcing > β International R&D collaboration:	$\chi^2 = 0.03$
β International R&D collaboration > β Domestic R&D outsourcing:	$\chi^2 = 5.37^{**}$
β International R&D collaboration < β Domestic R&D collaboration:	$\chi^2 = 22.37^{***}$
β Domestic R&D collaboration > β Domestic R&D outsourcing:	$\chi^2 = 77.57^{***}$
β Domestic internal R&D > β Offshore R&D outsourcing:	$\chi^2 = 11.27^{***}$
β Domestic internal R&D > β International R&D collaboration:	$\chi^2 = 36.61^{***}$
β Domestic internal R&D > β Domestic R&D outsourcing:	$\chi^2 = 89.02^{***}$
β Domestic internal R&D > β Captive R&D offshoring:	$\chi^2 = 1.96$

Significance levels: ***p<0.01, **p<0.05, *p<0.10.

Figure 9.2 contains a summary of the ranking of R&D governance modes and the innovation results of SMEs for the micro, small, and medium categories.

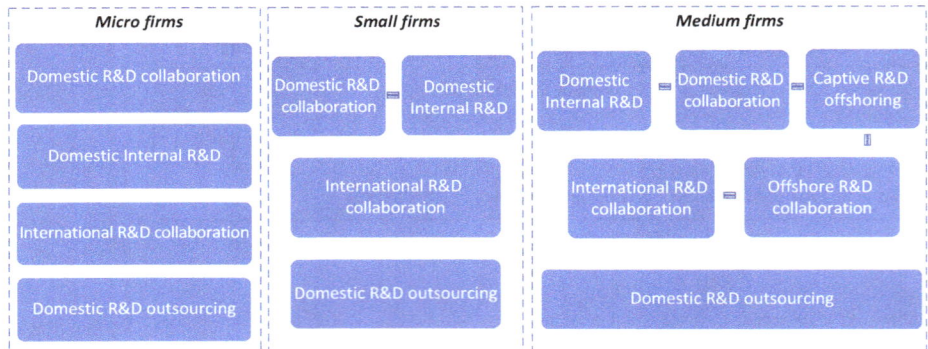

Figure 9.2: Ranking of R&D governance modes on innovation results for the micro, small, and medium categories.
Source: author's own framework based on the findings of this chapter. The governance modes are presented in accordance with their impact on innovation results – ordered from higher to lower impact when the difference is significant. When no significant difference exists between one or other governance mode, they appear at the same level with an equal sign between them (denoting the lack of significance in the Wald test). See Tables 9.5–9.7 for the results of the Wald tests.

Discussion and Conclusions

This chapter sets out to offer a comprehensive overview of different R&D governance modes – with particular attention paid to international R&D strategies – and to explore their relations with the competitiveness of SMEs in terms of innovation results. Offshore R&D activities present firms with an opportunity to acquire resources in different locations with conditions that are often better than those available in local markets. Such international strategies were considered to be limited to multinational and larger enterprises some 20 to 30 years ago, but today they are accessible and visible in firms of all types and sizes. Indeed, ever more SMEs have been turning to international markets all over the world in search of inputs. For this reason, it is now common to find firms that take advantage of location benefits by moving value-chain activities overseas – something that would have been unimaginable some years ago. The study of these cross-border R&D activities in SMEs is still in its infancy. As this chapter shows, however, SMEs use all three international governance modes analyzed: captive R&D offshoring; offshore R&D outsourcing; and international R&D collaboration.

The analysis in this chapter is based on a large sample of firms from the *Survey of Technological Innovation Panel* (PITEC) for the period 2008–2016. The findings obtained offer interesting insights on the relations of the different governance modes with the innovation results of SMEs. The empirical analyses show that all the governance modes are positively related with innovation achievements. Breaking the complete SME sample down by size into micro, small, and medium sub-samples, however, uncovers different patterns of behavior. An examination of these sub-samples reveals that captive modes and offshore outsourcing are not related with innovation achievements in the micro and small categories. In contrast, domestic and international collaboration, along with internal R&D in the home country, all boost innovation performance in the micro and small categories. The smaller size of these firms may hamper their ability to take advantage of international R&D strategies whose implementation requires larger capacities, though it may not prevent them from benefiting from cross-border knowledge obtained via collaborations with foreign partners. The differences between firms in these two categories regarding domestic outsourcing should be noted, however. Specifically, domestic outsourcing is negatively related with innovation performance in the micro sub-sample, but positively related in the small sub-sample. The small size of micro firms may exacerbate the risks of "hollowing out" that are inherent to R&D outsourcing strategies, to the point of negatively affecting the levels of innovation of these firms. For their part, the results for firms in the medium sub-sample indicate a positive relation between all governance modes and innovation results, in line with those for the complete sample of SMEs.

A ranking of the impact of the different governance options on innovation results reveals that substantial differences exist between them. For SMEs in general, three levels can be identified: (i) internal R&D and collaboration in the home country are the options that show the greatest levels of innovation – with no difference between them; (ii) setting up captive R&D centers abroad or collaborating with foreign partners; (iii) offshore R&D outsourcing modes and R&D outsourcing to suppliers in the home country, which are thus the governance modes related with the lowest levels of innovation. In sum, although all the R&D governance modes analyzed are related with the achievement of innovations, major differences exist among the six options.

Ranking the governance modes by the micro, small, and medium categories reveals that: (i) for micro, the strategy with the strongest relation to innovation achievement is collaborating with domestic partners, followed by internal R&D, and lastly by collaboration with foreign partners; (ii) for small, three levels can be observed, with domestic collaboration and internal R&D proving equally effective on the top level, with international collaboration on the second level, and domestic outsourcing on the third; (iii) for medium, no clear ranking emerges for the different options, though internal R&D and captive R&D offshoring appear to offer the most potential, closely followed by offshore outsourcing and international collaboration.

Theoretical Implications

This chapter contributes to the literature on R&D activities by extending in two ways our knowledge of different R&D governance modes in SMEs. First, most studies compare internal and external R&D governance modes in firms in general – not specifically in SMEs (Cuervo-Cazurra, 2018; Nieto & Rodríguez, 2011, 2022; Thakur-Wenz et al., 2020). This chapter, however, provides a comprehensive overview of R&D governance modes in SMEs by identifying six governance modes resulting from combinations of make, buy, and ally decisions, along with the dimension of location (in the home country or abroad). Second, these governance modes are also analyzed for three sub-categories of SMEs: micro, small, and medium. Previous studies of R&D governance modes in SMEs (Munjal et al., 2019; Rodríguez & Nieto, 2016) do not distinguish between these sub-categories. Thus, the more focused analysis described in this chapter generates interesting and highly novel insights in this research stream.

Managerial Implications

Managers of SMEs need to be cognizant of – and take advantage of – how these governance modes can make their firms more competitive. Knowledge of the potential benefits and difficulties related to each mode can help them make the correct decisions to achieve better innovation results. Given the unique resource endowments of SMEs, it is particularly important that their owners and managers are made aware of the key role overseas innovation activities can play in compensating for and overcoming their firms' limitations. These business leaders must be clear on how they can optimize their innovation strategies by: (i) setting up captive centers in countries with better conditions, skilled personnel, and advanced knowledge; (ii) collaborating with firms based overseas; and lastly (iii) outsourcing to a supplier (foreign or domestic). As this chapter has shown, all the governance modes analyzed can be useful for achieving innovations, although clear differences between their potential contributions to innovativeness exist. In sum, managers must take all this into account and choose the best strategies to find the necessary resources to innovate and be competitive, while always remaining conscious of their firms' capacities (which will vary depending on firm size).

Limitations and Future Research

The different governance modes have been analyzed in relation to their potential contributions to the competitiveness of SMEs in terms of innovation results. Other measures of performance (e.g., productivity, sales growth, etc.) could be analyzed by future research into SMEs. As this chapter does not delve into differences that may exist depending on the activity sector of the firm and its technological intensity, this would be another interesting area to examine. Lastly, given the interesting and valuable results that emerge for the micro and small sub-samples – and the different results obtained for the medium sub-sample – innovation strategies and internationalization in different types of firms merit further attention in future studies.

References

Abraham, F., & Schmukler, S.L. (2017). Addressing the SME finance problem. *World Bank Research and Policy Briefs* (120333).

Acs, Z.J., & Audretsch, D.B. (1990). *Innovation and small firms*. MIT Press.

Baier, E., Rammer, C., & Schubert, T. (2015). The impact of captive innovation offshoring on the effectiveness of organizational adaptation. *Journal of International Management, 21*(2), 150–165.

Balland, P.A., Boschma, R., & Frenken, K. (2013). Proximity and innovation networks: An evolutionary approach. In *Re-framing regional development* (pp. 204–218). Routledge.

Bertrand, O., & Mol, M.J. (2013). The antecedents and innovation effects of domestic and offshore R&D outsourcing: The contingent impact of cognitive distance and absorptive capacity. *Strategic Management Journal, 34*(6), 751–760.

Boschma, R. (2005). Proximity and innovation: A critical assessment. *Regional Studies, 39*(1), 61–74.

Boschma, R., & Frenken, K. (2010). The spatial evolution of innovation networks: A proximity perspective. In *The handbook of evolutionary economic geography*. Edward Elgar Publishing.

Cohen, W.M., & Klepper, S. (1996). Firm size and the nature of innovation within industries: The case of process and product R&D. *The Review of Economics and Statistics, 78*(2), 232–243.

Cuervo-Cazurra, A., Nieto, M.J., & Rodríguez, A. (2018). The impact of R&D sources on new product development: Sources of funds and the diversity versus control of knowledge debate. *Long Range Planning, 51*(5), 649–665.

Czarnitzki, D. (2006). Research and development in small and medium-sized enterprises: The role of financial constraints and public funding. *Scottish Journal of Political Economy*, *53*(3), 335–357.

Di Gregorio, D., Musteen, M., & Thomas, D.E. (2009). Offshore outsourcing as a source of international competitiveness for SMEs. *Journal of International Business Studies*, *40*(6), 969–988.

Ebersberger, B., & Herstad, S.J. (2013). The relationship between international innovation collaboration, intramural R&D and SMEs' innovation performance: A quantile regression approach. *Applied Economics Letters*, *20*(7), 626–630.

Ellram, L.M., Tate, W.L., & Billington, C. (2008). Offshore outsourcing of professional services: A transaction cost economics perspective. *Journal of Operations Management*, *26*(2), 148–163.

European Commission. (2020). *Entrepreneurship and small and medium-sized enterprises (SMEs)*. https://ec. europa.eu/growth/smes_es

Furman, J.L., Porter, M.E., & Stern, S. (2002). The determinants of national innovative capacity. *Research Policy*, *31*(6), 899–933.

Gherhes, C., Williams, N., Vorley, T., & Vasconcelos, A.C. (2016). Distinguishing micro-businesses from SMEs: A systematic review of growth constraints. *Journal of Small Business and Enterprise Development*, *23*(4), 939–963. https://doi.org/10.1108/JSBED-05-2016-0075

Grimpe, C., & Kaiser, U. (2010). Balancing internal and external knowledge acquisition: The gains and pains from R&D outsourcing. *Journal of Management Studies*, *47*(8), 1483–1509.

Hayek, F.A. (1945). The use of knowledge in society. *The American Economic Review*, *35*(4), 519–530.

Hervás-Oliver, J.L., Parrilli, M.D., Rodríguez-Pose, A., & Sempere-Ripoll, F. (2021). The drivers of SME innovation in the regions of the EU. *Research Policy*, *50*(9), 104316.

Hewitt-Dundas, N. (2006). Resource and capability constraints to innovation in small and large plants. *Small Business Economics*, *26*(3), 257–277.

Hossain, M., & Kauranen, I. (2016). Open innovation in SMEs: A systematic literature review. *Journal of Strategy and Management*, *9*(1), 58–73. doi.org/10.1108/JSMA-08-2014-0072

Jiang, R.J., Tao, Q.T., & Santoro, M.D. (2010). Alliance portfolio diversity and firm performance. *Strategic Management Journal*, *31*(10), 1136–1144.

Kapetaniou, C., & Lee, S.H. (2019). Geographical proximity and open innovation of SMEs in Cyprus. *Small Business Economics*, *52*(1), 261–276.

Kedia, B.L., & Mukherjee, D. (2009). Understanding offshoring: A research framework based on disintegration, location and externalization advantages. *Journal of World Business*, *44*(3), 250–261.

Kedia, B.L., & Lahiri, S. (2007). International outsourcing of services: A partnership model. *Journal of International Management*, *13*(1), 22–37.

Kogut, B. (1991). Country capabilities and the permeability of borders. *Strategic Management Journal*, *12*(S1), 33–47.

Khraishi, A., Huq, F., & Paulraj, A. (2020). Offshoring innovation: An empirical investigation of dyadic complementarity within SMEs. *Journal of Business Research*, *118*, 86–97.

Lasagni, A. (2012). How can external relationships enhance innovation in SMEs? New evidence for Europe. *Journal of Small Business Management*, *50*(2), 310–339.

Metters, R. (2008). A typology of offshoring and outsourcing in electronically transmitted services. *Journal of Operations Management*, *26*(2), 198–211.

Muhammad, H., Migliori, S., & Consorti, A. (2022). Corporate governance and R&D investment: Does firm size matter? *Technology Analysis & Strategic Management*, 1–15.

Munjal, S., Requejo, I., & Kundu, S.K. (2019). Offshore outsourcing and firm performance: Moderating effects of size, growth and slack resources. *Journal of Business Research*, *103*, 484–494.

Narula, R., & Martínez-Noya, A. (2015). International R&D alliances by firms: Origins and development. In *The handbook of global science, technology, and innovation*, 144–170.

Nieto, M.J., & Rodríguez, A. (2011). Offshoring of R&D: Looking abroad to improve innovation performance. *Journal of International Business Studies*, *42*(3), 345–361.

Nieto, M.J., & Rodríguez, A. (2022). Cross-border R&D sourcing strategies: Different governance modes and 'new' players. In D. Castellani, A. Perri, V. Scalera, and A. Zanfei (Eds.), *Cross-border innovation in a changing world. Players, places and policies* (pp. 215–239). Oxford University Press.

Nieto, M.J., & Santamaría, L. (2010). Technological collaboration: Bridging the innovation gap between small and large firms. *Journal of Small Business Management, 48*(1), 44–69.

Patel, P.C., Fernhaber, S.A., McDougall-Covin, P.P., & van der Have, R.P. (2014). Beating competitors to international markets: The value of geographically balanced networks for innovation. *Strategic Management Journal, 35*(5), 691–711.

Pisano, G.P. (1990). The R&D boundaries of the firm: An empirical analysis. *Administrative Science Quarterly*, 153–176.

Pisano, G. P., Russo, M. V., & Teece, D. J. (1988). Joint ventures and collaborative arrangements in the telecommunications equipment industry. In D. C. Mowery (ed.), International Collaborative Ventures in U.S. Manufacturing. Cambridge, MA: Ballinger, 23–70.

Rammer, C., Czarnitzki, D., & Spielkamp, A. (2009). Innovation success of non-R&D-performers: Substituting technology by management in SMEs. *Small Business Economics, 33*, 35–58.doi.org/ 10.1007/s11187-009-9185-7

Rammer, C., & Schmiele, A. (2008). Globalisation of Innovation in SMEs: Why they go abroad and what they bring back home. *Applied Economics Quarterly, 59*(Supplement), 173–212.

Raymond, L., & St-Pierre, J. (2010). R&D as a determinant of innovation in manufacturing SMEs: An attempt at empirical clarification. *Technovation, 30*(1), 48–56.

Rilla, N., & Squicciarini, M. (2011). R&D (re) location and offshore outsourcing: A management perspective. *International Journal of Management Reviews, 13*(4), 393–413.

Rodríguez, A., & Nieto, M.J. (2012). The internationalization of knowledge-intensive business services: The effect of collaboration and the mediating role of innovation. *The Service Industries Journal, 32*(7), 1057–1075.

Rodríguez, A., & Nieto, M.J. (2016). Does R&D offshoring lead to SME growth? Different governance modes and the mediating role of innovation. *Strategic Management Journal, 37*(8), 1734–1753.

Rodríguez, A., Nieto, M.J., & Santamaría, L. (2018). International collaboration and innovation in professional and technological knowledge-intensive services. *Industry and Innovation, 25*(4), 408–431.

Santamaría, L., Nieto, M.J., & Rodríguez, A. (2021). Failed and successful innovations: The role of geographic proximity and international diversity of partners in technological collaboration. *Technological Forecasting and Social Change, 166*, 120575.

Saunila, M. (2020). Innovation capability in SMEs: A systematic review of the literature. *Journal of Innovation & Knowledge, 5*(4), 260–265.

Tate, W.L., & Ellram, L.M. (2009). Offshore outsourcing: A managerial framework. *Journal of Business & Industrial Marketing, 24* (3/4), 256–268. doi.org/10.1108/08858620910939804

Thakur-Wernz, P., Bruyaka, O., & Contractor, F. (2020). Antecedents and relative performance of sourcing choices for new product development projects. *Technovation, 90*, 102097.

Torchia, M., & Calabrò, A. (2019). Open innovation in SMEs: A systematic literature review. *Journal of Enterprising Culture, 27*(2), 201–228.

Un, C.A., & Rodríguez, A. (2018). Learning from R&D outsourcing vs. learning by R&D outsourcing. *Technovation, 72*, 24–33.

Van Hemert, P., Nijkamp, P., & Masurel, E. (2013). From innovation to commercialization through networks and agglomerations: Analysis of sources of innovation, innovation capabilities and performance of Dutch SMEs. *The Annals of Regional Science, 50*(2): 425–452.

Weigelt, C. (2009). The impact of outsourcing new technologies on integrative capabilities and performance. *Strategic Management Journal, 30*(6), 595–616.

Zahoor, N., & Al-Tabbaa, O. (2020). Inter-organizational collaboration and SMEs' innovation: A systematic review and future research directions. *Scandinavian Journal of Management, 36*(2), 101109.

Katrin Kizilkan and Maximilian Wagenknecht

10 Lean Social Media Communication Strategies for SMEs

Exploring the Field of Risk-Adjusted Lean Social Media Communication Strategies in the Context of the Lean Startup Method for SMEs

Abstract: In the chapter titled "Lean Social Media Communication Strategies for SMEs – Exploring the Field of Risk-Adjusted Lean Social Media Communication Strategies in the Context of the Lean Startup Method for SMEs," Katrin Kizilkan and Maximilian Wagenknecht present how the Lean Startup Method can improve digital communication through active control of lean and targeted communication. This chapter provides a first attempt where parts of the Lean Startup Method are combined with social media communication to create a risk-adjusted lean communication strategy. The theoretical content of the chapter is developed by a systematic literature review and an inductive content analysis to connect these theoretical concepts. The results indicate that social media must be understood as an opportunity to actively interact with the core customers and as a tool that must be continuously evaluated and readjusted. Additionally, the benefits of a lean strategy can lead to cost reductions in market research and the preservation and control of the customer base. The most important findings are compiled in a risk-adjusted Lean Social Media Strategy framework for practitioners and future research.

Keywords: Customer Development Method, Lean Startup Method, Lean Communication, Persevere or Pivot, Social Media, Communication Theories, Small and Medium Enterprises, Risk Management

Introduction

It is essential for companies to show presence on social media and constantly interact with core customers (Ashley & Tuten, 2015; Ling et al., 2006). Targeted social media campaigns help connect with customers in a targeted manner and actively involve them in core processes. In this chapter, strategies derived from existing social media literature are outlined and analyzed. The focus lies on social media campaigns of small and medium enterprises (SME) in an early stage of development. All companies, irrespective of their size, must constantly realign themselves, their values, and product portfolios in line with the dynamic changes in the environment. This is especially true for SMEs, as their competitive advantage is characterized by effective solution-

Katrin Kizilkan, Maximilian Wagenknecht, Department of Entrepreneurship and Startup Management at the Leuphana University of Luneburg, Germany

https://doi.org/10.1515/9783110747652-011

oriented decision-making and more dynamic processes than in larger companies. A cost-effective way for SMEs to get in direct contact with customers is through social media communication. This type of communication in connection with hypothesis-driven and long-term strategic planning enables companies to check whether their product or service meets customer requirements and to generate new ideas directly from their target group. This book chapter deals with a possible structuring of digital communication by using lean and efficient methods. According to Kent and Li (2020), the social media sphere has received very little original theorizing, even if the social media topic is present in research and has tripled in the last few years.

Moreover, Kent and Li (2020) argue that existing theories are more likely to be applied and tested in the social media field than new approaches are developed. Application examples listed in further course refer mainly to the use of the social media network Instagram. It is precisely here that communication channels such as Facebook and Twitter have increasingly been examined in the literature to date. The importance of this topic results from the chances that arise from an intelligent usage of these social media networks.

However, as part of an inductive approach, this chapter addresses many research fields. The goal is to extend established concepts by new developments from the Lean Startup Method (LSM) area. To frame these communication and marketing theories, we aim to apply parts of the LSM to create a guideline on how to effectively and goal-oriented rethink the use of social media and form it into a risk-adjusted and lean strategy.

Stepping into the field of LSM, the method proposes a process of continuous iterative and agile validation cycles for verifying and testing a suitable business model (BM) and business strategies (Bocken & Snihur, 2020; Ghezzi & Cavallo, 2020; Silva et al., 2019). This method is not only used by startups but also SMEs and large companies (Chan et al., 2019; Clutterbuck et al., 2009). However, only parts of the LSM are often used since it consists of subordinated methods for different fields of application (Bortolini et al., 2018; Lizarelli et al., 2021; Ries, 2017).

A fundamental subordinated method is the Customer Development Method (CDM) (Blank, 2013; Melander, 2019). Further, agile development, the conscious implementation of lean processes, and the persevere or pivot strategy serve as additional foundations of this method (Blank, 2013; Leatherbee & Katila, 2020; Ries, 2017; Silva et al., 2019). In the context of these methods and practices, it can be stated that SMEs that use lean and hypothesis-driven processes often need an adapted communication strategy towards their customers (Kamboj & Sarmah, 2018; Seggie et al., 2017). Approaches in this field are justified because information and digital communication management, respectively social media, are already part of lean thinking (Müller et al., 2017; Redeker et al., 2019). LSM factors are used to improve the digital communication of SMEs. By connecting the outcomes with SMEs and the social media framework, we can significantly contribute to the mentioned research fields. For this purpose, we outline the chances and risks of Lean Social Media Communication (LSMC). In this context, the following research question (RQ) needs to be elaborated:

RQ1: What key factors derived from the Lean Startup Method can be applied to communication via social media platforms for SMEs?

In the second step of this process, the current state of motives and characteristics of customer engagement are analyzed (Hutton & Fosdick, 2011), which results in new insights for a more efficient social media strategy. The aim is to determine how digital communication can be improved through customer development (CD) and why a straightforward decision-making process in the context of a persevere or pivot strategy is of utmost relevance (Balocco et al., 2019; Colazo, 2020; Lizarelli et al., 2021). Thus, the second research question is dedicated to the concrete application possibilities of these LSM fields and potential risks that might occur:

RQ2: How can these identified key factors of lean communication be implemented in a risk-adjusted social media strategy for targeted customer communication?

This question is particularly relevant because the literature repeatedly points out that the choice of social media channels and the communication strategy must be geared to the appropriate customer segment (Melander, 2019; Santos et al., 2020). In this context, lean thinking can help avoid waste drivers and thus reduce financial and strategical risks. Addressing the gap in the literature, this study explores the combination of the two research fields theoretically. It aims to elaborate how human resources, financial capabilities, and a hypothesis-driven approach can be developed and implemented in a risk-adjusted LSMC-Strategy.

Theoretical Background – Digital Communication of SMEs

To date, several studies have investigated digital communication as a subarea of communication theories. The following theoretical accumulation concentrates on the subfield of digital communication, namely social media, focusing on SMEs' application. To derive the embedding of social media in communication theories, Fraccastoro et al. (2021) divide sales communication tools into three categories according to their digitalization level. The first one includes conventional communication tools like phone and post but also classic face-to-face conversation. The second tool category involves digital tools like e-mails, Search Engine Optimizing, websites, and online meeting tools like Zoom. The third category relates to social media. Social media offers many opportunities for organizational communication (Floreddu & Cabiddu, 2016).

Nowadays, a wide variety of social media channels can be an easy and, above all, cost-effective way to reach many potential customers, especially in comparison to more traditional communication tools (Wardati & Er, 2019). Thereby, social networks play a significant role in the consumer's purchase decision because they strengthen word-of-mouth and are more trusted than traditional advertising campaigns (Karimi & Naghibi, 2015). In addition, the number of users constantly increases (Shawky et al., 2020), and customers are directly involved in the processes through active dialog (Santos et al., 2020).

Especially for SMEs, these communication channels can win potential customers or involve existing customers in development processes. Therefore, it is necessary to determine which social media channels are preferred by the target group and reach out to them efficiently (Öztamur & Karakadilar, 2014). Loyal customers buy a product or service more quickly and might even get involved in a discourse with the companies (Elmadag & Peneklioglu, 2018). Here digital communication should be embedded in the companies' marketing strategy and form a social media strategy.

Customer engagement depends on the needs, desires, and goals of the customer group. This is related to the fact that on social media, they are not just recipients of the messages but actively participate in the communication (Schmitt, 2012).

Targeted social media use may result in an increase in traffic and engagement. It also helps to reduce the high costs of classic marketing campaigns. Implementing feedback loops and honest real-time communication with the customer can improve long-term customer relationships (Karimi & Naghibi, 2015). Mangold and Faulds (2009) point out that social media activities can also be harmful to companies, depending on how customers react to the content generated by them.

There is still a lack of guidance for employees to follow a stringent execution of content generation (Ashley & Tuten, 2015). Failures often occur in the communication structure due to the use of inappropriate language. This might create unattractive content and fail to attract customer awareness (Öztamur & Karakadilar, 2014). There is a great danger for SMEs in a nonstrategic use of social media.

Theoretical Background – Lean Startup Method

Lean companies that use parts of the LSM are characterized, among other things, by hypothesis-driven development processes combined with validated learning, lean process structures, and a focus on value-added and customer-oriented order fulfillment (Blank, 2013; Ries, 2017). Strategies that correspond to lean thinking can help achieve goals more efficiently and strategically (Eckert, 2017). The origins of the lean approach come from the Japanese car manufacturer Toyota (Shah & Ward, 2003). However, LSM goes beyond these explanations and uses only principles from the original approach (Bhamu & Singh Sangwan, 2014; Jesemann et al., 2020).

Established research articles connected with agile methods in all areas of the value chain analyzed the specifics of the method (see for example Balocco et al., 2019; Ghezzi, 2019; Ghezzi & Cavallo, 2020). The main goal is to develop and improve the BM through a continuous learning process. Osterwalder (2005) classifies five BM pillars: product, customer interface, infrastructure management, and financial aspects. In this context, LSM can be applied to all areas. However, just the first two pillars and four subordinate factors (validated learning, lean structures, customer development, and persevere or pivot) are of interest in the context of this study.

A Hypothesis-driven Development Process and Validated Learning

Especially in early company development phases, entrepreneurs ask themselves what requirements their customers have and how they can best develop their products and services in a targeted manner. In this context, LSM aims to make business creation and the search for a scalable and repeatable BM less risky and more efficient (Blank, 2013; Ries, 2017). Hypothesis-driven developments and continuous improvements can help understand customer needs faster and more efficiently (Newbert et al., 2020; Silva et al., 2019). Thereby, the hypotheses should correspond to a scientific structure and be falsifiable. The knowledge is validated and continuously integrated into the development process (Balocco et al., 2019; Frederiksen & Brem, 2017). Ries (2017) proposes continuously implementing learnings but simultaneously re-measuring and validating the new implementation (Build-Measure-Learn-Loop).

Lean Process Structures and Minimum Viable Products

Focused and planned development leads to more customer-oriented services and products (Eisenmann et al., 2011; Shepherd & Gruber, 2020). The aim is to keep the costs of the process as low as possible to efficiently drive forward further development through an experimental approach (Mansoori, 2017). In this context, a minimum viable product (MVP) can verify this early and collect valuable feedback. An MVP includes only a few critical features, and companies can develop it with minimal effort (Blank, 2013; Blank & Dorf, 2017; Tripathi et al., 2019). Such an MVP does not always have to exist in physical form but also as a described service description. Digital prototypes can already deliver customer feedback at an early stage (Shepherd & Gruber, 2020). The results must always be critically scrutinized during the validation process so that no wrong decisions are made based on examining the hypotheses (Eisenmann et al., 2011).

Customer Development Method

A fundamental subordinated method is the CDM (Blank, 2015; Melander, 2019). In the context of this method, it can be stated that companies that use lean and hypothesis-driven processes are often in need of an adapted communication and development strategy towards their customers (Kamboj & Sarmah, 2018). It builds on the previously described explanations and accentuates the importance of using a customer-centric approach (Blank, 2015; Melander, 2019).

The process is structured in four phases: 1. Customer Discovery; 2. Customer Validation; 3. Customer Creation; 4. Company Building (Blank, 2013). The first phase deals with identifying the customer's requirements for the service or product. Here it is essential to check whether there is a basic demand at all. Based on this question, a hypothesis-driven approach helps to analyze the situation. The second phase explores the customer's interest in greater depth and carries out validated learning steps. The goal is to elicit the positioning on the market to obtain or improve the MVP (Blank, 2015). The two subsequent phases will then support the establishment of the BM based on the data obtained (Blank, 2013).

Persevere or Pivot

After implementing ideas or procedures, the decision must be made if structures should be maintained (=persevere), only marginally improved or whether they should be fundamentally rethought (=pivot). This should be done continuously. Many studies have shown that companies which constantly adapt to new situations are usually more successful (Bajwa et al., 2016; Pillai et al., 2020).

Methodology

This study aims to extend and connect theoretical concepts and elaborate new assumptions within a conceptual, theoretical framework through a qualitative research approach (Ferreira et al., 2019). The goal is to figure out which derived key factors and procedures of the LSM can help reach and contact customers via social media in a lean-oriented manner.

The approaches are based on a systematic literature review (SLR) and an inductive content analysis (Bengtsson, 2016; Elo & Kyngäs, 2008). These two methods were chosen because it allows the systematic extraction and combination of relevant information from both research fields (Kraus et al., 2020).

The SLR is carried out using a multi-stage approach to systematically link the main literature from the core topics to obtain comprehensible results. Figure 10.1 shows the topics and the associated categories. These categories in connection to the topics were used as keywords for the searching process.

The following Figure 10.2 illustrates the finding process of the SLR. Four hundred and twelve articles were found by searching in different databases (Scopus, Web of Science, Google Scholar, Emerald, Springer, Elsevier, Wiley, and Science Direct). The

Research Fields and Key Words	
Lean Startup Method	Communication Theories
(SME) Innovation	
Customer Oriented Strategy	
Lean Structures	
Validated Learning	(SME) Social Media
Customer Development Method	(SME) Digitalization
Persevere or Pivot	(SME) Digital Marketing

Figure 10.1: Research fields and keywords.

search period was between 2001 and 2021 (=20 years). The keywords were used in the databases singularly and in various combinations with the other keywords.

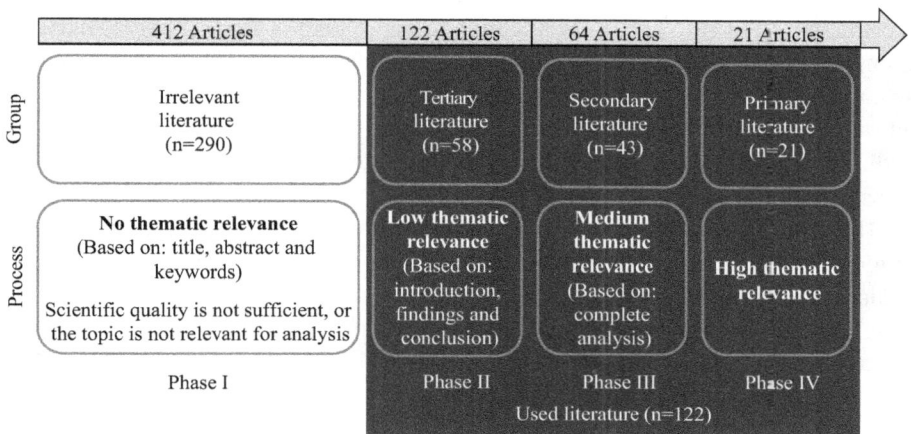

412 Articles	122 Articles	64 Articles	21 Articles

Group

Irrelevant literature (n=290)	Tertiary literature (n=58)	Secondary literature (n=43)	Primary literature (n=21)

Process

No thematic relevance (Based on: title, abstract and keywords) Scientific quality is not sufficient, or the topic is not relevant for analysis	**Low thematic relevance** (Based on: introduction, findings and conclusion)	**Medium thematic relevance** (Based on: complete analysis)	**High thematic relevance**
Phase I	Phase II	Phase III	Phase IV

Used literature (n=122)

Figure 10.2: Overview of the literature search process.

Within phase I, titles, abstracts, and keywords were analyzed by their reference to the main research areas. The literature was excluded if the scientific quality was not sufficient (for example, non-academic materials, book publications) or the topic was not relevant for the analysis. This step allowed us to exclude 290 articles.

In the second step (phase II), the main theoretical core statements were extracted and evaluated by analyzing the introductions and conclusions of the articles. Here, the authors carefully agreed on whether to exclude or include each article for the SLR. This reduced the number by 58 articles. In phase III, the articles were viewed holistically. If these texts had a significant overlap to the fields, they were identified as primary literature in the last phase (=21 articles). Otherwise, the articles were used as secondary literature (=64 articles). However, all 122 articles of the SLR were considered for the writing process according to their relevance.

The 21 articles within the primary literature were analyzed in-depth and key messages were extracted as part of the finding process. Within this process, references were made between the individual core statements by implementing four categories: "CDM," "lean structures," "validated learning," and " persevere or pivot." A systematic evaluation of the main findings in each field was conducted with the help of systematic content analysis. The chosen content analysis is a research method to analyze data within a contextual frame (Elo & Kyngäs, 2008). The framework of this kind of analysis is used for describing and evaluating a subject and extending it through new insights, interpretations, and a guide for action (Khirfan et al., 2020). The goal here is to create a multi-layered overview, categorize, and examine the concepts and categories that summarize the phenomenon or theory (Elo & Kyngäs, 2008).

As there are three different approaches of content analysis, namely conventional, directed, and summative, a decision had to be made on which one fits best (Hsieh & Shannon, 2005). The method, in general, is used to focus on characteristics of language as communication with particular attention to the content of the text being analyzed. In our approach, the results were also systematically categorized in a table. In this case, the categories are formed inductively, meaning they are not initially determined but rather emerge and are recognized during the analysis. The directed content analysis differs because there is already a solid body of literature on the subject area, but it needs further research to fill several gaps.

This content analysis approach aims to identify correlations and patterns of communication concepts with a lean orientation that can be transferred to the social media communication of SMEs. The most suitable variant of the content analysis here is the directed content analysis because there is a considerable corpus of existing literature for both topics. Still, there is very little literature connecting the topics. After this process, the primary objective within the discussion part is to clarify which of the main determinants should be included in a strategy of LSMC. The focus lies on both customer acquisition and communication with customers through social media.

Findings

To classify the findings from the systematic literature review in a structured way and relate the different research fields to each other, four subcategories are derived from the theoretical part on LSM. These serve to classify SMEs' information on social media use so that a lean social media communication strategy can be derived from it.

Figure 10.3 shows the age structure of the 122 articles for this research. What is striking is that there has been a sharp increase in publications in the last four years

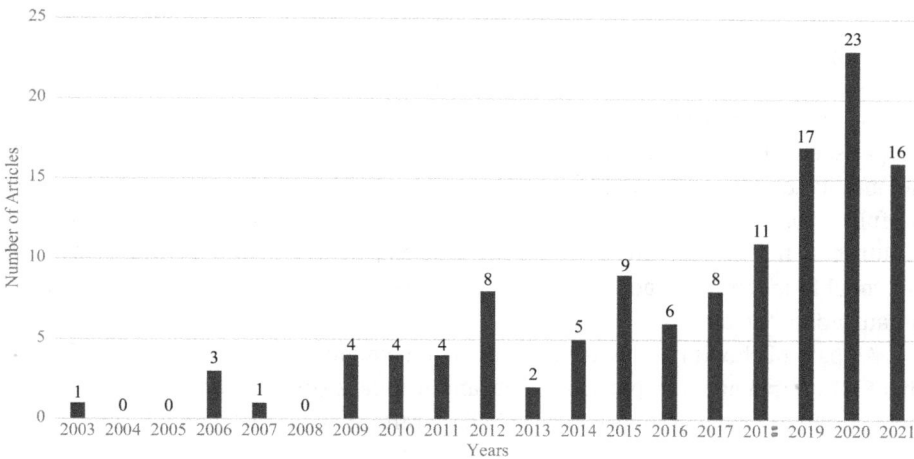

Figure 10.3: Age structure of the articles used.

(note: 2021 was only considered up to July 2021). The growing body of literature indicates the importance of the topic and the accompanying interest in the research area.

The growing importance of the subject is supported by Figure 10.10 in the appendix. It becomes clear that the subject area is primarily researched qualitatively, also shown by the fact that 93 of 122 articles have an inductive approach. Figure 10.11 illustrates how in this context the most popular research method used is a literature review, followed by case studies. However, due to the analysis, the articles might have two applied research methods, and the number is therefore 169 used research methods in 122 articles. Derived from the evaluation of the SLR, Figure 10.12 in the appendix also shows an overview of the most relevant journals in this field.

As shown in Figure 10.13 in the appendix, the articles were allocated to one or two topic areas of the research field. This enabled an assignment to the following four LSM fields for this findings part. Thirty of 122 articles dealt with social media, and 35 of 122 articles contained information from the LSM.

Tables 10.2 to 10.8 in the appendix show the key findings of the primary literature. These 21 articles have the highest subject relevance of the 122 articles and cover all subject areas. These texts serve as the basis for the findings and discussion, but insights from other articles supplement them.

Validated Social Media Learning

The basis for validated social media learning is the practical evaluation and analysis of digital customer feedback. Jesemann et al. (2021) emphasize that employees need to be well trained to engage with the customers via social media and understand their needs. Mangold and Faulds (2009) identify the potential risk of social media activities harming the company if employees are not sufficiently trained or do not know the campaign's goals and produce inappropriate content. Technology and tools evolve fast, so employees need to learn continuously (Eagleman, 2013). Before developing a proper social media strategy for the organization, employees need to accept the channel and its use. Alalwan (2018) measures the perceived ease of use and the perceived usefulness of the employees by adopting the Technology Acceptance Model. Lee et al. (2010) show that the perceived ease of use is strongly connected to the user's age, as it is probably much more accessible for digital natives to use social media within an organizational structure.

As part of this implementation process for validated learning, it is imperative that SMEs implement customer opinions and feedback correctly and through a structured process (Mangold and Faulds, 2009). Peralta et al. (2020) highlight the overall aim to deliver value to the customer. This approach can give SMEs, particularly, an advantage, even if they are weaker in their resources, such as finances, workforces, and organizational structure, than large corporations (Wardati & Er, 2019). Additionally, Wardati and Er (2019) emphasize the possibility of effective use of social media to build up networks in new markets at comparatively low costs and thus overcome limitations by using external resources to enrich and develop their communication. SMEs have a clear advantage in the absence of rigid structures and, if they know how to adapt dynamically, they can try things out and offer the customer enormous added value (Wardati & Er, 2019).

Validated learning means that through customer involvement, mainly marketing employees must also improve communication through active learning in the short term and derive a long-term strategy by aligning the suitable ideas with the general company vision (Jesemann et al., 2021). For a long-term strategy, Atanassova and Clark (2015) introduce the concept of dynamic capabilities (DCs) for a theoretical embedding that considers the dynamic adaptability of the environment of SMEs and explains the continuous learning process. To classify the further development of SMEs in the concept of DCs, it is represented by the ability of a company within a dynamic process to improve, expand, and rethink its resources, a reminder of the fundamental lean idea of build, measure, learn. Teece et al. describe DC as an organization's ability to adapt core competencies to a fast-evolving market (Teece et al., 1997). Knowledge and organizational learning form core DCs, especially when using social media for gaining customer knowledge easier (Eisenhardt & Martin, 2000). This continuous knowledge accumulation becomes a strategic resource for experimental learning (Atanassova & Clark, 2015).

Lean Social Media Structures

The knowledge about the conditions for using lean communication by applying parts of the LSM is not fully explored (De Cock et al., 2020). De Cock et al. (2020) point out that this might be related to the fact that it is often not easy to make the market information usable for the company. Soares and Teixeira (2014) list the benefits of LSM for every area, where these benefits can be mapped to each other, and how resources can be managed. The management of communication and information is a crucial part of lean thinking, and lean communication must be actively controlled and monitored because no relevant information should be lost (Redeker et al., 2019). But the processing and transfer of comments and opinions from customers are complex because the data is often just available in an unorganized form (Karimi & Naghibi, 2015). Planning in advance how to collect information in a lean and efficient manner is highly relevant (De Cock et al., 2020). But within the literature, there is no precise method or process for general improvements (Redeker et al., 2019).

One of the lean principles and, therefore, a communication rule is the elimination of waste, presented by Redeker et al. (2019). According to Redeker et al. (2019), seven types of waste in information exist: an overload of information, the use of too many systems, lack of integration between systems, too long period to wait for information, wrong information, and the information formats. Gifu and Teodorescu (2014) describe the waste drivers in communication that should be avoided for a communication strategy that follows the lean idea: insufficient information quality, ineffective communication, and unnecessary details.

Steinemann et al. (2012) relate lean communication to applying online tools and deriving recommendations for user utilization. Furthermore, reaction time plays a crucial role in customer service, and especially for social media applications, the answer is expected promptly (Steinemann et al., 2012). Karimi and Naghibi (2015) add here that this creates pressure on the one hand; on the other hand, it creates valuable real-time communication with the customer, whose feedback can be used immediately to improve communication strategies regarding the product portfolio.

Digital Customer Development

The current state of CD and empowerment has already been widely explored (Kamboj & Sarmah, 2018; Melander, 2019; Peralta et al., 2020; Santos et al., 2020). Customers are often deeply involved in the development process, especially in the industrial market and in the context of B2B communication (Melander, 2019). Melander (2019) points out that this can also be applied to the B2C context and less industrial-driven markets. Especially in social media, customer opinions are analyzed in a targeted manner to leverage real-time market knowledge (Atanassova & Clark, 2015). As social media contains the potential to interact and exchange with the customers efficiently, it is the perfect setting to gain insights from customers' needs and generate new ideas in interaction with them (Barlatier & Josserand, 2018).

In addition, Atanassova and Clark (2015) and Melander (Melander, 2019) raise the question of how many customers should actively influence product or service development. No consistent statements on this could be found in the selected literature. Nevertheless, it is crucial to determine in advance which of the available customers need to be involved in this process. Other authors like Santos et al. (2020) focus more on how customers can be identified as the primary target group and how to process expectations. Customer value is multidimensional, and value dimensions must be prioritized based on the market and customers (Santos et al., 2020).

Floreddu and Cabiddu (2016) recognize the opportunity that dialogs can reduce product or service failure risks in the long term. In terms of frequency of contact, regular interactions between the customer and the company strengthen the relationship (Floreddu & Cabiddu, 2016). Kamboj and Sarmah (2018) reveal that the customer's engagement is often motivated by the need for information. The variety of motivation derived from the customer needs to be explored by the company within their core community to develop customized communication and targeted products or services (Kamboj & Sarmah, 2018).

Further, Bharati et al. (2021) apply in their study of idea co-creation on social media platforms the social capital theory to the social media context and attempt to generate a theory of social ideation. This procedure can be connected to the subarea of the LSM, the customer development process. The theory implies the organizational strategies for the social exchange of information, knowledge, and ideas to generate new ideas or renew existing products or service offerings (Bharati et al., 2021). In this context, Ashley et al. (2015) focus on customer engagement and how companies can effectively align themselves. Therefore, creative social media content needs to be developed by the employees to get in touch with the customer (Ashley & Tuten, 2015).

Persevere or Pivot for a Successful Growth

Lean social media processes are, as often described in the literature, processes that run in loops and are pre-planned (Bortolini et al., 2018). Persevere or pivot are thus continuous factors of such a course of action (Balocco et al., 2019). In this context, Bortolini et al. (2018) point out that the adaptability and conscious decision for or against a particular direction can determine the existence of a company. The authors justify this by stating that the success of an organization is based on its ability to adapt its BM dynamically to new market developments. Lizarelli et al. (2021) indicate that waste should be avoided, and it is crucial to identify suitable areas where it makes sense to change processes and make them leaner at an early stage and with evaluated customer feedback. Otherwise, implementing lean structures without a long-term goal and plan can negatively influence performance (Lizarelli et al., 2021).

Atanassova and Clark (2015) argue that SMEs change and develop their marketing activities through social media use by gaining market intelligence. For them, social media might be a chance for SMEs to fill the resource gap that often exists to increase real-time market knowledge. Furthermore, Isari et al. (2016) describe that social media adapt to current trends and digital evolution. For instance, the younger generation intuitively uses lean communication because they are used to communicating with short text messages. Isari et al. (2016) also assert that the companies should continuously monitor and analyze customer communication. In addition, the companies should specifically adapt their communication strategy in the social media area to trends and current developments.

Pillai et al. (2020) indicate that companies that frequently conduct pivots and continuous scrutinization of current processes tend to be more successful than companies that have stuck to their first concept (Pillai et al., 2020). Such a pivot should be performed before the product/market fit is reached and based on empirical data (Maurya, 2012). Especially for fundamental adjustments, well-selected customer feedback is better than relying on the company's own intuition regarding customer needs (Balocco et al., 2019). However, caution is required if the core customers have not yet been identified and recommendations for action are derived from an undefined customer segment (Balocco et al., 2019).

Discussion

The discussion section is divided into three parts and intends to produce practical recommendations based on theoretical results. The first part deals with answering the first research question and shows the core factors of LSMC. The second part contains the chances of such a transition and how to implement the findings. Lastly, possible risks that could arise are discussed to look at the topic holistically.

Identified Key Factors Derived from the Lean Startup Method

The validated learning process of a lean digital communication strategy is first elaborated to answer the first research question.

RQ1: What key factors derived from the Lean Startup Method can be applied to communication via social media platforms for SMEs?

Previous research has pointed out that several strategies for SMEs are trying to improve efficiency (Öztamur & Karakadilar, 2014). Companies are not given a precise strategy here. For this reason, we will derive the key factors applicable to LSMC from our findings. Recent studies have shown that young companies in particular often do not know their digital customer base well enough, and a lack of focus within customer communication is the consequence (Appel et al., 2020).

The validated learning process, derived from lean thinking and applied to the social media context, implies several advantages, such as saving costs through an adapted learn-

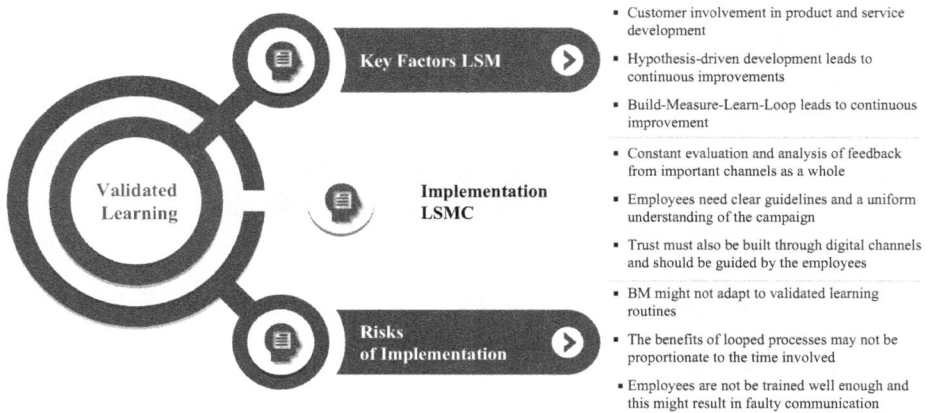

Figure 10.4: Key Factors LSM, Implication LSMC, and risks of validated learning.

ing strategy in combination with targeted customer communication. Figure 10.4 shows the most important findings and risks for validated learning.

As Ries (2017) indicates, limited resources lead to the need for long-term planning of targeted validated learning. Here the concept of DC can also be aligned with the subfield of validated learning as it facilitates renewing organizational resources through experiential learning, integrating new knowledge, reconfiguring, and developing capabilities to maintain competitiveness (Atanassova & Clark, 2015). Ries (2017) highlights the importance of adequately measuring the tested results to validate them and afterward implementing the gained insights. Hypothesis-driven learning routines can help to improve the BM and to generate trust in a targeted manner. In doing so, employees need a uniform understanding of the goals and strategies (Jesemann et al., 2021). Figure 10.5 shows some basics here, using the example of a strategic workflow for Instagram.

To determine the customer's needs, it is crucial to start with extending market research. In doing so, social media should stimulate consumer conversations about new ideas and developments (Mangold & Faulds, 2009). Therefore, the survey function on Instagram can be used. Companies can create a question and prepare answer options or ask an open question. With the second option, you usually get more extensive and more specific feedback in the present context. The companies can share the survey results with followers as a sign of appreciation for their engagement. The survey function was used by several companies very creatively and successfully in engaging their customer base. For example, regarding customer interaction in product development, different product variants can be illustrated (Chesbrough & Tucci, 2020). Here, users decide intuitively and spontaneously, and companies receive honest and fast feedback, which they can consider in product or service development.

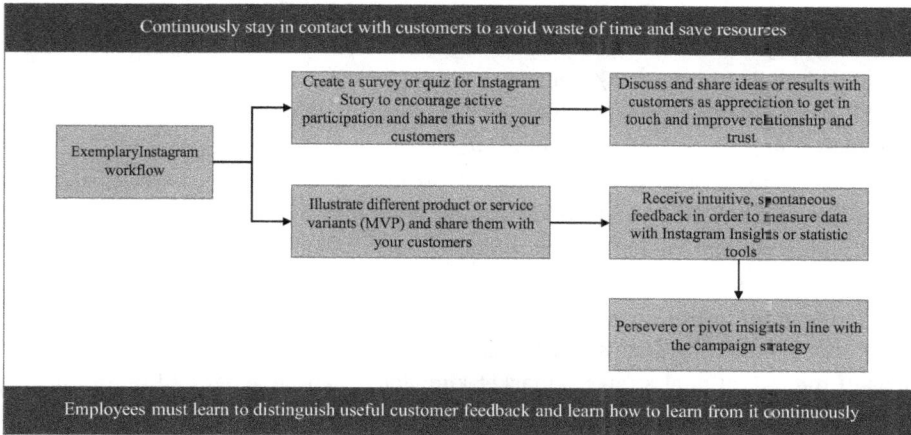

Figure 10.5: Exemplary Instagram workflow for validated learning.

However, validated learning is closely linked to the implementation by the employees and how well they make use of it. Therefore, sufficient training of the employees is highly relevant (Jesemann et al., 2021; Steinemann et al., 2012). Additionally, we suggest that companies must be actively willing to make fundamental changes based on customer data.

Lean structure in social media refers to the active controlling and monitoring of information and elimination of waste in communication.

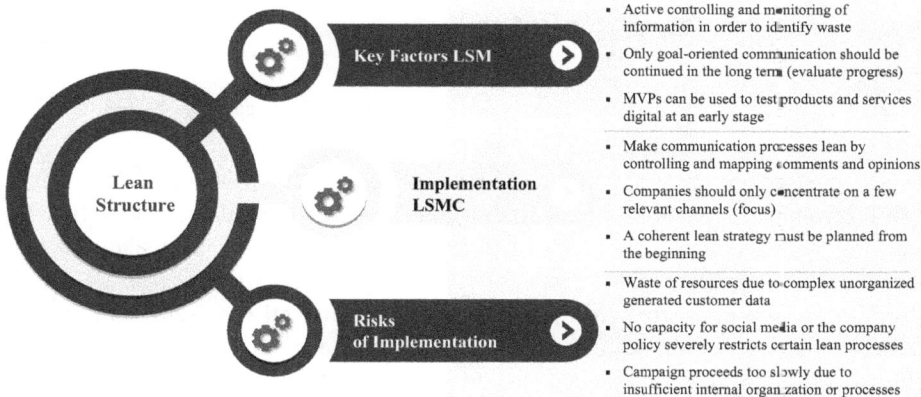

Figure 10.6: Key Factors LSM, Implication LSMC, and risks of lean structure.

Figure 10.6 shows the most important key factors and risks for a lean structure. One of the key factors here is the advanced information gathering and evaluation planning to identify waste drivers (Gifu & Teodorescu, 2014). Excessive accumulation of information and the use of inappropriate technology should be avoided, as this can hardly be handled by SMEs (Steinemann et al., 2012). In addition, too many channels should be avoided (Karimi & Naghibi, 2015); instead, they should be selected and supplied with content in a precisely planned and structured manner (Isari et al., 2016).

Lean communication processes mean controlling and mapping comments and insights with each other (Gifu & Teodorescu, 2014) and must be planned from the beginning. To accommodate lean thinking, creating a lean structure with the full potential of social media use must be exploited and implemented in an integrated strategy (Barlatier & Josserand, 2018).

In this context, the analysis of CD also shows that if customers are placed in the focus of the operational analysis, market knowledge can be generated more quickly (Atanassova & Clark, 2015).

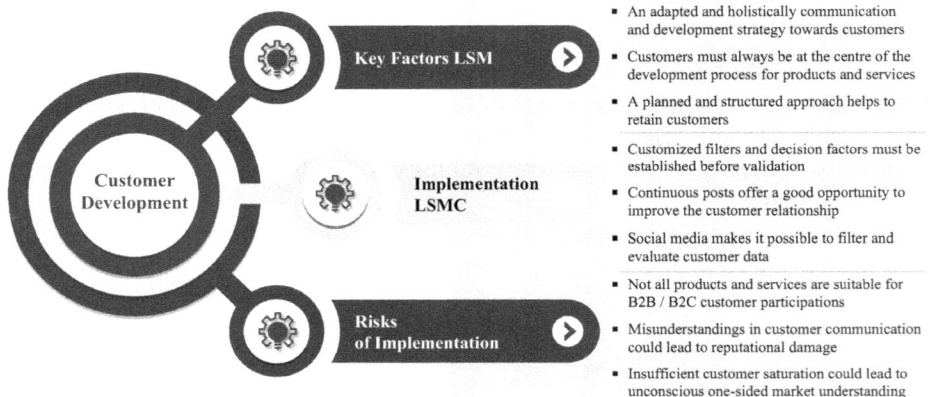

Figure 10.7: Key Factors LSM, Implication LSMC, and risks of customer development.

This is part of the customer discovery process (Blank, 2015; Carroll & Casselman, 2019). Figure 10.7 shows the main findings and risks. The results indicate that by working with hypotheses and critically reflecting on the continuously acquired customer data, this process makes sense for all markets (De Cock et al., 2020; Melander, 2019). It is essential to constantly generate content (Bharati et al., 2021) and at the same time synthesize the statements through filters. However, the application possibilities in product and service development are very different regarding the customer relationship (Ashley & Tuten, 2015). Here, for instance, it can be assumed that within the B2B sector, there are hardly any limitations for early customer participation regarding product or service development. It can also be anticipated that within the B2C sector, emotionalizing products and services (primarily not from industrial sectors) (Melander, 2019) are particularly suitable for early strong customer participation.

This is probably due to the generally more developed and easier to maintain customer relationships in the B2B area, especially in the digital communication processes.

As part of the customer validation process, it is crucial to determine at an early stage what kind of customers are the core customers and which are suitable for a contribution regarding a product or service development (Santos et al., 2020). The findings specify that the level of saturation for a social media campaign and the type of customers that should be included cannot be determined across the board for any kind of industry and adapt to the prevailing market environment with its unique characteristics.

The continuous evaluation of the current situation and the conscious decision for or against a particular course of the social media campaign is highly relevant. Here, the theoretical foundations of the persevere or pivot strategy from the LSM can provide helpful support. Figure 10.8 shows how to apply the results in a systematized way.

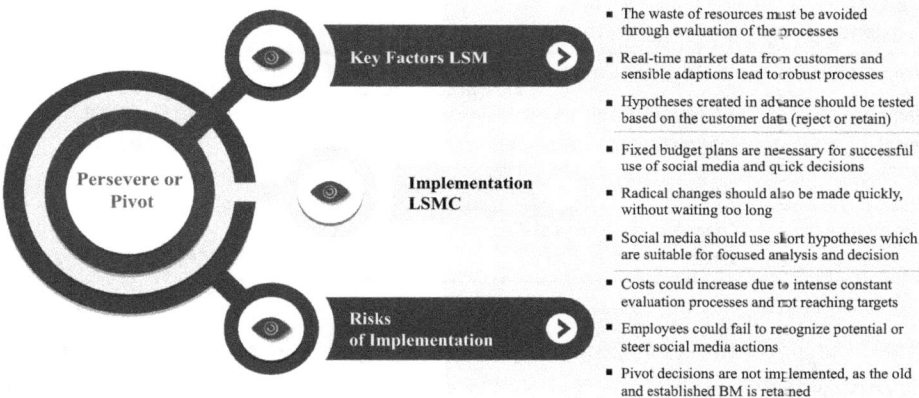

Figure 10.8: Key factors LSM, Implication LSMC, and risks of persevere or pivot.

The catalog of pivots proposed by Ries (2017) can be applied on several levels. The findings provide convincing evidence that in particular the first four of the mentioned pivots can significantly influence the direction of social media communication. If used as recommended with the application of targeted hypotheses, it might achieve a positive outcome.

Table 10.1, in association with the observations of Kim et al. (2018), illustrates that it is crucial to identify suitable areas where it makes sense to change processes and make them leaner. Often this is a looped process (Lizarelli et al., 2021).

The literature indicates that while generating customer data and intensifying the customer dialogue, significant changes should not automatically be integrated into operational processes. Additionally, the goals must be derived from the company's marketing campaign and continuously evaluated (Atanassova & Clark, 2015). They must be implemented in a targeted and evaluated manner and as a conscious decision (Kim et al.,

Table 10.1: Types of pivots (derived from Ries, 2017, pp. 172–176).

Type of Pivot	Information
Zoom-in Pivot	A single feature of a product becomes the whole product.
Zoom-out Pivot	A single feature of a product becomes a feature of a larger product.
Customer Segment Pivot	The product is solving a problem for a different customer than initially expected.
Customer Need Pivot	Customers have a different need than the planned product can deliver.
Platform Pivot	From application to a platform or vice versa.
Business Architecture Pivot	The company is switching its architectures (e.g., low to high volume).
Value Capture Pivot	Changes in value creation due to feedback.
Engine of Growth Pivot	A fundamental change of the growth engine (e.g., viral marketing campaign).
Channel Pivot	Change in sales channels and refocusing.
Technology Pivot	Change in the technical execution. The product or service remains the same.

2018). The aim is to revise existing hypotheses and generate new ones. But as market knowledge increases through real-time market data from customers, the BM becomes more robust over time, and adjustments can be implemented more quickly. No BM will ever be perfect and, according to the principles of lean thinking (Bhamu & Singh Sangwan, 2014), continuous improvement is the goal of such a campaign (Kim et al., 2018). Empirical evidence appears to confirm that companies which continuously adapt to market developments are often more successful in the long term (Bortolini et al., 2018).

Chances of Adapting a Lean Communication Strategy

Several scholars have provided empirical evidence supporting the chances which arise through the early and close customer relationship (Kamboj & Sarmah, 2018; Redeker et al., 2019). This empirical evidence leads us to our second research question:

RQ2: How can these identified key factors of lean communication be implemented in a risk-adjusted social media strategy for targeted customer communication?

If lean communication strategies are applied, products and services can be developed multidimensionally, promoting customer loyalty.

Social media offers an excellent opportunity to implement these adaptations in practice due to its high flexibility and almost worldwide availability (Dwivedi et al., 2021). Current studies appear to support the notion that social media is well suited for customization. A continuous aligning of the campaign to new requirements is mainly in the early stages of SMEs (Kamboj & Sarmah, 2018). This is an excellent opportunity as SMEs are more likely to have not yet fully developed structures and might still search for a sustainable BM (Atanassova & Clark, 2015).

The tools implemented in the social media channels to get in touch with customers and encourage them to interact, offer companies the chance to enter an honest, timely exchange and receive direct feedback. These approaches and procedures can reduce risks and failure in the long term and save money.

Targeted lean communication can develop and maintain a sincere relationship with the customer base. The shared information should not have to be decoded first but rather be communicated clearly and comprehensibly and visualized with appropriate images. For a good relationship with the customer and a high rate of interaction, it is essential to respond quickly to customers' questions, requests, and comments. The companies should work with guidelines on this to align the employees on one user level. We are firmly convinced that young SMEs in the early stages of their social media development have the most significant potential to benefit from a targeted LSMC strategy.

Risks of Adapting a Lean Communication Strategy

The most significant risk of such interactive processes is that the focus can get lost, and the continuous improvement process creates more costs than ultimately creating value. The literature review emanates from considering risks from two main actors: customers and the company itself.

On the one hand, communicating with customers digitally can be complex, leading to misunderstandings (Karimi & Naghibi, 2015). Companies should know their customers, for example, to choose the appropriate social media networks. This might also originate from the communication policy of the company. Insufficiently trained employees could fail to recognize potential pitfalls or steer social media actions in the wrong direction due to a lack of knowledge. It is vital to ensure that the discussion remains objective and actively managed (Gifu & Teodorescu, 2014).

On the other hand, risks could arise because many companies do not use the information gained through the customers because they are too attached to the original BM (Ghezzi, 2020). Related to the customer base, a lean social media strategy can only be successfully implemented if the correct number and right type of customers have been identified. It should be clear if these customers are the right customers for incremental changes within core parts of the BM (Chesbrough & Tucci, 2020).

Regarding lean structures, it is mainly for SMEs challenging to create sufficient personnel capacity for social media. Since some SMEs are rather sales-driven, there is a lack of structural planning. In addition, the easy-going character that characterizes social media could get lost through strategic planning that is too small in scope. Furthermore, von Krogh (2012) draws attention to the risks of losing competitive advantage. The knowledge shared in social media networks is accessible to everyone, as well as to other companies. By willingly presenting visions in public, competitors could transfer ideas to their concepts. We are convinced that companies can gain significant competitive advantages through direct interaction with their customers with the primary goal to optimize existing processes through customer feedback.

Framework

Figure 10.9 shows the main framework of this research. The framework includes all essential points for a comprehensive and risk-adjusted lean communication strategy.

Identifying the company's vision and selecting appropriate employees are located upstream of the cycle and are thus exempt from continual repetition. The whole strategy is embedded in a lean structure, which means that all aspects of the cycle described below should be based on lean thinking (Kim et al., 2018). Additionally, internal and external risks affect all processes and must be considered through the whole strategy-building process.

The validated learning cycle (left cycle) serves as a guideline for employees working with social media to improve their communication skills through continuous learning. Connected to this on the content level, creative contributions for generating new ideas can be sourced from the customer development method. Companies should always question the status quo. The BM should be dynamically and frequently adapted to customer needs and market conditions regarding products or service offerings (Ries, 2017).

The targeted hypothesis must be formulated regarding the lean customer development cycle (right cycle). Afterward, the MVP should be created or modified. During the posting process and dialog phase, the communication strategy must be coherent. In the context of the data analysis, the previously formulated hypotheses should be evaluated. After this step, the product or service insights must be aligned with the company vision before implementation.

Both cycles need to be repeated for continuous improvement, as customer requirements, customer segments, and external factors can change constantly. This is important for a successful social media campaign and a robust BM.

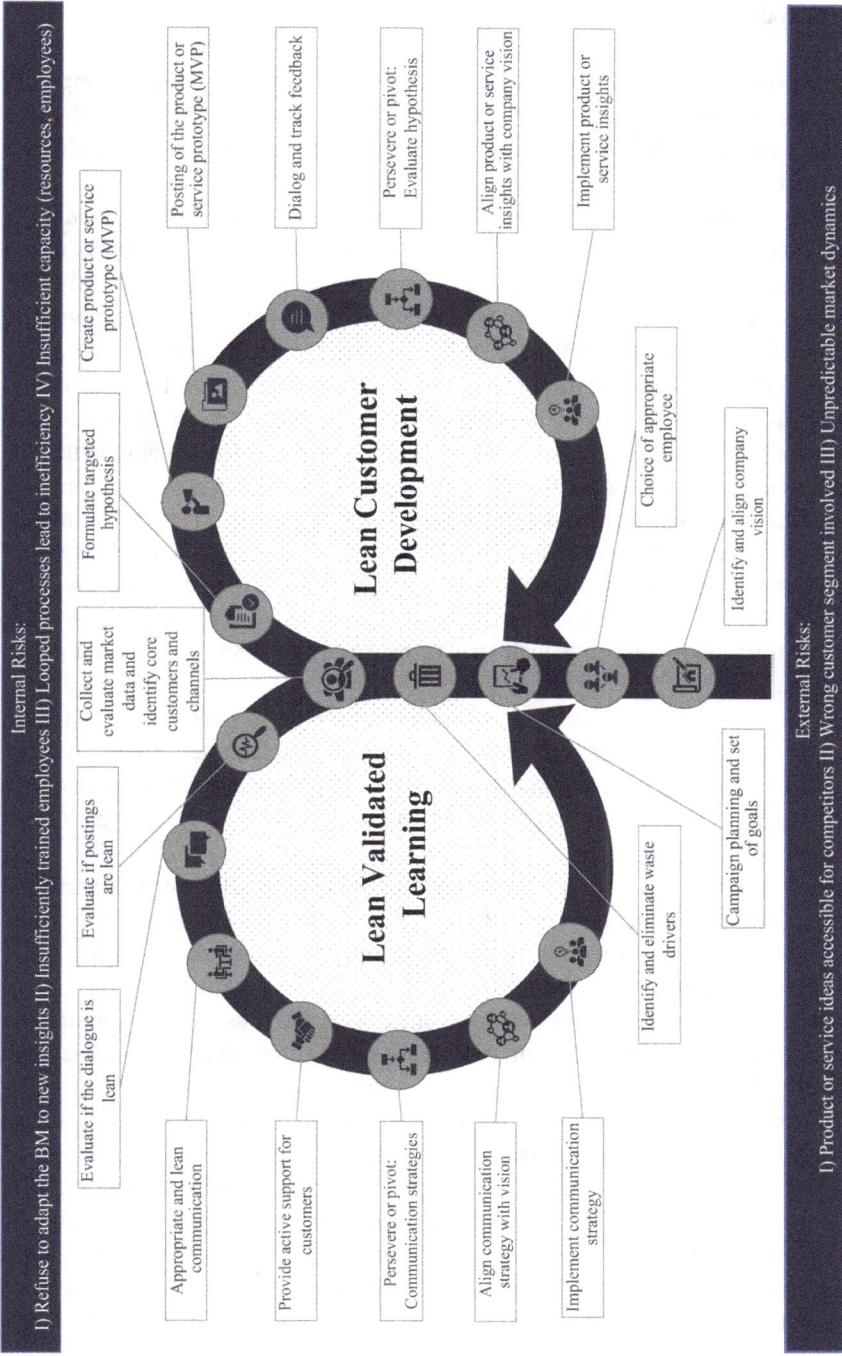

Internal Risks:
I) Refuse to adapt the BM to new insights II) Insufficiently trained employees III) Looped processes lead to inefficiency IV) Insufficient capacity (resources, employees)

External Risks:
I) Product or service ideas accessible for competitors II) Wrong customer segment involved III) Unpredictable market dynamics

Figure 10.9: Framework of a risk-adjusted lean social media communication strategy.

Conclusion

The chapter relates to new opportunities for SMEs and startups or larger companies regarding lean digital communication processes. It contributes to understanding the basics that are currently practiced in social media and reveals opportunities for improvement.

Through the evaluation of the core literature and the derived developments in the field of LSM and communication theory, it becomes apparent that parts of the LSM positively influence lean social media communication if applied correctly. The benefits can lead to cost reductions in research and development and the preservation and control of the customer base. LSMC is relevant for SMEs to counter the growing demands of digital communication and a better understanding of their customers.

The results indicate that social media must not only be understood as an advertising opportunity but as a place for targeted product and service development. The vital role of employees with a unified plan and positioning customers at the center of a social media campaign turns out to be essential for successful use of social media. The aim is to develop processes in a targeted manner and to evaluate them on an ongoing basis. It can be assumed that the successes of LSM can also be transferred to the early stages of SMEs. The necessary strategies can be linked to four identified core levels of LSM (validated learning, lean structures, customer development, and persevere or pivot).

Social media leads to a real-time increase of market data from customers. Through the analysis of validated learning, employees must be involved and know the campaign's goal to follow the unified plan. This is the best way employees can evaluate customer data in a targeted manner (reject or retain by hypotheses). Customer trust must be generated and maintained, especially in development processes.

Within the B2B sector, there are hardly any limitations for early customer participation regarding product or service development. In contrast to the B2C sector, emotionalizing products and services (primarily not from industrial sectors) are particularly suitable for early customer participation.

Lastly, the waste of resources and time must be avoided as early as possible by deciding exactly which processes or product specifications should be continued. Thereby the BM becomes more robust over time, and adjustments can be implemented more quickly. It is essential that the SMEs actively allow the BM to change dynamically because of insights gained from social media.

This book chapter has some limitations, especially regarding the methods. A SLR combined with content analysis is suitable for generating first knowledge insights by connecting established literature. The research focused only on secondary data without its empirical research. Thus, it limited the validation of the derived framework. Practical and hypothesis-driven testing is needed. Future studies should focus on the two cycles separately and in combination. This is important to determine how the two cycles influence each other. In addition, an industry-specific validation could verify the specific application areas of the individual frame parts. Already, it can be assumed that the framework cannot be fully applied to all use cases related to social media channels and industries.

Given the risks listed, it can be stated that both external and internal risks must be validated. Currently, the information is based on the selected literature. Future research should focus on individual aspects and expand the model if necessary. A long-term investigation of whether the results are feasible and transferable to a real case study might be vital, too. In addition, we focused on the social media network Instagram, which means that the results might not be transferred entirely to other social media networks.

Furthermore, lean communication on companies on social media was addressed here and summarized in a strategic framework. However, this does not consider the embedding in a cross-divisional marketing campaign, which may not only take place online.

In conclusion, as our conceptualization is justified merely by an SLR, future research should give a more comprehensive overview of this field by validating the findings through a quantitative study. All four mentioned LSM fields must be analyzed to validate the feasibility and benefits of implementations (individually and holistically).

Appendix

Table 10.2: Key findings of the primary literature (Part I).

Year	Authors	Title	LSM Field	Main Statements	Objective
2018	Kamboj, S. Sarmah, B.	Construction and validation of the customer social participation in brand communities scale	Customer Development	A) Social media is constantly developing and adapting to customer and company needs B) It is difficult to measure customer participation quantitatively or qualitatively to identify core customers C) Companies currently still have problems processing the disorganized information comprehensively and deriving strategies from it	This study aims to create a multidimensional scale to measure customer engagement in social media. In addition, many nfluencing parameters such as culture and geographic distribution are difficult to translate into a stringent strategy.

Table 10.2 (continued)

Year	Authors	Title	LSM Field	Main Statements	Objective
2014	Ashley, C. Tuten, T.	Creative strategies in social media marketing: An exploratory study of branded social content and consumer engagement	Customer Development	A) Social media content should be created creatively to build a strong relationship with the customer B) Social media gather customer information throughout the entire communication process, which can be monitored and implemented C) Customers will engage with the posted content on social media if it is done in a creative way D) With the generated ideas from the crowd, ideas for companies' products or services can be implemented	The article concludes several best proactive examples for customer engagement with best-practice ideas to generate creative content which stimulates the customer word-of-mouth marketing.
2019	Melander, L.	Customer involvement in product development: Using voice of the customer for innovation and marketing	Customer Development	A) Especially in industrial markets, customers should provide input for the product development process B) By using the voice of customer strategy, firms can improve their development processes and strengthen their customer relationships C) Cross-functional collaboration is the key for stable project involvement and pilot testing	Due to the case study approach, the author shows how customer involvement in product development can be achieved.

Table 10.3: Key findings of the primary literature (Part II).

Year	Authors	Title	LSM Field	Main Statements	Objective
2020	Santos, A. C. O. da Silva, C. E. S. Braga, R. A d. S., Corrêa, J. É. de Almeida, F. A.	Customer value in lean product development: Conceptual model for incremental innovations	Customer Development	A) The lean product development process has the goal to reduce waste and improve the value creation B) Customer value is multidimensional, and the dimensions of value must be prioritized based on the market and customers C) A problem for identifying customer expectations is that customers often struggle by formulating what their requirements are	This paper is based on a systematic literature review and aims to determine the customer value dimensions. The result is that several factors such as quality, cost, emotional, social, environmental, and innovation influence the value dimension.
2018	Barlatier, P. J. Josserand, E.	Delivering open innovation promises through social media	Customer Development	A) Social media is a valuable resource for idea creation within the process of open innovation B) Information and insights must be monitored and tracked in a coordinated way C) The collected ideas must be implemented in a lean manner	The study concludes best practice points for managers as an inspiration to involve their customers via social media in the innovation process.

Table 10.3 (continued)

Year	Authors	Title	LSM Field	Main Statements	Objective
2021	Bharati, P. Du, K. Chaudhury, A. Agrawal, N. M.	Idea co-creation on social media platforms: Towards a theory of social ideation	Customer Development	A) Social media is perfectly suitable for idea creation B) It is necessary to check if the company can process the gathered ideas C) Social media is an excellent tool for honest and frequent communication with the customer base	The study investigates the external impact of social media on idea creation.
2018	Alalwan, A. A.	Investigating the impact of social media advertising features on customer purchase intention	Validated Learning	A) Purchase intention has its predictors B) By analyzing social media advertisements, it is possible to predict purchase intention C) Parts of the unified theory of acceptance and use of technology applied to the social media context: performance expectancy connected to extrinsic motivation and hedonic motivation related to intrinsic motivation	The paper identifies the main factors to predict purchase intention in connection to social media by applying several fragments of the unified theory of acceptance and use of technology.

Table 10.4: Key findings of the primary literature (Part III).

Year	Authors	Title	LSM Field	Main Statements	Objective
2016	Floreddu, P. B. Cabiddu, F.	Social media communication strategies	Customer Development	A) Social media can be used at a meager cost and can be used easily B) Social media allows an interactive exchange between customer and company C) Through social media, the company can receive unfiltered feedback from the customer in real-time	The authors identify an effective social media communication strategy to exchange with the core customer and receive honest feedback.
2020	Peralta, C. B. d. L. Echeveste, M. E. Lermen, F. H. Marcon, A. Tortorella, G.	A framework proposition to identify customer value through lean practices	Lean Structure	A) For innovation management within firms generating customer value is the key B) 33 practices were found for supporting capturing customer value C) Often, by using a mix of methods, best results can be achieved	This paper's objective is to achieve customer value through lean practices and various customer relationship-building methods.
2014	Gifu, D. Teodorescu, M.	Communication process in a lean concept	Lean Structure	A) Communication is an integrated process and not a single event B) Waste drivers of communication are: deficient information quality, ineffective communication, unnecessary detail, and accuracy C) Distance affects the quality of information	The authors applied the systems theory to identify the continual stages of input, throughput (processing), and output, which demonstrate the concept of openness/closeness.

Table 10.4 (continued)

Year	Authors	Title	LSM Field	Main Statements	Objective
2012	Steinemann, A. Wampfler, S. Kennel, T. Kunz, A.	Definition and analysis of a lean communication theory	Lean Structure	A) Often, the choice of the communication tool to get in contact with the customer seems to be wrong B) Lean communication theory contains guidelines for the behavioral code for standard business communication C) Main problems are inadequate communication, the wrong technology choice, and bad timing	In this paper, the authors investigate the awareness of the correct use of communication tools and the optimization of communication behavior. To do so, the authors analyze the current behavior and offer an efficient lean communication theory.

Table 10.5: Key findings of the primary literature (Part IV).

Year	Authors	Title	LSM Field	Main Statements	Objective
2019	Redeker, G. A. Kessler, G. Z.Kipper, L. M.	Lean information for lean communication: Analysis of concepts, tools, references, and terms	Lean Structure	A) Lean communication and information processes aim to reduce waste and make general communication more efficient B) Within the literature, there is no precise method or process for general improvements C) Fixed communication rules and strategies help to make processes more efficient D) Waste drivers should be reduced within a learning communication process E) A method to implement lean information concepts is missing	This paper analyzes how lean information leads to lean communication by analyzing different articles quantitatively. Additionally, the researchers combine their findings with a case study. The authors identified a lack of a methodology for lean information concepts.

Table 10.5 (continued)

Year	Authors	Title	LSM Field	Main Statements	Objective
2020	De Cock, R Bruneel, J. Bobelyn, A.	Making the lean startup method work: The role of prior market knowledge	Lean Structure	A) The knowledge about conditions under which the lean startup method can be successful is not fully explored B) If the lean startup method is only used for product recurrence, this can lead to considerable problems C) One of the major problems is that it is often not easy to make market information usable for the company	Many growth-oriented ventures use the lean startup method for their development, but only parts of the method are often applied. This might lead to problems due to the limited market knowledge.
2015	Karimi, S. Naghibi, H. S.	Social Media Marketing (SMM) Strategies for small and medium Enterprises (SMEs)	Lean Structure	A) It is essential to use the right channel to reach the target group B) Success of campaigns can easily be tracked C) Creating good content is time-consuming and should be planned properly	The author presents concepts of social media as a marketing instrument. They explain the main reasons for using social media as a company and investigate with empirical analysis marketing techniques of SMEs.

Table 10.6: Key Findings of the primary literature (Part V).

Year	Authors	Title	LSM Field	Main Statements	Objective
2019	Wardati, N. K. Er, M.	The impact of social media usage on the sales process in small and medium enterprises (SMEs): A systematic literature review	Lean Structure	A) Social media is a helpful communication tool for organizations to achieve their goals. B) Facebook is the type of social media that's primarily investigated in the literature C) Products or services can be marketed more easily through social media	In this study, the authors analyzed the influence of the use of social media on the sales process with a focus on SMEs.
2021	Lizarelli, F. L. Torres, A. F. Antony, J. Ribeiro, R. Salentijn, W. Fernandes, M. M. Campos, A. T.	Critical success factors and challenges for lean Startup: A systematic literature review	Persevere or Pivot	A) Customer feedback should be obtained as early as possible within a development process B) Lean processes can deliver products and services better, faster, and reduce costs C) Companies should constantly evaluate what part of the venture can implement lean. Otherwise, a lean implementation might also be negative	The authors are pointing out that implementing lean processes and information flows can also negatively influence performance. It is crucial to identify suitable areas where it makes sense to change processes and make them leaner.

Table 10.6 (continued)

Year	Authors	Title	LSM Field	Main Statements	Objective
2019	Balocco, R. Cavallo, A. Ghezzi, A. Berbegal-Mirabent, J.	Lean business models change process in digital entrepreneurship	Persevere or Pivot	A) Business model change frequently occurs, especially in digital industries B) A lean framework can help through validated learning so that companies can develop and restructure processes in a more efficient way C) The environment is constantly changing, and by implementing a continuous customers' feedback process, business models can change in a customer-oriented manner	The article focuses on changing business models and innovation processes. The authors are suggesting that lean perspectives can be implemented in several areas.

Table 10.7: Key findings of the primary literature (Part VI).

Year	Authors	Title	LSM Field	Main Statements	Objective
2018	Bortolini, R. F. Cortimiglia, M. Danilevicz, A. d. M. F. Ghezzi, A.	Lean Startup: A comprehensive historical review	Persevere or Pivot	A) An essential factor for success is based on the companies' ability to adapt their business model dynamically and effectively B) Startups should adopt straightforward methods and processes that enable iterative development C) Lean and agile are two philosophies within the lean methodology	The article aims to present the lean startup methodology summarized from the literature. In doing so, all relevant parts of the method are addressed, and the principle of an agile and lean approach is fundamentally presented.
2021	Jesemann, I. Beichter, T. Constantinescu, C.Herburger, K. Rüger, M.	Investigation of the "lean startup" approach in large manufacturing companies towards customer driven product innovation in SMEs	Validated Learning	A) Lean startup methods can be used to adapt to changing market and customer need B) The goal of implementing agile methods is to reduce risks in the long term by flexibly adapting to markets C) Employees need to be well trained to engage with the customers and comprehend their needs and wishes	Customer-driven innovation is often used within manufacturing companies. When the development costs for a product are high, the return of investment for integrating customers into the development process can be achieved very fast.

Table 10.8: Key findings of the primary literature (Part VII).

Year	Authors	Title	LSM Field	Main Statements	Objective
2015	Atanassova, I. Clark, L.	Social media practices in SME marketing activities: A theoretical framework and research agenda	Validated Learning	A) SMEs can use social media to gain market intelligence B) Dynamic capabilities theory can be used to explain how organizations acquire new knowledge C) Day-to-day interactions become a resource of knowledge gained from social media D) Social media practices should always match with the marketing strategy E) Social media can be used to find resources outside and inside company boundaries F) Key is to build a strong relationship with the core customers and understand what they want and need	The study combines different topics such as SME marketing, social media, and dynamic capabilities to help SMEs develop and refine marketing practices.
2009	Mangold, W. G. Faulds, D. J.	Social media: The new hybrid element of the promotion mix	Validated Learning	A) Social media to stimulate consumer conversations about a new product to implement insights B) Storytelling in social media leaves a more accessible memorable message for the customer C) Companies should use social media as it becomes more and more critical for consumer purchase intention	The article aims to show the relevance of social media integration into integrated marketing communications of a company to managers.

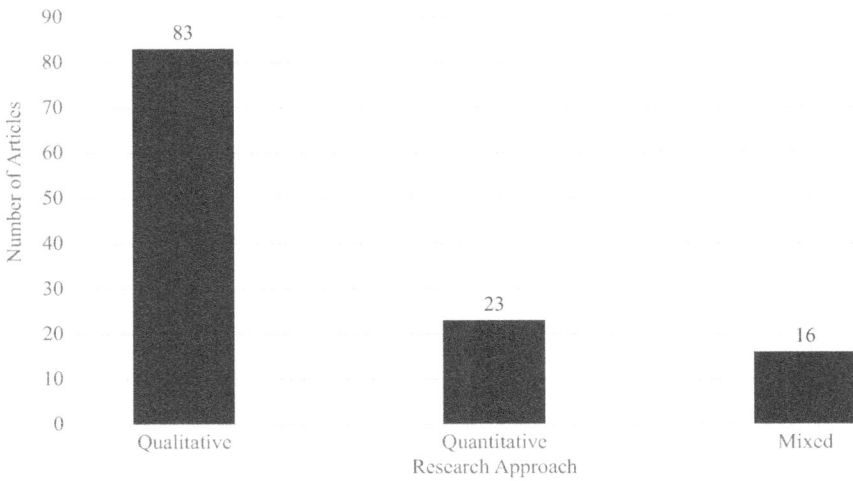

Figure 10.10: SLR – Distribution of qualitative, quantitative, or mixed-method articles.

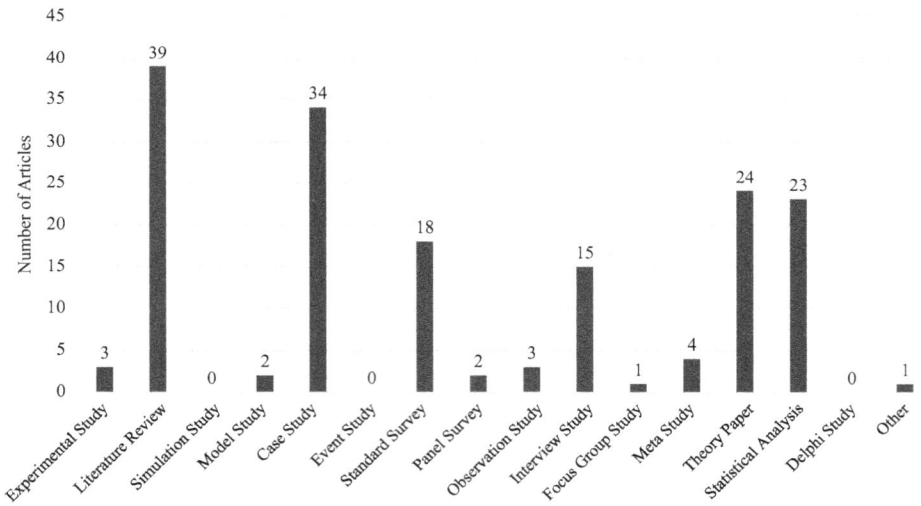

Figure 10.11: SLR – Used research methods (min. one max. two per article).

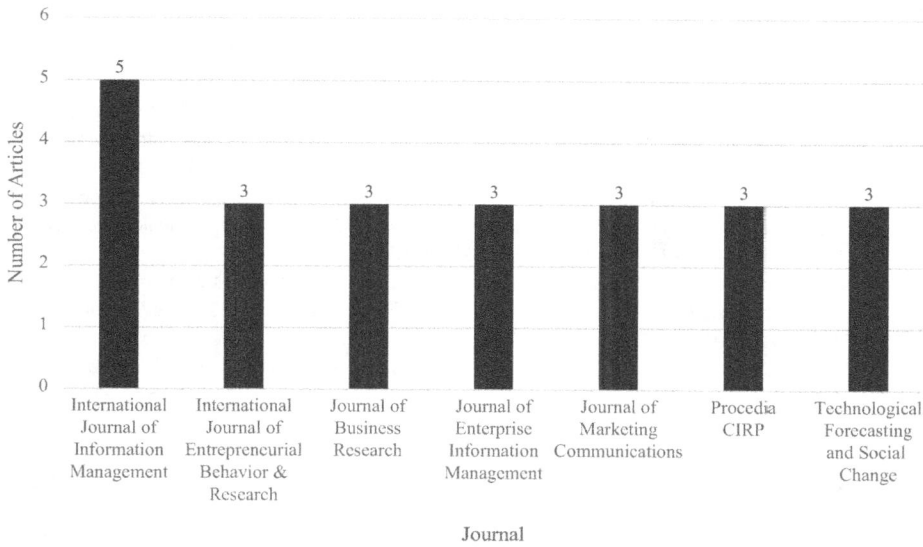

Figure 10.12: SLR – Most relevant journals for the topic.

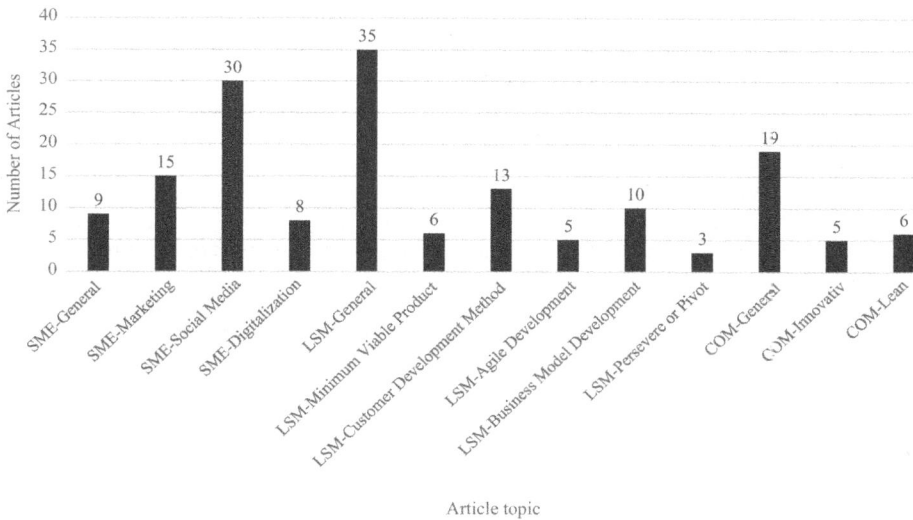

Figure 10.13: SLR – distribution of article topics (min. one max. two per article).

References

Alalwan, A.A. (2018). Investigating the impact of social media advertising features on customer purchase intention. *International Journal of Information, Business and Management, 42*, 65–77.

Appel, G., Grewal, L., Hadi, R., & Stephen, A.T. (2020). The future of social media in marketing. *Journal of the Academy of Marketing Science, 48*(1), 79–95. https://doi.org/10.1007/s11747-019-00695-1

Ashley, C., & Tuten, T. (2015). Creative strategies in social media marketing: an exploratory study of branded social content and consumer engagement: Creative strategies in social media. *Psychology and Marketing, 32*(1), 15–27. https://doi.org/10.1002/mar.20761

Atanassova, I., & Clark, L. (2015). Social media practices in SME marketing activities: A theoretical framework and research agenda. *Journal of Customer Behaviour, 14*(2), 163–183. https://doi.org/10.1362/147539215X14373846805824

Bajwa, S.S., Wang, X., Duc, A.N., & Abrahamsson, P. (2016). How do software startups pivot? Empirical results from a multiple case study. In A. Maglyas & A.–L. Lamprecht (Eds.), *Software business* (Vol. 240, pp. 169–176). Springer International Publishing. https://doi.org/10.1007/978-3-319-40515-5_14

Balocco, R., Cavallo, A., Ghezzi, A., & Berbegal-Mirabent, J. (2019). Lean business models change process in digital entrepreneurship. *Business Process Management Journal, 25*(7), 1520–1542. https://doi.org/10.1108/BPMJ-07-2018-0194

Barlatier, P.–J., & Josserand, E. (2018). Delivering open innovation promises through social media. *Journal of Business Strategy, 39*(6), 21–28. https://doi.org/10.1108/JBS-12-2017-0175

Bengtsson, M. (2016). How to plan and perform a qualitative study using content analysis. *NursingPlus Open, 2*, 8–14. https://doi.org/10.1016/j.npls.2016.01.001

Bhamu, J., & Singh Sangwan, K. (2014). Lean manufacturing: Literature review and research issues. *International Journal of Operations and Production Management, 34*(7), 876–940. https://doi.org/10.1108/IJOPM-08-2012-0315

Bharati, P., Du, K., Chaudhury, A., & Agrawal, N.M. (2021). Idea co-creation on social media platforms: Towards a theory of social ideation. *ACM SIGMIS Database: The DATABASE for Advances in Information Systems, 52*(3), 9–38. https://doi.org/10.1145/3481629.3481632

Blank, S.G. (2013). Why the lean start-up changes everything. *Harvard Business Review.*

Blank, S.G. (2015). The path to the epiphany: The customer development model. *Revista Cuatrimestral de Las Facultades de Derecho y Ciencias Económicas y Empresariales, 94*, 24.

Blank, S.G., & Dorf, R. (2017). *Das Handbuch für Startups* (K. Lichtenberg, Trans.; 2nd corrected reprint). O'Reilly.

Bocken, N., & Snihur, Y. (2020). Lean startup and the business model: Experimenting for novelty and impact. *Long Range Planning, 53*(4), 101953. https://doi.org/10.1016/j.lrp.2019.101953

Bortolini, R.F., Nogueira Cortimiglia, M., Danilevicz, A. de M. F., & Ghezzi, A. (2018). Lean startup: A comprehensive historical review. *Management Decision*, ahead-of-print. https://doi.org/10.1108/MD-07-2017-0663

Carroll, R., & Casselman, R.M. (2019). The lean discovery process: The case of raiserve. *Journal of Small Business and Enterprise Development, 26*(6/7), 765–782. https://doi.org/10.1108/JSBED-04-2019-0124

Chan, C.M.L., Teoh, S.Y., Yeow, A., & Pan, G. (2019). Agility in responding to disruptive digital innovation: Case study of an SME. *Information Systems Journal, 29*(2), 436–455. https://doi.org/10.1111/isj.12215

Chesbrough, H., & Tucci, C.L. (2020). The interplay between open innovation and lean startup, or, why large companies are not large versions of startups. *Strategic Management Review, 1*(2), 277–303. https://doi.org/10.1561/111.00000013

Clutterbuck, P., Rowlands, T., & Seamons, O. (2009). A case study of SME web application development effectiveness via agile methods. *The Electronic Journal Information Systems Evaluation, 12*(1), 13–26.

Colazo, J. (2020). Changes in communication patterns when implementing lean. *International Journal of Quality and Reliability Management, 38*(1), 296–316. https://doi.org/10.1108/IJQRM-10-2019-0323

De Cock, R., Bruneel, J., & Bobelyn, A. (2020). Making the lean start-up method work: The role of prior market knowledge. *Journal of Small Business Management, 58*(5), 975–1002. https://doi.org/10.1111/jsbm.12506

Dwivedi, Y.K., Ismagilova, E., Hughes, D.L., Carlson, J., Filieri, R., Jacobson, J., Jain, V., Karjaluoto, H., Kefi, H., Krishen, A.S., Kumar, V., Rahman, M.M., Raman, R., Rauschnabel, P.A., Rowley, J., Salo, J., Tran, G.A., & Wang, Y. (2021). Setting the future of digital and social media marketing research: Perspectives and research propositions. *International Journal of Information Management, 59.* https://doi.org/10.1016/j.ijinfomgt.2020.102168

Eagleman, A.N. (2013). Acceptance, motivations, and usage of social media as a marketing communications tool amongst employees of sport national governing bodies. *Sport Management Review, 16.*

Eckert, R. (2017). *Lean Startup in Konzernen und Mittelstandsunternehmen: Ergebnisse einer Expertenbefragung und Handlungsempfehlungen.* Springer Fachmedien Wiesbaden. https://doi.org/10.1007/978-3-658-15775-3

Eisenhardt, K.M., & Martin, J.A. (2000). *Dynamic capabilities: What are they?*

Eisenmann, T., Ries, E., & Dillard, S. (2011). Hypothesis-driven entrepreneurship: The lean startup. *Harvard Business School Entrepreneurial Management Case,* Case no. 812–095.

Elmadag, A.B., & Peneklioglu, O. (2018). Developing brand loyalty among SMEs: Is communication the key? *Small Enterprise Research, 25*(3), 239–256. https://doi.org/10.1080/13215906.2018.1522271

Elo, S., & Kyngäs, H. (2008). The qualitative content analysis process. *Journal of Advanced Nursing, 62*(1), 107–115. https://doi.org/10.1111/j.1365-2648.2007.04569.x

Ferreira, J.J.M., Fernandes, C.I., and Kraus, S. (2019). Entrepreneurship research: Mapping intellectual structures and research trends. *Review of Managerial Science, 13*(1), 181–205. https://doi.org/10.1007/s11846-017-0242-3

Floreddu, P.B., & Cabiddu, F. (2016). Social media communication strategies. *Journal of Services Marketing, 30*(5), 490–503. https://doi.org/10.1108/JSM-01-2015-0036

Fraccastoro, S., Gabrielsson, M., & Pullins, E.B. (2021). The integrated use of social media, digital, and traditional communication tools in the B2B sales process of international SMEs. *International Business Review, 30*(4). https://doi.org/10.1016/j.ibusrev.2020.101776

Frederiksen, D.L., & Brem, A. (2017). How do entrepreneurs think they create value? A scientific reflection of Eric Ries' Lean Startup approach. *International Entrepreneurship and Management Journal, 13*(1), 169–189. https://doi.org/10.1007/s11365-016-0411-x

Ghezzi, A. (2019). Digital startups and the adoption and implementation of lean startup approaches: Effectuation, bricolage and opportunity creation in practice. *Technological Forecasting and Social Change, 146,* 945–960. https://doi.org/10.1016/j.techfore.2018.09.017

Ghezzi, A. (2020). How entrepreneurs make sense of lean startup approaches: Business models as cognitive lenses to generate fast and frugal heuristics. *Technological Forecasting and Social Change, 161.* https://doi.org/10.1016/j.techfore.2020.120324

Ghezzi, A., & Cavallo, A. (2020). Agile business model innovation in digital entrepreneurship: Lean startup approaches. *Journal of Business Research, 110,* 519–537. https://doi.org/10.1016/j.jbusres.2018.06.013

Gifu, D., & Teodorescu, M. (2014). Communication process in a lean concept. *International Letters of Social and Humanistic Sciences, 28,* 119–127. https://doi.org/10.18052/www.scipress.com/ILSHS.28.119

Hsieh, H.-F., & Shannon, S.E. (2005). Three approaches to qualitative content analysis. *Qualitative Health Research, 15*(9), 1277–1288. https://doi.org/10.1177/1049732305276687

Hutton, G., & Fosdick, M. (2011). The globalization of social media: Consumer relationships with brands evolve in the digital space. *Journal of Advertising Research, 51*(4), 564–570. https://doi.org/10.2501/JAR-51-4-564-570

Isari, D., Pontiggia, A., & Virili, F. (2016). *Working with tweets: The effectiveness of lean communication in collaborative problem-solving.*

Jesemann, I., Beichter, T., Constantinescu, C., Herburger, K., & Rüger, M. (2021). Investigation of the "lean startup" approach in large manufacturing companies towards customer driven product innovation in SMEs. *Procedia CIRP, 99*, 711–716. https://doi.org/10.1016/j.procir.2021.03.095

Jesemann, I., Beichter, T., Herburger, K., Constantinescu, C., & Rüger, M. (2020). Migration of the lean-startup approach from high-tech startups towards product design in large manufacturing companies. *Procedia CIRP, 91*, 594–599. https://doi.org/10.1016/j.procir.2020.03.110

Kamboj, S., & Sarmah, B. (2018). Construction and validation of the customer social participation in brand communities scale. *Internet Research, 28*(1), 46–73. https://doi.org/10.1108/IntR-01-2017-0011

Karimi, S., & Naghibi, H.S. (2015). Social media marketing (SM) strategies for small and medium enterprises (SMEs). *International Journal of Information, Business and Management, 7*(4), 86–98.

Kent, M.L., & Li, C. (2020). Toward a normative social media theory for public relations. *Public Relations Review, 46*(1). https://doi.org/10.1016/j.pubrev.2019.101857

Khirfan, L., Peck, M., & Mohtat, N. (2020). Systematic content analysis: A combined method to analyze the literature on the daylighting (de-culverting) of urban streams. *MethodsX, 7*. https://doi.org/10.1016/j.mex.2020.100984

Kim, B., Kim, H., & Jeon, Y. (2018). Critical success factors of a design startup business. *Sustainability, 10*(9). https://doi.org/10.3390/su10092981

Kraus, S., Breier, M., & Dasí-Rodríguez, S. (2020). The art of crafting a systematic literature review in entrepreneurship research. *International Entrepreneurship and Management Journal, 16*(3), 1023–1042. https://doi.org/10.1007/s11365-020-00635-4

Leatherbee, M., & Katila, R. (2020). The lean startup method: Early-stage teams and hypothesis-based probing of business ideas. *Strategic Entrepreneurship Journal, 14*(4), 570–593. https://doi.org/10.1002/sej.1373

Lee, S., Park, G., Yoon, B., & Park, J. (2010). Open innovation in SMEs – An intermediated network model. *Research Policy, 39*(2), 290–300. https://doi.org/10.1016/j.respol.2009.12.009

Ling, K., Ludford, P., Wang, X., & Chang Klarissa. (2006). *Using Social Psychology to Motivate Contributions to Online Communities, 10*(4).

Lizarelli, F.L., Torres, A.F., Antony, J., Ribeiro, R., Salentijn, W., Fernandes, M.M., & Campos, A.T. (2021). Critical success factors and challenges for lean startup: A systematic literature review. *The TQM Journal*, ahead-of-print. https://doi.org/10.1108/TQM-06-2021-0177

Mangold, W.G., & Faulds, D.J. (2009). Social media: The new hybrid element of the promotion mix. *Business Horizons, 52*(4), 357–365. https://doi.org/10.1016/j.bushor.2009.03.002

Mansoori, Y. (2017). Enacting the lean startup methodology: The role of vicarious and experiential learning processes. *International Journal of Entrepreneurial Behavior and Research, 23*(5), 812–838. https://doi.org/10.1108/IJEBR-06-2016-0195

Maurya, A. (2012). *Running lean: Iterate from plan A to a plan that works* (2nd ed.). O'Reilly.

Melander, L. (2019). Customer involvement in product development: Using voice of the customer for innovation and marketing. *Benchmarking: An International Journal, 27*(1), 215–231. https://doi.org/10.1108/BIJ-04-2018-0112

Müller, R., Vette, M., Hörauf, L., Speicher, C., & Burkhard, D. (2017). Lean information and communication tool to connect shop and top floor in small and medium-sized enterprises. *Procedia Manufacturing, 11*, 1043–1052. https://doi.org/10.1016/j.promfg.2017.07.215

Newbert, S.L., Tornikoski, E.T., & Augugliaro, J. (2020). To get out of the building or not? That is the question: The benefits (and costs) of customer involvement during the startup process. *Journal of Business Venturing Insights, 14*. https://doi.org/10.1016/j.jbvi.2020.e00209

Osterwalder, A., Pigneur, Y., & Tucci, C.L. (2005). Clarifying business models: Origins, present, and future of the concept. *Communications of the Association for Information Systems, 16*. https://doi.org/10.17705/1CAIS.01601

Öztamur, D., & Karakadilar, İ.S. (2014). Exploring the role of social media for SMEs: As a new marketing strategy tool for the firm performance perspective. *Procedia – Social and Behavioral Sciences, 150,* 511–520. https://doi.org/10.1016/j.sbspro.2014.09.067

Peralta, C.B.d.L., Echeveste, M.E., Lermen, F.H., Marcon, A., & Tortorella, G. (2020). A framework proposition to identify customer value through lean practices. *Journal of Manufacturing Technology Management, 31*(4), 725–747. https://doi.org/10.1108/JMTM-06-2019-0209

Pillai, S.D., Goldfarb, B., & Kirsch, D.A. (2020). The origins of firm strategy: Learning by economic experimentation and strategic pivots in the early automobile industry. *Strategic Management Journal, 41*(3), 369–399. https://doi.org/10.1002/smj.3102

Redeker, G.A., Kessler, G.Z., & Kipper, L.M. (2019). Lean information for lean communication: Analysis of concepts, tools, references, and terms. *International Journal of Information Management, 47,* 31–43. https://doi.org/10.1016/j.ijinfomgt.2018.12.018

Ries, E. (2017). *The lean startup: How today's entrepreneurs use continuous innovation to create radically successful businesses* (Currency international edition). Currency.

Santos, A.C.O., da Silva, C.E.S., Braga, R.A.d.S., Corrêa, J.É., & de Almeida, F.A. (2020). Customer value in lean product development: Conceptual model for incremental innovations. *Systems Engineering, 23*(3), 281–293. https://doi.org/10.1002/sys.21514

Schmitt, B. (2012). The consumer psychology of brands. *Journal of Consumer Psychology, 22*(1), 7–17.

Seggie, S.H., Soyer, E., & Pauwels, K.H. (2017). Combining big data and lean startup methods for business model evolution. *AMS Review, 7*(3–4), 154–169. https://doi.org/10.1007/s13162-017-0104-9

Shah, R., & Ward, P.T. (2003). Lean manufacturing: Context, practice bundles, and performance. *Journal of Operations Management, 21*(2), 129–149. https://doi.org/10.1016/S0272-6963(02)00108-0

Shawky, S., Kubacki, K., Dietrich, T., & Weaven, S. (2020). A dynamic framework for managing customer engagement on social media. *Journal of Business Research, 121,* 567–577. https://doi.org/10.1016/j.jbusres.2020.03.030

Shepherd, D.A., & Gruber, M. (2020). The lean startup framework: Closing the academic–practitioner divide. *Entrepreneurship Theory and Practice.* https://doi.org/10.1177/1042258718899415

Silva, D.S., Ghezzi, A., Aguiar, R.B. de, Cortimiglia, M.N., & ten Caten, C.S. (2019). Lean startup, agile methodologies and customer development for business model innovation: A systematic review and research agenda. *International Journal of Entrepreneurial Behavior and Research,* ahead-of-print. https://doi.org/10.1108/IJEBR-07-2019-0425

Soares, S., & Teixeira, L. (2014). Lean information management in industrial context: An experience based on a practical case. *International Journal of Industrial Engineering and Management, 5*(2), 107–114.

Steinemann, A., Wampfler, S., Kennel, T., & Kunz, A. (2012). *Definition and analysis of a lean communication theory.* Ninth International Symposium on Tools and Methods of Competitive Engineering (TMCE 2012), Karlsruhe, Germany.

Teece, D.J., Pisano, G., & Shuen, A. (1997). Dynamic capabilities and strategic management. *Strategic Management Journal, 18*(7), 509–533.

Tripathi, N., Oivo, M., Liukkunen, K., & Markkula, J. (2019). Startup ecosystem effect on minimum viable product development in software startups. *Information and Software Technology, 114,* 77–91. https://doi.org/10.1016/j.infsof.2019.06.008

von Krogh, G. (2012). How does social software change knowledge management? Toward a strategic research agenda. *Journal of Strategic Information Systems, 21,* 154–164.

Wardati, N.K., & Er, M. (2019). The impact of social media usage on the sales process in small and medium enterprises (SMEs): A systematic literature review. *Procedia Computer Science, 161,* 976–983. https://doi.org/10.1016/j.procs.2019.11.207

Allan Villegas-Mateos

11 Challenges for Expatriate SMEs Entrepreneurs in a Rentier State Entrepreneurial Ecosystem

Abstract: This chapter aims to provide a micro-level analysis of the challenges of expatriates that have founded an SME in a rentier state entrepreneurial ecosystem, which in turn highlights the barriers in the local conditions and the nationality background influence to deal with them. To conduct the study, 15 in-depth semi-structured interviews were conducted in 2021 with expatriate SMEs entrepreneurs who have established a business within the last three years in Qatar, which is located in the Middle East and is part of the Gulf Cooperation Council states. The data was analyzed with a descriptive and data triangulation method. The findings suggest that being an expatriate is a disadvantage to accessing resources of the entrepreneurial ecosystem. Still, the economic and market conditions are attractive to pursue entrepreneurial opportunities despite the challenges. The literature on rentier states entrepreneurial ecosystems remains scarce, and these type of economies create an artificial environment for entrepreneurial activities.

Keywords: immigrant entrepreneurs, knowledge-based economy, entrepreneurial ecosystem, Middle East

Introduction

Several nations have recognized the importance of small and medium-sized enterprises (SMEs) and have formulated policies to encourage, support, and fund them (Okpara & Kumbiadis, 2008). The reason is that SMEs are considered the engines of worldwide economies and the primary sources of job creation (Wiklund et al., 2019). The evidence also shows that the impact of business creation and development on economic growth may be different across nations (Sternberg & Wennekers, 2005). Therefore, it is highly relevant to conduct regional and country comparative studies to understand how to support SMEs better. In this sense, the entrepreneurial ecosystem (EE) approach tries to understand the mechanisms underlying new firm creation dynamics and existing business support that helps to develop tools, public policies, and other support systems that enhance entrepreneurship activity outcomes (Villegas Mateos & Amorós, 2019; Cavallo et al., 2018). The EE literature has attracted particular attention from academics, entrepreneurial leaders, and policymakers that participate

Allan Villegas-Mateos, HEC Paris, Qatar

https://doi.org/10.1515/9783110747652-012

in the ecosystem (Stam, 2015). This growing focus on EEs has caused many unexplored and underexplored areas to emerge, so scholars have called for theoretical and empirical studies to help fill gaps in the literature (Alaassar et al., 2021; Audretsch et al., 2018; Brown & Mason, 2017; Spigel, 2017; Stam, 2015).

On the other hand, the EE literature focuses mainly on the structural and systemic conditions that enhance entrepreneurial activities (Stam, 2015). Consequently, it is common to find empirical studies of EEs based on secondary indicators at the country level trying to explain variations in entrepreneurship across countries (Chelariu et al., 2008), and, more recently, more studies based on primary data at regional levels have emerged (Fritsch, 2013; Tsvetkova, 2015; Bruns et al., 2017; Cavallo et al., 2018; Purbasari et al., 2019; Aljarwan et al., 2019; Villegas Mateos & Amorós, 2019; Villegas-Mateos, 2020). It seems that as research evolves the level of analysis that EEs require is passing from the macro-level to the meso-level and now to the micro-level. The macro-level studies focus on institutional factors that determine the structure, roles, and "rules of the game in a society" and influence individual behavior (North, 1990). While the meso-level in entrepreneurship studies the sub-national level of regions, suggesting it is the most appropriate spatial level to identify and measure EEs since the regional entrepreneurship literature provides striking evidence that entrepreneurship is primarily a regional (or local) event (Sternberg et al., 2019), the studies still focus on institutional factors. Finally, the micro-level research of EEs remains scarce when the evidence highlights the need for micro-level analyses that will advance our understanding of how the micro-level interplays with the macro-level (Cunningham & Menter, 2020). Therefore, this chapter focuses on studying the micro-level of EEs combined with the international context for which individual actors and how their actions, behaviors, and approaches are explored.

The individual actors on EEs are naturally the entrepreneurs (Villegas Mateos & Amorós, 2019; Villegas-Mateos, 2020). Thus, to address this explorative study, the author used a qualitative approach by gathering interviews of expatriate entrepreneurs that own an SME established in the State of Qatar. Expatriate entrepreneurs are privileged immigrants from abroad with lives with better conditions than in their country of origin (Fechter, 2016). It is appropriate because the role of SMEs in EEs should be researched not only from the macro-level, but also from the micro-level (Cunningham et al., 2019). It is relevant because of the role of SMEs on the economy, but to determine how the EE should support them one should first determine the barriers to their development. Previous studies suggest that SMEs often face barriers founding the market and, in the environment, management problems and financial barriers (Samitowska, 2011). In this case, the State of Qatar provides an incredible landscape to analyze at the micro-level the role of SMEs owned by expatriates because the unemployment rate has been historically below 1%. Also, Qatar is a rentier state creating a contradiction between the economic reform and the structural logic of the economy because it artificially changes some conditions of the EE and produces a gap in the experience that Qatari entrepreneurs have in comparison with non-Qatari entrepreneurs. It means that the economy relies on revenues from hydrocarbon resources which are redistributed to its citizens, and it produces a psychological condition under this rentier mentally (Mahdavy, 1970; Beblawi, 1990; Ben Hassen, 2020). Additionally, in 2017, some of the neighboring Gulf Cooperation Council (GCC) states of Qatar (the United Arab Emirates, Kingdom of Bahrain, and Kingdom of Saudi Arabia) and Egypt initiated a commercial blockade that finished at the beginning of 2021, so during this period the country was immersed in a crisis to satisfy the domestic demand for essential goods, but soon government and entrepreneurs invested in the local production of food, utilities, and services, among others. Therefore, considering that the literature lacks a holistic international lens that can widen our understanding of this phenomenon and pave a new way of thinking regarding the role of EEs in the global context (van Weele et al. 2018), this research is relevant since it studies an underexplored region in the literature of EEs from a perspective with even less visibility which is the micro-level of expatriate SMEs entrepreneurs.

The rest of the chapter is as follows. The next section, the theoretical development section, discusses the EE conditions and the status of the research and the case of rentier state ecosystems. The methodology section describes the sample, data collection, and analysis process. Then, the last three sections present the results, discussion, and implications, and limitations and future research, respectively.

Theoretical Development

Entrepreneurial Ecosystems (EEs)

"Entrepreneurial ecosystems have been recognized as an organized attempt made in line with the formation and establishment of environments that increase the success of newly developed ventures" (Mohammadi & Karimi, 2021). To study EEs, many different definitions have emerged without a clear consensus yet, but most of them agree on the combination or interaction of elements or conditions that together sustain entrepreneurial activities (De Brito & Leitão, 2020). Velt et al. (2020) classified the studies through a bibliometric clustering mapping the most relevant research on EEs, resulting in six research themes: complexity, context, governance, geography, agency, and network perspectives. According to that research, the complexity perspective in EEs is the most cited, and it means studying the infrastructure of entrepreneurship, not as an individual endeavor but as a collective effort of numerous entrepreneurs from the public and private sectors, who become the system's driving force (Van de Ven, 1993). The definitions under the complexity perspective of EEs reflect a different configuration of the micro-foundations and subsequently its resource dependency and resilience that require appropriate strategies to foster entrepreneurial activities (Roundy, 2019; Roundy & Bayer, 2019). To measure the micro-foundations of EEs some perceptual techniques have been used (Liguori et al., 2019; Roundy & Fayard, 2019;

Villegas Mateos & Amorós, 2019; Villegas-Mateos, 2020). Consequently, this chapter follows the complexity perspective to understand how the micro-level interplays with the macro-level by studying stakeholders' perceptions (Cunningham et al., 2019; Cunningham & Menter, 2020). Following the proposition by Villegas-Mateos (2021) of five types of conditions that encompass the most critical institutional factors recognized by most of the EEs models in the literature (Reynolds et al., 2005; Isenberg, 2011; Feld, 2012; WEF, 2013; Mason and Brown, 2014; Stam, 2015; Cavallo et al., 2018), this chapter aims to explore the conditions that represent barriers. The five conditions are:
1) Education
2) Finance
3) Government
4) Support organizations
5) Entrepreneurship competitions and sponsors

Therefore, the following research question was posed:

RQ1. Which entrepreneurial ecosystem conditions represent the major barriers for expatriate entrepreneurs willing to create a new SME?

Rentier State Economies and the Case of Qatar

The concept of the rentier state has been one of the more frequent and functional descriptions of the economic environment in the GCC region (Ennis, 2013). There are three fundamental characteristics of a rentier state that can affect the economic climate and entrepreneurship within a country. The first one is that the economy relies on external revenue from the renting of non-reproducible resources rather than its productive capacity (Mahdavy, 1970). The GCC economies (the United Arab Emirates, Kingdom of Bahrain, Kingdom of Saudi Arabia, Sultanate of Oman, the State of Qatar, and the State of Kuwait) depend and will continue to remain dependent on hydrocarbons for the foreseeable future, according to a critical report by Moody's Investor Service. The second characteristic is that the principal recipient of the external rent is the state's government, which in turn distributes the rent to its citizens (Ben Hassen, 2020). Consequently, it is customary to find strongly protective regulations to get citizenship to protect and keep the wealth among natives, leading to the third characteristic. A rentier mentality among citizens: a psychological condition with profound consequences for productivity where contracts are given as an expression of gratitude rather than as a reflection of economic rationale (Beblawi, 1990). Therefore, the economic environment conditions of a rentier state can be summarized in three main ways: (1) income and resources availability; (2) protectionist government and political power; and (3) business culture.

In recent times, the rentier states depending on hydrocarbons revenues are experiencing internal pressures with rising populations and a decrease in oil and gas revenues because of the drop in prices. Noreng (2004) highlighted that a possible decline in oil revenues would help provoke a more liberal and democratic trend in politics and strengthen the private sector over the rentier state. The expatriate population distribution is the majority in most GCC economies since they are attracting talent because of their strategy to transform towards knowledge-based economies and reduce the dependency on the hydrocarbon revenues before the end of their reserve. For the case of Qatar, a GCC and rentier state economy with one of the highest GDP per capita in the world, the expatriate population represents 85%, with a concentration of around 90% of the population living in the capital city, Doha (Villegas-Mateos, 2021), which means that only 15% are Qatari citizens receiving rents from the state. Additionally, Qatar had a commercial blockade from 2017 to the beginning of 2021, provoking heavy domestic investments in strategic sectors to cover the internal demand for products and services. However, the government support programs were targeting companies where Qatari partners owned 51% or more of the company. Since then, regulations have been changing, and more free zones have been created for establishing 100% foreign-owned companies in Qatar. Accordingly, with the Qatar Free Zone Authority, Qatar is strategically located in the Middle East, some six hours by airplane to 60% of the world's population between Africa, Asia, and Europe.

Therefore, the following research question was posed:

RQ2. Do the economic environmental conditions of a rentier state represent the same opportunity for expatriate SME entrepreneurs as for local citizen entrepreneurs?

Methodology

This chapter follows an exploratory qualitative case study of Qatar's entrepreneurial ecosystem. The approach is appropriate for the type of research questions posed in this chapter, considering the methodologies used for entrepreneurship research and that the EE literature is in an early stage of development (Dana & Dana, 2005). The Qatari context was chosen because it contains all the elements of an entrepreneurial ecosystem as described by Villegas-Mateos (2021), and it offers a notably different context from a less explored region, the Middle East and GCC economies where the rentier state has been one of the more frequent and functional descriptions of the economic environment in the region (Ennis, 2013). In this context, the data collected was primary through 15 in-depth semi-structured interviews conducted during 2021 with expatriate entrepreneurs that own an SME established in Qatar during the previous three years distributed equally among three of the main economic sectors: (1) construction and real estate; (2) food and agriculture; and (3) information and communication technologies.

The selection was carried out by exploring the incubation center's success stories and using a snowball technique based on the perspective of business actors. The interviews were transcribed for analysis, as well as the additional documents and reports collected from the institutional sites of the interviewed participants. With evidence of conducting descriptive research with data triangulation to study EEs (Purbasari et al., 2019, this study followed the same method.

Results

Barriers to the Entrepreneurial Ecosystem

In terms of education, expatriate entrepreneurs mostly have college degrees related to the business they have, from engineers founding information and communication technology SMEs to MBA graduates involved in food or manufacturing companies. This has proved that Qatar is investing in the transformation to a knowledge-based economy because many expatriate entrepreneurs came first when hired by a company sponsoring their visa and residence permit before becoming entrepreneurs. Few of the interviewed earned their degrees in Qatar and then worked, with the average age of 32 years for when such individuals became entrepreneurs. Qatar has brought eight international university satellite campuses into a multi-million-dollar complex called Education City, founded by Qatar Foundation to foster the innovation ecosystem (Villegas-Mateos, 2021). However the problem is not to create talent, but motivate individuals to become entrepreneurs and provide them with the conditions to scale their businesses. However, the findings suggest that in the three main sectors studied in this chapter (food and agriculture, construction and real estate, and information and communication technologies), the entrepreneurs were pursuing an opportunity rather than a necessity. However, in terms of the operation of their businesses, 90% of them have faced problems finding human capital. For the information and communication technologies sector, the required talent is for highly skilled professionals, with the costs very high to attract them and support their living expenses in Qatar. Therefore, one finding is that some companies have part of their teams operating abroad in cheaper ecosystems. This is not feasible for food and agriculture, nor the construction and real estate where they need individuals on site. In one case from the information and communication technologies sector, half of the employees of a company are based in Doha, Qatar, including the expatriate founder, and the other half are working remotely in India.

Regarding finance, the interviewed expatriate entrepreneurs agreed that despite the country's wealth, accessing financial sources is complicated. From opening a bank account for the company to requesting a loan and raising capital, they all have struggled. Forty percent of them have raised pre-seed funding, while the rest have bootstrapped their business. The entrepreneurs that have sought to raise funding have found limited options because their company ownership is not majority Qatari. The Qatar Development Bank offers many programs and incentives but so far these are for Qatari companies, and those include subsidies for land, services, and registration, while a non-Qatari has to look for different support mechanisms and/or pay more to start the same business activity. The evidence of Qatar's entrepreneurial ecosystem highlights the deficit in access to venture capital (Villegas-Mateos, 2021); so far, there haven't been stories of raising more than a Series A round: "It took me three months to finish my company registration in Qatar, while at the same time for the same business activity, I registered another company in Dubai (United Arab Emirates) in only two weeks."

This quote from an interview represents the general perception of the business enabling environment, including government bureaucracy, regulations, and legal framework. In the 2019 edition of the Ease of Doing Business Index of the World Bank, Qatar was at the bottom of the GCC list with a value of 77, whereas the United Arab Emirates (UAE) had 16. The evidence found that for the 33% of cases in the sample that have a Qatari partner, the process was smooth and easy but was done by the Qatari partner directly through the Ministry of Commerce and Industry, with the other 30% cases that went through a formal incubation program linked to registration in a free zone and hence also had a good and easy experience; however, the other 34% of cases went through more extended and more expensive processes just for being expatriate entrepreneurs without a local partner. As part of the Ease of Doing Business Index is the number of days required to start a business, Qatar takes an average of nine days, less than the Kingdom of Saudi Arabia (10) and the State of Kuwait (19), but more than the Kingdom of Bahrain (8), Sultanate of Oman, and the UAE (4 days respectively). Accordingly to the interviewed expatriates, this time could be longer when you are not a Qatari citizen or don't have at least one Qatari partner. The ownership rule did begin to change for some priority sectors with the creation of free zones supported by the Ministry of Commerce and Industry and Qatar's new Foreign Investment Law (2019). Still, its implementation was not wholly reflected in the government offices until 2021 (Villegas-Mateos, 2021). Another finding was that the incubated companies in the sample were in a government-supported incubation program.

The support organizations in Qatar include around 12 incubation and acceleration centers, with only one private incubator until 2020. By 2021 new private incubation centers emerged as a response to the need of entrepreneurs for higher-level support. The founders of SMEs incubated, got matched to local citizens for commercial registration, avoiding 100% foreign ownership. Despite the ownership ratio and incubation centers, the programs target technology and digital technologies. For food and agriculture, and construction and real estate, there have been no support organizations for expatriate entrepreneurs identified. As a result, 90% of the sample perceived it a disadvantage to be non-Qatari when starting and developing a business, and see having a Qatari partner as a strategy to facilitate access to finance, smoother regulation, and legal procedures, as well as access to business networks. However, during the interviews, the entrepreneurs were asked if they perceived an improvement in the EE conditions compared to the previous year and how they felt they will evolve in the years to come, and all agreed that the EE conditions are significantly improving year by year, and that is not impossible to have a successful business in Qatar.

Answering RQ1, education is not a problem, but attracting talent is according to the expatriate experiences. Access to finance seems complicated and could be because of the lack of entrepreneurial experience of angel investors, with venture capital funds remaining scarce to facilitate scaling businesses. At the same time, most of the available funding sources require a full-time commitment and/or a majority Qatari shareholding, which for non-Qataris is an additional constraint related to the immigration policies. In the 2020 Qatar Venture Investment Report of Qatar Development Bank, companies in Qatar reported raising a total of about six million USD (22 million Qatari riyals) in 2020, a 9% growth compared with 2019, but which is a low number for the Middle East and North of Africa region (654 million USD in total) where the prime position that year with regards to investment value was the UAE with 37.5 million USD raised. Entrepreneurs feel the government has a very active role in the entrepreneurial ecosystem; however, they feel that most of the programs are not suitable for the sectors they are in or for the ownership split of their companies. Finally, the support organizations and entrepreneurship competitions are almost mandatory to participate in because of the facilities related to incorporation and registration rather than for the added value for the business model validation and exploitation through funding, mentorship, and training.

The Challenges for Expatriate SMEs Entrepreneurs

Sixty-three percent of the interviewed expatriate SMEs' entrepreneurs did not face difficulties in registering the company, and instead they were incubated given those facilities, or they have a Qatari partner that helped them; nevertheless, the general perceptions are that regulations and legal framework to register a company are too bureaucratic and not suitable enough for expatriates. As previously quoted, the challenges are then related to the business's daily operations, where finding clients involves either selling directly to consumers or from business to business. A finding that explains the difficulty is that when the blockade started in 2017, the national culture changed to producing and consuming Qatari products over those imported: "Starting the company was not the problem, getting the projects was because established companies expect you to be a Qatari business." Until 2021, most registered businesses have majority ownership by Qatari citizens, and the shareholding is even higher in the strategic sectors. This means that having a company in the food and agriculture sector requires competing against or negotiating with the local community since the blockade converted them into one of the most priority sectors to overcome the crisis in demand for essential need products. At retail, you would find the products labeled as "Qatari product" to identify them quickly, an initiative of the Qatar Development Bank to cause local consumption, but even if originating in Qatar, the business cannot be majority owned by an expatriate. Elsewhere, in construction and real estate, the most significant infrastructure projects are from the government, where the story is similar, although the interviewed expatriate entrepreneurs highlighted that speaking Arabic helps them a lot to negotiate. Finally, in the information and communication technologies, the challenge is different because it depends on exactly which product or service you are offering, as detailed by an individual in the following case: "My business model relies on technology for banks, I need them, and they need me, but in many negotiations, we have not reached an agreement only because I don't have a Qatari partner, and 90% of the banks are Qatari-owned."

This is an example of the rentier state mentality impacting the economic productivity of the nation (Beblawi, 1990), the entrepreneur is losing contracts based on his nationality. One of the cases of a SME in the construction sector mentioned that he started the company because of a contract arranged with a big oil company before quitting his job, so he registered the business to focus on this contract, but when formalizing the deal it failed for undisclosed terms, and he had to spin off the idea and applied to an incubation program that helped him access clients and to validate his business model.

On the other hand, one individual reported to be operating in Dubai (UAE) developing his information technology business but got a direct invitation from an incubation program linked to Qatar Development Bank to move his headquarters to Qatar, and they would provide office space, registration, and seed investment. He moved, and his experience was outstanding as a wholly foreign company, and he has been operating in Qatar since 2020. Nevertheless, he has a digital product that requires scale to international markets, so keeping contracts with Dubai companies was difficult in the middle of the blockade, but not being a Qatari national turned out to be an advantage. By 2021, it was expected that the end of the commercial blockade would impact the internationalization strategies followed by SMEs that had already started and were growing within the national market of 2.5 million people, but in terms of ecosystem support, the government could have tried to foster those firms more intensively: "The small market size of Qatar can be the biggest constrain to grow although it is compensated by the higher purchase power of the population, although, if you want to scale your business you have to think about exporting soon and just now [it] is starting to become easier."

The interview results showed a relationship between the entrepreneur's background to his internationalization vision of the business. All the expatriate SMEs entrepreneurs answered that they have thought about bringing their business to their country of origin. Some of them don't know how to do the internationalization, and entrepreneurs or founders from construction and real estate SMEs feel it is very complicated for their sector. The general perception is that with the blockade, the options to expand internationally were not in the closest countries, but now they perceive more significant opportunities and have heard of at least one government program to help them do it. Additionally, analyzing other Qatari companies and entrepreneurs, it seems that everyone has similar opportunities to expand their business abroad. One case is established in one of the Qatar Free Zones, Ras Bufontas, next to the Hamad International Airport in Doha, with custom fees exemption, 100% ownership, and facilities to repatriate resources. He said his location is strategic and he has been exporting to Asia and Europe since 2019.

Answering RQ2, in terms of the economic climate conditions, the opportunities are perceived as almost equal to Qataris as to non-Qatari entrepreneurs; nevertheless, in the local business landscape, to access resources, navigate through regulations, gain contracts, and negotiate and enter sales channels, the expatriates have more significant challenges. The market size, available income, and city landscape make it easier to produce and deliver products or services directly to customers and grow fast, although all the interviewed entrepreneurs feel that the labor costs are expensive, which can increase the operating costs and struggle to attract talent. The rentier state's income and resources availability conditions are then perceived as leveraged between expatriates and citizens, although, in practice, some economic sectors could be unbalanced. This is linked also to the second condition of protectionist government and political power since it is openly shown that there is higher support for Qatari-owned SMEs than for expatriate-owned SMEs by the governmental institutions through funding, land, and registration, among others. Finally, 66.7% of the expatriate SMEs entrepreneurs have experienced at least once that their business creation and development has been more challenging because of their immigration status, which supports the argument that in rentier states the third economic environment condition is the business culture. Aspects related to the culture like nationality, language, physical appearance, and successful background could be constraints when dealing with negotiations, considering that a significant portion of the SMEs are Qatari-owned companies.

Discussion and Implications

Studying EEs at the micro-level is an emerging trend in the field, and this chapter contributes to filling the gap in studies at that level and in a less explored region, the Middle East and GGC economies. The findings of this exploratory study aimed to provide an outlook of how the entrepreneurs at the micro-level are dealing with the macro-level conditions (Cunningham & Menter, 2020). For the case of Qatar, the results aim to serve for public policies improvement related to business registration procedures and easiness of immigration status to facilitate new expatriates to come and invest in this country, or it is the case of having lived there and evaluating a career change as entrepreneurs. The chapter provides expatriates, policymakers, and Qatari nationals with the latest experiences of SMEs founded or co-founded by expatriates contributing to the local economic growth, aiming to formulate policies to encourage support and funding of SMEs (Okpara & Kumbiadis, 2008). The results can be extended to the comparative analysis of GCC economies where similar economic conditions are set for expatriates, given that the rentier states are the most common types of government in the GCC region (Ennis, 2013).

Limitations and Future Research

The study was limited to food and agriculture, construction and real estate, and information and communication technologies sectors. Accordingly, to the Ministry of Commerce and Industry, the priority sectors represent opportunities, especially for non-Qataris, because more facilities have been provided to facilitate investing in them and creating companies, besides the already studied are mining and energies, tourism, health, logistics services, cultural, sports and leisure services, and consultancy. To expand the understanding in the literature about expatriate entrepreneurship in a rentier state entrepreneurial ecosystem, future studies should aim to study and compare different sectors. Another limitation could be the sample size and selection; while the author relied on public information to approach the initial entrepreneurs, the snowball effect might create a bias in the perceptions evaluated. Avenues for future research should include incorporating different sectors, expanding the sample size, and conducting confirmatory studies of the findings that could consist of quantitative methodologies. Lastly, the growing trend of studies based on primary data at regional levels suggests expanding the analysis to other GCC economies (Fritsch, 2013; Tsvetkova, 2015; Bruns et al., 2017; Cavallo et al., 2018; Purbasari et al., 2019; Aljarwan et al., 2019; Villegas Mateos & Amorós, 2019; Villegas-Mateos, 2020).

References

Alaassar, A., Mention, A., & Helge Aas, T. (2021). Ecosystem dynamics: exploring the interplay within fintech entrepreneurial ecosystems. *Small Business Economics*, in press. https://doi.org/10.1007/s11187-021-00505-5

Aljarwan, A.A., Yahya, B.A., Almarzooqi, B.M., & Mezher, T. (2019). Examining the framework of entrepreneurial ecosystems: A case study on the United Arab Emirates. *International Journal of Entrepreneurship*, 23(3).

Audretsch, D., Mason, C., Miles, M.P., & O'Connor, A. (2018). The dynamics of entrepreneurial ecosystems. *Entrepreneurship & Regional Development*, 30(3–4), 471–474. https://doi.org/10.1080/08985626.2018.1436035

Beblawi, H. (1990). The rentier state in the Arab world. In G. Luciani (Ed.), *The Arab state* (pp. 85–98). Routledge.

Ben Hassen, T. (2020). The entrepreneurship ecosystem in the ICT sector in Qatar: Local advantages and constraints. *Journal of Small Business and Enterprise Development, 27*(2), 177–195. https://doi.org/10.1108/JSBED-04-2019-0119

Brown, R., & Mason, C. (2017). Looking inside the spiky bits: A critical review and conceptualisation of entrepreneurial ecosystems. *Small Business Economics, 49*(1), 11–30. https://doi.org/10.1007/s11187-017-9865-7

Bruns, K., Bosma, N., Sanders, M., & Schramm, M. (2017). Searching for the existence of entrepreneurial ecosystems: A regional cross-section growth regression approach. *Small Business Economics, 49*(1), 31–54. https://doi.org/10.1007/s11187-017-9866-6

Cavallo, A., Ghezzi, A., Colombelli, A., & Casali, G.L. (2018). Agglomeration dynamics of innovative start-ups in Italy beyond the industrial district era. *International Entrepreneurship and Management Journal, 16*(1), 1–24.

Chelariu, C., Brashear, T.G., Osmonbekov, T., & Zait, A. (2008). Entrepreneurial propensity in a transition economy: Exploring micro-level and meso-level cultural antecedents. *Journal of Business & Industrial Marketing, 23*(6), 405–415. https://doi.org/10.1108/08858620810894454

Cunningham, J.A., & Menter, M. (2020). Micro-level academic entrepreneurship: A research agenda. *Journal of Management Development* (ahead-of-print). https://doi.org/10.1108/JMD-04-2020-0129

Cunningham, J.A., Menter, M., & Wirsching, K. (2019). Entrepreneurial ecosystem governance: A principal investigator-centered governance framework. *Small Business Economics, 52*(2), 545-562.

Dana, L.P., & Dana, T.E. (2005). Expanding the scope of methodologies used in entrepreneurship research. *International Journal of Entrepreneurship and Small Business, 2*(1), 79–88.

De Brito, S., & Leitão, J. (2020). Mapping and defining entrepreneurial ecosystems: A systematic literature review. *Knowledge Management Research & Practice.* https://doi.org/10.1080/14778238.2020.1751571

Ennis, C.A. (2013). *Rentier 2.0: Entrepreneurship promotion and the (Re) imagination of political economy in the gulf cooperation council countries.* Unpublished PhD thesis, University of Waterloo, Ontario.

Fechter, A.M. (2016). *Transnational lives: Expatriates in Indonesia.* Routledge.

Feld, B. (2012). *Startup communities: Building an entrepreneurial ecosystem in your city.* John Wiley and Sons.

Fritsch, M. (2013). New business formation and regional development: A survey and assessment of the evidence. *Foundations and Trends in Entrepreneurship, 9*(3), 249–364. http://dx.doi.org/10.1561/0300000043

Isenberg, D. (2011). *The entrepreneurship ecosystem strategy as a new paradigm for economic policy: Principles for cultivating entrepreneurship.* Presentation at the Institute of International and European Affairs.

Liguori, E., Bendickson, J., Solomon, S., & McDowell, W.C. (2019). Development of a multi-dimensional measure for assessing entrepreneurial ecosystems. *Entrepreneurship and Regional Development, 31*(1–2), 7–21. https://doi.org/10.1080/08985626.2018.1537144

Mahdavy, H. (1970). The patterns and problems of economic development in rentier states: The case of Iran. In M.A. Cook (Ed.), *Studies in the economic history of the Middle East* (pp. 428–467). School of Oriental African Studies/Oxford University Press.

Mason, C., & Brown, R. (2014). *Entrepreneurial ecosystems and growth-oriented entrepreneurship.* Final Report to OECD, *30*(1), 77–102.

Mohammadi, N., & Karimi, A. (2021). Entrepreneurial ecosystem big picture: A bibliometric analysis and co-citation clustering. *Journal of Research in Marketing and Entrepreneurship.* https://doi.org/10.1108/JRME-10-2020-0141

Noreng, Ø. (2004). The predicament of the Gulf Rentier State. In D. Heradstveit and H. Hveem (Eds.), *Oil in the gulf: Obstacles to democracy and development* (p. 32), Routledge. https://doi.org/10.4324/9781315247779

North, D.C. (1990). *Institutions, institutional change and economic development.* Cambridge University Press.

Okpara, J.O., & Kumbiadis, N. (2008). SMEs export orientation and performance: Evidence from a developing economy. *International Review of Business Research Papers, 4*(5), 109–119.

Purbasari, R., Wijaya, C., & Rahayu, N. (2019). Interaction of actors and factors in entreprzneurial ecosystem: Indonesian creatives industries. *International Journal of Entrepreneurship, 3*(1S).

Reynolds, P.D., Bosma, N., Autio, E., Hunt, S., Bono, N.D., Servais, I., et al. (2005). Global entrepreneurship monitor: Data collection design and implementation 1998–2003. *Small Business Economics, 24*(3), 205–231. https://doi.org/10.1007/s11187-005-1980-1

Roundy, P. T. (2019). "It takes a village" to support entrepreneurship: Intersecting econoᴺic and community dynamics in small town entrepreneurial ecosystems. *The International Entrepreneurship and Management Journal, 15*(4), 1443–1475. https://doi.org/10.1007/s11365-018-0537-0

Roundy, P.T., & Bayer, M.A. (2019). Entrepreneurial ecosystem narratives and the micro-foundations of regional entrepreneurship. *International Journal of Entrepreneurship and Innovation, 20*(3), 194–208. https://doi.org/10.1177/1465750318808426

Roundy, P. T., & Fayard, D. (2019). Dynamic capabilities and entrepreneurial ecosystems: the micro-foundations of regional entrepreneurship. *The Journal of Entrepreneurship, 28*(1), 94–120.

Samitowska, W. (2011). Barriers to the development of entrepreneurship demonstrated by micro, small and medium enterprises in Poland. *Economics & Sociology, 4*(2), 42–49.

Spigel, B. (2017). The relational organization of entrepreneurial ecosystems. *Entrepreneurship Theory and Practice, 41*(1), 49–72. https://doi.org/10.1111/etap.12167

Stam, E. (2015). Entrepreneurial ecosystems and regional policy: A sympathetic critique. *European Planning Studies, 23*(9), 1759–1769. https://doi.org/10.1080/09654313.2015.1061484

Sternberg, R., & Wennekers, S. (2005). Determinants and effects of new business creation using global entrepreneurship monitor data. *Small Business Economics, 24*(3), 193–203. https://doi.org/10.1007/s11187-005-1974-z

Sternberg, R., Bloh, J. V., & Coduras, A. (2019). A new framework to measure entrepreneurial ecosystems at the regional level. *Zeitschrift für Wirtschaftsgeographie, 63*(2–4), 103–117.

Tsvetkova, A. (2015). Innovation, entrepreneurship, and metropolitan economic performance: Empirical test of recent theoretical propositions. *Economic Development Quarterly, 29*(4), 299–316. https://doi.org/10.1177/0891242415581398

Van De Ven, H. (1993). The development of an infrastructure for entrepreneurship. *Journal of Business Venturing, 8*(3), 211–230. https://doi.org/10.1016/0883-9026(93)90028-4

van Weele, M., van Rijnsoever, F.J., Eveleens, C.P., Steinz, H., van Stijn, N., & Groen, M. (2018). Start-EUup! Lessons from international incubation practices to address the challenges faced by Western European start-ups. *The Journal of Technology Transfer, 43*(5), 1161–1189.

Velt, H., Torkkeli, L., & Laine, I. (2020). Entrepreneurial ecosystem research: Bibliometric mapping of the domain. *Journal of Business Ecosystems, 2*(2). https://doi.org/10.4018/JBE.20200701.oa1

Villegas Mateos, A.O., & Amorós, J.E. (2019). Regional entrepreneurial ecosystems in Mexico: A comparative analysis. *Journal of Entrepreneurship in Emerging Economies, 11*(4). https://doi.org/10.1108/JEEE-02-2019-0024.

Villegas-Mateos, A. (2020). Regional entrepreneurial ecosystems in Chile: Comparative lessons. *Journal of Entrepreneurship in Emerging Economies, 13*(1), 39–63. https://doi.org/10.1108/JEEE-11-2019-0168

Villegas-Mateos, A. (2021). *Qatar's entrepreneurial ecosystem – 2021 Edition: Empowering the transformation* (pp. 1–100). HEC Paris. http://doi.org/10.5281/zenodo.4719075

WEF. (2013). *Entrepreneurial ecosystems around the globe and company growth dynamics.* World Economic Forum.

Wiklund, J., Nikolaev, B., Shir, N., Foo, M.D., & Bradley, S. (2019). Entrepreneurship and well-being: Past, present, and future. *Journal of Business Venturing, 34*(4), 579-588.

Manuel Bäuml and Thierry Volery

12 A Typology of Internet Functionalities to Develop Market Orientation in SMEs

Abstract: This study investigates how small and medium-sized enterprises (SMEs) leverage internet technology to overcome inherent challenges in being market oriented. In comparison to large firms, the competitive advantage of SMEs stems from maximizing customer intelligence and their agility in responding to customer needs. However, SMEs often struggle to gather market intelligence beyond existing customers. We identify four roles of internet functionalities which can help SMEs develop their market orientation: (1) increasing brand knowledge; (2) identifying market trends; (3) identifying new customer needs; and (4) streamlining processes. We conclude with seven propositions that drive the adoption of internet-enabled technologies for each role.

Keywords: Market orientation, internet, digital, marketing, digitalization

Introduction

Over the past three decades, market orientation has been recognized as one of the key drivers for maintaining a competitive advantage (Jaworski & Kohli, 1993; Kumar et al., 2011). Because customer needs and expectations constantly evolve over time, firms are required to continuously monitor and respond to changing marketplace needs, i.e., being market oriented. In this vein, Kohli and Jaworski (1990) define market orientation in terms of three dimensions: the collection of information about current and future customer needs; the dissemination of such information across organizational departments; and the development and implementation of strategies in response to the information. The vast literature on market orientation examines the extent to which enterprises behave in accordance with this marketing concept (see Kirca et al., 2005 for a review).

Market orientation is particularly important in smaller companies because it complements a SME's entrepreneurial orientation and ultimately affects firm performance (Baker & Sinkula, 2009; Kara et al., 2005). SMEs typically share three distinctive characteristics: scarcity of human resources; the central role of the owner-manager; and limited capital resources (Zor et al., 2019), all of which are likely to affect their market orientation in two ways. First, SMEs are generally recognized to display an intrinsic customer orientation (Keskin, 2006), a high flexibility in responding to customer requests and a focus on opportunities (Carson et al., 1995). This suggests that

Manuel Bäuml, Swiss Institute of Small Business and Entrepreneurship, University of St.Gallen
Thierry Volery, School of Management & Law, Zurich University of Applied Sciences (ZHAW)

https://doi.org/10.1515/9783110747652-013

SMEs are strong in disseminating information internally and in responding to customer needs. Second, SMEs are often described as being close to their customers and able to maintain more personal relationships with them (Kara et al., 2005). This behavior indicates that SMEs are generally adept at gathering information from existing customers.

In today's digital era, SMEs can leverage internet-enabled technology to improve their market orientation. Although it is widely recognized that the internet has significantly affected the way SMEs conduct their marketing activities (Mazzarol, 2015; Saura et al., 2021), there is a paucity of research about how SMEs use internet-enabled technologies to develop their market orientation. As de Swaan et al. (2014) remarked: "Though social and digital media have changed what marketers do to engage customers almost beyond recognition, in most firms the organization of the marketing function has hardly evolved in the past decades" (p. 56). This research gap is remarkable as SMEs form the backbone of most economies in terms of employment and value-added. By capitalizing on internet-enabled technology and overcoming the challenges in being market oriented, SMEs are likely to substantially increase their competitive advantage (Celuch & Murphy, 2010; Doern, 2009).

In this study, we investigate how SMEs use internet features and functionalities to overcome the inherent challenges in being market oriented. Drawing from the literature on ICT and marketing, we develop a typology of internet functionalities which can sustain market orientation, before examining empirically the antecedents affecting the use of internet enabled functionalities to optimize market orientation. Building on the work of Saura et al. (2021) and Trainor et al. (2013), we define internet functionalities as digital technologies used to access and provide hypermedia content in a distributed computer-mediated network. For example, internet functionalities enable firms to gather information about prospective buyers, conduct market research, and facilitate customization of products.

This study contributes to the literature on market orientation in three ways. First, we develop a typology around four major roles that internet features and functionalities can play in achieving market orientation in the context of SMEs. Second, while previous research has established several general and marketing-specific characteristics of SMEs (Harrigan et al., 2012), this study reveals that the specific challenges that SMEs face in being market-oriented lies in gathering information beyond existing customers. Lastly, this study provides further insight into the adoption of new technologies in the context of SMEs. To this end, we go beyond the inception of new technologies in general, also referred to as "technological opportunism" (Mazzarol, 2015), to highlight which supplier and customer variables drive the promotion of certain types of internet-enabled technologies to realize each of the four roles identified.

Review of the Literature

The Challenges for SMEs to Develop a Market Orientation

There are a variety of factors which differentiate SMEs from large companies. In addition to the size of the organization, the ownership structure of SMEs is often characterized by the central role of the owner-manager (Zor et al., 2019). Other distinctive characteristics of SMEs include the owner's attitude and capabilities (Garengo et al., 2005), limited capital resources (Doern, 2009), and a scarcity of human resources (Doole et al., 2006). As shown in Table 12.1, these typical SME characteristics are likely to affect their market orientation. For example, SMEs tend to have a strong customer orientation (Slotte-Kock & Coviello, 2010), closer and more personal relationships with their customers (Jack et al., 2010; Moreno & Casillas, 2008), and the flexibility to react to customer needs (Carson & Gilmore, 2000).

Table 12.1: SME characteristics and their effect on market orientation.

Defining criteria	Distinctive SME characteristics	Further SME characteristics	Effect on market orientation[a]		
			Information gathering	Information dissemination	Responsiveness
Ownership structure/ central role of owner	Owner-manager attitude and capabilities (Garengo et al., 2005; Mazzarol, 2015)	1. Inherent customer orientation (Slotte-Kock & Coviello, 2010)	+	+	+
		2. Lack of marketing expertise (Carson et al., 1995)	−	−	−
		3. Focus on operational activities rather than on marketing (Sousa et al., 2006)	−	+	+
		4. Informal, dynamic strategies (Berry, 1998)	−	0	+

Table 12.1 (continued)

Defining criteria	Distinctive SME characteristics	Further SME characteristics	Effect on market orientation[a]		
			Information gathering	Information dissemination	Responsiveness
	Limited capital resources (Doern, 2009) and inability to secure additional sources of funding (Zor et al., 2019)	5. Low IT capabilities and reliance on simple IT technology (Peltier et al., 2009)	–	0	0
		6. Reliance on a small number of customers and operating in niche markets (Appiah-Adu & Singh, 1998)	+/–[b]	+	+
Firm size ≤ 250 FTE	Scarcity of human resources (Doole et al., 2006)	7. Scarcity of human resources (Doole et al., 2006)	–	+	–
		8. Flat structures and flexible processes (Cho & Tansuhaj, 2013)	0	+	+
		9. Reactive, fire-fighting mentality (Mazzarol, 2015)	0	+	+
		10. Focus on simple marketing approaches (O'Dwyer et al., 2009)	–	0	0
		11. Marketing by networking (Keskin, 2006)	+/–[b]	0	0
		12. Closeness to customers (Moreno & Casillas, 2008)	+/–[b]	+	+
		13. More personal relationships (Jack et al., 2010)	+/–[b]	+	+

Table 12.1 (continued)

Defining criteria	Distinctive SME characteristics	Further SME characteristics	Effect on market orientation[a]		
			Information gathering	Information dissemination	Respon-siveness
		14. Easy access to market information (Hills et al., 2008)	+/−[b]	0	+
		15. Flexibility to customer needs (Carson and Gilmore, 2000)	0	+	+

[a]Qualitative assessment: + indicates a positive effect, − a negative effect, 0 no effect.
[b]Depending on existing customers (+) or beyond existing customers, particularly in new geographic and/or product markets (−)

However, other factors such as management emphasis and organizational design can have a negative effect on a firm's market orientation (Kirca et al., 2005). In the context of SMEs, we suggest that their inherent characteristics reduce the business capability to gather intelligence beyond existing customers, and, conversely, enhance intelligence dissemination and responsiveness.

Intelligence Gathering

Market intelligence refers to the analysis of exogenous factors that affect the needs and preferences of customers (Jaworski & Kohli, 1993). Large companies differ to SMEs with regards to their managerial focus on marketing in general and information gathering and market screening capabilities. Large firms often have institutionalized roles with dedicated resources in their organizations. SMEs are said to develop closer and more personal relationships with customers (Jack et al., 2010; Moreno & Casillas, 2008), which allows them to draw on their network for information (Keskin, 2006).

However, SMEs tend to put less emphasis on gathering market intelligence beyond existing customers. For example, few SMEs have dedicated resources that proactively screen markets for changes in regulation and changes in customer needs. SME characteristics such as scarcity of human resources (Doole et al., 2006), lack of marketing expertise (Carson et al., 1995), and low IT capabilities (Peltier et al., 2009) result in a low focus on gathering market intelligence beyond existing customers. Market intelligence is particularly important, because SMEs have fewer financial resources (Loern, 2009) to buffer the effects of unforeseen changes in regulation, shifts in demand patterns or competitor actions.

Overall, past research suggests that SMEs tend to maximize customer intelligence but focus less on gathering market intelligence beyond existing customers and with regards to exogenous factors. Information gathering is particularly challenging when SMEs expand to new geographic or product markets.

Intelligence Dissemination

Reacting to market needs requires an efficient internal communication of market intelligence to relevant departments and individuals in the organization (Jaworski & Kohli, 1993). Several SME characteristics contribute to the dissemination of intelligence. Flat organizational structures (Cho & Tansuhaj, 2013) as well as short and informal communication (Berry, 1998) facilitates the rapid and efficient spread of information. In addition, decision-making is pragmatic and concentrated in the hands of the owner-manager. Overall, the efficient dissemination of intelligence is a key strength of SMEs.

Responsiveness

Superior performance can only be achieved by a timely and efficient response to customers' ever-changing needs. Thus, once the marketers have gathered, processed, and disseminated market information internally, then it is time to develop action plans. Responsiveness is an organization's ability to react to market needs based on intelligence gathered and disseminated (Jaworski & Kohli, 1993). The literature provides substantial evidence for high levels of responsiveness in smaller firms. For example, SMEs are said to focus on opportunities, be highly attuned to customer needs, and be willing to try new approaches (Hills et al., 2008; O'Dwyer et al., 2009). As a result, they show high innovation potential (Saura et al., 2021). In sum, several intrinsic characteristics of SMEs point to a high responsiveness to market needs, which in turn constitutes a competitive advantage for this type of enterprise.

Roles of Internet Functionalities to Sustain Market Orientation of SMEs

Internet-enabled technologies have transformed marketing strategy and operations (Kohli, 2017; Nguyen et al., 2015). Typical internet features and functionalities include, for example, websites, search engines, social media platforms, and/or content sharing platforms. These technologies are important because over one-third of the world's population is online, and users are increasingly willing to share information (Ye et al., 2022).

In this technological environment, abilities for market players to interact (Trainor et al., 2013) and to personalize information has greatly advanced (Lin et al., 2021). Interactivity refers to the degree which internet-enabled interactions between an organization and other market players are perceived by each entity to be bidirectional, timely, mutually controllable, and responsive (Yadav and Varadarajan 2005). For example, a low level of interactivity occurs when a firm uses internet-enabled media for mass communication, which transmits information to many market players in a one-way interaction (Nguyen et al., 2015). Personalization is the degree to which an organization recognizes, approaches, and treats its market players as individuals, using personalized information (Montgomery & Smith, 2009). For instance, a company may use emails with personalized content to approach a specific group of customers. Personalization requires the integration of specific content based on research or previous interactions with the customer. Although personalization of services remains the holy grail of marketing, Yoganarasimhan (2020) recently put forward a machine learning framework to rank recommendations using personalized data in many settings.

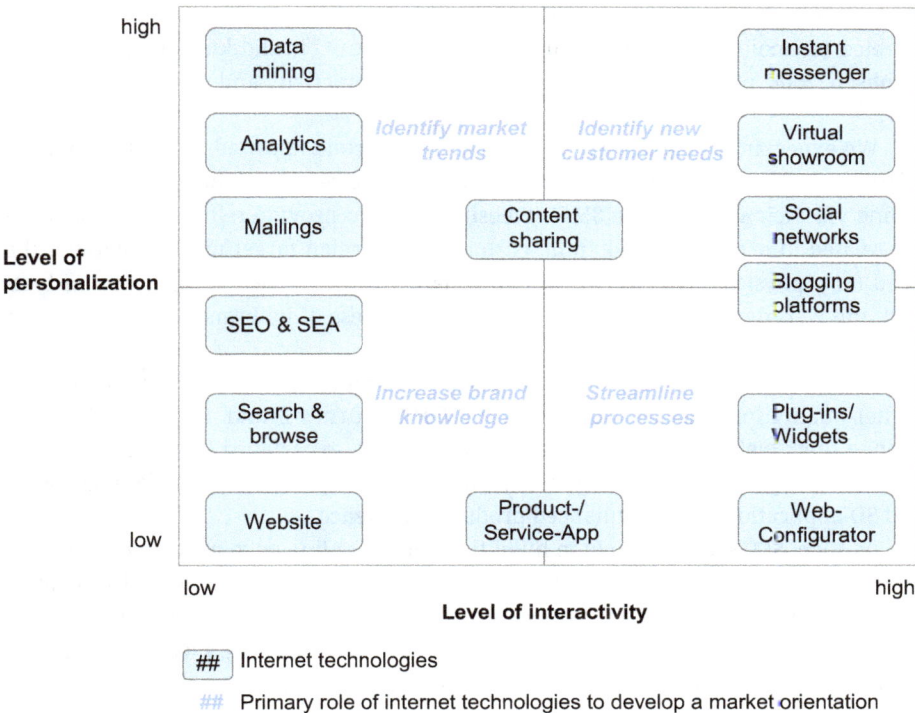

Figure 12.1: A typology of internet functionalities to develop a market orientation.

As depicted in Figure 12.1, the different archetypes of internet functionalities can be classified according to their level of personalization and interactivity. In this matrix, this relates to the extent to which technology is used for personalization and interactivity to derive four primary roles which can contribute to the development of a market orientation: (1) increasing brand knowledge; (2) identifying market trends; (3) identifying new customer needs; and (4) streamlining processes. Please refer to Appendix 12.1 for a definition and an example of the constructs used in the typology outlined hereafter.

Increase Brand Knowledge

The notion of gathering information suggests that firms actively search for customer information. However, preliminary discussions with managers of B2B SMEs suggested that many of them use internet-enabled technologies primarily to increase awareness and understanding of the brand identity, to provide product-related information, and in the attempt to gather customer information. Overall, this suggests that internal-enabled technologies contribute to the development of "brand knowledge" (Mizik & Jacobson, 2008, p. 16). However, both the level of interactivity and personalization are low.

We expect internet-enabled media to increase brand knowledge in two ways. For example, SMEs can significantly enhance geographic reach and build brand identity online via their website. The SME's website serves to provide relevant firm or product-related information to potential customers in foreign target markets without the need for a physical presence. As this information can be accessed regardless of location, the website enables a SME to increase awareness of its brand in all geographic markets.

In the same vein, internet-enabled media enables SMEs to provide more and higher-quality information, which better reflects a firm's brand. For example, firms change their websites to create a compelling online experience (Lin et al., 2021) by producing more intuitive navigation logic, embedding video clips, reference cases, and 3D-applications for an enhanced product experience.

As such, SMEs aim not only to build their brand online or to provide information on their product, but also to signal competence to prospective customers. This competence supports trust-building, which is particularly important in the digital world (Bart et al., 2005). Overall, internet functionalities can help SMEs, including B2B companies, in raising their brand profile, and ultimately attracting new customers.

Identify Market Trends

The internet has increased the amount of information accessible. New technologies enable SMEs to enhance their gathering of information about market trends through systematic data mining approaches. Data mining and analytics techniques enable SMEs to identify market trends if the respective information is shared online. We acknowledge that data mining is not an internet technology per se. Rather this concept is broadly defined as "a business process for exploration and analysis of large quantity of data in order to discover meaningful patterns" (Linoff & Berry, 2011, p. 2). However, we contend that by tapping into the vast quantity of data generated by consumers online SMEs can improve their ability to form learning relationships with their customers. As data is increasingly available everywhere and in copious amounts, SMEs can build data mining algorithms to identify market trends and patterns about subscribers, web visitors, and on customer behaviour.

It might nevertheless be more difficult for specialized B2B SMEs that supply second- or third-tier suppliers to predict exactly the impact of emerging trends. For example, a SME that is specialized in producing the covers of lithium batteries relies on the specific requirements of the battery manufacturer, who itself supplies a major car manufacturer. Tracking publicly available information on sales of cars with batteries will help the SME to better understand major trends, especially regarding volume, but less on predicting changes in detailed product requirements. Overall, the use of internet-enabled technologies to predict market trends depends heavily on quality and quantity of data information available. To increase data usefulness the SME needs to gather relevant and therefore personalized information that is specific to its products and/or services.

Identify New Customer Needs

Internet-enabled media can create new pools of customer information for SMEs which enable them to identify new customer needs. Pools of information refer to platforms that enable customer-to-customer discussions about suppliers, and suppliers to access these platforms for information gathering. For example, SMEs may use YouTube to share their latest product developments. In doing so, they also enable existing or prospective customers to express and exchange opinions about products or the supplier (e.g., by using the commentary field). However, it seems that expressing frustration via public social media platforms depends heavily on the relationship strength between businesses and consumers. For example, customers who have bought an expensive piece of equipment would be less likely to express frustration publicly on a platform. Instead, they are more likely to approach their supplier directly to modify certain product features as part of the after-sales service. In sum, digital platforms can be a new source for SMEs to gather relevant customer information such as product feedback and increase their responsiveness to changing customer needs. This role of internet-enabled media requires high levels of both personalization and interactivity.

Streamline Processes

Internet-enabled media allows SMEs to lower their searching, bargaining, and processing costs (Cho & Tansuhaj, 2013). These three types of costs form the core elements of "transaction costs," and their level depends on the extent to which a firm's approach towards market orientation is personalized and interactive. We posit that, in a B2B business environment, internet-enabled functionalities can primarily help SMEs in reducing their bargaining and processing costs, and, to a lesser extent, in lowering their searching costs.

Searching costs refer to the costs associated with gathering relevant market information. A search for companies that match the SME's target customer profile typically requires high levels of personalization to customize the search and generally entails a low level of interaction between the SME and the customer. Internet-enabled media helps to obtain information on potential customers quickly, and without the need for physical presence. For example, searching for firms in online directories or for information on firm websites allows SMEs to identify potential customers. Similarly, it is a simple matter for a business to track the browsing behavior of a given customer, and, based on that, make inferences about the customer's preference structure and likely interest in a host of products and services (Kohli, 2017). Additionally, it has become easier and cheaper to hunt for new product and service ideas from individual customers across the globe (crowdsourcing).

However, finding relevant sources and obtaining pertinent customer information can be challenging, even with internet-enabled media (Cho & Tansuhaj, 2013). Data mining may be less suitable for some SMEs as they often lack the relevant capabilities and/or customers do not provide relevant information online. In addition, the use of electronic marketplaces to lower their searching costs (Cho & Tansuhaj, 2013) may be less suited in a B2B context where personal relationships are often essential.

Bargaining and processing costs refer to the costs associated with information dissemination in the organization and with responding to customer requests. As such, the level of interactivity with customers is high. The level of personalization is moderate, depending on the willingness and flexibility of a SME to accommodate customer requests that do not match existing product and/or service characteristics. SMEs use internet-enabled media to improve responsiveness to customer requests. For example, in the manufacturing sector, SMEs can typically adopt web-configurators (web-based platforms that allow customers to provide their specific product application characteristics such as material type, physical dimensions, location, and type of drillings). The web-configurator then translates these application characteristics into a (modularized) product that best suits the customer's application needs. As a result, a SME's capability to disseminate information and to provide a timely response increase.

Overall, internet-enabled media can provide several advantages for SMEs. First, this technology can reduce bargaining costs. Second, it supports the integration of the customer during the bargaining process. Clear definition of requirements, customization, and integration of the customer is likely to positively affect solution effectiveness (Tuli et al., 2007). Third, it helps to institutionalize and centralize know-how. In many SMEs, process-specific know-how is often in the heads of employees rather than in processes. Consequently, critical know-how can be unavailable or get lost when experienced employees are absent or resign. Internet-enabled media can help to institutionalize this know-how by embedding it in formalized processes. Lastly, internet-enabled media can reduce processing costs. This allows SMEs to create automated end-to-end processes by linking customer-facing processes to internal ones. This lowers the effort required to process customer requests.

Method

We adopted a grounded theory approach for this study because of the relative paucity of research on internet-enabled technology to enhance SMEs' market orientation. The extant literature lacks an established theoretical framework that integrates the various perspectives outlining the role of internet towards the development of SMEs' market orientation. Accordingly, we aimed to develop an emergent theoretical framework which is shaped by the views of the participants who are involved in the process (Strauss & Corbin, 1998). Given this, we believe a better understanding of the complex issues related to internet-enabled technologies for marketing can be obtained by directly talking with people who are involved in strategic marketing, and "allowing them to tell their stories unencumbered by what we expect to find or what we have read in the literature" (Creswell 2007, p. 40). The grounded theory approach helped us to understand the context and the settings within which the issues related to marketing strategy making are addressed (Malshe & Sohi, 2009), thereby providing further insight into the internet-enabled media roles derived in our review of the literature. This is of particular importance for SMEs because, as we have previously discussed, their context and organization differ significantly from large enterprises.

Sample

We conducted a series of structured interviews with 66 SME owner-managers and managing directors based in Switzerland. The interviews lasted between 30 and 110 minutes each. The study participants played a significant role in their organizations and were best suited to oversee and to shape management practices (Waldman et al., 2012), and therefore to detail their company's marketing strategy and operations. Our sample comprised of 35 (53%) medium-sized enterprises with 50 to 250 employees, 27 (41%) small enterprises with 10 to 49 employees, and four (6%) micro enterprises with less than 10 employees, from the precision engineering and machinery industry. Virtually all the SMEs (96%) in the sample were established before the 2000s. By selecting companies with similar characteristics in terms of industry background and age, we aimed to diminish heterogeneity in our sample and facilitate cross-case comparison. These companies tend to operate in mature business environments and are therefore likely to have more sophisticated internal systems and procedures for market orientation (Golann, 2006). Consequently, we expect companies in our sample to have more mature information gathering processes.

Data Collection and Analysis

We conducted in-depth interviews using a semi-structured questionnaire in 2016–2017. The questionnaire provided a general interview structure and was followed up with additional questions to clarify statements, to elaborate on interesting ideas, and to ask for concrete examples. Participants declined requests to record interviews because of confidentiality reasons. Therefore, we took detailed interview notes and sent them to each interviewee afterwards for confirmation.

Like Tuli et al. (2007), we used a dual filter approach to identify meaningful ideas that apply beyond a single firm-specific context: (1) Is the idea or insight applicable beyond a specific context, such as firm or industry?; and (2) Does the idea go beyond the "obvious" to provide more interesting and useful conclusions? This textual analysis served to identify first-order constructs in the first step (Malshe & Sohi, 2009). The identified themes are depicted in Table 12.2.

Table 12.2: Frequency of themes mentioned by interviewees (multiple responses).

	Theme	Frequency	
		Abs.	%
Increase brand knowledge	Website	10	15
	Professionalization	7	11
	Localization	3	5
	Search-Engine-Marketing	3	5
	Search Engine Advertising (SEA)	2	3
	Search Engine Optimization (SEO)	3	5
	3D product/service application	2	3

Table 12.2 (continued)

	Theme	Frequency	
		Abs.	%
Identify market trends	Mailings	4	6
	Virtual showroom	2	3
	Data mining	1	2
Streamline processes	Web-configurator	2	3
Identify new customer needs	Social media	3	5
	Facebook	1	2
	YouTube	1	2
	Digital platforms (not specified)	1	2
	Instant messaging	1	2

Next, we reassembled the data to identify relationships between and among the categories to form second-order constructs. The latter are abstract, theoretically distinct constructs developed for academia (Nag & Gioia, 2012). After blending themes that emerged from this field research and ideas in extant literature, we identified four roles that internet-enabled media play in market orientation of SMEs.

Results

Our field research suggests that SME owner-managers sense opportunities to increase their market orientation that emerge from the rise of internet-enabled technologies. However, given the plurality of technological solutions, many struggle to find the best solution suited to their specific needs. As the owner-manager of a medium-sized temperature and control technology manufacturer remarked: "Formerly, everyone simply exhibited and visited fairs. Today, the internet plays a crucial role. Potential customers use the internet to identify suppliers. We still struggle with these technologies, and we might need to be more active in future, but only if it is meaningful in our B2B business."

Figure 12.2 depicts the key variables that emerged from our field research as predictors for the specific role that a SME pursues when adopting internet-enabled technologies. It is structurally consistent with the mounting research with a co-creation perspective (e.g., Tuli et al., 2007; Vargo & Lusch, 2004) and therefore includes both variables referring to characteristics of the adopting SME and its (potential) customers.

SME variables
P₁: Internationalization emphasis
P₂: Brand orientation
P₃: Niche orientation
P₄: Formalization emphasis
P₅: Analytical orientation

Customer variables
P₆: Operational counselling
P₇: Virtual presence

Role of internet-enabled technologies
1. Increase brand knowledge
2. Identify market trends
3. Identify new customer needs
4. Streamline processes

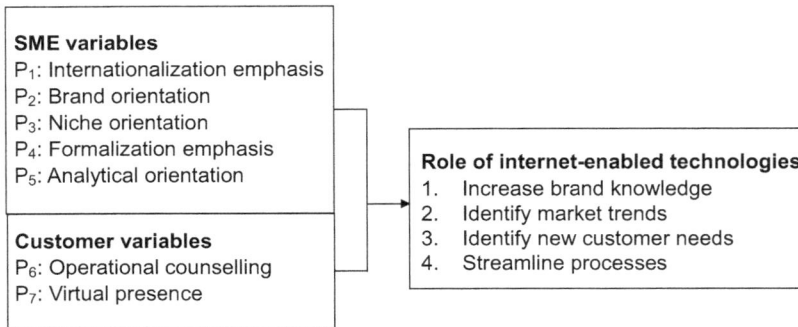

Figure 12.2: Variables affecting the use of internet functionalities to develop a market orientation.

SME-related Dimensions

As the field study progressed, it became clear that SMEs aim for specific roles of internet-enabled technologies. For example, some suppliers were particularly interested in web-configurators that helped them to streamline their information gathering processes. At the same time, this technology was perceived less meaningful for other SMEs. Several supplier variables emerge from this field study that encourage pursuing specific types of roles, as discussed in the following.

Internationalization Emphasis

SMEs with higher market orientation in general, and capabilities in information gathering, show higher international competitiveness (Armario et al., 2008). Discussions with SME leaders indicated that a firm's internationalization emphasis primarily shows in adopting internet-enabled technologies that are related to brand knowledge and therefore increase reach and awareness of their brand. These technologies show low levels of personalization and interactivity. As the operations manager of a mid-sized netting solution manufacturer pointed out: "We try to use new technologies as part of our internationalization and export efforts. One important dimension is branding, especially in new target countries. We believe in professionalization of our website and aim to make potential new customers aware of us."

In this example, the interviewee emphasized the supporting role of internet-enabled technologies in increasing brand knowledge in their internationalization efforts. In contrast to traditional fair visits or sales activities abroad, SMEs leverage new technologies such as Search Engine Optimization (SEO) and Search Engine Advertising (SEA) to increase the reach of their brand to foreign markets without the need for costly activities abroad such as fair visits. However, limitations of these technologies exist as, in many organizations, trust and commitment (Morgan & Hurt, 1994) are essential for business relationships. The development of such relationships may not be fully ensured by internet-enabled technologies.

For example, internationalization emphasis is likely to be reflected in adopting technologies that allow SMEs to one-way communicate their brand profile and product information. This supports the companies to increase reach and awareness of existing products and services in new geographic markets without interactivity in the first step. Hence:

P1: The greater a SME's internationalization emphasis, the greater its use of internet-enabled technologies to increase brand knowledge (low interactivity/low personalization).

Brand Orientation

Brand orientation refers to the extent to which a firm focuses on developing its brand in terms of brand differentiation, esteem, relevance, and energy. Several SME leaders noted the opportunity of internet-enabled technologies to develop their brand. Their observations mirror the importance of transferring a brand to the digital world (Quinton, 2013). Notably, the digital footprint of the firm was seen as important, even in cases where SME leaders considered marketing activities as less relevant to their business. As the managing director of a medium-sized precision motion simulator manufacturer remarked: "I do not see marketing as part of our core activities. Much more important is to maintain relationships with our existing customers and to identify new customers. However, in our view the attractiveness of our website is crucial. Therefore, we invest in professionalizing our website."

The attractiveness of the website refers to a compelling online experience with regards to technical functionality such as intuitive navigation (Lin et al., 2021) and reflecting brand characteristics in the digital world (Quinton, 2013). For example, a leading manufacturer of stamping machines has worked together with a marketing agency to improve intuitive navigation on its website, and to redesign its website to reflect the firm's brand values of "reliability," "technological leadership," and "we care mentality," by embedding high-end pictures, 3D-animations, and providing personal contacts. The respective communication is one-way and provides general information about the firm and its products. Therefore, the technologies show low levels of interactivity with market players. As such, they are likely to aim primarily for increasing brand relevance, differentiation, esteem, and energy and less for identifying customer needs or market trends. The implication is that:

P2: The greater a SME's brand orientation, the greater its use of internet-enabled technologies to increase brand knowledge (low interactivity/low personalization).

Niche Orientation

Niche orientation refers to the extent to which a SME's strategy focuses on products and services offered for a small number of customers and provided from a small number of suppliers. Niche orientation affects the role of internet-enabled technologies as suppliers rely on a relatively small number of customers and vice versa (Appiah-Adu & Singh, 1998). Consequently, awareness of players in the niche and importance of relationships tends to be higher (Jack et al., 2010). For example, an owner-manager of a medium-sized thermoplastic powders manufacturer said: "Marketing and therefore also marketing-related technologies are of low priority for us for three reasons: we operate in a B2B business providing expensive products, we operate in a niche market, and we do have long customer relationships."

We expect that niche orientation decreases the use of internet-enabled technologies to identify customer needs. A greater niche orientation translates into focusing on a smaller number of existing and potential customers. Many SMEs rely on marketing by networking (Keskin, 2006). With a smaller niche size, the interdependence between customer-supplier organizations increases. As a result, both customer and seller are likely to increase relationship-specific investments to increase trust and commitment (Palmatier et al., 2007). As SMEs tend to have personal and close relationships with their customers (Jack et al., 2010; Moreno & Casillas, 2008) it is likely that they gather in-depth information in personal talks and focus on strengthening their relationship. Internet-enabled technologies, however, assist to gather a broader set of information from a wide range of potential customers. We therefore expect that:

P3: The greater a SME's niche orientation, the lower its use of internet-enabled technologies to identify new customer needs (high interactivity/high personalization).

Formalization Emphasis

Formalization emphasis refers to the extent to which SMEs have established process procedures and organizational standards (Golann, 2006; Terziovski, 2010). Several SME leaders noted the importance of formalizing processes and reported major benefits from adopting internet-enabled technologies that support streamlining of information gathering processes. For example, a web-configurator assists SMEs in gathering details on a specific customer product inquiry by which internal pre-sale processing complexity is reduced. Consider the experience of a supplier of precision laser machines: "The web-configurator helps us to formalize know-how such as price and cost calculation by extracting it from the head of our employees into a formal system."

When formalization emphasis is high, SMEs are more likely to implement internet-enabled technologies with high levels of interactivity and low levels of personalization for two reasons. First, internet-enabled technologies support realizing the associated benefits of formalization, i.e., lower bargaining and processing costs as well as bundling of know-how. Higher formalization is reflected in defined processes and greater standardization of procedures. Both are prerequisites to automate processes. Automation is likely to be the goal of SMEs that adopt internet-enabled technologies with low personalization but high interactivity because they help to reduce processing and bargaining complexity. In addition, several SMEs try to formalize their know-how. Specifically, they aim to transfer process, product, and pricing knowledge from the heads of employees into formal systems as described previously. Internet-enabled technologies can be the systems that help SMEs to operationalize this bundling of know-how

Second, formalization increases transparency for customers, which reduces perceived seller opportunistic behavior and ultimately improves customer trust. New technologies enable firms to integrate the customers into internal processes that provide standardized information but allow high interactivity. For example, formalized internal processes provide standard information regarding price-product feature combinations and a web-based interface enables interactivity of the communication process. The preceding discussion suggests that:

P4: The greater a SME's formalization emphasis, the greater its use of internet-enabled technologies that support streamlining of processes (high interactivity/low personalization).

Analytical Orientation

In recent times, data-driven business models have emerged, especially in the online retail market (Ye et al., 2022). These enterprises show high levels of analytical orientation. Analytical orientation refers to the extent to which the company bases its market development and operational decisions on quantitative information. Analytical orientation is likely to increase the use of internet-enabled technologies that assist in identifying market trends. Analytical oriented SMEs use technologies such as data mining or analytic tools to identify specific market trends related to their products or services. These technologies tend to show low levels of interactivity but are highly personalized to identify relevant information from large amounts of data. Thus, we posit that:

P5: The greater the analytical orientation of an SME, the greater its use of internet-enabled technologies that assist in identifying market trends (low interactivity/high personalization).

Customer-related Dimensions

Operational Counseling

Operational counseling refers to "the extent to which a customer provides information and guidance about its operations to a supplier" (Tuli et al. 2007, p. 12). It allows a
supplier to anticipate and to gather information about changes that customers demand from existing products and to identify the need for new products. Information
of interest is those that concern operational processes and technological specifications
of potential customers. Therefore, operational counseling requires a SME to use internet-enabled technologies with high interactivity and personalization of information.
In the words of the owner-manager of a small-sized manufacturer of laser machines:
"We have implemented a virtual showroom. A potential customer can send in his
specifications of the technical application. We then produce his application on our
machines and can discuss and understand details about the customer's process and
subsequent use of the application in the web-session. The advantage compared to a
physical showroom in the customer's country is that the risk is lower that a potential
customer shows up with an application that we can't produce on our machines, and it
is [a] much cheaper option for us."

Clarification of goals and specifications helps the supplier to gather information
about potential customers and the unique elements of their operations. Sharing and
gathering of personalized information therefore constitutes a relationship-specific investment from both suppliers and customers (Palmatier et al., 2007). In addition, it
lowers the risk of reducing customer trust by making unrealistic promises. This is a
situation which can easily occur when suppliers use agent networks.

Finally, the associated costs for potential new customers when using internet-
enabled technologies to get in contact and interact with a supplier are relatively low.
For example, an interested customer does not need to invest in a trip to visit the supplier's headquarters. Potential new customers are more likely to approach and to test the
products of the supplier. Therefore, operational counseling assists SMEs in anticipating
changes in customer needs, in adapting existing products, and in innovating. Hence:

P6: The greater the customer's operational counseling, the greater a SME's use of internet-enabled technologies that assist in identifying new customer needs (high inter-
activity/high personalization).

Virtual Presence

Virtual presence refers to customers using internet-enabled technologies for business
purposes. Several SME leaders emphasized that internet-enabled technologies were
not important for their market orientation. We expect the use of these technologies,

especially in respect to reach and awareness, to depend on the extent to which customers use internet-enabled technologies such as digital platforms for information sharing. Consider the experience of the managing director of a leading stamping machine manufacturer: "The social media platform Facebook, for example, is not important to us. [On the] contrary, I noticed that several relationships have emerged via my LinkedIn and Xing profiles. Typically, these were contacts of my contacts or contacts that I have met once but back then no immediate leads had evolved. It seems that the actual usage of these platforms for business purposes by potential customers is crucial."

Consequently, these platforms may be less frequently used in B2B environments and when personal relationships between suppliers and customers are required. As such, SME managers in B2B manufacturing think of how to maximize the use of social media to increase their market orientation. An owner-manager of a medium-sized temperature and control technology manufacturer said: "We need to be more active in [the] future and may use Facebook or Twitter for instance. We will only adopt these technologies when this is really meaningful in our B2B business."

A supplier can greatly increase its brand reach and awareness by means of internet-enabled technologies. For example, accessing the social media business networks where a supplier's employees are active increases the likelihood that respective potential customers belong to the same or associated industries. The implication is that:

P7: The greater the customers' presence, the greater a SME use of internet-enabled technologies to increase brand knowledge (low interactivity/low personalization).

Conclusion

This study focuses on theory development rather than theory testing. It combines the market orientation view in SMEs with internet-enabled technologies and contributes to the field with the development of a conceptual framework. Drawing on the level of personalization and the level of interactivity as the two central dimensions, our framework encompasses a wide range of internet-enabled media archetypes which essentially fulfill four roles: (1) increasing brand knowledge; (2) identifying market trends; (3) identifying new customer needs; and (4) streamlining processes. Our study thus contributes to the wider literature of ICT in small business management (Mazzarol, 2015). Most small business operators are time poor and have short planning horizons. They will need to see the benefits of any investment in ICT, and they will need to better understand the costs, risks, and benefits of doing so.

Our findings suggest that internet-enabled technologies can help SMEs to reduce the challenges they face in their attempt to develop a market orientation. However, given the plurality of technological solutions many struggle to find the best solution suited to their specific needs. We identified a series of SME-related variables (internationalization emphasis, brand orientation, niche orientation, formalization emphasis, and analytical orientation), as well as customer-related variables (operational counselling and virtual presence) which are likely to affect the roles of the internet in developing a market orientation.

Implications

This study has significant implications for SMEs and their leaders. First, SME owner-managers need to have a clear vision of the pursued role that these technologies are supposed to play for their firm. Is the goal to reduce internal complexity, to improve information dissemination and responsiveness? Is it to build relationships with new customers? Or is it to raise customers' awareness of the firm and its products in new target markets? Once the role has been defined, our conceptual framework provides SME decision-makers with useful pointers to narrow down the list of potential technologies, and to determine the required degree of personalization of information and level of interactivity with market players.

Second, the variables we have identified, and which affect the pursued roles, are largely under the control of the SME. Still, it is important for SME managers to be aware that technologies which work well for one firm might not be suitable for another firm. For example, social media might be much more attractive for SMEs that cater to B2C markets with mainly young customers. Conversely, the same technologies are of little use for SMEs if their customers are not present in social media, which is often the case in many established B2B markets. As such, the SMEs need to also be aware of customer variables – such as virtual presence and operational counseling – when adopting a specific technology.

Finally, the adopted technologies need to be integrated into organizational procedures and processes, and be part of the strategic agenda. Internet-enabled technologies can enhance SMEs' market orientation capabilities despite their inherent resource constraints. Although the implementation, usage, and maintenance of new technologies nevertheless require resources, a higher market orientation can be achieved with relatively fewer resources compared to traditional approaches. The technologies need to be embedded into existing procedures and processes with an adequate level of resources. In addition, an adequate level of senior executive commitment and managerial attention is necessary to avoid the risk that the project will be pushed aside in favor of more pressing daily operational issues. This is particularly important for technologies with high personalization of communication, which tend to require more resources and are less suited for automation.

Suggestions for Future Research and Limitations

Much work remains to be done to develop a better understanding of the contribution that internet-enabled technologies make in marketing. We would like to point out three major avenues for further research.

First, industry variables may define the scope for using internet-enabled technologies. Therefore, the moderating effect of industry variables such as maturity and competitive intensity requires further attention in future studies. For example, it might be more conducive for mature industries to focus on technologies that help to identify new market trends. It could be argued that SMEs in mature industries are more pressured to investigate and to exploit new opportunities to drive business. In particular, market leaders with well-organized internal processes are likely to have both financial and labor resources to focus on new topics compared to firms that struggle to manage their operational tasks. In contrast, young industries are likely to have more young entrepreneurs that assess new ways of increasing market orientation.

Second, we suggest putting a greater emphasis on customer experience in future research. SME owner-mangers tend to emphasize the importance of personal relationships with existing and prospective customers. At the same time, resource constraints and the required investments to nurture personal relationships confine SMEs in their internationalization efforts, which, in turn, aid the spread of internet-enabled technologies for market orientation. In this vein, the role of customer experience when interacting with SMEs using new technologies is an important field of research. For example, several owner-mangers mentioned that personal relationships remain important despite having adopted internet-enabled technologies. Interestingly, all owner-mangers who emphasized the importance of personal relationships had relatively high product pricing compared to others within their domain. Therefore, it would be useful to investigate the necessary conditions and the customer experience during the different phases of the interaction when SMEs adopt internet-enabled technologies.

Third, assessing the effectiveness of marketing-related efforts presents an intriguing challenge for SMEs. Empirical evidence with an in-depth analysis of SMEs that have adopted internet-enabled technologies would greatly contribute to understanding both objective and subjective benefits. This would complement the views presented in this paper and provide evidence of the conditional effects when a certain type of technology is advisable. In addition, further research could elaborate on ways to implement and to integrate technologies in organizational structures.

It should be noted, as a limitation to our study, that our results may not be generalized to the entire population of SMEs because our sample mainly comprises established SMEs from the precision engineering and machinery industry. Most of our SMEs were launched two or three decades ago and have long established customer databases which can give them an edge in streamlining their market orientation.

Appendix 12.1 Overview of Constructs

	Definition	Variation of value	Example	Source
Internet-enabled media	Digital technologies used to access and to provide hypermedia content in a distributed computer-mediated network	Dichotomous	Website, search engine, social media platform, content sharing platform	Celuch and Murphy (2010); Trainor et al. (2013)
Market orientation	Organization wide generatioṅ of market intelligence pertaining to current and future customer needs, dissemination of the intelligence across departments, and organization wide responsiveness to it	Continuous from zero to high market orientation	Actively monitoring regulatory changes and competition that influence the needs and preferences of customers	Jaworski and Kohli (1993); Kohli (2017)
Interactivity with market players	Degree to which internet-enabled interactions between an organization and other market players is perceived by each entity to be bidirectional, timely, mutually controllable, and responsive	Continuous from zero to high interactivity	Mass one-way communications with same content to many receivers (low interactivity)	Yadvac and Varadarajan (2005)
Personalization of information	Degree to which an organization recognizes, approaches, and treats its market players as individuals using personalized information	Continuous from zero to high personalization	Communication to selected target group and adapting content considering the group's specific needs and previous communications	Montgomery and Smith (2009)

References

Appiah-Adu, K., & Singh, S. (1998). Customer orientation and performance: A study of SMEs. *Management Decision*, *36*(6), 385–394.

Armario, J., Ruiz, D., & Armario, E. (2008). Market orientation and internationalization in small and medium-sized enterprises. *Journal of Small Business Management*, *46*(4), 485–511.

Baker, W., & Sinkula, J. (2009). The complementary effects of market orientation and entrepreneurial orientation on profitability in small business. *Journal of Small Business Management, 47*(4), 443–464.

Bart, Y. Shankar, V., Sultan, & Urban, G.L. (2005). Are the drivers and role of online trust the same for all web sites and consumers? A large-scale exploratory empirical study. *Journal of Marketing, 69*(4), 133–152.

Berry, M. (1998). Strategic planning in small high-tech companies. *Long Range Planning, 31*(3), 455–466.

Carson, D., Cromie, S., McGowan, P., & Hill, J. (1995). *Marketing and entrepreneurship in SMEs: An innovative approach.* Prentice Hall.

Carson, D., & Gilmore A. (2000). SME marketing management competencies. *International Business Review, 9*(3), 363–382.

Celuch, K, & Murphy, G. (2010). SME internet use and strategic flexibility: The moderating effect of IT market orientation. *Journal of Marketing Management, 26*(1–2), 131–145.

Cho, H., & Tansuhaj, P. (2013). Becoming a global SME: Determinants of SMEs' decision to use e-intermediaries in export marketing. *Thunderbird International Business Review, 55*(5), 513–530.

Creswell, J. (2007). *Qualitative Inquiry and Research Design,* 2nd ed. Sage.

De Swaan Arons, M., van Driest, F., & Weed, K. (2014). The ultimate marketing machine. *Harvard Business Review, 92*(7/8), 55–63.

Doern, R. (2009). Investigating barriers to SME growth and development in transition environments: A critique and suggestions for developing the methodology. *International Small Business Journal, 27,* 275–305.

Doole, I., Grimes, T., & Demack, S. (2006). An exploration of the management practices and processes most closely associated with high levels of export capability in SMEs. *Marketing Intelligence and Planning, 24*(6), 632–647.

Garengo, P., Biazzo, S., & Bititci, U. (2005). Performance measurement systems in SMEs: A review for a research agenda. *International Journal of Management Reviews, 7*(1), 25–47.

Golann, B. (2006). Achieving growth and responsiveness: Process management and market orientation in small firms. *Journal of Small Business Management, 44*(3), 369–385.

Harrigan, P., Ramsey, E., & Ibbotson, P. (2012). Exploring and explaining SME marketing: Investigating e-CRM using a mixed methods approach. *Journal of Strategic Marketing, 20*(2), 127–163.

Hills, G., Hultman, C., & Miles, M. (2008). The evolution and development of entrepreneurial marketing. *Journal of Small Business Management, 46,* 99–112.

Jack, S., Moult, S., Anderson, A.R., & Dodd, S. (2010). An entrepreneurial network evolving: Patterns of change. *International Small Business Journal, 28*(4), 315–337.

Jaworski, B., & Kohli, A. (1993). Market orientation: Antecedents and consequences. *Journal of Marketing, 57*(3), 53–70.

Kara, A., Spillan, J., & DeShields, O. (2005). The effect of a market orientation on business performance: A study of small-sized service retailers using MARKOR scale. *Journal of Small Business Management, 43*(2), 105–118.

Keskin, H. (2006). Market orientation, learning orientation and innovation capabilities in SMEs: An extended model. *European Journal of Innovation Management, 9*(4), 396–417.

Kirca, A., Jayachandran, S., & Bearden, W. (2005). Market orientation: A meta-analytic review and assessment of its antecedents and impact on performance. *Journal of Marketing, 69*(2), 24–41.

Kohli, A. (2017). Market orientation in a digital world. *Global Business Review, 18*(3), S203–S205.

Kohli, A., & Jaworski, B. (1990). Market orientation: The construct, research propositions, and managerial implications. *Journal of Marketing, 54*(2), 1–18.

Kumar, V., Jones, E., Venkatesan, R., & Leone, R. (2011). Is market orientation a source of sustainable competitive advantage or simply the cost of competing? *Journal of Marketing, 75*(1), 16–30.

Lin, J., Luo, Z., Benitez, J., Luo, X., & Popovič, A. (2021). Why do organizations leverage social media to create business value? An external factor-centric empirical investigation. *Decision Support Systems*, 113628.

Linoff, G., & Berry, M. (2011). *Data mining techniques: for marketing, sales, and customer relationship management*. John Wiley & Sons.

Malshe, A., &. Sohi, R. (2009). What makes strategy making across the sales-marketing interface more successful? *Journal of the Academy of Marketing Science*, *37*(4), 400–421.

Mazzarol, T. (2015). SMEs' engagement with E-commerce, E-business, and E-marketing. *Small Enterprise Research*, *22*(1), 79–90.

Mizik, N., & Jacobson, R. (2008). The financial value impact of perceptual brand attributes. *Journal of Marketing Research*, *45*(1), 15–32.

Montgomery, A., & Smith, M. (2009). Prospects for personalization on the internet. *Journal of Interactive Marketing*, *23*(2), 130–137.

Moreno, A., & Casillas, J. (2008). Entrepreneurial orientation and growth of SMEs: A causal model. *Entrepreneurship Theory and Practice*, *32*, 507–528.

Morgan, R., & Hunt, S. (1994). The commitment-trust theory of relationship marketing. *Journal of Marketing*, *58*(3), 20–38.

Nag, R., & Gioia, D. (2012). From common to uncommon knowledge: Foundations of firm-specific use of knowledge as a resource. *Academy of Management Journal*, *55*(2), 421–457.

Nguyen, B., Yu, X., Melewar, T., & Chen, J. (2015). Brand innovation and social media: Knowledge acquisition from social media, market orientation, and the moderating role of social media strategic capability. *Industrial Marketing Management*, *51*, 11–25.

O'Dwyer, M., Gilmore, A., & Carson, D. (2009). Innovative marketing in SMEs. *European Journal of Marketing*, *43*(1/2), 46–61.

Palmatier, R., Dant, R., & Grewal, D. (2007). A comparative longitudinal analysis of theoretical perspectives of interorganizational relationship performance. *Journal of Marketing*, *71*(4), 172–194.

Peltier, J., Schibrowsky, J., & Zhao, Y. (2009). Understanding the antecedents to the adoption of CRM technology by small retailers: Entrepreneurs vs. owner-managers. *International Small Business Journal*, *27*(3), 307–336.

Quinton, S. (2013). The community brand paradigm: A response to brand management's dilemma in the digital era. *Journal of Marketing Management*, *29*(7/8), 912–932.

Slotte-Kock, S., & Coviello, N. (2010). Entrepreneurship research on network processes: A review and ways forward. *Entrepreneurship Theory and Practice*, *34*(1), 31–57.

Saura, J., Palacios-Marqués, D., and Ribeiro-Soriano, D. (2021). Digital marketing in SMEs via data-driven strategies: Reviewing the current state of research. *Journal of Small Business Management*, 1–36.

Sousa, S., Aspinwall, E., & Rodrigues, A. (2006). Performance measures in English small and medium enterprises: Survey results. *Benchmarking: An International Journal*, *13*(1/2), 120–134.

Strauss, A., & Corbin, J. (1998). *Basics of qualitative research: techniques and procedures for developing grounded theory*. Sage Publications.

Terziovski, M. (2010). Innovation practice and its performance implications in small and medium enterprises (SMEs) in the manufacturing sector: A resource-based view. *Strategic Management Journal*, *31*(8), 892–902.

Trainor, K.J., Andzulis, J.M., Rapp, A., & Agnihotri, R. (2013). Social media technology usage and customer relationship performance: A capabilities-based examination of social CRM. *Journal of Business Research*, *67*(6), 1201–1208.

Tuli, K., Kohli, A., & Bharadwaj, S. (2007). Rethinking customer solutions: From product bundles to relational processes. *Journal of Marketing*, *71*(3), 1–17.

Vargo, S., & Lusch, R. (2004). Evolving to a new dominant logic for marketing. *Journal of Marketing*, *68*(1), 1–17.

Waldman, D., de Luque, M., & Wang, D. (2012). What can we really learn about management practices across firms and countries? *Academy of Management Perspectives, 26*(1), 34–40.

Yadav, M., & Varadarajan, R. (2005). Interactivity in the electronic marketplace: An exposition of the concept and implications for research. *Journal of the Academy of Marketing Science, 33*(4), 585–603.

Ye, Y., Yu, Q., Zheng, Y., & Zheng, Y. (2022). Investigating the effect of social media application on firm capabilities and performance: The perspective of dynamic capability view. *Journal of Business Research, 139*, 510–519

Yoganarasimhan, H. (2020). Search personalization using machine learning. *Management Science, 66*(3), 1045–1070.

Zor, U., Linder, S., & Endenich, C. (2019). CEO characteristics and budgeting practices in emerging market SMEs. *Journal of Small Business Management, 57*(2), 658–678.

Filippo Ferrari

13 Mimetic Isomorphism, Pluralistic Ignorance, and Entrepreneurial Decision-making in SMEs: A Socio-psychological Approach Explaining the Collective Diffusion of "Bad Practices" in an Organizational Field

Abstract: Empirical evidence shows that inter-organizational imitative behaviors with negative outcomes for innovation are a common occurrence in SMEs. This chapter aims to provide an explanation for the widespread diffusion of such managerial practices within an organizational field (manufacturing district, firms' network, local communities). In order to explain this diffusion, a socio-psychological approach can be very useful in addition to a managerial one. This paper also aims to provide suggestions for the prevention of these types of dysfunctional organizational innovation.

Keywords: mimetic isomorphism, SMEs, organizational innovation, pluralistic ignorance, metamanagement

Purpose of the Chapter

Every period of crisis, especially the present one of unusual length, is characterized by the perception of an uncertain future. In this complex scenario, the decision of the single actor frequently occurs within a cybernetics process typical of highly complex and uncertain decisions (Cyert & March, 1963; Minciu et al., 2020). The decision is based on perceived utility ("it works"/ "does not work"). Moreover, the decision is often based on the reinforcement principle characterizing the imitation processes, thus defining the social basis of thought and action (Bandura, 1986). This situation of ambiguity affects all corporate decision makers, but SME entrepreneurs especially (Koudstaal et al., 2019). The purpose of this chapter is to explain how, under uncertainty, SME entrepreneurs can rely on imitative mechanisms, adopting practices that prove to be dysfunctional for their business. More specifically, this chapter aims to present and discuss the socio-psychological mechanisms underlying such dysfunctional imitative processes, in particular pluralistic ignorance (Allport, 1933; Bjerring

Filippo Ferrari, University of Bologna, Bologna, Italy

https://doi.org/10.1515/9783110747652-014

et al., 2014; Monin & Norton, 2003; Perkins & Berkowitz, 1986; Sargent & Newman, 2021), and how to avoid it.

Psychological literature applied to entrepreneurship (Amato, 2012; Koudstaal et al., 2019; Simon, 1955, 1962) underlines how, in periods of uncertainty, the small entrepreneur adopts spontaneous tools and an intuitive and bounded rationality in order to make strategic decisions. Furthermore, the decision is usually guided by heuristics, that is based on the collection of incomplete information and overconfidence (Åstebro & Elhedhli, 2006; Busenitz & Barney, 1994; Gigerenzer & Gaissmaier, 2010; Weathers et al., 2005). The assumption of bounded rationality is particularly relevant to smaller firms (Lloyd-Reason & Sear, 2007). These firms have fewer resources devoted to strategic analysis than their larger competitors, and they are also characterized by higher levels of risk aversion (Di Gregorio et al., 2009). Hence, their success is critically linked to their ability to access relevant external knowledge and overcome the limits of a small size and less appetite for risk (Bruneel et al., 2010).

In accordance with a neo-institutional approach, the limited rationality of the choice processes is not only considered at the level of the single actor/decision-maker, but rather within an organizational field, i.e. a system of organizations, including competitors (Di Maggio & Powell, 1983). Social psychology has also shown that, in conditions of uncertainty and ambiguity, other people become a guide for the decision-making process (Halbesleben et al., 2007; Sargent & Newman, 2021), thus widening the focus from the single actor to the organizational field in which the company operates. Lipparini (in Pasini, 2005) underlines that, in an economic crisis in a specific sector, there is a shared responsibility between companies and the context to which they belong. In a production context which requires an intensive level of knowledge, the critical elements that characterize (both positively and negatively) such a situation of potential "contagion" can be identified by some factors. First, the complexity of the competitive context enhances the role of knowledge in facing competition that sees some actors penalized from a cost point of view. Second, through relationships, companies broaden this knowledge, adding learning from interaction to that obtained from experience. Finally, the positive relationship between common infrastructures, component suppliers and innovation (process and product), labor availability and cost efficiency is documented. All the aforementioned factors can be traced back to intangible elements, both intellectual and relational, which emphasize the role of knowledge and the dissemination of information and ideas in a given context (Lipparini, 2002; Rullani, 2004).

Indeed, entrepreneurial decision-making can result in managerial "bad practices," practices that are often the result of imitative mechanisms among entrepreneurs and their stakeholders, and generate disutility in terms of efficiency, effectiveness, fairness, and organizational reliability. Available empirical evidence suggests that imitative behaviors with negative outcomes for organizational performance are common. For example, they often occur in the noncritical adoption of franchise ownership structures (Stanworth et al., 2014), in the adoption of ISO 9000 Quality procedures (Heras-

Saizarbitoria & Boiral, 2015), in internationalization (Wood et al., 2011; Brouthers et al., 2005; Fernhaber & Li, 2010), and finally in the choice of business strategies (Meek & Wood, 2015). The available literature highlights that imitative behavior is activated mainly in conditions of uncertainty (where the future is not predictable in a clear and precise way) and ambiguity (when the available information is not complete).

The literature highlights two imitative mechanisms in particular that can be activated in conditions of uncertainty: mimetic isomorphism (Canello, 2021; Di Maggio & Powell, 1983) and pluralistic ignorance (Duffy & Lafky, 2020; also see Sargent & Newman, 2021 for a recent literature review). The first mechanism in itself does not necessarily lead to negative decisions, while the second presents more criticalities in the quality of the decision.

This chapter explains how, under uncertainty, SME entrepreneurs can rely on imitative mechanisms, adopting practices that prove to be dysfunctional for their business. Therefore, in studying these dynamics, this chapter contributes to the theory and practice of SME entrepreneurship in several ways.

First, imitative mechanisms are well-known, but their causes are not yet so clear. This chapter clarifies the socio-psychological and cognitive causes of mimetic isomorphism, thus responding to a recent call from empirical literature (Canello, 2021).

Second, this better knowledge of the socio-psychological and cognitive causes of mimetic isomorphism helps scholars and practitioners to improve the entrepreneur's decision making, generating greater utility in conditions of uncertainty and ambiguity.

Finally, by identifying the role of the meta-manager as a factor preventing the pluralistic ignorance, this study addresses local government policies towards a more specific target of action.

Theoretical Background: Ambiguity and Imitative Processes

Scholars have shared the opinion that, since the 1980s, work organizations have become extremely flexible, fragmented, and individualized over time, generating difficulties both in terms of strategic planning and day-to-day management. The difficulties encountered within the world of organizations are best identified by the term "VUCA" (Bennis & Nanus, 1985). The acronym indicates an environment characterized by:

Volatility (V) where the context is characterized by continuous and sudden changes.

Uncertainty (U) where the future is not predictable in a clear and precise way.

Complexity (C) where the context is difficult to analyze concretely.

Ambiguity (A) where, for example, the incompleteness of information does not allow for the adequate decoding of a situation under examination, generating negative responses in the subject (Peters & McKewen, 2015).

Lockdown, and other limitations due to the Covid-19 pandemic, is an excellent example of this scenario: until mid-February 2020, nobody in the world would have imagined such a profound reorganization of work and daily activities.

In a situation characterized by ambiguity and uncertainty, both an institutionalist approach (Di Maggio & Powell, 1983) and the existing literature on strategic groups (Schendel & Hofer, 1979; Thomas & Venkatraman, 1988) support the idea that the imitation of other entrepreneurial subjects can help a firm to address its own entrepreneur's limited rationality (Simon, 1955, 1962). Small businesses often lack the resources to activate internal strategic assessment procedures (Zhu et al., 2012), which often rely on the exchange of knowledge with their peers (Baum et al., 2015; Di Gregorio et al., 2009). Research has shown that, for smaller companies, the most common target group is peers located in the same region of origin (Fernhaber & Li, 2013; Milanov & Fernhaber, 2014). Furthermore, imitation can facilitate complex decisions, prepare strategic actions, and increase the legitimacy of the entrepreneur, who will therefore have easier access to external resources, such as investors or financiers (Meyer & Rowan, 1977; Peteraf & Shanley, 1997).

However, the two aforementioned approaches differ in their identification of the motivation behind this imitation. Following institutionalist theory, the largest or most prestigious companies in their field are often imitated: companies that are salient for their profitability (Haveman, 1993), their level of innovation (Semadeni & Anderson, 2010), and those that generate a high return on investment of their own capital (Haunschild & Miner, 1997). On the other hand, according to the strategic groups approach, companies perceived as more similar to their own are more likely to be imitated (Porac et al., 1995). In this case the dimensions an entrepreneur most frequently resorts to for identifying (consciously or not) a subject to imitate include organizational characteristics such as: size or reputation (Haveman, 1993); business networks to which they belong (Beckman & Haunschild, 2002); the type of product/service delivered (Porac et al., 1989; Yang & Hyland, 2006); and the geographical location (Greve, 1998; Kim & Miner, 2007). The available empirical evidence seems to confirm both hypotheses, but with the predominance of similarity, particularly for SMEs (for a review, see Yang & Hyland, 2012). For both approaches, the final result is an imitative mechanism, which can take the form of mimetic isomorphism (Canello, 2021), or pluralistic ignorance (Sargent & Newman, 2021), and the second phenomenon can help explain why the first occurs, as clarified in the paragraphs below.

Mimetic Isomorphism

The organizational processes that are most frequently imitated are; the acquisition of other companies (Baum, Li, & Usher, 2000; Yang & Hyland, 2006), the formation of alliances (Garcia-Pont and Nohria, 2002), governance and ownership structures (Lee &

Pennings, 2002), remuneration practices (Porac et al., 1999), and internationalization strategies (Canello, 2021; Xia et al., 2008). Literature presents many models to explain these imitative processes (Arkan, 2010; Gentry et al., 2013), but the best-known model is proposed by Di Maggio and Powell (1983; Di Maggio, 1997). They have provided theoretical tools to describe and explain inter-organizational imitative processes, in particular what they call mimetic isomorphism. According to this mechanism, in a situation of environmental uncertainty, organizations spontaneously activate imitative processes. In this case, imitative innovation acts as a surrogate for certainty. In the entrepreneur's vision, if all the operators present in an organizational field (district, sector, territory), in particular within companies with certain characteristics of similarity or ideality, act in a certain way it means that they have information that the entrepreneur lacks, and therefore it may seem useful to the entrepreneur to comply with it. Recent empirical investigation (Canello, 2021) suggests that mimetic isomorphism decreases the risk of cost estimation errors, driving SMEs to make better locational choices and to establish more durable relationships with foreign suppliers.

Previous findings instead supported the detrimental effects of mimetic isomorphism (Mitsuhashi, 2011). Moreover, research suggests that SMEs are often engaged in "inertial imitation" (Albertoni et al., 2019) and highlighting latent factors that can lead to negative decision-making outcomes (Heimeriks, 2010; Zollo, 2009). However, to date it is not clear in which conditions would mimetic isomorphism lead to positive versus negative consequences. Current literature therefore lacks a definitive point of view for explaining the heterogeneity of the outcomes of imitative processes. This represents a theoretical gap to which the chapter tries to provide an explanation and new insights.

In addition, mimetic isomorphism in itself is not negative, as it could also facilitate the dissemination of good managerial practices. Mimetic isomorphism is activated through contact and comparison between operators active in an organizational field. The entrepreneur's final decision is therefore taken after a process of exchange and comparison, within which theory should reduce the possibility of error. Of course, there is no deterministic relationship between situation uncertainty and mimetic isomorphism, as the available evidence supports (Canello, 2021; Yang & Hyland, 2012) that within the same organizational field the response of each single firm to isomorphism can be different. As the complexity (in terms of variety) of the context increases, the system can respond by equipping itself with adequate cognitive variety to cope with it, namely the Law of Requisite Variety (Ashby, 1952; 1960). There are some moderating variables explaining these differences, such as the past experience of the entrepreneur/ decision maker and the company's ability to absorb uncertainty (for example, because it is equipped with market analysis tools (see Haleblian et al., 2006; Haunschild & Sullivan, 2002; Li & Rowley, 2002; Miner et al., 2003). However, it is also possible that the decision process happens without a direct and explicit discussion with industry peers, and that decisions are made based on the motivation attributed to peers. In this case the decision is not due to mimetic isomorphism itself, but to the so-called pluralistic ignorance. It is therefore possible that mimetic isomorphism is due to pluralistic ignorance, a socio-cognitive mechanism that activates and directs it, which is presented in the next paragraph.

Pluralistic Ignorance

Situations in which an entrepreneur decides to adopt a chosen strategy due to the fact that he/she believes the majority of peers will act in that way are different from mimetic isomorphism, and have been investigated less in empirical research. Such a situation is made possible by the so-called pluralistic ignorance, which can favor the spread of "bad practices" in an organizational field. Social psychology has described this mechanism extensively (Allport, 1933; Bjerring et al., 2014; Monin & Norton, 2003; Perkins & Berkowitz, 1986; for a recent review, see Sargent & Newman, 2021). Pluralistic ignorance is the belief that one's attitude toward a problem (for example, innovation or the use of offshoring) is different from that of other group members, although everyone's behavior is identical (Allport, 1933). Following the existing literature on strategic groups (Schendel & Hofer 1979; Thomas & Venkatraman 1988), it is in fact assumed that, in a situation characterized by ambiguity, an entrepreneur decides how to behave by observing the behavior of other entrepreneurs, and therefore conforming to the aim of reducing this ambiguity (Perkins & Berkowitz, 1986). However, this phenomenon applies to all entrepreneurs in the field of analysis, and the result is that each entrepreneur perceives themselves to be the only one without full knowledge of the situation. The paradoxical result is that a group behavior discrepant from the beliefs of each member emerges (Bjerring et al., 2014). This is possible because observing does not mean interacting: the reasons for the behavior of others are inferred, and not verified. Moreover, the diffusion of an observed phenomenon can be vitiated by the observed sample, and subject to statistical error. In other words, pluralistic ignorance is activated whenever an actor attributes a certain motivation for a behavior to another actor in the same organizational field, without verifying this attribution, and without worrying about the statistical significance of the observed behavior (Sargent & Newman, 2021). A group member is assumed to infer group norms by observing the behavior of other members, and then conforming because they believe the others have information they lack (Perkins & Berkowitz, 1986). Furthermore, Monin and Norton (2003) emphasize the importance of consensus on what is right and what is wrong in a given situation. If each entrepreneur (singularly) develops a personal critical position toward the adoption of a certain organizational practice, but during a discussion between peers no one mentions their personal position, most entrepreneurs will adopt this practice, and in the end each entrepreneur will come to the conclusion that it is not an anomaly, but "good" practice. This is the way pluralistic ignorance has its effect.

Empirical Evidence Supporting the Theoretical Model: The Offshoring Decision

An example of the imitative dynamic is the decision, common to many companies in the same sector, to relocate production activities by moving abroad (offshoring). This decision has had an extremely significant and negative impact on the local economy in the mid-term, and therefore becomes a case study very suitable for investigating imitative processes.

In the early nineties, many large companies from around the world moved their businesses abroad. This is due to the increased competitiveness of Eastern European countries, whose labor and property costs were more advantageous than in Western Europe. They were also driven by the imitation of competitors, also active in the opening of company branches in Eastern Europe (Di Mauro et al., 2018). As for Italy, many studies show that the sector most affected by the offshoring phenomenon is manufacturing. To understand why the manufacturing sector moved abroad, it is enough to think about the production of clothing, fabrics, and the processing of leather goods. These types of production processes are so-called "labor-intensive" and as already mentioned it is easy to understand the reason for moving production abroad where labor has a lower cost. However, after a few years these companies decided to return to their homeland, abandoning the initial project and incurring backshoring costs. According to the December 2017 annual report conducted by the Studies and Research Department of Banca Intesa San Paolo entitled "Economics and finance of industrial districts," the most well-known cases of backshoring that have occurred in recent years have involved renowned fashion brands such as Louis Vuitton, Prada, Ferragamo, Ermenegildo Zegna, Bottega Veneta, Geox, Benetton and manufacturers of bags and suitcases such as Piquadro and Nannini. The need to shorten the production chains to make them more sustainable and resistant to the impacts of any future crises has therefore prompted more and more companies to think about repayment plans of which, as regards Italy, there were already 175 in April 2020 (Fratocchi et al., 2014).

According to a model of absolute rationality, in making a decision to relocate the company, an entrepreneur should evaluate the economic and organizational feasibility of any operation, by analyzing the scenario and calculating costs and risks. Despite this, however, the forecasted scenario does not always coincide with the actual scenario (Canello, 2021). Many companies, after having relocated, suffer the negative events brought about by the operation itself that had not been adequately assessed. Some companies have failed in the activity of relocation because, for example, they had not taken into consideration whether offshoring was really an opportunity that could be adapted to their business model, or, alternatively, because they had not made the right considerations regarding suppliers, or because they had decided to outsource at all costs, not taking into account the complexity of their value chain (Baronchielli, 2008).

Informal interactions with the external environment can increase awareness of international opportunities, facilitating the process of acquiring knowledge (for a review, see Dabić et al., 2020; Johanson & Mattsson, 2015), but at the same time also favor the spread of "bad practices." Indeed, research highlights that misjudgments are more common among smaller firms, which often rely on incomplete and inefficient assessment methods and lack systematic location planning and forecasting capabilities (Kinkel, 2014; Kinkel et al., 2007). Other empirical research has already highlighted episodes of pluralistic ignorance in the fashion and footwear sector (Ferrari, 2015a; 2015b; 2015c). In particular, in a study conducted by Ferrari (2019), a panel of 12 entrepreneurs was involved in a series of focus groups aimed at understanding the reasons for their original decision to relocate, a decision that turned out to be negative from a strategic point of view. In fact, the 12 entrepreneurs were chosen from among those who made backshoring choices at a later time. It emerged that all entrepreneurs had experienced one or more negative factors related to the offshoring decision. During the focus groups, it also emerged that all the entrepreneurs had formulated hypotheses on why the decision to relocate was taken, and on the positive and negative consequences. However, it also emerged that four entrepreneurs (of 12) had carried out a methodologically-based scenario analysis before the decision to relocate. Ten had talked to their accountant, and all had inquired at the Chamber of Commerce, the Industrial Association or other institutions. However, and this is the most significant data qualitatively, only two had dealt directly with other competing entrepreneurs who had already relocated, and had tried to gather information on how to relocate, not on why or on the consequences of the decision. In other words, their decision to relocate was mainly based on their own hypotheses attributed to other economic actors in the same organizational field; these hypotheses had a good level of agreement and homogeneity, but no one had verified the empirical basis of these hypotheses. Given these characteristics, this scenario is configured as a case of pluralistic ignorance that has favored the spread of bad practices in an organizational field (for more details on this study, see Ferrari, 2019).

Further evidence appears to support these mechanisms. Investigating the mechanisms underlying the strategic decision of offshoring and, subsequently, backshoring, Canello (2021) highlighted that the imitative processes are activated more frequently in the offshoring decision, but fail in the subsequent backshoring one. This suggests that the driver of the first decision is imitation, and experiential learning of the second (Canello, 2021). The same study suggests that imitative behaviors are activated when there is a local peer community, but not when the entrepreneur decides on the basis of direct contact with suppliers. The negative outcomes of strategic decisions may therefore be due to, at least in part, pluralistic ignorance. By making the most of real knowledge (i.e. not simply observed and/or perceived as such) available in an organizational field, managers can increase their propensity to anticipate the "hidden costs" of the decision (Larsen, 2016; Manning, 2014), moderating the risk of facing unforeseen challenges in the short term. Theoretical reflection is at this point called on to question how to prevent the spread of bad practices as a consequence of imitative mechanisms based on a perceived and not real decision-making mainstream. The literature suggests that for this purpose it is appropriate to activate a subject with a metamanagerial role within a specific organizational field.

The Metamanagerial Governance of the Organizational Field

The literature in both the economic-organizational and socio-psychological areas suggests that environmental ambiguity is the most direct antecedent of mimetic isomorphism and pluralistic ignorance. Furthermore, the literature provides evidence of the importance of business networks in generating imitative behaviors (Gentry et al., 2013; Galaskiewitcz & Burt, 1991). Therefore, any strategy with the aim of preventing this degeneration must reduce ambiguity through the circulation of information. Canello (2021) suggests that politicians can improve these mechanisms, leveraging the role of local industry associations and promoting both the dissemination of opportunities and the establishment of new forms and informal relations within the region (Costa et al., 2015).

To this end, the literature supports the importance of an actor (e.g. an organization) that plays a metamanagerial role in the governance of the organizational field and in the evaluation of value generation processes (Ferrari & Emiliani, 2007; Lipparini, 2002; Visconti, 2002). The absence of a strategic decision-making center risks constituting an element of weakness in the district, or more generally, in an organizational field (Brusco, 1990; Dimitriadis et al., 2010; Norman, 1979). However, what actually is a metamanager? Metamanagement is a role (or a set of roles) whose fundamental task is to ensure that the system adapts to changes in the environmental context. Naturally, in order not to fall into an inappropriate deterministic logic, the metamanager is subject to influence by the actors in the system, and experiences change in the course of their action (for mutual causations see among others Senge, 2006). Literature (Bhaumik et al., 2012; Dimitriadis et al., 2010), does not support a greater a priori rationality of the metamanager, nor a top-down model of dissemination of good practices, but rather a model of participatory design. For example, Ferrari and Emiliani (2007) report a case study that provides a good example of metamanagerial action. In the nineties, in the sports shoe sector in the north-east of Italy, the offshoring practices adopted by many companies had negative effects on the local economy. In such cases, the domestic supply chain is likely to collapse, and negatively affects the stability of informal social networks (see also Baraldi et al., 2018). High schools abandoned their educational path addressing footwear studies and no longer graduated students with the necessary skills. When the backshoring phenomenon began, companies could no longer find the necessary professionalism and skills on the job market. Furthermore, reshoring firms might face resistance, lack of commitment or distrust, as they might be perceived as unfaithful to the local domestic community (Baraldi et al., 2018). The metamanagerial role was then played by the local association of entrepreneurs (Associazione degli Industriali) in the "control room" with the Regional Government, which financed and activated professional training courses within schools; at the same time, training courses were financed not for single companies but for entrepreneurs in the supply chain, in order to reactivate customer-supplier partnerships. Finally, funds and contributions were allocated to favor the new productive settlements, as the previous structure had been abandoned.

In a scenario of spontaneous dissemination of knowledge and innovative practices, deriving from the interrelationships between entrepreneurs, it is necessary to aim for the conception of regulatory mechanisms in contexts that do not arise from the hierarchy or from the market (Williamson, 1985). The focus may be on the transaction, that is, the exchange of goods and services between two technically separable interfaces, such as the entrepreneur and his/her supplier (Ouchi, 1980). In the case of knowledge, the market in which these transactions take place is a network made up of companies and their knowledge suppliers (universities, research institutions, learning agencies, consultants). Visconti (2002) stresses that entrepreneurship is a widespread resource in a company or in a territory, can be carried out by several subjects, and is not necessarily attributable to individuals or coinciding with the ownership of the company.

In other words, it is useful to define the metamanager, the subject who, in a given economic context, plays the leading role in the system. A subject who does not directly carry out the action, but who takes on the responsibility of creating the conditions so that others (companies) can produce and undertake said action. Naturally, a metamanager is not personally endowed with a rationality superior to those of the actors in the organizational field, but often has a broader vision that allows them to activate, in a participatory manner, the expertise necessary to deal with the spread of "bad practices." Some further empirical evidence available (Dimitriadis et al., 2010; Ferrari et al., 2007; Ferrrari & Emiliani, 2007; Ferrari et al., 2006) suggests that the heterogeneity of skills and the direct emanation from the organizational field help the metamanager reduce ambiguity, and at the same time direct the action of the actors in the organizational field.

The Focus of Metamanagement: Intangible Asset Development

Metamanagement actions can take place in various areas, such as the creation and improvement of infrastructures, the formulation of development visions, external communication, the enhancement of synergies and interrelationships, and finally the development of intangible assets (Visconti, 2002). Referring more specifically to mimetic isomorphism, the concomitance of typical characteristics of entrepreneurship (Amato, 2012) and psychosocial phenomena direct metamanagerial action toward formative logic, that is, the development of intangible capital. The development of intangible assets, training policies, and the creation and dissemination of knowledge in the organizational field are of fundamental importance: the cognitive dimension is in fact a pivotal factor for understanding the reasons for entrepreneurial success and for evaluating the development potential. Where knowledge and skills are usually tacit and contextual in nature, they are difficult to transfer and subject to obsolescence. Furthermore, they are prone to distortions related to the limited rationality of decision makers, pluralistic ignorance and the above-described imitative processes. A powerful tool for hindering the spread of "bad practices" is the development of a "culture of evidence," objectivity and quantitatively appreciable and measurable results among the players in the organizational field. In other words, an important metamanagerial function is to provide decision makers with "antibodies" to defend themselves against the contagion of "bad practices." The specific objective of the metamanager is therefore to activate the appropriate information bases, and help the managerialization of SMEs.

Who Can be a Metamanager?

The aforementioned scarce empirical experiences makes it premature to try to identify metamanagers definitely. Nevertheless, the question remains: who can be a metamanager? It is possible to identify different organizations that can carry out a metamanagement role (Visconti, 2002). In Italy there are the so-called *Comitati di Distretto* (Cluster Committees), identified by Law 347/91. Universities, which can offer a contribution to the development and functioning of the economic system, are still, in reality, actually rather scarce, acting as metamanagers of the intellectual capital of the territory. Elsewhere, the Chambers of Commerce, Industry, Agriculture, and Crafts (CCIAA), with Law 580/93, assume ample autonomy in defining political-institutional guidelines and their services. Local banks have historically contributed to the system by offering various financial stimuli, although not training stimuli. Business associations aggregate, select, defend, and promote the interests of their members. Finally, the Learning Agencies have traditionally played a role of assisting in the production of knowledge, and being rooted in a territory/sector. The research carried out (Ferrari et al., 2007; Ferrrari & Emiliani, 2007; Ferrari et al., 2006) suggests that it is this latter subject (i.e. the Learning Agencies), often in the "control room" with one or more of the others such as a potential metamanager, who are able to contribute to creating the conditions for the development of intellectual capital in a given territory or sector.

Regarding the working methods of the metamanager, empirical evidence supports an approach based at the same time on both a top-down and a bottom-up logic for the dissemination of good practices. To this end, the analysis of training needs to be linked to innovation, in order to achieve specific territorial/sector training plans, and is an essential practice to help reach a balance between the top-down logic and the enhancement of the needs of individual entrepreneurs. For the latter, in fact, it is very difficult to establish a priori which innovation should be imitated and which not. Since the metamanager is not the bearer of an innovation proposal per se, but creates the conditions of context, the "good" innovation must arise from a participatory process (Iscoe & Harris, 1984; Lewin, 1946), of which the metamanager is the director.

In summary, the metamanager should be inspired by management principles appropriate to the complexity of the system (Ashby, 1960). They should focus more on interconnections than on structures: knowing the networks of competence (the people who hold the know-how), trust or communication, allows us to understand the real functioning of the production context and to identify the changes that improve its organization.

It should also build generative contexts: complexity requires flexibility and speed of action by all members of the organization. To this end, the metamanager is not the one who decides the strategy, defines the action plans, and checks that others do. The metamanager is transformed into a constructor of generative contexts that leave autonomy to entrepreneurs but at the same time guide collective behaviors towards the objectives of the local economy.

Finally, it should develop cognitive redundancy: as suggested by Ashby (1960), through his Law of Requisite Variety, to govern a complex system it is necessary to have a complexity (understood as a variety of possible behaviors) similar to or superior to that system. In this sense, imitative behaviors could reduce the behavioral variety of the system.

Conclusions and Future Research Directions

Some empirical evidence (Dimitriadis et al., 2010; Ferrari et al., 2007; Ferrrari & Emiliani, 2007) suggests that the heterogeneity of skills and the territorial proximity help the metamanager to reduce ambiguity, and at the same time to direct the action of the actors in the organizational field. In the light of what has emerged from literature (Yang & Hyland, 2012), and according to the Law of Requisite Variety especially (Ashby, 1952, 1960), it is necessary for the metamanagerial action to focus on an and provide the services to an extremely specific target group of companies, i.e. groups of homogeneous companies for geographical location, size, product/service created. This approach refers to the Law of Requisite Variety: as the complexity (in terms of variety) of the context increases, the system must equip itself with adequate cognitive variety to cope with it (Ashby, 1952, 1960). This approach leads to a reduction of pluralistic ignorance (Ferrari et al., 2006).

The metamanager is therefore a methodologist, not a content expert. The role and contribution of the experts (researchers, consultants) becomes crucial, as they are called on by the metamanager to carry out the delicate task of providing entrepreneurs with the elements to distinguish between "perceived diffusion and motivation" and "real diffusion and motivation" of a strategic decision in an organizational field, but also between "good practices" and "bad practices." The novelty with respect to the traditional proliferation of consultancy is that the action of the expert must be based on the principle of scientific evidence (evidence-based management), a principle sometimes disregarded by the experts themselves (see the example of "use of common sense in human resource management," Rynes et al., 2002). Another ever-present problem is that of financial sustainability. Based on the theoretical arguments illustrated, and given the lack of empirical data deriving from "bad" innovation, the creation of a territorial metamanager is not justified solely by the need to prevent non-rational behavior by members of the local system. The metamanagerial action does not result in the creation of new jobs, but in the application of a working method by subjects who are already operating in a territory (learning agencies, consultants, researchers).

In order to broaden the discussion, a promising line of future research could focus on information socialization practices that do not require the presence of a metamanager. For example, beyond the problem of pluralistic ignorance discussed in this article, the literature indicates some critical issues that have recently emerged, which cast doubt on the original hypotheses that supported collective rationality in decision-making processes. Some studies (Lorenz et al., 2011) seem to indicate that the socialization of information with peer-to-peer logic in the time of social networks weakens collective rationality, as has been identified since Galton's pioneering studies (1907). It is increasingly questioned that a collective value judgment (such as the average of individual valuations) is more reliable than single individual valuations. Future research will therefore be able to investigate alternative mechanisms for pluralistic ignorance in order to explain (and prevent) "bad" innovation.

Finally, the research (and the practice adopted by consultants) will have to focus on the resistance that the metamanager has to face in its action. This resistance can be identified in a scarce diffusion and lack of attention to "evolved" managerial practices in the SME system (Biasetti et al., 2009). Research is called upon to provide the "access keys" to effectively intervene and tackle these obstacles to the dissemination of good managerial practices.

Bibliography

Albertoni, F., Elia, S., & Piscitello, L. (2019). Inertial vs. mindful repetition of previous entry mode choices: Do firms always learn from experience? *Journal of Business Research, 103*, 530–546. https://doi.org/10.1016/j.jbusres.2018.02.034

Allport, G. (1933). *Institutional behavior*. University of North Carolina Press.

Amato, C. (2012). *Psicologia dell'imprenditorialità*. Armando Armando Editore.

Arkan, A. (2010). Regional entrepreneurial transformation: A complex systems perspective. *Journal of Small Business Management, 48*(2), 152–173.

Ashby, W.R. (1952). *Design for a Brain*. John Wiley.

Ashby, W.R. (1960). *An introduction to cybernetics*. Chapman & Hall.

Åstebro, T., & Elhedhli, S. (2006). The effectiveness of simple decision heuristics: Forecasting commercial success for early-stage ventures. *Management Science, 52*(3), 395–409. https://doi.org/10.1287/mnsc.1050.0468

Bandura, A. (1986). *Social foundation of thought and action*. Prentice-Hall.

Baraldi, E., Ciabuschi, F., Lindahl, O., & Fratocchi, L. (2018). A network perspective on the reshoring process: The relevance of the home-and the host-country contexts. *Industrial Marketing Management, 70*, 156–166. https://doi.org/10.1016/j.indmarman.2017.08.016

Baronchielli G., (2008), *"La delocalizzazione nei mercati internazionali. Dagli IDE all'offshoring"*, LED Edizioni Universitarie.

Baum, J., Li, S., & Usher, J. (2000). Making the next move: How experiential and vicarious learning shape the locations of chains' acquisition. *Administrative Science Quarterly, 45*(4), 766–801. https://doi.org/10.2307%2F2667019

Baum, M., Schwens, C., & Kabst, R. (2015). A latent class analysis of small firms' internationalization patterns. *Journal of World Business, 50*(4), 754–768. https://doi.org/10.1016/j.jwb.2015.03.001

Beckman, C.M., & Haunschild, P.R. (2002). Network learning: The effects of partners' heterogeneity of experience on corporate acquisitions. *Administrative Science Quarterly* (47), 92–124. http://dx.doi.org/10.2307/3094892

Bennis, W., & Nanus, B. (1985). *Leaders: Strategies for taking charge*. Harper & Row.

Bhaumik, S.K., Dimova, R., Kumbhakar, S.C., & Sun, K. (2012). *Does institutional quality affect firm performance? Insights from a semiparametric approach*. IZA DP No. 6351.

Biasetti, C., Ferrari, F., Franciosi, F., & Venturelli, M.C. (2009). *Il futuro della mia impresa. Pratiche manageriali per garantire la longevità del business nelle PMI*. Franco Angeli.

Bjerring, J.C., Hansen, J.U., & Pedersen, N.J.L.L. (2014). On the rationality of pluralistic ignorance. *Synthese* (191), 2445–2470.

Bonesso, S., Gerli, F., & Scapolan, A. (2014). The individual side of ambidexterity: Do individuals' perceptions match actual behaviors in reconciling the exploration and exploitation trade-off? *European Management Journal, 32*(3), 392–405. https://doi.org/10.1016/j.emj.2013.07.003

Brouthers, L.E., O'Donnell, E., & Hadjimarcou J. (2005). Generic product strategies for emerging market exports into triad nation markets: A mimetic isomorphism approach. *Journal of Management Studies, 42*(1), 225–245. https://doi.org/10.1111/j.1467-6486.2005.00495.x

Bruneel, J., Yli-Renko, H., & Clarysse, B. (2010). Learning from experience and learning from others: How congenital and interorganizational learning substitute for experiential learning in young firm internationalization. *Strategic Entrepreneurship Journal, 4*(2), 164–182. https://doi.org/10.1002/sej.89

Brusco, S. (1990). The idea of the industrial district: Its genesis. In F. Pike, G. Becattini, & W. Sengenberger (Eds.), *Industrial districts and interfirm cooperation in Italy*. International Institute for Labor Studies.

Busenitz, L.W., & Barney, J.B. (1994). Biases and heuristics in strategic decision making: Differences between entrepreneurs and managers in large organizations. *Proceedings*, 85–89. https://doi.org/10.5465/ambpp.1994.10341736

Cagliano, R., & Spina, G. (2000). *Pratiche gestionali e successo competitivo nella piccola impresa e nell'artigianato*. Franco Angeli.

Canello, J. (2021). Mimetic isomorphism, offshore outsourcing and backshoring decisions among micro and small enterprises. *Regional Studies*. http://dx.doi.org/10.1080/00343404.2021.1937596

Costa, E., Soares, A. L., & de Sousa, J. P. (2015). *A new insight in the SMEs internationalization process*. In Camarinha-Matos, L., Bénaben, F., & Picard, W. (Eds.), *Risks and resilience of collaborative networks*.

PRO-VE 2015 (IFIP Advances in Information and Communication Technology Vol. 463). Springer. https://doi.org/10.1007/978-3-319-24141-8_36

Cyert, R.M., & March, J.J. (1963). *A behavioral theory of the firm*. Prentice Hall.

Dabić, M., Maley, J., Dana, L.P., et al. (2020). Pathways of SME internationalization: A bibiometric and systematic review. *Small Business Economics*, *55*, 705–725. https://doi.org/10.1007/s'1187-019-00181-6

Di Gregorio, D., Musteen, M., & Thomas, D.E. (2009). Offshore outsourcing as a source of international competitiveness for SMEs. *Journal of International Business Studies*, *40*(6), 969–988. https://doi.org/10.1057/jibs.2008.90

Di Maggio, P.J. (1997). Culture and cognition. *Annual Review of Sociology* (23), 263–287. https://doi.org/10.1146/annurev.soc.23.1.263

Di Maggio, P.J., & Powell, W.W. (1983). The iron cage revisited – institutional isomorphism and collective rationality in organizational fields. *American Sociological Review*, *48*(2), 147–160. https://doi.org/10.2307/2095101

Di Mauro, C., Fratocchi, L., Orzes, G., & Sartor, M. (2018). Offshoring and backshoring: A multiple case study analysis. *Journal of purchasing and supply management*, *24*(2), 108–134. https://doi.org/10.1016/j.pursup.2017.07.003

Dimitriadis, N., Simpson, M., & Andronikidis, A. (2010). Knowledge diffusion in localised economies of SMEs: The role of local supporting organisations. *Environment and Planning C: Government and Policy* (23), 799–814.

Duffy, J., & Lafky, J. (2020). Social conformity under evolving private preferences available at SSRN. https://ssrn.com/abstract=3226057 or http://dx.doi.org/10.2139/ssrn.3226057

Fernhaber, S.A., & Li, D. (2010). The impact of interorganizational imitation on new venture international entry and performance. *Entrepreneurship Theory and Practice*, *34*(1), 1–30.

Fernhaber, S.A., & Li, D. (2013). International exposure through network relationships: Implications for new venture internationalization. *Journal of Business Venturing*, *28*(2), 316–334. https://doi.org/10.1016/j.jbusvent.2012.05.002

Ferrari, F. (2009). La Gestione del Capitale Relazionale. In C. Biasetti, F. Ferrari, F. Franciosi, & M.C. Venturelli, *Il futuro della mia impresa. Pratiche manageriali per garantire la longevità del business nelle PMI'*. Franco Angeli.

Ferrari, F. (2009). La Gestione del Capitale Relazionale. In C. Biasetti, F. Ferrari, F. Franciosi, & M.C. Venturelli (Eds.), *Il futuro della mia impresa. Pratiche manageriali per garantire la longevità del business nelle PMI'*. Franco Angeli.

Ferrari, F. (2015a, October 30–31). *The back-shoring process and its impact on Human Resources Management practices. First empirical evidence and some issues for the future research agenda*. Paper presented at the AIB Conference *Breaking up the global value chain: Possibilities and consequences*, Milano, Italy.

Ferrari, F. (2015b, September 24–25). *Isomorfismo mimetico e diffusione di pratiche disfunzionali nelle PMI. La cattiva innovazione di processo nel fronteggiamento della crisi*. Paper presented at the 4° Workshop – Re-positioning of SMEs in the Global Value System, Urbino, Italy.

Ferrari, F. (2015c, July, 2–4). *Re-shoring and skill mismatch. Training needs analysis in school-to-work transition*. Paper presented at the 27th Annual Meeting of the Society for the Advancement of Socio-Economics, London.

Ferrari, F. (2019). Global labor market, "re-shoring" dynamics, and skill mismatch: An exploratory study at a job-specific level. In B. Christiansen, I. Sysoeva, A. Udovikina, & A. Ketova (Eds.), *Emerging economic models for global sustainability and social development* (pp. 125–143). IGI Global. https://doi.org/10.4018/978-1-5225-5787-6.ch007

Ferrari, F., & Emiliani, E. (2007). *Percorsi di sviluppo nei distretti multipolari. La gestione delle risorse umane per l'innovazione*. Franco Angeli.

Ferrari, F., Timoncini, B., & Conzatti, S. (2007). *Piani Formativi di Settore: la formazione per lo sviluppo locale. Una proposta a sostegno dello sviluppo delle Cinque Valli Bolognesi.* MPRA Paper n. 20624, University Library of Munich.

Ferrari, F., Timoncini, B., Conzatti, S., & Teglia, E. (2006). *Quaderno di lavoro del "Progetto di sviluppo territoriale della Comunità Montana Cinque Valli Bolognesi".* MPRA Paper n. 20628, University Library of Munich.

Fitzsimmons, M. (2006). The problem of uncertainty in strategic planning. *Survival, 48*(4), 131–146. DOI: 10.1080/00396330601062808

Fratocchi L., Di Mauro C., Barbieri P., Nassimbeni G., Zanoni A. (2014). When manufacturing moves back: Concepts and questions. *Journal of Purchasing and Supply Management,* 20, 1, 54–59. https://doi.org/10.1016/j.pursup.2014.01.004

Galaskiewicz, J., & Burt, R.S. (1991). Interorganization contagion in corporate philanthropy. *Administrative Science Quarterly, 36*(1), 88–105.

Galton, F. (1907). Vox Populi. *Nature, 75,* 450–451. https://doi.org/10.1038/075450a0

Garcia-Pont, C., & Nohria, N. (2002). Local versus global mimetism: The dynamics of alliance formation in the automobile industry. *Strategic Management Journal, 23*(4), 307–321.

Gentry, R.J., Dalziel, T., & Jamison, M.A. (2013). Who do start-up firms imitate? A study of new market entries in the CLEC industry. *Journal of Small Business Management, 51*(4), 525–538. DOI: 10.1111/jsbm.12055

Gigerenzer, G., & Gaissmaier, W. (2010). Heuristic decision making. *Annual Review of Psychology, 62*(1), 451–482. https://doi.org/10.1146/annurev-psych-120709-145346

Greve, H.R. (1998). Managerial cognition and the mimetic adoption of market positions: What you see is what you do. *Strategic Management Journal, 19*(10), 967–988. http://www.jstor.org/stable/3094172

Halbesleben, J.R.B., Wheeler, A.R., & Buckley, M.R. (2007). Understanding pluralistic ignorance in organizations: Application and theory. *Journal of Managerial Psychology, 22*(1), 65–83. https://doi.org/10.1108/02683940710721947

Haleblian, J., Kim, J., & Rajagopalan, N. (2006). The influence of acquisition experience and performance on acquisition behavior: Evidence from the US commercial banking industry. *Academy of Management Journal, 49*(2), 357–70. http://dx.doi.org/10.5465/AMJ.2006.20786083

Haunschild, P.R., & Miner, A. (1997). Modes of interorganizational imitation: The effects of outcome salience and uncertainty. *Administrative Science Quarterly, 42*(3), 472–500.

Haunschild, P., & Sullivan, B. (2002). Learning from complexity: Effects of prior accidents and incidents on airlines' learning. *Administrative Science Quarterly, 47*(4), 609–43.

Haveman, H.A. (1993). Follow the leader – Mimetic isomorphism and entry into new markets. *Administrative Science Quarterly, 38*(4), 593–627.

Heimeriks, K.H. (2010). Confident or competent? How to avoid superstitious learning in alliance portfolios. *Long Range Planning, 43*(1), 57–84. https://doi.org/10.1016/j.lrp.2009.10.004

Heras-Saizarbitoria, I., & Boiral, O. (2015). Exploring the dissemination of environmental certifications in high and low polluting industries. *Journal of cleaner production* (89), 50–58.

Koudstaal, M., Sloof, R., & Praag, M. (2019). Entrepreneurs: Intuitive or contemplative decision-makers? *Small Business Economics, 53*(4), 901–920. DOI: 10.1007/s11187-018-0109-2

Iscoe, I., & Harris, L.C. (1984). Social and community interventions. *Annual Review of Psychology Social and Community Interventions, 35,* 333–60. doi: 10.1146/annurev.ps.35.020184.002001

Intesa San Paolo. (2018). *Economia e finanza dei distretti industriali – Rapporto annuale n. 10 – 2018.* https://group.intesasanpaolo.com/content/dam/portalgroup/repository-documenti/research/it/economia-e-finanza-dei-distretti/10_Economia%2e%20finanza%20dei%20distretti%20industriali.pdf

Johanson, J., & Mattsson, L.G. (2015). *Internationalisation in industrial systems – A network approach.* In M. Forsgren, U. Holm, & J. Johanson (Eds.), *Knowledge, networks and power.* Palgrave Macmillan. https://doi.org/10.1057/9781137508829_5

Kinkel, S. (2014). Future and impact of backshoring – some conclusions from 15 years of research on German practices. *Journal of Purchasing and Supply Management, 20*(1), 63–65. https://doi.org/10.1016/j.pursup.2014.01.005

Kinkel, S., Lay, G., & Maloca, S. (2007). Development, motives and employment effects of manufacturing offshoring of German SMEs. *International Journal of Entrepreneurship and Small Business, 4*(3), 256–276. https://doi.org/10.1504/IJESB.2007.013251

Kim, J., & Miner, A. (2007). Vicarious learning from the failures and near-failures of others: Evidence from the US commercial banking industry. *Academy of Management Journal* (50), 687–714. https://journals.aom.org/doi/abs/10.5465/amj.2007.25529755

Larsen, M.M. (2016). Failing to estimate the costs of offshoring: A study on process performance. *International Business Review, 25*(1), 307–318. https://doi.org/10.1016/j.ibusrev.2015.05.008

Lee, K., & Pennings, J.M. (2002). Mimicry and the market: Adoption of a new organizational form. *Academy of Management Journal, 45*(1), 144–162. https://journals.aom.org/doi/abs/10.5465/3069289

Lewin, K. (1946). Action research and minority problems. *Journal of Social Issues* (2), 34–35.

Li, S., & Rowley, T. (2002). Inertia and evaluation mechanisms in interorganizational partner selection: Syndicate formation among US investment banks. *Academy of Management Journal, 45*, 1104–19. https://journals.aom.org/doi/abs/10.5465/3069427

Lipparini, A. (2002). *La gestione strategica del capitale intellettuale e del capitale relazionale.* Il Mulino.

Lloyd-Reason, L., & Sear, L. (2007). *Trading places–SMEs in the global economy: A critical research handbook.* Edward Elgar.

Lorenz, J., Rauhutb, H., Schweitzera, F., & Helbing, D. (2011). How social influence can undermine the wisdom of crowd effect. *PNAS, 108*(22), 9020–9025.

Manning, S. (2014). Mitigate, tolerate or relocate? Offshoring challenges, strategic imperatives and resource constraints. *Journal of World Business, 49*(4), 522–535. https://doi.org/10.1016/j.jwb.2013.12.006

Meek, W.R., & Wood, M.S. (2016). Navigating a sea of change: Identity misalignment and adaptation in academic entrepreneurship. *Entrepreneurship Theory and Practice, 40*(5), 1093–1120. https://doi.org/10.1111/etap.12163

Meyer, J.W., & Rowan B. (1977). Institutionalized organizations: Formal structure as myth and ceremony. *American Journal of Sociology, 83*(2), 340–363.

Milanov, H., & Fernhaber, S.A. (2014). When do domestic alliances help ventures abroad? Direct and moderating effects from a learning perspective. *Journal of Business Venturing, 29*(3), 377–391. https://doi.org/10.1016/j.jbusvent.2013.05.004

Minciu, M., Berar, F.A., & Dobrea, R.C. (2020). New decision systems in the VUCA world. *Management & Marketing. Challenges for the Knowledge Society, 15*(2), 236–254. DOI: 10.2478/mmcks-2020-0015

Miner, A., Haunschild, P., & Schwab, A. (2003). Experience and convergence: Curiosities and speculation. *Industrial and Corporate Change, 12*(4), 789–813.

Mitsuhashi, H. (2011). Almost identical experience biases in vicarious learning. *Industrial and Corporate Change, 21*(4), 837–869. https://doi.org/10.1093/icc/dtr068

Molteni, M., & Sainaghi, R. (1997). Il metamanagement di un distretto turistico. *Economia e Management* (6), 159–82.

Monin B., & Norton, M.I. (2003). Perceptions of a fluid consensus: Uniqueness bias, false consensus, false polarization, and pluralistic ignorance in a water conservation crisis. *Personality And Social Psychology Bulletin, 29*(5), 559–567.

Normann, R. (1979). *Le condizioni di sviluppo dell'impresa*, Etas Libri.

Ouchi, W.G. (1980). Markets, bureaucracies, and clans. *Administrative Science Quarterly, 25*(2), 129–141.

Pasini, F. (Ed.). (2005). *I sistemi produttivi locali nell'economia della conoscenza.* Franco Angeli.

Perkins, H.W., & Berkowitz, A.D. (1986). Perceiving the community norms of alcohol use among students: Some research implications for campus alcohol education programming. *International Journal of the Addictions*, *21*(9/10), 961–976. https://psycnet.apa.org/doi/10.3109/10826088609077249

Peteraf, M., & Shanley, M. (1997). Getting to know you: A theory of strategic group identity. *Strategic Management Journal* (18), 165–186. https://doi.org/10.1002/(SICI)1097-0266(199707)18:1+%3C165::AID-SMJ914%3E3.0.CO;2-%23

Peters, A., & McEwen, B.S. (2015). Stress habituation: Body shape and cardiovascular mortality. *Neuroscience Biobehavioural Review* (56), 139–150. https://doi.org/10.1016/j.neubiorev.2015.07.001

Porac, J.F., Thomas, H., & Baden- Fuller, C. (1989). Competitive groups as cognitive communities: The case of scottish knitwear manufacturers. *Journal of Management Studies (*26), 397–416.

Porac, J.F., Thomas, H., Wilson, F., Paton, D., & Kanfer, A. (1995). Rivalry and the industry model of Scottish knitwear producers. *Administrative Science Quarterly*, *40*(2), 203–227. https://doi.org/10.2307/2393636

Porac, J., Wade, J., & Pollock, T. (1999). Industry categories and the politics of the comparable firm in CEO compensation. *Administrative Science Quarterly*, *44*(1), 112–144. https://doi.org/10.2307%2F2667033

Rullani, E. (2004). *La fabbrica dell'immateriale*. Carocci.

Rynes, S.L., Colbert, A.E., & Brown, K.G. (2002). HR professionals' beliefs about effective human resource practices: Correspondence between research and practice. *Human Resource Management*, *41*(2), 149–174. https://psycnet.apa.org/doi/10.1002/hrm.10029

Sargent, R.H., & Newman, L.S. (2021). Pluralistic ignorance research in psychology: A scoping review of topic and method variation and directions for future research. *Review of General Psychology*, *25*(2), 163–184. https://doi.org/10.1177/1089268021995168

Schendel, D., & Hofer, C. (1979). *Strategic management: A new view of business policy and planning*. Little, Brown & Company.

Semadeni, M., & Anderson, B. (2010). The follower's dilemma: Innovation and imitation in the professional services industry. *Academy of Management Journal*, *53*(5), 1175–1193. https://doi.org/10.5465/amj.2010.54533232

Senge, P.M. (2006). *La quinta disciplina*. Sperling & Kupfer.

Simon, H.A. (1955). A behavioral model of rational choice. *The Quarterly Journal of Economics* (69), 99–118.

Simon, H.A. (1962). The architecture of complexity. *Proceedings of the American Philosophical Society* (106), 467–482.

Stanworth, J., Stanworth, C., Watson, A., Purdy, D., & Healeas, S. (2004). Franchising as a small business growth strategy: A resource-based view of organizational development. *International Small Business Journal*, *22*(6), 539–559. https://doi.org/10.1177/0266242604047409

Thomas, H., & Venkatraman, N. (1988). Research on strategic groups: Progress and prognosis. *Journal of Management Studies*, *25*(6), 537–555. https://doi.org/10.1111/j.1467-6486.1988.tb00046.x

Visconti, F. (2002). *Il governo dei distretti industriali. Strategie, strutture e ruoli*. EGEA.

Weathers, D., Sharma, S., & Niedrich, R.W. (2005). The impact of the number of scale points, dispositional factors, and the status quo decision heuristic on scale reliability and response accuracy. *Journal of Business Research*, *58*(11), 1516–1524. https://doi.org/10.1016/j.jbusres.2004.08.002

Williamson, O.E. (1985). L'economia Dell'organizzazione: Il Modello Dei Costi Di Transazione. In R.C.D. Nacamulli & A. Rugiadini (Eds.), *Organizzazione & Mercato*. Il Mulino.

Wood, E., Khavul, S., Perez-Nordtvedt, L., Prakhya, S., Velarde Dabrowski, R., & Zheng, C. (2011). Strategic commitment and timing of internationalization from emerging markets: Evidence from China, India, Mexico, and South Africa. *Journal of Small Business Management* (324), 252–282. https://doi.org/10.1111/j.1540-627X.2011.00324.x

Xia, J., Tan, J., & Tan, D. (2008). Mimetic entry and bandwagon effect: The rise and decline of international equity joint venture in China. *Strategic Management Journal*, *29*(2), 195–217. https://doi.org/10.1002/smj.648

Yang, M., & Hyland, M.A. (2006). Who do firms imitate? A multilevel approach to examining sources of imitation in the choice of mergers and acquisitions. *Journal of Management, 32*(3), 381–399. https://doi.org/10.1177%2F0149206305280790

Yang, M., & Hyland, M.A. (2012). Re-examining mimetic isomorphism. *Management Decision, 50*(6), 1076–1095. http://dx.doi.org/10.1108/00251741211238346

Zhu, H., Eden, L., Miller, S.R., Thomas, D.E., & Fields, P. (2012). Host-country location decisions of early movers and latecomers: The role of local density and experiential learning. *International Business Review, 21*(2), 145–155. https://doi.org/10.1016/j.ibusrev.2011.02.004

Zollo, M. (2009). Superstitious learning with rare strategic decisions: Theory and evidence from corporate acquisitions. *Organization Science, 20*(5), 894–908. https://doi.org/10.1287/orsc.1090.0459

Agus Syarip Hidayat and Wee Ching Pok

14 Modelling the Collaborative Advantage of SMEs in Pursuit of Competitiveness: An Emerging Economy Case

Abstract: This paper examines the effect of collaborative advantage (CA) on the performance of small-and-medium-sized enterprises (SMEs). It also explains the mediation effect of a firm's capability in this relationship. Prior to examining this effect, the conceptualization of the CA model is investigated. Based on a questionnaire survey from the Indonesian SMEs, the analysis is conducted using PLS-SEM two-stage reflective-formative Hierarchical Component Model (HCM). By taking into account the unique features of SMEs, CA is conceptualized in eight constructs (collaborative commitment, collaborative efficiency agreement, collaborative risk-sharing, collaborative planning, collaborative resource sharing, collaborative relational capital, collaborative information-knowledge sharing, collaborative synchronized response) and further re-categorized into three pillars (inter-firm trust, dynamic synchronization, and resources investment). The empirical findings show that CA is positively affecting SMEs' performance, and the effect is stronger when the firm's capability is taken into account. This study contributes to the theory of CA by reformulating the constructs that fit for SMEs to strengthen inter-firm trust building and to synchronize the firm's response to changing external factors. In addition, this study also brings a new insight by incorporating relational capital as a non-price factor in motivating firms to share wider access to resources. This study also has a managerial implication that could help firm owners and/or managers to design a framework of collaboration with their peers that provides mutual benefits for all members.

Keywords: small-and-medium-sized enterprises (SMEs), collaborative advantage, firm performance, Hierarchical Component Model (HCM)

Introduction

Establishing collaborations with peers and also along the supply chain is imperative as interdependency among firms is also becoming higher (Dyer, 2000; Li. et al., 2015; Nilsson & Göransson, 2021). This interdependence is a reflection of the inadequacy of firms acting alone in acquiring competitiveness in a dynamic marketplace. Collabora-

Agus Syarip Hidayat, Research Centre for Economic of Industry, Trade, and Services - National Research and Innovation Agency (BRIN), Indonesia
Wee Ching Pok, Flinders University

https://doi.org/10.1515/9783110747652-015

tion can offer mutual benefits from this interdependence if managed well. Managing collaboration, however, requires specific strategies in order to allocate resources efficiently and effectively to produce valuable, inimitable, and affordable products and services. Firms that have good collaboration can improve their performance by improving efficiency through reducing transaction costs (Lavie, 2006; Lin & Lin, 2015), minimising opportunistic behaviors, and reducing monitoring costs (Cao & Zhang, 2011). Firms could also gain by expanding their access to resources (Ehrenhard & Hoffmann, 2014; Tanriverdi, 2006), new information, and knowledge (Dyer, 2000; Nilsson & Göransson, 2021; Sheu et al., 2006). In addition, collaboration could also offer firms a way to minimize their risks and vulnerabilities (Christopher & Lee, 2004; Nilsson & Göransson, 2021; Tang, 2006).

Dyer (2000) introduces the term collaborative advantage (CA) to describe networking between firms and their peers. This research will operationally use the term CA to represent the way firms create competitive advantages through effective inter-firm collaboration in order to achieve strategic benefits/outcomes (Cao & Zhang, 2011; Dyer, 2000; Huxham & Vangen, 2004; Jap, 2001; Kanter, 1994). According to Dyer (2000) there are three important pillars of CA: (1) inter-firm trust building; (2) resources investment (Dyer refers to this as dedicated asset investment); and (3) knowledge sharing. Each of the pillars is supported by different constructs. Inter-firm trust building uses constructs such as commitment, free assistance to improve productivity, and efficiency. Constructs such as sharing resources for physical assets, sites, and human specializations are applied to resources investment. For knowledge sharing, constructs such as exchange of technical information are applied. In my study, in order to conceptualize a CA model that fits SMEs, we will adapt Dyer's model by incorporating new constructs into each of Dyer's CA pillars.

The extant literatures of CA have been evolving around the underlying constructs with different emphasis. While many researches focus on examining a particular individual construct of CA, for example risk information sharing and risk sharing mechanism (Li et al., 2015), information sharing (Wu et al., 2014), and trust building (Chen et al., 2017; Herczeg et al., 2018), others exploit CA as a bundle of constructs that interrelate to each other (Cao & Zhang, 2011; Dyer, 2000; Huxham & Vangen, 2005; Simatupang & Sridharan, 2005). However, these models were designed mainly for large firms in developed economies, hence their proposed CA models might not be fully applicable for SMEs in developing economies.

To conceptualize the constructs of the CA model that fits SMEs in developing economies, and in particular SMEs in the automotive component industry,[1] adaption

---

[1] The main consideration of choosing the sample from automotive components manufacturers is that the automotive component products are part of the 12 Priority Integration Sectors of ASEAN Economic Community (AEC). In addition, SMEs producing automotive components could become generators for establishing collaboration through both forward and backward linkages with other related manufacturing sectors.

of the generic CA model is necessary. This new model will capture the unique features of SMEs operating in developing economies. These features include SMEs offering more relational capital, which is lacking in large enterprises (Manimala et al., 2019; Welbourne & Pardo-del-val, 2009) and how this culture of social support provides additional advantages for SEMs (Welter & Kautonen, 2005), and that SMEs are more sensitive to the changing external environment (Prajogo & McDermott, 2014; Sahiti, 2019).

The main objective of this study is to examine the effect of CA on the performance of small medium enterprises (SMEs) in the automotive component industry. It also explains the mediation effect of a firm's capability in this relationship. To achieve this objective, it is necessary to address the following research questions: (1) To what extent does collaborative advantage affect SMEs' performance and firm capability?; (2) Which relevant mechanisms can be identified?; and (3) Does firm capability mediate a positive relationship between CA and firm performance?

This paper proceeds as follows. Section 2 provides a literature review and the hypothesis' development. Section 3 describes the data and descriptive statistics. Section 4 explains the method of analysis. Section 5 presents the results and discussion, before a conclusion in Section 6.

Literature Review and Hypothesis Development

While there is a consensus that the heart of CA is joint working among firms (Cao & Zhang, 2011; Dyer, 2000; Flynn et al., 2010; Huxham & Vangen, 2005; Nilsson & Göransson, 2021; Simatupang & Sridharan, 2005), the literature provides different views on how CA should be constructed. Simatupang and Sridharan (2005) suggest that a reciprocal approach is a more appropriate concept to describe collaboration between firms. Based on this approach, they propose five constructs of CA: a collaborative performance system, information sharing, decision synchronization, incentive alignment, and an integrated supply chain process. Cao and Zhang (2011) also develop five constructs of CA, but with different features. They are process efficiency, offering flexibility, business synergy, product quality, and innovative activities. In this study, we define CA as the way firms create competitive advantages through effective inter-firm collaboration in order to obtain strategic benefits/outcomes.

The Conceptual Development of a CA Model for SMEs

Designing a CA model that fits SMEs, especially in developing economies, will require some modification to suit the unique features of SMEs. Three unique features that need to be addressed in designing a CA model are related to the nature of SMEs operating in the developing economies: containing higher risks (Jüttner, 2005); acknowledging relational capital (Welbourne & Pardo-del-val, 2009); and being sensitive to external changes as the markets of developing economies become more integrated.

Table 14.1: Constructs of collaborative advantage.

Pillars	Constructs	Citations
Inter-firm trust building	Collaborative commitment	Grafton and Mundy (2016), I.-L. Wu et al. (2014), Gundlach, Achrol, and Mentzer (1995); Huxham and Vangen (2005), Angle and Perry (1981); Dwyer, Schurr, and Oh (1987)
	Collaborative efficiency agreements	Cao and Zhang (2011), Huxham and Vangen (2005), Simatupang and Sridharan (2005), Frohlich and Westbrook (2001), Herczeg et al. (2018)
	Collaborative risk sharing	G. Li et al. (2015), Ghadge, Dani, and Kalawsky (2012), Cao and Zhang (2011), Ellegaard (2008), Tang (2006), Christopher and Lee (2004), Dyer (2000), Lorenzoni and Lipparini (1999), Nilsson and Göransson (2021)
Resources investment	Collaborative planning	Flynn et al. (2010), Simatupang and Sridharan (2005), Barratt and Oliveira (2001), Frohlich and Westbrook (2001)
	Collaborative resource sharing	Cao and Zhang (2011), Flynn et al. (2010), Doven Lavie (2006b), Dyer (2000)
	Collaborative relational capital	Lin and Lin (2015); McAdam, Miller, and McSorley (2019) Z. Wu and Pullman (2015) Davis and Golicic (2010), J. Li and Matlay (2006), Huxham and Vangen (2005)
Dynamic synchronization	Collaborative information and knowledge sharing	Cao and Zhang (2011), Sheu et al. (2006), Min, Roath, Daugherty, Genchev, and et al. (2005), Simatupang and Sridharan (2005), Davenport, Harris, De Long, and Jacobson (2001), Dyer (2000)
	Collaborative synchronizing of responses	Huxham and Vangen (2005)

Inter-Firm Trust Building

Inter-firm trust building is a prerequisite for successful CA (Dania et al., 2018; Dyer, 2000; Huxham & Vangen, 2005). Dyer (2000) states that, without trust, firms will not be willing to share information and invest their assets in the collaboration. Trust will exist in a collaboration if a firm has confidence in their peer's reliability and integrity (Morgan & Hunt, 1994). Thus, willingness to cooperate based on high trust could help to maintain the collaboration in the long-term. Well-established trust among collaborators can also be regarded as an effective instrument to minimize transaction costs, even more effective than legal contracts (Dyer, 2000). Therefore, we propose three constructs to support the inter-firm trust building pillar: a) collaborative commitment; b) collaborative efficiency agreements; and c) collaborative risk sharing.

Resources Investment

Resources investment is investment allocated by the firm in the value chain to increase productivity in the production network. Dyer (2000) suggests firms should pursue three different types of asset investment, namely, site specialization, physical specialization, and human specialization. Many researchers such as Cao and Zhang (2011), Flynn et al. (2010) and Dyer (2000) suggest that, under a collaboration, members could share their physical assets. These include machinery and related equipment, human resources, technical supports, financial assistance, and site specialization. Resources sharing enables collaboration members to assess inventory-level data (Cao & Zhang, 2011) and to lower inventory-associated costs, transportation costs, and communication costs (Dyer, 2000).

While much research has mostly focused on dedicated asset investment in terms of tangible assets, the non-tangible assets embedded in the price factors have been neglected. Collaborative relational capital can be regarded as an intangible asset, which can influence organizational ethics, collaborative members' behaviour, and/or employees' working style (Davis & Golicic, 2010; Huxham & Vangen, 2005; McAdam et al., 2016). The importance of addressing collaborative relational capital in resources investment is strongly related to the working style in the firm collaboration itself, in which the working process involves people from various backgrounds, such as different professional expertise, organizational cultures, objectives, cultural norms, and values.

The power of collaborative relational capital relies on its embedded values, which can affect the dynamics of supply chain networks (Wu & Pullman, 2015). Collaborative relational capital can also have a strategic role in empowering collaboration members through its intrinsic motivation (McAdam et al., 2019). McAdam et al. (2019) call this a support culture.[2] This study exploits collaborative relational capital in the form of a socially supportive culture (SSC). The characteristics of SSC are a high level of humane orientation and a low level of assertiveness (Semrau et al., 2016), a positive social environment in which people support each other (Thai & Turkina, 2014), collective identity, reliance on informal networks, and tolerance for failure (House et al., 2004). In the context of Indonesia, the country where this research was conducted, it

---

2 According to McAdam et al. (2019) there are four typologies of culture in relation to collaboration empowerment: (a) role culture, which focuses on procedure, hierarchy, and status; (b) power culture, which focuses on the dominant and authoritative person in charge with mainly informal rules; (c) achievement culture, which focuses on task and purpose and participatory orientation; and (d) support culture, which focuses on an empowering environment with high levels of intrinsic motivation.

is called "kekeluargaan." It is similar to "guanxi" (personal network relationship) in Chinese terminology (Li & Matlay, 2006; Lin & Lin, 2015).

In this study, the pillar of resources investment consists of three constructs: a) collaborative planning; b) collaborative resource sharing; and c) collaborative relational capital.

Dynamic Synchronization

Dynamic synchronization refers to the process by which collaboration members are able to bring into line the sharing of information among the collaboration members and to synchronize their responses to external shocks. In this study, the pillar of decision synchronization consists of two constructs: collaborative information and knowledge sharing, and collaborative synchronized responses.

Synthesizing the existing constructs of the CA model and considering the importance of incorporating SMEs' unique features, this study proposes eight constructs which support the three pillars of CA, as described in Table 14.1. These constructs are: (a) collaborative commitment; (b) collaborative efficiency agreements; (c) collaborative risk sharing; (d) collaborative planning; (e) collaborative resource sharing; (f) collaborative relational capital; (g) collaborative information and knowledge sharing; and (h) collaborative synchronized responses. Further, these are categorized into three pillars, namely inter-firm trust building, resources investment, and dynamic synchronisation.

Hence, we hypothesize:

Hypothesis H1a collaborative commitment has a positive effect on CA.
Hypothesis H1b collaborative efficiency agreement has a positive effect on CA.
Hypothesis H1c collaborative risk sharing has a positive effect on CA.
Hypothesis H1d collaborative planning has a positive effect on CA.
Hypothesis H1e collaborative resource sharing has a positive effect on CA.
Hypothesis H1f collaborative relational capital has a positive effect on CA.
Hypothesis H1g collaborative information and knowledge sharing has a positive effect on CA.
Hypothesis H1h collaborative synchronized has a positive effect on CA.

CA and Firm Performance

Cao and Zhang (2011) contend that cooperation under a collaboration framework can lead to a positive sum game. Ehrenhard and Hoffmann (2014), Park et al. (2004), Tanriverdi (2006) and Dyer (2000) believe that networking helps firms to secure wider access to resources. Handfield and Bechtel (2002), Lavie (2006), Lin and Lin (2015), Sheu et al. (2006) and Dyer (2000) suggest that having a collaborative relationship with suppliers can reduce transaction costs. Collaboration can also minimize opportunism and monitoring costs as well as incompetence activities that arise in the integration process and market transactions (Cao & Zhang, 2011; Croom, 2001; Dyer, 2000). These benefits eventually lead to improved firm performance such as efficiency, productivity, sales, and profitability.

Even though many studies support the positive effect of collaboration on firm performance, a collaboration that is not properly designed could also adversely affect firm performance (Eisenhardt & Tabrizi, 1995; Fabbe-Costes & Jahre, 2008; Koufteros et al., 2005; Liker et al., 1996). For instance, a collaboration that is not well designed could affect the effectiveness of product development (Eisenhardt & Tabrizi, 1995) and increase the complexity of coordinating a firm's decisions (Liker et al., 1996). This, in turn, affects a firm's ability to respond effectively to changing market dynamics.

The above two contrasting effects of collaboration on firm performance indicate that the process of achieving better firm performance may require efforts to improve the firm's capability. Considering the above-mentioned views, in this study a firm's capabilities are reflected in four indicators: a) the firm's ability to respond to changes in the marketplace (adaptability); b) the firm's ability to fulfil various customer demands efficiently (flexibility); c) the firm's ability to offer product differentiation (differentiation); and d) the firm's ability to produce products at a competitive price (affordability).

In some studies such as Flynn et al. (2010), Beamon (1999), Murphy et al. (1996) and Venkatraman and Ramanujam (1986), firm capability is indicated by operational performance, which reflects the key operational success factors such as introduction of new products, product quality, marketing effectiveness, and technological efficiency. Success in operational performance may lead to better firm performance, especially achieving financial goals. In other words, operational performance can be treated as a mediator variable for achieving better firm performance. Therefore, this study hypothesizes:

Hypothesis H2: CA has a positive effect on firm performance.
Hypothesis H3: CA has a positive effect on firm capability.
Hypothesis H4: Firm capability mediates a positive relationship between CA and firm performance.

Data and Descriptive Statistics

The data for this study was collected in 2017 using a survey of Indonesian SMEs engaged in automotive components manufacturing and located in four provinces, namely Jakartai, West Java, Central Java, and East Java, Republic of Indonesia. These four provinces are the centre of Indonesia's manufacturing industries, including the automotive components industry.

The questionnaires were distributed to 500 SMEs using stratified random sampling. We received 201 responses to the questionnaire. The response rate of respondents in East Java was the highest (41.6%), followed by Central Java (41.3%), West Java (31.00%),and Jakarta (24.00%). Respondents in the small firm category provided a higher response rate (41.89%) than that in the medium firm category (30.67%). After screening, 177 responses were usable and the remaining 24 responses are unused (mostly with incomplete answers). The majority of the questionnaires (97%) were collected through direct visit to factories. In this case, almost all of the questionnaires were filled by the firm owners. We also distributed some questionnaires through posting to the firm owners or firm managers. In addition, we also developed online questionnaires and sent the website link to the firms by email.

The validity of the questions in the questionnaire was discussed and checked with several parties. First, we conducted discussions with leaders of two SME associations, Gabungan Industri Alat-alat Mobil dan Motor (GIAMM) (Automotive Parts & Components Industry Association) and Perkumpulan Industri Kecil-Menengah Komponen Otomotif (PIKKO) (Automotive Components Small-Medium Industry Association), to gather their views on the relevance of the questions in the questionnaire to the current context of SMEs. Second, the questionnaire was also discussed and reviewed by economic researchers at Lembaga Ilmu Pengetahuan Indonesia (the Indonesian Institute of Sciences/LIPI). Third, at the proposal stage, the questionnaire was reviewed by academics at Flinders University through a series of discussions. In addition, we had also pre-tested the questionnaire with seven SME entrepreneurs. The questionnaire was also translated into the Bahasa Indonesia and verified by two Indonesian native speakers.

The statistics in Table 14.2 show that the median and mean of the three constructs (collaborative commitment, collaborative efficiency agreement, and collaborative risk sharing) under the pillar of inter-firm trust building vary significantly. Collaborative commitment has a median of 4 with an aggregate mean of nearly 4, indicating that more than 50% of the firms had a high level of agreement that it was important to commit to collaboration. While the firms also looked at collaborative efficiency agreements, especially for production cost per unit (EFA 1) and level of productivity (EFA 2), as important indicators of collaboration with peers, firms expressed less concern about collaborative risk sharing.

Under the pillar of resources investment, firms placed high importance on the collaborative planning construct, with a median and aggregate mean of 3.5 each. This construct measures the planning and integrating of product design, raw material procurements, inspection of plants, and delivery time. The importance given to the relational capital construct among the firms was also relatively high, where members of a collaboration build cooperation, resolve conflicts, and help each other based on kinship. In the construct of collaborative resource sharing, except for the indicator of ex-

Table 14.2: Descriptive statistics of CA and firm performance.

Constructs	Indicators		Observations	Mean	St dev	Min	Median	Max
Collaborative commitment	1	CCM 1	177	4.181	0.798	1	4	5
	2	CCM 2	177	4.017	0.980	1	4	5
	3	CCM 3	177	3.616	1.138	1	4	5
	4	CCM 4	177	3.695	1.049	1	4	5
Collaborative efficiency agreement	5	EFA 1	177	4.141	0.817	1	3	5
	6	EFA 2	177	3.028	1.346	1	4	5
	7	EFA 3	177	3.023	1.548	1	3	5
	8	EFA 4	177	2.831	1.388	1	3	5
Collaborative risk sharing	9	RSK 1	177	2.480	1.366	1	2	5
	10	RSK 2	177	2.226	1.150	1	2	5
	11	RSK 3	177	1.384	0.790	1	2	5
	12	RSK 4	177	2.243	1.073	1	1	5
Collaborative planning	13	CPL 1	177	4.107	0.932	1	4	5
	14	CPL 2	177	3.147	1.248	1	4	5
	15	CPL 3	177	3.028	1.130	1	3	5
	16	CPL 4	177	4.023	0.859	1	3	5
Collaborative resource sharing	17	RSS 1	177	2.028	1.189	1	4	5
	18	RSS 2	177	2.644	1.217	1	2	5
	19	RSS 3	177	2.740	0.989	1	3	5
	20	RSS 4	177	2.763	1.252	1	3	5
Collaborative relational capital	21	CRC1	177	3.469	1.163	1	2	5
	22	CRC 2	177	3.774	1.069	1	4	5
	23	CRC 3	177	3.350	1.221	1	4	5
Collaborative information and knowledge sharing	24	IKS 1	177	1.983	1.175	1	4	5
	25	IKS 2	177	2.390	1.220	1	1	5
	26	IKS 3	177	2.802	1.168	1	2	5
	27	IKS 4	177	3.096	1.132	1	3	5
	28	IKS 5	177	2.339	1.196	1	3	5

Table 14.2 (continued)

Constructs	Indicators		Observations	Mean	St dev	Min	Median	Max
Collaborative synchronised responses	29	EXR 1	177	2.881	1.366	1	2	5
	30	EXR 2	177	2.401	1.366	1	3	5
	31	EXR 3	177	2.017	1.170	1	2	5
	32	EXR 4	177	2.192	1.166	1	2	5
Firm performance		FPF 1	177	3.232	0.721	1	3	5
		FPF 2	177	3.051	0.848	1	3	5
		FPF 3	177	3.356	0.955	1	4	5
		FPF 4	177	3.260	1.000	1	4	5
Firm capability		FCB 1	177	3.463	0.691	1	4	5
		FCB 2	177	3.311	0.783	1	3	5
		FCB 3	177	3.401	0.848	1	4	5
		FCB 4	177	3.469	0.971	1	4	5

Source: primary data, 2017.

tending financial assistance in emergency situations (RSS 2), firms' dedication to investment sharing with their peers was relatively high.

The median and mean for collaborative information and knowledge sharing and collaborative synchronized response under the dynamic synchronization pillar are at about 2.5, which is the lowest among the eight CA constructs. The firms on average had good firm capability, with the median of all the indicators nearly 4 and the mean at about 3.4. Moreover, the firms also showed good performance.

Methodology

This study employs Partial Least Squares-Structural Equation Modelling (PLS-SEM) for modelling CA. There are several reasons of employing this method: first, PLS-SEM is appropriate for a study in which the goal is to establish new constructs for a new model (Hair, 2010). In addition, PLS-SEM can accommodate a relatively small sample size. We follow the "10 times rule" by Barclay et al. (1995) to determine the eligibility of using PLS-SEM and whether our sample meets the requirement.

The analysis of a PLS path modelling consists of two parts, namely (1) measurement model (outer model) and (2) structural model (inner model). The measurement model examines the relationship between the CA constructs and its indicators. The structural model tests the effect of CA on firm performance. While we can examine the effect of the structural model directly, literature suggests that it could also be examined indirectly through a mediating variable. The analyses of direct and indirect effects are illustrated in a framework as shown in Figure 14.1.

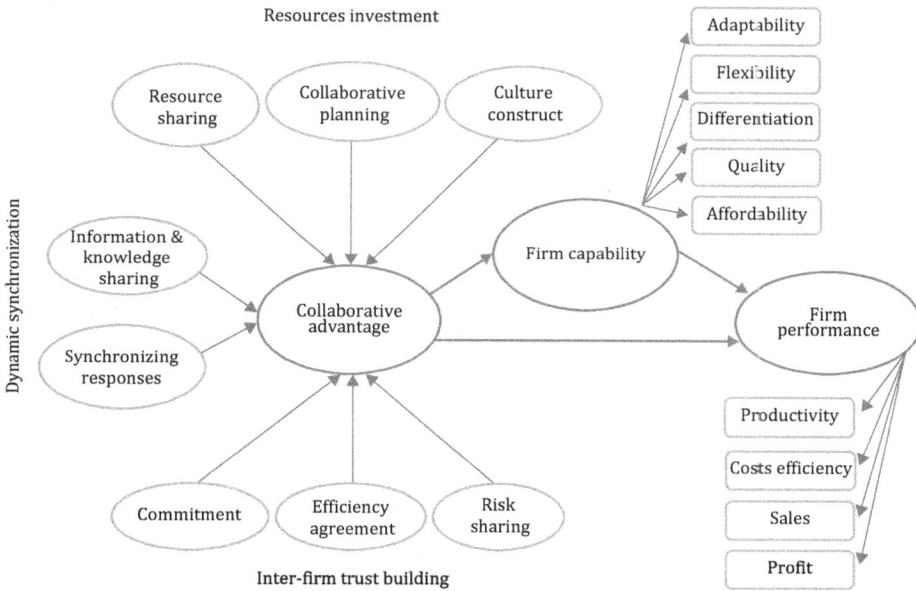

Figure 14.1: Structural and measurement model of CA, firm capability, and firm performance.

CA is conceptualized as a formative second order model, in which each indicator captures a specific aspect of the construct domain. The basic assumption is that causal indicators form the construct of linear combination. While PLS-SEM does not require the assumption of normality regarding the data distribution, the data we used in this study are normally distributed. In PLS-SEM, conceptualizing the eight constructs and the CA either in formative or reflective form is important because it is related to their conceptual meaning (Diamantopoulos & Winklhofer, 2001; Jarvis et al., 2003; Podsakoff et al., 2003). To measure the effect of CA on firm performance, it is estimated using Hierarchical Component Models (HCMs). Considering the nature of the eight constructs and CA, this study uses a reflective-formative measurement model. When using a reflective-formative model, it is important to use a combination of repeated indicators approaches in Lower Order Constructs (LOC) and to use latent scores in Higher Order Constructs (HOC) (Hair et al., 2017). The benefit of this approach is it prevents over-explaining the variance of HOC as compared to if the model is estimated only through a repeated indicator approach.

In the LOC measure, following Becker et al. (2012), the repeated indicator approach mode B is used to obtain the latent scores for the LOCs. This is because mode B produces better parameter estimates than mode A in terms of root mean square error (RMSE) and mean absolute relative bias (MARB).[3] An unbiased result can be achieved if the number of indicators in each construct does not vary greatly (Hair et al., 2018). My LOCs measure of the eight constructs fulfils this requirement.

The latent scores obtained from the LOC are used as manifest variables in the HOC measurement model. Prior to measuring the HOC, the LOCs measurement model has to satisfy all the assessment criteria for reliability and validity. If some indicators of LOCs are found to deviate significantly from the assessment criteria, a scale purification process has to be applied to improve the results. Purification is a process of eliminating indicators to improve the reliability and validity of the newly developed LOCs (Churchill, 1979; Wieland et al., 2017).

We have created a preliminary list of 32 measurement indicators for the eight constructs of CA. These cover the constructs of collaborative commitment (four indicators), collaborative efficiency agreement (five indicators), collaborative risk sharing (four indicators), collaborative planning (four indicators), collaborative resource sharing (four indicators), collaborative relational capital (three indicators), collaborative information and knowledge sharing (four indicators), and collaborative synchronizing response (four indicators). As shown, the number of indicators in each construct is almost same, except for collaborative efficiency agreement and collaborative relational capital.

Results and Discussion

Assessment Results of LOCs

The assessment of convergent validity for the LOCs' indicator reliability test showed that, among 32 indicators, there are 24 indicators with loading value greater than 0.7, which is the cut-off threshold for this indicator reliability test (Hair et al., 2017), except for eight indicators with loading scores below the threshold, in which their scores

---

3 RMSE measures the difference between the predicted value and observed value. MARB is the average of the simple absolute deviations between the true parameter and the estimated parameter divided by the true parameter and the root mean squared error (Becker et al., 2012).

vary between 0.5 and 0.6. However, bootstrapping estimates show that all 32 indicators' loadings are statistically significant at a 1% level. While indicator reliability is not satisfactory for some, all constructs have an average variance extracted (AVE) greater than 0.5, suggesting an adequate convergent validity.

Literatures allow us to retain the indicators loading with a value of 0.4 to 0.7 in the model and continue the estimation to the second stage (Hair et al., 2017; Hulland, 1999). However, instead of taking such a shortcut, purification of the LOCs' measurement was taken in order to meet the basic assessment criteria of the reflective measurement model.

Assessment Results of LOCs after Purification

Purification of the LOCs was conducted based on statistical and theoretical judgment (Wieland et al., 2017). After the purification process, the model now has 29 indicators measuring eight constructs of CA. Table 14.3 shows the assessment results for LOCs after purification.

Table 14.3: LOCs results after purification.

Constructs	Indicators	Factor loadings	Internal consistency	Convergent validity		Discriminant validity		
			Composite reliability	AVE	Cross-loading indicator	Fornell-Larcker criterion	HTMT (< 0.9)
Collaborative commitment	1 CCM1	0.835	0.881	0.711	Yes	Yes	Yes
	2 CCM2	0.834					
	3 CCM3	0.861					
Collaborative efficiency agreement	4 EFA1	0.523	0.858	0.610	Yes	Yes	Yes
	5 EFA2	0.807					
	6 EFA3	0.907					
	7 EFA4	0.833					
Collaborative risk sharing	8 RSK1	0.888	0.863	0.679	Yes	Yes	Yes
	9 RSK2	0.865					
	10 RSK3	0.708					
Collaborative planning	11 CPL1	0.628	0.816	0.532	Yes	Yes	Yes
	12 CPL2	0.858					
	13 CPL3	0.813					
	14 CPL4	0.586					

Table 14.3 (continued)

Constructs	Indicators	Factor loadings	Internal consistency	Convergent validity		Discriminant validity	
			Composite reliability	AVE	Cross-loading indicator	Fornell-Larcker criterion	HTMT (< 0.9)
Collaborative resource sharing	15 RSS1	0.552	0.842	0.578	Yes	Yes	Yes
	16 RSS2	0.813					
	17 RSS3	0.797					
	18 RSS4	0.843					
Collaborative relational capital	19 CRC1	0.882	0.896	0.741	Yes	Yes	Yes
	20 CRC2	0.842					
	21 CRC3	0.858					
Collaborative information and knowledge sharing	22 IKS1	0.811	0.908	0.711	Yes	Yes	Yes
	23 IKS2	0.871					
	24 IKS3	0.819					
	25 IKS4	0.869					
Collaborative synchronized responses	26 EXR1	0.858	0.873	0.636	Yes	Yes	Yes
	27 EXR2	0.891					
	28 EXR3	0.783					
	29 EXR4	0.633					

Source: author's calculation.

Statistically, we found that the LOCs after purification met all the assessment criteria. The indicators loading as a measure of indicator reliability show that 24 out of 29 indicators have a loading value greater than 0.7. The five indicators that are retained in the model have a loading value of between 0.5 and 0.6. Estimation through bootstrapping shows that all indicators' loadings are significant at a 1% level. Overall, the purification leads to more robust LOCs.

The evaluation of internal consistency through composite reliability yielded satisfactory results with a range of 0.8 to 0.9. In addition, measuring internal consistency using Cronbach's alpha also produced model consistency as indicated by its value of between 0.7 and 0.8. Evaluation of convergent validity through average variance extracted (AVE) indicated that all constructs have a value greater than 0.5. In examining the discriminant validity, the Fornell-Larcker criterion, cross-loading and HTMT validated that discriminant validity is established for the model. The results from the three tests confirm that the LOCs to be used for the next phase are valid and reliable.

Assessment Results of the HOC

The HOC measurement model is conceptualized as a formative model. To estimate CA, the latent scores of each of the eight LOCs are used as manifest indicators in the HOC (Figure 14.2).

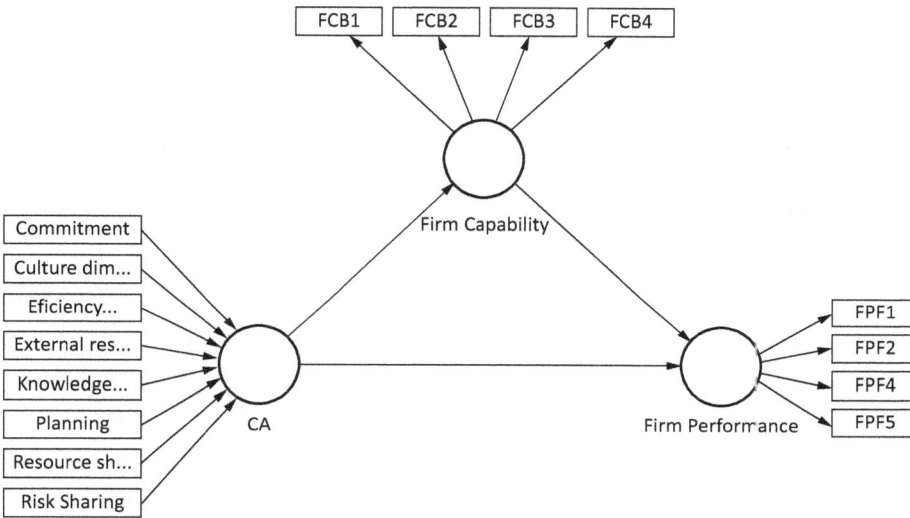

Figure 14.2: HOC process.

All latent constructs from LOCs will now be referred to as manifest indicators. Under the HOC, the manifest indicators are expected to have a low level of indicator correlations with each other. A high level of indicator correlations between manifest indicators will be problematic in terms of methodological issues and interpretation of the path coefficient (Hair et al., 2017) and also lead to difficulties separating the distinct influence of individual indicators (Diamantopoulos & Winklhofer, 2001).

Table 14.4 reports the results of the collinearity and the level of loading weight significance of the HOC measurement.

The estimation results show that the VIF for the manifest indicators ranges from 1.953 to 3.253, which is below the suggested threshold of 5 for PLS-SEM (Hair et al., 2017). Therefore, the HOC model is free from collinearity problems.

The statistical significance of the indicators' weight provided very useful information in the formative model as it measured the relative importance of each manifest indicator (Cenfetelli & Bassellier, 2009). The bootstrapping estimation with 1,000 sub-samples revealed that four out of eight manifest indicators (collaborative planning, collaborative risk sharing, collaborative information and knowledge sharing, and collaborative resource sharing) have statistically significant weights at a 1% level. How-

Table 14.4: Assessment results of the HOC.

Indicators	VIF	Indicator weight		Indicator loading	
		Coefficient	Standard error	Coefficient	Standard error
Collaborative commitment	1.999	0.132	0.103	0.689***	0.076
Collaborative efficiency agreement	2.443	−0.186	0.137	0.615***	0.079
Collaborative risk sharing	2.080	0.305***	0.091	0.773***	0.050
Collaborative planning	2.226	0.267***	0.105	0.810***	0.050
Collaborative resource sharing	1.624	0.208***	0.082	0.717***	0.054
Collaborative relational capital	1.994	0.116	0.097	0.691***	0.059
Collaborative information and knowledge sharing	3.253	0.421***	0.110	0.886***	0.042
Collaborative synchronized responses	2.850	−0.048	0.123	0.673***	0.061

Source: author's calculation
*Significant at 10%, **Significant at 5%, ***Significant at 1%

ever, we also found insignificant weights for the other four manifest indicators (collaborative commitment, collaborative efficiency agreement, collaborative relational capital, and collaborative synchronized responses). Even though these three manifest indicators are not significant, the estimation shows that the loading values of these three indicators are above 0.6 and statistically significant at a 1% level of significance.

The insignificant indicator weights of some LOCs indicates that those constructs make a smaller contribution to a formatively measured construct. This, however, should not be interpreted as meaning that the quality of the formative model is poorly established (Cenfetelli & Bassellier, 2009; Hair et al., 2017). Instead, it can be viewed comprehensively by looking at the absolute contribution of those manifest indicators through their formative indicator's outer loading. Moreover, it is also recommended not to drop formative indicators with lower weight from the model as this may possibly alter the empirical meaning of the construct (MacKenzie et al., 2005). These results support hypothesis H1 (a to h), which posits that collaborative commitment, collaborative efficiency agreements, collaborative risk sharing, collaborative planning, collaborative resource sharing, collaborative relational capital, collaborative information and knowledge sharing, and collaborative synchronized responses have positive effects on CA.

Assessment of the HOC after Purification

The above-mentioned HOC results are evidence that the manifest indicators are sufficient to represent manifest indicators in the CA model for SMEs. However, since some manifest indicators have a relative contribution and some others have an absolute contribution, the aggregation of the CA concept might be in question, especially when connecting it to a firm's capability and performance. Therefore, in explaining the effect of CA on firm capability and firm performance in the structural model, a purification process may be needed to improve the reliability of the structural model.

Cenfetelli and Bassellier (2009) suggest three prescriptions to treat insignificant weights: (1) re-categorize the manifest indicators into two or more constructs, resulting in a smaller number of constructs; (2) do the same as above and include an aggregate construct of the HOC; or (3) retain all manifest indicators with insignificant weights but have an acceptable and significant loading value, and analyze its absolute contribution.

In this study, we applied the second prescription to purify the insignificant weights of some manifest indicators (Figure 14.3). The manifest indicators were re-categorized into three different constructs: (1) inter-firm trust building; (2) dynamic synchronization; and (3) resources investment. This decision is justified by relevant theory. As explained above, the eight constructs are grouped into three different pillars, namely inter-firm trust building, resources investment, and dynamic synchronization. Following my framework, the three pillars were constructed. The HOC examines the structural model for hypothesis testing.

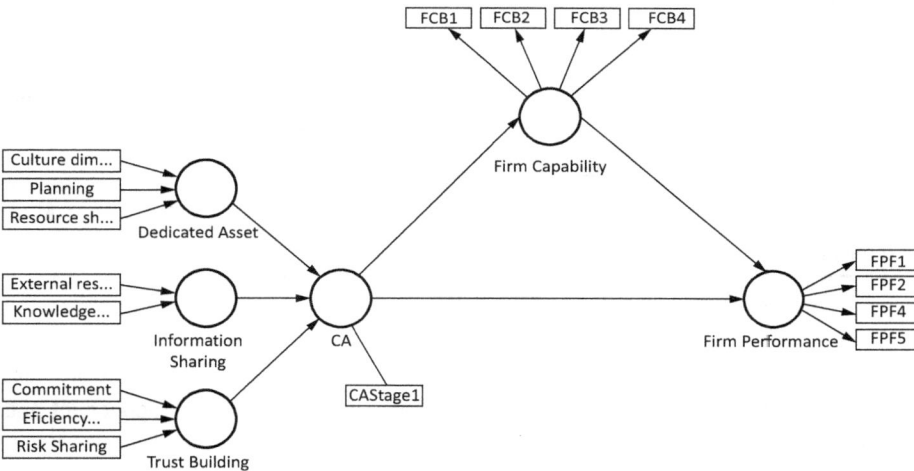

Figure 14.3: HOC process after purification.

Table 14.5 reports the results of the significant level of the HOC's indicator weights after purification and the significance level of the three pillars as well as their level of collinearity.

The HOC estimation results show that there is no multicollinearity issue in the structural model. This is indicated by VIF values of the outer and inner model that are under the threshold of 5. The test results for multicollinearity under the threshold can also be

Table 14.5: Assessment results of the HOC after purification.

Indicator weights			Constructs			
	Coefficient	Standard error		Coefficient	Standard error	Inner VIF
Collaborative commitment to inter firm trust building	0.390***	0.043	**Inter-firm trust building**	0.378***	0.014	3.137
Collaborative efficiency agreement to inter firm trust building	0.431***	0.044				
Collaborative risk sharing to inter firm trust building	0.398***	0.047				
Collaborative planning to resources investment	0.517***	0.049	**Resources investment**	0.387***	0.013	2.334
Collaborative resource sharing to resources investment	0.361***	0.049				
Collaborative relational capital to resources investment	0.319***	0.049				
Collaborative information & knowledge sharing to dynamic synchronization	0.678***	0.056	**Dynamic synchronization**	0.331***	0.014	3.100
Collaborative synchronizing response to Dynamic synchronization	0.392***	0.058				

*Significant at 10%, **Significant at 5%, ***Significant at 1%

an indication that the model is not contaminated by the common method bias problem (Kock, 2015). Common method bias can occur when the data for both independent and dependent variables are obtained from the same respondent in the same measurement context using similar indicators and characteristics (Podsakoff et al., 2003).

A bootstrapping estimation on the HOC reveals that all eight manifest indicators after purification have statistically significant weights, as shown in Table 14.5. The three manifest indicators (collaborative efficiency agreement, collaborative relational capital, and collaborative synchronized responses) that previously had insignificant weights now have significant weights at a 1% level of significance. This indicates that the three pillars as theorized in the literature review are a reliable way to represent CA.

CA and Firm Performance

The above-mentioned assessment results of LOCs and the HOC indicate that all the models meet the requirements of the reliability and validity tests. In addition, we also found that the mediator construct meets all the reliability tests (internal consistency, convergent validity, and discriminant validity) of reflective measurement. Therefore, we proceeded to evaluate the structural model. The results of the structural model are presented in Table 14.6.

Table 14.6: Results of the structural model.

Path	Coefficients	Standard error		f^2
CA to firm performance	0.170	0.074**	0.026	
CA to firm capability	0.707	0.032***	1.001	
Firm capability to firm performance	0.541	0.064***	0.267	
Indirect effect of	0.383	0.048***		
CA to firm capability-firm performance				
Total effect of	0.553	0.054***		
CA to firm performance				
Adjusted R^2 firm capability	0.497			
Adjusted R^2 firm performance	0.446			

*Significant at 10%, **Significant at 5%, ***Significant at 1%

In the structural model, we found that the path coefficient of CA to firm performance is 0.170, which is statistically significant at the 5% level. This means that increasing CA by 1% is estimated to increase firm performance by 0.170%. This supports the hypothesis that CA has a positive effect on firm performance. Hence, this supports hypothesis H2. The value of coefficient determination (adjusted R^2) of firm performance of 0.446 indicates that it has a moderate predictive power. The blindfolding test for cross-validated redundancy shows that the predicative power (Q^2) value for all endogenous constructs is above zero. The Q^2 values are 0.969, 0.279, and 0.331 for CA, firm performance, and firm capability respectively.

The evidence of the positive direct relationship between CA and firm performance has been validated by the hierarchical component model (HCM) tests. This finding is consistent with previous research that links CA directly to firm performance (Cao & Zhang, 2010; Chang et al., 2016; Flynn et al., 2010). We, however, found that the direct effect of CA on firm performance has a small effect size (only 0.025). The path coefficient of CA on firm performance is relatively low (0.170) compared to other path coefficient results. Previous research by Cao and Zhang (2010) found the direct effect is about 0.72. Interpreting the total effect of CA on firm performance in many cases is not straightforward. CA may also affect firm performance indirectly through the mediating variable of firm capability. My estimation results showing small effect size of

CA on firm performance seem to support the importance of the mediating variable in this relationship. We are taking into account this important view and examining the effect of CA on firm performance through firm capability as a mediating variable. Firm capability captures four indicators that address adaptability, flexibility, differentiation, and affordability.

We observe that the path coefficient of CA to firm capability is 0.707, which is statistically significant at the level of 1%. In comparison to the effect on firm performance, CA's effect on firm capability is substantially higher with an effect size of 1.001. In addition, firm capability has a positive and significant effect on firm performance with a path coefficient of 0.541 and effect size of 0.267. This shows that firm performance is not only affected by CA, but also indirectly by firm capability. These results confirm the hypothesis that CA has a positive effect on firm capability. Hence, hypothesis H3 is confirmed.

A mediating effect is established if the coefficient of indirect effect from CA to firm capability and the coefficient from firm capability to firm performance are both significant. As shown in Table 14.6, both coefficients from CA to firm capability as well as firm capability to firm performance are significant at a 1% level. This confirms the hypothesis that firm capability mediates a positive relationship between CA and firm performance. Hence, hypothesis H4 is confirmed. Referring to the calculation of the VAF value = 0.383/0.553 = 0,693, we conclude that firm capability partially mediates the relationship between CA and firm performance.

The estimation results show empirical support for the important mediating role of firm capability in the relationship between CA and firm performance. This implies that firm capability helps to increase the contribution of CA to firm performance. Evidently, the magnitude of the indirect effect of CA on firm performance through the mediator variable (0.383) is twice as large as its direct effect (0.170). Overall, the total effect of CA on firm performance is quite pronounced (0.553).

For Indonesian SMEs, adaptability can be particularly associated with their ability to survive pressure from competitors under regional economic integration. This is particularly related to the implementation of the ASEAN-China Free Trade Agreement (ACFTA) since 2010 and the ASEAN Economic Community (AEC) since 2015. Under ACFTA and AEC, the flow of goods and services within China and ASEAN countries is affected by the very minimum of protective policies such as tariffs. This promotes higher competition in the markets and hence pushes firms to adjust their competition strategy. The entrepreneurs in automotive component SMEs are some of the market actors who actively adapt to these market dynamics because their products are included as part of a priority integration sector under the AEC framework.

If Indonesian automotive component SMEs are flexible in terms of fulfilling changes in customer requests efficiently, they can adjust to the growing markets in ACFTA and AEC member countries. For the Indonesian market itself, flexibility is required to deal with two demand factors. First is flexibility in response to demand from the growing middle class. The middle-class population is growing rapidly in Indonesia and hence pushes a high demand for secondary and tertiary goods including automotive products. The Asian Development Bank (2011) predicts that Indonesia will have a middle class population of about 220 million by 2030 and this is considered the largest number in ASEAN and the third largest number in the world.

Second is flexibility in response to changing seasonal demand. According to the SME entrepreneurs, the peak demand for automotive components occurs at the end of the year. OEMs, car producers, request more automotive components to increase car production at the end of the year to prepare for high car demand in the following year. This happens because they need to adjust the car supply with the behavior of car buyers who tend to purchase cars in the New Year or several months after, but not at the end of the year. In addition, the interview results with SME entrepreneurs reveal that the demand for automotive components also tends to increase when approaching the celebration of Eid al-Fitr, an important religious holiday for Muslims, and also one of the major national holidays in Indonesia.

SMEs' ability to produce various products (differentiation) with reasonable prices (affordability) also contributes significantly to CA and firm performance Improvement of these abilities is crucial for SMEs to compete with various competitors' products, especially those entering the market under ACFTA and AEC. Among the participating member countries of these two free trade agreements, China and Thailand are considered the main competitors. While China's automotive component producers are price competitive, Thai producers rely on design and quality as means to compete in the market. On the other hand, Indonesian automotive component SMEs seem to have not strongly established any form of competitive advantage. Empowering SMEs to improve the four capabilities (adaptability, flexibility, differentiation, and affordability) would substantially improve the CA and therefore also firm performance.

Since the eight constructs of CA consist of combining resources originating from inside the firm and its networks, these results are in line with the extended resources-based view (ERBV) of Lavie (2006). The theory suggests that a firm's internal resources and external resources can be combined to improve firm performance. These findings expand the literature on CA as well as the ERBV by incorporating culture as a non-price factor in tandem with mainstream price factors, especially in designing a well-established firm collaboration.

Conclusion

In this paper, we investigated the conceptualization of collaborative advantage (CA) and examined its effect on SMEs' performance. Empirical testing of a hierarchical component model (HCM) using a two-stage approach validated eight constructs of CA: collaborative commitment, collaborative efficiency agreements, collaborative risk sharing, collaborative planning, collaborative resource sharing, collaborative relational capital, collaborative information and knowledge sharing, and collaborative synchronized responses. The process of producing these constructs was assessed in the LOC's measurement model with purification as suggested by Wieland et al. (2017) and Hair et al. (2017). Since some constructs had insignificant weight in the second step, the eight constructs were classified into three pillars, namely inter-firm trust building, resources investment, and dynamic synchronization. This treatment was taken to increase the reliability of the model, as suggested by Cenfetelli & Bassellier (2009). Reliable constructs in the LOC and HOC measurements established a strong basis for estimating the structural model.

The estimation of the structural model confirmed that CA has a positive direct effect on firm performance. The effect size of this relationship, however, is relatively small, suggesting that the effect of CA on firm performance is not straightforward and is substantially captured through a mediation process. By using firm capability as a mediator, the estimation results showed the importance of the mediating role of firm capability. The magnitude of the indirect effect of CA on firm performance through the mediator variable is twice as large as its direct effect. This implies that firm capability helps increase the contribution of CA to firm performance.

By taking into account the important features of SMEs, my study makes three contributions to the literature on CA. First, it reformulates the CA constructs that fit SMEs, namely strengthening inter-firm trust building and synchronization of firms' responses to changes in external factors. Second, it incorporates collaborative relational capital as a non-price factor in resources investment, which offers an additional perspective to the existing literature on CA that is dominated by price factors. Third, it enriches the transaction costs literature by examining the synchronization of responses to external shocks as one instrument to reduce transaction costs efficiency. In addition, this study also has a managerial implication that could help firm owners and/or managers to design a framework of collaboration with their peers that provides mutual benefits for all members.

The main limitation of this study is related to the fact that the data were collected from only a single respondent in each firm to represent collaboration that might vary across different divisions or departments of a firm. This may have meant that some biased perspectives were collected.

References

Angle, H. L., & Perry, J. L. (1981). An empirical assessment of organizational commitment and organizational effectiveness. *Administrative Science Quarterly*, *26*(1), 1–14.
Asian Development Bank. (2011). *Realizing the Asian Century*. www.adb.org
Barclay, D., Higgins, C., & Thompson, R. (1995). The partial least squares (PLS) approach to causal modeling: Personal computer adoption and use as an illustration. *Technology studies*, *2*(2), 285–309. doi:citeulike-article-id:5760069

Barratt, M., & Oliveira, A. (2001). Exploring the experiences of collaborative planning initiatives. *International Journal of Physical Distribution & Logistics Management, 31*(4), 266–289.

Beamon, B. M. (1999). Measuring supply chain performance. *International Journal of Operations & Production Management, 19*(3), 275–292.

Becker, J.-M., Klein, K., & Wetzels, M. (2012). Hierarchical latent variable models in pls-sem: Guidelines for using reflective-formative type models. *Long Range Planning, 45*(5), 359–394. doi:https://doi.org/10.1016/j.lrp.2012.10.001

Cao, M., & Zhang, Q. (2010). Supply chain collaborative advantage: A firm's perspective. *International Journal of Production Economics, 128*(1), 358–367. doi:http://dx.doi.org/10.1016/j.ijpe.2010.07.037

Cao, M., & Zhang, Q. (2011). Supply chain collaboration: Impact on collaborative advantage and firm performance. *Journal of Operations Management, 29*(3), 163–180. doi:http://dx.doi.org/10.1016/j.jom.2010.12.008

Cenfetelli, R.T., & Bassellier, G. (2009). Interpretation of formative measurement in information systems research. *MIS Quarterly, 33*(4), 689–707. http://ezproxy.flinders.edu.au/login?url=http://search.ebscohost.com/login.aspx?direct=true&db=bth&AN=44986346&site=ehost-live

Chang, W., Ellinger, A.E., Kim, K., & Franke, G.R. (2016). Supply chain integration and firm financial performance: A meta-analysis of positional advantage mediation and moderating factors. *European Management Journal, 34*(3), 282–295. doi:http://dx.doi.org/10.1016/j.emj.2015.11.008

Chen, L., Zhao, X., Tang, O., Price, L., Zhang, S., & Zhu, W. (2017). Supply chain collaboration for sustainability: A literature review and future research agenda. *International Journal of Production Economics, 194*, 73–87. doi:https://doi.org/10.1016/j.ijpe.2017.04.005

Christopher, M., & Lee, H. (2004). Mitigating supply chain risk through improved confidence. *International Journal of Physical Distribution & Logistics Management, 34*(5), 388–396.

Churchill, G.A., Jr. (1979). A paradigm for developing better measures of marketing constructs. *Journal of Marketing Research, 16*, 64–73.

Croom, S. (2001). Restructuring supply chains through information channel innovation. *International Journal of Operations & Production Management, 21*(4), 504–515.

Dania, W. A. P., Xing, K., & Amer, Y. (2018). Collaboration behavioural factors for sustainable agri-food supply chains: A systematic review. *Journal of Cleaner Production, 186*, 851–864. doi:https://doi.org/10.1016/j.jclepro.2018.03.148

Davenport, T.H., Harris, J.G., De Long, D.W., & Jacobson, A.L. (2001). Data to knowledge to results: Building an analytic capability. *California Management Review, 43*(2), 117–138.

Davis, D.F., & Golicic, S.L. (2010). Gaining comparative advantage in supply chain relationships: The mediating role of market-oriented IT competence. *Journal of the Academy of Marketing Science, 38*(1), 56–70. doi:10.1007/s11747-008-0127-8

Diamantopoulos, A., & Winklhofer, H.M. (2001). Index construction with formative indicators: An alternative to scale development. *Journal of Marketing Research, 38*(2), 269–277.

Dwyer, F.R., Schurr, P.H., & Oh, S. (1987). Developing buyer-seller relationships. *Journal of Marketing, 51*(2), 11–27.

Dyer, J.H. (2000). *Collaborative advantage: Winning through extended enterprise supplier networks.* Oxford University Press.

Ehrenhard, M., & Hoffmann, P. (2014). Better off alone?: SME preferences for joining a cooperative purchasing group. *Academy of Management Proceedings* (1). doi:10.5465/AMBPP.2014.17748abstract

Eisenhardt, K.M., & Tabrizi, B.N. (1995). Accelerating adaptive processes: Product innovation in the global computer industry. *Administrative Science Quarterly, 40*(1), 84–110.

Ellegaard, C. (2008). Supply risk management in a small company perspective. *Supply Chain Management, 13*(6), 425–434. doi:http://dx.doi.org/10.1108/13598540810905688

Fabbe-Costes, N., & Jahre, M. (2008). Supply chain integration and performance: A review of the evidence. *International Journal of Logistics Management, 19*(2), 130–154. doi:http://dx.doi.org/10.1108/09574090810895933

Flynn, B.B., Huo, B., & Zhao, X. (2010). The impact of supply chain integration on performance: A contingency and configuration approach. *Journal of Operations Management, 28*(1), 58–71. doi:http://dx.doi.org/10.1016/j.jom.2009.06.001

Frohlich, M.T., & Westbrook, R. (2001). Arcs of integration: an international study of supply chain strategies. *Journal of Operations Management, 19*(2), 185–200. doi:http://dx.doi.org/10.1016/S0272-6963(00)00055-3

Ghadge, A., Dani, S., & Kalawsky, R. (2012). Supply chain risk management: Present and future scope. *International Journal of Logistics Management, 23*(3), 313–339. doi:http://dx.doi.org/10.1108/09574091211289200

Grafton, J., & Mundy, J. (2016). Relational contracting and the myth of trust: Control in a co-opetitive setting. *Management Accounting Research, 36*, 24–42. doi:http://dx.doi.org/10.1016/j.mar.2016.07.008

Gundlach, G.T., Achrol, R.S., & Mentzer, J.T. (1995). The structure of commitment in exchange. *Journal of Marketing, 59*(1), 78–92.

Hair, J.F., Hult, G.T.M., Ringle, C.M., & Sarstedt, M. (2017). *A primer on partial least squares structural equation modeling* (2nd ed.). Sage.

Hair, J.F., Sarstedt, M., Ringle, C.M., & Gudergan, S. (2018). *Advanced issues in partial least squares structural equation modeling*. SAGE Publications, Inc.

Handfield, R.B., & Bechtel, C. (2002). The role of trust and relationship structure in improving supply chain responsiveness. *Industrial Marketing Management, 31*(4), 367–382.

Herczeg, G., Akkerman, R., & Hauschild, M.Z. (2018). Supply chain collaboration in industrial symbiosis networks. *Journal of Cleaner Production, 171*, 1058–1067. doi:https://doi.org/10.1016/j.jclepro.2017.10.046

House, R.J., Hanges, P.J., Javidian, M., Dorfman, P.W., & Gupta, V.E. (2004). *Culture, leadership, and organizations: The GLOBE study of 62 societies*. SAGE.

Hulland, J. (1999). Use of partial least squares (PLS) in strategic management research: A review of four recent studies. *Strategic Management Journal, 20*(2), 195.

Huxham, C., & Vangen, S. (2005). *Managing to collaborate: The theory and practice of collaborative advantage*. Routledge.

Huxham, C., & Vangen, S.I.V. (2004). Realizing the advantage or succumbing to inertia? *Organizational Dynamics, 33*(2), 190–201. doi:https://doi.org/10.1016/j.orgdyn.2004.01.006

Jap, S. D. (2001). Perspectives on joint competitive advantages in buyer-supplier relationships. *International Journal of Research in Marketing, 18*(1–2), 19–35. doi:http://dx.doi.org/10.1016/S0167-8116(01)00028-3

Jarvis, C.B., MacKenzie, S.B., & Podsakoff, P.M. (2003). A critical review of construct indicators and measurement model misspecification in marketing and consumer research. *Journal of Consumer Research, 30*(2), 199–218. doi:10.1086/376806

Jüttner, U. (2005). Supply chain risk management. *International Journal of Logistics Management, 16*(1), 120–141. doi:http://dx.doi.org/10.1108/09574090510617385

Kanter, R.M. (1994). Collaborative advantage: The art of alliances. *Harvard Business Review of Economic Dynamics, July-August*, 96–108.

Kock, N. (2015). Common method bias in PLS-SEM: A full collinearity assessment approach. *International Journal of E-Collaboration, 11*(4), art. 1. doi:10.4018/ijec.2015100101

Koufteros, X., Vonderembse, M., & Jayaram, J. (2005). Internal and external integration for product development: The contingency effects of uncertainty, equivocality, and platform strategy. *Decision Sciences, 36*(1), 97–133.

Lavie, D. (2006). The competitive advantage of interconnected firms: An extension of the resource-based view. *Academy of Management Review, 31*(3), 638–658.

Li, G., Fan, H., Lee, P.K.C., & Cheng, T.C.E. (2015). Joint supply chain risk management: An agency and collaboration perspective. *International Journal of Production Economics, 164*, 83–94. doi:http://dx.doi.org/10.1016/j.ijpe.2015.02.021

Li, J., & Matlay, H. (2006). Chinese entrepreneurship and small business development: An overview and research agenda. *Journal of Small Business and Enterprise Development, 13*(2), 248–262. doi:http://dx.doi.org/10.1108/14626000610665953

Liker, J.K., Sobek, D.K., Ward, A.C., & Cristiano, J.J. (1996). Involving suppliers in product development in the United States and Japan: Evidence for set-based concurrent engineering. *IEEE Transactions on Engineering Management, 43*(2), 165–178. doi:10.1109/17.509982

Lin, F.-J., & Lin, Y.-H. (2015). The effect of network relationship on the performance of SMEs. *Journal of Business Research, 69 (5)*, 1780–1785. doi:http://dx.doi.org/10.1016/j.jbusres.2015.10.055

Lorenzoni, G., & Lipparini, A. (1999). The leveraging of interfirm relationships as a distinctive organizational capability: A longitudinal study. *Strategic Management Journal, 20*(4), 317–338. doi:10.1002/(SICI)1097-0266(199904)20:4<317::AID-SMJ28>3.0.CO;2-3

MacKenzie, S.B., Podsakoff, P.M., & Jarvis, C.B. (2005). The Problem of measurement model misspecification in behavioral and organizational research and some recommended solutions. *Journal of Applied Psychology, 90*(4), 710–730. doi:10.1037/0021-9010.90.4.710

Manimala, M.J., Wasdani, K.P., & Vijaygopal, A. (2019). *Transnational entrepreneurship issues of SME internationalization in the Indian context* (1st ed.): Springer Singapore: Imprint: Springer.

McAdam, R., Miller, K., & McSorley, C. (2016). Towards a contingency theory perspective of quality management in enabling strategic alignment. *International Journal of Production Economics*. doi: https://doi.org/10.1016/j.ijpe.2016.07.003

McAdam, R., Miller, K., & McSorley, C. (2019). Towards a contingency theory perspective of quality management in enabling strategic alignment. *International Journal of Production Economics, 207*, 195–209. doi:https://doi.org/10.1016/j.ijpe.2016.07.003

Min, S., Roath, A.S., Daugherty, P.J., Genchev, S.E. et al. (2005). Supply chain collaboration: What's happening? *International Journal of Logistics Management, 16*(2), 237–256. doi:http://dx.doi.org/10.1108/09574090510634539

Morgan, R.M., & Hunt, S.D. (1994). The commitment-trust theory of relationship marketing. *Journal of Marketing, 58*(3), 20–38. http://ezproxy.flinders.edu.au/login?url=http://search.ebscohost.com/login.aspx?direct=true&db=bth&AN=9408160246&site=ehost-live

Murphy, G.B., Trailer, J.W., & Hill, R.C. (1996). Measuring performance in entrepreneurship research. *Journal of Business Research, 36*(1), 15–23. doi:https://doi.org/10.1016/0148-2963(95)00159-X

Nilsson, F., & Göransson, M. (2021). Critical factors for the realization of sustainable supply chain innovations – Model development based on a systematic literature review. *Journal of Cleaner Production, 296*, 126471. doi:https://doi.org/10.1016/j.jclepro.2021.126471

Park, N.K., Mezias, J.M., & Song, J. (2004). A resource-based view of strategic alliances and firm value in the electronic marketplace. *Journal of Management, 30*(1), 7–27.

Podsakoff, P.M., MacKenzie, S.B., Jeong-Yeon, L., & Podsakoff, N.P. (2003). Common method biases in behavioral research: A critical review of the literature and recommended remedies. *Journal of Applied Psychology, 88*(5), 879–903. doi:10.1037/0021-9010.88.5.879

Prajogo, D., & McDermott, C.M. (2014). Antecedents of service innovation in SMEs: Comparing the effects of external and internal factors. *Journal of Small Business Management, 52*(3), 521. do :10.1111/jsbm.12047

Sahiti, F. (2019). *The growth of firms in less-developed countries lessons from Kosovo* (1st ed.). Springer International Publishing: Imprint: Palgrave Macmillan.

Semrau, T., Ambos, T., & Sascha, K. (2016). Entrepreneurial orientation and SME performance across societal cultures: An international study. *Journal of Business Research, 69*(5), 1928–1932. doi:http://dx.doi.org/10.1016/j.jbusres.2015.10.082

Sheu, C., Yen, H.R., & Chae, D. (2006). Determinants of supplier-retailer collaboration: Evidence from an international study. *International Journal of Operations and Production Management, 26*(1), 24–49.

Simatupang, T.M., & Sridharan, R. (2005). An integrative framework for supply chain collaboration. *International Journal of Logistics Management, 16*(2), 257–274. doi:http://dx.doi.org/10.1108/09574090510634548

Tang, C.S. (2006). Perspectives in supply chain risk management. *International Journal of Production Economics, 103*(2), 451–488. doi:https://doi.org/10.1016/j.ijpe.2005.12.006

Tanriverdi, H. (2006). Performance effects of information technology synergies in multibusiness firms. *MIS Quarterly, 30*(1), 57–77.

Thai, M.T.T., & Turkina, E. (2014). Macro-level determinants of formal entrepreneurship versus informal entrepreneurship. *Journal of Business Venturing, 29*(4), 490–510. doi:https://doi.org/10.1016/j.jbusvent.2013.07.005

Venkatraman, N., & Ramanujam, V. (1986). Measurement of business performance in strategy research: A comparison of approaches. *Academy of Management Review, 11*(4), 801–814. doi:10.5465/AMR.1986.4283976

Welbourne, T.M., & Pardo-del-val, M. (2009). Relational capital: Strategic advantage for small and medium-size enterprises (SMEs) through negotiation and collaboration. *Group Decision and Negotiation, 18*(5), 483–497. doi:http://dx.doi.org/10.1007/s10726-008-9138-6

Welter, F., & Kautonen, T. (2005). Trust, social networks and enterprise development: Exploring evidence from East and West Germany. *International Entrepreneurship and Management Journal, 1*(3), 367–379. doi:http://dx.doi.org/10.1007/s11365-005-2601-9

Wieland, A., Durach, C.F., Kembro, J., & Treiblmaier, H. (2017). Statistical and judgmental criteria for scale purification. *Supply Chain Management: An International Journal, 22*(4), 321–328. doi:doi:10.1108/SCM-07-2016-0230

Wu, I.-L., Chuang, C.-H., & Hsu, C.-H. (2014). Information sharing and collaborative behaviors in enabling supply chain performance: A social exchange perspective. *International Journal of Production Economics, 148*, 122–132. doi:https://doi.org/10.1016/j.ijpe.2013.09.016

Wu, Z., & Pullman, M.E. (2015). Cultural embeddedness in supply networks. *Journal of Operations Management, 37*, 45–58. doi:http://dx.doi.org/10.1016/j.jom.2015.06.004

Britta Boyd, Alexander Brem, and Silke Tegtmeier

15 Sustainable Collaborative Business Models for Energy Efficient Solutions – An Exploratory Analysis of Danish and German SMEs

Abstract: The growing dynamics of innovation and productivity are challenges that are met by companies with the constant development of new technologies and business models – the logic with which they create and capture value. Especially in the face of the grand challenge of climate change, looking for energy efficient solutions offers opportunities not only for big companies in metropolitan areas, but also for small and medium sized companies in rural areas. This study therefore investigates similarities and differences of SMEs in an energy intensive industry that are situated in a specific, geographic border region regarding dependencies between networks, energy efficiency, and success. These three dimensions are analyzed in a qualitative study leading to implications for energy efficient solutions. This study contributes to existing research on sustainable collaborative business models by suggesting the inclusion of cross border networking and circular economy aspects.

Keywords: business models, collaborative business models, sustainable development, sustainability, energy efficiency, Danish and German manufactures, SMEs, qualitative case analysis, NVivo, business model canvas

Introduction

At least since the "Fridays for Future" protests by pupils have diffused all over the world, the challenge of climate change has made it into the news again. As a decisive factor for sustainable development, i.e. a "development that meets the needs of the present without compromising the ability of future generations to meet their own needs" (WCED, 1987, p. 41), fighting against climate change has become an important aim worldwide.

In this context, the importance of improving the energy efficiency of production equipment, processes, and products was stressed by the World Commission on Environment and Development three decades ago (WCED, 1987). However, due to the political situation in many countries, not many measures have been introduced so far or are to

Britta Boyd, Witten/Herdecke University
Alexander Brem, University of Stuttgart, Germany
Silke Tegtmeier, University of Southern Denmark

https://doi.org/10.1515/9783110747652-016

be expected, nor are measures that have been taken of sufficient impact. In contrast, public pressure to address this issue with new products and processes or by revising existing ones increases. In this context, technological developments can be beneficial to facilitate innovation and continuous improvement. Renewable energies, which have already grown to a high market share, e.g. in Germany, are a leading area. The capacities for renewable energies are now even higher than for conventional energy (EMR, 2018). As many emerging technologies do not make it to the market or do not achieve market success (Hjorth & Brem, 2016), more attention is directed towards improving processes in companies, especially in the area of energy efficiency.

On a micro-level, sustainable business models (SBM) have been investigated by many scholars from different angles (Schaltegger et al., 2012; Willard et al., 2014; Bocken et al., 2014; Joyce & Paquin, 2016; Kurucz et al., 2017; Evans et al., 2017; Brehmer et al., 2018). In this context, "collaborative business models" are discussed to underline the need for cooperation among diverse parties in view of the entire value chain. Cooperation with competitors can be particularly important to achieve the goal of environmental sustainability because many organizations, specifically SMEs, may not be able to build up new infrastructure (e.g. recycling or renewable energy facilities) on their own. It can be more effective to split the investments between different stakeholders to develop solutions not only for individual organizations but for the entire system. Such coopetition endeavors are especially challenging for SMEs lacking experience and networks in this regard (Gast et al., 2019). Finally, Schaltegger et al. (2016) sum up this discussion by concluding that "little is known about the dynamic role of business models for sustainable entrepreneurship processes aiming at upscaling ecologically and socially beneficial niche models or sustainability upgrading of conventional mass market players" (p. 264).

Therefore, knowledge about the role of sustainable business models to upscale ecological benefits is still scarce. To the best of our knowledge, there is no previous research that analyzes the existence and concrete form of collaborative business models in the energy sector. With the following explorative study, we tap into this research gap. In particular, for SMEs in an energy intensive industry a sustainable and collaborative business model could help to gain competitive advantage. The above described research gap, along with the discussed literature, was considered when formulating the following research questions:

1. How should a collaborative business model be conceptualized to be successful in terms of sustainable development?
2. In which way do existing SMEs need to transform their business models in order to become successful as sustainable businesses?
3. What are the key challenges that collaborative business models impose upon the processes in SMEs?
4. Why are the companies acting the way they do with regard to reaching higher energy efficiency?
5. Why are networks not utilized sufficiently in order to reach higher energy efficiency?

To answer the first two research questions, we explore theoretical approaches that combine collaborative business model approaches considering sustainable development as a success factor. The last three research questions will be answered later when analyzing the results of the empirical dataset. This study focuses on the energy sector and its collaborative business model collaborations. Denmark and Germany are the research subjects since these neighboring countries are both strong in the energy industry, especially in renewable energies (Lipp, 2007), and both went through an intensive transition process in recent years.

The reminder of this chapter is as follows: the upcoming section deals with the theoretical grounding as well as previous research about the topic under investigation. In the following, we outline the method of the investigation before we document the analysis and results. The final part of the chapter discusses both results and its implications. Limitations and prospects for future research are discussed before the chapter culminates with a conclusion.

Theoretical Background and Literature Review

In the following, we introduce the concept of sustainable business models as a baseline for our empirical work.

Sustainability and Business Models

Sustainability goals call for a radical transformation of organizations toward a genuine sustainable development of our countries, societies, and the world (Bolton & Hannon, 2016; Eller et al., 2020; Loorbach et al., 2010). In-depth research needs to reveal if modified existing business models or rather completely new business models can create financially viable as well as environmentally and socially valuable solutions for the future. In this context, it will be key to either reduce negative or to create positive external effects (Boons & Lüdeke-Freund, 2013; Schaltegger et al., 2012; Schaltegger et al., 2016; Stubbs & Cocklin, 2008).

Based on two case studies, Stubbs and Cocklin (2008) conceptualized a Sustainability Business Model derived from a set of normative principles. In this way, they came up with an ideal type of a sustainability business, which includes several structural as well as cultural characteristics of an organization. Among these characteristics are: drawing on economic, environmental, as well as social aspects of sustainability, using a Triple Bottom Line (TBL) approach to measure performance, and treating nature as a stakeholder while promoting environmental stewardship.

Recent research yielded further approaches towards sustainable business models, such as the sustainable business canvas (Fichter & Tiemann, 2018) or the Strongly Sustainable Business Model canvas (Kurucz et al., 2017; Upward, 2013; Upward & Jones, 2016). Both approaches are based on the business model canvas introduced by Osterwalder and Pigneur (2010) that has widely been referenced for the definition of business models and that serves as a visual design method.

The sustainable business canvas adds three components to the basic model: business model – vision and mission, competitors, and relevant stakeholders. Customer segments, relationships, and channels were summed up as customers. This tool extension is based on several sustainability concepts, such as the normative claim for the Triple Bottom Line, the stakeholder perspective, and strong sustainability (Fichter & Tiemann, 2015). For all parts of the sustainable business canvas, classical economic, but also sustainability-related, questions that a new business model should be able to answer have been developed.

Normative requirements for such relevant elements of sustainable business models are also of great importance, besides the above-mentioned approaches. They provide ecological, social or economic values for the value proposition and they ground the business infrastructure in principles that are related to sustainable supply chain management. Managers need to improve flexibility and agility levels in the supply chain to meet faster technological developments, shorter product life cycles, and increased global competition (Gharaei et al., 2019). Further, sustainable business models enable close relationships with diverse stakeholders in order to take responsibility not only for production, but also for consumption systems of the customer interface. For the financial model, they distribute economic gains and costs equitably among the actors involved (Boons & Lüdeke-Freund, 2013).

Recent research started to analyze how existing organizations can be transformed to rely on sustainable business models. Gauthier and Gilomen showed that this transformation couldn't necessarily be reached within one single organization. In fact, this may call for collaborative business models, which in turn may have an impact on urban districts or regions if not the entire economy. Focusing on energy efficiency projects, the authors elaborate on multi-actor collaborations in the context of business model innovations. Their work reveals that energy efficiency and financial returns on investment can go along with multiple win-win potentials (Gauthier & Gilomen, 2016).

Future research needs to unveil the role of collaboration in making sustainable business models successful. This may include cooperative arrangements, learning-action networks, but also struggles between different stakeholder groups regarding their political power (Schaltegger et al., 2016). The current study builds upon a growing body of research concerning business models with a major focus on companies' processes of greening their business models.

In their case-based work concerning industrial manufacturing, Rajala and colleagues focus on how companies can adjust their business models on the organizational level in order to become more environmentally sustainable. They outline the importance of managerial agency in organizational identity generation and its impact on greening the business ecosystem. According to their findings, business model greening requires a major change of the business ecosystem and needs to be regarded as a multi-layered process (Rajala et al., 2016).

In line with this, Abdelkafi and Täuscher (2016) propose a system dynamic perspective and argue that the entire business logic needs to be transformed in order to create value for the manifold stakeholders of the business as well as the natural environment. In a multilevel model, they propose installing a feedback loop between the value created for the customer, the value made by the company, and the value in terms of the natural environment.

In contrast, Al-Saleh and Mahroum (2015) focus on policy instruments that foster green business models. Instead of the more common technology-push perspective, they investigate the behavior of businesses related to these policy instruments and find some merit in pure awareness campaigns. Bocken (2015) raises another key issue through her work on sustainable venture capital. As major success factors, she names business model innovation, collaboration, as well as a strong business case. Her work confirms that practical idealism and disagreement with the status quo are motivators, while a strong incumbent industry and adverse investor mind-sets are hindering factors.

Hatak et al. (2015) focus on small and medium-sized enterprises that face particular challenges when relating their business to sustainable development. This is because SMEs need to manage limited resources even more than other businesses. This work reveals that there is still a high level of uncertainty when it comes to realizing sustainable opportunities in companies. As a key issue, the authors stress the owner's attitude towards sustainability.

Based on linguistic variables, Doukas et al. (2014) develop a multi-criteria framework for policy to assess firms' energy and environment related corporate policies. Their study reveals that SMEs, which follow systematic environmental practices, show a higher performance than others. This is mainly the case for countries that implement CSR concepts. Using data from the Global Reporting Initiative that includes a variety of industries, they apply the following criteria: management commitment, monitoring the progress and related impact, participation in dissemination activities, promotion of renewable energy, promotion of energy efficiency, as well as waste and water management.

Collaborative Business Model Approaches

With focus on the entire supply or value chain, the term "collaborative business model" is used to underline the need to cooperate among diverse parties in the collaborative business (Chen & Cheng, 2010; Sroka and Jablonski, 2013). Nowadays, collaborative business models are becoming more and more essential in many industries, such as the steel industry (Sroka and Jablonski, 2013), the automotive industry (Ward et al., 2016, chemistry (Lozano et al., 2013), pharmacy (Garnsey & Leong, 2008), mobile communications (Chen & Cheng, 2010), or web-based solutions (Hinz & Spann, 2008).

Cooperation with competitors can be of particular importance to achieve the goal of environmental sustainability since many organizations, specifically SMEs, may not be able to invest in the required new infrastructure (e.g. recycling or renewable energy facilities). Thus, sharing investments between different stakeholders may be more effective. This may also involve that stakeholders develop solutions not only for individual organizations, but for the entire system (Stubbs & Cocklin, 2008). Earlier work suggests that a collaborative approach can make the whole supply chain sustainable in the long run (Stubbs & Cocklin, 2008; Hawkins, 1993). For example, in the case of chemistry, collaborative business models can lead to a reduction in the use of dangerous chemicals. Thus, society and environment can benefit simultaneously from this cooperation and partners gain economic benefits (Lozano et al., 2013). Together with improved resource allocation on the network level (Garnsey & Leong, 2008), partner companies can profit from collaboration in terms of cost efficiencies, access to new markets, and quicker marketing for products (Ward et al., 2016).

However, a key challenge for installing collaborative business models among companies is to develop collaborative business processes. A well-defined business process management system is required, which not only refers to all the complex interactions of one single company, but also the process interfaces of all partners joining the collaborative business model (Lazarte et al., 2009). Installing interfaces between systems and processes of the diverse partners likely goes along with more intensive maintenance and operation costs (Ward et al., 2016).

In recent years, business model innovation research showed a tendency towards graphical ways of showing the linkages between different aspects of a business model. Our further analysis is mainly focused on identifying key models in the context of collaboration and sustainability that address the social business model aspects, as highlighted by Yunus et al. (2010).

Bocken et al. (2014) took a first step to integrate technological, social, and organizational perspectives into business model archetypes (see Figure 15.1). With this view, the different directions for business model thinking become apparent: archetypes are driven by specific mechanisms and solutions. They argue that specific archetypes maximize material and energy efficiency, create value from "waste," substitute existing solutions with renewable and natural processes, deliver functionality rather than ownership, adopt a stewardship role, encourage sufficiency, re-purpose the business for society/ environment, and develop scale-up solutions. Evans et al. (2017) support the creation of such sustainable business models and lay a foundation to support organizations in investigating and experimenting with alternative new business models.

Recently, a triple-layered business model ontology was introduced by Joyce and Paquin (2019). The rationale behind this approach is that business models consist of three layers: an economic layer, an environmental life cycle-layer, and a social layer. The first one refers to the well-known basic business model understanding that originated from

Groupings	Technological			Social			Organisational	
Archetypes	Maximise material and energy efficiency	Create value from waste	Substitute with renewables and natural processes	Deliver functionality rather than ownership	Adopt a stewardship role	Encourage sufficiency	Repurpose for society/ environment	Develop scale up solutions
Examples	Low carbon manufacturing/ solutions Lean manufacturing Additive manufacturing De-materialisation (of products/ packaging) Increased functionality (to reduce total number of products required)	Circular economy, closed loop Cradle-2-Cradle Industrial symbiosis Reuse, recycle, re-manufacture Take back management Use excess capacity Sharing assets (shared ownership and collaborative consumption) Extended producer responsibility	Move from non-renewable to renewable energy sources Solar and wind-power based energy innovations Zero emissions initiative Blue Economy Biomimicry The Natural Step Slow manufacturing Green chemistry	Product-oriented PSS - maintenance, extended warrantee Use oriented PSS- Rental, lease, shared Result-oriented PSS- Pay per use Private Finance Initiative (PFI) Design, Build, Finance, Operate (DBFO) Chemical Management Services (CMS)	Biodiversity protection Consumer care - promote consumer health and well-being Ethical trade (fair trade) Choice editing by retailers Radical transparency about environmental/ societal impacts Resource stewardship	Consumer Education (models); communication and awareness Demand management (including cap & trade) Slow fashion Product longevity Premium branding/ limited availability Frugal business Responsible product distribution/ promotion	Not for profit Hybrid businesses, Social enterprise (for profit) Alternative ownership: cooperative, mutual, (farmers) collectives Social and biodiversity regeneration initiatives ('net positive') Base of pyramid solutions Localisation Home based, flexible working	Collaborative approaches (sourcing, production, lobbying) Incubators and Entrepreneur support models Licensing, Franchising Open innovation (platforms) Crowd sourcing/ funding "Patient / slow capital" collaborations

Figure 15.1: Sustainable business models archetypes by Bocken et al., 2014, p. 48.

Osterwalder and Pigneur (2010). This internally oriented view is complemented by an external view of the impact of the new business, which is the second layer focusing on environmental impacts. The last layer is the potential social impact (see Figure 15.2).

Upward and Jones developed a detailed sustainable business model ontology that includes a detailed critique of the original business model canvas as well as an elaboration on the definition of business success. This ontology includes three contexts as well as three perspectives: the sustainable business model includes the environment (physical, chemical, biological), society (social, technological), and the financial economy (monetary). It adopts a process perspective, a stakeholder perspective, as well as a measurement perspective, all of which include a variety of constructs/ components. For practical use, the so-called flourishing business canvas has originated from this ontology (Upward & Jones, 2016; Upward, 2013). Figure 15.3 shows a graphic overview of this approach.

The flourishing business canvas was found to be most useful for this study of sustainable collaborative business models because it focuses on environmental, societal, and economic contexts in an integrated model. These contexts are further divided into 16 components according to which Elkington and Upward (2016) developed 16 questions (see Appendix 15.1). These contexts and components are critical for building competitive advantages in SMEs that act in energy intensive industries.

Economic Business model Canvas

Partners	Activities	Value Proposition	Customer Relationship	Customer Segments
	Resources		Channels	

Costs	Revenues

Environmental Life Cycle Business model Canvas

Supplies and Out-sourcing	Production	Functional Value	End-of-Life	Use Phase
	Materials		Distribution	

Environmental Impacts	Environmental Benefits

Social stakeholder Business model Canvas

Local Communities	Governance	Social Value	Societal Culture	End-User
	Employees		Scale of Outreach	

Social Impacts	Social Benefits

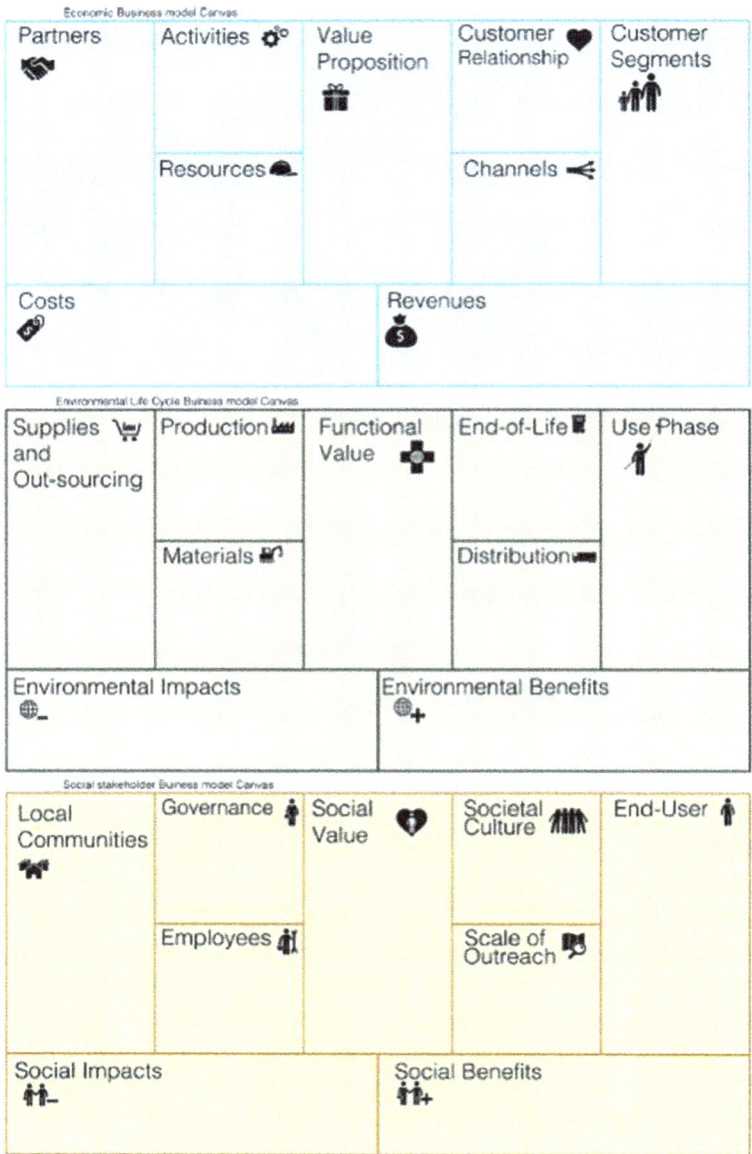

Figure 15.2: Overview of the triple layered business model canvas by Joyce and Paquin, 2016, p. 10.

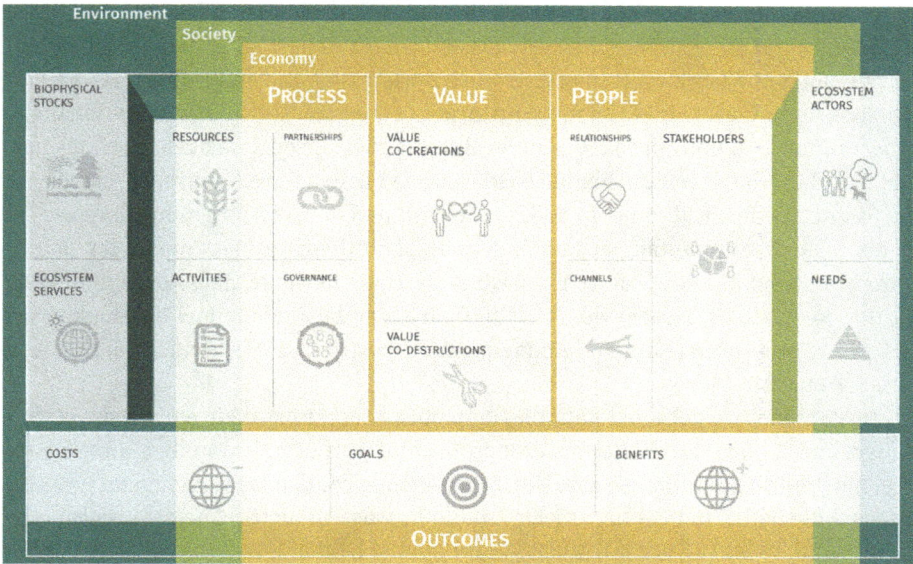

Figure 15.3: The flourishing business canvas (Elkington and Upward, 2016, p. 132).

Method

Research Design and Setting

We explore potential collaborations and business models in the energy sector in the Danish-German cross-border region. We have chosen the energy sector since this is one of the system critical industries, and economically a key industry as well. This industry went through dramatic changes in recent years through the so-called "Energiewende" (Giones et al., 2019). Denmark and Germany are two very suitable countries for this purpose, because for many years they have been world-leading in the development of renewable energies (Lipp, 2007), and they are neighboring countries. A more recent study, which compares regional initiatives to reduce emissions implemented in Denmark, indicated that the Sønderborg region scored best in the Carbon Regional Index (Straatman et al., 2018). As Sønderborg is situated close to the German border, we focus on this border region by comparing Northern German and Southern Danish companies.

We were aiming to receive a comprehensive view of the whole phenomenon under investigation by mainly addressing "how" and "why" questions. Therefore, we regard an in-depth, interpretive case study approach as highly valuable (Edmondson & McManus, 2007; Eisenhardt, 1989; Eisenhardt & Graebner, 2007; Yin, 2009). This approach then allows us to discover new knowledge by inductively content analyzing our data. As a synthesis, we come up with implications that contribute to building a preliminary theory from the cases we investigated (Eisenhardt & Graebner, 2007).

We build our work on former literature by assessing the applicability of the proposed sustainable business models in terms of a successful sustainable business. Thus, the focus of our approach is on evaluating the concepts and relationships provided in these models. For this purpose, we need a structured approach, which we can test in an empirical setup. In addition, we wanted to take a longitudinal approach: do the businesses maintain sustainability values in their business model for five or more years, and do these values increase or decrease in the business over time? (Upward & Jones, 2016). Hence, we used the flourishing business model ontology based on Upward and Jones (2016) and Elkington and Upward (2016) introduced earlier as a basis for our interviews.

In step one, we collected data on companies concerning their emissions, performance, and innovation. Hence, as an approach of purposeful sampling, a first-stage screening of Southern Danish and Northern German companies in the metal industry that could benefit from energy efficient solutions was conducted. The data reveal relevant cases that are further investigated through the help of interviews (step two) with company representatives regarding stakeholder networks and business models. In that second stage, qualitative interviews based on the business model concept were carried out. About 30 companies were identified to explain their energy efficient solutions and collaborative business models. In total, nine companies were willing to take part in the more intense interview study and were investigated in more detail. The questions for the semi-structured interviews were derived from the flourishing business canvas (Elkington & Upward, 2016) and adapted according to the requirements of the study and of the investigated companies, i.e. SMEs. The adapted version of the 16 questions from Elkington & Upward (see Appendix 15.1) and the final questionnaire (see Appendix 15.2) were pre-tested with a company in Northern Germany.

Sample

For many years, both Denmark and Germany have been world-leading in the development of renewable energies (Lipp, 2007). According to The International Energy Efficiency Scorecard Report, Germany is also number one worldwide in energy efficiency (Kallakuri et al., 2016). Denmark is investing high amounts to increase its energy efficiency, already with some remarkable successes. For instance, more than two percent per year of the Danish manufacturing industry's energy intensity has been reduced in the last ten years (Danish Energy Agency, 2016). In addition, both countries have similar annual growth rates of renewable energy consumption compared to non-renewables, as well as a similar average annual real GDP growth (Bhattacharya et al., 2016).

In the border region Danish and German manufacturing companies and initiatives successfully started to develop clean technologies and reduce carbon emissions.

The idea of developing an energy network with existing initiatives and companies in the region to facilitate more energy efficient solutions seems to pay off. News items in media like *The Guardian* show that there is supra-regional attention on this issue (The Guardian, 2015).

There are several reasons why the Danish-German border region is an appropriate subject for this research. Both sides of the border have in common that they are peripheral regions in their respective country. This implies less political attention, because not as many people are living in these areas compared to ones that are more central. However, this does not necessarily imply a low economic performance. World-leading companies such as Danfoss or Krones AG are located in this border region. However, the majority of companies are small and medium sized, which offers an interesting research background: 99% of all companies in Europe are SMEs (European Union, 2018). We specifically focus our study on SMEs because for these companies the transition to more sustainable business models is infinitely more difficult, not least because of resource constraints in daily operations. Further, a region where many SMEs are located can be an interesting starting point to investigate collaborative business models in particular. Finally, earlier research also highlights the role of cross-border regional innovation systems, which can be found in the Danish-German border region (Trippl, 2010; Makkonen, 2015), also in an energy-industry context (Jensen et al., 2016).

Data Collection

To empirically investigate our research questions, we did purposeful sampling of 30 companies and interviewed the nine companies from the German-Danish border region out of those which were willing to join our study. This region is proactively seeking climate neutrality. The Sønderborg commune joined "project zero," which aims to attain climate neutrality for Sønderborg by the end of 2029. One of the main foci of "project zero" is the smart use of energy to reduce energy consumption by 40% compared to the baseline in 2007 (Project Zero, 2018). The importance of this goal is also supported by the bi-annual conference "100% Climate Neutrality" that stems from a collaboration between universities, municipalities, and innovation actors in the Danish-German border region (SDU Mads Clausen Institute, 2018). Similarly, the "Sylter Declaration" aims at rendering the German-Danish Wadden Sea region climate neutral by 2030 (Werner, 2010). This is further supported by Schleswig-Holstein's ambition to become climate neutral by 2050 (Schleswig-Holstein, 2018). By choosing this region, we are able to investigate companies that should be extremely inclined to focus on energy efficiency and saving.

Furthermore, we focus on the metal building industry, which is very energy intensive (Eurostat, 2018) and therefore has a significantly high potential for energy saving. For this purpose, we investigate extreme cases that can unveil the reasons, challenges, resistances, shortcomings, and advancements in the process of energy saving.

The data collection is based upon nine in-depth semi-structured interviews with company representatives such as managers and owners. Therefore, our interviewees were highly knowledgeable informants (Eisenhardt & Graebner, 2007) as they view the phenomenon from different perspectives and have comprehensive knowledge of all areas of their businesses due to their leading role.

The interview guideline (see Appendix 15.2) was developed along the lines of the business model approach according to Osterwalder and Pigneur (2010). It was further refined and adopted regarding sustainability goals based on the flourishing business canvas, according to Upward (2013). The conceptualization followed the work of El-kington and Upward (2016) with individual questions for each area of the canvas. The business model approach unveils the companies' logic to create and capture value and this allows us to discover energy-related attitudes and intentions of the investi-gated companies. For transcription, as well as coding and further analysis of the data, we used the NVivo 11 software.

Characterization of the Sample

1. Company 1 was founded in 1991 and is located close to Flensburg but operates all over Germany and other European countries. With around 50 employees they also work in the on-site workshop and execute orders in their closer surrounding. With their skilled workers they operate on the cutting edge of technical development. The company, which is specialized in pipeline constructions, plant and mechanical engineering, offers their customers solutions for a wide range of tasks in all metal construction segments. The company produces fine-mechanic components as well as complete pipelines and large refrigeration systems. Inspection work on various plant systems also belongs to their scope of activities (AMB, 2018).
2. Company 2 had operated since 1972, is close to Flensburg, and firmly rooted in the region. With 10 employees they trade hard metal tools specialized in grinding and sharpening saws, chainsaws, drills, but also domestic kitchen cutlery. Moreover, the company offers producing or replacement services for special tools in the in-dustry, craft, and hobby segments. They used over 40 years to continuously develop themselves and their machines to offer a high-quality standard (Hartmetall-Werkzeuge-Nord, 2018).
3. Company 3, a specialist in processing metals, is located near Flensburg. In total 25 employees work in the company, mostly in production of and operating high-tech machines. Long training is needed for turning, milling, drilling, gear cutting, and balancing as well as laser and water jet technology. Therefore, every worker has the skills to run just one or a few machines on their own. Company 3 is a subsidi-ary that grew out of another company nearby, which produces machines for out-side applications (e.g. wood chipping and milling machines) and purchases metal

components from company 3. They believe that customers value their expertise, flexibility, and reliability that have grown over 130 years (Jensen, 2018).

4. Company 4 located in Hamburg operates in the plant construction sector with specialization in automation. Seventy employees currently work for company 4 and most of them are electrical engineers. The products, such as switch cabinets, are drafted on the computer and subsequently manufactured in the company's own workshop. They offer complete solutions for production plants in the food industry but also for other sectors such as shipbuilding and the pharmaceutical industry. Company 4 has a close partnership with Siemens AG and provides services such as building frequency converters for their partner.

5. Company 5 operates in the plant construction sector with a specialization in air-conditioning technology, ventilation systems, and fire protection for different industries. With around 200 employees, the firm also assembles pipeline constructions in ships, ranging from planning and construction to the installation. For very big orders, external personnel is recruited to do the installation on-site. The company is active in different associations, such as the ship-builders association, windmills association, and chamber of commerce.

6. Company 6 started in 1961 producing a simple steel plate grinding mill which led to further developments. With its head office in Sønderborg, the company is now owned by the second generation. The main area of activity is within machines for cattle feeding, straw processing machinery, and biomass technology.

7. Company 7 has more than 35 years of experience as an extrusion, stamping, deep drawing, and metal plate working subcontractor. Based in Nordborg, company 7 was formed through the merger of two companies. About 90 employees are working on 25 fully automated production lines that facilitate the production from single-unit series to larger-scale series of up to 15 million units per year (DFT Presswork, 2018).

8. Company 8, situated in Sønderborg, is a leading developer and manufacturer of prestressing tool systems and tool assembly presses, based on the strip winding technology. Company 8 has also taken a leading position in the development of a robot system for the surface polishing of tools and molds with high-quality requirements. They are furthermore engaged in developing and delivering special machinery and equipment solutions for selected customers (Strecon, 2018).

9. Company 9 was founded in 1934 and has been continuously modernized, as their production methods have been optimized as well as automated. In addition, new machines have been installed. Company 9 complies with strict environmental regulations through new wastewater treatment plants and methods. Through competent staff and qualified management, they want to ensure that they are regarded as one of the most reputable and valued companies in the industry and that their galvanic surface refinement contributes to modern development with intelligent solutions (Sønderborg Fornikling, 2018).

The questionnaire was pretested twice to develop and validate a suitable interview guideline. The nine interviews were conducted in spring and summer 2017. The interview length varied between 30 and 60 minutes each. The total of six hours and five minutes resulted in transcripts of 70 pages. All interviews were conducted in the native language of the interviewee (Danish or German), and later translated into English to enable a sound analysis and comparison of the interviews. Table 15.1 gives an overview of the sample firms and available figures:

Table 15.1: Company description (sources: interviews, homepages of the companies, and other publicly available material).

Company	Industry	Date of incorporation	Location	Turnover in 2016/17 USD	Number of employees
1	Metal construction	1991	Schleswig-Holstein	5,065,792	ca. 50
2	Metal processing	1972	Schleswig-Holstein	556,565	10
3	Metal processing	2006	Schleswig-Holstein	1,741,920	ca. 25
4	Plant construction	n.a.	Hamburg	n.a.	ca. 70
5	Plant construction	n.a.	Hamburg	n.a.	ca. 200
6	Metal processing	1981	Sønderborg	558,505	24
7	Metal processing	2000	Nordborg	1,247,295	ca. 90
8	Metal- and tool processing	2001	Sønderborg	688,027	18
9	Metal processing	2012	Sønderborg	848,370	ca. 20

Data Analysis

We apply an inductive, qualitative approach according to the work of Eisenhardt (1989) to code and analyze the data we collected. Our methodological procedure is systematic, accurate, and rigorous (Eisenhardt & Graebner, 2007). Therefore, the main purpose of our study is to reveal the relevant concepts related to energy efficiency, networking behavior, and success of the companies. We follow the guidelines to generate theory, which were suggested in "grounded theory" approaches (Glaser & Strauss, 1967; Lincoln & Guba, 1985; Strauss & Corbin, 1998). The qualitative case analysis with the NVivo software considers connections between the following three dimensions: networks, energy efficiency, and success. Table 15.2 depicts the initial codes

Table 15.2: List of themes and concepts.

List of initial codes		
ENERGY	**SUCCESS**	**NETWORKING**
Awareness of energy efficiency	Optimization	Commitment in organizations
Costs	Overall company success and future expectations	Communication
Ecological aspects	Relationship networking and success	Partnership with companies
Energy saving (economical)	Relationship energy and success	Resistance to associations
Energy saving (environmental)		
Implemented energy efficiency measures		
Present state and outlook on the future		
Resources		
List of Themes		
Relation success & networking	Relation networking & energy	Relation energy & success

and key concepts derived from the analysis. A comparison of the cases shows which differences and similarities exist among the companies.

As we take a social constructivist perspective (Hammersley, 1992; Huberman & Miles, 2002; Sandberg 2005), we oppose inter-rater reliability, which is a measure from positivist approaches proposing there was a right or wrong way of labelling data (Burr, 2015; Kleine et al., 2019; Ritchie and Lewis 2014). Instead, we apply the Quality Management Process Model introduced by Walther et al. (2013) and use several strategies to assure the validity and reliability of our study. Such qualitative approaches were also applied by other researchers evaluating sustainable business models, e.g. in the energy industry (Leisen et al., 2019).

Results

We conducted an in-depth analysis of each interview through the lens of our main research questions:

What are the key challenges that collaborative business models impose upon the processes in SMEs?

Why are the companies acting the way they do with regards to reaching higher energy efficiency?

Why are networks not utilized sufficiently in order to reach higher energy efficiency?

We started the analysis without theoretical preferences or any a priori hypotheses. The interviews were analyzed independently to receive a comprehensive picture of each company. We were therefore able to identify the theoretical concepts, relationships, and process patterns regarding our research questions within the case and, later, across cases. Furthermore, by means of NVivo, we used several tables and graphs to facilitate our analyses (Miles and Huberman, 1994).

Industry Analysis

In the study we discovered that the three themes, success, energy efficiency, and networks are relevant for the metal working industry. In this energy intensive industry, the potential to save energy is very high. Steel, for example, has superior environmental characteristics and advantages through life cycle thinking. The demand for steel is at the end of a rare cycle but global scrap availability is expected to grow strongly. The steel industry can increase its use of ferrous scrap considerably in the medium and long-term. In general, the steel industry has shown considerable improvements in productivity and reductions in environmental impact (Worldsteel Association, 2017).

Because steel is infinitely recyclable, it makes the industry integral to the global circular economy and, thus, a sustainable future. The circular economy describes a move from linear business models to circular business models where products or parts are repaired, re-used, returned, and recycled instead of manufactured from raw materials, used, and then discarded (see Braungart et al.'s (2007) cradle-to-cradle concept). The circular economy concept is fundamental to the triple bottom line, which focuses on the interplay between environmental, social, and economic factors (Geissdoerfer et al., 2017; Korhonen et al., 2018; Worldsteel Association, 2018).

The economic relevance of the Danish steel industry can be considered as small. The sector is not very big with 83 companies and had an aggregated employment of 2,723 in 2006 (Eurofound, 2018). In Germany, 4,400 steel and metalworking companies employ around 440,000 people. The metal industry is predominantly medium-sized, except for some leading international companies such as Thyssen-Krupp AG or MAN AG. The total turnover of the industry in the year 2003 cumulated to 715.312 million Euro (Statista, 2018).

Company Analysis

The importance of the topics was described as follows by the interviewed companies:
Networking in general contributes to the success of a company. It secures potential clients and creates a certain stability among companies. The result is that they do not need to worry and fight for customers because through reliability and good service they gain the customers' trust, which creates increasing demand for favours and services (DE_Interview_1).
However, lower energy costs affect business success. In this context, the recent implementation of LED lighting and new building insulation contributed to the firm's success (DE_Interview_2).
The success of a company depends on the customers. Nowadays, due to the tremendous price rivalry from Eastern Europe, western countries are not able to compete with the low prices that are offered in Poland or the Czech Republic. Surprisingly, this is not due to material prices or energy – which are almost equal between western and eastern countries – but due to much lower wages for employees (DK_Interview_9).

Looking at the three themes in detail, the results reveal that there is no significant distinction between the statements of Danish and German representatives. The values, issues, and considerations that are primarily important for companies are similar. Economic considerations have priority over environmental concerns. Success is tightly connected to networking and customer satisfaction. Difficulties in the market arise from Eastern European competitors. Associations are seen as a possibility to gain free consultancy, especially legal advice. The same can be observed when comparing the Danish to the German companies.

Comparison of Danish and German Companies

A comparison of the German and Danish companies considers, more precisely, how they combine the three dimensions of energy, success, and networking. After analyzing nine interviews (five companies from Northern Germany and four from Southern Denmark), several general conclusions can be drawn. However, there is no significant distinction between the representatives from those two countries, because the values, issues, and considerations that are important for these companies are alike and can be traced back to the fact that all companies are of smaller size. Economics take priority over environmental considerations and success is tightly connected to networking and customer satisfaction. Moreover, difficulties in being competitive and attractive in the market nowadays are increasing due to the prices Eastern European markets are offering. All companies regard optimization and introduction of energy saving potential more from the economic point of view rather than from the environmental.

Some companies are more devoted to being part of associations, yet the main reason is to gain free consultation or to broaden their network to acquire more customers.

Overall, it can be said that the three dimensions influence each other, yet all companies strive to achieve one major goal which is the financial benefit of the company. However, besides the similarities that the SMEs in the metal working industry share, the following differences were observed:

Germany (Companies 1, 2, 3, 4, and 5):
The companies are aware of the environmental aspects of energy efficiency, but in all instances the economic part always comes first. This is because clients do not expect products provided by companies to be more environmentally friendly; it is usually most important that the price is low and appropriate.

The costs of implementing changes in energy efficiency need to break even after a specific timeframe (2–3 years), otherwise no companies will decide to invest in such changes. Once a company decides to implement the energy saving means and it works, they claim to have positive effects. The majority observe a tight relation between the companies' success and energy efficient means.

Cooperation with other companies affects the company's success positively. Yet, networking in general does not necessarily lead to positive effects for the companies and can even lead to a potential waste of employee working hours.

"Participation in associations is related with devoting a lot of time for it" (DE_Interview_5). This is what one German company stated and they do not want to participate in more than the obligatory associations due to lack of time.

Companies in the wider Hamburg area experience more success than those in the north due to better financial situations and company size.

Denmark (Companies 6, 7, 8, and 9):
Whilst the German companies from Schleswig consider the LED implementation a huge success and contribution to energy efficiency and saving, Danish companies see the implementation of LED as a necessary change nowadays. This shows how this technology has been perceived differently.

The implemented changes should pay off after two and a half years, otherwise the companies would resist investing in improvements. That confirms that it is of utmost importance for Danish companies that investments pay off, more than it is for the German companies.

To be able to survive on the market, the Danish companies invest a lot of money in machinery. For future development they try to find a way to be both profitable and innovative at the same time. One company suggests a "learning by doing approach to be able to see the energy potential and simultaneously achieve a success" (DK_Interview_6).

One company is dependent on Danfoss regarding compressed air delivery and therefore has a close relationship with Danfoss.

The Danish companies see the advantage of using external consultancies, which broadens the knowledge and perspectives regarding new implementation and energy saving potential in general. Moreover, they stress the importance of maintaining good customer services as this ensures profits and further leads to the success of the company. Participation in organizations is used as another method to build and extend networks.

Clients in this industry do not require greener or more eco-friendly products; as one Danish company mentions, "it is not like selling coffee on Østerbro in Copenhagen" (DK_Interview_8).

Companies claim that taxation should be more appropriately adjusted regarding energy costs. For example, it should be possible to buy energy cheaper at night. One Danish company proposes a change in managing costs of energy per kWh.

Cooperation with other companies provides a good customer experience. If there is an inquiry that cannot be resolved in Denmark, the problem can be solved more easily through networking and cooperation with other companies. Moreover, one company pointed out the utmost importance of employees' health for being successful.

In summary, minor differences between the companies located north and south of the border can be identified. Danish companies in the metal working industry are slightly more advanced in energy efficiency, stricter in cost management, and more positive towards diverse networks. The bigger German companies were positive towards using the advice of external consultants and being open to changes. Due to a lack of resources, smaller companies were generally more reserved to introduce changes and energy efficient solutions.

Discussion and Further Research

Answering the first research question of how a collaborative business model should be conceptualized to be successful in terms of sustainable development, we have referred to the flourishing business canvas (Elkington & Upward, 2016). The questions referring to the canvas have been the basis of this study. After pretesting, the questions were reformulated to make them better understandable for the owners or managers of the investigated SMEs. Therefore, we conclude that a business model should be easy to use for practitioners or should at least be transformed into an understandable language.

The second research question, which asked in what way existing SMEs need to transform their business models in order to become successful as a sustainable business, can follow up on the previous considerations. The investigated SMEs all lack time and experience to think about their business model. They rather collaborate with associations and other networks to get access to free consulting than thinking about their strategy themselves. Therefore, it can be concluded that the companies need to transform their business model towards greater collaboration in order to become successful as a sustainable business.

The last three research questions were answered in the analysis part where an industry analysis as well as a more detailed investigation and comparison of the companies were conducted:

In the industry analysis, we discovered that the three themes, success, energy efficiency, and networks are relevant for the metal working industry. In this energy intensive industry, the potential to save energy is very high. Therefore, the third research question can be answered by looking at what challenges the industry faces – such as innovation, energy saving, and recycling. As discussed in the industry analysis, the companies need to think about the direction of the circular economy concept (Geissdoerfer et al., 2017; Korhonen et al., 2018) and focus on the interplay between environmental, social, and economic factors. Moreover, future discussions on sustainable collaborative business models need to include the concept of a global circular economy.

Research question four investigated why the companies are acting the way they do, regarding the goal of higher energy efficiency. The investigated SMEs in the metal industry revealed that the conditions in the industry have become more difficult. Competition from Eastern Europe is increasing and products can be offered at a lower price level because of cheaper labor (interviews 3 and 9). Companies in southern Germany can offer better working conditions in larger companies in the metal working industry (interviews 2 and 3), which makes it difficult for the investigated SMEs to employ qualified engineers. Moreover, the aspect of a circular economy should be considered because of the high energy saving potential in the metal working industry. As the Worldsteel Association (2017) stated, considerable improvements in productivity and reductions in environmental impact can be gained, e.g. by using and recycling ferrous scrap in the metal working industry. This could be a success factor countering the growing competition.

The last research question considered why networks were not utilized sufficiently in order to reach higher energy efficiency. Regarding networks, the companies prefer to seek advice from consultants because they bring more values and profits than advice from associations. This means that the companies rather pay for valuable advice, especially in legal issues, than getting it for free. This resistance towards associations stems from the belief that issues discussed in associations are not relevant for their company. Thus, they would rather not participate in private networks that focus on energy efficiency issues (interviews 1 and 2). Personal networks and past experience with clients are seen as important because they can provide the company with new customers.

All companies know what energy efficiency means and that a solution capable of increasing energy efficiency would usually imply the need for new equipment. The problem is that they often do not have enough capital to replace or improve old machines. Moreover, they prefer investments that potentially pay off in the near future instead of energy saving solutions that might result in extra profit at a much later stage. An exception is company 7 that mentioned that investing in heating change and lighting paid off. Other companies implemented energy saving changes with regard to heating and energy usage (interviews 1 and 2). From the industry and company analysis it can be concluded that the companies could gain a competitive advantage by utilizing the potential of energy saving and networking more intensively.

Overall, the companies mentioned that turnover was a crucial issue while implementing energy efficiency means. They are not willing to accept waiting time for energy efficient solutions as this will not bring quick benefits to the company. Therefore, a conclusion for the investigated SMEs in the metal processing industry is that their primary focus is on the success of the company and less on time consuming networking and energy efficiency. This needs to be changed towards a more sustainable collaborative business model, which was discussed in this study.

Theoretical Implications

Based on the flourishing business canvas from Elkington and Upward (2016), a questionnaire was designed for SMEs in the metal working industry. Expanding the scope of existing literature, our contribution is to transform the business model as mostly used in larger companies in a way to be beneficial for smaller companies. Therefore, we think that the development of collaborative business models in general should be adapted to the businesses to which they are addressed. Consequently, the general thinking in collaborative business models should be adapted to the needs of SMEs. For this, the existing business model frameworks need to be revisited to the needs of SMEs with their special characteristics like having short decision processes but lacking resources and competences. Hence, the following theoretical implications could be discussed.

The three contexts and 16 components presented in the flourishing business canvas from Elkington & Upward (2016) were in a first step adapted and simplified (see Appendix 1). In a second step, the final questionnaire could be developed to address SMEs in the metal working industry. Here we assigned the questions resulting from our adaptation into three relevant themes: success, energy efficiency, and networks. These themes can be related to the three contexts of economy, environment, and society as presented in the flourishing business canvas. With our adaptation we stress the importance of networks and collaboration for SMEs in this specific industry.

As Rajala and colleagues (2016) pointed out, a greening of the business ecosystem requires a major change of the business ecosystem, an adjustment of the business model on an organizational level, and needs to be regarded as a multi-layered process. With our study, we showed how this process can be adapted for SMEs and that collaborative elements are of vital importance for sustainable business models.

Managerial Implications

Implications for smaller companies in border regions can be necessary to implement networks across borders. From our findings, we can confirm the theoretical suggestions that collaboration across geographical boundaries can help to solve problems. Moreover, especially in energy intensive industries, the circular economy concept needs to be considered when thinking about new strategic pathways. Future research should therefore focus on developing collaborative sustainable business models further in order to facilitate energy efficient solutions.

The results reveal that the outcome of a project depends on collaboration with companies in the region. Based on the findings of this study, open, and collaborative business models are suggested. The expected outcome of new collaborative business models could be in the area of a circular economy, resource efficiency or energy storage. The project is a starting point to increase interdisciplinary research in this domain and ultimately export solutions to other regions of the world. As a final result, we derived implications for further research regarding the investigated processes and policies.

Limitations and Future Research

This chapter is not free of several limitations, which offer potentials for future research. First, data was collected in a specific border region in Europe. Future research needs to unveil how results would change for other European border regions, but also in other regions all over the world. Furthermore, the focus was on SMEs, which usually face specific challenges, though larger companies might have different opportunities and challenges to report. While purposefully sampling a similar number of SMEs of the energy sector in the Danish-German cross-border region, we had to rely on those identified SMEs that were willing to join our study. As SMEs face daily challenges that prevent them from taking part in research, the selection of the nine companies out of the 30 companies identified was made by convenience. Future research might be able to avoid potential biases, which might have been resulting from this approach. Finally, longitudinal studies over several years might allow for a different perspective and insights.

Appendix 15.1

The 16 questions introduced by Elkington and Upward in their flourishing business model (2016, pp. 134–135)

(1) Goals: What are the goals of this business that its stakeholders have agreed? What is this business's definition of success: environmentally, socially, and economically?

(2) Benefits: How does this business choose to measure the benefits that result from its business model (environmentally, socially, economically), each in relevant units?

(3) Costs: How does this business choose to measure the costs incurred by its business model (environmentally, socially, economically), each in relevant units?

(4) Ecosystem actors: Who and what may have an interest in the fact that this business exists? Which ecosystem actors may represent the needs of other humans, groups, organizations, and non-humans?

(5) Needs: What fundamental needs of the ecosystem actors is this business intending to satisfy or may hinder? See Max-Neef et al. (1991) for an introduction to "fundamental human needs" and their "satisfiers."

(6) Stakeholders: How is each ecosystem actor involved in this business? What roles does each ecosystem actor take? Examples: customer, employee, investor, owner, supplier, community, and regulator.

(7) Relationships: What relationships with each stakeholder must be established, cultivated, and maintained by this business via its channels? What is the function of each relationship in each value co-creation or value co-destruction relevant for each stakeholder?

(8) Channels: What channels will be used by this firm to communicate and develop relationships with each stakeholder (and vice versa)? Examples: retail, face-to-face, Internet, phone, email, mail, transport.

(9) Value co-creations: What are the (positive) value propositions of this business? What value is co-created with each stakeholder, satisfying the needs of the associated ecosystem actor, from their perspective (world-view) now and/ or in the future?

(10) Value co-destructions: What are the (negative) value propositions of this business? What value is co-destroyed for each stakeholder, hindering the satisfaction of the needs of the associated ecosystem actor, from their perspective (world-view), now and/ or in the future?

(11) Governance: Which stakeholders get to make decisions about: who is a legitimate stakeholder, the goals of this business, its value propositions, and its processes?

(12) Partnerships: Which stakeholders are formal partners of this business? To which resources do these partners enable this business to gain preferred access? Which activities do these partners undertake for this business?

(13) Resources: What tangible (physical materials from one or more biophysical stocks, including fixed assets, raw materials, and human beings) and intangible resources

(energy, relationship equity, brand, tacit and explicit knowledge, intellectual property, money–working capital, cash, loans, etc.) are required by this business's activities to achieve its goals?

(14) Biophysical stocks: From what ultimate stocks are the tangible resources moved, flow, and/ or transformed by this business's activities to achieve its goals? As per laws of conservation of matter, all tangible resources remain biophysical stocks somewhere on our single shared planet irrespective of this business's activities (past, present, and anticipated future).

(15) Activities: What value adding work, organized into business processes, is required to design, deliver, and maintain the organization's value co-creations and value co-destructions to achieve this business' goals?

(16) Ecosystem services: Ecosystem services are processes powered by the sun that use biophysical stocks to create flows of benefits humans need: clean water, fresh air, vibrant soil, plant, and animal growth, etc. Which flows of these benefits are required by, harmed or improved by this business' activities? For an introduction, see World Business Council for Sustainable Development (WBCSD)'s Corporate Ecosystem Service Review v2.0 (Hansonetal, 2012).

Adapted 16 questions from Elkington & Upward (2016) for the study of SMEs in the metal working industry:

(1) Goals: What common goal does the business follow? How do you define success: environmentally, socially, and economically?

(2) (3) Benefits/ costs: How do you measure the benefits and costs (environmentally, socially, and economically)?

(4) Ecosystem actors: Who and what may have an interest in the fact that this business exists?

(5) Needs: What fundamental needs are satisfied with your business?

(6) Stakeholders: What roles do customer, employee, investor, owner, supplier, community, and regulators play?

(7) (8) Relationships/ Channels: Can you describe the relationships and communication with each of these stakeholders?

(9) (10) Value co-creations/ value co-destructions: What are the (positive or negative) values co-created with each stakeholder now and in the future?

(11) (12) Governance/ Partnerships: Which of the stakeholders are formal partners and make decisions about business goals?

(13) (14) Resources/ Biophysical stocks: What tangible (physical materials including fixed assets, raw materials, and human beings) and intangible resources (energy, relationship equity, brand, tacit and explicit knowledge, intellectual property, money–working capital, cash, loans, etc.) are required and/ or transformed to achieve the business goals?

(15) Activities: What activities are required to design, deliver, and maintain the organization's values and goals?
(16) Ecosystem services: Does your company provide benefits for humans' need (clean water, fresh air, vibrant soil, plant and animal growth, etc.)?

Appendix 15.2 Final Questionnaire

Collaboration

1) Does your company have any special relationships that go beyond the so-called "standard" relations (e.g. with other companies, suppliers, customers)? Do you use them to achieve common goals?
2) Do your employees have a good, sort of "private," networking community? Does that contribute to the overall development of the firm, e.g. acquiring new customers?
3) What networks/ associations is your company a member of? Do you consider the participation useful for the development of your company?
4) How dedicated are you towards the listed networks and associations (e.g. how will you deal with pieces of information (retrieved, read, evaluated); personal engagement; regular participation in meetings; preparation of documents for the association etc.)?
5) What does the flow of communication in networks/ associations look like (e.g. emails, personal relationships, regularity, decent vs. fugitive relations)?
6) Could you imagine being more active in these networks/ organizations? If so, what topics would be relevant to you?

Energy management

7) Are aspects such as energy consumption, price, and political regulation with respect to energy relevant for your company?
8) Do you think there is a scope for improvement for saving energy in your company? If so, what would it be?
9) Is energy management attractive for your company purely out of economic reasons (such as cost savings) or also due to environmental aspects (e.g. customers demanding compliance with certain environmental aspects)?
10) Do you keep track of your energy consumption? If so, how do you measure it (e.g. energy input per ton of steel)?
11) Do you currently dispose of any human resources and/ or money available for information gathering and the introduction of energy-efficient measures?

12) Do you see any problems or barriers in introducing energy-efficient measures (e.g. founding, staff capacities, access to information, etc.)?
13) Would you say that being a member of a network or organization will, to a certain extent, contribute to the general issue of energy saving?
14) Have you ever engaged any consultants' assistance regarding energy topics or can you imagine using this kind of service? Would you prefer networks/ associations or consultants to improve the company's energy efficiency?

Success

15) How would you assess the success of the company?
16) Have investments contributed to the company's success? If so, in which sectors were the investments completed?
17) Did cooperation with other parties contribute to the company's overall success?
18) Would you say that energy-efficient measures affect the company's success? Or do you think it will be moderately the case in the future?

References

Abdelkafi, N., & Täuscher, K. (2016). Business models for sustainability from a system dynamics perspective. *Organization & Environment, 29*(1), 74–96.

Al-Saleh, Y., & Mahroum, S. (2015). A critical review of the interplay between policy instruments and business models: greening the built environment a case in point. *Journal of cleaner production, 109*, 260–270.

AMB. (2018). *Wir über uns.* https://amb-soerup.de/wir.htm.

Bhattacharya, M., Paramati, S.R., Ozturk, I., & Bhattacharya, S. (2016). The effect of renewable energy consumption on economic growth: Evidence from top 38 countries. *Applied Energy, 162*, 733–741.

Bocken, N.M., Short, S.W., Rana, P., & Evans, S. (2014). A literature and practice review to develop sustainable business model archetypes. *Journal of Cleaner Production, 65*, 42–56.

Bocken, N. M. (2015). Sustainable venture capital–catalyst for sustainable start-up success? *Journal of Cleaner Production, 108*, 647–658.

Bolton, R., & Hannon, M. (2016). Governing sustainability transitions through business model innovation: Towards a systems understanding. *Research Policy, 45*(9), 1731–1742.

Boons, F., & Lüdeke-Freund, F. (2013). Business models for sustainable innovation: state-of-the-art and steps towards a research agenda. *Journal of Cleaner production, 45*, 9–19.

Brehmer, M., Podoynitsyna, K., & Langerak F. (2018). Sustainable business models as boundary-spanning systems of value transfers. *Journal of Cleaner Production, 172*, 4514–4531.

Braungart, M., McDonough, W., & Bollinger, A. (2007). Cradle-to-cradle design: creating healthy emissions–a strategy for eco-effective product and system design. *Journal of Cleaner Production, 15* (13–14), 1337–1348.

Burr, V. (2015). *Social constructionism.* Routledge.

Chen, P. T., & Cheng, J. Z. (2010). Unlocking the promise of mobile value-added services by applying new collaborative business models. *Technological Forecasting and Social Change, 77*(4), 678–693.

Danish Energy Agency. (2016). *The Danish energy model.* https://ens.dk/sites/ens.dk/files/Globalcoopera tion/the_danish_energy_model.pdf

DFT Presswork. (2018). *About us – profile.* http://www.dft-presswork.dk/en/profile.html

Doukas, H., Tsiousi, A., Marinakis, V., & Psarras, J. (2014). Linguistic multi-criteria decision making for energy and environmental corporate policy. *Information Sciences, 258,* 328–338.

Edmondson, A.C., & McManus, S.E. (2007). Methodological fit in management field research. *Academy of Management Review, 32,* 1246–1264.

Eisenhardt, K.M. (1989). Building theories from case study research. *Academy of Management Review, 32,* 532–550.

Eisenhardt, K.M., & Graebner, M.E. (2007). Theory building from cases: Opportunities and challenges. *Academy of Management Journal, 50,* 25–32.

Elkington, R., & Upward, A. (2016). Leadership as enabling function for flourishing by design. *Journal of Global Responsibility, 7*(1), 126–144.

Eller, F., Gielnik, M., Wimmer, H., Thölke, C., Holzapfel, S., Tegtmeier, S., & Halberstadt, J. (2020). Identifying business opportunities for sustainable development: Longitudinal and experimental evidence contributing to the field of sustainable entrepreneurship. *Business Strategy and the Environment, 29,* 1387–1403.

EMR. (2018). *Energy monitoring report 2018.* Published by the Bundesnetzagentur and the Bundeskartellamt. https://www.bundesnetzagentur.de/SharedDocs/Pressemitteilungen/EN/2018/20181128_Monitoringbericht.html

Eurofound. (2018). *Representativeness of the European social partner organizations: Steel industry–Denmark.* https://www.eurofound.europa.eu/publications/report/2009

European Union. (2018). *SME Definition.* https://ec.europa.eu/growth/smes_de

Eurostat – European Commission. (2018). *Energy balance sheets – 2016.* Publications Office of the European Union.

Evans, S., Vladimirova, D., Holgado, M., Van Fossen, K., Yang, M., Silva, E.A., & Barlow, C.Y. (2017). Business model innovation for sustainability: Towards a unified perspective for creation of sustainable business models. *Business strategy and the environment, 26*(5), 597–608.

Fichter, K., & Tiemann, I. (2018). Factors influencing university support for sustainable entrepreneurship: Insights from explorative case studies. *Journal of Cleaner Production, 175,* 512–524.

Garnsey, E., & Leong, Y. Y. (2008). Combining resource-based and evolutionary theory to explain the genesis of bio-networks. *Industry and Innovation, 15*(6), 669–686.

Gauthier, C., & Gilomen, B. (2016). Business models for sustainability: Energy efficiency in urban districts. *Organization & Environment, 29*(1), 124–144.

Gast, J., Kallmünzer, A., Kraus, S., Gundolf, K., & Arnold, J. (2019). Coopetition of small-and medium-sized family enterprises: Insights from an IT business network. *International Journal of Entrepreneurship and Small Business, 38*(1/2), 78–101.

Geissdoerfer, M., Savaget, P., Bocken, N.M., & Hultink, E.J. (2017). The circular economy–A new sustainability paradigm?' *Journal of Cleaner Production, 143,* 757–768.

Gharaei, A., Hoseini Shekarabi, S.A., Karimi, M., Pourjavad, E., & Amjadian, A. (2019). An integrated stochastic EPQ model under quality and green policies: Generalised cross decomposition under the separability approach. *International Journal of Systems Science: Operations & Logistics.*

Glaser, B.G., & Strauss, A. (1967). *The discovery of grounded theory: Strategies for qualitative research.* Aldine Publishing Co.

Giones, F., Brem, A., & Berger, A. (2019). Strategic decisions in turbulent times: Lessons from the energy industry. *Business Horizons, 62*(2), 215–225.

Hammersley, M. (1992). *What's wrong with ethnography? Methodological explorations.* Routledge.

Hartmetall-Werkzeuge-Nord. (2018). *Über uns.* https://www.hw-nord.de/ueber-uns/

Hatak, I., Harms, R., & Fink, M. (2015). Age, job identification, and entrepreneurial intention. *Journal of managerial psychology, 30*(1), 38–53.

Hawkins, M., Pope, B., Maciver, S. K., & Weeds, A. G. (1993). Human actin depolymerizing factor mediates a pH-sensitive destruction of actin filaments. *Biochemistry, 32*(38), 9985–9993.

Hinz, O., & Spann, M. (2008). The impact of information diffusion on bidding behavior in secret reserve price auctions. *Information Systems Research, 19*(3), 351–368.

Hjorth, S., & Brem, A.M. (2016). How to assess market readiness for an innovative solution: The case of heat recovery technologies for SMEs. *Sustainability, 8*(11), 1152.

Huberman, A.M., & Miles, M.B. (2002). *The qualitative researcher's companion*. Sage.

Jensen. (2018). *About us – More than 130 years of experience in development and engineering woodchippers*. http://www.jensen-service.de/eng/about-us.php

Jensen, M.B., Møller, J., & Scheutz, C. (2016). Comparison of the organic waste management systems in the Danish–German border region using life cycle assessment (LCA). *Waste Management, 49*, 491–504.

Joyce, A., & Paquin, R.L. (2016). The triple layered business model canvas: A tool to design more sustainable business models. *Journal of Cleaner Production, 135*, 1474–1486.

Kallakuri, C., Vaidyanathan, S., Kelly, M., & Cluett, R. (2016). *The 2016 international energy efficiency scorecard*. American Council for an Energy-Efficient Economy http://aceee.org/research-report/e1602

Kleine, K., Giones, F., & Tegtmeier, S. (2019). The learning process in technology entrepreneurship education-insights from an engineering degree. *Journal of Small Business Management, 57*(S1), 94–110.

Korhonen, J., Nuur, C., Feldmann, A., & Birkie, S.E. (2018). Circular economy as an essentially contested concept. *Journal of Cleaner Production, 175*, 544–552.

Kurucz, E.C., Colbert, B.A., Luedeke-Freund, F., Upward, A., & Willard, B. (2017). Relational leadership for strategic sustainability: Practices and capabilities to advance the design and assessment of sustainable business models. *Journal of Cleaner Production, 140*, 189–204.

Lazarte, I. M., Chiotti, O., & Villarreal, P. D. (2009). Transforming collaborative process models into interface process models by applying an MDA approach. In *Software Services for e-Business and e-Society: 9th IFIP WG 6.1 Conference on e-Business, e-Services and e-Society, I3E 2009, Nancy, France, September 23–25, 2009. Proceedings 9* (pp. 301–315). Springer Berlin Heidelberg.

Leisen, R., Steffen, B., & Weber, C. (2019). Regulatory risk and the resilience of new sustainable business models in the energy sector. *Journal of cleaner production, 219*, 865–878. https://doi.org/10.1016/j.jclepro.2019.01.330

Lincoln, Y.S., & Guba, E.G. (1985). *Naturalistic inquiry*. Sage Publications.

Lipp, J. (2007). Lessons for effective renewable electricity policy from Denmark, Germany and the United Kingdom. *Energy Policy, 35*(11), 5481–5495.

Loorbach, D., van Bakel, J.C., Whiteman, G., & Rotmans, J. (2010). Business strategies for transitions towards sustainable systems. *Business Strategy and the Environment, 19*(2), 133–146.

Lozano, R., Lukman, R., Lozano, F. J., Huisingh, D., & Lambrechts, W. (2013). Declarations for sustainability in higher education: becoming better leaders, through addressing the university system. *Journal of Cleaner Production, 48*, 10–19.

Makkonen, T. (2015). Scientific collaboration in the Danish–German border region of Southern Jutland-Schleswig. *Geografisk Tidsskrift-Danish Journal of Geography, 115*(1), 27–38.

Miles, M.B., & Huberman, A.M. (1994). *Qualitative data analysis: An expanded sourcebook* (2nd ed.). Sage.

Osterwalder, A., & Pigneur, Y. (2010). *Business model generation: A handbook for visionaries, game changers, and challengers*. Wiley.

Project Zero. (2018). *Bright green business – project zero*. http://www.projectzero.dk/

Rajala, R., Westerlund, M., & Lampikoski, T. (2016). Environmental sustainability in industrial manufacturing: re-examining the greening of Interface's business model. *Journal of Cleaner Production, 115*, 52–61.

Ritchie, J., & Lewis, J. (2014). *Qualitative research practice: A guide for social science students and researchers*, 2nd ed.

Sandberg, J. (2005). How do we justify knowledge produced within interpretive approaches? *Organizational research methods, 8*(1), 41–68.

Schaltegger, S., Lüdeke-Freund, F., & Hansen, E. G. (2012). Business cases for sustainability: The role of business model innovation for corporate sustainability. *International Journal of Innovation and Sustainable Development, 6*, 95–119.

Schaltegger, S., Lüdeke-Freund, F., & Hansen, E.G. (2016). Business models for sustainability: A co-evolutionary analysis of sustainable entrepreneurship, innovation, and transformation. *Organization & Environment, 29*(3), 264–289.

Schleswig-Holstein. (2018). *Klimaschutz*. https://www.schleswig-holstein.de/DE/Themen/K/klimaschutz.html

SDU Mads Clausen Institute. (2018). *100% Climate neutrality*. https://www.climateneutral.eu/

Sønderborg Fornikling. (2018). *Om os – historie*. http://www.sdbg-fornikling.dk/pages/id29.asp

Sroka, W., Jabłoński, A., & Jabłoński, M. (2013). Cooperative business models in steel enterprises in Poland. *Metalurgija, 52*(4), 565–568.

Statista. (2018). *Forecast: Manufacture of metal structures revenue in Germany 2010–2022*. https://www.statista.com/forecasts/353807/manufacture-of-metal-structures-revenue-in-germany

Stubbs, W., & Cocklin, C. (2008). Conceptualizing a "sustainability business model". *Organization & environment, 21*(2), 103–127.

Straatman, B., Boyd, B., Mangalagiu, D., Rathje, P., Eriksen, C., Madsen, B., Stefaniak, I., Jensen, M., & Rasmussen, S. (2018). A consumption-based, regional input-output analysis of greenhouse gas emissions and the carbon regional index. *International Journal of Environmental Technology and Management, 21*(1–2), 1–36.

Strauss, A., & Corbin, J. (1998). *Basics of qualitative research: Techniques and procedures for developing grounded theory* (2nd ed.). Sage Publications, Inc.

Strecon. (2018). *About us*. http://www.strecon.com/en/about-us/

The Guardian. (2015). *Sønderborg: The little-known Danish town with a zero carbon master plan*. http://www.theguardian.com/sustainable-business/2015/oct/22/denmark-sonderborg-danish-town-trying-to-be-carbon-neutral

Trippl, M. (2010). Developing cross-border regional innovation systems: Key factors and challenges. *Tijdschrift voor Economische en Sociale Geografie, 101*, 150–160. doi:10.1111/j.1467- 9663.2009.00522.x

Upward, A. (2013). Towards an ontology and canvas for strongly sustainable business models: A systemic design science exploration. Masters of Environmental Studies/Graduate Diploma in Business + Environment, York University, Faculty of Environmental Studies and Schulich School of Business. http://hdl.handle.net/10315/20777

Upward, A., and Jones, P. (2016). An ontology for strongly sustainable business models: Defining an enterprise framework compatible with natural and social science. *Organization & Environment, 29*(1), 97–123.

Walther, J., Sochacka, N. W., & Kellam, N. N. (2013). Quality in interpretive engineering education research: Reflections on an example study. *Journal of engineering education, 102*(4), 626–659.

Ward, J., Stratil, P., Uhl, A., & Schmid, A. (2016). Smart Mobility: An Up-and-Down Ride on the Transformation Roller Coaster. In *Business Transformation Essentials* (pp. 77–94). Routledge.

WCED. (1987). World Commission on Environment and Development. *Our common future, 17*(1), 1–91.

Willard, B., Kendall, G., Leung, P., Park, C., Rich, M., & Upward, A. (2014). *Future fit business benchmark*. The Natural Step Canada and 3D Investment Foundation.

Werner, A. (2010). *Sylter Erklärung – Wattenmeer soll bis 2030 klimaneutral sein*. https://www.shz.de/regionales/schleswig-holstein/panorama/wattenmeer-soll-bis-2030-klimaneutral-sein-id2081416.html

Worldsteel Association. (2017). *Fact sheet: Energy use in the steel industry*. https://www.worldsteel.org/publi
cations/fact-sheets.html
Worldsteel Association. (2018). *Steel's contribution to a low carbon future*. https://www.worldsteel.org/publi
cations/position-papers/steel-s-contribution-to-a-low-carbon-future.html
Yin, R. K. (2009). *Case study research: Design and methods* (Vol.5).sage.
Yunus, M., Moingeon, B., & Lehmann-Ortega, L. (2010). Building social business models: Lessons from the
Grameen experience. *Long Range Planning*, *43*(2–3), 308–325.

Part 3: **Processes and Performance of SMEs**

Magdalena Marczewska and Marzenna Anna Weresa

16 The Digital Transformation of SMEs

Abstract: In the constantly digitalizing world, digital transformation is seen as one of the ways for businesses to stay competitive. However, as many studies have pointed out, SMEs still lag behind larger, especially international companies in their digital transition and this gap negatively impacts their productivity and operations. Such scenario creates a need for policymakers to address this issue by appropriate policy measures and constantly monitoring digital transformation of SMEs in order to appropriately tailor the policies and support measures.

The chapter offers an overview of opportunities, challenges, and barriers associated with digital transformation of SMEs. It sheds the light on the background for digital transformation of SMEs and reflects on the need to monitor the digitalization patterns tracing how an organization integrates ICT deployment with people and the processes to change business performance. It concludes with a conceptual framework of digital transformation of SMEs that links objectives, resources, impact, outcomes, and metrics, followed by implications for management practice and policymakers.

Keywords: digital transformation, SMEs, business model, digitalization

Introduction

There are various dimensions of digital transformation of production processes, such as the Internet of things, artificial intelligence adoption, new digital technologies adoption such as digital twins, big data analytics, and use in production and management, automation, robotization or cloud computing (Kagermann et al., 2013; Schwab, 2016; Kostrzewski et al., 2020). The digital transformation of enterprises is based on the adoption of information and communication technologies (ICT). A new techno-economic paradigm emerging in connection with digitalization has diverse consequences for business models and management practices of small and medium enterprises (SMEs) leading to systemic, social, and cultural changes (Russmann et al., 2015). In order to face competition SMEs need to implement digital technologies and adapt their production, processes, and management practices. Digital transformation allows the distance between the producer and the customer to be shortened and, thus, products can be better adapted to consumers' needs (Porter & Heppelmann, 2014). However, to improve their efficiency and competitiveness SMEs are forced to boost the speed of adjusting to changing demand and increase their operational flexibility. At

Magdalena Marczewska, Faculty of Management, University of Warsaw
Marzenna Anna Weresa, World Economy Research Institute, SGH Warsaw School of Economics

https://doi.org/10.1515/9783110747652-017

the same time, entrepreneurs experience the growing flow of information. In order to be competitive, they should speed up the process of acquiring, processing, and using information and new knowledge in their business activity. Furthermore, market success is more and more dependent on innovations that are digital or data driven. The COVID-19 pandemic has strengthened the need for digital transformation of SMEs, and thus up to 70% of SMEs have started to use digital technologies more frequently (OECD, 2021a, p. 34). However, as many studies have pointed out, SMEs still lag in the digital transition and this digital gap negatively impacts their productivity and creates a need for policymakers to address this issue by appropriate policy measures (Weresa et al., 2018; Pelletier & Cloutier, 2019; OECD, 2021a).

Digital transformation is regarded as a diffuse multidimensional concept which combines managerial and technological aspects at macro and micro levels (Kraft et al., 2022). An overview of existing research on digital transformation in the field of business and management shows that both internal and external perspectives can be applied to analyze this new phenomenon. The first one is rooted in a resource-based view, whilst the latter takes into account a structural change and its impact on in the way the value is created (Kraus et al., 2022). Digital transformation causes a shift of value creation from tangible to intangible sources and impacts the relationship between technology and people as well as tools used by managers and employees to fulfill their tasks. It breaks boundaries function, distance, and time, leading to a fundamental change in business models and ways of value creation (Garzella et al., 2021; Kraft et al., 2022). Because of the complexity of digital transformation, general management theories and models do not fully capture all different dimensions of this process. In this paper we make an attempt to combine internal (resource-based) and external (value-based) perspectives linking objectives, resources, impact, and outcomes of digital transformation.

The aim of this chapter is to study how small and medium size enterprises adopt digital technologies and to identify barriers to their digital transformation. The research question that is addressed is related to mechanisms through which digital technologies drive productivity of SMEs. The chapter presents a review of relevant theoretical concepts and empirical literature related to the digital transformation of SMEs along with a comparative analysis of available data. It concludes with a conceptual framework illustrating the digital transformation processes within an SME including a list of indicators that could be considered by SMEs to measure the success of digital transformation. Finally, implications for policy and management practice are discussed.

Method

The two-step research method applied in this chapter includes an umbrella review, followed by an overview of relevant empirical studies results. The aim of the umbrella review was to present a range of previously research issues related to digital transformation of SMEs and develop recommendations for future research (Grant & Booth, 2009). Digital transformation of companies has been widely studied so far, however, with regards to SMEs the research is still fragmental, limited, and incomplete. The review of reviews focused directly on SMEs and their digital transformation allows the topics already explored to be mapped so as to then draw conclusions related to future research directions relevant to this specific types of companies (Aromataris et al., 2014; Faulkner et al., 2022).

This umbrella review is based on records obtained from Scopus database. The database search included the following keywords: search 1 – digital transformation, SME; search 2 – digital transformation, SME, review. The initial search resulted in 413 records, which were then limited to "reviews" (document type) or papers that included the word "review" in its title and checked for duplicates. As a result, 54 documents were screened based on abstracts and references and 37 of them were excluded due to topic mismatch, irrelevant research methods used, or type of publication. Finally, 17 full-text articles were assessed for eligibility based on the following criteria: topic relevance, clear research problem and objectives, data sources clearly reported, adequate review methods used, clear presentation of research results. The eligibility check allowed a list of nine reviews of previous research to be developed that were further studied in this umbrella review (Figure 16.1). Seven papers were not relevant for our umbrella review in terms of research methods used. An umbrella review includes published systematic reviews and meta-analyses as the analytical unit of the review (Grant & Booth, 2009; Faulkner et al., 2022) while these seven papers offered mixed-method reviews supported by some empirical research, and they were therefore excluded from our umbrella analysis.

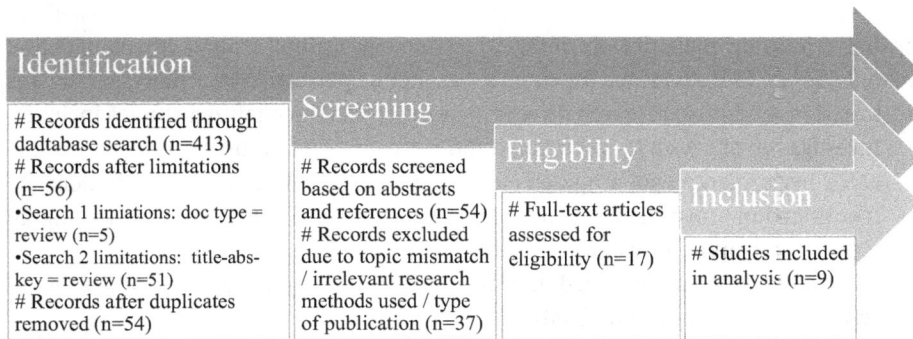

Identification	Screening	Eligibility	Inclusion
# Records identified through dadtabase search (n=413) # Records after limitations (n=56) •Search 1 limiations: doc type = review (n=5) •Search 2 limitations: title-abs-key = review (n=51) # Records after duplicates removed (n=54)	# Records screened based on abstracts and references (n=54) # Records excluded due to topic mismatch / irrelevant research methods used / type of publication (n=37)	# Full-text articles assessed for eligibility (n=17)	# Studies included in analysis (n=9)

Figure 16.1: Umbrella review – research steps (compiled by authors).

A synthesis of relevant empirical studies focused on digital transformation is a second research step, a follow-up built on the research results of the umbrella review. The digital transformation of SMEs is one of the emerging research topics, especially with the ongoing COVID-19 pandemic that is constantly pushing companies to digitalize (OECD, 2021a). Therefore, a synthesis of existing evidence provides an insight into the mechanisms of the digital transformation of SMEs already identified in the empirical studies. The integration of the umbrella literature review with results of empirical studies allows a conceptual framework of digital transformation of SMEs to be proposed, which links its objectives, resources, impact, outcomes, and the potential metrics of this process.

Synthetizing the Research on Digital Transformation of SMEs: An Umbrella Review Approach

Digitalization rapidly goes across all spheres of all business activities and the volume of literature pertinent to digital transformation is growing at an increasing rate. To provide a better sense of research directions and propose a conceptual approach to SMEs digital transformation, this paper offers the umbrella review of existing systematic reviews and meta-analysis of the literature. In this umbrella review we specifically attempt to answer the following questions:
- What has already been found on digital transformation in SMEs research?
- What are the potential future research directions and research opportunities that could enhance current knowledge on digital transformation of SMEs?

Table 16.1 summarizes the results of systematic review focused on digital transformation of SMEs. It appears that systematic review studies focus on a variety of specific sub-topics related to digital transformation of SMEs that are analyzed separately. These sub-topics can be grouped into three categories: SMEs capabilities needed for the digital journey; main drivers of digital technologies adoption; and impact of digital technologies on SMEs' various functions or economic performance. The research gaps illustrated in the future research directions proposed in the analyzed studies include:
- Investigation of causal-logical relationship between digital technologies adoption and SMEs' performance with proposed measurement of added value of digitalization;
- Identification of barriers to SMEs' digital transformation in integrating the digital technologies in their business models;
- Elaboration of a standardized approach to both conceptualization and empirical research on digitalization of SMEs;
- Conducting of further empirical qualitative studies in order to investigate a more context-specific view on SMEs' digital transformation;
- The development of a comprehensive strategic roadmap of digital technologies adoption.

Our research addresses three of these gaps and aims at providing a conceptual framework illustrating the process of digital transformation within an SME from both input and output perspectives along with a list of indicators that could be considered by SMEs to measure the success of digital transformation.

Table 16.1: An umbrella review of research on SMEs digital transformation (compiled by authors based on the literature indicated in the first column of the table).

Study	Research focus	Method	Main findings	Future research directions indicated in the study
Chavez et al., 2020	Managerial capabilities for the deployment of digitalization in SMEs	A narrative (traditional) literature review supported by a case study of one Swedish SME in manufacturing	A sequence of four managerial capabilities (monitoring, control, optimization, autonomy) was found as important for successful deployment of digital solutions by SMEs	Empirical tests of the path for deploying all managerial capabilities for digitalization Examining challenges faced by the implementation of the I4.0 concept related to the robustness and resilience of the manufacturing production system
Dethine et al., 2020	Digitalization and the internationalization capability of SMEs	An extensive exploratory literature review of 21 articles and cross analysis of review results	Main areas of impact of digitalization on export practices (i.e. firm's strategic vision, the customization of its offerings, network dynamics, firm's internal structure) were identified	Resources and skills of SMEs' influencing acceptability of the digital facilitators deployed Study on impacts of digital solutions on other internationalization modes, more advanced than exports Specificity of digitalization of "born-global" SMEs

Table 16.1 (continued)

Study	Research focus	Method	Main findings	Future research directions indicated in the study
González-Varona et al., 2020	The digital challenges faced by SMEs, and digital capabilities development	An in-depth literature review of 90 papers indexed in Scopus and Web of Science Semi-structured interviews with six experts	The importance of organizational learning and knowledge for the digital transformation of SMEs was confirmed A model of organizational competence for digital transformation of SMEs was developed	Identifying the causal-logical relationship between the elements of SMEs' competence and their development during the organizational learning process Elaborating guidelines for management to identify the capabilities for digital transformation
Menon & Shah, 2020	Digital transformation of SMEs' supply chain in manufacturing	Literature review of 32 papers extracted using the Harzing Publish and Perish database analytical tool	Research gaps related to digital transformation of supply chain functions in SMEs in the field of inventory management, quality control, customer satisfaction, and returns were identified	Developing a comprehensive strategic roadmap for digital transformation of SMEs Identification of how barriers faced by SMEs such as resource limitation, high degree of specialization, and inclination toward a niche influence the process of integrating the digital technologies into supply chain

Table 16.1 (continued)

Study	Research focus	Method	Main findings	Future research directions indicated in the study
Chavez et al., 2022	The degree of SMEs' digitalization and digital transformation practice	A systematic literature review of 16 qualitative and quantitative studies published in 2015–2019, supplemented with the review of an additional eight papers selected using backward snowballing approach	A premature stage of SMEs' digital transformation was confirmed Low costs were identified as a primary driver of SMEs' digitalization Practical digital applications rather than framework conditions were found to predominate in SMEs' digital transformation	Developing a standardized approach to both conceptualization and empirical research on digitalization of SMEs Investigating impacts of digital solutions on changes in management and control in SMEs as well as their organizational excellence Resilience and sustainability related to deployment of digital solutions
Pfister & Lehmann, 2021	The impact of digitization on SMEs' business performance	A systematic literature review of 124 papers published in 2009–2019 in peer-reviewed journals indexed in EBSCOhost, Emerald, ResearchGate, and ScienceDirect	Key strategic and financial benefits of digital transformation for SMEs were identified (i.e. efficiency, cost reduction, productivity growth, customer satisfaction, competitive advantage).	Measurement of digital transformation and its added value Investigating recent technology trends and their potential impact on SMEs Conducting qualitative studies to investigate a more context-specific view on SMEs' digital transformation and its impact on firms' performance

Table 16.1 (continued)

Study	Research focus	Method	Main findings	Future research directions indicated in the study
Sufian et al., 2021	The transition of manufacturing SMEs into smart factories	A systematic literature review of 46 journal articles and conference proceedings, five books, 79 industrial reports, and 38 online electronic articles	Six stages of SMEs' transformation into smart factories were identified (strategy, connectivity, integration, analytics, AI, scale); a roadmap for adoption of digital solutions was proposed	The development of a comprehensive strategic roadmap of digital technologies adoption in other industrial sectors
			Challenges of digital transformation for manufacturing SMEs were identified	
Yasiukovich & Haddara, 2020	Adoption of cloud enterprise resource planning (ERP) solutions by SMEs	A systematic review of 74 articles published between 1 January 2010 and 30 June 2019	Previous research on cloud ERP solutions by SMEs was found to focus mainly on the adoption decision phase	Examining risks and benefits of cloud ERP during later stages of this solution adoption (i.e. acquisition, implementation, use, and maintenance)
Zide & Jokonya, 2022	Factors affecting the adoption of data management by SMEs	A systematic review of relevant articles published in the period of 2008–2020 using a quantitative content analysis	The technology security, organizational costs, and government regulations were found to most affect the adoption of data management by SMEs	Empirical research on factors affecting the adoption of data management by SMEs

Digital Transformation and SMEs: Empirical Studies Perspective

The digital era raises various challenges for all business sectors. In order to stay competitive, companies need to respond to these challenges and adapt to the digitalizing world. The use of the Internet, social media, and various available digital technologies is significant to market expansion and encouraging the innovation capabilities of

SMEs (Fachrunnisa et al., 2020). Oswald and Kleinemeier (2017) claim that digitalization is not only an opportunity that may help to develop business, but rather an obligatory step. Moreover, digital technologies are becoming more accessible and less costly, and thus more available for smaller organizations such as SMEs.

Digital transformation is the utilization of novel digital technologies to allow major business improvements (Fitzgerald et al., 2014). It is also seen as an organizational transformation integrating business processes with digital technologies (Liu et al., 2011). Rogers (2016) argues that digital transformation of a company relates more to its strategy than the technology itself. It is a set of comprehensive actions based on strategic decisions that allow to exploit the opportunities and avoid the threats related to digitalization (Singh & Hess, 2017). From the managerial perspective, it is about the changes that digital technologies can cause to companies' business models, which in turn lead to changes in products, organizational structures, and automation of processes (Hess et al., 2016). Thus, digital transformation should be treated as "organizational change that is triggered and shaped by the widespread diffusion of digital technologies" (Hanelt et al., 2021, p. 1160).

Digital transformation of an organization should be distinguished from IT-related organizational change due to its different key activities and outcomes. The former is related to utilizing digital technologies to define or redefine a value proposition and organizational identity, whereas the latter focuses on using these technologies to support existing business activity (Wessel et al., 2021).

Digital transformation of an SME relies on its capabilities to utilize digital technologies, such as technology absorption, development, transfer, use, creation, and dissemination (De Mori et al., 2016; Cannas, 2021). According to Warner and Wäger (2019) the micro foundations of companies' capabilities fundamental to their digital transformation relate to managing various tensions that accompany navigating innovation ecosystems, redesigning internal structures, and improving digital maturity. The process model conceptualizing building dynamic capabilities for digital transformation, based on the framework of sensing, seizing, and transforming capabilities developed by Teece (2018), consists of external triggers and core internal enablers and barriers. The main external triggers associated with building dynamic capabilities for digital transformation are changing consumer behaviors, disruptive digital competitors, and disruptive digital technologies. Core internal enablers include cross-functional teams, fast decision making, and executive support, whereas barriers include rigid strategic planning, change resistance, and a high level of hierarchy (Warner & Wäger, 2019). The analysis by Warner and Wäger (2019) led to the conclusion that digital transformation of companies concerns agility in strategic renewal of their business models, collaborative approach, and culture. IT-enabled dynamic capabilities, supported by organizational agility, facilitates firms' competitive performance (Mikalef & Pateli, 2017). This agility is important because digital transformation improves performance of SMEs primarily thanks to changing their business models (Loebbecke & Picot, 2015; Bouwman et al., 2019), i.e., adapting their elements or designing completely new ones (Wirtz et al., 2010).

Digital transformation is a high-priority management challenge and one of the challenges that companies face nowadays (Hess et al., 2016). An exemplary approach that SMEs should take towards their successful digital transformation starts with the analysis of their corporate strategy, objectives, and environment in light of contribution that digital transformation can make to achieve set objectives effectively and efficiently (Nwaiwu, 2018; Stich et al., 2020). Digital transformation of companies may serve different objectives, such as: transforming the business; increasing sales; improving productivity, quality, and transparency; making new markets; uncovering latent supply; addressing unmet demand; increasing efficiency; improving innovation; building new value propositions; improving customer experience and engagement; introducing novel forms of interactions with customers; improving business decision making; changing brand market value; and transforming the workplace (Kane et al., 2015; Dawson et al., 2016; Yucel, 2018). These detailed objectives relate to leveraging existing knowledge to comprehensively change the core of company including its management strategy, technological mix, operational setup, and culture (Savić, 2019). By setting these objectives, SMEs address the question: why transform? The next step is to indicate what to transform by assessing the current state and defining the anticipated future level of transformation of key areas of business that can be digitally transformed, i.e.: business model, structure, people, processes, IT capability, offerings, and engagement model (Wade, 2015). Then, the measures for a successful digital transformation (such as adaptive production and logistic planning; IT competence of the employees; implementation of ERP; IT integration; modern sales channels) classified under four structural areas – resources, information systems, organizational structure, and culture – should be considered and specified (Schuh et al., 2017; Stich et al., 2020). Finally, chosen measures should be agilely and harmoniously developed and implemented in each structural area (Wade, 2015; Mikalef & Pateli, 2017; Warner & Wäger, 2019). Such a path leads SMEs to the development of their roadmaps for digital transformation, which should ideally and additionally ensure cost reductions and increase of sustainability (Stich et al., 2020). Thus, the success of a company's digital transformation relies upon its strategy, rather than technology (Kane at al., 2015). Implementation of digital transformation strategy may change SMEs' activity in various ways, for example, increasing their productivity, facilitating decision-making processes, ensuring time-to-market reduction, establishing a new role of the customer in doing business, contributing to environmental sustainability, raising product quality, and processing efficiency. Interestingly, although in general digitalization and sustainability are positively related, SMEs in the process of internationalization struggle to pursue both simultaneously (Denicolai et al., 2021).

SMEs during their digital transformation may face several obstacles related to, among others, introduction of new technologies, supply of necessary hardware and computing capacity, data protection and cybersecurity, employee attitudes towards changes being implemented, employee flexibility, adaptability and skills, and feasibility of digitalization in the workplace (Orellana, 2017; Soto-Acosta & Cegarra-Navarro, 2016). In order to overcome risks associated with obstacles listed above, SMEs should take well-planned, thorough actions enforcing their digital transformation comprehensively with support of effectively used cultural change (Bauer & Groll, 2020). The latter one is crucial in order to introduce new forms of communication and collaboration, push for intellectual agility, deal with employee resistance to change, shape their positive attitudes towards digital transformation, and thus facilitate its implementation (Davis et al., 2015; Dabić et al., 2021). To succeed SMEs should omit a too strong focus on pure digital technologies, and rather concentrate their efforts on introducing comprehensive strategies and reconsidering how employees work (McConnell, 2015; Savić, 2019; Kraus et al., 2021).

Barriers and Challenges to Digital Transformation of SMEs

Digital transformation brings the challenge of integrating digital and physical systems in business activity. Enterprises have indicated a number of barriers that impede their digital transition. Possible barriers to digital transformation of SMEs can be of a technical nature, since digital technologies are diverse and complex, encompassing the Internet of things, big data and analytics, cloud computing, robotics, additive manufacturing, augmented reality, artificial intelligence etc. Moreover, digital operations need to be supported by reliable technical infrastructure, which requires development of uniform standards and integration and synchronization of various types of systems with production processes (Peillon & Dubruc, 2019). Technical challenges may also be related to ensuring cybersecurity, including control information deluge as well as selection and delivery of relevant information required for a specific manufacturing process. For example, key digital twin barriers for manufacturing SMEs can be grouped into the following areas related to: connectivity, data, modelling, deployment, security, application programming interface (API), regulation and the law, innovation and business models, digital skills and competences (Pileggi, 2021). These barriers are mainly of a technical and organizational nature, but they are interconnected. There are also financial and social barriers. The digital transformation is a huge challenge for SMEs as they are usually more constrained than large firms in terms of finance. Difficulties occur in financing investments necessary to implement digital solutions. Expenditure on digital technologies can be returned in the future thanks to operational cost reduction when the efficiency increases, but access to capital might be a constraint for SMEs as investment is necessary at the start of the digital transition (Weresa et al., 2018).

Social barriers to digitalization of SMEs are related to firms' human resources and relations with suppliers and customers. Digitalization increases the need for new competences and skills. Lack of ability of using digital technology in an effective way may be an important barrier for SMEs as digital competences are regarded as a prerequisite for digital transformation. A need for employment restructuring due to digital technologies deployment may also be a challenge for SMEs. Requirements for a new technical qualification profile of employees that combines knowledge of engineering, IT, mechatronics, and economics as well as problem-solving skills may also constitute a barrier (Peillon & Dubruc, 2019), in particular when it is coupled with labor shortages and market constraints. Digital transformation of business activity represents a radical change, therefore unwillingness of employees to change may be the most important cultural barrier. Collaboration with various partners, including customers and suppliers, assuring transaction sustainability, and putting in place technology integration systems may be a challenge, given the uneven level of digital transformation development of collaborating partners (Okfalisa et al., 2021). Table 16.2 shows various challenges and barriers to the digital transformation of SMEs identified in the literature.

Table 16.2: Classification of key barriers to digital transformation of SMEs (compiled by authors, based, among others, on Abel-Koch et al., 2019; European Investment Bank, 2019, 2021; Kilimis et al., 2019; Okfalisa et al., 2021; Peillon & Dubruc, 2019; Pileggi, 2021; Uvarova, 2021; Weresa, et al., 2018).

Type	Barriers
Technological	– Necessity to synchronize different systems and elements of the production process – Lack of uniform standards enabling integration of systems – Digital security issues – Problems with access to technical infrastructure
Financial	– Limited capability to finance digital investments – Difficulties in accessing external financing – Return on investment risk
Organizational	– Lack of access to skilled personnel – Lack of programming knowledge and competencies in analyzing complex data – Insufficient skills to manage digital projects
Social	– Necessity to re-design collaboration culture – Resistance to change

Surveys conducted among European SMEs allow prioritizing the barriers according to their burden. The SMEs from France, Germany, Poland, Spain, and the UK surveyed in 2019 reported a wide range of barriers and challenges to digitalization and indicated that insufficient digital infrastructures, cybersecurity concerns, and the lack of digital skills among their employees were key obstacles for digital transformation of SMEs in all five countries (Abel-Koch et al., 2019). However, the importance of these barriers varies across countries. In Germany SMEs complained about slow internet speeds (reported by 27% of survey respondents), the lack of employees with IT skills (24%), as well as the shortage of IT experts that can be hired on the external labor market (23%). In Poland the key problems are related to IT security issues (28%), insufficient digital skills of employees (27%), and internal resistance to change (26%). Similar barriers were also reported as the top three obstacles in Spain. The most severe obstacles to digitalization faced by French SMEs were low speed of Internet connection (29%), IT security issues (28%), and insufficient skills for going digital (28%). In the UK, apart from IT security problems, the most important barriers were related to the access to digital talents. Insufficient digital skills of employees and shortage of IT specialists were identified by around a third of British SMEs as a hindrance to digital transformation (Abel-Koch et al., 2019). A study on the digitalization gaps between Italian SMEs and the EU peers identified financial barriers as important ones hampering their willingness to go digital (European Investment Bank, 2021). Limited access to financing was the primary barrier for SMEs' digitalization in Ireland. In particular, this obstacle is severe for large-scale digital transformation programs. It is a result of the high cost of funding, low profitability of Irish SMEs, as well as insufficient expertise in the banking sector in financing projects with strong digital and artificial intelligence components (European Investment Bank, 2019).

Financial barriers are harsher in emerging economies, where government resources to help small businesses in their digital transformation are limited. This was confirmed by an empirical study on digital transformation in the time of the COVID-19 pandemic covering six developing countries, i.e. Armenia, Azerbaijan, Belarus, Georgia, Moldova, and Ukraine. The study found that SMEs from these countries sped up the process of their digital transformation due to the pandemic outbreak, having however huge problems in redirecting financial and human resources towards digitalization in most cases (Uvarova, 2021).

Looking at barriers to SMEs' digital transformation from a sectoral perspective brings a slightly different picture of the importance of various obstacles. The exploratory study on digital servitization in French manufacturing SMEs revealed that the most significant barriers were customer-related, such as deployment and use of customer relationship management software, monitoring the customer use of the equipment in its production process, and securing data exchanges (Peillon & Dubruc, 2019). An evaluation of the implementation of digital technologies in Brandenburg by Kilimis et al. (2019) based on a survey among 50 SMEs and supported by multi-case studies from manufacturing, metal-processing, and service sectors confirmed that the type of barriers to digitalization is sector specific and depends on the sector's technical advancement and already existing infrastructure.

Monitoring Digital Transformation of SMEs

Digital transformation of SMEs is a multidimensional and complex process (Matt et al., 2015; Pelletier & Cloutier, 2019). Digitalization has been changing the way companies communicate with the market. It also stimulates the emergence of new business models.

Therefore, there is a need to monitor the digitalization patterns tracing how an organization integrates ICT deployment with people, and the processes to change business performance. This means that methodology and indicators for measuring progress in digital transformation should also be adapted accordingly. To assess the level of digitalization of SMEs, several metrics can be taken into consideration. Indicators should reflect key dimensions of digital transformation allowing comparisons to be made across countries and pinpoint differences and their drivers. The availability of data in longer time series is another key element that needs to be considered when selecting the indicators. There are many attempts to assess and compare digitalization in different countries, however, to get a complete picture, indicators across a wide range of areas need to be mapped. These areas include for instance innovation and transformative technologies, education and training, trade, data flows, finance, etc. Basic indices that describe the various aspects of digitalization are given in absolute values and are further used as the basis for composite indicators. New approaches to the composite indicators design include indices measuring digitalization at various levels. The national level is covered by the Digital Intelligence Index (DII) (Chakravorti et al., 2020) and Digital Economy and Society Index (DESI) (European Commission, 2021). There are also some attempts to measure and benchmark digitalization of regions (Sidorov & Senchenko, 2020), while digitalization of sectors is measured by the Digital Intensity of sectors (Calvino et al., 2018; OECD, 2019) or Network Readiness Index (NRI) (Dutta & Lanvin, 2020). However, all these approaches to measure digitalization are rather general and do not focus on SMEs and their digital transformation. As SMEs differ from large companies not only by size, but also by strategies and ways of doing business, there is a need to propose a framework for assessing the level of their digital advancement and monitor progress in implementation of digital solutions by SMEs. Measurement of SMEs' digitalization is essential for effective support of their digital transition. Digital solutions, when introduced in an enterprise, are innovations and their implementation impacts the whole activity of the enterprise. The planning of digital transformation includes the identification of a set of objectives that digitalization is expected to achieve as well as resources needed for such transition. Value creation is an implicit goal of digitalization, however, it cannot be achieved automatically on an *ex ante* basis because outcomes of digital transformation are uncertain and can be heterogeneous. Value-related measures are also important for understanding the impacts of digitalization on enterprises' activity, which eventually leads to intended and unintended outcomes. Measuring the digitalization of SMEs requires the subject-based approach, which (opposite to the object-based approach) focuses on the firm (the subject) and employs data on its digital activities and performance. The OECD database (OECD, 2021a, 2021b) allows a digital divide to be measured between SMEs and large firms. The database contains 51 indicators of enterprises' digitalization selected on the basis of the second revision of the OECD Model Survey on ICT Access and Usage by Businesses (OECD, 2015). The survey was created to monitor the digital uptake of all sizes of businesses across the OECD countries. Core indicators are grouped into nine categories: connectivity, websites, information, management tools, e-commerce, digital security, e-government, use of cloud computing, ICT skills, and use of social media. The data are collected through surveys and come from an OECD data collection and the Eurostat statistics (OECD 2021a, p. 20). The data shows that there is a digital divide between SMEs and large firms. The digital gap is the largest in the area of enterprise resource planning, customer relationship management, and radio frequency identification. General administration and marketing operations are business functions in which SMEs are relatively more strongly digitalized. Business-to-government interactions, electronic invoicing, and social media usage as well as selling online belong to the activities where the smallest divide in digital technology adoption can be observed between SMEs and large companies (OECD, 2021a, p. 24).

The COVID-19 pandemic accelerated the process of SMEs' digital transformation, and in particular a sharp increase in online sale has been observed. The OECD estimates that since the beginning of the pandemic up to 70% of SMEs have increased their use of digital technologies, although there are huge differences in this respect between sectors and countries (OECD, 2021a, p. 34). Furthermore, the COVID-19 pandemic has caused a 20% rise of SME online platforms, which allow various activities to be pursued, such as mobile payments, online marketplaces, etc. without physical proximity, while platform use has declined by 70% in other areas that offer services in the sectors affected by the pandemic (tourism, transportation). Again, the use of online platforms varies across countries and regions due to differences in access to digital infrastructure. These space-based disparities have also had some impact on digital technologies adoption by SMEs (OECD, 2021a, p. 115).

Although many SMEs have digital ambitions, little has been said about digital transformation success metrics that can be used by SMEs to measure their performance. The assessment process of digital transformation requires a consistent approach to: (a) the evaluation of resources used for going digital; and (b) the evaluation of impacts of digital solutions, which are reflected in the company's outcome. The impacts are transmitted to the economic mechanisms such as costs and prices, but digitalization also affects the behavior of managers and other employees, which also may contribute to a firm's performance. Revenue from digital operations is regarded as a key metric showing how digitalization has changed the business. However, as the literature points out, digital transformation goes beyond the economic dimension. Its impact can be also seen in three interconnected areas: economic, social, and environmental (ecological) (Figure 16.2).

The distribution of the potential costs and of the benefits of the digital transformation with respect to the business size can be analyzed quantitatively and qualitatively, taking into account direct and indirect effects. The direct benefits of digital transformation include possible impacts on innovation, competition, market structure, efficiency, improvements of working conditions, increased business agility, reduction of environmental burden etc. They can be reflected in reduced costs of doing business in the short or medium term. Indirect benefits related to a new collaboration approach enabled by digitalization or behavioral and cultural change can appear in

Objectives of digital transformation	Resources for digital transformation	Main types of impact	Outcome

Outcome

Competitive performance change

New products introduction

Business models (re)definition

Organizational identity (re)definition

Virtual networks development

Collaboration approach (re)defined

Behavioral & cultural change

Increasing resource and information efficiency

Change in environmental footprint due to resource and energy use

Objectives of digital transformation

Change the core of a company (technological mix, management strategy, operational setup, culture)

More efficient use of existing resources

Resources for digital transformation

Financial capital

Human capital & digital skills

Technology & digital infrastructure

Main types of impact

Economic impact

Social impact

Environmental impact

Examples of digital transformation metrics for SMEs – input perspective

- Increase in R&D expenditures related to digital technologies development/adoption
- Expenditures on upgrading of skills of staff or the recruitment of new staff with digital capacities
- Financial contribution to the creation of digital culture (awareness raising, events, information diffusion etc.)
- Costs of the introduction/spread of new standards
- Investment in digital infrastructure
- Expenditures on ensuring safety and security in wireless devices

Examples of digital transformation metrics for SMEs – output perspective

- Revenue attributed to digital adoption as a share of total company's revenue
- Productivity index for digital operations
- Share of transactions executed through digital platforms
- Share of employees with advanced digital skills
- Share of employees using advanced digital tools and methods
- Share of collaborative initiatives initiated remotely (including social media)
- Share of employees taking part in training on digital technology use
- The decrease in costs of waste due to digital activity
- Corporate ecological footprint index for digital operations

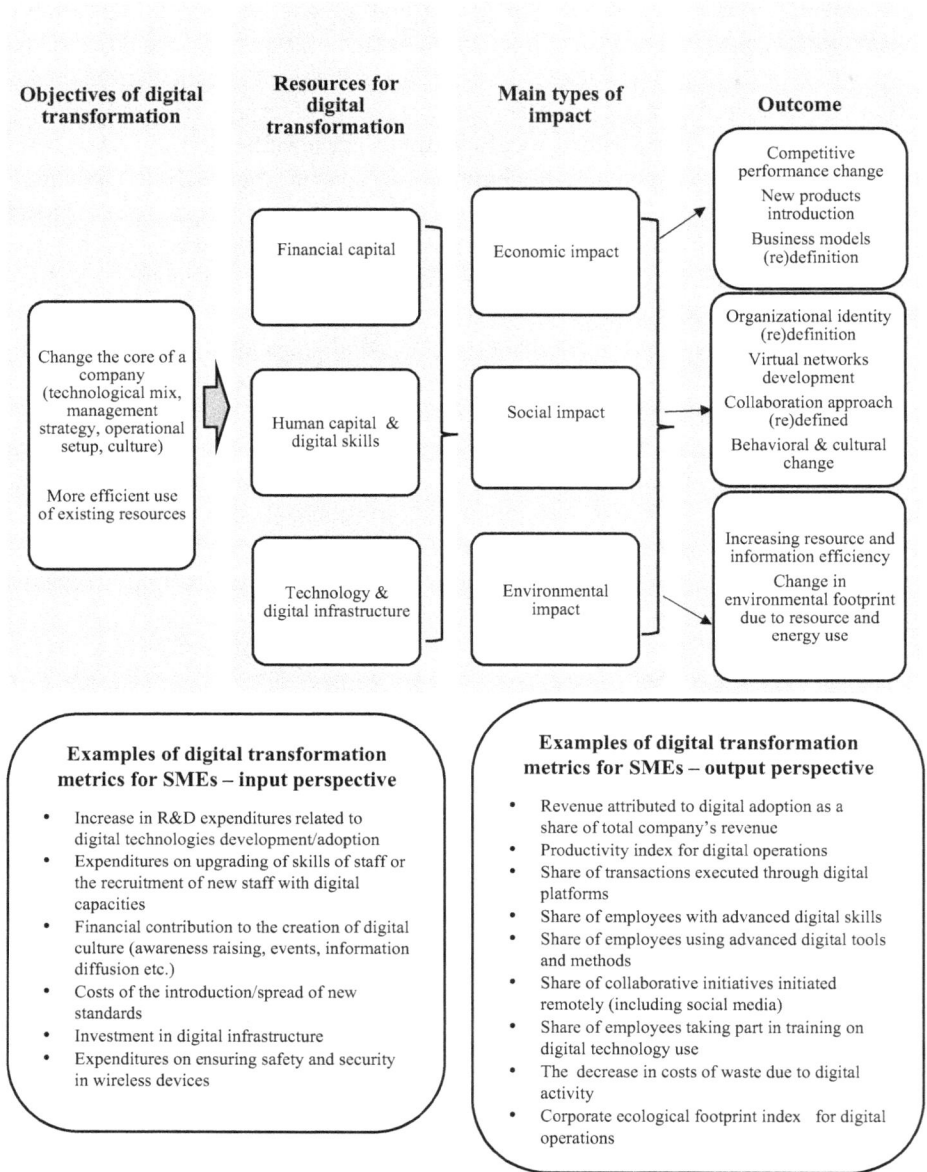

Figure 16.2: A conceptual framework of digital transformation of SMEs: linking objectives, resources, impact, outcomes, and metrics (compiled by authors based on the results of the umbrella review and a synthesis of empirical literature).

the medium and long run and they are not easily measurable. Yet, these benefits cannot occur without covering various costs related to digital transformation, notably the purchase of technology, licenses, new equipment, acquiring new resources for handling digital operations or managing data and information, training of staff, and accessing digital infrastructure. Both input and output sides of digital transformation need to be measured. Figure 16.2 provides a non-exhaustive list of indicators that could be considered by SMEs to measure the success of digital transformation. The choice of specific metrics to use should be made on a case-by-case basis given the heterogeneity of SMEs and industry characteristics.

Implications for Management Practice and Policymakers

Unleashing the potential of digital technologies for SMEs and speeding up the processes of their digital transformation can be facilitated by actions undertaken at both micro and macro levels. Looking from the firm perspective, a key success factor is a well-designed digitalization strategy, which goes beyond new technologies adoption or upgrading of current systems. One of the biggest challenges for a small firm could be the initiation of the digital journey. Such a journey can start when a firm has awareness of market competition changes and the ability to come up with and develop its clear digital transformation objectives to answer market needs. Thus, technological knowledge along with digital capabilities and digital skills and competencies of employees seem to be crucial to identify and fully exploit digital opportunities. Decision-making based on knowledge and information related to digital transformation implies strategic renewal of the firm's business models, collaborative approach, and culture and leads to the increase of the organization's competitive advantage and business growth. In order to be successful in the dynamically changing environment managers should work towards ensuring the agility of operations and fast execution of set objectives.

Our analysis of existing literature on digital transformation leads to the conclusion that in order to describe this process in a comprehensive way, technological, socio-economic, and environmental aspects need to be integrated. We proposed a framework for managing digital transformation of SMEs, which links objectives, resources, impact, and outcomes of digital transformation and we identified the input and output metrics of its success.

SMEs have growing digital ambitions, but many of them have no sufficient metrics to monitor success of digital transformation. Therefore, when initiating the process of digital transformation, managers need to establish key performance indicators to track progress of the digital journey of their companies, keeping in mind not only economic but also social and environmental impacts of digitalization. The most promising direction for managers should be to design digital strategies taking into account sustainability goals. The necessity to connect digital and green innovations has been already noticed by the leading European SMEs, which supported The European Green

Digital Coalition declaration launched in 2021 promoting sustainable digitalization (see box below). The success of sustainable digital transformation highly depends on leadership mindsets and the culture of managers at all management levels.

The pace of digital transformation of SMEs is both country- and industry-specific, thus when it comes to policy recommendations a one-size-fits-all approach does not apply. However, there are general recommendations that should be followed, keeping in mind that the priorities of countries and industries differ, in order to increase the speed of digital transformation of SMEs.

Example of initiatives supporting sustainable digital transformation of SMEs

The European DIGITAL SME Alliance is the nonprofit international network representing about 45,000 digital SMEs. The Alliance carries out research, promotes exchange of experiences, know-how, and best practices in the ICT sector, and offers training programs, seminars, and conferences in issues relating to ICT development, standardization, etc. It also supports sustainable digitalization focusing on digital sovereignty and analyzing the impact of ICT (both positive and negative) on the environment.

Source: https://www.digitalsme.eu/about/european-digital-sme-alliance/https://www.digitalsme.eu/blog/2020/11/23/greener-technologies-innovative-smes-lead-the-fight-against-the-throwaway-economy/

The European Green Digital Coalition (EGDC) declaration was launched in 2021 to support enterprises in their sustainable digitalization journey. It is an initiative by the European Parliament, implemented by the European Commission aimed at connecting top digital and green innovators in order to share their experience in sustainable digitalization. Forty-five digital SMEs had already joined this initiative at its launching stage and others are following. This platform for sharing best practices can be an inspiration for other SMEs to go digital and sustainable.

Source: https://digital-strategy.ec.europa.eu/en/news/companies-take-action-support-green-and-digital-transformation-eu

The Digital Volunteers Pilot Program aims to support digital transformation of European SMEs by growing digital competences of their employees and digitalizing business activities. Mentors from larger businesses offer advice for SMEs in development of digital marketing, co-designing content management systems or customer relationship management.

Source: https://digital-strategy.ec.europa.eu/en/news/leading-european-companies-support-digitalisation-smes-digital-volunteers-pilot-programme

---

It seems that the connectivity issue along with the access to broadband internet and its affordability is still a challenge. Thus, the first step towards assuring SMEs' willingness to go digital is to ensure relevant infrastructure for a digital ecosystem and high-speed network coverage. These improvements will significantly diminish the barriers of digital transformation for SMEs related to connectivity and costs. Such improvements, along with available e-government services and safety-ensuring, efficient and reliable digital financial services provide an inviting institutional setting for SMEs to engage in digital transformation.

SMEs, especially the smaller ones, often face a digital skills gap of their employees and change resistance. Thus, the efforts of policymakers should be targeted towards investments in education at every level accompanied by training of digital skills and providing lifelong learning opportunities to ensure the flexibility of employees with established careers. Training for digital talents and targeted coaching initiatives seem to be crucial for SMEs in order to pursue the implementation of their digital strategies.

There are many initiatives aimed at supporting SMEs in their digital transformation. The Digital Volunteers Pilot Program can serve as an example of the collaborative initiative of SMEs and large companies created to support digital transformation of European SMEs through mentoring and collaboration. It is aimed at growing digital competences and digitalizing SMEs' business activities (see box above). SMEs themselves are aware of the need to collaborate and share experience regarding their digitalization. Some of them already have established international networks, such as The European DIGITAL SME Alliance to collaborate in shaping digital talents through various training courses, seminars or conferences (see box above).

Policies aimed at ensuring digital transformation of SMEs should not only be oriented towards stimulating the use of novel information technologies and accompanying digital services, such as machine learning, big data, Internet-of-Things, smart services, social media, artificial intelligence, or the smart industry, but more importantly should focus on incentivizing SMEs to implement new strategies and adopt new business models raising from the opportunities provided by digital ecosystems. The holistic approach towards supporting SMEs seems to be crucial in order to ensure digital transformation instead of digitalization of SMEs.

References

Abel-Koch, J., Al Obaidi, L., El Kasmi, S., Acevedo, M.F., Morin, L., & Topczewska, A. (2019). *Going digital. The challenges facing European SMEs*. Bank Gospodarstwa Krajowego, Bpifrance, British Business Bank, Instituto de Crédito Oficial, KfW Bankengruppe. https://www.british-business-bank.co.uk/wp-content/uploads/2019/11/going-digital-the-challenges-facing-european-smes-european-sme-survey–2019_2.pdf

Aromataris, E., Fernandez, R., Godfrey, C., Holly, C., Khalil, H., & Tungpunkom, P. (2014). Methodology for JBI umbrella reviews. In *Joanna Briggs Institute reviewers' manual: 2014 edition / Supplement* (pp. 1–34). The Joanna Briggs Institute.

Bauer, T., & Groll, T. (2020). Digitalization of collaboration and communication in German SMEs: Using design thinking methods to develop strategic thrust for a digital transformation. *Regensburg Papers in Management and Economics*, 4. https://www.oth-regensburg.de/fileadmin/media/fakultaeten/bw/Projekte/publikationen/Regensburg_Papers_in_Management_and_Economics_No._4.pdf

Bouwman, H., Nikou, S., & de Reuver, M. (2019). Digitalization, business models, and SMEs: How do business model innovation practices improve performance of digitalizing SMEs? *Telecommunications Policy*, *43*(9), article 101828. https://doi.org/10.1016/j.telpol.2019.101828

Calvino, F., Criscuolo, Ch., Marcolin, L., & Squicciarini, M. (2018). A taxonomy of digital intensive sectors. *OECD Science, Technology and Industry Working Papers*, 2018/14. https://doi.org/10.1787/f404736a-en

Cannas, R. (2021). Exploring digital transformation and dynamic capabilities in agrifood SMEs. *Journal of Small Business Management.* https://doi.org/10.1080/00472778.2020.1844494

Chakravorti, B., Chaturvedi, R.S., Filipovic, C., & Brewer G. (2020). *Digital in the times of COVID. Trust in the digital economy and its evolution across 90 economies as the planet paused for a pandemic.* Institute for Business in the Global Context, The Fletcher School at Tufts University. https://sites.tufts.edu/digital planet/files/2021/03/digital-intelligence-index.pdf

Chavez, Z., Baalsrud Hauge, J., & Bellgran, M. (2020). A conceptual model for deploying digitalization in SMEs through capability building. In B. Lalic, V. Majstorovic, U. Marjanovic, G. von Cieminski, & D. Romero (Eds.), *Advances in production management systems. Towards smart and digital manufacturing. APMS 2020. IFIP Advances in Information and Communication Technology* (pp. 108–116), vol 592. Springer. https://doi.org/10.1007/978-3-030-57997-5_13

Chavez, Z., Hauge, J.B., & Bellgran, M. (2022). Industry 4.0, transition or addition in SMEs? A systematic literature review on digitalization for deviation management. *International Journal of Advanced Manufacturing, 119,* 57–76. https://doi.org/10.1007/s00170-021-08253-2

Dabić, M., Stojčić, N., Simić, M., Potocan, V., Slavković, M., & Nedelko, Z. (2021). Intellectual agility and innovation in micro and small businesses: The mediating role of entrepreneurial leadership. *Journal of Business Research, 123,* 683–695. https://doi.org/10.1016/j.jbusres.2020.10.013

Davis, J.R., Richard, E.E., & Keeton, K.E. (2015). Open Innovation at NASA: A new business model for advancing human health and performance innovations. *Research Technology Management, 58*(3), 52–58. https://doi.org/10.5437/08956308X5803325

Dawson, A., Hirt, M., & Scanlan, J. (2016). The economic essentials of digital strategy. McKinsey Quaterly. https://www.mckinsey.com/business-functions/strategy-and-corporate-finance/our-insights/the-economic-essentials-of-digital-strategy

De Mori, C., Batalha, M.O., & Alfranca, O. (2016). A model for measuring technology capability in the agri-food industry companies. *British Food Journal, 118*(6), 1422–1461. https://doi.org/10.1108/BFJ-10-2015-0386

Denicolai, S., Zucchella, A., & Magnani, G. (2021). Internationalization, digitalization, and sustainability: Are SMEs ready? A survey on synergies and substituting effects among growth paths. *Technological Forecasting and Social Change, 166*(C). https://doi.org/10.1016/j.techfore.2021.120650

Dethine, B., Enjolras, M., & Monticolo, D. (2020). Digitalization and SMEs' export management: Impacts on resources and capabilities. *Technology Innovation Management Review, 10*(4), 18–34. https://doi.org/10.22215/TIMREVIEW/1344

Dutta, S., & Lanvin, B. (Eds.) (2020). *The Network Readiness Index 2020. Accelerating digital transformation in a post-COVID global economy.* Portulans Institute. https://joserobertoafonso.com.br/wp-content/up loads/2021/02/NRI-2020-V8_28-11-2020.pdf

European Commission. (2021). *International digital economy and society index 2020.* Directorate-General of Communications Networks, Content and Technology. https://doi.org/10.2759/757411

European Investment Bank. (2019). *The digitalisation of small and medium-sized enterprises in Ireland. Models for financing digital projects.* Department of Business, Enterprise and Innovation and the European Investment Advisory Hub, Luxembourg. https://www.eib.org/attachments/thematic/digitalisation_of_smes_in_ireland_summary_en.pdf

European Investment Bank. (2021). *The digitalisation of small and medium-sized enterprises in Italy. Models for financing digital projects.* Innovation Finance Advisory (IFA), EIB Advisory Services. https://www.eib.org/en/publications/the-digitalisation-of-smes-in-italy-summary-report

Fachrunnisa, O., Adhiatma, A., Lukman, N., & Majid, M.N.A. (2020). Towards SMEs' digital transformation: The role of agile leadership and strategic flexibility. *Journal of Small Business Strategy, 30*(3), 65–85.

Faulkner, G., Fagan, M.J., & Lee, J. (2022). Umbrella reviews (systematic review of reviews). *International Review of Sport and Exercise Psychology, 15*(1), 73–90. https://doi.org/10.1080/1750984X.2021.1934888

Fitzgerald, M., Kruschwitz, N., Bonnet, D., & Welch, M. (2014). Embracing digital technology: A new strategic imperative. *MIT Sloan Management Review, 55*(2), 1–12.

Garzella, S., Fiorentino, R., Caputo, A., & Lardo, A. (2021). Business model innovation in SMEs: The role of boundaries in the digital era. *Technology Analysis and Strategic Management, 33*(1), 3–43.

González-Varona, J.M., López-Paredes, A., Poza, D., & Acebes, F. (2021). Building and development of an organizational competence for digital transformation in SMEs. *Journal of Industrial Engineering and Management, 14*(1), 15–24. https://doi.org/10.3926/jiem.3279

Grant, M.J., & Booth, A. (2009). A typology of reviews: An analysis of 14 review types and associated methodologies. *Health Information & Libraries Journal, 26*, 91–108. https://doi.org/10.1111/j.1471-1842.2009.00848.x

Hanelt, A., Bohnsack, R., Marz, D., & Antunes Marante, C. (2021). A systematic review of the literature on digital transformation: Insights and implications for strategy and organizational change. *Journal of Management Studies, 58*(5), 1159–1197. https://doi.org/10.1111/joms.12639

Hess, T., Matt, C., Benlian, A., & Wiesböck, F. (2016). Options for formulating a digital transformation strategy. *MIS Quarterly Executive, 15*(2), 103–119.

Kagermann, H., Helbig, J., Hellinger, A., & Wahlster, W. (2013). *Recommendations for implementing the strategic initiative INDUSTRIE 4.0: Securing the future of German manufacturing industry.* Final report of the Industrie 4.0 working group, Forschungsunion.

Kane, G.C., Palmer, D., Phillips, A.N., Kiron, D., & Buckley, N. (2015). *Strategy, not technology, drives digital transformation.* MIT Sloan Management Review and Deloitte University Press. https://www2.deloitte.com/content/dam/insights/us/articles/digital-transformation-strategy-digitally-mature/15-MIT-DD-Strategy_small.pdf

Kilimis, P., Zou, W., Lehmann, M., & Berger, U. (2019). A survey on digitalization for SMEs in Brandenburg, Germany. *IFAC PapersOnLine, 52*–13, 2140–2145. https://doi.org/10.1016/j.ifacol.2019.11.522

Kostrzewski, M., Marczewska, M., Chamier-Gliszczynski, N., & Woźniak, W. (2020). Digital twins as innovation in the era of Industry 4.0. *Proceedings of the 36th International Business Information Management Association (IBIMA)*, November 2020.

Kraft, C., Lindeque, J.P., & Peter, M.K. (2022). The digital transformation of Swiss small and medium-sized enterprises: Insights from digital tool adoption. *Journal of Strategy and Management.* https://doi.org/10.1108/JSMA-02-2021-0063

Kraus, S., Jones, P., Kailer, N., Weinmann, A., Chaparro-Banegas, N., & Roig-Tierno, N. (2021). Digital transformation: An overview of the current state of the art of research. *SAGE Open*, 1–15. https://doi.org/10.1177/21582440211047576

Kraus, S., Durst, S., Ferreira, J.J., Veiga, P., Kailer, N., & Weinmann, A. (2022). Digital transformation in business and management research: An overview of the current status quo. *International Journal of Information Management, 63*, 102466.

Liu, D.Y., Chen, S.W., & Chou, T.C. (2011). Resource fit in digital transformation. *Management Decision, 49*(10), 1728–1742.

Loebbecke, C., & Picot, A. (2015). Reflections on societal and business model transformation arising from digitization and big data analytics: A research agenda. *The Journal of Strategic Information Systems, 24*(3), 149–157. https://doi.org/10.1016/j.jsis.2015.08.002

Matt, C., Hess, T., & Benlian, A. (2015). Digital transformation strategies. *Business & Information Systems Engineering, 57*(5), 339–343. https://doi.org/10.1007/s12599-015-0401-5

McConnell, J. (2015). The company cultures that help (or hinder) digital transformation. *Harvard Business Review Digital Articles*, 2–5. https://hbr.org/2015/08/the-company-cultures-that-help-or-hinder-digital-transformation

Menon, S., & Shah, S. (2020). Growth of digital supply chains for SME transformation. *Paper presented at the 2020 IEEE International Conference on Technology Management, Operations and Decisions, ICTMOD 2020.* https://doi.org/10.1109/ICTMOD49425.2020.9380603

Mikalef, P., & Pateli, A. (2017). Information technology-enabled dynamic capabilities and their indirect effect on competitive performance: Findings from PLS-SEM and fsQCA. *Journal of Business Research*, *70*, 1–16. https://doi.org/10.1016/j.jbusres.2016.09.004

Nwaiwu, F. (2018). Review and comparison of conceptual frameworks on digital business transformation. *Journal of Competitiveness*, *10*(3), 86–100. https://doi.org/10.7441/joc.2018.03.06

OECD. (2015). *The OECD model survey on ICT usage by businesses: 2nd Revision*. OECD.

OECD. (2019). *Measuring the digital transformation: A roadmap for the future*. OECD Publishing. https://doi.org/10.1787/9789264311992-en

OECD. (2021a). *The digital transformation of SMEs, OECD studies on SMEs and entrepreneurship*. OECD Publishing. https://doi.org/10.1787/bdb9256a-en

OECD. (2021b). *ICT Access and use by businesses (edition 2020)*. OECD Telecommunications and Internet Statistics (database). https://doi.org/10.1787/851be3c1-en

Okfalisa, O., Anggraini, W., Nawanir, G., Saktioto, S., & Wong, K.Y. (2021). Measuring the effects of different factors influencing on the readiness of SMEs towards digitalization: A multiple perspectives design of decision support system. *Decision Science Letters*, *10*, 425–442. https://doi.org/10.5267/J.DSL.2021.1.002

Orellana, S. (2017). Digitalizing collaboration. *Research Technology Management*, *60*(5), 12–14.

Oswald, G., & Kleinemeier, M. (2017). *Shaping the digital enterprise*. Springer International Publishing.

Peillon, S., & Dubruc, N. (2019). Barriers to digital servitization in French manufacturing SMEs. *Procedia CIRP*, *83*, 146–150. https://doi.org/10.1016/j.procir.2019.04.008

Pelletier, C., & Cloutier, L.M. (2019). Conceptualising digital transformation in SMEs: an ecosystemic perspective. *Journal of Small Business and Enterprise Development*, *26*(6/7), 855–876. https://doi.org/10.1108/JSBED-05-2019-0144

Pfister, P., & Lehmann, C. (2021). Returns on digitisation in SMEs – a systematic literature review. *Journal of Small Business and Entrepreneurship*. https://doi.org/10.1080/08276331.2021.1980680

Pileggi, P. (2021). *Overcoming 9 digital twin barriers for manufacturing SMEs. Position paper*. https://www.change2twin.eu/wp-content/uploads/2021/04/Change2Twin_Position-Paper_Overcoming-9-Digital-Twin-Barriers-for-manufacturing-SMEs–.pdf

Porter M.E., & Heppelmann, J. (2014). How smart connected products are transforming competition. *Harvard Business Review*, *2014/11*.

Rogers, D. (2016). *The digital transformation playbook: Rethink your business for the digital age*. Columbia University Press.

Russmann, M., Lorenz, M., Gerbert, P., Waldner, M., Justus, J., Engel, P., & Harnisch, M. (2015). *Industry 4.0.: The future of production and growth in manufacturing industries*. Boston Consulting Group.

Savić, D. (2019). From digitization, through digitalization, to digital transformation. *Online Searcher*, *43*(1), 36–39.

Schuh, G., Anderl, R., Gausemeier, J., ten Hompel, M., & Wahlster, W. (Eds.). (2017). *Industrie 4.0 maturity index. Managing the digital transformation of companies (acatech STUDY)*. Herbert Utz Verlag.

Schwab, K. (2016). *The fourth industrial revolution*. World Economic Forum.

Sidorov, A., & Senchenko, P. (2020). Regional digital economy: Assessment of development levels. *Mathematics*, *8*(12), Article 2143. https://doi.org/10.3390/math8122143

Singh, A., & Hess, T. (2017). How chief digital officers promote the digital transformation of their companies. *MIS Quarterly Executive*, *16*(1).

Soto-Acosta, P., & Cegarra-Navarro, J. (2016). New ICTs for knowledge management in organizations. *Journal of Knowledge Management*, *20*(3), 417–422. https://doi.org/10.1108/JKM-02-2016-0057

Stich, V., Zeller, V., Hicking, J., & Kraut, A. (2020). Measures for a successful digital transformation of SMEs. *Procedia CIRP*, *93*, 286–291. https://doi.org/10.1016/j.procir.2020.03.023

Sufian, A.T., Abdullah, B.M., Ateeq, M., Wah, R., & Clements, D. (2021). Six-gear roadmap towards the smart factory. *Applied Sciences*, *11*(8). https://doi.org/10.3390/app11083568

Teece, D.J. (2018). Business models and dynamic capabilities. *Long Range Planning, 51*(1), 40–49. https://doi.org/10.1016/j.lrp.2017.06.007

Uvarova, O. (2021). *SMEs Digital transformation in the EaP countries in COVID-19 time: Challenges and digital solutions.* Eastern Partnership Civil Society Forum, Brussels. https://eap-csf.eu/wp-content/uploads/SMEs-digital-transformation-in-the-EaP-countries-during-COVID-19.pdf

Wade, M. (2015). *Digital business transformation. A conceptual framework.* Global Center for Digital Business Transformation. https://www.imd.org/contentassets/d0a4d992d38a41ff85de509156475caa/framework

Warner, K.S.R., & Wäger, M. (2019). Building dynamic capabilities for digital transformation: An ongoing process of strategic renewal. *Long Range Planning, 52*(3), 326–349. https://doi.org/10.1016/j.lrp.2018.12.001

Weresa, M.A., Kowalski A.M., & Mackiewicz, M. (2018). Innovation policy for SMEs in the era of Industry 4.0: Policy measures to strengthen innovation capacity of SMEs. In *2017/18 Knowledge Sharing Program with Visegrad Group: Innovation policy for SMEs in the era of Industry 4.0* (pp. 244–282). Ministry of Economy and Finance & Korea Development Institute.

Wessel, L.K., Baiyere, A., Ologeanu-Taddei, R., Cha, J., & Jensen, T.B. (2021). Unpacking the difference between digital transformation and IT-enabled organizational transformation. *Journal of the Association for Information Systems, 22*(1), 102–129. https://doi.org/10.17705/1jais.00655

Wirtz, B.W., Schilke, O., & Ullrich, S. (2010). Strategic development of business models: Implications of the web 2.0 for creating value on the internet. *Long Range Planning, 43*(2/3), 272–290. https://doi.org/10.1016/j.lrp.2010.01.005

Wollscheid, S., & Tripney, J. (2021). Rapid reviews as an emerging approach to evidence synthesis in education. *London Review of Education, 19*(1). https://doi.org/10.14324/LRE.19.1.32

Yasiukovich, S., & Haddara, M. (2020). Tracing the clouds. A research taxonomy of cloud-ERP in SMEs. *Scandinavian Journal of Information Systems, 32*(2), 237–304. https://aisel.aisnet.org/sj s/vol32/iss2/9

Yucel, S. (2018). Estimating the benefits, drawbacks and risk of digital transformation strategy. *2018 International Conference on Computational Science and Computational Intelligence (CSCI,.* https://doi.org/10.1109/csci46756.2018.00051

Zide, O., & Jokonya, O. (2022). Factors affecting the adoption of data management as a service (DMaaS) in small and medium enterprises (SMEs). *Procedia Computer Science, 196*, 340–347. https://doi.org/10.1016/j.procs.2021.12.022

Jadranka Švarc and Marina Dabić

17 Are the "Guys who Play Games" Shaping our Economic Future? The Croatian Economy's Potential for Digital Transformation

Abstract: "Croatia is hit by a technological fever" read one of the headlines in the public media following the sale of game development company Nanobit to the Swedish Stillfront group in 2020 for a billion HRK ($148 million). Croatia is one of the least developed EU member states, with many of its companies operating in low and medium-tech sectors. As such, the purpose of this research is to explore whether digital transformation can contribute to recovering such a low-tech service-based economy, or if this is just media hype. The research is explorative and includes an analysis of structural factors (the potential of the ICT sector), institutional factors (socio-economic environment), and the relationship between them. The findings suggest that Croatia has promising prospects in terms of its digital transformation. Digital transformation can also facilitate a potentially obstructive institutional environment, rooted in crony capitalism and state paternalism, as a result of the distinct character of business models brought by frontier digital technologies.

Keywords: Croatia, digital transformation, ICT sector, SMEs, unicorns, political economy, institutional factors, crony capitalism

Introduction

"Croatia is hit by a technological fever" read one of the headlines in the public media following the sale of game development company Nanobit to the Swedish Stillfront group in 2020 for a billion HRK ($148 million). This came as a great surprise as, prior to this, Nanobit was not considered an established industry and, secondly, few companies in Croatia are sold for one billion kunas. Nanobit, together with Infobit (the first Croatian unicorn,[1] with a valuation over $1 billion), and Rimac autombili (see Case 1),

---

[1] A "unicorn" is a start-up company that is not listed on the stock exchange but is valued as over $1 billion. Infobit was included in the Global Unicorn Club in September 2020. This is available at: https://www.cbinsights.com/research-unicorn-companies [September 2, 2021]

Jadranka Švarc, Institute of Social Sciences Ivo Pilar, Zagreb, Croatia
Marina Dabić, University of Zagreb, Faculty of Economics and Business, Croatia

https://doi.org/10.1515/9783110747652-018

producer of electric super cars which have attracted the interest of global players such as Bugatti and Porsche, make a popular trio of companies that are often used to illustrate Croatia's admittance into the digital economy. These companies are the first real examples of Croatian "garage" companies: start-ups which achieved global market success through the model "from garage to a billion dollars in less than 15 years." They are also a vivid illustration of how digital technologies, increasingly coupled with artificial intelligence, have seriously shaken the world of traditional entrepreneurship and exiting entrepreneurship theories (Ferreira et al., 2019), necessitating new business models and organizational cultures, new sorts of products or services, and new types of customer service.

The essential characteristic of these companies, in contrast to companies in conventional industries, is that they are "born global" and "born digital" (Vadana et al., 2019), meaning that their business strategy is orientated towards international markets through their incentives, while their business models rely on information and communication technology (ICT) and digitalization.

It is well known that digitally and industrially advanced economies tend to derive larger socio-economic benefits from digitalization and Industry 4, creating a larger share of their GDP from the ICT sector (Chakravorti et al., 2020). Therefore, the main research question of this study is: can digital transformation and the development of the ICT sector help to recover less developed and low-tech service-based economies, such as that of Croatia?

Croatia became the last (twenty-eighth) EU member in 2013 and is one of the least developed EU member states, falling behind its eastern peers (e.g., Poland, Czech Republic, and Hungary) with many companies operating in low and medium-tech sectors, remarkably in trade and tourism. This also affects the levels of innovation and business spending in research and development, which are currently low at around a mere 0.5% of GDP.

The decline in economic progress suggests that a shift in technology and economic policy, based on ICT and digital transformation, is needed. Therefore, the purpose of this study is to understand the challenges which confront the concepts of digital transformation and entrepreneurship in Croatia. Because the structure of the ICT sector and policy factors can explain the differences in the adoption of ICT (Andrews et al., 2018, p. 6), two analogous factors have been identified in order to play a decisive role in digital transformation. These will be discussed in this article. The first is a structural factor which comprises the strengths of the ICT sector, while the business and socio-political environment and governance (government actions, policies, laws, and regulations) build contextual and institutional factors together that determine the pace of progress towards the digital economy.

This leads to the following two questions: firstly, does the ICT sector have the potential to provide solutions for a deep socio-economic stalemate, driving economic growth in Croatia; and secondly, can Croatia, in the given socio-economic regime, make a turn towards the policy support and institutional landscapes that support digitalization and the ICT sector?

This research sheds additional light on the ongoing debates about the potential of the ICT sector in Croatia, which is a precondition for digital transformation. Discussions regarding the relationships between digital transformations and the institutional factors that hinder economic development contribute to scholarly literature in the fields of political economy and sociology. Although the results of this study are mainly limited to Croatia, they can assist policymakers and practitioners in understanding the difficulties and advantages of digital transformation in countries that are similarly lagging in terms of technological development.

Following the presentation of the methodology in Section 2, Section 3 clarifies the importance of digital technologies for economic progress on a global scale. The potential of the ICT sector in Croatia is outlined in Section 4, and the limitations of the institutional context for digital transformation are described in Section 5. The impact of digital transformation on political contexts is presented in Section 6. Section 7 provides conclusions and recommendations.

Methodology

The methodology of this study is made up of two stages. The first stage is focused on the assessment of the current state of the ICT sector in Croatia as a prerequisite for digital transformation. It involves the analysis of nine assessment studies of the ICT sector, of which four were carried out on an international level, three at a European level, and two at a national level (Table 17.1). The next stage is primarily explorative and is based on institutional theory, facilitating an understanding of the contextual and governance determinants for digital transformation in Croatia. It combines the theory of digital innovation with selected studies pertaining to the institutional socio-economic context of Croatia to demonstrate how advanced digital entrepreneurship can provide an alternative to socio-political frameworks' aversion to digital transformation.

Why are ICT and Digital Technologies Important?

Many economists suggest that ICT is still not visible in productivity statistics, pointing to Solow's productivity paradox (Solow, 1987) that questions ICT as a driver of economic growth (van Ark, 2016). Despite the fact that "ICT is everywhere except for the productivity statistics," to paraphrase Solow, many scholars argue that the benefits of the new digital economy are mismeasured and are hardly visible in the "installation phase" of the major techno-economic restructuring brought about by ICT (Brynjolfsson et al., 2017). The intangible capital needed to complement ICT progress – primarily through innovations like organizational changes, business models, adjustments of costs, and new skills – is not developed and implemented to support transformation. Some respectable global studies (WEF, 2017; OECD, 2017) argue that digital technologies contribute towards increases in productivity and employment, as well as better economic performance. In this vein, a number of scholars argue that there is no doubt that digital technologies will completely transform our "life, business and economy" (Makridakis, 2017) and that digitalization and robotization will revolutionize society as electricity once did (Brynjolfsson & McAfee, 2014; Ford, 2015).

Despite scholarly disputes and doubts regarding the contribution of ICT to long term economic growth, it is rather important to understand why digitalization and ICT are unavoidable attributes of our future development. The answer lies in the radically changed nature of innovation; its transformation from industrial and material types of innovation based on classical, mainly in-house, research; and its development into digital or "smart" innovations that produce products and services with disembodied or digital materiality (Švarc, 2021). Digital materiality or intangibility (Yoo et al., 2010), such as digital sensors or software designs, afford new functions to common things, such as cars, books, and touristic or bank services, considerably improving product planning, design, production, and distribution, changing products from the industrial era (Yoo et al., 2010). No industries or companies within the current economic sector can ignore the alterations made to the nature of innovation, nor can they escape the process of digital transformation. This essentially assumes the merging of digital technologies and business processes (Nambisan et al., 2019; Warner & Wäger, 2019), which should eventually lead to the establishment of the digital entrepreneurship ecosystem (Elia et al., 2020) and Industry 4, in which industrial devices can optimize or accomplish the manufacturing process themselves (with no human interference) using cyber-physical communication systems (Schwab & Davis, 2018). Therefore, digital technologies can open up new sectors in traditional economies that are globally competitive, allowing for the gradual restructuring and revival of the economy (D'Ippolito, 2019), or even a leapfrog into new technological sectors (Lee, 2019).

Digital transformation involves the application of digital innovations (e.g., big data, cloud computing, IoT, etc.) and further upgrades through cutting-edge technologies, such as robotics, deep learning, or artificial intelligence. A systemic literature review (Gong & Ribiere, 2021; Kraus et al., 2021) revealed that there was no consensus around the concept, and that the definition of digital transformation differs. Gong and Ribiere (2021, p. 12) therefore proposed that, based on the 134 well-received, published definitions, the unified definition of digital transformation should be: "A fundamental change process, enabled by the innovative use of digital technologies accompanied by the strategic leverage of key resources and capabilities, aiming to radically improve an entity and redefine its value proposition for its stakeholders" (where, an entity could be an organization, a business network, an industry, or a society).

Digital transformation also requires a new management paradigm and new business models that integrate all business processes into one interacted value chain, involving cultural transformation at an organizational or company level, as well as at a societal level, embracing digital technologies through the wider population (Caputo et al., 2021). This, therefore, presents a great challenge for both individual companies and national economies. Due to the globalized character of the present value chains, most of the world's economy will be compelled to use digital technologies sooner or later. This therefore presents a great challenge for both individual companies and national economies.

However, today's advanced digital production (ADP) technologies are primarily concentrated on a handful of countries and companies (UNIDO, 2019). Even technologically advanced countries can hardly keep pace with digital forerunners. The reliance of the companies in the EU on mostly US digital platforms, like Google, Microsoft, or Amazon, is a trivial example of how European technology development and growth can be threatened or slowed down simply because it failed to take part in building the major digital platforms. For example, "United States and China account for 90% of the market capitalization value of the world's 70 largest digital platforms while Europe's share is 4%" (UNCTAD, 2019, p. xvi).

This raises a dilemma: can technological followers like Croatia take advantage of digital technologies as a path to economic revitalization and growth, or is this just an ungrounded illusion stemming from exaggerated publicity created by the media? Therefore, the aim of the next section is to gain some insights into the state of the ICT sector as a basis for the digital transformation of the Croatian economy.

The Potential of the ICT Sector in Croatia

A range of studies and analyses have tried to assess the size and growth of the Croatian ICT sector and its contribution to the overall Croatian economy. The studies are carried out on international and European levels for the sake of countries' comparisons, while domestic studies are focused on the in-depth assessment of national achievements (Table 17.1).

However, accurately gathering data on the contribution of ICT and digitalization on economic development is a rather challenging task due to the different methodological approaches and the measurements of available studies and statistical data. Nevertheless, all analyses converge in agreeing that ICT is one of the most propulsive sectors in Croatia, with significant potential in terms of its ability to spur economic growth. For example, McKinsey and Company's (2020, p. 3) study of the digital potential of 10 countries in Central and Eastern Europe (CEE) (Poland, Hungary, Lithuania, Bulgaria, Czechia, Latvia, Slovenia, Croatia, Romania, and Slovakia) classified countries in terms of them being "Digital Challengers," revealing that digitalization could act as the next driver of sustainable growth in the region, potentially contributing €200 billion of additional GDP by 2025. The contribution of digitalization to the

Table 17.1: Selected studies on the level of digitalization in Croatia.

International Studies	European Studies	Domestic Studies
Industrializing in the digital age (UNIDO, 2019)	Digital economy and society index (EC, 2020a)	Analysis of the Croatian ICT industry 2014–2019 (Žitnik & Subotičanec (2020)
Digital challengers in the next normal (McKinsey and Company, 2020)	European Digital Transformation Scoreboard (EC, 2018a)	Croatia digital index (Apsolon, 2020)
IMD World Competitiveness digital ranking 2020 (IMD, 2021).	EC Country Report, Croatia (EC, 2020b)	
Digital Intelligence Index (Chakravorti et al., 2020)		

economy's growth in Croatia is estimated to reach up to €8.3 billion in GDP by 2025 (additional €2,000 GDP per capita) (McKinsey and Company, 2018).

In line with these estimates, UNIDO (2019, p. 29) places Croatia, along with 23 other countries, as followers of advanced digital production (ADP) technologies. Because the remaining 88 countries are classified as "laggards," Croatia is positioned rather well on the global digital scale as a country which is actively involved in ADP and could adopt and develop technological advances generated mainly in only 10 digital frontrunners led by China, France, and Germany.

According to the EU digital transformation scoreboard (EC, 2018a, p. 54) "[t]he IT sector in Croatia has grown drastically in the last five years, with an increase in the capacity of data centres and a growing use of mobile applications and big data analytics." The analysis of the Croatian ICT industry between 2014 and 2019 (Žitnik & Subotičanec, 2020) supports this assessment, as the Croatian ICT industry generated a total revenue of €3.6 billion in 2019, with an annual growth of 12.4%. The average annual growth rate (AAGR) in the last five years (2014–2019) reached 11.2%, largely due to exports because the total income realized on foreign markets was, according to the compound annual growth rate (CAGR), around 15%, with 11.4% from the domestic market.

In the last five years, exports have been growing at a rate of 18.6%, compared to the growth of the country's total exports of services of 9.9%. As much as 70.6% of total revenue is made up of ICT services, such as programming or consulting. The newly created value achieved by the Croatian ICT industry last year reached over €1 billion (with an annual growth of 15.2%) and achieved 2.1% of GDP. The ICT industry has grown four times faster than Croatia's GDP and is the flagship of our economy (Žitnik & Subotičanec, 2020, p. 7).

While this data is encouraging, comparisons between EU countries shows that the Croatian ICT industry, by the number of companies, total revenue, and the value of exports, is at the bottom of the European scale (Žitnik & Subotičanec, 2020). McKinsey and Company (2020) suggest that digital technologies are not sufficiently exploited in Croatia, which leads to its significant digital lag. It is quite obvious that the Croatian IT sector is growing, but not fast enough to catch up not only with developed countries but also its CEE peers. For example, the share of the ICT sector in GDP is 4.45%, which is much worse than that of Bulgaria, Hungary, Czechia, and even Serbia (Figure 17.1). Croatia also lags behind the majority of CEE in ICT turnover (five years CAGR[2] 2014–2019) and in ICT personnel (Figure 17.1).

The Croatian ICT industry is driven mostly by escalating global demand for software development and the swift response of the Croatian' developers to those demands. A new wave of hundreds of fast-growing software export-orientated companies in Croatia has arisen. These are largely foreign-owned and their annual turnover and exports often exceed 50% (Žitnik & Sobotičanec, 2020). However, software programmes of global importance are offered by a relatively small number of companies – about 20 in total – such as GDI Gisdata, Ericsson Nikola Tesla, Infobip, Photomath, etc.

However, many other Croatian companies have seen rapid growth too, such as Ars Futura, AG04 Innovative Solutions, Delta Reality etc., of which a number are included on Deloitte's list of the 50 fastest growing technology companies in Central Europe[3] (Electrocoin, Bazzar, Agrivi, Include, Eco mobile) and/or the Financial Times' list of Europe's fastest-growing companies (Infinum, Microblink, Agrivi, Q, Serengeti) (MEEC, 2019). The most technologically disruptive company, which has become globally known as a "company whose new electric car turns upside down everything known about cars" (Index.hr, 2021), is Rimac Automobili (Case 1).

Case 1: Mate Rimac's electric hypercars: The future is already here
"What an incredible day! What a journey!" posted Mate Rimac, CEO of Rimac Automobili on his Facebook page on July 6, 2021, to announce another major milestone in the company's history when Bugatti – the archetypical auto brand – became a new partner in a recent joint venture between Rimac and Porsche. Rimac Automobili started in a garage in 2009 with an idea for an electric-powered sportscar. In the ten years since then, the company has become a globally recognized developer in the electric vehicle industry, designing and manufacturing high-performance electric supercars and setting technological benchmarks for others. The company expanded rapidly. In just two years, employee numbers doubled from 500 in 2019 to 1,000 in 2020. However, the plans for business growth are fascinating, as the grounds of the new campus – with 200,000 square meters for 2,500 employees – have already been elaborated upon. Mate Rimac's future plans include robotaxis: driverless vehicles that might attract hundreds of millions of euros in investments. If the project succeeds, the first robotaxis could be tested on Zagreb streets in 2024. Rimac Automobili proved that great innovations can be developed anywhere with ambitious and creative people who believe in themselves and their ideas.

Sources: personal visit to the company; various Internet and media news.

---

2 CAGR – Compound annual growth rate.
3 Available at: https://www2.deloitte.com/content/dam/Deloitte/ce/Documents/fast50/ce-technology-fast-50-results-report-2020.pdf [September 12th, 2021]

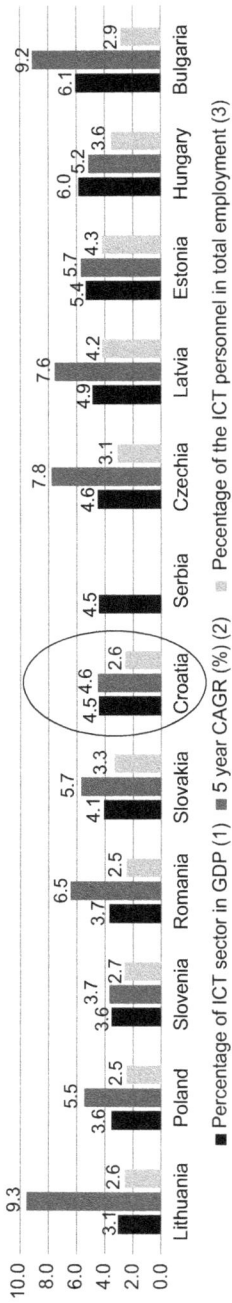

Figure 17.1: Comparisons between Croatia and CEE peers in selected indicators of the ICT sector in 2018.

Sources:

(1) Eurostat

(2) https://www.nationmaster.com/nmx/ranking/turnover-of-ic

(3) Eurostat, [isoc_bde15ap]

Data extracted: 1 September, 2021.

Although the innovation performance of Croatian companies has improved over the last couple of years (EC 2021), the business research and development expenditure of 0.5% of GDP is among the lowest in the EU, leaving Croatia with internationally un-competitive products. European Structural funds have helped, however, to establish several centers for advanced robotic technologies, primarily in medicine (Case 2), and they have also helped technical universities in Zagreb – primarily Faculty of Electrical Engineering and Computing (FER) and the Faculty of Mechanical Engineering and Naval Architecture (FSB) – to establish research facilities for advanced ICT. The most prominent is the Innovation Centre Nikola Tesla (ICENT) at FER, with six institutes fo-cusing on ICT, robotics, transport, energy, automation, and biomedical engineering. Smaller universities, like the University of Rijeka and the University of Dubrovnik, have also established facilities in the area of intelligent autonomous systems. A comprehen-sive list of research facilities is provided by MEEC (2019).

Case 2: RONNA – the first Croatian robot for neurosurgical operations
It took 16 years for Prof. Bojan Jerbić, from the Faculty of Mechanical Engineering and Naval Architecture (FSB) in Zagreb, and Dr. Darko Chudyj, from the Dubrava Clinical Hospital, to move from the robotic neuro-navigation system prototype (RONNA) to the first robotic neurosurgical operation in 2016. This was the first operation of its kind in this part of Europe. Since the launch of the project in 2008, supported by modest funds from the Ministry of Science, four generations of the RONNA system have been developed, and the fifth is in progress to enable a fully autonomous surgical system. Today, more than 4,000 robots operate in the world, and Croatia is slowly catching up with these trends.

Following the experience of RONNA, in June 2021 FSB established the Regional Centre of Excellence in Robotic Technology (CRTA) for development and education in the field of artificial intelligence and robotics.

Sources: various Internet and media news.

European funds also supported local initiatives through the Interreg-IPA project (2014–2020) for the development of digital innovative hubs in small cities (Gradiška, Daruvar, and Lipik) in different regions. The genuine local initiative is the campus for the gaming industry in Novska and the Osijek Software City (Case 3) in Slavonia. The latter can be used to show the "best practices" for how to promote digital technologies at a regional level.

Case 3: Osijek Software City
The Osijek Software City project was launched in early 2012 by individuals and several Osijek ICT companies who wanted to make changes in Slavonia: a region that was among the most devastated following the Homeland War and its transition to capitalism. In an age of hopelessness due to growing poverty, rural exo-dus, and unemployment, enthusiasts have launched an association in Osijek, the administrative and univer-sity centre of Slavonia, to support the developer as a profession, improve its market competitiveness, and advance ICT entrepreneurship. Their vision was to build the Croatian "Silicon valley" and employ 300 people in the ICT sector over 5 years. This idea has been met with ridicule, and today it is far exceeded. The city currently has around 90 members (30 companies and 60 individuals) and has further expansion prospects. It is estimated that around 150 companies with over 1,000 employees are linked to the city.

Source: https://softwarecity.hr/ and various Internet and media news.

According to the Digital Economy and Society Index (DESI) (EC, 2020a), Croatian enterprises are progressively integrating digital technologies into their business. Croatia ranks twelfth among EU countries and, with 23% of enterprises at a high or very high level of digital intensity (use of different digital technologies at enterprise level), Croatia is slightly below the EU average of 26%. However, the rather low rankings of other DESI components (e.g., human capital, connectivity, etc.) places Croatia fairly low on the EU digital scale, ranking twentieth of 28 EU member states.

The good level of digitalization in Croatian companies is also confirmed by the European Digital Transformation Scoreboard (EC, 2018a), on which Croatia is slightly below the EU average, ahead of 10 countries, including Bulgaria, Estonia, Greece, Hungary, Italy, and Poland, among others. However, according to the same source, Croatia is the third worst country in the EU Digital Transformation Enablers' Index, as only Latvia and Romania are performing worse. This emphasizes the need for Croatia to invest serious efforts in "digital enablers," such as access to finance, digital infrastructure, and the demand and supply of skills and categories that have been in decline since 2016.

It is interesting to note that the European Country Report for Croatia 2020 (EC, 2020b, p. 46) contradicts the optimistic estimations of DESI (EC, 2020a) and the Scoreboard (EC, 2018a) with regards to the good levels of digitalization in Croatian companies. The Report suggests "Croatian enterprises are slowly taking up digital technologies," with an integration score below the EU average (15.5% versus 18%). Small businesses are especially behind, as less than 20% of small firms are highly digitalized, compared to 47% of large companies.

In a similar way, some other international studies also express criticism, estimating that Croatian achievements in the digital economy are fairly modest and unsatisfactory. According to the IMD-World Digital Competitiveness Ranking 2020 (IMD, 2021), Croatia is ranked rather low, at fifty-fifth out of 64 leading world economies in 2020. Its future prospects are estimated to be rather weak because its readiness for future digitalization is ranked in sixtieth place. Also, the Digital Intelligence Index (Chakravorti et al., 2020) scored Croatia at forty-third on the "Digital evolution state" and seventy-seventh in terms of "Digital Momentum" (future perspectives) out of 90 countries. Croatia belongs to the "Watch out" countries, like Hungary, Uganda, Ethiopia, Nigeria, or Brazil, which maintain more skeptical attitudes toward digitalization. On the other hand, they have the potential to use digitalization to leapfrog by transforming their economies.

Finally, it is rather surprising that, according to the EU Digital Transformation Scoreboard (EC, 2018a), Croatia's highest score is in the field of entrepreneurial culture (which is traditionally low in Croatia), falling just below the Netherlands and Portugal, which are the best-performing European countries in terms of "entrepreneurial culture." Croatia is also solid in e-leadership, mainly due to the provision of regular training for ICT specialists and good internet connection for employees. These estimations do not comply with the results of the Croatian Digital Index, carried out by Apsolon (2020), a leading consultative firm in Croatia for digital transformation, which measures the readiness of companies for digital transformation. Their survey on 300 firms revealed that only 17.7% of companies (mostly large ones) have developed a strategy of digital transformation. Around 57% of companies intend to make such a strategy, while around 25% have no intention of doing so. Digital transformation is one of the top priorities in only 37% of companies. This suggests that our companies do not develop systemic approaches to new businesses management based on digital technologies. This myopic mindset could threaten competitiveness in a growingly digitalized global economy.

The reasons behind this slow digitalization can be deduced from many different factors: primarily in the lack of digital skills on the labor market and limited progress in broadband connectivity (EC, 2020a; McKinsey and Company, 2020; EC, 2018a). IMD (2021) finds obstacles in the lack of training, education, and scientific concentration, and Apsolon (2020) in the shortage of financial resources, time, and willingness to deviate from conventional business models. As summarized by McKinsey and Company (2018), the following five factors are critical for digital transformation: ICT infrastructure, education system, entrepreneurial environment, digital skills, and entrepreneurial environment.

Institutional Context

The removal of these structural obstacles for faster digitalization is largely dependent on socio-cultural and political contexts, i.e., on the "invisible hand" of the institutional factors that determine the speed and efficiency of institutional change. Since P. Hall's (1993) seminal work on policy paradigms explained the role of social learning in policymaking, a growing number of authors in the social sciences have sought to explore the role of institutions (defined as the "the basic rules of the game" by North (1990)) in policy change, especially those that can alternate existing policy discourses to spur socio-economic progress. According to Hinings et al. (2018), digital transformation brings out novel structures, actors, and values that require novel institutional and socio-cultural arrangements, changing the existing rules of the game. In short, institutions provide moral or cognitive patterns for governance, policy actions, and decision-making, which influence the path and speed of developments, including digital transformation.

Croatia's economic development, following the demise of socialism in 1990 and the country's transition to a market economy, has been unsuccessful and disappointing (Jurčić, 2019; Švarc & Dabić, 2019), illustrating that institutions have not created the socio-political and cultural context supportive of economic progress. Today, Croatia is among the worst EU countries economically in terms of GDP growth and business competitiveness. It seriously lags behind countries that it has outperformed in the past. It remains an upper middle-income country, with a GDP per capita of €12.186 in 2020,[4] which achieved around 64% of the EU-28 average. Croatia has remained around the same distance from the EU average for more than ten years, indicating that it has made no real convergence with the EU. After the end of the Homeland War for independence in 1995, Croatia's GDP per capita (GDP p/c) was only lower than Slovenia and the Czech Republic. In contrast, in 2020, only Bulgaria had a lower GDP p/c than Croatia (and Greece, which has meanwhile declined[5]). Membership in the EU since July 1, 2013, has assisted Croatia's economic growth and prosperity, but far less so than for other new EU members from the previous Eastern bloc. Croatia had numerous advantages over those countries during the 1990s in terms of its reformed banking system, foreign trade, and price liberalization (Uvalić, 2018). This was the legacy from ex-Yugoslavia, when Croatia was one the most developed of the republic, aside from Slovenia, with a reasonably strong industrial base and advanced technological services in certain sectors, which were exported to foreign (mostly Arab) countries (Radošević, 1994).

Although the economic and technological decline can be partly attributed to the destabilizing effects of the Homeland War (1991–1995), Croatia had only one period of growth after gaining its independence: from 2003 to 2008 (Jurčić, 2019). This inevitably raises questions concerning the efficiency of economic policies, state governance, and management in economy restructuring, from the socialist self-management system to a liberal market economy. The harsh disputes surrounding the reasons behind the sluggish economic recovery and highly restrictive business environment, with limited market competition and held back investments, are still ongoing.

However, many scholars from social sciences, primarily political economists, believe that a distorted political economy developed during the transition known as "crony capitalism" is one of the main barriers to economic progress and innovation (Švarc, 2017). This still shapes the political economy framework of modern Croatia. It is featured by institutional deficits defined by "a specific environment in which corruption, lack of transparency, lack of accountability, and high taxes coexist" (Vuković, 2017). Crony capitalism relies on conservative populism and consists essentially of systemic clientelism and corruption (Čepo, 2020; Franičević & Bićanić, 2007), which derogate the values of democracy and social justice in favor of particular interest groups protected by the corrupted political elites. This compromised the rule of law and faith in honest work and merit-based success (Franičević & Bićanić, 2007), which are fundamental prerequisites for a healthy business climate that facilitates the market competition needed for economic growth. This socio-cultural and political context is deepened by the rise of conservative civil movements, the Catholic Church's strong impact on

---

4 https://www.hnb.hr/statistika/glavni-makroekonomski-indikatori [September 2nd, 2021]
5 https://ec.europa.eu/eurostat/statistics-explained/index.php?title=File:Volume_indices_per_capita,_2018–2020,_(EU%3D100)_v2.png#filehistory [September 2nd, 2021]

civil life (e.g., educational reform), and the 500,000 registered veterans who strive to protect their collective rights by weakening media freedom and democratic values (Čepo, 2020). The socio-economic environment adverse to business development is largely enabled by the slow, unpredictable, and often unfair system of the judiciary. According to Transparent International, Croatia remained a highly corrupt country in 2020, with only Romania, Hungary, and Bulgari more corrupt in the EU.

Economists mainly hold the neoliberal growth model responsible, along with macroeconomic policies based on financial discipline and the restriction of public sector spending, excessive servitization of the economy, and the collapse of manufacturing (Jurčić, 2019). The enormous decline of industrial sectors in the 1990s, mainly due the privatization of state-owned companies by corrupted tycoons who "sucked out" the companies' substance (Županov, 2001), is considered to be one of the most devastating consequences when it comes to techno-economic progress. Similar processes in other post-socialist countries, like Hungary, Poland, or Slovenia, were moderated by their incorporation into the EU's techno-economic networks, due to their prior EU membership.

There is also a range of other socio-economic deficiencies, like having the lowest activity rate of the population in the EU (except Italy), due to the early retirement of war veterans, confused health and pension systems, low productivity rates, aging of the population, etc. There is a lack of strategic thinking and political will for managing these deficits: there are many strategies and action plans, but reforms are few and far between. Croatia still has one of the largest and most underperforming sectors of state-owned enterprises (SOE), with a value of 47.2% of the GDP in 2019 (OECD, 2021) and hundreds of other firms operating mostly with the state. The companies under state paternalism lack incentives for genuine market competition, diverting their business focus from technology and export-driven strategies towards political protection and clientelistic networks.

At the turn of twenty-first century, Croatia remained without a meaningful development strategy (except for monetary and fiscal policy), and relied on its traditional low-skilled, low-income service sectors, dominated by tourism and trade. The structure of the economy has remained relatively unchanged over the last 15 years, with no shift towards more knowledge-intensive sectors (EC, 2018b, p. 275). The large reliance on tourism (around 25% of GDP) not only contributes to the downfall of other relevant industries, but also creates the "rent-based" economic culture in which innovation and technologically driven entrepreneurship play a tiny role. High emigration rates reveal the unfortunate fact that a large number of citizens are looking for a better life outside of Croatia. The need for a turnaround in economic and social policy is becoming critical, along with the opening of new technology trajectories and models in business management.

Given that the reforms and policy actions taken so far have not yielded significant results, it seems that the changes should be implemented at the individual level, i.e. at the level of the entrepreneurs themselves. In support of this is the fact that Croatia suffers from weak entrepreneurial capital and spirit due to the inheritance of socialism when private ownership was largely discouraged (Švarc & Dabić, 2019). Therefore, one of the most promising policy actions would be leverage of entrepreneurial education which is indicated as one of the main barriers to booster economic development (Rialti et al., 2017). Entrepreneurial education can stimulate the birth of new firms and facilitate business internalisation, which is very important in the digital global economy. An important aspect of entrepreneurial education is fostering digital competences and literacy that are needed for digital transformation, which can change a growth paradigm and in parallel create a new institutional socio-economic context.

Can Digital Transformation Create a New Political Economy?

A certain number of ICT companies have departed from the institutional context shaped by crony capitalism and established over the last decade. They seem to be developing in a rather specific way, detached from the rest of the economy. These companies can be considered "digitally transformed," as their leadership and employees are familiar with advanced ICT and shape business operations accordingly. At least four factors make these companies distinct.

First of all, the majority of these ICT companies are orientated towards international markets ("born global"), rendering them independent from the domestic market and, at the same time, free from political and economic elites which shape the "rules of the game" inclined to protect the interests of a networked minority at the expanse of the entrepreneurial majority.

Secondly, these companies are characterized by a new generation of managers who acquire significant wealth solely through their work and knowledge, in contrast to the managers of state-dependent companies and those that profit from companies' privatization.

Thirdly, digital companies have acquired needed capital investments from foreign and/or private stakeholders, who are driven by their interest in making a profit, rather than clientelistic group interests. Therefore, this new class of managers are liberated from the majority of the ill-shaped institutions, ranging from public administration (e.g., ministries) and various public agencies, over financial and judiciary institutions, to the notorious privatization of companies.

Fourthly, the managers of digitally transformed companies understand new digital business models and build new organizational cultures that are quite different from standard management practices, especially those modelled by clientelistic relations. New business models integrate new technologies (e.g., software development, sensors, artificial intelligence, robots, big data, etc.) with company management, daily operations, and strategies. Many experts, including current political and economic elites, face difficulties in understanding the paradigm shift in business management (marketing, economics, information systems, operations, strategy, etc.) brought about by digital transformation (Nambisan et al., 2019). Like blockchain technology, which remains a mystery to many, cutting-edge digital technologies are also in uncharted territory, falling under the radar of restrictive bureaucracy and the vested interest of local strongman (e.g., majors), enabling "digital managers" to take advantage of their unique expertise and knowledge for their own prosperity and common good. Their social function is still inconclusive. Over time, they can turn into the desirable archetypes of the new digital entrepreneurs, or can, on the other hand, deepen the social gap between successful "game players," similar entrepreneurs, and most others trapped using old, less profitable technologies.

However, digital entrepreneurs ("digipreneurs") differ significantly and the concept remains inconclusive (Bandera & Passerini, 2020). By studying the hospitality sector in Greece, Pappas et al. (2021) identified four types of owners/managers according to their willingness to adopt IoT technologies since IoT is able to the redefine business model: (a) rational – evaluates risk and opportunities; (b) enthusiast – seeks to offer breakthrough innovations for revolutionizing the business model; (c) cautious – emphasizes risks and barriers to innovate; and (d) futurist – anticipate futures and reengineers operational steps. The analysis of IT companies in Croatia in the last 10 years (Žitnik & Subotičanec, 2020) has shown that it is possible to identify seven types of companies or entrepreneurs/managers (Table 17.2) of which very few belong to the category of enthusiasts or futurists who truly have the potential to change economic sectors.

Table 17.2: Structure of IT service companies by type, 2008–2017 (total income in %).

Company type	2008	2017
System integrators	62.9	41.5
Value-Added Reseller	10.5	8.7
IT Repair and Maintenance	3.8	3.5
Software Developers	13.7	33.3
Application Implementers	7.3	6.2
Data Centers	0.7	5.7
Digital platforms	1.1	1.1
Total	100	100

Source: Žitnik & Subotičanec, 2020, p. 40.

The most common type of companies in both 2008 and 2017 is system integrators, which are "old" type companies offering classical IT services. Meanwhile, software developers experienced the largest increase. They include national software champions like Infinum, Pet minuta, Nanobit, and Serengeti etc. However, the majority of these type of companies have up to four employees and are foreign-owned, which suggests that software development is a kind of "loan-job" in which domestic developers are small subcontractors for foreign large companies.

Therefore, different IT companies or their mangers/owners contribute to digital transformation in different ways depending on their own individual preferences and circumstances. However, many of them, especially those oriented to foreign markets, build digital transformation that might have a significant positive influence on creating an institutional environment that is supportive for economic growth. This is in harsh contrast to the political economy shaped by crony relationships and clientelistic networks. Advanced digital businesses are largely independent from political nomenclature and its narrow and vested interests, enabling these companies to develop according to their own logic, inspiring others to try to follow their model of business success. This can open up new sectors of the economy away from low-profit traditional sectors, state-dependent businesses, or rent-seeking economies, such as tourism. Such sectors can build their own "political economy" based on new business models and organizational culture, where transparency, work, and merit all play decisive roles, rather than state paternalism and personal connections.

Conclusions

This short overview of the selected studies reveals that estimations of Croatia's potential for digital transformation differ in many aspects. Nevertheless, the majority of the studies reviewed perceive Croatia to be a digital follower, with promising prospects in digitalization. The long-term trends of ICT indicators reveal a desirable growth pattern and a more significant contribution to GDP than some traditionally important economic sectors, such as agriculture or transport (Keček et al., 2019).

Some scholars suggest, on the other hand, that the growing Croatian technological optimism around digital unicorns, start-ups, and gazelles is a mere techno-utopia and a simple media bubble that has no foothold in reality (Bičanić, 2021). The dilemma remains as to whether the ICT sector can be a driver of the Croatian economy, as the share of those engaged in digital technologies is negligible in national accounts. Indeed, there are only around 4,000 active IT firms, with around 33,000 employees as of 2019. This represents 3.4% of the total number of employees in the non-financial industry (Žitnik & Subotičanec, 2020.) It is clear then that, in terms of volume, it is not yet possible to talk about the significant impact of the ICT sector on the national GDP or the labor market. However, there are many experts who believe that the statistics of the ICT sector do not depict the sector appropriately as ICT is measured only by one NACE sector (sector J – information and communication). However, ICT is a general-purpose technology spread throughout the economy. However, these effects are not taken into account in statistical measurement since they are not covered by the J sector. Besides, capturing the ICT sector is not only a matter of measurement, but also a substance of understanding what activities make up the sector. General consensus on this has not yet been reached. Unlike conventional technologies, whose impact on productivity are more easily discernible, the impact of WhatsApp, online meetings, or mobile phones on productivity is difficult to measure. There substantial empirical evidence reveals that companies that do not embrace digital technologies usually perish and exit the market, suggesting that digital transformation is not an option but rather an obligation required in order to survive (Windpassinger, 2017).

Analysis of the structure of the ICT sectors suggests that Croatia's substantial progress towards digital transformation as a new techno-economic paradigm is rather fragile. This hinders its potential to leapfrog into new sectors and industries (Lee, 2019) and limits frontier digital technologies on random and a reduced number of cases, some of which are presented in the frames. However, such initiatives are of great importance for future development because they pave the way for new, emerging, and promising economic sectors, certain niches of which are not occupied by other international players like China and are not dominated by eastern European countries integrated into the European value chains (e.g., the automotive industry). This contributes to the gradual restructuring of economy. It is clear that Croatia has developed over the last 10 years a certain "islands of excellence" in digital technologies but, in order to have an impact on economic growth, the development of complementary competences is required. These include digital capital or the development of the overall average of digital literacy, along with new business models and infrastructures, to enable these advanced technologies to spread.

Digital capital is also very important when it comes to changing the growth paradigm. Digital entrepreneurship can facilitate or even escape the obstructive socio-economic environment rooted in clientelistic types of economy as a result of the distinct characteristics of new types of managers, jobs, skills, business models, and culture, all brought about by digitalization. Digital transformation can ease the negative influence of institutional contexts shaped by crony capitalism in business development and can open up new perspectives for socio-economic development by building new types of political economy, based on individual merit and achievements. This aspect of digital transformation, which can help to drive economic growth, certainly deserves rigorous investigation in the future.

The main limitation of this research is its lack of systematic and comprehensive data and the absence of the strategic and policy analyses which could serve as a reliable input for the broader estimation of Croatia's potential for digital transformation. Since this research is more focused on digital elite ("born global") companies, a deeper analysis of different actors in digital transformation (e.g., digital "loan" jobs, digital merchants, digital adapters of technology to local circumstances, digital maintainers, etc.) should be pursued. Future research should also explore the role of the state in accelerating digital transformation due to its complexity and its large infrastructure requirements.

Finally, digital transformation is an integral part of Europe's strategic development, as promoted by the European Green Deal (COM(2019) 640 final), the Strategy on Shaping Europe's Digital Future (COM(2020) 67 final), and the new Industrial Strategy (COM(2020) 102 final), which focus on twin, digital, and ecological transitions or the integration of digital transformation in efforts to prevent climate change. Following European strategic plans, the Croatian National Development Strategy for 2030 (Development direction 3) (OG 13/2021) and the National Recovery and Resilience Plan (NRRP) both include the green and digital transition as development priorities at a national level. The NRRP serves as a prerequisite for receiving funds from the European Recovery and Resilience Facility (RRF), worth around €6.3 billion, 20% of which should be allocated to projects dedicated to digital transition. For example, Rimac Automobili (Frame 1) will receive around €200,000 for the development of a new urban mobility system integrated with public transport in Zagreb. As a part of the Next Generation EU (NGEU) recovery instrument, the RRF marks a turning point in public policies to support the digitalization of companies – both start-ups and incumbents – and can contribute to creating new market niches for digital transformation.

Our title question is: are the "guys who play games" shaping our economic future? The answer can be both positive and negative. It is negative if we consider only the gaming industry as a driver of growth, but it is positive if we understand the gaming industry to be symbolic of Croatia's ability to build the digital capital needed for a new paradigm of development, based on digital and green technologies.

References

Andrews, D., Nicoletti, G., & Timiliotis, C. (2018). *Digital technology diffusion: A matter of capabilities, incentives or both?* OECD Working paper no. 1476. OECD, Geneva.

Apsolon. (2020). Digital transformation in Croatia 2020. Apsolon (in Croatian). https://apsolon.com/publikacije/

Bandera, C., & Passerini, K. (2020). Personality traits and the digital entrepreneur: Much of the same thing or a new breed? *Journal of the International Council for Small Business*, 1(2), 81–105, DOI: 10.1080/26437015.2020.1724838

Bičanić, I. (2021). Croatian techno-utopia. The productivity paradox will not disappear. Ideje.hr, June 15, 2021. https://ideje.hr/hrvatska-techno-utopia-paradoks-produktivnosti-nece-nestati/ (in Croatian). [September 22, 2021].

Brynjolfsson E., & McAfee A. (2014). *Race against the machine: How the digital revolution is accelerating innovation, driving productivity, and irreversibly transforming employment and the economy.* W. W. Norton and Company, Inc.

Brynjolfsson, E., Rock, D., & Syverson, C. (2017). *Artificial intelligence and the modern productivity paradox: A clash of expectations and statistic*s. NBER working paper series, working paper 24001.

Caputo, A., Pizzi, S., Pellegrini, M.M., & Dabić, M. (2021). Digitalization and business models: Where are we going? A science map of the field. *Journal of Business Research*, 123, 489–501.

Chakravorti, B., Chaturvedi, R.S., Filipovic, C., & Brewer, G. (2020). *Digital intelligence index*. Tufts University.

Čepo, D. (2020). Structural weaknesses and the role of the dominant political party: Democratic backsliding in Croatia since EU accession. *Southeast European and Black Sea Studies*, 1–19, DOI: 10.1080/14683857.2020.1709721.

D'Ippolito, B. (2019). Archetypes of incumbents' strategic responses to digital innovation. *Journal of Intellectual Capital*, *20*(5), 662–679. DOI: 10.1108/JIC-04-2019-0065.

EC. (2018a). *Digital transformation scoreboard 2018*. Publications Office of the European Union, Luxembourg. https://ec.europa.eu/growth/tools-databases/dem/monitor/. [September 22, 2021].

EC. (2018b). *European science, research and innovation performance of the EU 2018: Strengthening the foundations for Europe's future*. European Commission. https://ec.europa.eu/info/sites/info/files/srip-report-full_2018_en.pdf. [June 11, 2020].

EC. (2020a). *Digital economy and society index (DESI) 2020 Croatia*. European Commission. https://file:///C:/Users/Korisnik/Downloads/10_desi_2020_-_croatia_-_eng_CB8F75A3-90CF-F710-6D05B5E904BB0FFA_66908.pdf. [September 23, 2021].

EC. (2020b). *Country report Croatia 2020*. (2020 European Semester). European Commission Brussels, 26.2.2020, SWD (2020) 510 final.

EC. (2021). *European innovation scoreboard (EIS)*. Publications Office of the European Union.

Elia, G., Margherita, A., & Passiante, G. (2020). Digital entrepreneurship ecosystem: How digital technologies and collective intelligence are reshaping the entrepreneurial process. *Technological Forecasting and Social Change*, *150*, 119791. DOI: 10.1016/j.techfore.2019.119791.

Ferreira, J.J., Fernandes, C.I., & Kraus, S. (2019). Entrepreneurship research: Mapping intellectual structures and research trends. *Review of Managerial Science*, *13*(1), 181–205.

Ford, M. (2015). *Rise of the robots: Technology and the threat of a jobless future*. Basic Books.

Franičević, V., and Bićanić, I. (2007). EU accession and Croatia's two economic goals: Modern economic growth and modern regulated capitalism. *Southeast European and Black Sea Studies*, *7*, 637–663. DOI: 10.1080/14683850701726104.

Gong, C., & Ribiere, V. (2021). Developing a unified definition of digital transformation. *Technovation*, *102*, 102217.

Hall, P. (1993). Source policy paradigms, social learning, and the state: The case of economic policymaking. *Comparative Politics*, *25*(3), 275–296.

Hinings, B., Gegenhuber, T., & Greenwood, R. (2018). Digital innovation and transformation: An institutional perspective. *Information and Organization*, *28*(1), 52–61. DOI: 10.1016/j.infoandorg.2018.02.004

IMD. (2021). *World competitiveness yearbook 2021, Digital 2020, talent 2020: Summaries, country profile Croatia*. MD-World Digital Competitiveness Ranking. https://file:///C:/Users/Korisnik/Downloads/HR.pdf

Index.hr. (2021). Top Gear reviewed Nevera: Forget everything you knew about hypercars, https://www.index.hr/vijesti/clanak/top-gear-objavio-veliku-recenziju-rimac-nevere/2280437.aspx [September 27, 2021].

Jurčić, Lj. (2019). Croatia's stagnation in the EU. *Ekonomski Pregled*, *70*(6), 902–938 (in Croatian).

Keček, D., Boljunčić, V., & Mikulić, D. (2019). Hypothetical extraction approach for measuring total economic effects of Croatian ICT sector. *Croatian Operational Research Review*, *10*(1), 131–140, DOI: 10.17535/crorr.2019.0012.

Kraus, S., Jones, P., Kailer, N., Weinmann, A., Chaparro-Banegas, N., & Roig-Tierno, N. (2021). Digital transformation: An overview of the current state of the art of research. *SAGE Open*, *11*(3), DOI: https://21582440211047576.

Lee, K. (2019). *Economics of technological leapfrogging*. United Nations Industrial Development Organization (UNIDO), Working paper 17/2019.

Makridakis, S. (2017). The forthcoming artificial intelligence (AI) revolution: Its impact on society and firms. *Futures, 90*, 46–60. DOI: http://dx.doi.org/10.1016/j.futures.2017.03.006.

MEEC. (2019). *Croatia – Industry 4.0.* Ministry of Economy, Entrepreneurship and Crafts.

Nambisan, S., Wright, M., & Feldman, M. (2019). The digital transformation of innovation and entrepreneurship: Progress, challenges and key themes. *Research Policy, 48*(8), Article 103773.

McKinsey and Company. (2018). *Croatia – emerging digital challenger: Digitization as the new growth engine for Croatia.* https://digitalchallengers.mckinsey.com/files/Digital-Challengers-Perspective-on-Croatia.pdf [September 22, 2021].

McKinsey and Company. (2020). *Digital challengers in the next normal: Central and eastern europe on a path to digitally-led growth.* McKinsey and Company.

North, Douglass A. 1990. *Institutions, institutional change and economic performance.* Cambridge University Press.

OECD. (2017). *Key issues for digital transformation in the G20.* Report prepared for a joint G20, German Presidency/OECD conference, Berlin, Germany, 12 January 2017.

OECD. (2021). *OECD review of the corporate governance of state-owned enterprises: Croatia.* https://www.oecd.org/corporate/soe-review-croatia.htm [September 22, 2021]

Pappas, N., Caputo, A., Pellegrini, M.M., Marzi, G., & Michopoulou, E. (2021). The complexity of decision-making processes and IoT adoption in accommodation SMEs. *Journal of Business Research, 131*, 573–583.

Radosević, S. (1994). Strategic technology policy for Eastern Europe. *Economic Systems, 18*(2), 87–116.

Rialti, R., Pellegrini M.M., Caputo A., & Dabić M. (2017). Entrepreneurial education and internationalisation of firms in transition economies: A conceptual framework from the case of Croatia. *World Review of Entrepreneurship, Management, and Sustainable Development, 13*(2–3), 290–313.

Schwab, K., & Davis, N. (2018). *Shaping the future of the fourth industrial revolution: A guide to building a better world.* Penguin Random House.

Solow, R.M. (1987). We'd better watch out. *New York Times*, July 12, Book Review, No. 36.

Švarc, J. (2017). Socio-political approach in exploring the innovation culture in post-socialist countries: The case of Croatia. *Post-Communist Economies, 29*(3), 359–374. DOI: 10.1080/14631377.2017.1315001.

Švarc, J. (2021). Prolegomena to social studies of digital innovation. *AI and Society*, 1–13. DOI: https://df10.1007/s00146-021-01220.

Švarc, J., & Dabić, M. (2019). The Croatian path from socialism to European membership through the lens of technology transfer policies. *The Journal of Technology Transfer, 44/5*, 1476–1504, DOI: 10.1007/s10961-019-09732-1.

Uvalić, M. (2018). The rise and fall of market socialism in Yugoslavia DOC Research Institute, special report. https://doc-research.org/2018/03/rise-fall-market-socialism-yugoslavia/. [September 22, 2021].

Vadana, I.I., Torkkeli, L., Kuivalainen, O., Saarenketo, S. (2019). The Internationalization of Born-Digital Companies. *The Academy of International Business*, 199–220. DOI: 10.1007/978-3-030-03931-810.

Vuković, V. (2017). The political economy of local government in Croatia: Winning coalitions, corruption, and taxes. *Public Sector Economics, 41*(4), 387–420.

UNCTAD. (2019). *Digital economy report 2019.* United Nations.

UNIDO. (2019). *Industrial development report 2020. Industrializing in the digital age. Overview.* United Nations Industrial Development Organization.

van Ark, B. (2016). The productivity paradox of the new digital economy. *International Productivity Monitor, 31*, 1–15.

Warner, K.S.R., & Wäger, M. (2019). Building dynamic capabilities for digital transformation: An ongoing process of strategic renewal. *Long Range Planning, 52*(3), 326–349.

WEF. (2017). *White paper: Technology and innovation for the future of production: Accelerating value creation*. World Economic Forum.

Windpassinger, N. (2017). *Digitize or die.* IoT Hub.

Yoo, Y., Henfridsson, O., & Lyytinen, K. (2010). Research commentary: The new organizing logic of digital innovation: An agenda for information systems research. *Information Systems Research, 21*(4), 724–735. https://www.jstor.org/stable/23015640 [September 22, 2021].

Žitnik, B., & Subotičanec, D. (2020). *Analysis of the Croatian IT industry 2014 – 2019*. Croatian Chamber of Commerce (in Croatian).

Županov, J. (2001). The industrializing and de-industrializing elite in Croatia in the second half of the 20th century. In D. Čengić & I. Rogić (Eds.), *Ruling elites within an analytic perspective* (pp. 11–37). Institute of Social Sciences Ivo Pilar (in Croatian).

Tin Horvatinovic, Mihaela Mikic, and Sanel Jakupović

18 Should Entrepreneurs Effectuate? A Conceptual Examination on the Effects of Effectuation on Firm Performance

Abstract: In this study, a theoretical analysis was conducted of empirical papers that tested the influence of effectuation on business performance. The results show that such research has gained prominence in recent years and that the general effect of effectuation on business performance is positive. However, a diverse set of statistical procedures has been utilized and the aforementioned effect alters between effectuation principles. These results have implications for additional research on this topic and bring about practical recommendations as well.

Keywords: effectuation, business performance

Introduction and Theoretical Background

Effectuation theory, an emerging and pragmatic theory of entrepreneurship (Fisher, 2012; Perry et al., 2012), has become a highly researched topic in recent years (Grégoire & Cherchem, 2020; Matalamäki, 2017). It was established by Sarasvathy in 2001 and since then it has challenged the traditional way scholars think about entrepreneurial behavior, what Sarasvathy calls causation. In a causal approach, entrepreneurs try to achieve a predetermined goal by collecting resources and deciding on the use of these based on the criteria of maximizing expected returns. In addition, entrepreneurs view other firms as competitors, give priority to preexisting knowledge, and attempt to predict the future, which is theoretically possible in stable environments (Sarasvathy, 2001). In contrast, the effectual entrepreneur strives to control the future, not to predict it. The main reason for this practice is the postulate that most entrepreneurs operate in uncertain environments in the Knightian sense (Knight, 1921; Sarasvathy, 2001). Predicting the future in such environments is untenable. What entrepreneurs should do is devote their attention to controllable aspects of the future. They will consider other firms as partners and through such partnerships they try to reduce uncertainty. Because some level of uncertainty is inevitable, entrepreneurs must be equipped with the capabilities of exploiting unforeseen future situations and create many options for future actions using the principle of affordable loss (Sarasvathy, 2001).

Tin Horvatinovic, Mihaela Mikic, Department for Managerial Economics, Faculty of Economics and Business, University of Zagreb, Zagreb, Croatia
Sanel Jakupović, "APEIRON", Banja Luka, Bosnia and Herzegovina

https://doi.org/10.1515/9783110747652-019

Given this unique deviation from the processes of formal business planning, it is not surprising that researchers would congregate and test the effects of an effectual approach to entrepreneurship on business performance. Analyzing studies that tested this effect is the topic of this paper. In other words, the subject matter of this paper is to conceptually examine and evaluate the state of such research. By conducting such an analysis, the authors are exploring an important component of highly influential creation and network theories in the entrepreneurship field (Ferreira et al., 2019).

The research questions of the paper are stated as follows:

RQ1: What is the status, in terms of quantity and quality, of papers that test the impact of effectuation on business performance?

RQ2: Based on the current findings, can the application of an effectual approach to entrepreneurship be recommended to real-world entrepreneurs?

To address these questions, all empirical papers that are published and accepted for publication, in two prominent scientific databases, on the topic of the effect of effectuation on business performance were probed. The results show that there is an increase in publications, that most samples were drawn in developed countries, and that various approaches to hypothesis development and testing were used. Furthermore, the effect of the overall use of effectuation on business performance is positive but varies between effectual principles.

The paper is structured as follows. In the next section, the applied research methodology is laid out. In section three, the results of the analysis are displayed and scrutinized. Lastly, the discussion and concluding remarks are made in section four.

Research Methodology

The research methodology that was employed in this study is in line with the procedures and objectives of a semi-systematic literature review. In other words, the overarching goal of this research methodology is to critically examine the subject matter in question by identifying and synthesizing all relevant research that has been conducted on the topic (Snyder, 2019). Many methods can be classified as a semi-systematic literature review, but for this paper the specific method that was utilized is vote counting. This approach was chosen because of the research question stated in the introduction and state of the research field on the effect of effectuation on business performance. The former relates to the sole use of quantitative studies in the review analysis which then excludes methods that are designed to analyze the text of the articles, such as narrative inquiry or discourse analysis. The latter is related to the assessment of the field, by the authors of this paper, as having a small to large study population, medium to high study samples, and low to high consensus of the measurement of the effectuation construct. Because of these characteristics, vote counting is the most appropriate method (Newbert et al., 2014).

The process of gathering the data for the analysis began with identifying the key characteristics that the study must have to be eligible for the final sample. The criteria are: 1) the study must be published or accepted for publication in a scientific journal; and 2) the study must explicitly and quantitatively test the impact of effectuation on the business performance of a firm using primary data. According to the first criteria, studies such as conference papers, working papers, and book chapters were excluded. Following the second criteria, papers such as case studies and review articles were also excluded. Furthermore, a broad view of business performance was taken, meaning that various measures (such as business model innovation and process efficiency) were deemed acceptable for the analysis alongside explicit business performance variables. Finally, papers that tested multi-firm performance (Fischer et al., 2021) or that examined the performance impact by not using empirical data, such as the study of Welter & Kim (2018) that employed simulations, were excluded from the sample.

After establishing these two criteria, journal articles were searched in the Web of Science and Scopus database using the search term "effectuation." All articles that came up in the search were individually examined by the authors to assess whether or not the two criteria were met. In other words, using this broad search criterion for effectuation, all 773 articles in the Web of Science database and all 622 articles in the Scopus database were assessed. After this screening process was finished, the final sample of this study come out to 37 articles. This relatively small percentage of articles attests to the fact that effectuation is a highly encompassing theory that can be examined in numerous ways, both theoretically and empirically.

Results

The full list of papers is given in Table 18.1 and the dynamics of the article publication can be found in Figure 18.1. In the vast majority of these studies, the authors sampled only small and medium-sized enterprises (SMEs). There were also some studies that used a composite sample of predominantly SMEs and a smaller number of large firms, while only a handful of studies focused exclusively on large firms.

Figure 18.1 shows that it took about ten years since the publication of the foundational paper of effectuation theory (Sarasvathy, 2001) for researchers to start testing the effects of effectuation on business performance. This is not surprising since the research of many theories in business economics did not immediately surge after the publication of the article that founded those theories (Perry et al., 2012). In addition, empirical measures of effectuation were not being put forward which undoubtedly slowed down the progress of effectuation research. Brettel et al. (2012), who were the

Table 18.1: Studies that were used for the analysis.

Brettel et al., 2012	Futterer et al., 2018	Vanderstraeten et al., 2020
Blauth et al., 2014	Smolka et al., 2018	Wu et al., 2020
Mthanti & Urban, 2014	Yu et al., 2018	Yang et al., 2020
Urban & Heydenrych, 2015	Guo, 2019	Alzamora-Ruiz et al., 2021a
Guo et al., 2016	Xia et al., 2019	Alzamora-Ruiz et al., 2021b
Parida et al., 2016	Deligianni et al., 2020	Deng et al., 2021a
Roach et al., 2016	Furlotti et al., 2020	Deng et al., 2021b
Cai et al., 2017	Pacho & Mushi, 2020	Long et al., 2021
Eijdenberg et al., 2017	Peng et al., 2020	Pati et al., 2021
Jisr & Maamari, 2017	Ruiz-Jiménez et al., 2020	Shirokova et al., 2021
Laskovaia et al., 2017	Shirokova et al., 2020	Yoon & Cho, 2021
de la Cruz et al., 2018	Szambelan & Jiang, 2020	
Eyana et al., 2018	Szambelan et al., 2020	

Source: compiled by the authors.

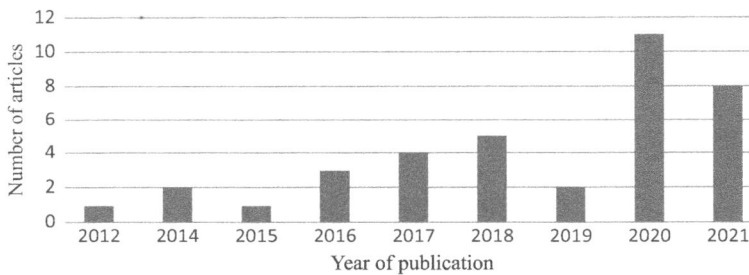

Figure 18.1: Article publication by year.
Source: compiled by the authors.
Note: some articles have not yet published but have been accepted for publication. These articles have been entered into 2021 column.

first to examine the effectiveness of effectuation, had to develop their methodology for measuring effectuation.

Each year from 2012 to 2019, except in 2013, at least one paper was published on the topic and during that period there was a steady increase in published works. In 2019, however, there was an unexpected decline in published articles but in 2020 and 2021 there was a substantial increase. In 2020, eleven articles were published and in 2021 (at the time of writing this chapter) eight articles were published or accepted for publication. Whether or not this amount of research will be published in high-quality scientific journals in the future remains to be seen but this is a promising sign.

It is also important to identify the most influential articles in the sample by looking at the number of citations. The rankings are constructed using the total number of citations in Web of Science and Scopus database. Utilizing this metric, Table 18.2 shows the 10 most prominent articles. As can be anticipated, most articles published one or two years ago are not highly cited. Looking individually at the current status, Brettel et al. (2012) is by far the most cited article in both Web of Science and Scopus database, followed by Smolka et al. (2018) and Futterer et al. (2018).

Table 18.2: Top 10 most cited articles in Web of Science and Scopus database.

Authors	Web of Science citations	Scopus citations
Brettel et al., 2012	220	193
Smolka et al., 2018	85	78
Futterer et al., 2018	68	63
Roach et al., 2016	69	57
Cai et al., 2017	62	54
Laskovaia et al., 2017	51	47
Blauth et al., 2014	51	35
Guo et al., 2016	39	34
Yu et al., 2018	33	26
Mthanti & Urban, 2014	23	23

Source: compiled by the authors.

Looking at the distribution of articles classified by the journals they are published in, most journals, a total of 19, have published one article. *Journal of Business Research* published the highest number of articles with five, followed by *Journal of Small Business Management* and the *Technology Analysis & Strategic Management* with five. A full list of journals that published the articles in this analysis is displayed in Figure 18.2.

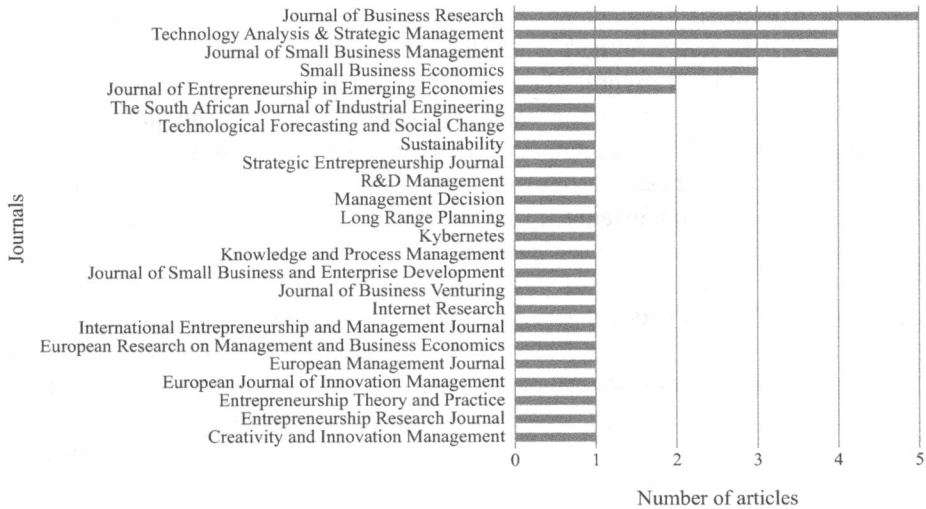

Figure 18.2: Article publication by journal.
Source: compiled by the authors.

Concerning the country from which the studies drew their samples, China is the most frequent one with 11 followed by Germany with five and Spain with four, as can be seen in Table 18.3. Only three studies used multiple countries in their sample and their sample sizes were consequently much higher than those that drew samples from one country. The average sample size of these three studies was 2,957 while the average sample size for the other 34 studies was 221. Besides having larger sample sizes, accumulating samples from multiple countries results in a more nuanced examination of the effect of effectuation on business performance.

Table 18.3: Countries from which the samples were collected.

Country	Frequency
China	11
Germany	5
Spain	4
Multiple countries and South Africa	3
Belgium, Burundi, Ethiopia, Greece, India, Lebanon, Netherlands, Russia, Sweden, Tanzania, and United States of America	1

Source: compiled by the authors

Developing a hypothesis, using the process of theory building, is a requirement for almost all scientific articles. Since this mechanism is essential, each sampled study was examined to see how they developed their hypothesis. More concretely, each hypothesis in the sampled studies was examined and categorized. In theory construction literature, hypothesis development can take many distinctive forms (Pawar, 2009; Reynolds, 1976). However, authors in practice commonly combine various approaches to build a hypothesis. Therefore, a judgement was made on which form and approach had the most prominent role in the process of each hypothesis development.

Using Reynolds' (1976) categorization, each sampled study mostly utilized a causal process form of hypothesis development. They used interconnected definitions and statements, of equal importance, to describe situations and mechanisms through which effectuation affects business performance. A similar but more expanded classification can be found in the work of Pawar (2009). Adopting a slightly modified version of Pawar's (2009) categories, hypotheses in 18 sampled studies predominantly were based on existing conceptual literature and empirical findings, ten were based on an existing model or theoretical perspective, and four used premises mostly based on definitions and assumptions. What is interesting is that the remaining five studies did not develop and put forward a hypothesis on the effect of effectuation on business performance even though they displayed the statistical results of this effect.

Looking more narrowly at the construction of the hypothesis in the research context (Table 18.4), most hypotheses (11) were developed from their own literature of each effectuation principle or set of means. Next, eight hypotheses heavily relied on

the results from the previous literature of the impact of effectuation on business performance, seven hypotheses were established thorough the foundational literature of effectuation theory, while six hypotheses borrowed from the theory and findings of the
dependent variable to make the connection with effectuation. Lastly, only four hypotheses utilized other theoretical perspectives as the foundation for the subsequent results.

Table 18.4: Theoretical perspectives used for hypothesis development.

Theoretical perspective	Frequency
Each principle/ set of means from own literature	11
From the previous literature of the impact of effectuation	8
From the effectuation literature	7
From the literature of the dependent variable	6
None because it was not a hypothesis	5
Social construction theory, absorptive capacity, resource-based view, learning school approach	1

Source: compiled by the authors.
Note: the total frequency exceeds the total number of articles because
some articles used different approaches for different hypothesis.

Effectuation can be measured in many ways, but the two most dominant approaches
in the whole effectuation literature are those developed by Chandler et al. (2011) and
Brettel et al. (2012) (McKelvie et al., 2020). These two methods are the most utilized in
the sampled studies, but the methodology that Chandler et al. (2011) used was by far
the most dominant approach. Their approach can be found in 24 studies, while five
studies used the approach by Brettel et al. (2012). It is interesting to note that four
studies developed their methodology even though the measures of effectuation as presented by Chandler et al. (2011) and Brettel et al. (2012) were already well established
and accepted in the effectuation literature. Their methodologies were not used by subsequent studies. The full list of methodologies for measuring effectuation is displayed
in Table 18.5.

Table 18.5: Method of measuring effectuation.

Method	Frequency
Chandler et al., 2011	24
Brettel et al., 2012	5
Own method	4
Appelhoff et al., 2016	2
Werhahn et al., 2015	2

Source: compiled by the authors.
Note: Brettel et al., 2012 developed their own method and this was
accounted for in Brettel et al., 2012, not in "Own method."

After looking at the method for measuring effectuation, the next step in the analysis is to examine what analytical methods scientists used to test the impact of effectuation on business performance. The most dominant analytical method, as presented in Table 18.6, was hierarchical linear regression (13) followed by ordinary least squares regression (9). Structural equation modelling was also heavily used with total usage of seven for a covariance-based approach and four for a variance-based approach. Looking at the chronological order, early studies did not employ hierarchical linear regression often. It was not until 2018 when it became the leading method. This is intriguing for two reasons.

Reason number one relates to the inherent limitations that pertain to hierarchical linear regression. Hierarchical linear regression is one type of variance partitioning where, through the model, the researcher incrementally divides the coefficient of determination (R2) into chunks with each chunk attributed to a variable or a block of variables (Pedhazur, 1997). Relying on the coefficient of determination is problematic in social research since this measure is sample-specific and it is difficult to generalize the results of the model of the sample to the population (Pedhazur, 1997). Furthermore, it is difficult to judge the superiority of one model against others using the coefficient of determination (Berk, 1983) and it is not designed to give real-world pragmatical recommendations (Cain & Watts, 1970). These are the reasons why other analytical methods, such as structural equation modelling, are preferable to hierarchical linear regression (Keith, 2015). In addition, effectuation is conceptualized as a latent variable in approaches by Chandler et al. (2011) and Brettel et al. (2012). Latent variables are more suited for structural equation modelling than for hierarchical linear regression (Keith, 2015). Given these arguments, it is perplexing to notice a rise in the use of hierarchical linear regression in the sampled studies. One possible reason is that researchers could inflate the statistical significance of the effectuation variable. This could be done by manipulating the order of entry. In other words, the first block of variables that are entered into hierarchical regression has a higher chance of being statistically significant (Keith, 2015). Fortunately, the argument that this is the reason for the use of hierarchical linear regression must be dismissed because none of the sampled studies used the effectuation variable in the first block of variables entered into the analysis. Lastly, because the order of entry is important in hierarchical linear regression, researchers must develop a criterion for how variables are put into the model. One possible criterion is time (Keith, 2015), but none of the sampled studies put forward a criterion or a discussion on this issue.

Reason number two concerns the compatibility of the chosen method of measuring effectuation with the chosen analytical method for testing hypotheses. More specifically, most studies, as was mentioned previously, used the questions from Chandler et al. (2011) to measure effectuation. However, according to Chandler et al. (2011), effectuation is a second-order reflective-formative construct. This is important when discussing the analytical method that researchers use because most methods are not designed to accommodate formative constructs. The method that is recommended in those situations is a partial least squares structural equation modelling or PLS-SEM (Hair et al., 2017) which was used only four times in the sampled studies. Out of the 24 studies that choose the methodology of Chandler et al. (2011), eight applied hierarchical linear regression while only two used PLS-SEM. In other words, in studies where the method of Chandler et al. (2011) was selected and where PLS-SEM was not adopted, effectuation was not conceptualized as a reflective-formative construct. This finding is puzzling and there seems to be no explanation for this development. One can possibly point to the early claimed shortcomings (e.g. Antonakis et al., 2010) of PLS-SEM as a reason for this observation. However, criticisms of this sort have been answered and the use of PLS-SEM is growing in other business disciplines (Hair et al., 2011, 2012, 2017, 2019). It is worth mentioning that only one of the sampled studies (Urban & Heydenrych, 2015) that used the measurement of Chandler et al. (2011) aand did not use PLS-SEM put forward a discussion or gave reasons for not conceptualizing effectuation as a reflective-formative construct.

Table 18.6: Analytical methods that were utilized in the studies.

Analytical method	Frequency
Hierarchical linear regression	13
Ordinary least squares regression	9
Covariance-based structural equation modelling	7
Partial least squares structural equation modelling	4
Hierarchical linear modeling, Logistic regression, Multiplicative heteroscedasticity regression, and Multivariate linear regression	1

Source: compiled by the authors

The final step in the analysis consists of looking at the actual results of the effect of effectuation and its principles on business performance. These results are displayed in Table 18.7.

It is not surprising that effectuation as a whole is the most tested in the sampled studies. The vast majority that examined this relation (21 studies) found that effectuation has a positive impact on business performance, while 14 studies did not test this relationship at all. Most of the studies that did not test for this effect did not do so because of the method of measuring effectuation. In other words, the methods that were utilized, for instance, Brettel et al. (2012), in most of these studies only conceptualized principles of effectuation, not the whole effectual logic. This approach, of only testing the principles, has a drawback when looking through the lens of effectuation theory since effectuation theory is more than a collection of principles. Effectuation theory has implications for questions that go beyond principles and business performance, questions such as whether or not the external environment of the entrepreneur is risky or uncertain and whether or not the entrepreneurial opportunities are created or discovered (Sarasvathy, 2001, 2009; Sarasvathy & Dew, 2005). This is the reason why it is advisable to further modify methods that do not conceptualize effectuation as a whole, for instance how Futterer et al. (2018) adapted the approach of

Brettel et al. (2012) to achieve a single effectuation variable. By doing so, practical recommendations are more easily achieved since it is not clear whether or not an effectual approach to entrepreneurship can be advised to real-world entrepreneurs if, for instance, a study looks at only principles of effectuation and finds that two principles are statistically significant while the other two are not. What this recommendation does not imply is that future studies should not test for individual effects of various principles. Rather it means that effectuation as a whole should be examined and that in the next steps authors should look at which principle has the most predominant effect.

When looking at the sole principles, exploitation of contingencies/ flexibility is the most examined and the one that has the most empirical support of having a positive effect on business performance. Other principles have more erratic effects on business performance. For instance, affordable loss seems to have the most dubious impact on business performance given that only four out of the 16 studies found that it has a positive effect on business performance while five studies reported this effect to be negative. Partnerships/ pre-commitment and experimentation do not have that many confirmed negative effects, but a high percentage of studies found that they had no statistically significant effect. Means/questions of effectuation were statistically significant in most studies that reported this effect, whereas controlling the future was the least studied principle of effectuation.

All these effects were tested on cross-sectional data, or put differently none used longitudinal data. What is interesting is that 28 out of the 37 sampled studies recommended future studies to collect and examine longitudinal data. This could mean that researchers are aware of the importance of further enhancing the validity of the causal effect of effectuation on business performance but due to procedural or methodological difficulties are unable to conduct such inquiry.

Table 18.7: Effects of effectuation on firm performance.

Variables	Frequency			
	Positive	Negative	Not significant	Not tested
Effectuation	21	2	5	14
Exploitation of contingencies/ flexibility	10	2	5	24
Affordable loss	4	5	7	23
Partnerships/ pre-commitment	7	1	6	25
Means/ questions of effectuation	8	1	3	27
Experimentation	5	–	3	31
Controlling the future	1	–	–	36

Source: compiled by the authors.
Note: the total frequency of some variables exceeds the total number of articles because some articles used more than one dependent variable.

Discussion and Conclusions

This paper tried to analyze the current status of scientific research on the effect of an effectual approach to entrepreneurship on business performance. Through the use of tools regularly employed in semi-systematic literature reviews, this goal was accomplished by examining quantitative studies in the Web of Science and Scopus database that tested that effect. In other words, this paper aims to congregate the extant knowledge and to scrutinize the state of research on the effectuation-business performance topic.

The overall contribution of this study is to improve the understanding of cumulative and unarranged scientific knowledge by carefully mapping the dynamics and the structure of the aforementioned topic. More specifically, the contribution lies in the identification and detection of emerging research trends in the field, the most used publication outlets, the most examined context, the quality of the theoretical underpinning, the appropriateness of statistical procedures and the predominant outcomes. Moreover, avenues for future research and practical implications are proposed.

The analysis shows that the research on this topic is gaining ground in high-quality scientific journals and that publications are not clustered in a few of these journals. The vast majority of these articles used samples of SMEs and collected their samples from only one country with China being the dominant country from where the sampled firms were drawn. Articles that have been published two years ago or less have not yet emerged as being influential, in terms of the total number of citations, in the field.

Theoretical perspectives of hypothesis development were examined next. Like most scientific social research, every sampled study employed a causal process form of hypothesis development. It can be estimated that the quality of hypothesis development is high since most studies used existing conceptual literature and empirical findings, either in the effectuation literature or in a related field of research to effectuation, as a theoretical grounding for their hypotheses. Only a few studies predominantly relied on definitions and assumptions. Examining all the hypotheses individually, most hypotheses were based on the literature of each principle/set of means, followed by the previous literature of the impact of effectuation on business performance and from the effectuation literature.

The methods of the measurement of effectuation were in line with the trends of the literature. What was surprising is the finding that hierarchical linear regression became the most used statistical method to test the significance of the effect of effectuation on business performance. Two reasons were given on why this approach is suboptimal.

Lastly, the results of the sampled studies were examined. Effectuation, in most studies, displayed a positive effect on business performance. The picture gets murkier with individual principles of effectuation. Some principles seem to have a positive effect on business performance, while for others it can be said that this effect is not significant or even negative.

Limitations of the Study

Like all scientific research, this study has certain limitations. The first limitation pertains to the chosen databases. Web of Science and Scopus, although highly influential, are not the only databases that effectuation research is published in. Studies published in other databases, such as Google Scholar, might have added a more nuanced picture of this emerging field. Secondly, this study bundled all effectuation-business performance research into one category. It is possible that the theoretical setting and the results of the studies are dependent on some contingent factor. For example, the conceptual framework for postulating that effectuation has an impact on business performance, as well as the outcomes of that relationship, could change depending on the type and structure of the industry where entrepreneurs operate in. The third limitation is the sole use of a snapshot of published studies. Put differently, the dynamics of the use of methodologies and results of the studies are neglected. It is possible that those, and other factors as well, changed through time.

Implications for Future Research

With regard to scientific explorations, a set of recommendations for future research can be put forward. Firstly, as was mentioned, most studies acquired their sample from one country. Future research should accumulate samples from multiple countries since this can result in a more nuanced examination of the effect of effectuation on business performance. Moreover, examining the impact of context change can be accomplished through sampling entrepreneurs in multiple countries.

Second, even though it is to be expected that over the passage of time more and more studies will mainly use the previous literature on the impact of effectuation on business performance, we advise the authors to try to expand the theoretical basis of this relationship in subsequent studies since it could yield more stimulating philosophical discussion and empirical investigations. Furthermore, some studies did not develop a hypothesis for the effect of effectuation on business performance. While respecting every author's freedom to conceptualize their own articles, it is advisable in this stage of research on effectuation to try to conceptualize novel ways of understanding the aforementioned effectuation-business performance relationship.

Third, authors in subsequent research should consider the statistical method they will use in their studies. Other statistical methods are more appropriate than hierarchical linear regression in the context of this topic given the nature of the effectuation variable and the limitations of this method. In addition, there appear to be inconsistencies with employing hierarchical linear regression and the method of measuring effectuation that conceptualize it as a reflective-formative construct. In those situations, partial least squares structural equation modelling is to be preferred.

Lastly, because of these inconsistencies in the results and the fact that effectuation theory is more than just the sum of its principles, the recommendation for future studies is to test the effect of effectuation as a whole. This recommendation holds even for studies that use methods of measuring effectuation through principles only. There are examples in the current literature of how modifying this method can yield such results.

Practical Implications

To answer the question posed by the title of this article one needs to look at the whole process of testing and the sheer number of results on the impact of effectuation on business performance. In the current state of research, effectuation as a whole should be recommended, with caution, as a way of thinking and running the business of real-world entrepreneurs. The reasons it should be recommended are related to the strengths of the analyzed articles. As a whole, the studies are mostly published in high-quality scientific journals and they display a generally high level of hypothesis building, consistent use of measurement of effectuation, and considerable congruence on the effect of effectuation on business performance. But they also have some limitations, which is why the term "with caution" was used. These refer to the neglect of cultural context, use of suboptimal statistical procedures, and lack of consistency in the findings on the effects of individual effectual principles on business performance.

By further providing quality research results this recommendation could be made with more confidence.

References

Alzamora-Ruiz, J., del Mar Fuentes-Fuentes, M., & Martinez-Fiestas, M. (2021a). Together or separately? Direct and synergistic effects of effectuation and causation on innovation in technology-based SMEs. *International Entrepreneurship and Management Journal.*

Alzamora-Ruiz, J., Fuentes-Fuentes, M. del M., & Martinez-Fiestas, M. (2021b). Effectuation or causation to promote innovation in technology-based SMEs? The effects of strategic decision-making logics. *Technology Analysis & Strategic Management, 33*(7), 797–812.

Antonakis, J., Bendahan, S., Jacquart, P., & Lalive, R. (2010). On making causal claims: A review and recommendations. *The Leadership Quarterly, 21*(6), 1086–1120.

Appelhoff, D., Mauer, R., Collewaert, V., & Brettel, M. (2016). The conflict potential of the entrepreneur's decision-making style in the entrepreneur-investor relationship. *International Entrepreneurship and Management Journal, 12*(2), 601–623.

Berk, R.A. (1983). Applications of the general linear model to survey data. In P. Rossi, J. Wright & A. Anderson (Eds.), *Handbook of survey research* (pp. 495–546). Elsevier.

Blauth, M., Mauer, R., & Brettel, M. (2014). Fostering creativity in new product development through entrepreneurial decision making: Fostering creativity in new product development. *Creativity and Innovation Management, 23*(4), 495–509.

Brettel, M., Mauer, R., Engelen, A., & Küpper, D. (2012). Corporate effectuation: Entrepreneurial action and its impact on R&D project performance. *Journal of Business Venturing, 27*(2), 167–184.

Cai, L., Guo, R., Fei, Y., & Liu, Z. (2017). Effectuation, exploratory learning and new venture performance: Evidence from China. *Journal of Small Business Management, 55*(3), 388–403.

Cain, G.G., & Watts, H.W. (1970). Problems in making policy inferences from the Coleman report. *American Sociological Review, 35*(2), 228–242.

Chandler, G.N., DeTienne, D.R., McKelvie, A., & Mumford, T.V. (2011). Causation and effectuation processes: A validation study. *Journal of Business Venturing, 26*(3), 375–390.

de la Cruz, M.E., Verdú Jover, A.J., & Gómez Gras, J.M. (2018). Influence of the entrepreneur's social identity on business performance through effectuation. *European Research on Management and Business Economics, 24*(2), 90–96.

Deligianni, I., Sapouna, P., Voudouris, I., & Lioukas, S. (2020). An effectual approach to innovation for new ventures: The role of entrepreneur's prior start-up experience. *Journal of Small Business Management,* 1–32.

Deng, C., Yang, J., Loh, L., & Mu, T. (2021a). Exploring the antecedents and consequences of effectuation in NPD: The moderating role of firm size. *Technology Analysis & Strategic Management,* 1–15.

Deng, C., Yang, J., Su, Z., & Zhang, S. (2021b). The double-edged sword impact of effectuation on new product creativity: The moderating role of competitive intensity and firm size. *Journal of Business Research, 137,* 1–12.

Eijdenberg, E.L., Paas, L.J., & Masurel, E. (2017). Decision-making and small business growth in Burundi. *Journal of Entrepreneurship in Emerging Economies, 9*(1), 35–64.

Eyana, S.M., Masurel, E., & Paas, L.J. (2018). Causation and effectuation behaviour of Ethiopian entrepreneurs: Implications on performance of small tourism firms. *Journal of Small Business and Enterprise Development, 25*(5), 791–817.

Ferreira, J.J.M., Fernandes, C.I., & Kraus, S. (2019). Entrepreneurship research: Mapping intellectual structures and research trends. *Review of Managerial Science, 13*(1), 181–205.

Fischer, D., Greven, A., Tornow, M., & Brettel, M. (2021). On the value of effectuation processes for R&D alliances and the moderating role of R&D alliance experience. *Journal of Business Research, 135,* 606–619.

Fisher, G. (2012). Effectuation, Causation, and Bricolage: A Behavioral Comparison of Emerging Theories in Entrepreneurship Research. *Entrepreneurship Theory and Practice, 36*(5), 1019–1051.

Furlotti, M., Podoynitsyna, K., & Mauer, R. (2020). Means versus goals at the starting line: Performance and conditions of effectiveness of entrepreneurial action. *Journal of Small Business Management, 58*(2), 333–361.

Futterer, F., Schmidt, J., & Heidenreich, S. (2018). Effectuation or causation as the key to corporate venture success? Investigating effects of entrepreneurial behaviors on business model innovation and venture performance. *Long Range Planning, 51*(1), 64–81.

Grégoire, D.A., & Cherchem, N. (2020). A structured literature review and suggestions for future effectuation research. *Small Business Economics, 54*(3), 621–639.

Guo, R. (2019). Effectuation, opportunity shaping and innovation strategy in high-tech new ventures. *Management Decision, 57*(1), 115–130.

Guo, R., Cai, L., & Zhang, W. (2016). Effectuation and causation in new internet venture growth: The mediating effect of resource bundling strategy. *Internet Research, 26*(2), 460–483.

Hair, J.F., Ringle, C.M., & Sarstedt, M. (2011). PLS-SEM: Indeed a silver bullet. *Journal of Marketing Theory and Practice, 19*(2), 139–152.

Hair, J.F., Sarstedt, M., & Ringle, C.M. (2019). Rethinking some of the rethinking of partial least squares. *European Journal of Marketing*, *53*(4), 566–584.

Hair, J.F., Sarstedt, M., Ringle, C.M., & Mena, J.A. (2012). An assessment of the use of partial least squares structural equation modeling in marketing research. *Journal of the Academy of Marketing Science*, *40*(3), 414–433.

Hair, J., Hult, T., Ringle, C., & Sarstedt, M. (2017). *A primer on partial least squares structural equation modeling (PLS-SEM)* (2nd ed.). Sage.

Jisr, R.E., & Maamari, B.E. (2017). Effectuation: Exploring a third dimension to tacit knowledge. *Knowledge and Process Management*, *24*(1), 72–78.

Keith, T.Z. (2015). *Multiple regression and beyond: An introduction to multiple regression and structural equation modeling* (2nd ed.). Routledge.

Knight, F. (1921). *Risk Uncertainty and Profit*. Houghton Mifflin.

Laskovaia, A., Shirokova, G., & Morris, M.H. (2017). National culture, effectuation, and new venture performance: Global evidence from student entrepreneurs. *Small Business Economics*, *49*(3), 687–709.

Long, D., Wang, H., & Wang, P. (2021). Built to sustain: The effect of entrepreneurial decision-making logic on new venture sustainability. *Sustainability*, *13*(4), 2170.

Matalamäki, M.J. (2017). Effectuation, an emerging theory of entrepreneurship – towards a mature stage of the development. *Journal of Small Business and Enterprise Development*, *24*(4), 928–949.

McKelvie, A., Chandler, G.N., DeTienne, D.R., & Johansson, A. (2020). The measurement of effectuation: Highlighting research tensions and opportunities for the future. *Small Business Economics*, *54*(3), 689–720.

Mthanti, T.S., & Urban, B. (2014). Effectuation and entrepreneurial orientation in high-technology firms. *Technology Analysis & Strategic Management*, *26*(2), 121–133.

Newbert, S.L., David, R.J., & Han, S.-K. (2014). Rarely pure and never simple: Assessing cumulative evidence in strategic management. *Strategic Organization*, *12*(2), 142–154.

Pacho, F.T., & Mushi, H. (2020). The effect of effectuation set of means on new venture performance: Flexibility principle as a mediating factor. *Journal of Entrepreneurship in Emerging Economies*.

Parida, V., George, N.M., Lahti, T., & Wincent, J. (2016). Influence of subjective interpretation, causation, and effectuation on initial venture sale. *Journal of Business Research*, *69*(11), 4815–4819.

Pati, R., Ghobadian, A., Nandakumar, M.K., Hitt, M.A., & O'Regan, N. (2021). Entrepreneurial behavior and firm performance: The mediating role of business model novelty. *R&D Management*.

Pawar, B. (2009). *Theory building for hypothesis specification in organizational studies*. Sage.

Pedhazur, E.J. (1997). *Multiple regression in behavioral research: Explanation and prediction* (3rd ed.). Harcourt Brace College Publishers.

Peng, X.B., Liu, Y.L., Jiao, Q.Q., Feng, X.B., & Zheng, B. (2020). The nonlinear effect of effectuation and causation on new venture performance: The moderating effect of environmental uncertainty. *Journal of Business Research*, *117*, 112–123.

Perry, J.T., Chandler, G.N., & Markova, G. (2012). Entrepreneurial effectuation: A review and suggestions for future research. *Entrepreneurship Theory and Practice*, *36*(4), 837–861.

Reynolds, P. (1976). *A primer in theory construction*. Bobbs – Merrill Co.

Roach, D.C., Ryman, J.A., & Makani, J. (2016). Effectuation, innovation and performance in SMEs: An empirical study. *European Journal of Innovation Management*, *19*(2), 214–238.

Ruiz-Jiménez, J.M., Ruiz-Arroyo, M., & del Mar Fuentes-Fuentes, M. (2020). The impact of effectuation, causation, and resources on new venture performance: Novice versus expert entrepreneurs. *Small Business Economics*.

Sarasvathy, S. (2001). Causation and effectuation: Toward a theoretical shift from economic inevitability to entrepreneurial contingency. *The Academy of Management Review*, *26*(2), 243–263.

Sarasvathy, S. (2009). *Effectuation: Elements of entrepreneurial expertise*. Edward Elgar.

Sarasvathy, S.D., & Dew, N. (2005). New market creation through transformation. *Journal of Evolutionary Economics*, *15*(5), 533–565.

Shirokova, G., Morris, M.H., Laskovaia, A., & Micelotta, E. (2021). Effectuation and causation, firm performance, and the impact of institutions: A multi-country moderation analysis. *Journal of Business Research*, *129*, 169–182.

Shirokova, G., Osiyevskyy, O., Laskovaia, A., & MahdaviMazdeh, H. (2020). Navigating the emerging market context: Performance implications of effectuation and causation for small and medium enterprises during adverse economic conditions in Russia. *Strategic Entrepreneurship Journal*, *14*(3), 470–500.

Smolka, K.M., Verheul, I., Burmeister-Lamp, K., & Heugens, P.P.M.A.R. (2018). Get it together! Synergistic effects of causal and effectual decision-making logics on venture performance. *Entrepreneurship Theory and Practice*, *42*(4), 571–604.

Snyder, H. (2019). Literature review as a research methodology: An overview and guidelines. *Journal of Business Research*, *104*, 333–339.

Szambelan, S., Jiang, Y., & Mauer, R. (2020). Breaking through innovation barriers: Linking effectuation orientation to innovation performance. *European Management Journal*, *38*(3), 425–434.

Szambelan, S.M., & Jiang, Y.D. (2020). Effectual control orientation and innovation performance: Clarifying implications in the corporate context. *Small Business Economics*, *54*(3), 865–882.

Urban, B., & Heydenrych, J. (2015). Technology orientation and effectuation – links to firm performance in the renewable energy sector of South Africa. *The South African Journal of Industrial Engineering*, *26*(3), 125–136.

Vanderstraeten, J., Hermans, J., van Witteloostuijn, A., & Dejardin, M. (2020). SME innovativeness in a dynamic environment: Is there any value in combining causation and effectuation? *Technology Analysis & Strategic Management*, *32*(11), 1277–1293.

Welter, C., & Kim, S. (2018). Effectuation under risk and uncertainty: A simulation model. *Journal of Business Venturing*, *33*(1), 100–116.

Werhahn, D., Mauer, R., Flatten, T.C., & Brettel, M. (2015). Validating effectual orientation as strategic direction in the corporate context. *European Management Journal*, *33*(5), 305–313.

Wu, L., Liu, H., & Su, K. (2020). Exploring the dual effect of effectuation on new product development speed and quality. *Journal of Business Research*, *106*, 82–93.

Xia, L., Luo, B., & Sun, Y. (2019). How can entrepreneurs achieve success in chaos?: The effects of entrepreneurs' effectuation on new venture performance in China. *Kybernetes*, *49*(5), 1407–1428.

Yang, T., Hughes, K.D., & Zhao, W. (2020). Resource combination activities and new venture growth: Exploring the role of effectuation, causation, and entrepreneurs' gender. *Journal of Small Business Management*, 1–29.

Yoon, J.H., & Cho, E. (2021). Effectuation (EF) and causation (CS) on venture performance and entrepreneurs' dispositions affecting the reliance on EF and CS. *Entrepreneurship Research Journal*, 20200054.

Yu, X., Tao, Y., Tao, X., Xia, F., & Li, Y. (2018). Managing uncertainty in emerging economies: The interaction effects between causation and effectuation on firm performance. *Technological Forecasting and Social Change*, *135*, 121–131.

Hary Febriansyah, Zulaicha Parastuty, and Dieter Bögenhold

19 How do SMEs Perform in Developing Countries? The Case of Indonesia

Abstract: This study aims to explore how Small and Medium-sized Enterprises (SMEs) manage their businesses, recognize the importance of resources inside the organization, and manage changes. It examines growth factors for SMEs in Indonesia through the lens of internal and external factors by adopting the framework of the Four Dimension Conceptual Model (FDCM) by Salder et al. (2020) methodologically using a multi-case analysis. The data were gathered by in-depth interviews and then cross-case analysis was used to interpret the data. Four dimensions have emerged as critical pillars for understanding which factors influence SME performance and growth. The focus lies on an integrated framework of determinants rather than individual units by exploring both internal and external factors in the context of SME growth in Indonesia. Awareness of such factors is an opportunity to arrive at a more adequate understanding of SME growth in developing countries such as Indonesia. The study answers the question of how owners manage the visions and daily operations of their businesses, with the most critical dimensions being strategies and the environment. Finally, a few implications are drawn for policymakers and business practices.

Keywords: Small and Medium Enterprises, growth, business strategy, Indonesia

Introduction

Indonesia has a growing number of Small and Medium-sized Enterprises (SMEs) with some 26 million SMEs in 2016 (Badan Pusat Statistik, 2019). SMEs employ 97 percent of the workforce and contribute 63 percent to the country's GDP, the highest value in Southeast Asia (ADB, 2018). According to Griffiths et al. (2009) and Gamidulleva et al. (2020), the growth of SMEs has a positive effect on local, regional, and national economic growth. Their impact can also be seen in the form of job creation, competitive-

Acknowledgements: We would like to express a Highest Appreciation to Professor Mark Gilman (University of Derby Regional Economic Observatory, the United Kingdom), a Principal Researcher while conducting this joint research (the call sign is Promoting Sustainable Performance for Small Medium Enterprises) for the concept preparation and data collection.

Hary Febriansyah, Center of Knowledge for Business Competitiveness (CK4BC), School of Business and Management, Bandung Institute of Technology (ITB), Indonesia
Zulaicha Parastuty, Department of International Management at the Johannes Kepler University Linz, Austria; University of Klagenfurt, Austria
Dieter Bögenhold, University of Klagenfurt, Austria

https://doi.org/10.1515/9783110747652-020

ness, and a reduction in regional inequalities (Zhao & Thompson, 2019). Given their significance, this is an interesting research area and it is worth exploring the growth of SMEs in Indonesia more deeply.

Growth determination has been conceptualized in many ways. The most common viewpoints of the determinants of SME growth by previous researchers are based on internal (e.g. Cowling et al., 2015; El Shoubaki et al., 2020) and external factors (e.g. Love & Roper, 2015; Nkawabi & Mboya, 2019) or a combination of the two (Kraja & Osmani, 2015). Internal factors include labor, learning capabilities, marketing strategies, levels of innovation, and technological investments (Cowling et al, 2015) while external factors include financial support, laws and regulations, business location, competition, globalization, and management as well as other trade barriers (Love & Roper, 2015). In other words, internal factors can represent structural and behavioral characteristics that shape SMEs' performance (Dobbs & Hamilton, 2007) while external factors can serve as catalysts for new capabilities and resources (Bager et al., 2015). In fact, resources are among the most important assets for driving SMEs' success because managerial ties have a positive impact on performance both directly and indirectly (Zulu-Chisanga et al., 2021).

This study explores both internal and external determinants of growth in the Indonesian SME context in order to gain a contextual understanding of growth theory (Ipinnaiye et al., 2017), thus contributing to potential developments in the growth process of SMEs in the contextual setting of an emerging market, i.e. Indonesia, and including implications for policymakers and business practices. This study follows the conceptual framework proposed by Salder et al. (2020) which consists of internal growth as a resource-based view (RBV) and external factors as a network-based view (NBV). The RBV focuses on internal resources and capabilities, while the NBV explains more about innovation or knowledge-based networks. Growth factors are explored through the lens of internal and external factors by adopting the framework of the Four Dimensions Conceptual Model (FDCM) by Salder et al. (2020). The remainder of this paper has the following structure. The theoretical background of growth theories is discussed in Section two and the research design is outlined in Section three. Section four then describes the findings of the study of all growth factors in Indonesian SMEs, with Section five providing a detailed discussion of the data analysis. The conclusion, limitations, and future research are summarized in the last section.

Literature Review

Resource-Based View

The resource-based view (RBV) is the most influential paradigm for interpreting strategic management since it focuses on internal resources and capabilities to define and maintain a business's competitive advantage and performance (Runyan et al., 2006;

Eniola & Ektebang, 2014). The company's resources and capabilities are important because they are the foundation of the company's competitiveness and performance, including all the assets, organizational processes, information, and knowledge that allow the company to devise and implement a strategy to grow and to make strategic decisions when competing in an external business environment (Barney, 1991). Competitive advantages are used to allow an organization to maintain the advantages gained by their superior resources. Wernerfelt (1984) explains that the RBV also addresses an organization's competitive advantage in terms of its tangible or intangible assets. Tangible resources include financial capital (e.g. equity capital, debt capital, retained earnings) and physical capital (e.g. machinery and buildings), access to capital and location (among others) while intangible resources consist of the organization's culture, learning, networks, and reputation among others (Winter, 1987). Yet, the RBV argues that not all resources have the potential to create competitive advantages (Runyan et al., 2006). Barney (1991) defined four main characteristics that a resource must provide in order to have a sustainable competitive advantage: it must be valuable, scarce, mobile, and non-substitutable.

The RBV has become a foundational concept in SME analysis, focusing on firm-based acquisition, activation, and management of resources capable of offering sustained competitive advantage (Barney et al., 2011). The RBV explores the potential of a firm's resources and generates sustained competitive advantage to achieve growth (Barney, 1991). It suggests that there can be heterogeneity among firms to sustain competitive advantage as well as to deploy key resources (Barney, 1991). Thus, the impact of the RBV on SME creation debates has been central (Sadler, et al., 2020). For small business owners, entrepreneurial orientation and social capital are management skills, i.e. resources which lead to competitive advantages (Runyan et al., 2006). Strategic management is frequently asserted to be especially important just for a firm, and it often happened that SMEs did not pay sufficient attention to their strategic management (Eniola & Ektebang, 2014). Therefore, the RBV analysis of SME growth describes resources not within the firm but within the context of the firm, incorporating a number of sub- and supra-firm-level resources through dynamic capabilities to understand the changing external environment (Salder et al., 2020). Such internal resources and capabilities are crucial, particularly in SMEs where their limitations remain a recognized barrier to growth (Teece et al., 1997).

Network-Based View

The network-based view explains the importance of focusing explicitly on processes over determinants but also leads to a transition in how the functioning of a firm is conceptualized from resource-based to network-based views (Sadler et al., 2020). Network-based approaches to regional studies and economic development that focus on innovation or knowledge-based networks as an important component in building an entrepreneurial and resilient regional economy are becoming more popular (Huggins & Thompson, 2013). Network capital, which consists of relational assets in the form of strategic and calculative inter-organizational networks specifically designed to facilitate knowledge flow and innovation, better explains how economically beneficial knowledge is accessed. These inter-organizational networks are concerned with the interactions, relationships, and ties that exist between firms and may arise as a result of the need to access new technology, skills, or expertise in order to compete. Network interactions facilitate internationalization, moderate perceptions of the risk of entering foreign markets, reduce investment costs and the time span of integration processes (Chaney & Lin, 2007), are relevant to economic growth, and improve performance (Huber et al., 2011). The network perspective provides the best explanation for modern business models which focus on high-level technology and worldwide marketing (Hosseini & Dadfar, 2012). Regions are increasingly considered important sources for economic and organizational development in a global economy; likewise, entrepreneurship, and the innovation it has the capacity to spawn, is increasingly considered to be a key factor underpinning the future growth trajectories of regions (Huggins & Thompson, 2015).

In an era of increasing start-up activity, accelerating technological interaction, barrier reductions, and ongoing vertical disintegration of production activities, networks have become more prominent (Sadler et al., 2020). Network capital is vital for entrepreneurial companies as they seek to access and source knowledge (Huggins & Thompson, 2015). Inter-organizational networks established by entrepreneurs and their companies give them access to the knowledge they require to innovate and grow and may also ultimately contribute to creating and sustaining innovation and growth in the region in which they are located (Huggins & Thompson, 2015) Inter-organizational networks and knowledge sources are also important assets for competitiveness (Lechner & Dowling, 2003). In creating a competitive advantage, the relationship between resources and the creation, utilization, and exploitation of networks is important in response to specific market challenges (Barney, 1991).

The Four Dimensions Conceptual Model

The growth of SMEs is supported by internal factors such as human capital, capital, innovation, and infrastructure as well as by the external conditions of the company such as industry growth, technology, and regulations (Ipinnaiye et al., 2017; Bilal et al., 2016; Nkawabi & Mboya, 2019). An organization's internal factors require company-related factors that influence its capacity to achieve the specified goals and execute viable strategies that lead, consequently, to its success (Oluwadare & Oni, 2015). Meanwhile, an external factor environment is a factor outside a company's control that may impact the company's performance (Ontorael & Suhadak, 2017). The internal factors of a company can be emphasized through the RBV for formulating management strategies so that the company can achieve a sustainable competitive advantage in its markets and industries (Freiling, 2008; Barney et al., 2011). It is necessary for the SME growth process not only to see it within the context of the firm but also to increase its capabilities of sensing and understanding change in the external environment. Therefore, the concept from a resource-based to a network-based view to create a distinctive response to specific market challenges is required to accelerate technological interaction, barrier reductions, and ongoing vertical disintegration of production activities (Barney, 1991).

Resources are classified in four distinct forms or dimensions adapted from Salder et al. (2020), namely characteristics, assets, strategy, and environment. The characteristics dimension is defined as a set of structural characteristics, including age, size, industry, and ownership, which determine the firms' capacity for, ability in, and commitment to growth. The acquisition and embedding of organizational resources, such as finance, intellectual property, and human capital (Hayton, 2005), are a company-internal asset dimension to shape the growth process. The strategy dimension is found in multiple forms at firm- and sub-firm-level representing planned and behavioral responses to evolving environmental conditions (Chebo & Kute, 2019), contributing toward improvements in resources and capabilities to meet environmental challenges. Regional, national, and global economic trajectories impact SME growth, changing the critical resource environments dimension and providing human and social capital, knowledge and communications infrastructures, and cultural-economic institutions (Love & Roper, 2015). Characteristics and the environment are significant factors that support the growth of SMEs (Sadler et al., 2020).

Research Design

Multi-Case Study

The study makes use of exploratory research. An exploratory study is a broad, objective, structured, pre-arranged undertaking aimed at maximizing the discovery of generalizations that lead to the explanation and analysis of the phenomena (Stebbins, 2001). The exploratory analysis technique used here is the qualitative research method. Qualitative analysis is a holistic approach including discovery. Creswell (1994) defines a qualitative study as an effective model that occurs in a natural setting that allows the researcher to establish a level of detail from a high degree of involvement in the actual experience.

The authors carried out their qualitative analysis using a multi-case study approach (Yin, 2018). A case study approach investigates phenomena in their natural context, using various data collection techniques to obtain knowledge from one or more entities (people, groups, or organizations). This research involves a within-case and cross-case analysis to clarify the case study. Through within-case and cross-case analyses, the phenomena may be observed in their natural environment, allowing a clearer understanding of the nature of the phenomenon to be studied in its natural setting, thereby facilitating a better understanding of the nature of the phenomenon and enabling exploratory inquiries (Yin, 2018). In addition, the authors present a preliminary questionnaire in the form of descriptive analysis to strengthen the qualitative findings.

Data Collection

First, an online survey was conducted using a structured questionnaire. The results of this online survey were used to select the participants for the in-depth interviews based on the firm's age, i.e. older than five years, and firm size, i.e. more than 10 employees. We then contacted the individuals in the firms who were responsible for their daily operation such as the business owner or general manager. We developed an interview protocol to guide a more structured interview. This study analyzed four SMEs owned by a resident of Indonesia. They are run with or without a legal body by a person or business institution with maximum net assets excluding land and buildings. Their annual total revenue is less than IDR 50 billion (approx. USD 356,000), which means they are categorized as small companies according to Indonesian classifications.

We conducted interviews from January to October 2020 by teleconferencing or phone. In-depth interviews were conducted with one of the decision makers in each SME, such as the director, chief executive officer, supervisor, or human resources manager. Interview topics related to business development, human resource management, business strategies, and operation. The interviews were recorded, transcribed, and translated. The informants involved in this study were invited to join business workshops and mentoring programs run by Bandung University.

The first phase of the research focused on a within-case analysis (Yin, 2018) which included reading the transcripts of the interview in order to understand each case. The authors then performed a cross-case study (Yin, 2018) to determine similarities and differences, depending on the research topics, in order to classify determinants of growth in SMEs. This research uses three steps of data analysis: reduction, display, and conclusion drawing/verification (Miles & Huberman, 1994). Data reduction should result in a condensed description of the original data which is much smaller in quantity but retains its quality. Table 19.1 shows the respondent characteristics in this research.

Table 19.1: Characteristics of respondents.

Company name ID	Location	Year of foundation	Total employees	Revenue (USD)	Main Activities
A	Jakarta	2015	18	8,500	Leather craft
B	Bandung	2012	35	3,500	Interior design – IT
C	Malang	2011	10	106,000	Software – IT
D	Surabaya	2001	12	68,000	Leather craft

Data Analysis

Case Study Narrative – Company A

Company A is a leather craft brand from Jakarta that grew out of a hobby of creating personalized genuine leather preferences into a commercial business that has been in existence for five years. Its growth revenue and profit tend to increase by 3–5 percent per year. Not only looking for profit, they also educate buyers about raw leather and fine leather. Based on its size, this company is a micro business. In the face of dynamic business changes, companies tend to react to change as it occurs because they want to keep innovating but do not want to reduce the quality of the products they produce. In running this business, the owner is always open-minded and customer oriented.

The company currently has a total of 18 employees and it is predicted that it will need 3–5 percent more to support company growth. The company uses internal funds to conduct its business which are allocated to business operations, from purchasing raw materials to producing consumer products. Its revenue is made up of 20 percent from newly marketed products, 60 percent from products that the company has just developed, and the last 20 percent from products that have been marginally modified. The company tries to maintain communication with vendors and suppliers, who have pointed out that it needs rebranding to match the segmentation and target market that fits with the company's vision and mission so that it can achieve more significant growth. The company is building a network with several vendors because they play a vital role in running the company's business.

The company defines its strategies as developing business and increasing its market share. In its daily business activities, the company conducts market analysis and develops new products every three months which are executed directly by the internal team. The company also develops process innovations carried out in-house. Its marketing innovations relate to making new designs, promotions, and product placements. The company applies profit-related pay strategies and teamwork to motivate employees to work.

The market condition for leather crafts tends to be inconsistent; therefore, the company utilizes the latest technology to deal with those conditions in the form of social media for marketing and selling activities, software applications for monitoring and managing human resources and vendors, and an internal information management system for company data. Networks built with vendors help the company to fill the missing human capital when needed.

Case Study Narrative – Company B

Company B is a service-based interior designer and contractor with a home base in Bandung that has been operating for eight years. It provides bespoke solutions for its clients. Its purpose is to educate consumers about the world of interior design and architecture as well as to improve team members' prosperity. The business started off mending leaky roofs and so did not go directly into interior design. However, over time, thanks to many requests from customers, it finally focused more on interior and exterior design. In running his business the owner maintains integrity and trust, with integrity standing for responsibility, a professional attitude towards doing business, persistence, and mutual respect, etc. The three entrepreneurial competencies that the owner upholds are resilience, ambition, and a willingness to learn.

The company currently has a total of 35 employees. In 2019, its revenue was IDR 50,000,000 with a market diversification of 70 percent inside the province and 30 percent outside. The company's revenue and profit in 2019 increased by 5 percent over the previous year, with projected employee needs that were also higher. The owner is more interested in the substance that can be achieved and felt meaningfully by the company's employees. In managing human resources, Company B believes in the dreams of each employee and hopes that the company has the vehicle to achieve them. For payroll workers, the system is freelance on a daily basis and professional in nature: they are not bound by a contract, so the payment is based on the project being worked on. Training in relation to architecture is provided as and when opportunities arise, both for the owner and the core team. Customers and key suppliers are the most critical assets and the backbone for Company B. In order to have a good reputation with customers, the business has to maintain time efficiency, price reductions, flexibility in terms of payment, and quality control. This should also enable long-term customer sales with potential repeat orders. At the same time, clients can market and recommend the company's services to colleagues or relatives. With suppliers, especially of materials, the goal is to build long-term partnerships.

Company B defines its strategy as a step-by-step effort to achieve its goals, endeavoring to make every destination or step of the journey seen and clearly visible in terms of purpose and direction. The strategy used is carrying out in-depth consultations from the outset to synchronize the desires of consumers with their budget and to commit to the deadline. Each project is unique and challenging. Therefore, the team always undergoes evaluations of their work at the beginning and end of a project. Internally and in the shorter term, there is a structural evaluation every three and six months for the core team and craftsmen. In addition to that, long term goals are defined at the beginning of the year such as marketing and sales targets. The source of funding is mainly from private capital. The advantage is more time efficiency and quality control that is highly regarded because of the level of complexity and size of projects. The bigger the project, the greater the risk. In order to maintain quality control and demonstrate well-coordinated commitment, the company sets a timeline and puts limits on the quality of specifications. Company B really illustrates the effort of focusing on the process to keep their assets and maintain profits. To keep up with strong prices and the competition, direct surveys in the field are used, such as what products are trending at the moment, what furniture is being sought by the public, and what kind of design is preferred by the public. The company also follow competitors' developments to identify their innovations and problems so as to develop the business and be more vigilant to improve internally. For Corporate Social Responsibility, they try to use eco-friendly raw materials such as plywood and reduce waste.

In order to gain more information and expand their network, Company B has joined several associations such as KIDI, an Indonesian interior design community, and the Kampung Architect Forum to get to know other business people in the same sector and exchange information or share experiences. Then the benefits can be shared in relation to vendor information and a database on the interior design business. Over the past three years the number of projects has indeed increased. From 2012 to the present, interior trends have become increasingly important in Indonesia so that interior design has an impact on increasing market potential. Company B has anticipated and mapped the market for what is happening over the next few months or years so that they will be ready to face any threats in the future.

Case Study Narrative – Company C

Company C is a digital creative company in Malang, East Java, which has been operating for nine years. It is currently providing apps for the internet and smartphones. It started as an online tour and shuttle booking service and then transferred into web production. The shifts that are taking place in the industry are due to very competitive circumstances and internally the company is unable to overcome competitors to meet market demand. However, as they turn into a software app company, it is a crucial move forward to react to key takeaways.

The company is now running with 10 employees on sales of IDR 1,500,000,000 with a growth in revenues and profits of between 2 and 5 percent over the last year and a forecast increase of 2 to 4 percent in employee needs. Because of the company's transformation, the old team learned how to carry out business research, analyzed their internal capabilities, and built up a new team that could learn new knowledge before establishing the business idea to maintain their performance. The owner always emphasizes democracy to ensure harmonious cooperation when making decisions; his core competencies are openness and kinship when it comes to running the company. The capital comes from internal capital and grants. The owner includes employees when crafting company strategies because he feels that many things are not noticed when the strategy is created top down. Involving all employees in drawing up strategies helps the company to ensure they are understood by employees and cover the situation in the field. In addition, there is an indirect impact on transparency and synergy between employees and the company. The company has a good reputation in the eyes of its clients so it has a good brand image, connections in the IT community of Malang City for obtaining future projects, and qualified human resources for completing projects. These three assets help the company grow. The company fosters cooperation with its main customers and suppliers because these parties also help the company to grow. It has managed to retain its existing customers, who are satisfied with the performance the company provides. This has an impact on the sustainability of its future projects and provides a reference to the network that needs the company's services. The role of suppliers also plays an important role in company growth because they help invest considerable resources in supporting the company's business.

The strategy is aimed at the company's sustainability so that it can continue honing its performance, for example with software on selling activities (using recording software for selling to simplify the recording process and follow up on potential clients), purchasing (payments using a payment gateway), product design (an application tool for design and planning), and finance management (company cash flow accounting). In general, the purpose of the strategy is a marketing plan, creating the company's sales target, developing, operational activities and developing technology. Each quarter the company prioritizes the implementation of one of the strategies. In the last year, it focused on business strategies for developing new markets within the local region, developing new markets outside the local region, introducing new or significantly improved goods or services, intensifying or improving the marketing of goods and services, increasing its flexibility or responsiveness, and building alliances with other enterprises or institutions.

The IT industry is developing at a rapid pace so that competitors can quickly rise to the challenge to recruit new employees who have qualifications matching the standards set by them. That is why the company decided to join several communities on a regional and national scale to overcome such challenges. The benefits the company gains by joining the communities are sharing experiences on business in the IT sector, updates on product development and information about potential clients, fostering product innovation from the point of view of several business sectors, and identifying new markets for company business.

Case Study Narrative – Company D

Company D, a family business, focuses on leather souvenirs for weddings and pilgrimage customs and is based in Surabaya, the capital city of East Java. Its purpose is driven by two factors: first, preserving the family's business heritage and earning income; and second, to fulfill market demand, which is influenced by the external environment of a leather crafts village. Company D performs advertising, tracks manufacturing processes, determines the selling prices, and manages human capital in order to accomplish these goals. The company has been operating for 19 years. In 2019, its revenue was IDR 96,000,000 with a market diversification of 80 percent inside the province and 20 percent outside the province. The company's revenue and profit in 2019 increased by around 2–3 percent compared to the previous year with projected employee needs that were the same as the previous year.

The company currently has a total of 12 employees. In running the business, the owner always prioritizes its employees and being customer oriented. The three entrepreneurial competencies are clear communication, openness, and attention to detail. Human resource management is a crucial element in managing the company, ensuring that workers are satisfied with their employment and maximizing employees' work capacity. Employees are inspired at work if incentives and bonuses are offered. The organization therefore employs such strategies relevant to results based on its performance. In addition to defining the training needs of the company, it also looks into business demand if workers require expertise in art or management skills. The owner attends weekly meetings to monitor the work of the workers. The business is a family inheritance so 100 percent of the company's ownership and management is handled by the family. Therefore, family members jointly determine the targets and operational activities of the company. In the short and long term, there is no interference from staff in the development of company plans because the owners do not want any outside intervention in the operation of their company. The company obtains capital to run the business from the family and bank loans. It has also built several partnerships with major customers (e.g. tours and travel and a wedding agency) and suppliers. Building a partnership with the main customers is beneficial because they buy a large number of products. In addition to high profit margins, the company can also predict the amount of raw material that must be purchased and stored in the warehouse for the production process. Furthermore, suppliers help provide raw materials that are of suitable quality for consistent production standards. In terms of CSR, this company makes an effort to filter waste, which creates not only advantages for the environment but also for the company's credibility and purpose.

Company D's defined strategies are to maximize its annual profits. Several strategic activities that could be done to maximize profits are ensuring the quality of products, decreasing expenses, and maintaining customer satisfaction. In order to achieve these goals over the last three years, the company has introduced innovative products, improved product quality, and expanded into new markets outside the company's region. However, none of the strategies has been laid down in writing. The company has assets in the form of new machines and a workforce which has hard skill competencies related to craft. In addition, the efficiency of using the new machinery and innovative marketing activities (e.g. promotions, new design, loyalty programs) are three competitive advantages for this business. Unfortunately, the company still uses conventional ways of managing its day-to-day business, customer relationship management, and marketing activities. For instance, when networking to attract new customers, they still focus on warm relations and building consumer trust. The company carries out product innovation strategy, developed in-house, as one of the steps involved in facing strong price competition, strong competition on product quality, reputation, and a lack of demand. Process innovation in a company is a method of manufacturing or producing goods which is carried out by the company itself. Meanwhile, the company's product innovation involves conducting design innovation, marketing, and promotion venues.

By doing so, the company earns 30 percent of its total revenue from new products and 70 percent from old products.

The craft industry is undergoing a downward trajectory because of the pandemic. Business is considerably affected because several of the company's business partners have been forced to stop trading. For example, one of their partners organizes tours and travel for the Umrah and Hajj. Company D is usually responsible for making suitcases for these pilgrimages. Since these activities are forbidden, it is no use manufacturing the products usually demanded by the tour and travel company which collaborates with them. So, companies have to gather early insights into their rivals and potential market opportunities in order to face competitive and unpredictable circumstances, particularly in the light of the waning pandemic. For example, businesses are attempting to exploit the digital opportunity market by taking part in restricted physical business practices. This is related to how companies change management approaches to anticipate necessary change.

Cross-Case Analysis

We adopted a multi-case study approach to perform a cross-case analysis of sample cases from four different companies, aiming to present some interesting patterns across the case studies to understand growth factors among SMEs in Indonesia (Table 19.2). The cross-case analysis presents several findings based on the FDCM framework covering characteristics, assets, strategy, and environment.

Characteristics Analysis (Structural and Behavioral)

The first dimension of how SMEs grow and become sustainable is related to their characteristics. Characteristics include structural (age, size, sector) and behavioral (learning, networking, and innovation) factors (Sadler et al., 2020). The characteristics dimension also influences business owners in creating their vision and day-to-day management (Reid, 1993. The businesses concerned are engaged in the creative sector. The age of the business does not determine its size; rather its size is determined by the total assets owned by the business and the criteria that define them.

Behavioral characteristics cover how businesses deal with learning, networking, and innovation processes (Sadler et al., 2020). The findings showed that the creative industry has the same strategy of responding to market changes and uncertainties. However, the size of business has an effect on its responses. Small businesses still stick to the main plan and are open to minor improvements while micro businesses are more reactive and innovative in response to changing trends, preparing to anticipate necessary and unpredicted changes, and are more flexible toward market and client demands.

Table 19.2: Cross-Case analysis.

Four Dimensions Concept Model	Determinant	Company A	Company B	Company C	Company D
Characteristics (structural and behavioral)	Structural: age	5 years	8 years	9 years	19 years
	Structural: size	Micro	Micro	Small	Micro
	Structural: sector	Creative industry (craft based)	Creative industry (IT based)	Creative industry (IT based)	Creative industry (craft based)
	Behavioral: learning	Being reactive towards changes such as trends when they occur frequently in order to keep innovating without sacrificing the quality of the materials	Pre-planning and being ready to anticipate necessary and unprecedented changes in the future that may cause business setbacks	Sticking to the main plan which has been approved by stakeholders; however, it is still open to minor improvements and changes to make the strategy easier to track and minimize the cost	Being reactive and more flexible towards market and client demands
Assets (tangible and intangible determinants within a firm's control)	Human resources	18 employees at present Predicted increase: 3–5% in the following year	35 employees at present Predicted increase: 5–10% in the following year	10 employees at present Predicted increase: 3–5% in the following year	12 employees at present No predicted increase in the following year
	Finance	Source of funding is mainly from internal capital	Source of funding is mainly from internal capital	Sources of funding are from internal capital and grants	Funding is from family and bank loans

Table 19.2 (continued)

Four Dimensions Concept Model	Determinant	Company A	Company B	Company C	Company D
	Tacit knowledge	Tacit knowledge is obtained when the owner collaborates with business partners to create innovative products.	Skills and knowledge are gained through various client projects with some evaluation. In addition, team progression and internal dynamics have shaped the company for the past two years.	Knowledge is gained to analyze business strategies and market needs and how to handle crises as the company shifts to become a software apps company.	Trial and error process from customer demands in each project. Also learning from mistakes to find a suitable pattern in order to achieve progress
	Network relations	The company did not join the community to widen its network. The network built by the company is only with vendors.	The company joined several interior design communities.	The company joined several communities on a regional and national scale.	The company is established in the craft village community; thus, the networking relation is mostly around people who have the same business and revenue.
Strategy (management plans and aptitude development)	Product development	Goods innovation which is fresh on the market and developed by the company.	Service innovation which is based on client requests and developed by the company	Goods innovation which is fresh on the market and developed by the company	Goods innovation which is fresh on the market and developed by the company

Table 19.2 (continued)

Four Dimensions Concept Model	Determinant	Company A	Company B	Company C	Company D
	Process development	New methods for creating new products. This development process is carried out in-house.	New methods for creating new products. This development process is carried out in-house.	New methods for creating new products. This development process is carried out in-house.	New methods for creating new products, shipping processes, and supporting processes. This development process is carried out in-house.
	Personnel development	No personnel development applied.	Identify needs for personnel development based on market needs and the problems faced by the company.	Identify needs for personnel development as a result of monthly meeting discussions.	Identify needs for personnel development based on market needs, employee skill gaps, and the products to be produced
Environment (extra-firm determinants)	Infrastructure/ Innovations	Using technology to carry out marketing activities, manage employees, monitor vendor performance, and maintain the company's internal database	Using technology to carry out business activities. For marketing and selling activities, the company uses local social networks. For production activities, the company uses design software.	Using social media and websites to introduce the company to potential clients. Recording selling app to monitor and follow up on prospective and existing clients.	Using technology to produce products (e.g. material cutting machines, sewing machines) and distributing goods in collaboration with third parties

Table 19.2 (continued)

Four Dimensions Concept Model	Determinant	Company A	Company B	Company C	Company D
			Lastly, the company uses several computer programs to analyze the company's condition (e.g., using Excel to store sales data and interpret company conditions).	Payment gateway implemented for the purchasing process. Doing design and planning software development	
	Regulation/ Support	There are no specific regulations or support that support company growth.	There are no specific regulations or supports that support company growth.	Companies get support from government funding. The company has legal problems, so it is difficult to develop several business activities.	There are no specific regulations or supports that support company growth.
	Market/ Industry	Inconsistent market industry.	The market for this company is currently growing. However, there is a strong price competition among business players.	The market is currently growing.	The craft industry is currently in decline due to the uncertain pandemic conditions.
	Human resources recruitment strategies	A third party assists to recruit employees to facilitate the selection of staff with suitable qualifications.	Having difficulty getting suitable employees.	Having difficulty getting employees who have the needed competencies.	Having difficulty getting employees who are competent in crafting.

Assets Analysis (Tangible and Intangible within Firm's Control)

Assets consist of how the business manages human capital, finance, tacit knowledge, and network relations. Human capital is important because it is the foundation of the company's competitiveness and performance (Barney, 1991). Each business has its own strategy in managing resources. The authors found that all respondents within these cases in the creative industry sector, whether micro or small businesses, still depend on internal capital and bank loans/ grants to fund their businesses.

The creative industry (craft based) learns by trial and error from collaborating with business partners and customers' demands to gain and develop their knowledge. They learn from their mistakes to find a suitable pattern and achieve progress to create innovative products. In network relations they focus on vendors and people who have the same business. The IT-based creative industry, in contrast, needs to follow IT developments and market needs for technology. They have to update their skills and knowledge to handle the challenges in terms of technological developments. They also actively join several communities on a regional and national scale to enhance relations.

Strategy (Management Plans and Aptitude Development)

The strategy dimension consists of product development, process development, and personal development. The authors found that the creative industry always pursues product development with good innovations and service innovations which are fresh on the market based on client requests and market demand but also developed by the company itself. They always pay attention to the development process. Starting from the initial process of creating the product, to the shipping process, new methods for creating the new product are developed by internal processes.

The creative industry tries to support their employees with personal development based on market needs, employee skill gaps, and the products to be produced. Other than that, employees have evaluations in work at the beginning and at the end of projects. Building networks to attract new customers, they still focus on warm relations and building consumer trust.

Environment (Extra-firm Determinants)

Environmental dimensions are divided into Infrastructure/ Innovations, Regulations/ Support, Market/ Industry, and Human/ Cultural Capital. The craft industry uses technology to produce the product, distribute it, and collaborate with others. They also use technology to support business activities such as marketing, managing employees, monitoring business processes, and analyzing the company's internal database. The IT industry also uses technology to support business activities, in addition to technology being the main business innovation. The findings show that all respondents stated that there are no specific regulations or support in favor of company growth. The craft sector is supported and regulated by the Ministry of Tourism and Creative Economy and the IT sector by the Ministry of Research and Technology.

The creative industry (craft based) found that there were inconsistent market industries and niche markets. The craft industry is currently in flux due to the uncertainties of the pandemic while the IT industry is needed at this time. This market is currently growing along with an increasing number of competitors and strong price competition among business players. The findings also show that all respondents in the creative industry have difficulties finding human capital that suit their company and have the competencies that match company needs. Companies thus use third-party assistance to recruit employees to facilitate the selection of staff with suitable qualifications.

Discussion

In our research on SMEs applying within-case and cross-case analyses, our first question addressed the internal and external factors that make SMEs in Indonesia grow, using the FDCM framework to impartially subdivide the growth determinants into Characteristics, Assets, Strategy, and Environment. The second question sought to understand how the internal and external factors affect SMEs' growth in Indonesia.

Based on the analysis, the most critical dimensions relating to how businesses face changing trends, create a competitive advantage to compete with their competitors, and attain growth and sustainability are strategy and environment. However, all four dimensions emerged as critical pillars for understanding what influences SME growth (Sadler et al., 2020).

The identification of characteristics rarely defines SMEs as an individual body, but rather as a set of structural characteristics that determine their behavior and growth (Sadler et al., 2020; Cowling et al., 2015; Dobbs & Hamilton, 2007; Covin & Slein, 1991). The characteristics become part of the internal factors that make businesses grow in terms of the initial innovation by the business owner to running the business. Structural and behavioral factors, including learning and innovation, are the main factors behind SMEs running a business, growing, and becoming sustainable.

The analysis of assets covered human capital, finance, tacit knowledge, and network relation factors (Sadler et al., 2020). Asset dimensions are part of the internal factors that influence business growth. The company's resources and capabilities are important because they are the foundation of its competitiveness and performance, including all assets, organizational processes, information, and knowledge that allow the company to devise and implement strategies to grow and to make strategic decisions when competing in an external business environment (Barney, 1991). Human resource management is a crucial element when managing the company: companies ensure that workers are satisfied with their employment and maximize employees' work capacity. Talent management is one of the solutions when companies have problems with resources, building on the human capital's capacity in the process of managing change (Lawler, 2008). The SMEs in our study obtained their financial capital from internal capital and grants. Finally, network capital is very prominent for entrepreneurial companies as they seek to access and source knowledge (Huggins & Thompson, 2015). For SMEs to grow in a business capacity, creating advantageous relationships between resources and internal company capabilities as well as exploring networks are important in response to market challenges.

The strategy dimension is the next critical dimension that influences SMEs' growth. Product development, process development, and personal development are the determinants of a company's internal capability and performance. Strategic management is frequently asserted to be especially important for a successful business, and it often happens that the SMEs did not pay adequate attention to strategic management (Eniola & Ektebang, 2014). Strategy as a step-by-step effort helps achieve company goals, prepare for the company's sustainability, and maximize their profit.

The analysis of the environment dimension, or factors outside a company's control that may impact the company's performance (Ontorael & Suhadak, 2017), focuses on infrastructure/ institutions, regulation/ support, market/ industry and human/ cultural capital. The environment is the most crucial dimension externally to influence business growth. External conditions of the company include industry growth, technology, and regulations (Ipinnaiye et al., 2017; Bilal et al., 2016; Nkawabi & Mboya, 2019). The companies in our study undertook attempts to join several communities on a regional and national scale to overcome challenges. The benefits the company gains by joining the community are sharing experience on business, updates on product development and information about potential clients, obtaining product innovation from the point of view of several business sectors, and gaining a new market for the company business. In Indonesia, the development of SMEs is supported and regulated by the Ministry of Cooperatives and Small and Medium Enterprises of the Republic of Indonesia based on Law No. 20 of 2008.

Conclusions, Limitations, and Future Research

This paper analyzed determinants of growth in SMEs in Indonesia using qualitative case studies. It performed both within- and cross-case analyses to explore critical findings which may benefit not only researchers but also owners of SMEs and policy makers. The Four Dimensions Conceptual Model covers internal and external factors that influence the growth of SMEs in Indonesia. This study has critical implications for much research into and interpretation of SMEs' practices informed by RBV and NBV theory as well as the application of the four dimensions of characteristics, assets, strategy, and environment.

The conclusion of this research is that owners or managers of SMEs have different ways of managing companies, which then influences how the vision is formed as well as day-to-day operational management. Thus, in general every SME has different approaches to implementing strategies within the company. All the respondents recognized that human resource management plays a pivotal role in the company. However, the authors found that there are still very few SMEs that have managers or roles which are fully responsible for HR. This is why the majority of SMEs have not implemented talent management optimally. The condition of uncertain business dynamics requires companies to be able to adapt so that they can improve their sustainability performance. The majority of respondents chose to adapt or make slight changes instead of introducing preventive business changes.

This research provides several solutions for SME decision makers and policymakers on how to support SME growth in Indonesia, for example in relation to human resource management practices to enhance employees' capabilities in the company. The limitation of this research is to only analyze SMEs engaged in the craft and IT industries in four regions in Indonesia. Further research should cover other industries in different regions. It would also be possible to use a quantitative or mixed method approach to enrich this research, including more tools and techniques capable of integrating the SMEs themselves in the research process. Finally, the proposed solutions are end-to-end talent management practice.

References

ADB (Asian Development Bank) (2018). *GDP Growth in Asia and the Pacific, Asian Development Outlook (ADO)*. https://data.adb.org/dataset/gdp-growth-asia-and-pacific-asian-development-outlook

Anggadwita, G., Luturlean, B.S., Ramadani, V., & Ratten, V. (2017). Socio-cultural environments and emerging economy entrepreneurship: Women entrepreneurs in Indonesia. *Journal of Entrepreneurship in Emerging Economies*, 1(9), 85–96. https://doi.org/10.1108/JEEE-03-2016-0011

Badan Pusat Statistik. (2019). *Potensi Peningkatan Kinerja Usaha Mikro Kecil*. https://www.bps.go.id/publica tion/2019/03/05/66912048b475b142057f40be/analisis-hasil-se2016-lanjutan-potensi-peningkatan-kinerja-usaha-mikro-kecil.html

Baidoun, S.D., Lussier, R.N., Burbar, M., & Awashra, S. (2018). Prediction model of business success or failure for Palestinian small enterprises in the West Bank. *Journal of Entrepreneurship in Emerging Economies*, 1(10), 60–80. https://doi.org/10.1108/JEEE-02-2017-0013

Bager, T. E., Jensen, K. W., Nielsen, P. S., & Larsen, T. A. (2015). Enrollment of SME managers to growth-orientated training programs. *International Journal of Entrepreneurial Behaviour & Research*, 21(4), 578–599. https://doi.org/10.1108/IJEBR-12-2014-0224

Barney, J. (1991). Firm resources and sustained competitive advantage. *Journal of Management*, 17(1), 99–120. https://doi.org/10.1177/014920639101700108

Barney, J.B., Ketchen, D.J., & Wright, M. (2011). The future of resource-based theory: Revitalization or decline? *Journal of Management*, 37(5), 1299–1315. https://doi.org/10.1177/0149206310391805

Bilal, A.R., Khan, A.A., & Akoorie, M.E.M. (2016). Constraints to growth: A cross country analysis of Chinese, Indian and Pakistani SMEs. *Chinese Management Studies, 10*(2), 365–386. https://doi.org/10.1108/CMS-06-2015-0127

Chebo, A.K., & Kute, I. M. (2019). A Strategic process and small venture growth: The moderating role of environmental scanning and owner-CEO. *Journal of Small Business Strategy, 29*(3), 60–77. https://libjournals.mtsu.edu/index.php/jsbs/article/view/1002

Claudiu, C., Ion, P., Corina, M., & Simona, C.S. (2019). Determinants of SMEs' performance: Evidence from European countries. *Economic Research-Ekonomska Istraživanja, 32*(1), 1602–1620. https://doi.org/10.1080/1331677X.2019.1636699

Cowling, M., Liu, W., Ledger, A., & Zhang, N. (2015). What really happens to small and medium-sized enterprises in a global economic recession? UK evidence on sales and job dynamics. *International Small Business Journal, 33*(5), 488–513. https://doi.org/10.1177/0266242613512513

Covin, J. G., & Slevin, D. P. (1991). A Conceptual Model of Entrepreneurship as Firm Behavior. *Entrepreneurship Theory and Practice, 16(1)*, 7–26. https://doi.org/10.1177/104225879101600102

Creswell, J. W. (1994). Research design: Qualitative & quantitative approaches. Sage Publications, Inc.

Dobbs, M. and Hamilton, R.T. (2007). Small business growth: recent evidence and new directions", International Journal of Entrepreneurial Behavior & Research, 13(5), pp. 296–322. https://doi.org/10.1108/13552550710780885

Delmar, F. (2006). Measuring growth: methodological considerations and empirical results. In R. Donckels & A. Miettinen (Eds.), *Entrepreneurship and SME research: On its way to the next millennium*, 199–216. Ashgate.

Do, H., & Shipton, H. (2019). High-performance work systems and innovation in Vietnamese small firms. *International Small Business Journal, 37*(7), 732–753. https://doi.org/10.1177/0266242619863572

El Shoubaki, A., Laguir, I., & den Besten, M. (2020). Human capital and SME growth: The mediating role of reasons to start a business. *Small Business Economics, 54*(3), 1107–1121. https://doi.org/10.1007/s11187-018-0129-y

Eniola, A.A., & Ektebang, H. (2014). SME firms performance in Nigeria: Competitive advantage and its impact. *International Journal of Research Studies Management, 2*(2), 75–86. https://doi.org/10.5861/ijrsm.2014.854

Fatima, T., & Bilal, A.R. (2020). Achieving SME performance through individual entrepreneurial orientation: An active social networking perspective. *Journal of Entrepreneurship in Emerging Economies, 12*(3), 399–411. https://doi.org/10.1108/JEEE-03-2019-0037

Freiling, J. (2008). RBV and the road to the control of external organizations. *Management Revue, 19*(1/2), 33–52. http://www.jstor.org/stable/41783570

Games, D., Soutar, G., & Sneddon, J. (2021). Personal values and SME innovation in a Muslim ethnic group in Indonesia. *Journal of Entrepreneurship in Emerging Economies, 13*(5), 1012–1032. https://doi.org/10.1108/JEEE-01-2020-0008

Gamidullaeva, L.A., Vasin, S.M., & Wise, N. (2020). Increasing small- and medium-enterprise contribution to local and regional economic growth by assessing the institutional environment. *Journal of Small Business and Enterprise Development, 27*(2), 259–280. https://doi.org/10.1108/JSBED-07-2019-0219

Griffiths, M.D., Gundry, L., Kickul, J., & Muñoz Fernandez, A. (2009). Innovation ecology as a precursor to entrepreneurial growth: A cross-country empirical investigation. *Journal of Small Business and Enterprise Development, 16*(3), 375–90. https://doi.org/10.1108/14626000910977116

Hayton, J.C. (2005). Competing in the new economy: The effect of intellectual capital on corporate entrepreneurship in high-technology new ventures. *R&D Management, 35*(2), 137–55. https://doi.org/10.1111/j.1467-9310.2005.00379.x

Hosseini, M., & H. Dadfar (2012). 'Network-base theories and internalization of firms. Application to empirical studies'. Paper presented at International Trade and Academic Research Conference (ITARC). London.

Huber, M., Lechner, M., Wuncsh, C, & Walter, T. (2011). 'Do German welfare-to-work programmes reduce welfare dependency and increase employment?. *German Economic Review, 12(2)*, 182–204. https://doi.org/10.1111/j.1468-0475.2010.00515.x

Huggins, R., & Thompson, P. (2015). Entrepreneurship, innovation and regional growth: a network theory. *Small Business Economics, 45(1)*, 103–128. http://www.jstor.org/stable/43553080

Kraja, Y.B., & Osmani, E. (2015). Importance of external and internal environment in creation of competitive advantage to SMEs (case of SMEs, in the northern region of Albania). *European Scientific Journal, 11*(13), 120–130. https://eujournal.org/index.php/esj/article/view/5641

Kussudyarsana, K., Soepatini, S., Maimun, M.H., & Vemuri, R. (2020). Examining formal and relational governance in family small medium enterprises: Evidence from Indonesia. *Journal of Entrepreneurship in Emerging Economies, 12*(2), 231–257. https://doi.org/10.1108/JEEE-10-2018-0108

Lawler, E.E., (2008). Make Human Capital a Source of Competitive Advantage. *Marshall School of Business Working Paper*, No. MOR 16–09, http://dx.doi.org/10.2139/ssrn.1311431

Lechner, C. & Dowling, M. (2003). Firm networks: external relationships as sources for the growth and competitiveness of entrepreneurial firms. *Entrepreneurship & Regional Development, 15(1)*, 1–26, https://doi.org/10.1080/08985620210159220

Love, J.H., & Ropper, S. (2015). SME innovation, exporting and growth: A review of existing evidence. *International Small Business Journal, 33*(1), 28–48. https://doi.org/10.1177/0266242614550190

Chaney, I. M., & Lin, K. (2007). The Influence of Domestic Interfirm Networks on the Internationalization Process of Taiwanese SMEs. *Asia Pacific Business Review, 13*(4), 565–584.

Mamun, A.A., Nawi, N.B.C., Permarupan, P.Y., & Muniady, R. (2018). Sources of competitive advantage for Malaysian micro-enterprises. *Journal of Entrepreneurship in Emerging Economies, 10*(2), 191–216. https://doi.org/10.1108/JEEE-05-2017-0037

Mariyono, J. (2019). Micro-credit as catalyst for improving rural livelihoods through agribusiness sector in Indonesia. *Journal of Entrepreneurship in Emerging Economies, 11*(1), 98–21. https://doi.org/10.1108/JEEE-06-2017-0046

Miles, M. B., & Huberman, A. M. (1994). Qualitative data analysis: An expanded sourcebook (2nd ed.). Sage Publications, Inc.

Musteen, M., Francis, J. and Datta, D.K. (2010) The Influence of International Networks on Internationalization Speed and Performance: A Study of Czech SMEs. Journal of World Business, 45, 197–205. http://dx.doi.org/10.1016/j.jwb.2009.12.003.

Nkawabi, J.M., & Mbboya, L.B. (2019). A review of factors affecting the growth of small and medium enterprises (SMEs) in Tanzania. *European Journal of Business and Management, 11*(33). 1–8. https://doi.org/10.7176/EJBM/11-33-01

Ipinnaiye, O., Dineen, D., & Lenihan, H. (2017). Drivers of SME performance: A holistic and multivariate approach. *Small Business Economics, 48*, 883–911. https://doi.org/10.1007/s11187-016-9819-5

Isaga, N., Masurel, E., & Van Montfort, K. (2015). Owner-manager motives and the growth of SMEs in developing countries: Evidence from the furniture industry in Tanzania. *Journal of Entrepreneurship in Emerging Economies, 7*(3), 190–211. https://doi.org/10.1108/JEEE-11-2014-0043

Nyikos, Gy., Béres, A., Laposa, T., & Závecz, G. (2020). Do financial instruments or grants have a bigger effect on SMEs' access to finance? Evidence from Hungary. *Journal of Entrepreneurship in Emerging Economies, 12*(5), 667–685. https://doi.org/10.1108/JEEE-09-2019-0139

Oluwadare A., & Oni, I. (2015). The effect of internal environment on the performance of small and medium scale enterprise in Kano metropolis. *International Journal of Management and Commerce Innovations, 3*(2), 120–126.

Ontorael, R., & Mawardi, M.K. (2017). Analysis of the influence of external and internal environmental factors on business performance: A study of micro small and medium enterprises of food and beverage. *Russian Journal of Agricultural and Socio-Economic Sciences, 6*(66), 47–56. https://doi.org/10.18551/rjoas.2017-06.05

Panjaitan, J.M., Timur, R.P., & Sumiyana, S. (2021). How does the government of Indonesia empower SMEs? An analysis of the social cognition found in newspapers. *Journal of Entrepreneurship in Emerging Economies, 13*(5), 765–790. https://doi.org/10.1108/JEEE-04-2020-0087

Phillips, C., & Bhatia-Panthaki, S. (2007). Enterprise development in Zambia: Reflections on the missing middle. *Journal of International Development, 19*(6), 793–804. https://doi.org/10.1002/jid.1402

Rafiki, A. (2020). Determinants of SME growth: An empirical study in Saudi Arabia. *International Journal of Organizational Analysis, 28*(1), 205–225. https://doi.org/10.1108/IJOA-02-2019-1665

Reid, G.C. (1993). Small business enterprise. An economic analysis. Psychology Press.

Runyan, R.C., Huddleston, P., & Swinney, J.L. (2006). Entrepreneurial orientation and social capital as small firm strategies: A study of gender differences from a resource-based view. *Entrepreneurship Management, 2*, 455–477. https://doi.org/10.1007/s11365-006-0010-3

Salder, J., Gilman, M., Raby, S., & Gkikas, A. (2020). Beyond linearity and resource-based perspectives of SME growth. *Journal of Small Business Strategy, 30*(1), 1–17.

Sheehan, M. (2014). Human resource management and performance: Evidence from small and medium-sized firms. *International Small Business Journal, 32*(5), 545–570. https://doi.org/10.1177/0266242612465454

Stebbins, R.A. (2001). *Exploratory research in the social sciences*. Sage Publications, Inc.

Teece, D.J., Pisano, G., & Shuen, A. (1997). Dynamic capabilities and strategic management. *Strategic Management Journal, 18*(7), 509–533. https://www.jstor.org/stable/3088148

Zhao, Y., & Thompson, P. (2019). Investments in managerial human capital: Explanations from prospect and regulatory focus theories. *International Small Business Journal: Researching Entrepreneurship, 37*(4), 365–394. https://doi.org/10.1177/0266242619828264

Wernerfelt, B. (1984). A resource-based view of the firm. *Strategic Management Journal, 5*(2), 171–180. https://www.jstor.org/stable/2486175

Winter, S. (1987). Knowledge and Competence as Strategic Assets, in Teece, D. (ed.), *The Competitive Challenge: Strategies for Industrial Innovation and Renewal*, New York: Harper & Row, Ballinger Division.

Yin, R. K. (2018). *Case Study Research Design and Methods (6th Ed.)*. Thousand Oaks, CA: Sage Publishing.

Zimon, G. (2018). Influence of group purchasing organizations on financial situation of Polish SMEs. *Oeconomia Copernicana, 9*(1), 87–104. https://doi.org/10.24136/oc.2018.005

Zulu-Chisanga, S., Chabala, M., & Mandawa-Bray, B. (2021). The differential effects of government support, inter-firm collaboration and firm resources on SME performance in a developing economy. *Journal of Entrepreneurship in Emerging Economies, 13*(2), 175–195. https://doi.org/10.1108/JEEE-07-2019-0105

Léo-Paul Dana and Aidin Salamzadeh

20 The Role of Culture and Entrepreneurial Opportunities in SME Entrepreneurship: A Systematic Literature Review

Abstract: Entrepreneurs use their innovative mindset to change societies. They take various actions to create value and ensure the socio-economic development of societies. Besides, SME entrepreneurs have to consider SME and entrepreneurship related policies simultaneously while acting in any context. Then, the context, in general, and the culture, more specifically, could play a vital role in their survival and success. Although the cultural factors have been widely studied in entrepreneurship research, this domain has remained overlooked while studying SME entrepreneurship. Therefore, this chapter focuses on how culture and entrepreneurial opportunities are investigated in SME entrepreneurship research. The authors conducted a systematic literature review that includes publications indexed in Scopus between 1995 and 2021. Thus, general trends are discussed, and the chapter provides a big picture for those interested in researching this area. Findings revealed that most publications have implicitly paid attention to this issue despite its importance, and culture has been used as a control variable or a general measure to categorize the findings. Finally, it is noteworthy that future researchers could focus on opening the black box of culture and its relationships with SME entrepreneurship instead of considering it purely as a contextual factor.

Keywords: SME Entrepreneurship, culture, entrepreneurial opportunities, systematic literature review

Introduction

The relationship between entrepreneurship and culture is debatable from two perspectives. On the one hand, the results of entrepreneurship affect society, and on the other hand, the entrepreneurial process and the culture that governs it, in addition to being influenced by a society's culture, can also bring about fundamental changes in any society (Dana, 1993; Qureshi et al., 2021). Then, entrepreneurship is an essential precondition for promoting the culture of a society by creating job opportunities, generating wealth, and improving economic conditions (Cui et al., 2006; Salamzadeh et al., 2019). By meeting the basic needs of livelihood, the ground is prepared to address higher-level human needs, and if this work is directed in the right direction, it

Léo-Paul Dana, ICD Business School, Paris, France
Aidin Salamzadeh, University of Tehran

https://doi.org/10.1515/9783110747652-021

will lead to the prosperity and excellence of human beings and society (Tur-Porcar et al., 2018; Abdulghaffar & Akkad, 2021). In addition, innovation, which is one of the fundamental characteristics of entrepreneurship, leads to the production of newer and more diverse products and services. Thus, it increases the choice power of the people, and by improving people's level of well-being, comfort, and leisure, more opportunities for cultural activities are created. In addition, understanding how entrepreneurship is formed requires us to use special rules based on specific beliefs and values (Kirby & Ibrahim, 2011). The set of these rules and beliefs can be considered as culture. Any entrepreneurial process is embedded in a particular culture (García-Rodríguez et al., 2017). This culture can be considered the one that governs small entrepreneurial firms, and it includes a set of common concepts, values, beliefs, and rules that govern a venture (Stuetzer et al., 2018). Parsons, a well-known American sociologist who has expressed his views on the four biological, cultural, social, and religious systems, sees the development of a culture of creativity and initiative as the product of a social system influenced by family and school (Davey et al., 2016). In his famous study *The Protestant Ethic and the Spirit of Capitalism*, Max Weber argues that what led to the formation of capitalism in the West was influenced by a particular conception of Christianity, namely Calvinism or reformed Protestantism (Brouwer, 2002). Calvinism, by expressing insights about life in this world, God's salvation and mercy, strengthened and further developed the entrepreneurial spirit and culture to create prosperity in this world and, consequently, led to the accumulation of wealth (Landes, 1949; Light & Dana, 2020; Grytten, 2021).

Taking all these into account, one might conclude that SME entrepreneurship is a contextual phenomenon that deals with exploring, evaluating, and exploiting entrepreneurial opportunities (EOs) by small and medium-sized enterprises (Gilmore et al., 2013). Then, culture and SMEs' approach toward entrepreneurial opportunities could be critical in their success or failure (Dana, 1995, 2013, 2015). This phenomenon is not investigated explicitly using the SME entrepreneurship approach despite the existing literature on the relationships between culture, entrepreneurial opportunities, and entrepreneurship (Eniola & Dada, 2019; Eniola, 2020; Liñán et al., 2020). Culture and contextual factors could profoundly affect the performance or even the existence of SMEs in various economies. Furthermore, subjective and objective entrepreneurial opportunities might also be variously explored, evaluated, and exploited by SMEs. Besides, there are controversial issues to be discussed in this chapter. For instance, there are several differences between SME and entrepreneurship policies (Lundstrom & Stevenson, 2005), further discussed in this chapter. Then, this chapter contributes to the extant literature by providing an integrative and comprehendible view of the subject matter. It also offers insights for future researchers as it provides them with the mainly studied or overlooked topics and areas in this regard.

In sum, this chapter is focused on answering three main questions, i.e. (i) how has the role of culture and entrepreneurial opportunities in SME entrepreneurship been developing in the literature?; (ii) what is the state of the art knowledge in this field?, and (iii) what are the key trends and research streams in this area of knowledge? Therefore, the chapter is structured as follows. First, the authors have briefly reviewed the theoretical background, and the research method is discussed accordingly. Then, the findings are highlighted, and the chapter concludes with some remarks and directions for future research.

Theoretical Background

The history of SME entrepreneurship and its relevant debates goes back to the 1980s, when the word was used to clarify how SMEs act entrepreneurially (Krasniqi, 2007). Although the concept was coined earlier, only a few scholars emphasized it before 2000 (Eniola, 2020). For almost two decades, debates on SME entrepreneurship have continued, and many controversial aspects have remained. While a group of scholars believe that the idea is a breakthrough, many have challenged it, as they distinguished SMEs from entrepreneurial ventures (Guiliani & Torrès, 2018). On the one hand, the domain has remained controversial. On the other hand, many relevant topics have been highlighted by its proponents. One of these critical concepts is culture (Abdullahi et al., 2018; Bunagan & Sison, 2019; Anning-Dorson, 2021).

Creating and strengthening entrepreneurial values, attitudes, and behaviors, as entrepreneurial culture, is one of the main components of governments' strategies in SME entrepreneurship development (Salamzadeh et al., 2015). This goal is mainly pursued in policies and educational incentive programs at all levels and social strata (Krueger et al., 2013). The cultures in question take place in the context of public-private partnerships. There are few programs in different countries related to cultural issues in SME entrepreneurship, the main burden of which could be considered deficiencies in the educational systems and mass media (Katz, 1991; Guerrero et al., 2014; Duman et al., 2015).

Due to its esoteric complexities and subtleties, culture requires the participation of strata and individuals more than any other component in the broader entrepreneurship strategy to institutionalize cultural diversity and positive values embedded in subcultures (Jenssen & Kristiansen, 2004; Valliere, 2019). Entrepreneurial culture advocates creativity, innovation, risk-taking, open communications, and disruptive visions and supports entrepreneurial leaders (Dabić et al., 2018; Salamzadeh et al., 2022). These characteristics in a team create a powerful force that shapes the culture of entrepreneurship in any society. Hofstede's study of societies' culture and cultural dimensions led to studies on the relationship between his four cultural dimensions and entrepreneurship and entrepreneurial activities (Hofstede et al., 2004; Puumalainen et al., 2015; Dheer et al., 2019). Since then, several studies have been conducted to discuss the relationship between culture and entrepreneurship and business. Many of these studies were based on or similar to Hofstede's approach (e.g.,

Ulijn & Salamzadeh, 2022). Although the connection between entrepreneurship and culture was studied extensively in the extant literature, the relationship between SME entrepreneurship and culture has remained overlooked. It is noteworthy that the authors have used Shane and Venkataraman's (2001) approach and Lundström and Stevenson's (2005) framework to analyze the extant literature and elaborate on the findings.

Research Method

This study is focused on a series of research questions, as follows: (i) RQ1. How has the role of culture and entrepreneurial opportunities in SME entrepreneurship been developing in the literature?; (ii) RQ2. What is the state of the art knowledge in this field?; and (iii) RQ3. What are the key trends and research streams in this area of knowledge? A systematic literature review (SLR) is performed to answer the above questions. The authors used a multi-stage review protocol in this study that includes the following stages, according to de Araújo Lima et al. (2020):

(i) Literature investigation: At this stage, the authors reviewed the existing literature on the role of culture and entrepreneurial opportunities in SME entrepreneurship. Due to the search results, several relevant publications that have implicitly or explicitly paid attention to this issue were studied. First, we searched for SME Entrepreneurship as a construct in the Scopus database. The results revealed that there were only 145 references, which were written in English, and just 117 were published in journals. This result witnessed the novelty of this field.

(ii) Research questions definition: After a primary search, the authors defined the main research questions (RQ1, RQ2, and RQ3).

(iii) Research strategy definition: The authors used SCOPUS ((TITLE-ABS-KEY ("small firm" OR "SME" OR "small and medium*") AND TITLE-ABS-KEY ("entrepreneur*") AND TITLE-ABS-KEY ("Cultur*"))) as the primary databases for finding relevant publications. The searching and selecting processes were performed accordingly. The authors created a database to initiate the systematic literature review process.

(iv) Selection criteria determination: This stage narrowed down the results (Dabić et al., 2019). The authors considered a series of filters in this research and excluded editorial materials, notes, proceedings papers, reviews, data papers, and non-English results. Four hundred and forty-three search results were found in Scopus and assessed qualitatively in the next stage. This data was used to analyze the existing trends.

(v) Quality assessment: The authors independently controlled the titles, keywords, and abstracts to fine-tune the results before the data extraction and analysis. Also, the authors read the abstracts and removed the results that: (i) were not relevant to the research questions, (ii) had less than six pages, and (iii) followed non-scientific approaches. At this stage, 69 papers were selected accordingly. The authors used this group of articles to scrutinize and analyze the role of culture and entrepreneurial opportunities in SME entrepreneurship.

(vi) Data extraction and analysis: After constructing the database, descriptive and bibliometric analyses were conducted to identify and analyze the key variables, and then the content analysis was performed based on the framework of the analysis.

The authors followed the procedure used by Caputo et al. (2016), and the stepwise protocol and the results are summarized in the following table accordingly (see Table 20.1).

Table 20.1: Stepwise protocol and results (compiled by authors).

Step	Description	Total articles
0	Articles retrieved from SCOPUS (excluding editorial materials, notes, proceedings papers, reviews, data papers, and non-English results)	443
1	Articles with relevant title	132
2	Articles with relevant abstract	92
3	Articles with relevant text	69

Findings

As discussed earlier, we aimed to answer three main questions that could provide a comprehensive understanding for those interested in SME entrepreneurship and how this phenomenon relates to culture and entrepreneurial opportunities. For the sake of simplicity, we considered the existence of entrepreneurial opportunities in any entrepreneurial activity (Holcombe, 2003; Mueller, 2007; Alvarez & Barney, 2010; Davidsson, 2015). Besides, we read the selected manuscripts to ensure that the references were relevant. The authors searched for a feasible area of knowledge to highlight the possible relationship between three primary constructs, i.e. culture, entrepreneurial opportunities, and SME entrepreneurship.

The search results revealed that the first relevant publication was published in 1985; however, the major trend initiated in the 2000s. The number of publications was increased incrementally in the past two decades, and the number quadrupled from 2000 until 2021 (see Figure 20.1). It implies an emerging focus on the topic, although it does not explicitly mean that scholars have simultaneously paid more attention to these constructs.

As illustrated in Figure 20.2, a small number of the mentioned publications were published in a few journals. It shows that there might be a need for special issues, thematic approaches, or maybe a more relevant call for papers. Besides, most of the

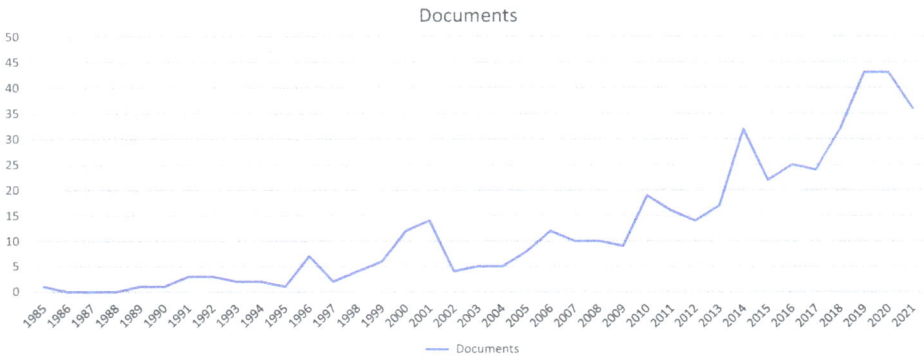

Figure 20.1: Documents published in each year.
Source: compiled by authors.

publications were published in entrepreneurship and small business journals. Such an approach might be due to cultural studies scholars' lack of attention or interest (Lundström & Stevenson, 2005; Welter, 2009; Marchesnay, 2011). It was evident while the authors were reviewing the selected papers. Cultural aspects were marginalized or less studied in almost all of the papers (Smith, 2021).

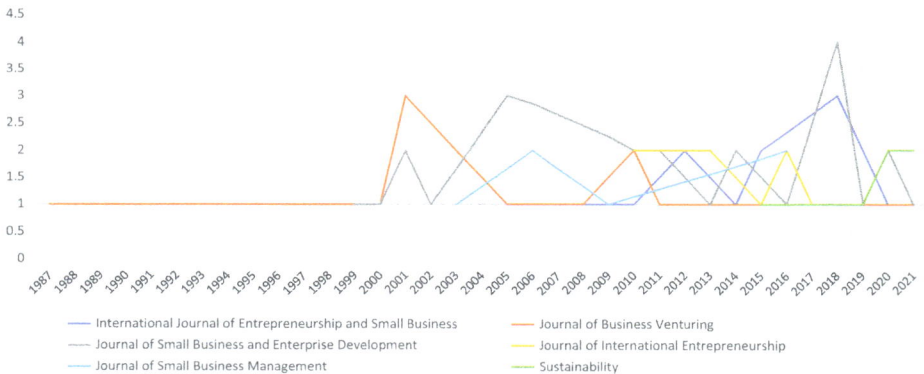

Figure 20.2: Documents published in top journals.
Source: compiled by authors.

Surprisingly, authors from Malaysian universities paid more attention to these constructs (e.g., Ahmad et al., 2011; Hanifah et al., 2019; Ratnasingam et al., 2021) (see Figure 20.3). The authors noticed a major focus on business ethics, sustainable development, social responsibility, and some other relevant concepts in Malaysian universities, primarily focused on the cultural aspects of SME entrepreneurship (e.g. Pedrini et al., 2016).

Documents

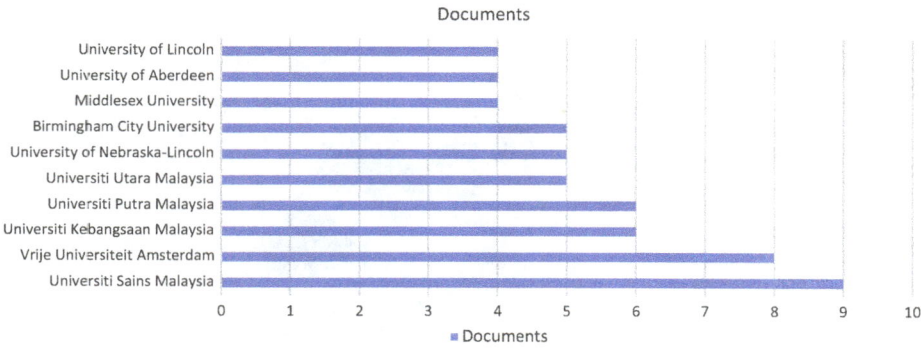

Figure 20.3: Published documents by authors' affiliations (compiled by authors).

Although many authors were affiliated with the Malaysian universities, Malaysia was in third place, standing after the United Kingdom and the United States. Indonesia, Italy, Australia, Canada, the Netherlands, Pakistan, and China stand respectively in the following places (see Figure 20.4).

Documents

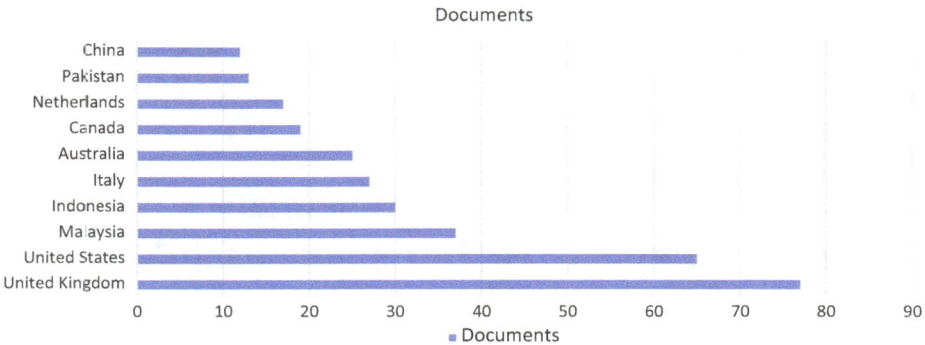

Figure 20.4: Documents published in top ten countries.
Source: compiled by authors.

In terms of subject, most of the research papers were published respectively in journals categorized under (i) Business, Management and Accounting, (ii) Social Sciences, and (iii) Economics, Econometrics, and Finance. A significant number of publications were also published in other fields, which shows the diversity of publications (see Figure 20.5).

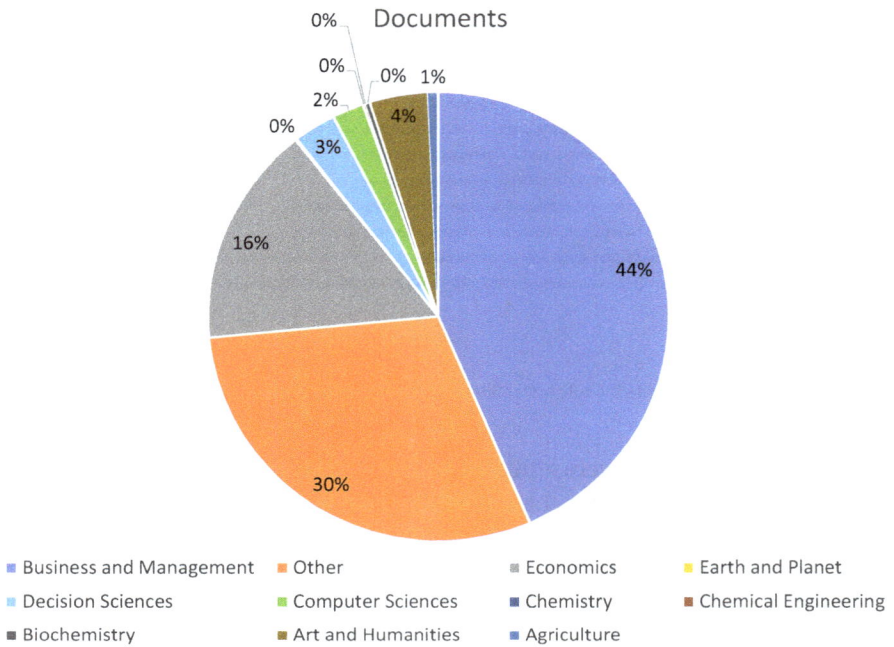

Figure 20.5: Category of the published documents.
Source: compiled by authors.

How Could Culture and Entrepreneurial Opportunities Affect SME Entrepreneurship?

Culture plays a vital role in shaping entrepreneurship. Many scholars have previously highlighted the impacts of culture itself and cultural factors in creating an entrepreneurial environment (Achim et al., 2021). On the one hand, cultural factors could facilitate or hinder entrepreneurial activities (Aparicio et al., 2021; Xia & Liu, 2021), making them an Achilles' heel if policymakers, practitioners, and entrepreneurs do not consider it well. On the other hand, exploring, evaluating, and exploiting entrepreneurial opportunities might not be possible without considering cultural factors. Thus, we took advantage of an implicitly proposed framework suggested by Shane and Venkataraman (2001), based on the notion of individual-opportunity nexus. This approach has been widely used in the entrepreneurship literature, and, therefore, the authors used it as a stepping stone to discuss how culture and entrepreneurial opportunities could affect SME entrepreneurship (Ratten, 2014; Zanella et al., 2019).

Based on this approach, the main actor, i.e. the entrepreneur, is a typical SME. Whenever the SME faces an entrepreneurial opportunity, the entrepreneurial journey begins. Then, simply put, SME Entrepreneurship is shaped based on exploring, evaluating, and exploiting entrepreneurial opportunities. Besides, the playgrounds and rules of the game [formal and informal institutions] are defined by culture (Su et al., 2017). This framework helped the authors integrate the extant literature (see Figure 20.6).

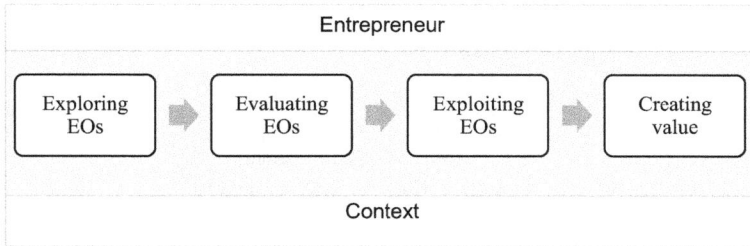

Figure 20.6: General framework.
Source: authors' elaboration, based on Shane and Venkataraman (2001).

According to the framework, the entrepreneur refers to SME entrepreneur, the context implies Culture, and the mentioned process addresses Entrepreneurial Opportunities. Therefore, the suggested framework is illustrated below (see Figure 20.7).

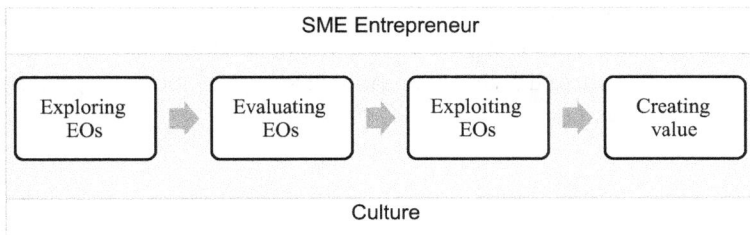

Figure 20.7: Proposed framework.
Source: authors' elaboration.

According to the literature review, the concept of SME Entrepreneurship was implicitly studied in terms of culture. Even when it was explicitly mentioned in the literature, it was mostly discussed at a corporate level. Only a few studies have focused on the national level. For instance, Ahmad et al. (2011) proposed a cross-cultural approach to investigating SME entrepreneurs' competency mix in two selected countries, i.e. Malaysia and Australia. Most of the extant literature focused on SMEs' cultural aspects or how those aspects might affect or moderate entrepreneurial behavior. It is crystal clear that culture's direct or indirect impact had not been studied by the time this study was conducted. The annexed table (Appendix 1) shows which aspects have been implicitly (I) or explicitly (X) mentioned in the portfolio of reviewed papers.

The following Figure shows the distribution of studies focusing on various aspects of the framework (see Figure 20.8). As illustrated below, most publications referred to SME entrepreneurs explicitly, while the cultural aspects were considered mainly implicitly. Besides, exploiting and exploring [entrepreneurial] opportunities were mentioned explicitly while evaluating [entrepreneurial] opportunities and value creation were studied implicitly.

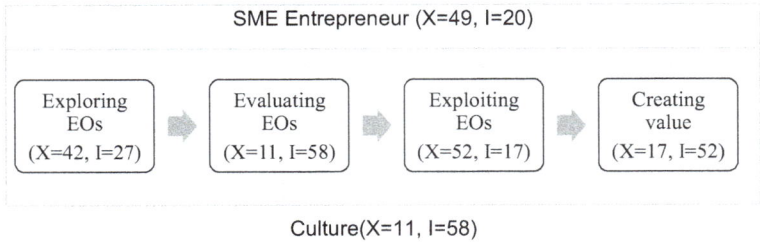

SME Entrepreneur (X=49, I=20)

| Exploring EOs (X=42, I=27) | Evaluating EOs (X=11, I=58) | Exploiting EOs (X=52, I=17) | Creating value (X=17, I=52) |

Culture(X=11, I=58)

Figure 20.8: Distribution of studies according to the proposed framework.
Source: authors' elaboration.
Note: X=Explicit; I=Implicit.

According to the following figure, the main keywords used in these studies are illustrated (see Figure 20.9). As it is shown, culture is the most frequently used in these studies, while performance (e.g. Laforet, 2016) and innovation (e.g. Semrau et al., 2016) are also among the most repeated terms. This shows that cultural aspects of the phenomenon are primarily discussed at an organizational level, e.g., such as organizational performance and innovation.

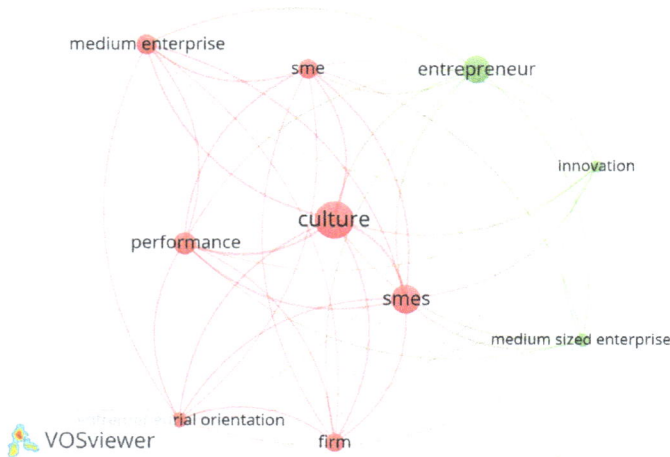

Figure 20.9: The main keywords used in the selected publications.
Source: compiled by authors.

The literature review reveals that the idea of considering how culture and entrepreneurial opportunities could impact SME entrepreneurship has been overlooked. It might be due to controversial discussions among proponents of the distinction between SME-related and entrepreneurship-related policies and approaches (e.g., Smallbone, 2016; Mamman et al., 2019; Fotopoulos & Storey, 2019), which have been raised many years ago by various authors such as Lundström and Stevenson (2005). Although such views have been further developed and sometimes criticized, the slow growth rate of publications in this field might indicate such controversies. Looking through their perspective, one could notice that SME Entrepreneurship deals mainly with the startup phase, which has been marginally studied in the investigated literature (see Figure 20.10). The reason might be focusing on SMEs as more mature entities which search for entrepreneurial business models. Table 20.2 shows the number of studies at each stage. It provides a more integrated understanding of how cultural issues have been studied in SME entrepreneurship research.

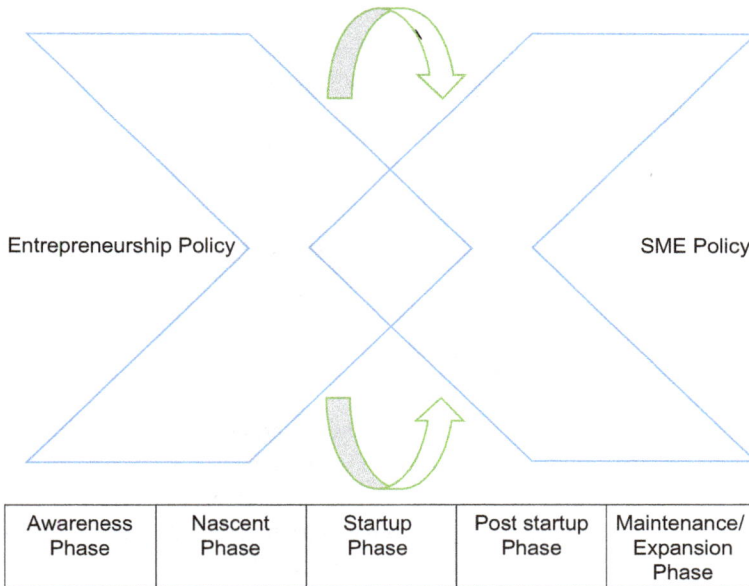

| Awareness Phase | Nascent Phase | Startup Phase | Post startup Phase | Maintenance/ Expansion Phase |

Figure 20.10: Entrepreneurship policy and SME policy (Lundström & Stevenson, 2005).

Table 20.2: Number of studies at each stage.

Phase	Awareness	Nascent	Startup	Post startup	Maintenance/ Expansion
Frequency	2	3	6	32	26
Percent	2.90	4.35	8.70	46.38	37.68

Source: compiled by authors

Conclusion

SME entrepreneurship is an emerging field of research that has been developed primarily during the last decade. Although one could witness periods of debates and controversies in this area, the topic has remained interesting (e.g., see, Lundström & Stevenson, 2005; Eniola, 2020). While a significant body of the literature has been focused on distinguishing SME and entrepreneurship policies, proponents of another stream still believe that SME entrepreneurship is necessary for socio-economic development. Given this fact, using a systematic literature review, the present study investigated the connection between culture, [entrepreneurial] opportunities, and SME entrepreneurship. We borrowed the approach proposed by Shane and Venkataraman (2001) to analyze the findings. Then, we categorized the literature into two groups: (i) those that have explicitly mentioned a relationship between culture and SME entrepreneurship; and (ii) the ones who have implicitly mentioned it. The findings revealed that although culture is an integral part of any entrepreneurial activity, it has been studied explicitly in the realm of SME entrepreneurship. Besides, most publications related to exploiting and exploring [entrepreneurial] opportunities were mentioned explicitly while evaluating [entrepreneurial] opportunities and value creation were studied implicitly. According to our review, culture has been mainly studied as a black box that needs to be opened and interpreted in more detail to better understand how it affects SME entrepreneurship. Only a few studies have scrutinized the cultural aspects of SME entrepreneurship, and most publications have used it as a contextual factor or a measure to categorize SME entrepreneurial activities.

Directions for Future Research

The authors tried to shed more light on the role of culture and entrepreneurial opportunities in promoting SME entrepreneurship. According to the results of this study, the connection between culture, entrepreneurial opportunities, and SME entrepreneurship needs more explanation, as previous researchers have marginally scrutinized these relationships. Then, there is a need to measure the impact of culture or cultural factors on promoting SME entrepreneurship. This is also the case while reviewing the papers related to entrepreneurial opportunities and SME entrepreneurship. Another interesting domain to be studied by future researchers might be the controversies about SME and entrepreneurship policies and how these two could be connected. It has led to controversial discussions between entrepreneurship scholars, as some believe that SME and entrepreneurship policies are different in nature. Besides, according to this study, there is a lack of sufficient research about culture and SME entrepreneurship at the awareness, nascent, and startup stages, while most studies are related to the post-startup and maintenance/expansion stages. Finally, future researchers might use qualitative, quantitative or mixed research designs to answer various aspects of the mentioned relationship. The authors believe that using Interpretive Structural Modeling (ISM) or Grounded Theory (GT) could pave the way for future research, while adding more explanations and insights by testing the relationships could also be of paramount importance.

Appendix

Table 20.1A: The focus of selected references.

Reference	Title	SE	CU	EO
Virglerova et al. (2021)	Selected factors of internationalization and their impact on the SME perception of the market risk	I	I	X
Khan et al. (2021)	Factors affecting women entrepreneurs' success: A study of small- and medium-sized enterprises in emerging market of Pakistan	X	I	X
Games et al. (2021)	Personal values and SME innovation in a Muslim ethnic group in Indonesia	X	X	I
Omeihe et al. (2021)	Trusting in indigenous institutions: Exporting SMEs in Nigeria	X	X	I
Parasotskaya et al. (2021)	Comparative analysis of small and medium-sized businesses and its impact on the development of tourism	X	I	X
Ratnasingam et al. (2021)	Success factors of small and medium enterprises in the Malaysian furniture industry: Discerning the growth of entrepreneurs	X	I	X
Bashir et al. (2021)	Rural micro, small and medium enterprises development in emerging markets: The case of Punjab, Pakistan	X	I	I
Karia, N. (2021)	A comparative benchmark model for SMEs: Viable entrepreneur emotional intelligence	X	X	I
Gunawan et al. (2021)	The adoption of ecopreneurship practices in Indonesian craft SMEs: value-based motivations and intersections of identities	X	I	X
Sawaean et al. (2021)	Entrepreneurial leadership and organizational performance of SMEs in Kuwait: The intermediate mechanisms of innovation management and learning orientation	X	I	X
Tefera, O., & Dlamini, W. (2021)	Effect of innovation, knowledge sharing and trust culture on hotels' SMEs growth in Eswatini	X	X	I

Table 20.1A (continued)

Reference	Title	SE	CU	EO
Venter, E., & Hayidakis, H. (2021)	Determinants of innovation and its impact on financial performance in South African family and non-family small and medium-sized enterprises	X	I	X
Krobbuaban et al. (2021)	The influence of organizational culture and entrepreneurial orientation on organizational performance: Organizational innovation as a mechanism in Thailand SMES	X	X	I
Sawaean, F.A.A., & Ali, K.A.M. (2021)	The nexus between learning orientation, TQM practices, innovation culture, and organizational performance of SMEs in Kuwait	X	X	I
Hamdan, Y., & Alheet, A.F. (2020)	Influence of organizational culture on pro-activeness, innovativeness and risk taking behaviour of SMEs	X	X	I
Jardon, C.M., & Martinez-Cobas, X. (2020)	Culture and competitiveness in small-scale Latin-American forestry-based enterprising communities	X	X	I
Khedhaouria et al. (2020)	The relationship between organizational culture and small-firm performance: Entrepreneurial orientation as mediator	I	X	I
Şahin, F., & Gürbüz, S. (2020)	Entrepreneurial orientation and international performance: The moderating role of cultural intelligence	I	X	I
Bhatti et al. (2020)	Organizational capabilities mediates between organizational culture, entrepreneurial orientation, and organizational performance of SMEs in Pakistan	X	X	I
Abadli et al. (2020)	Entrepreneurial culture and promotion of exporting in Algerian SMEs: Perception, reality and challenges	X	X	I
Roopchund, R. (2020)	SMEs in Mauritius: Economic growth, employment and entrepreneurial culture	X	X	I
Prasannavadanan et al. (2020)	Regional cultural diversities amongst small business entrepreneurs in India	X	X	I
Soomro, B.A., & Shah, N. (2019)	Determining the impact of entrepreneurial orientation and organizational culture on job satisfaction, organizational commitment, and employee's performance	I	X	I
Győri et al. (2019)	Innovation, financial culture, and the social-economic environment of SMEs in Hungary	X	X	I
Hanifah et al. (2019)	Emanating the key factors of innovation performance: Leveraging on the innovation culture among SMEs in Malaysia	X	I	X

Table 20.1A (continued)

Reference	Title	SE	CU	EO
Kadam et al. (2019)	Impact of cultural intelligence on SME performance: The mediating effect of entrepreneurial orientation	X	X	I
Toubes et al. (2019)	Cross-cultural analysis of Japanese and Mediterranean entrepreneurs during the global economic crisis	I	X	I
Lee et al. (2019)	Organizational culture and entrepreneurial orientation: An orthogonal perspective of individualism and collectivism	I	X	I
Baghel, D., & Parthasarathy, D. (2019)	Knowledge generation for innovation in ayurvedic cosmetics MSMEs: Investigating entrepreneur's cultural and symbolic capital	X	X	I
Mutiara et al (2019)	Exploring cultural orientation on the entrepreneur competencies in the globalization era	I	X	I
Del Carmen Vásquez Torres et al. (2018)	The organizational culture of family enterprises and their relationship with innovation in the municipality of Cajeme, Mexico	I	I	I
Tanyavutti et al. (2018)	An idea generation tool harnessing cultural heritage for design-driven entrepreneurs	I	X	I
Villena-Manzanares et al. (2018)	Entrepreneurial culture, corporate imagen and export performance: An empirical study	I	X	I
Maelah, R., & Nor Yadzid, N.H. (2018)	Budgetary control, corporate culture and performance of small and medium enterprises (SMEs) in Malaysia	X	I	I
Thampi et al. (2018)	Revisiting Hofstede in the Indian context: Understanding the influence of entrepreneurial culture on performance of micro, small and medium enterprises	X	X	I
Ali et al. (2017)	The effect of entrepreneurial orientation, market orientation, total quality management and organizational culture on the SMEs performance: A theoretical framework	X	X	I
Cherchem, N. (2017)	The relationship between organizational culture and entrepreneurial orientation in family firms: Does generational involvement matter?	I	X	I
Sulhaini, S. (2017)	Assessing value co-creation and new product success from cultural orientations and relationship marketing perspectives	I	X	X
Hanifah et al. (2017)	Understanding the innovation culture towards innovation performance among Bumiputera SMEs	X	X	I
Anggadwita et al. (2017)	Socio-cultural environments and emerging economy entrepreneurship women entrepreneurs in Indonesia	I	X	I

Table 20.1A (continued)

Reference	Title	SE	CU	EO
Naidu, S., & Chand, A. (2017)	National culture, gender inequality and women's success in micro, small and medium enterprises	X	I	I
Dimitratos et al. (2016)	SME internationalization: How does the opportunity-based international entrepreneurial culture matter?	X	I	X
Pedrini et al. (2016)	The impact of national culture and social capital on corporate social responsibility attitude among immigrants entrepreneurs	I	X	I
Laforet, S. (2016)	Effects of organizational culture on organizational innovation performance in family firms	I	X	I
Semrau et al. (2016)	Entrepreneurial orientation and SME performance across societal cultures: An international study	X	X	I
Aliyu et al. (2015)	Knowledge management, entrepreneurial orientation and firm performance: The role of organizational culture	I	X	I
Brettel et al. (2015)	How organizational culture influences innovativeness, proactiveness, and risk-taking: Fostering entrepreneurial orientation in SMEs	X	X	I
Charoensukmongkol, P. (2015)	Cultural intelligence of entrepreneurs and international network ties: The case of small and medium manufacturing firms in Thailand	X	X	I
Thampi et al. (2015)	Cultural characteristics of small business entrepreneurs in India: Examining the adequacy of Hofstede's framework	I	X	I
Gnizy et al. (2014)	Proactive learning culture: A dynamic capability and key success factor for SMEs entering foreign markets	X	X	I
Shehu, A.M., & Mahmood, R. (2014)	The mediating effect of organizational culture on the relationship between entrepreneurial orientation and firm performance in Nigeria	I	X	I
Harbi et al. (2014)	Innovation culture in small Tunisian ICT firms	X	X	I
Felício et al. (2013)	Cross-cultural analysis of the global mindset and the internationalization behavior of small firms	X	X	I
Singh et al. (2013)	Interplay between entrepreneurial characteristics, organizational structure, corporate culture and SME performance: Empirical results from Fiji Islands	X	X	I
Wolf et al. (2012)	Exploring innovating cultures in small and medium-sized enterprises: Findings from central Switzerland	X	X	I
Ahmad et al. (2012)	A cross-cultural insight into the competency-mix of SME entrepreneurs in Australia and Malaysia	X	X	X

Table 20.1A (continued)

Reference	Title	SE	CU	EO
Altinay, L., & Wang, C.L. (2011)	The influence of an entrepreneur's socio-cultural characteristics on the entrepreneurial orientation of small firms	X	X	I
Minai et al. (2011)	The moderating effect of culture on small firm performance: Empirical evidence	I	X	I
Chalhoub, M.S. (2011)	Culture, management practices, and the entrepreneurial performance of small and medium enterprises: Applications and empirical study in the Middle East	X	X	I
Kreiser et al. (2010)	Cultural influences on entrepreneurial orientation: The impact of national culture on risk taking and proactiveness in SMEs	X	X	I
Walczak-Duraj, D. (2010)	Model of entrepreneurship and social-cultural and market orientation of small business owners in Poland	X	I	I
Jack et al. (2006)	Small entrepreneurial ventures culture, change and the impact on HRM: A critical review	X	I	I
Yetim, N., & Yetim, U. (2006)	The cultural orientations of entrepreneurs and employees' job satisfaction: The Turkish small and medium sized enterprises (SMEs) case	X	X	I
Hung, C.M., & Katsioloudes, M.I. (2002)	Cultural context and the Vietnamese-American entrepreneurial experience	I	X	I
Minguzzi, A., & Passaro, R. (2001)	The network of relationships between the economic environment and the entrepreneurial culture in small firms	X	X	I
Choueke, R., & Armstrong, R. (2000)	Culture: A missing perspective on small- and medium-sized enterprise development?	X	X	I
Raffo et al. (2000)	Teaching and learning entrepreneurship for micro and small businesses in the cultural industries sector	X	I	I
Gibb, A. (1999)	Creating an entrepreneurial culture in support of SMEs	X	X	I
Gibb, A. (1993)	Enterprise culture and education: Understanding enterprise education and its links with small business, entrepreneurship and wider educational goals	X	X	I

Note: SME Entrepreneurship=SE; Culture=CU; Entrepreneurial Opportunities=EO; X=Explicit; I=Implicit.

References

Abdulghaffar, N.A., & Akkad, G.S. (2021). Internal and external barriers to entrepreneurship in Saudi Arabia. *Digest of Middle East Studies*, *30*(2), 116–134.

Abdullahi, M.A., Mohamed, Z., Shamsudin, M.N., Sharifuddin, J., & Ali, F. (2018). Effects of top leadership culture and strategic sustainability orientation on sustainable development among Malaysian herbal-based SMEs. *Business Strategy & Development*, *1*(2), 128–139.

Achim, M.V., Borlea, S.N., & Văidean, V.L. (2021). Culture, entrepreneurship and economic development. An empirical approach. *Entrepreneurship Research Journal*, *11*(1).

Ahmad, N.H., Wilson, C., & Kummerow, L. (2011). A cross-cultural insight into the competency-mix of SME entrepreneurs in Australia and Malaysia. *International Journal of Business and Management Science*, *4*(1), 33–50.

Alvarez, S.A., & Barney, J.B. (2010). Entrepreneurship and epistemology: The philosophical underpinnings of the study of entrepreneurial opportunities. *Academy of Management Annals*, *4*(1), 557–583.

Anning-Dorson, T. (2021). Organizational culture and leadership as antecedents to organizational flexibility: Implications for SME competitiveness. *Journal of Entrepreneurship in Emerging Economies*, *13*(5), 1309–1325.

Aparicio, S., Urbano, D., & Stenholm, P. (2021). Attracting the entrepreneurial potential: A multilevel institutional approach. *Technological Forecasting and Social Change, 168*, 120748.

Brouwer, M.T. (2002). Weber, Schumpeter and Knight on entrepreneurship and economic development. *Journal of evolutionary economics*, *12*(1), 83–105.

Bunagan, V.D., & Sison, M.S.M. (2019). Entrepreneurial culture and orientations of SME owners/managers in the kingdom of Bahrain. *Journal of Small Business and Entrepreneurship*, *7*(1), 60–70.

Caputo, A., Pellegrini, M.M., Dabic, M., & Dana, L.P. (2016). Internationalization of firms from Central and Eastern Europe: A systematic literature review. *European Business Review*, *28*(6), 630–651.

Cui, A.S., Griffith, D.A., Cavusgil, S.T., & Dabic, M. (2006). The influence of market and cultural environmental factors on technology transfer between foreign MNCs and local subsidiaries: A Croatian illustration. *Journal of World Business*, *41*(2), 100–111.

Dabić, M., Lažnjak, J., Smallbone, D., & Švarc, J. (2018). Intellectual capital, organizational climate, innovation culture, and SME performance: Evidence from Croatia. *Journal of Small Business and Enterprise Development*, *26*(4), 522–544.

Dabić, M., Maley, J., Dana, L.P., Novak, I., Pellegrini, M.M., & Caputo, A. (2019). Pathways of SME internationalization: A bibliometric and systematic review. *Small Business Economics*, *85*, 1–21.

Dana, L.P. (1993). An inquiry into culture and entrepreneurship: Case studies of business creation among immigrants in Montreal. *Journal of Small Business & Entrepreneurship*, *10*(4), 16–31.

Dana, L.P. (1995). Entrepreneurship in a remote sub-Arctic community. *Entrepreneurship Theory and Practice*, *20*(1), 57–72.

Dana, L.P. (2013). Is the identification of opportunity for entrepreneurship objective or is opportunity identification tinted by culture? Inaugural Address spoken in abbreviated form at the public acceptance of the professorship at Open Universiteit of the Netherlands, Heerlen, on 31 October, 2013 by Prof. dr. Léo-Paul Dana, Heerlen: Open University of the Netherlands.

Dana, L.P. (2015). Indigenous entrepreneurship: an emerging field of research. *International Journal of Business and Globalisation*, *14*(2), 158–169.

Davey, T., Hannon, P., & Penaluna, A. (2016). Entrepreneurship education and the role of universities in entrepreneurship: Introduction to the special issue. *Industry and higher education*, *30*(3), 171–182.

Davidsson, P. (2015). Entrepreneurial opportunities and the entrepreneurship nexus: A re-conceptualization. *Journal of business venturing*, *30*(5), 674–695.

de Araújo Lima, P.F., Crema, M., & Verbano, C. (2020). Risk management in SMEs: A systematic literature review and future directions. *European Management Journal*, *38*(1), 78–94.

Dheer, R.J., Li, M., & Treviño, L.J. (2019). An integrative approach to the gender gap in entrepreneurship across nations. *Journal of World Business*, *54*(6), 101004.

Duman, L., Bedük, A., Köylüoğlu, A.S., & Ay, K. (2015). Entrepreneurship culture at SMEs: A case study in konya. *Procedia-social and behavioral sciences*, *207*, 492–501.

Eniola, A.A. (2020). Entrepreneurial self-efficacy and orientation for SME development. *Small Enterprise Research*, *27*(2), 125–145.

Eniola, A.A., & Dada, D.A. (2019). Entrepreneurial self-efficacy, institutional environment, and entrepreneurial orientation for SME: A review. *International Journal of Research*, *8*(2), 11–22.

Fotopoulos, G., & Storey, D.J. (2019). Public policies to enhance regional entrepreneurship: Another programme failing to deliver? *Small Business Economics*, *53*(1), 189–209.

García-Rodríguez, F.J., Gil-Soto, E., Ruiz-Rosa, I., & Gutiérrez-Taño, D. (2017). Entrepreneurial process in peripheral regions: The role of motivation and culture. *European Planning Studies*, *25*(11), 2037–2056.

Gilmore, A., McAuley, A., Gallagher, D., Massiera, P., & Gamble, J. (2013). Researching SME/entrepreneurial research: A study of journal of research in marketing and entrepreneurship (JRME) 2000–2011. *Journal of Research in Marketing and Entrepreneurship*, *15*(2), 87–100.

Grytten, O.H. (2021). Is there really a relationship between protestantism and economic growth. In *The legacy of Hans Nielsen Hauge. Puritan economics, entrepreneurship, and management*. Bodoni forlag.

Guerrero, M., Urbano, D., & Salamzadeh, A. (2014). Evolving entrepreneurial universities: Experiences and challenges in the Middle Eastern context. In *Handbook on the Entrepreneurial University*. Edward Elgar Publishing.

Guiliani, F., & Torrès, O. (2018). Entrepreneurship: an insomniac discipline? An empirical study on SME owners/directors. *International Journal of Entrepreneurship and Small Business*, *35*(1), 81–101.

Hanifah, H., Halim, H.A., Ahmad, N.H., & Vafaei-Zadeh, A. (2019). Emanating the key factors of innovation performance: Leveraging on the innovation culture among SMEs in Malaysia. *Journal of Asia Business Studies*, *13*(4), 559–587.

Hofstede, G., Noorderhaven, N.G., Thurik, A.R., Uhlaner, L.M., Wennekers, A.R., & Wildeman, R.E. (2004). Culture's role in entrepreneurship: Self-employment out of dissatisfaction. *Innovation, entrepreneurship and culture: The interaction between technology, progress and economic growth*, 162203.

Holcombe, R.G. (2003). The origins of entrepreneurial opportunities. *The Review of Austrian Economics*, *16*(1), 25–43.

Jenssen, J.I., & Kristiansen, S. (2004). Sub-cultures and entrepreneurship: The value of social capital in Tanzanian business. *The journal of Entrepreneurship*, *13*(1), 1–27.

Katz, J.A. (1991). The institution and infrastructure of entrepreneurship. *Entrepreneurship Theory and Practice*, *15*(3), 85–102.

Kirby, D.A., & Ibrahim, N. (2011). Entrepreneurship education and the creation of an enterprise culture: Provisional results from an experiment in Egypt. *International Entrepreneurship and Management Journal*, *7*(2), 181–193.

Krasniqi, B.A. (2007). Barriers to entrepreneurship and SME growth in transition: The case of Kosova. *Journal of Developmental Entrepreneurship*, *12*(01), 71–94.

Krueger, N., Liñán, F., & Nabi, G. (2013). Cultural values and entrepreneurship. *Entrepreneurship & Regional Development*, *25*(9–10), 703–707.

Laforet, S. (2016). Effects of organizational culture on organizational innovation performance in family firms. *Journal of Small Business and Enterprise Development*, *23*(2), 379–407.

Landes, D.S. (1949). French entrepreneurship and industrial growth in the nineteenth century. *The Journal of Economic History*, *9*(1), 45–61.

Light, I., & Dana, L.P. (2020). *Entrepreneurs and capitalism since Luther: Rediscovering the moral economy*. Lexington Books.

Liñán, F., Paul, J., & Fayolle, A. (2020). SMEs and entrepreneurship in the era of globalization: Advances and theoretical approaches. *Small Business Economics*, *55*(3), 695–703.

Lundström, A., & Stevenson, L. (2005). *Entrepreneurship policy: Theory and practice* (Vol. 9). Springer.

Mamman, A., Bawole, J., Agbebi, M., & Alhassan, A.R. (2019). SME policy formulation and implementation in Africa: Unpacking assumptions as opportunity for research direction. *Journal of business research*, *97*, 304–315.

Marchesnay, M. (2011). Fifty years of entrepreneurship and SME: A personal view. *Journal of Small Business and Enterprise Development*, *18*(2), 352–365.

Mueller, P. (2007). Exploiting entrepreneurial opportunities: The impact of entrepreneurship on growth. *Small Business Economics*, *28*(4), 355–362.

Pedrini, M., Bramanti, V., & Cannatelli, B. (2016). The impact of national culture and social capital on corporate social responsibility attitude among immigrants entrepreneurs. *Journal of Management & Governance*, *20*(4), 759–787.

Puumalainen, K., Sjögrén, H., Syrjä, P., & Barraket, J. (2015). Comparing social entrepreneurship across nations: An exploratory study of institutional effects. *Canadian Journal of Administrative Sciences/Revue Canadienne des Sciences de l'Administration*, *32*(4), 276–287.

Qureshi, M.I., Parveen, S., Abdullah, I., & Dana, L.P. (2021). Reconceptualizing the interventions of open innovation systems between the nexus of quadruple organization cultural dynamics and performance. *Quality & Quantity*, *55*(5), 1661–1681.

Ratnasingam, J., Ab Latib, H., Mariapan, M., Othman, K., Amir, M.A., & Liat, L.C. (2021). Success factors of small and medium enterprises in the malaysian furniture industry: Discerning the growth of entrepreneurs. *BioResources*, *16*(3), 5586–5600.

Ratten, V. (2014). Future research directions for collective entrepreneurship in developing countries: A small and medium-sized enterprise perspective. *International Journal of Entrepreneurship and Small Business*, *22*(2), 266–274.

Salamzadeh, A., Farsi, J.Y., Motavaseli, M., Markovic, M.R., & Kesim, H.K. (2015). Institutional factors affecting the transformation of entrepreneurial universities. *International Journal of Business and Globalisation*, *14*(3), 271–291.

Salamzadeh, A., Radovic Markovic, M., & Masjed, S.M. (2019). The effect of media convergence on exploitation of entrepreneurial opportunities. *AD-minister*, *34*, 59–76.

Salamzadeh, Y., Farzad, F.S., Salamzadeh, A., & Palalić, R. (2022). Digital leadership and organizational capabilities in manufacturing industry: A study in Malaysian context. *Periodicals of Engineering and Natural Sciences*, *10*(1), 195–211.

Semrau, T., Ambos, T., & Kraus, S. (2016). Entrepreneurial orientation and SME performance across societal cultures: An international study. *Journal of Business Research*, *69*(5), 1928–1932.

Shane, S., & Venkataraman, S. (2001). Entrepreneurship as a field of research: A response to Zahra and Dess, Singh, and Erikson. *Academy of Management Review*, *26*(1), 13–16.

Smallbone, D. (2016). Entrepreneurship policy: Issues and challenges. *Small Enterprise Research*, *23*(3), 201–218.

Smith, H.L. (2021). Entrepreneurs, entrepreneurship policy and regional innovation systems. In *Unlocking Regional Innovation and Entrepreneurship*. Edward Elgar Publishing.

Stuetzer, M., Audretsch, D.B., Obschonka, M., Gosling, S.D., Rentfrow, P.J., & Potter, J. (2018). Entrepreneurship culture, knowledge spillovers and the growth of regions. *Regional Studies*, *52*(5), 608–618.

Su, J., Zhai, Q., & Karlsson, T. (2017). Beyond red tape and fools: Institutional theory in entrepreneurship research, 1992–2014. *Entrepreneurship Theory and Practice*, *41*(4), 505–531.

Tur-Porcar, A., Roig-Tierno, N., & Llorca Mestre, A. (2018). Factors affecting entrepreneurship and business sustainability. *Sustainability*, *10*(2), 452.

Ulijn, J., & Salamzadeh, A. (2022). Investigating the influence of cultural factors in the disclosure of corporate strategies in annual reports by 100 European firms: Does context matter? *International Journal of Business and Globalisation*, forthcoming.

Valliere, D. (2019). Refining national culture and entrepreneurship: The role of subcultural variation. *Journal of Global Entrepreneurship Research, 9*(1), 1–22.

Welter, F. (2009). On the road to a "culture of entrepreneurship"? In *Public policies for fostering entrepreneurship* (pp. 181–195). Springer.

Xia, T., & Liu, X. (2021). Cultural values and innovation: The mediating role of entrepreneurial learning capacity. *Journal of International Management, 27*(1), 100812.

Zanella, G., Solano, D.B.C., Hallam, C.R., & Guda, T. (2019). The role of the organization in the entrepreneur-opportunity nexus. *International Journal of Entrepreneurial Behavior & Research, 25*(7), 1537–1562.

Tatiana Beliaeva, Vincent Mangematin, and Agnès Guerraz[†]

21 Emerging Artificial Intelligence Methods for Predicting SME Growth: Opportunities and Challenges

Abstract: While SME growth has attracted substantial interest and massive empirical research, the results of existing studies are inconclusive and have low predictive power, calling for exploiting of new methodologies. The explosion in available data and advances in artificial intelligence for predictive analytics have a potential to provide novel perspectives to growth studies. In this chapter, we combine the literature on SME growth with AI-based studies in entrepreneurship and suggest how growth research may advance by the application of AI methods. Opportunities and challenges of AI methods are compared with traditional methods in terms of growth prediction. The analysis also provides the research agenda to guide scholars willing to leverage AI in growth research.

Keywords: SME growth, data science, artificial intelligence, big data, prediction, methodology

Introduction

The importance of entrepreneurship and small and medium-sized enterprises (SMEs) for the economy (Ferreira et al., 2019) and considerable variance in their growth rates have generated numerous studies seeking to explain why some firms experience more growth than others. Existing growth models suggest that new venture growth factors include their strategy, resources, the industry involved, their organizational structure and systems, and the entrepreneur characteristics (Gilbert et al., 2006).

Despite extensive research into firm growth, however, empirical analyses of growth factors report low predictive power (Coad et al., 2013; McKelvie & Wiklund, 2010). Coad et al. (2013, p. 616) theorized "the growth and survival of new businesses by referring to a gambler playing a game of chance." The authors observed "the diversity of growth patterns and the fact that firms have an almost equal probability of

---

[†] This author is deceased

Tatiana Beliaeva, Skopai France; Université Catholique de Lyon/ESDES Lyon Business School, Unité de Recherche "Confluence: Sciences et Humanités", Institute of Sustainable Business and Organizations, France
Vincent Mangematin, KEDGE Business School, France; Université Catholique de Lyon/ESDES Lyon Business School, Unité de Recherche "Confluence: Sciences et Humanités", Institute of Sustainable Business and Organizations, France
Agnès Guerraz, Skopai, France

https://doi.org/10.1515/9783110747652-022

exhibiting any of these growth paths" (Coad et al., 2013, p. 623). In a later exchange, Derbyshire and Garnsey (2014, 2015) and Coad et al. (2015) reflected on the firm growth debate. The former showed that randomness can reflect the methods used, and suggested analyzing firms as if they were complex adaptive systems, which "requires a whole new set of methods and theoretical logic" (Derbyshire & Garnsey, 2014, p. 11). Recently, van Witteloostuijn and Kolkman (2019) capitalized on the data science revolution (Chen et al., 2012; McAfee & Brynjolfsson, 2012) to improve the performance of firm growth models. The authors compared regression with a machine learning (ML) technique and found that the latter yielded a much higher goodness-of-fit, indicating that "perhaps firm growth is less random than suggested by traditional regression analysis" and "machine learning can be of value to firm growth research" (van Witteloostuijn & Kolkman, 2019, p. 1).

In recent years, the explosion in available data and advances in data science have enabled the processing of large amounts of information, offering new opportunities for businesses and researchers (Chen et al., 2012; Obschonka & Audretsch, 2020; Schwab & Zhang, 2019). Artificial intelligence (AI) and ML have made it possible to collect fine-grained information about micro-events in real-time and to make predictions based on hundreds of different variables. As a result, companies are increasingly integrating digital technologies in their business models (Bouncken et al., 2021). Moreover, scholars have started to rely on ML algorithms to provide novel insights into entrepreneurship and firm growth research (e.g., Coad & Srhoj, 2020; Weinblat, 2018).

Over the last few years, several high-quality reviews of different kinds of literature on firm growth have contributed to a re-structuring of the knowledge in the field (e.g., Dobbs & Hamilton, 2007; Gilbert et al., 2006; McKelvie & Wiklund, 2010). In addition, a number of valuable contributions have been made as a result of reviewing the literature on the use of AI in business (e.g., Vlačić et al., 2021; Zeba et al., 2021). However, the role of AI as a method of research is underexplored in entrepreneurship literature. Scholars have recently called for the integration of data science methods into entrepreneurship phenomena research, in order to extend the research scope and relevance (Lévesque et al., 2020). This is particularly relevant in the context of the firm growth debate. Yet, there is a lack of understanding as to how emerging methods that are based on massive amounts of data may contribute to firm growth prediction. This chapter aims to fill this gap by synthesizing the existing knowledge base on SME growth, comparing AI-based methods with traditional methods, and proposing avenues for future research.

It addresses the following research questions: (1) what is the current state of SME growth research and how are data science and AI methods used to study SME growth?; (2) what are the relative advantages and disadvantages of emerging data science methods when compared with traditional methods of firm growth research?; and (3) what are the promising research directions for scholars willing to leverage AI methods in their growth studies? We conduct a literature review of SME growth studies and analyses of data science and AI-driven research approaches in entrepreneurship and management. The qualitative analysis focuses on theories, data, methods, model performance, and main contributions. The results highlight the opportunities and challenges that are presented by big data and AI when predicting SME growth. The benefits include an enhanced ability to predict and extrapolate by means of a data-driven approach. In a highly dynamic environment, AI methods enable samples to be updated with the new data and may produce many more predictors than traditional statistical methods. The challenges relate to the theoretical explanations behind these predictions. Furthermore, the results suggest promising research avenues for analyzing SME growth using data science methods.

The chapter proceeds as follows. In the following section, we present the research design. We then discuss SME growth models, and the emergence of an AI-driven approach to growth prediction. We then go on to compare current AI methods with traditional methods and end with a research agenda to help guide future SME growth investigations that apply data science methods.

Research Design

We conducted a qualitative literature review to examine SME growth explanations and predictions. Given the different stages of development of SME growth and AI-based research, we performed two literature searches. The research design is presented in Figure 21.1.

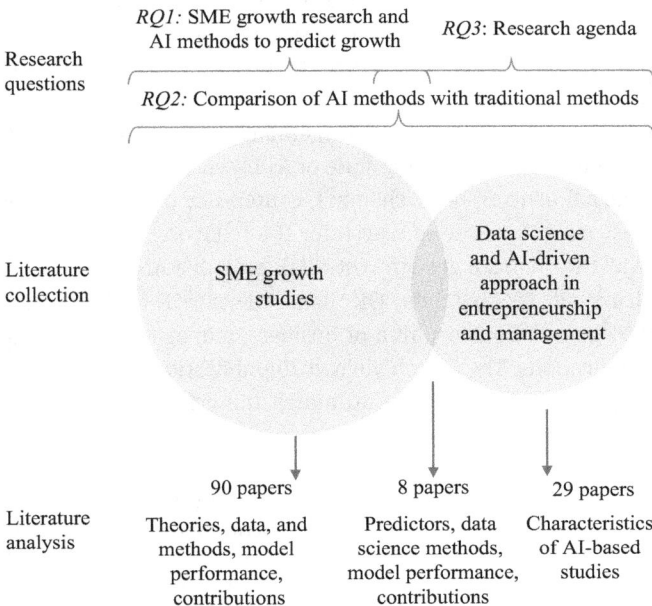

Figure 21.1: Research design.

First, we drew together the empirical studies that have analyzed SME growth using traditional methods. Following the recommendations made by Short (2009), we examined the relevant literature published in the leading management, entrepreneurship, and small business journals. We used the *Financial Times* (FT) list of 50 journals[1] and the 2021 *Academic Journal Guide* (AJG) of Chartered Association of Business Schools (CABS)[2] to select the journals. We limited our search to journals ranked 4*, 4, and 3 according to AJG to ensure high standards of quality and transparency (Kraus et al., 2020). We searched the *Academy of Management Journal*, the *Academy of Management Review*, the *Administrative Science Quarterly*, *Entrepreneurship & Regional Development*, *Entrepreneurship Theory and Practice*, the *International Small Business Journal*, the *Journal of Business Venturing*, the *Journal of Management*, the *Journal of Management Studies*, the *Journal of Small Business Management*, *Management Science*, *Organization Science*, *Small Business Economics*, the *Strategic Entrepreneurship Journal*, and the *Strategic Management Journal*. These journals are recognized globally by high-quality publications, generally have the highest impact factors, and are appropriate means of disseminating information on management and entrepreneurship issues given the SME growth topic. We used the search terms "firm growth" OR "business growth" OR "venture growth" OR "SME growth," which resulted in 142 articles in 13 journals. To meet the inclusion criteria, the articles needed to be empirical quantitative studies, focusing on SMEs and analyzing growth as a dependent variable. Furthermore, one of the authors manually reviewed the titles, abstracts, and, where necessary, text of the articles and selected those sources that were relevant to the inclusion criteria. This produced 90 articles, published between 1989 and 2022. Whilst analyzing the articles, we examined and discussed theories and research designs to structure the literature, as well as contributions and model performance.

Second, we brought together studies that applied AI methods to the investigation of the growth phenomenon. Considering the emerging state of AI-based research in entrepreneurship, we included journal articles, book chapters, conference papers, and discussion papers. We used the Scopus database to search for the following terms: ("firm growth" OR "business growth" OR "venture growth" OR "SME growth") AND ("artificial intelligence" OR "machine learning" OR "big data" OR "data science" OR "AI") in titles, abstracts, and keywords. We chose the subject area of business, management, and accounting amongst English publications. The search yielded 29 publications. In addition, one of the authors manually screened the papers to match the criteria of the SME

---

1 The FT list includes 50 journals used by the Financial Times to compile the FT Research rank, which is included in the Global MBA, EMBA, and Online MBA rankings. More information about the FT list is available at https://www.ft.com/content/3405a512-5cbb-11e1-8f1f-00144feabdc0.

2 The AJG classifies journals as follows: 4* (journals of distinction), 4 (top journals), 3 (highly regarded journals), 2 (well regarded journals), 1 (journals publishing research of a recognized, but more modest standard). More information about AJG methodology is available at https://charteredabs.org/academic-journal-guide-2021/.

growth study and the AI research method. Only three papers met the inclusion criteria, whereas most other papers examined the use of AI in a business setting. We then performed an additional search using the reference lists and included five other papers. In total, this produced eight publications on SME growth and AI methodology, affirming the emerging state of research. We examined growth predictors, data science methods, contributions, and the performance of predictive models. Furthermore, we complemented the review with studies on data science and an AI-driven research approach in entrepreneurship and management in general. Mindful of how niche this field is, we searched reference lists of the relevant conceptual and empirical studies (e.g., George et al., 2016; Obschonka & Audretsch, 2020) and added 29 papers. In these papers, almost half of which are conceptual, we analyzed the characteristics of AI-based entrepreneurship research.

Understanding SME Growth and its Determinants

Growth Models

Firm growth is among the key topics in entrepreneurship research, and massive empirical research and conceptual developments have been published to date. Growth is a complex, multidimensional, and heterogeneous construct (Leitch et al., 2010). The most frequently suggested indicators of growth include a change in sales, employment, and market share (Gilbert et al., 2006).

To address the first part of the first research question about the current state of SME growth research, we categorized the SME growth publications according to the theoretical perspectives used to explain firm growth and the empirical data used to test the models. The theories and data used to understand growth are vast and vary substantially (McKelvie & Wiklund, 2010). The studies explain growth using individual-level, firm-level, and environmental-level theoretical perspectives, or their combination. This classification is consistent with Baum et al. (2001), who used multiple levels (entrepreneurs, competitive strategy, and environment) to explain venture growth. Similarly, Davidsson and Wiklund (2000) proposed the motivation perspective, the resource-based perspective, and the strategic adaptation perspective, and Wright and Stigliani (2013) examined the effects of entrepreneurs, resource orchestration, and contextual-level factors on entrepreneurial growth. In terms of data sources, we classified studies according to whether they use survey data, national statistics and business registers, or other databases. Additionally, we analyzed the focus, main contributions, and performance of econometric models. Table 21.1 summarizes the theoretical perspectives and data sources of traditional SME growth methods-based studies.

The review showed how diverse and pluralistic the theoretical perspectives and models used for studying SME growth are. The individual-level variables explain firm

Table 21.1: Theoretical perspectives and data sources of traditional SME growth methods-based studies.

Theoretical perspectives / Data sources	Individual-level: psychological, cognitive, motivation, upper echelons, lifespan, feminist perspectives	Firm-level: economic, resource-based, human capital, social capital, network, strategic management perspectives	Environmental level: institutional, contingency, fit, macroeconomic perspectives	Integrative models: a combination of individual-level, firm-level, and/or environmental level perspectives
Survey	9 papers (e.g., Baum & Bird, 2010; Delmar & Wiklund, 2008; Moen et al., 2016)	18 papers (e.g., Altinay et al., 2016; Bruton & Rubanik, 2002; Nason et al., 2019; Premaratne, 2001)	1 paper (Covin et al., 2000)	9 papers (e.g., Baum et al., 2001; Koeller & Lechler, 2006; Wiklund et al., 2009)
National statistics and business registers	1 paper (Bird & Zellweger, 2018)	16 papers (e.g., Davidsson et al., 2002; Greve, 2008; Yang & Tsou, 2020)	6 papers (e.g., Ang, 2008; Garsaa & Levratto, 2015; Martín-García & Morán Santor, 2021)	7 papers (e.g., Kangasharju, 2000; Peric & Vitezik, 2016)
Other databases (e.g., Bureau van Dijk)	2 papers (e.g., Yamakawa et al., 2015)	19 papers (e.g., Barroso-Castro et al., 2022; Roper, 1997; Schoonjans et al., 2013)	3 papers (e.g., Cainelli & Ganau, 2019; Eberhart et al., 2017)	3 papers (e.g., Castrogiovanni & Justis, 2002)
Focus and main contributions	Focus is on how individuals and their actions affect firm growth. The importance of the entrepreneur's personality and psychology to the venture success	Focus is on how firms, and their competitive strategies and resources, explain firm growth. The role of a unique combination of resources and capabilities in the development of business activities and growth	Focus is on how industry-specific factors and the external environment affect firm growth. The role of competitive intensity, institutions, and the environment in firm growth opportunities	Building comprehensive, multilevel models of firm growth by simultaneously considering the constructs from different perspectives and examining their relationships to produce a more complete understanding of firm growth
R^2	Low	Low to medium	Low	Low to medium

Notes: Data sources are not mutually exclusive, and papers combining multiple datasets belong to multiple cells.

growth in 12 of the studies analyzed. The studies focus on individuals and their characteristics and apply psychological theories such as cognitive and motivation theories to explain the differences in growth rates (e.g., Moen et al., 2016; Yamakawa et al., 2015). The firm-level analyses represent the largest group of studies analyzed (50 studies). They focus on firm-specific resources, capabilities, and strategies to explain SME growth from resource-based, human capital, social capital, network, and strategic management perspectives (e.g., Altinay et al., 2016; Bruton & Rubanik, 2002; Schoonjans et al., 2013). The early economic models that analyzed firm characteristics such as firm age and size also fall into this group (e.g., Wagner, 1992). The environmental level perspective with regard to firm growth (nine studies) focuses on understanding the role of industry-specific factors as well as the broader institutional and macroeconomic environment (e.g., Ang, 2008; Martín-García & Morán Santor, 2021). Integrative models of firm growth combine multilevel growth factors (19 studies) and develop a "big picture" by simultaneously considering multiple factors and the relationships between them to arrive at a more complete understanding of growth (e.g., Baum et al., 2001; Castrogiovanni & Justis, 2002; Wiklund et al., 2009).

With regard to data sources, individual-level studies predominantly collected data using a survey. On the other hand, studies in the environmental level group mostly used national statistics and other databases that provide industry and macro-level data. Firm-level and integrative models relied on both primary survey and secondary databases. The methodology used in modeling firm growth relied on statistical methods such as multiple regression, logistic regression, structural equation modeling (SEM), partial least squares (PLS), cluster analysis, analysis of variance (ANOVA), and discriminant analysis. In general, the analyzed studies show low to medium coefficient of determination R^2 values of SME growth models, which is consistent with several other observations (e.g., Coad, 2009; Dobbs & Hamilton, 2007; Wright & Stigliani, 2013).

The Need for Higher Predictive Power in Growth Research

The extensive number and variety of perspectives around the study of firm growth have provided valuable contributions to the theoretical explanations of growth. However, studies have recognized that theoretical models have been of limited use in predicting the phenomenon, and the message has emerged that growth largely seems to be a random process (Coad, 2009; Coad et al., 2013). Despite the use of numerous theoretical models and a wide variety of empirical data and methods to tackle the problem, ranging from survey data to large panel datasets, econometric analysis appears to be inconclusive regarding the determinants of growth. Empirical studies have been unable to isolate variables that have a consistent effect on firm growth (Shepherd & Wiklund, 2009). There is a high heterogeneity among high-growth firms, which complicates the identification of common characteristics.

Studies also emphasize the fragmented knowledge base and recognize, in some cases, the weaknesses of the empirical work to date. There have been discussions about how the study of firm growth should be approached, levels of analysis, and the appropriateness of matching theory with methods. In terms of furthering the development of entrepreneurship and growth studies, Leitch et al. (2010, p. 252) pointed out that "the production of rich, in-depth knowledge requires researchers to adopt diverse ontological and epistemological positions." The authors emphasized the importance of recognizing that the traditional approach to methodology is less adapted to the study of ephemeral, indefinite, and irregular phenomenon of entrepreneurship and growth. Hence, it has been proposed that greater methodological diversity and plurality should be applied to growth studies which focus on a multilevel approach, incorporating microfoundations, and dynamics (Wright & Stigliani, 2013), which would help to capture the diversity and complexity of firm growth.

Recent studies have attempted to reflect on the debate about firm growth and randomness by exploiting new methodologies. For example, van Witteloostuijn and Kolkman (2019) used ML to improve firm growth models' goodness-of-fit, when compared with the traditional regression models. Coad and Srhoj (2020, p. 541) investigated whether high-growth firms are hard to predict "because firm growth is fundamentally random, or because previous investigations had only a small number of (the wrong type of) explanatory variables." The authors examined the latter explanation by using datasets with an extensive number of time-variable predictors and by applying big data techniques. In the following section, we review the emerging AI-driven approach to growth and entrepreneurship research to better understand the role of data science methods in the prediction of firm growth, while comparing them with traditional methods.

Artificial Intelligence Methodologies for Growth Prediction

AI Methodology-based Studies in Entrepreneurship

Data are expanding dramatically in every sphere of society and business. It may stem from a variety of sources, including the internet, social media, mobile phones, user-generated content, sensors, or business transactions. Big data have several attributes, which are often referred to as the "Vs": volume (the sample size and number of variables), velocity (the speed of data collection and analysis in real or near real-time), and variety (the plurality of structured and unstructured data sources) (George et al., 2016; McAfee & Brynjolfsson, 2012). Besides these three core attributes, recently, other "Vs" were also added, such as veracity and value (Jin et al., 2015). Given the explosion in data and the advances in data science, such as data mining, data visualization, and

ML, there is an increasing reliance on algorithms to structure and analyze the data. AI can broadly refer to the development of computer systems that are capable of performing tasks and solving problems that normally require human intelligence. It is an overarching term that incorporates ML as a subset. AI is applied in various disciplines, such as biology, medicine, and climate studies. It is also growing in importance in economics, management, innovation, and psychology (Obschonka & Audretsch, 2020).

In recent years, there has been an increasing interest in the application of AI and big data to entrepreneurship research. Schwab and Zhang (2019, p. 843), in their editorial in *Entrepreneurship Theory and Practice* on a new methodological frontier in entrepreneurship research, encourage "entrepreneurship scholars to consider big data research" and offer guidance for the design and execution of empirical studies. In another editorial, Lévesque et al. (2020, p. 1) argue that "it is time for the entrepreneurship field to come to terms with leading-edge artificial intelligence" and suggest integrating AI with theory building and testing. In 2020, a special issue devoted to big data, AI, and entrepreneurship was published in *Small Business Economics*, in which the editors predicted that "AI and big data will disrupt both entrepreneurship research and practice," and "the way research and practice interact with each other" (Obschonka & Audretsch, 2020, pp. 530–531). Recently, AI-based studies have been published on such topics as the personality characteristics of entrepreneurs (Obschonka et al., 2017), the demand for entrepreneurial skills (Prüfer & Prüfer, 2020), and new venture survival (Antretter et al., 2019).

To advance the understanding of AI methods' role in the field of SME growth, and address the second part of the first research question, we summarize the characteristics of SME studies that predict growth using AI methodologies (Table 21.2). The studies have been published over the last five years and have used ML techniques to identify key growth predictors and forecast high-growth firms. They examined different variables, which are mostly related to financial and demographic firm information but also to macroeconomic indicators (Zhou & Gumbo, 2021) and business model patterns (Böhm et al., 2017), with the number of predictor variables ranging from 30 to 403. Most studies relied on company databases as data sources and compared the performance of traditional methods (OLS, logistic, stepwise regression) with ML methods (RFA, LASSO, ANN, SVM, boosted regression). Established measures of growth were used, such as sales, employment, assets, or profits growth. When estimating the performance of the models, the R^2 reached 23% in the random forest model, compared to 6% in the regression model (van Witteloostuijn & Kolkman, 2019). The share of correct predictions (accuracy) of the ML models reached 94% in the papers analyzed (Coad & Srhoj, 2020). ML techniques were generally found to perform better than regressions in predicting firm growth (Zhou & Gumbo, 2021) and enabled the identification of the most predictive variables (Weinblat, 2018; Zekić-Sušac et al., 2016). However, the goodness-of-fit indices ranged depending on the data, measures, and model selected. For example, McKenzie and Sansone (2017) noted that ML meth-

Table 21.2: Studies that use AI methodologies to predict SME growth.

Author(s)	Predictors of growth	Data collection	Methods	Growth measure	R²	Main contributions
Zhou & Gumbo (2021)	Financial (total assets, sales), demographic (e.g., firm age, location, registration, employees, owner's gender and age), digital (website, digital marketing), macroeconomic (GDP, unemployment rate, Purchasing Managers Index (PMI))	191 manufacturing SMMEs from South Africa over three years	Comparison of logistic regression and two ML techniques, artificial neural network (ANN) and support vector machine (SVM)	Growth dummy variable = 1 if a firm registered sales growth for two years	N/A (Logit) (accuracy: 75.4%; sensitivity: 98.9%; specificity: 0%); N/A (ML) (accuracy: 75.9–76.3%; sensitivity: 93.4–100%; specificity: 0–13%)	ML techniques performed better than logistic regression in predicting firm growth. The variable importance showed the extent to which factors contribute to SMME growth prediction
Coad & Srhoj (2020)	172 (Croatian sample) and 403 (Slovenian sample) variables: financial (balance sheet, profit and loss statements, export, import), demographic (e.g., firm age, employees, capital region, economic activity)	Croatian Financial Agency (FINA), 2003–2006; 212,769 observations (45,465 firms); Slovenian Agency for Public Legal Records and Related Services (AJPES), 2007–2014; 35,758 observations (14,096 firms)	Least absolute shrinkage and selection operator (LASSO)	Eurostat-OECD high-growth firms dummy, calculated for growth of either sales or employment	Pseudo-R²: 0.092–0.157 (accuracy: 72.86–94.47%; sensitivity: 32.94–58.22%; specificity:74.30–95.43%)	Identification of most relevant variables for prediction of high-growth firms

van Witteloostuijn & Kolkman (2019)	113 variables: financial (e.g., total assets, total equity, working capital, current ratio, solvency ratio), demographic (e.g., firm age, employees, country, industry)	Graydon dataset over six years; 451,432 observations (168,055 firms) from Belgium and the Netherlands	Comparison of random forest analysis (RFA) and regression (ordinary least squares (OLS) and forward stepwise regression)	Growth rate as an index of total assets growth	R^2 (regression): 0.05–0.06; R^2 (RFA): 0.16–0.23	RFA achieved a much higher goodness-of-fit and indicated that perhaps firm growth is less random than suggested by traditional regression analysis
Weinblat (2018)	30 variables: financial (e.g., debt ratio, ROA, ROS, sales per employee ratio, fixed assets ratio, equity fixed assets ratio, liquidity ratio), demographic (e.g., firm age, firm size, legal form, employees, sector)	Amadeus database; 179,970 firms from nine European countries, 2004–2014	RFA	High-growth firms dummy, Schreyer growth indicator	N/A (accuracy: 63.02–90.16%); depending on the country, the algorithm was able to determine up to 39% of all HGFs	Identification of variable importance ranking. The results enable cross-national comparisons
Böhm et al. (2017)	Business model (55 patterns, cluster, scope, focus, industry, physical assets, firm age), involved people (industry/foundation experts, investors, founding team size, education of founders, location), start-up idea (closeness to science and patents, competition, innovativeness)	Mattermark dataset, Crunchbase-Insights, Deadpool, autopsy.io, web, survey; 181 start-ups from the USA and Germany	Cluster analysis and SVM	Revenue growth	N/A (accuracy: 58.4–66.8%)	Identification of business model clusters with different growth expectations

(continued)

Table 21.2 (continued)

Author(s)	Predictors of growth	Data collection	Methods	Growth measure	R^2	Main contributions
McKenzie & Sansone (2017)	393 variables: e.g., gender, age, education, region, marital status, family composition, language, internal migrant, business background, outside employment, experience abroad, risk aversion, motivation, self-confidence, registration, assets, sector, employee education, tax paid, loans, business challenges, projected outcomes	2,506 participants in business plan competition in Nigeria over three years	Comparison of OLS and ML methods (Post-LASSO, SVM, boosted regression)	Three-year employment, sales, and profits among business plan competition participants	Adjusted R^2 (OLS): 0.011–0.125; Adjusted R^2 (ML): 0.001–0.13 (accuracy: 80.5–85.3%; sensitivity: 9–27.6%)	ML methods do not offer noticeable improvements in predicting average performance but have a role in identifying the top tail of performance

Study	Variables	Data	Methods	Dependent variable	Results	Findings
Miyakawa et al. (2017)	200 variables: firm characteristics (e.g., employees, firm age, CEO age, establishments), financial data, geography and industry variables (e.g., industry, sales growth of firms in the same city/industry); supply-chain network variables (e.g., centrality, suppliers' and customers' characteristics); TSR solvency score	TSR database; 1,700,000 firms from Japan, 2006–2014	LASSO, weighted RFA	Sales growth, profit growth	N/A (sensitivity: 22–25%)	Improved predictions of sales and profit growth; the practical usage of ML methods in firm performance prediction
Zekić-Sušac et al. (2016)	111 variables: e.g., liquidity, turnover, leverage, and profitability ratios, industry sector	Croatian Financial Agency (FINA); 1,492 firms, 2008–2013	Comparison of logistic regression and ANNs	High-growth firms = 1 if a firm's annualized asset growth exceeded 20% over a three-year period	N/A (Logit) (accuracy: 69.66%); N/A (ANNs) (accuracy: 71.03%)	Neural networks produced a higher classification accuracy in the model with all variables. Identification of the variable importance for SME growth

Notes: N/A denotes "not available."

ods allowed for better prediction of the top tail of performance when compared with the prediction of average performance.

The Added Value and Challenges of AI for Growth Research

Big data and AI methods are well suited to addressing numerous research questions and provide new research opportunities. They enable old questions to be investigated in new ways, address emerging practice needs, examine new questions, and improve science by making it possible for theories and models to be tested and retested, verified, and updated (Tonidandel et al., 2018). In addition to the aforementioned, researchers have emphasized that there are numerous challenges to conducting AI-based studies in entrepreneurship and highlighted that new data analytics is reconfiguring the scientific research process (George et al., 2016; Jin et al., 2015; Kitchin, 2014; Sivarajah et al., 2017).

Based on the literature on SME growth and the AI-driven approach in management and entrepreneurship research, we compare AI-based methods with traditional methods in terms of the different steps in the research process: research objective, epistemological approach, data collection and variables measurement, data analysis, and the theoretical and practical implications. Table 21.3 outlines the main advantages and disadvantages of AI compared with traditional methods in terms of growth prediction, which are discussed below and refer to the second research question.

Table 21.3: Advantages and disadvantages of AI-based methods compared with traditional methods of growth prediction.

Research process	Traditional research methods	AI research methods
Research objective	Explanation of a phenomenon; Selected determinants of growth explained by theories; formulation and testing of hypotheses; Difficult for studying emerging phenomena for which the theory doesn't exist	Prediction of an event; Discovering and forecasting growth without much regard for testing theories or causal models; Suited to investigating non-obvious patterns in the data, dynamic processes, and micro-events, for which models do not exist;
Epistemological approach	Deductive, theory-driven approach moving from theoretical causal models to empirical verification; Explanatory studies; Based on theories and defined profiles and characteristics of firms	Inductive, data-driven approach investigating patterns in the data and forecasting events; Quantitative exploratory studies; Based on similarities in firm profiles, adaptative and integrates many characteristics

Table 21.3 (continued)

Research process	Traditional research methods	AI research methods
Data collection and variables measurement	Data are collected in order to address a specific research question; Primary (surveys) and secondary (databases) data collection; Retrospective, more stable data; A more systematic structure in the raw data; Smaller volume of observations and variables; Lower level of data heterogeneity; Objective and self-reported measures	Big data are collected for reasons other than research (e.g., operational) and utilized for empirical investigations; Data collection that does not necessarily include conducting primary research; Real or near real-time observations, less stable data; Lack of overall systematic structure in the raw data, integration of data from a large and varied number of sources; Larger volume of observations and variables; Higher level of data heterogeneity; Numeric and non-numeric data for quantitative analysis
Data analysis	OLS regression, logistic regression, SEM, PLS, cluster analysis, ANOVA, discriminant analysis; General assumptions of linearity; Statistical significance tests; Lower predictive power; Interpretation and explanation of significant results by confirming, refining, or rejecting theoretical hypotheses	Supervised and unsupervised ML, RFA, LASSO, ANN, SVM, boosted regression; Easier incorporation of nonlinearity; Statistical significance tests are of less value for large sample sizes; Generally higher predictive power; Requires interpretation and distinguishing between the theoretically interesting results and the relatively unimportant significant results
Theoretical and practical implications	Extension and refinement of existing theories; Identification of boundary conditions of theories and context-specific relationships; Easier to define public policy due to the explanation of a phenomenon	Revealing of new patterns in the dataset which become the basis for the development of new theories; Enhancing generalizability of findings from traditional research; Higher accuracy of prediction and practical relevance

Research Objective

The scope and granularity of big data allow scholars to develop new research questions and generate better answers to established questions (George et al., 2016). AI-based methods enable analysis of patterns and the accurate prediction of future events based on a rich and comprehensive dataset, while minimizing human biases (George et al., 2014; Shmueli, 2010). Whereas traditional methods are more focused on the explanation of a phenomenon based on theoretical assumptions, AI methods discover patterns and forecast events without much regard for testing theories (Schwab & Zhang, 2019). Hence, they may be particularly helpful in cases where there is not enough knowledge to formulate hypotheses or where such knowledge is tacit and hard to formalize (van Witteloostuijn & Kolkman, 2019). AI methods have the capacity to uncover non-obvious patterns in the data, dynamic processes, and micro-events, and are useful in terms of their ability to address a number of policy-relevant prediction problems as opposed to causal inference questions (McKenzie & Sansone, 2017). For example, Böhm et al. (2017) combined data mining approaches with the business model concept to predict the success of start-ups, which enables empirically informed strategic and investment decisions to be made. Coad and Karlsson (2022) used Swedish total population data to map the distribution of high-growth firms, which included any combination of firm size and age and provided a rich non-parametric representation using contour maps.

Epistemological Approach

AI and ML are strongly associated with prediction that is based on empirical characteristics and similarity of firm profile. The number and types of predictors are typically broad. Their inclusion is limited by how much data are available rather than theoretical considerations. Traditional quantitative growth studies generally adopt a deductive, theory-driven approach and focus on theoretical explanation and empirical verification of the hypothesized relationships. In contrast, AI studies are often of an exploratory and data-driven nature, which makes the formulation of hypotheses premature. By engaging in fact-finding quantitative exploratory research and analyzing generic modeling using a wide range of predictors, AI-based studies challenge the field of entrepreneurship, which is dominated by the deductive approach, and call for a new way of framing growth studies (Coad & Srhoj, 2020). Kolkman and van Witteloostuijn (2019, p. 4) note that in social sciences, occupied with explanation, ML algorithms are less widespread since they offer "increased predictive accuracy at the cost of explanatory insight." According to the authors, prediction is as important as explanation and forms a foundation for solution-oriented science. Furthermore, researchers may consider combining the inductive, data-driven approach of AI studies with deductive techniques. In doing so, research complements theory-building and theory-testing practices, which fit within the abduction approach.

Data Collection and Variables Measurement

Given the characteristics of big data, data collection, cleanup, and integration tend to be of a different quality and scale than traditional datasets. For example, big data are often collected for other purposes than addressing a specific research question and primary research is not necessarily conducted. Moreover, data mining and web scraping techniques enable the collection of data in real or near real-time, in contrast to retrospective studies. Big datasets are also less stable than traditional datasets, and tend to require updates on a regular basis. In addition, big data are often only available in unstructured and textual form, which requires a researcher to extract meaningful categories and transform the data into a more structured form (Schwab & Zhang, 2019). AI-based studies often integrate data from a large variety of different sources such as high-dimensional publicly available financial reports, company websites, and social media. As such, they have a higher level of data heterogeneity and include a greater number of observations and variables, when compared with studies that employ traditional quantitative methods, which rely on a smaller set of variables and aggregation methods for data reduction. For example, Coad and Srhoj (2020) analyzed 172 and 403 predictors of high-growth firms based on comprehensive Croatian and Slovenian datasets.

Data Analysis

Analyzing the data using AI-based methods is also different from traditional methods of analysis. There is a range of specialized techniques for analyzing big data, which stem from several disciplines, including statistics, computer science, applied mathematics, and economics (George et al., 2014). Hence, interdisciplinary research is important and is encouraged as it produces high-quality big data and AI studies (Jin et al., 2015). Besides generally offering higher predictive accuracy compared with traditional methods, ML techniques are also adaptive, due to their capacity to continuously learn from the data and improve prediction results (Zhou & Gumbo, 2021). Modern data analytic methods also often eschew traditional assumptions around linearity and instead allow researchers to better incorporate and detect nonlinear relationships (Tonidandel et al., 2018). While statistical significance tests are the basis for traditional methods, they are of less value when it comes to large datasets. Given the large number of predictors in AI-based studies, there is a need to distinguish between theoretically meaningful and relatively unimportant results. Furthermore, non-parametric methods in ML do not produce the β-coefficients and p-values commonly used in traditional quantitative studies. Hence, it becomes more difficult to argue about the significance of results (Kolkman & van Witteloostuijn, 2019).

Theoretical and Practical Implications

Given the peculiarities of research objectives, epistemology, data collection, and data analysis, AI studies may potentially contribute to entrepreneurship and growth literature in a different way to traditional forms of modeling. Specifically, AI methods can handle big data collected from a variety of different sources, improve the accuracy of predictions, explore new or non-obvious patterns in large and complex data, and offer inputs for developing new theories (Kolkman & van Witteloostuijn, 2019; Shmueli, 2010). Furthermore, using a larger volume of observations and variables, the results of AI studies can potentially be more generalizable than those results obtained from traditional research, which often focus on context-specific relationships and identifying boundary conditions for existing theories. However, a potential downside of AI methods is the incomprehensive causal mechanism of transforming input into output (Kolkman & van Witteloostuijn, 2019). AI-generated predictions remain a "black box" that offer high predictive power without interpretative insight. Hence, producing more explainable AI research has been one of the challenges faced by the research community to date.

In terms of practical implications, explaining a phenomenon using traditional research makes it easier to establish arguments and define public policy. Although AI methods per se produce less information about theoretically causal relationships between the predictors and the outcome, their high predictive ability plays an important role in boosting targeted policies and solving practical tasks that require high predictive accuracy (Bargagli-Stoffi et al., 2021). Since variables drawn from big data are situated in the real world and closely represent the phenomenon of interest, AI-based analysis helps enhance research relevance and aids scrutiny of issues that various stakeholders are interested in (Lévesque et al., 2020). For example, Zekić-Sušac et al. (2016) suggested a model that may support investors and policymakers in identifying SMEs with growth potential. Miyakawa et al. (2017) constructed ML predictions of future firm performance that outperformed the credit score assigned by the credit reporting agency based on survey results and interviews with firms.

A Research Agenda

AI methodology "has not received much scrutiny in contemporary entrepreneurship research so far" (Obschonka & Audretsch, 2020, p. 529). AI-based studies on firm growth have only just begun to emerge, and the publications review enabled a better understanding of the potential avenues for future research, which forms the basis of our third research question.

The added value of AI methods is their ability to enable better predictions, but one of their main drawbacks remains the lack of theoretical explanations for these predictions. The main challenge today is adjusting theoretical approaches in order to enhance our understanding of start-ups and SME growth.

One of the directions for future research concerns methodological improvements. Several studies suggest that firm growth prediction remains a challenge (Coad & Srhoj, 2020; McKenzie & Sansone, 2017). Hence, developing ML models that use a richer set of predictors as well as more advanced algorithms might improve the predictive quality and accuracy of the models (McKenzie & Sansone, 2017; Weinblat, 2018). For example, in addition to financial and demographic predictors, it might be interesting to include other variables such as activity around investment, importation, exportation, productivity, research and development, and founder characteristics (Weinblat, 2018; Zekić-Sušac et al., 2016). Furthermore, the models that use other measures of firm growth might provide additional insights into the field (van Witteloostuijn & Kolkman, 2019).

Another avenue of research involves exploring various large datasets from different countries. Further investment in data-scraping opportunities has been encouraged in order to obtain richer information about firms and their environment (Kolkman & van Witteloostuijn, 2019). For instance, applying Google Trends data may provide valuable insights into the growth dynamics of new technology-based ventures (Malyy et al., 2021). It is a comprehensive data source that shows how often a specific term has been searched, of which the time and location is noted, and can serve as a basis for building models and forecasting the growth or decline of firms.

Furthermore, revealing the importance ranking of the growth predictors, and understanding which of them are the most relevant and which have a marginal effect on firm growth, is valuable for theoretical development and for better informing public policy (Bargagli-Stoffi et al., 2021). With the rise in various ML applications and the need to explain the results produced by complex models, there has been growth in the field of explainable AI (Mathews, 2019; Rai, 2020). Explainable AI aims to create techniques that provide visibility of how the algorithm makes predictions and decisions. It enables more explainable models to be produced, as well as maintaining a high degree of accuracy.

Finally, how to build a theoretical contribution based on the results from AI methodology is a question that requires future investigation and has the potential to accelerate the adoption of AI methods by entrepreneurship researchers. Lévesque et al. (2020) suggested approaches that involve integrating AI with theory testing and theory building to create stronger linkages between entrepreneurship theory and practice. The authors proposed a series of zones in which AI could be applied in entrepreneurship research: a safe zone (applying AI to test the relationships prescribed by the theoretical model and enhancing the generalizability of the findings), a bold zone (applying AI in order to discover patterns with a view to developing new theories or enriching existing ones), and an entrepreneurial zone (applying AI to both theory building and theory testing). Combining AI with traditional econometric techniques may also provide further opportunities to better understand the growth phenomenon (van Witteloostuijn & Kolkman, 2019). ML is a quantitative method of induction, the results of which may serve as inputs for subsequent deductive techniques. New patterns identified in complex data can "inspire theory development, with the associated hypotheses being deductively tested by using well-known parametric techniques" (Kolkman & van Witteloostuijn, 2019, p. 24). Both emerging AI methods and traditional methods have complementary strengths for researching firm growth. AI provides a set of methods that enable traditional methods to be augmented with new insights and applied to new research tasks, as opposed to tools that replace traditional methods.

Conclusion

Firm growth research is one of the most extensively researched fields in entrepreneurship. However, despite the important contributions provided by conceptual and empirical studies, it is generally argued that the determinants of growth are inconclusive, and the results yield low predictive power. In this chapter, we reviewed empirical studies on SME growth and outlined emerging AI methodologies to approaching growth prediction.

This chapter contributes to the entrepreneurship and growth literature in several ways. First, by reviewing the SME growth studies that embrace traditional and AI methods, the existing knowledge base in the field is synthesized and the firm growth debate highlighted. It focuses on the emerging AI methods and shows how they have contributed to firm growth prediction. The results indicate that ML techniques generally improve growth prediction, yet studies differ in terms of how the models perform. Second, the chapter compares and contrasts AI methods with traditional quantitative methods utilized in SME growth research. The results show the added value and challenges of using AI methods pertaining to research objective, epistemological approach, data collection, variables measurement, data analysis, and theoretical and practical implications. Third, this chapter outlines the research agenda for entrepreneurship scholars willing to leverage AI and big data in SME growth research. Future research points in the direction of establishing the relationship between AI methodology and the theoretical development of growth studies.

Companies, investors, and governments should consider integrating ML in order to support their decision-making, forecast performance, and develop targeted SME policies. Investors may use algorithms to help scout for new firms that have the potential for high growth. Predicting firm performance and growth may allow policymakers to allocate funds to those projects that have the potential to be most profitable in the future. Understanding which factors are the most predictive for firm growth is also beneficial for entrepreneurs as it provides a direction for goal setting and resource deployment. Predictive analytics may also automate business forecasts due to the availability of real-time data and help reduce risks. However, although data are becoming a strategic resource, AI is a resource-intensive activity which requires specialized infrastructure to provide high computational power. Hence, a trade-off between the benefits of AI and the costs required to process large amounts of data should be considered. Different tools exist, such as cloud computing, end-user and open source software, which increase the accessibility of big data analytics for SMEs (Wang & Wang, 2020). Achieving a more cost effective way of handling big data is one of the challenges that needs to be met in the research field and in practice.

One of the limitations of this chapter is that we only selected articles published in a pre-defined list of top-tier academic journals in order to analyze SME growth studies. The inclusion of publications from other more niche journals might identify additional theoretical perspectives and data sources used to examine firm growth. Another limitation is that we searched for publications in the field of management in order to analyze AI-based growth studies. Extending our search to publications from the data science research field may yield fascinating results. This chapter focused on quantitative methodologies as a means of examining firm growth. Future studies that compare AI methods with both quantitative and qualitative methods provides another means of understanding the prediction and explanation of growth more deeply. Future reviews are also suggested once further entrepreneurship studies that integrate AI methods have been published, to evaluate the development of this research field. It is our hope that the discussion of and ideas for future research presented in this chapter will help stimulate continued innovative investigation using new methodologies and advance the understanding of a growth phenomenon that is so vital to practitioners, policymakers, and academics.

References

Altinay, L., Madanoglu, M., De Vita, G., Arasli, H., & Ekinci, Y. (2016). The interface between organizational learning capability, entrepreneurial orientation, and SME growth. *Journal of Small Business Management, 54*(3), 871–891. http://doi.org/10.1111/jsbm.12219

Ang, S.H. (2008). Competitive intensity and collaboration: Impact on firm growth across technological environments. *Strategic Management Journal, 29*(10), 1057–1075. http://doi.org/10.1002/smj.695

Antretter, T., Blohm, I., Grichnik, D., & Wincent, J. (2019). Predicting new venture survival: A Twitter-based machine learning approach to measuring online legitimacy. *Journal of Business Venturing Insights, 11*, e00109. https://doi.org/10.1016/j.jbvi.2018.e00109

Bargagli-Stoffi, F.J., Niederreiter, J., & Riccaboni, M. (2021). Supervised learning for the prediction of firm dynamics. In S. Consoli, D. Reforgiato Recupero, & M. Saisana (Eds.), *Data science for economics and finance: Methodologies and applications* (pp.19–41). Springer.

Barroso-Castro, C., Domínguez-CC, M., & Rodríguez-Serrano, M.Á. (2022). SME growth speed: The relationship with board capital. *Journal of Small Business Management, 60*(2), 480–512. http://doi.org/10.1080/00472778.2020.1717293

Baum, J.R., & Bird, B.J. (2010). The successful intelligence of high-growth entrepreneurs: Links to new venture growth. *Organization Science, 21*(2), 397–412. http://doi.org/10.1287/orsc.1090.0445

Baum, J.R., Locke, E.A., & Smith,K.G. (2001). A multidimensional model of venture growth. *Academy of Management Journal, 44*(2), 292–303. https://doi.org/10.5465/3069456

Bird, M., & Zellweger, T. (2018). Relational embeddedness and firm growth: Comparing spousal and sibling entrepreneurs. *Organization Science, 29*(2), 264–283. http://doi.org/10.1287/orsc.2017.1174

Böhm, M., Weking, J., Fortunat, F., Müller, S., Welpe, I., & Krcmar, H. (2017). The business model DNA: Towards an approach for predicting business model success. In J.M. Leimeister, & W. Brenner (Eds.), *Proceedings der 13. Internationalen Tagung Wirtschaftsinformatik* (pp. 1006–1020).

Bouncken, R.B., Kraus, S., & Roig-Tierno, N. (2021). Knowledge-and innovation-based business models for future growth: Digitalized business models and portfolio considerations. *Review of Managerial Science, 15*(1), 1–14. https://doi.org/10.1007/s11846-019-00366-z

Bruton, G.D., & Rubanik, Y. (2002). Resources of the firm, Russian high-technology startups, and firm growth. *Journal of Business Venturing, 17*(6), 553–576. https://doi.org/10.1016/S0883-9026(01)00079-9

Cainelli, G., & Ganau, R. (2019). Related variety and firm heterogeneity. What really matters for short-run firm growth? *Entrepreneurship and Regional Development*, *31*(9–10), 768–784. http://doi.org/10.1080/08985626.2019.1571636

Castrogiovanni, G.J., & Justis, R.T. (2002). Strategic and contextual influences on firm growth: An empirical study of franchisors. *Journal of Small Business Management*, *40*(2), 98–108. https://doi.org/10.1111/1540-627X.00043

Chen, H., Chiang, R.H.L., & Storey, V.C. (2012). Business intelligence and analytics: From big data to big impact. *MIS Quarterly*, *36*(4), 1165–1188. https://doi.org/10.2307/41703503

Coad, A. (2009). *The growth of firms: A survey of theories and empirical evidence*. Edward Elgar.

Coad, A., Frankish, J., Roberts, R.G., & Storey, D.J. (2013). Growth paths and survival chances: An application of Gambler's Ruin theory. *Journal of Business Venturing*, *28*(5), 615–632. https://doi.org/10.1016/j.jbusvent.2012.06.002

Coad, A., Frankish, J.S., Roberts, R.G., & Storey, D.J. (2015). Are firm growth paths random? A reply to "Firm growth and the illusion of randomness." *Journal of Business Venturing Insights*, *3*, 5–8. https://doi.org/10.1016/j.jbvi.2014.11.001

Coad., A., & Karlsson, J. (2022). A field guide for gazelle hunters: Small, old firms are unlikely to become high-growth firms. *Journal of Business Venturing Insights*, *17*, e00286. https://doi.org/10.1016/j.jbvi.2021.e00286

Coad, A., & Srhoj, S. (2020). Catching gazelles with a lasso: Big data techniques for the prediction of high-growth firms. *Small Business Economics*, *55*, 541–565. https://doi.org/10.1007/s11187-019-00203-3

Covin, J.G., Slevin, D.P., & Heeley, M.B. (2000). Pioneers and followers: Competitive tactics, environment, and firm growth. *Journal of Business Venturing*, *15*(2), 175–210. https://doi.org/10.1016/S0883-9026(98)00015-9

Davidsson, P., Kirchhoff, B., Hatemi, J.A., & Gustavsson, H. (2002). Empirical analysis of business growth factors using Swedish data. *Journal of Small Business Management*, *40*(4), 332–349. https://doi.org/10.1111/1540-627X.00061

Davidsson, P., & Wiklund, J. (2000). Conceptual and empirical challenges in the study of firm growth. In D. Sexton & H. Landström (Eds.), *The Blackwell handbook of entrepreneurship* (pp. 26–44). Blackwell.

Delmar, F., & Wiklund, J. (2008). The effect of small business managers' growth motivation on firm growth: A longitudinal study. *Entrepreneurship Theory and Practice*, *32*(3), 437–457. https://doi.org/10.1111/j.1540-6520.2008.00235.x

Derbyshire, J., & Garnsey, E. (2014). Firm growth and the illusion of randomness. *Journal of Business Venturing Insights*, *1–2*, 8–11. https://doi.org/10.1016/j.jbvi.2014.09.003

Derbyshire, J., & Garnsey, E. (2015). Are firm growth paths random? A further response regarding Gambler's ruin theory. *Journal of Business Venturing Insights*, *3*, 9–11. https://doi.org/10.1016/j.jbvi.2014.12.001

Dobbs, M., & Hamilton, R.T. (2007). Small business growth: Recent evidence and new directions. *International Journal of Entrepreneurial Behavior and Research*, *13*(5), 296–322. https://doi.org/10.1108/13552550710780885

Eberhart, R.N., Eesley, C.E., & Eisenhardt, K.M. (2017). Failure is an option: Institutional change, entrepreneurial risk, and new firm growth. *Organization Science*, *28*(1), 93–112. http://doi.org/10.1287/orsc.2017.1110

Ferreira, J.J., Fernandes, C.I., & Kraus, S. (2019). Entrepreneurship research: Mapping intellectual structures and research trends. *Review of Managerial Science*, *13*(1), 181–205. https://doi.org/10.1007/s11846-017-0242-3

Garsaa, A., & Levratto, N. (2015). Do labor tax rebates facilitate firm growth? An empirical study on French establishments in the manufacturing industry, 2004–2011. *Small Business Economics*, *45*(3), 613–641. http://doi.org/10.1007/s11187-015-9653-1

George, G., Haas, M., & Pentland, A. (2014). From the editors: Big data and management. *Academy of Management Journal, 57*(2), 321–326. http://dx.doi.org/10.5465/amj.2014.4002

George, G., Osinga, E., Lavie, D., & Scott, B. (2016). Big data and data science methods for management research. *Academy of Management Journal, 59*(5), 1493–1507. https://doi.org/10.5465/amj.2016.4005

Gilbert, B.A., McDougall, P.P., & Audretsch, D.B. (2006). New venture growth: A review and extension. *Journal of Management, 32*(6), 926–950. https://doi.org/10.1177/0149206306293860

Greve, H.R. (2008). A behavioral theory of firm growth: Sequential attention to size and performance goals. *Academy of Management Journal, 51*(3), 476–94. https://doi.org/10.2307/20159522

Jin, X., Wah, B., Cheng, X., & Wang, Y. (2015). Significance and challenges of big data research. *Big Data Research, 2*(2), 59–64. https://doi.org/10.1016/j.bdr.2015.01.006

Kangasharju, A. (2000). Growth of the smallest: Determinants of small firm growth during strong macroeconomic fluctuations. *International Small Business Journal, 19*(1), 28–43. https://doi.org/10.1177/0266242600191002

Kitchin, R. (2014). Big data, new epistemologies and paradigm shifts. *Big Data and Society.* https://doi.org/10.1177/2053951714528481

Koeller, C.T., & Lechler, T.G. (2006). Economic and managerial perspectives on new venture growth: An integrated analysis. *Small Business Economics, 26*(5), 427–437. https://www.jstor.org/stable/40229479

Kolkman, D., & van Witteloostuijn, A. (2019). Data science in strategy: Machine learning and text analysis in the study of firm growth. *Tinbergen Institute Discussion Paper 2019-066/VI.* http://dx.doi.org/10.2139/ssrn.3457271

Kraus, S., Breier, M., & Dasí-Rodríguez, S. (2020). The art of crafting a systematic literature review in entrepreneurship research. *International Entrepreneurship and Management Journal, 16*, 1023–1042. https://doi.org/10.1007/s11365-020-00635-4

Leitch, C., Hill, F., & Neergaard, H. (2010). Entrepreneurial and business growth and the quest for a "comprehensive theory": Tilting at windmills? *Entrepreneurship Theory and Practice, 34*(2), 249–260. https://doi.org/10.1111/j.1540-6520.2010.00374.x

Lévesque, M., Obschonka, M., & Nambisan, S. (2020). Pursuing impactful entrepreneurship research using artificial intelligence. *Entrepreneurship Theory and Practice.* http://doi.org/10.1177/1042258720927369

Malyy, M., Tekic, Z., & Podladchikova, T. (2021). The value of big data for analyzing growth dynamics of technology-based new ventures. *Technological Forecasting and Social Change, 169*, 120794. https://doi.org/10.1016/j.techfore.2021.120794

Martín-García, R., & Morán Santor, J. (2021). Public guarantees: A countercyclical instrument for SME growth. Evidence from the Spanish Region of Madrid. *Small Business Economics, 56*(1), 427–449. http://doi.org/10.1007/s11187-019-00214-0

Mathews, S.M. (2019). Explainable artificial intelligence applications in NLP, biomedical, and malware classification: A literature review. In K. Arai, R. Bhatia, & S. Kapoor (Eds.), *Intelligent computing. CompCom 2019. Advances in intelligent systems and computing, 998* (pp. 1269–1292). Springer. https://doi.org/10.1007/978-3-030-22868-2_90

McAfee, A., & Brynjolfsson, E. (2012). Big data: The management revolution. *Harvard Business Review, 90*, 61–67.

McKelvie, A., & Wiklund, J. (2010). Advancing firm growth research: A focus on growth mode instead of growth rate. *Entrepreneurship Theory and Practice, 34*(2), 261–288. https://doi.org/10.1111/j.1540-6520.2010.00375.x

McKenzie, D., & Sansone, D. (2017). Man vs. machine in predicting successful entrepreneurs: Evidence from a business plan competition in Nigeria. *Policy Research Working Paper Series 8271.* The World Bank.

Miyakawa, D., Miyauchi, Y., & Perez, C. (2017). Forecasting firm performance with machine learning: Evidence from Japanese firm-level data. Technical report, Research Institute of Economy, Trade and Industry (RIETI). Discussion Paper Series 17-E-068. https://www.rieti.go.jp/jp/publications/dp/17e068.pdf

Moen, O., Heggeseth, A.G., & Lome, O. (2016). The positive effect of motivation and international orientation on SME growth. *Journal of Small Business Management, 54*(2), 659–678. http://doi.org/10.1111/jsbm.12163

Nason, R.S., Wiklund, J., McKelvie, A., Hitt, M., & Yu, W. (2019). Orchestrating boundaries: The effect of R&D boundary permeability on new venture growth. *Journal of Business Venturing, 34*(1), 63–79. http://doi.org/10.1016/j.jbusvent.2018.05.003

Obschonka, M., & Audretsch, D. (2020). Artificial intelligence and big data in entrepreneurship: A new era has begun. *Small Business Economics, 55*, 529–539. https://doi.org/10.1007/s11187-019-00202-4

Obschonka, M., Fisch, C., & Boyd, R. (2017). Using digital footprints in entrepreneurship research: A Twitter-based personality analysis of superstar entrepreneurs and managers. *Journal of Business Venturing Insights, 8*, 13–23. https://doi.org/10.1016/j.jbvi.2017.05.005

Peric, M., & Vitezic, V. (2016). Impact of global economic crisis on firm growth. *Small Business Economics, 46*(1), 1–12. http://doi.org/10.1007/s11187-015-9671-z

Premaratne, S.P. (2001). Networks, resources, and small business growth: The experience in Sri Lanka. *Journal of Small Business Management, 39*(4), 363–371. https://doi.org/10.1111/0447-2778.00033

Prüfer, J., & Prüfer, P. (2020). Data science for entrepreneurship research: Studying demand dynamics for entrepreneurial skills in the Netherlands. *Small Business Economics, 55*, 651–672. https://doi.org/10.1007/s11187-019-00208-y

Rai, A. (2020). Explainable AI: From black box to glass box. *Journal of the Academy of Marketing Science, 48*, 137–141. https://doi.org/10.1007/s11747-019-00710-5

Roper, S. (1997). Product innovation and small business growth: A comparison of the strategies of German, U.K. and Irish Companies. *Small Business Economics, 9*, 523–537. https://doi.org/10.1023/A:1007963604397

Schoonjans, B., Van Cauwenberge, P., & Vander Bauwhede, H. (2013). Formal business networking and SME growth. *Small Business Economics, 41*(1), 169–181. http://doi.org/10.1007/s11187-011-9408-6

Schwab, A., & Zhang, Z. (2019). A new methodological frontier in entrepreneurship research: Big data studies. *Entrepreneurship Theory and Practice, 43*(5), 843–854. https://doi.org/10.1177/1042258718760841

Shepherd, D., & Wiklund, J. (2009). Are we comparing apples with apples or apples with oranges? Appropriateness of knowledge accumulation across growth studies. *Entrepreneurship: Theory and Practice, 33*(1), 105–123. http://doi.org/10.1111/j.1540-6520.2008.00282.x

Shmueli, G. (2010). To explain or to predict? *Statistical Science, 25*(3), 289–310. https://doi.org/10.1214/10-STS330

Short, J. (2009). The art of writing a review article. *Journal of Management, 35*(6), 1312–1317. https://doi.org/10.1177/0149206309337489

Sivarajah, U., Kamal, M., Irani, Z., & Weerakkody, V. (2017). Critical analysis of big data challenges and analytical methods. *Journal of Business Research, 70*, 263–286. https://doi.org/10.1016/j.jbusres.2016.08.001

Tonidandel, S., King, E., & Cortina, J. (2018). Big data methods: Leveraging modern data analytic techniques to build organizational science. *Organizational Research Methods, 21*(3), 525–47. https://doi.org/10.1177/1094428116677299

van Witteloostuijn, A., & Kolkman, D. (2019). Is firm growth random? A machine learning perspective. *Journal of Business Venturing Insights, 11*, e00107. https://doi.org/10.1016/j.jbvi.2018.e00107

Vlačić, B., Corbo, L., Costa e Silva, S., & Dabić, M. (2021). The evolving role of artificial intelligence in marketing: A review and research agenda. *Journal of Business Research, 128*, 187–203. https://doi.org/10.1016/j.jbusres.2021.01.055

Wagner, J. (1992). Firm size, firm growth, and persistence of chance: Testing GIBRAT's law with establishment data from Lower Saxony, 1978–1989. *Small Business Economics, 4*, 125–131. https://doi.org/10.1007/BF00389853

Wang, S., & Wang, H. (2020). Big data for small and medium-sized enterprises (SME): A knowledge management model. *Journal of Knowledge Management, 24*(4), 881–897. https://doi.org/10.1108/JKM-02-2020-0081

Weinblat, J. (2018). Forecasting European high-growth firms – A random forest approach. *Journal of Industry, Competition and Trade, 18*, 253–294. https://doi.org/10.1007/s10842-017-0257-0

Wiklund, J., Patzelt, H., & Shepherd, D.A. (2009). Building an integrative model of small business growth. *Small Business Economics, 32*(4), 351–374. http://doi.org/10.1007/s11187-007-9084-8

Wright, M., & Stigliani, I. (2013). Entrepreneurship and growth. *International Small Business Journal, 31*(1), 3–22. https://doi.org/10.1177/0266242612467359

Yamakawa, Y., Peng, M.W., & Deeds, D.L. (2015). Rising from the ashes: Cognitive determinants of venture growth after entrepreneurial failure. *Entrepreneurship: Theory and Practice, 39*(2), 209–236. http://doi.org/10.1111/etap.12047

Yang, C.H., & Tsou, M.W. (2020). Globalization and firm growth: Does ownership matter? *Small Business Economics, 55*(4), 1019–1037. http://doi.org/10.1007/s11187-019-00170-9

Zeba, G., Dabić, M., Čičak, M., Daim, T., & Yalcin, H. (2021). Technology mining: Artificial intelligence in manufacturing. *Technological Forecasting and Social Change, 171*, 120971. https://doi.org/10.1016/j.techfore.2021.120971

Zekić-Sušac, M., Šarlija, N., Has, A., & Bilandžić, A. (2016). Predicting company growth using logistic regression and neural networks. *Croatian Operational Research Review, 7*(2), 229–248. http://doi.org/10.17535/crorr.2016.0016

Zhou, H., & Gumbo, V. (2021). Comparative analysis of a traditional and machine learning techniques in predicting SMMEs growth performance. *Academy of Entrepreneurship Journal, 27*(3), 1–12.

Part 4: **Entrepreneurial Capital, Gender, and SMEs**

Thierry Levy and Mouhoub Hani

22 Entrepreneurial Teams and Collective Dynamics: Toward an Eco(systemic) Perspective

Abstract: Extent literature has abundantly addressed the question of how the entrepreneurial team emerges with two main approaches, namely: a resource-based view and a logic of homophily. However, the issue of why and how entrepreneurial team founders clash (with exit members) still remains rarely explored. This chapter aims at enriching current work by borrowing a systemic modeling approach of teams' dynamics that could also apply to collective involvement of small firms in networked ecosystems and platforms. Entrepreneurial team modelling considers the entrepreneurial team as digital platforms and social networks which are systems with essentially four dimensions that need to be articulated: (1). *Affectio Societatis*; (2). Synergy; (3). Commitment; and (4). Shared vision. Finally, if one these dimensions is missing or irrelevant with the rest, then the entrepreneurial team functioning becomes critical.

Keywords: entrepreneurial team, collective dynamics, ecosystems, platforms, systemic lens

Introduction

Most new ventures are the product of teams of entrepreneurs, not individual ones (Kamm et al. 1990). According to Lazar et al. (2020), the entrepreneurial team is defined as "two or more individuals who pursue a new business idea, are involved in its subsequent management, and share ownership" (p. 29). The entrepreneurial team has become a growing field of research and interest (Ben-Hafaiedh, 2017). Extent literature has focused on how the entrepreneurial team emerges with two main options: a resource-based view in which a leader tasks partners with developing a firm's capability resources; and a logic of homophily (the co-entrepreneurs decide to start business together because of affinities and socio-cognitive proximity (Ruef et al., 2003). Similarly in this second option, firm's growth and external performance pressures make competence a very important criterion in assembling teams and we would expect universalistic norms to govern recruitment. These teams exemplified many of the desired characteristics identified by

---

Note: This reflection is based on the PhD dissertation of Nisrine Miliani-Mosbah supervised by one of the authors.

Thierry Levy, Mouhoub Hani, Paris 8 Vincennes Saint-Denis University

https://doi.org/10.1515/9783110747652-023

the "rational process" models of entrepreneurial team formation: adequate size, skill diversity, shared prior experiences, and high human capital (Aldrich & Kim, 2007).

However, this literature does not (or rarely – Cardon et al., 2017; Gregori & Parastuty, 2021) examine why and how entrepreneurial team founders clash (with exit members). These few studies recently put forward some reasons why new venture team members exit their teams and organizations, for example, when the incongruence between a new venture team member's entrepreneurial passion and the team entrepreneurial passion is irreconcilable. More importantly, research on collective efficacy is less well developed than on self-efficacy but is nonetheless telling in this domain (Shepherd & Krueger, 2002). A significant and growing focus in the study of entrepreneurship is more about the genesis of entrepreneurial thinking (Shepherd & Krueger, 2002). These scientific efforts allowed a better understanding of the entrepreneurial behaviors. Consequently, we have learned that corporate entrepreneurship is not necessarily about the individual entrepreneur inside the organization but much more about building an organization that behaves entrepreneurially (Shepherd & Krueger, 2002). This work advocates for the benefit of collective dynamics of the entrepreneurial team.

In sum, this chapter aims at proposing such a systemic modeling of teams' dynamics that could also apply to collective involvement of small firms in networks and platforms, and even ecosystems. Our modeling is based on systemic approach and considers that entrepreneurial teams such as digital platforms and social networks are systems with essentially four dimensions that need to be articulated. These four elements are: a. *Affectio Societatis* (meaning that all members wish to collaborate at the same level); b. Synergy (following Luecke, 2004; Amason & Sapienza, 1997; Ucbasaran et al., 2003, p. 110); c. Commitment (Vohora et al., 2004); and d. Shared vision (Carland & Carland, 2012).

This chapter is structured as follow. First, we analyze the existing literature on the entrepreneurial team that can be categorized on two main blocs. On one hand, literature about the entrepreneurial team is fundamentally interested in the formation process through rational, irrational, and relational mechanisms. On the other hand, this literature has endeavored to explain the extent to which the entrepreneurial team affects the firm's performance that is contingent upon the external environment, the entrepreneurial team composition, and its processes. Second, we develop an evolutionary and dynamic view of interaction by (re)defining the entrepreneurial team (and probably more generally collective entrepreneurship, for instance in the context of interorganizational networks or collaborative platforms) as a system. Such a system is characterized by four dimensions that need to be articulated: *Affectio Societatis*; Synergy; Commitment and Shared vision. Last, we propose platforms and ecosystems as an extension of the entrepreneurial team before outlining some implications for further research for entrepreneurship scholarship.

Existing Literature on the Entrepreneurial Team

The entrepreneurial team is one of the old themes in entrepreneurship scholarship. However, the scientific efforts undertaken do not seem to reach a consensus in stabilizing the concept by providing a clear and precise definition of what an entrepreneurial team is. Through their recent review on the concept of a startup team, Knight and his colleagues (2020) assert that the entrepreneurship theorists use dozens of terms to describe a group of people working together to advance a new venture: terms such as "startup team" (Franke et al., 2008), "entrepreneurial team" (Kamm et al., 1990), "new venture team" (Klotz et al., 2014), "founding team" (Beckman, 2006), and "entrepreneurial top management team" (Ferguson et al., 2016). In this chapter, we borrow the Schjoedt and Sascha's (2009) definition through which, "an entrepreneurial team consists of two or more persons who have an interest, both financial and otherwise, in and commitment to a venture's future and success; whose work is interdependent in the pursuit of common goals and venture success; who are accountable to the entrepreneurial team and for the venture; who are considered to be at the executive level with executive responsibility in the early phases of the venture, including founding and pre-startup; and who are seen as a social entity by themselves and by others." (p. 515).

This stream of research has flourished over the past two decades (Patzelt et al., 2021) leading to a growing body of research on various intertwined dimensions. These scientific efforts are articulated around two main fields of research. On one hand, prior studies have tried to explain the factors leading to the entrepreneurial team formation (Aldrich & Kim, 2007; Lazar et al., 2020; Forbes et al., 2006). On the other hand, research has attempted to see how an entrepreneurial team, through the dimensions of its formation, influences the performance of its members (Francis & Sandberg, 2000; Schjoedt & Kraus, 2009; Uy et al., 2021; Jin et al., 2017).

Entrepreneurial Team Formation

Many previous studies have addressed the issue of entrepreneurial team formation. These studies highlighted some rational, irrational, and relational antecedents of the formation mechanisms. First, from a social network perspective, some authors as Aldrich & Kim (2007) have tried to explain the formation of an entrepreneurial team (in terms of exit and entry of team members) through the concept homophily which occurs in some categories such as team size (Chandler et al., 2005), firm age (Ucbasaran et al., 2003), gender diversity (Tenner & Hörisch, 2021) and member disagreements (Cardon et al., 2017). Second, from an intentions-based perspective, authors (among many others) such as Shepherd & Krueger (2002) have highlighted the importance of perceptions of desirability and feasibility from the team as well as the individual perspective. Third, work from the rich and broad social cognition literature gives us several new insights into how to develop an entrepreneurship-friendly "cognitive infrastructure" at the collective level. This stream of research recognizes that friendship as an interpersonal relation may affect a group's dynamics, hold teams together, and stimulate heroic efforts during difficult times (Francis & Sandberg, 2000). Last, a more recent point of view from an affective perspective highlights the importance of collective passion in the entrepreneurial team convergence and formation (Drnovsek et al., 2009; Cardon et al., 2017). Drnovsek et al. (2009) define collective passion "as the combined entrepreneurial passion experienced by members of a team of entrepreneurs, including potential differences in the level and focus of each member's individual passion" (p. 2). According to them, the exploration of collective passion is important for two reasons: (1) entrepreneurial passion has been argued to be a powerful motivational resource that leads to attainment of entrepreneurial goals despite formidable obstacles; and (2) there is an evident gap in extant research surrounding how entrepreneurial passion works within teams, especially where a lead entrepreneur not only needs to manage his/ her own passion but must also work with the various potential configurations of passion among team members. Similarly, other authors (Cardon et al., 2017) reveal that a team's diversity along two identity-based affective dimensions (focus and intensity) may combine to influence the emergence of team-level effect. In the next section, we present the extent to which the characteristics of entrepreneurial team composition (i.e., aggregated, heterogeneity, team size) affect new venture performance (Jin et al., 2017). Accordingly, entrepreneurial teams exemplified many of the desired characteristics identified by the "rational process" models of entrepreneurial team formation: adequate size, skill diversity, shared prior experiences, and high human capital (Aldrich & Kim, 2007). Last, the entrepreneur's human capital explains their involvement in the entrepreneurial team, especially through their educational level and their intrapreneurial experience. In others words, entrepreneurs with higher levels of education and intrapreneurial experience are more likely to be involved in the entrepreneurship process as members of teams (Pinzón et al., 2021).

Entrepreneurial Team Performance

Previous literature highlighted that the entrepreneurial team's performance is contingent upon the external environment, the entrepreneurial team composition, and its processes (Schjoedt & Kraus 2009). For example, a recent study (Lazar et al., 2020) showed that using dual (or even collective) formation strategies accelerates the team's ability to develop learning systems for superior performance early on more than single strategies. Experiencing team progress facilitated passion convergence, whereas experiencing team setbacks did not have a significant impact on passion convergence. Teams with members converging on a high level of passion positively predicted team performance. Additionally, it was predicted that brokerage role diversity as a specific and particularly important case of structural role complementarity will enhance entrepreneurial teams' functioning and outcomes (Aven & Hillmann, 2018). These results indicate that both internal and external social networks have marginally positive impacts on a new venture's innovative capability, and trust within entrepreneurial teams is found to be as important a moderator for the relationship between external social networks and innovative capability (Chen & Wang, 2008). Also, team sizes in all fields increased over time, reflecting the growing complexity of the fields and external performance pressures. Clearly, competence was a very important criterion in assembling teams and we would expect universalistic norms to govern recruitment (Aldrich & Kim, 2007). Similarly, peer pressure is common among established agile teams and it negatively influences the innovative output of the agile teams. Moreover, the magnitude of the effect of peer pressure is contingent on control mechanisms at higher levels within the organization (Khanagha et al., 2021).

Some recent work (Cardon et al., 2017; Uy et al., 2021) argues that experiencing team progress facilitated passion convergence, which consequently leads to positive team performance. In this vein, diversity of entrepreneurial passions may influence emergence of a collective passion within the team and affects team-related processes as well as the venture's performance (Uy et al., 2021). Relatedly, the three entrepreneurial orientation diversity dimensions – proactiveness, risk taking, and innovativeness diversity – affect the entrepreneurial team performance, although they belong to the same diversity type and even belong to a common superordinate construct (Kollmann et al., 2017). Precisely, environmental orientation is not dependent on the share of female members, but rather on the gender diversity of the founding team (Tenner & Hörisch, 2021).

Moreover, friendship is also conducive to decision-making processes that enhance the team's effectiveness in solving "wicked" problems (Francis & Sandberg, 2000). In parallel, team cohesion and cognitive conflict will be high and relationship conflict will be low because all team members feel passion for the same role identity. In a balanced entrepreneurial passion team, team cohesion, cognitive conflict, and relationship conflict will all be moderate. Additionally, it seems that a mixed passion team is likely to face low team cohesion, moderate cognitive conflict, and high relationship conflict (Drnovsek et al., 2009). Through an identity-based approach to an affective construct – passion – these contributions showed how a team's diversity along two identity-based affective dimensions (focus and intensity) may combine to influence the emergence of team-level affect (Cardon et al., 2017). Relatedly, the collective cognition's structural characteristics that are differentiation and integration strongly explain firm performance (West, 2007). Finally, teams with autonomy over choosing either ideas or team members outperform teams in the baseline treatment as measured by pitch deck performance. The effect of choosing ideas is significantly stronger than the effect of choosing teams. However, the performance gains vanish for teams that are granted full autonomy over choosing both ideas and teams (Boss et al., 2021)

Table 22.1 details the findings of studies that are representative of research into the entrepreneurial team field (please see also Knight et al. (2020) and Lazar et al (2021) for a broader review of entrepreneurial team). A common theme across these studies is that the entrepreneurial team differs from the sum of its members.

Table 22.1: Main research on the entrepreneurial team.

Article	Research question	Key concept	Theoretical perspectives	Main contributions
Shepherd & Krueger (2002)	How the team differs from the sum of its members?	Social cognition (perceptions)	Intentions-based Perspective	The importance of perceptions of desirability and feasibility from the team as well as the individual perspective.
Khanagha et al. (2021)	How control mechanisms affect innovative output of self-managing team?	Control mechanisms (peer pressure)	Multi-level perspective	Peer pressure is common among established agile teams and it negatively influences the innovative output of the agile teams. Moreover, the magnitude of the effect of peer pressure is contingent on control mechanisms at higher levels within the organization.
Aldrich & Kim (2007)	(1) To what extent is the social world organized into local clusters of densely connected individuals who interact primarily with one another? (2) What is the average path length between individuals in the network, conceptualized as the average number of intermediaries it takes to connect any two randomly chosen individuals?	ET Formation (homophily)	Social network perspective	The principle of small world networks reveals the tension hidden in calls for nascent entrepreneurs to "use networking" to build entrepreneurial teams and seek opportunities. Being embedded in dense clusters of social relations that have emerged through homophily and propinquity creates a highly circumscribed world for entrepreneurs. Local clusters of family, friends, work, and neighborhoods will serve as the pool of people available for recruitment into entrepreneurial teams, if nascent entrepreneurs follow the principle of interpersonal relations in team building. The great majority of entrepreneurial teams emerge out of the local clusters described by small world networks but without the bridging ties necessary to reduce the social distance to strangers qualified for team membership.

Study	Research question	Concept	Perspective	Findings
Francis & Sandberg (2000)	How does friendship affect the team's behavior and the performance of the venture?	ET Formation & performance (Friendship)	*Gemeinschaft* perspective	Friendship facilitates the formation of ET and thereby improves their early performance. Friendship is conducive to decision-making processes that enhance the team's effectiveness in solving "wicked" problems.
Chen & Wang (2008)	(1) Will the internal social networks and external social networks of entrepreneurial teams have positive impacts on a new venture's innovative capability? 2) Will trust within the entrepreneurial teams moderate the relationship between social networks and innovative capability in new ventures?	Innovative Capability Trust	Social network perspective	The results indicate that both internal and external social networks have marginally positive impacts on a new venture's innovative capability, and trust within the entrepreneurial teams is found to be as important a moderator for the relationship between external social networks and innovative capability. Moreover, results reveal that a higher level of trust between entrepreneurial team members can reduce the external social networks spanning the boundaries of the new venture and therefore may cause a "not invented here" syndrome which will reduce its innovative capability.
Aven & Hillmann (2018)	How do the abilities between team members' act as network brokers change?	Structural role complementarity (brockerage)	Structural embeddedness perspective	Variation among team members' brokering ability significantly predicts the starting capital raised by their firm. The effect is moderated by the team's average brokering potential. Entrepreneurial teams with greater brokerage role diversity among the founding partners realize higher capital.

(continued)

Table 22.1 (continued)

Article	Research question	Key concept	Theoretical perspectives	Main contributions
Yang & Aldrich (2014)	How do inequalities arise among autonomous groups pursuing economic goals?	Gender inequality	Structural embeddedness perspective	Gender stereotypes of leaders pervasively constrain women's access to power positions, and gender's effect intensifies when spousal relationships are involved. Women have reduced chances to be in charge if they co-found new businesses with their husbands, and some family conditions further modify women's chances, such as husbands' employment and the presence of children.
Schjoedt & Sascha (2009)	How do factors influence ET performance and, in turn, new venture performance?	ET performance	–	ET performance is contingent upon the external environment, ET composition, and ET processes.
Lazar et al. (2020)	Why, how, when, and where are entrepreneurial teams formed?	ET formation	Economic, psychology, and sociology perspectives	The dynamic nature of the formation process, the origins of new venture teams, primary formation strategies used to initiate cofounding relations, and their effects on team characteristics, processes, and performance
Lazar et al. (2021)	How does using single versus dual formation strategies accelerate or impede the team's ability to develop learning systems for superior performance early on? How are learning systems influenced by the founding teams formation process?	Transactive memory systems	Economic, psychology, and sociology perspectives	Teams formed based on a dual strategy raised greater seed funding on Kickstarter, a leading crowdfunding platform, were more successful in a prestigious entrepreneurial competition, and gained more profits from selling their initial products.

Pinzón et al. (2021)	Why do some individuals get involved in entrepreneurship through a team rather than alone?	Involvement	Multilevel approach	The entrepreneur's human capital explains their involvement in the ET, especially through their educational level and their intrapreneurial experience. Entrepreneurs with higher levels of education and intrapreneurial experience are more likely to be involved in the entrepreneurship process as members of teams.
Tenner & Hörisch (2021)	How does the gender of founding teams influence the environmental orientation of entrepreneurial ventures?	Diversity (gender)	Entrepreneurial approach	The level of environmental orientation is not dependent on the share of female members, but rather on the gender diversity of the founding team. We conclude that gender diversity within the entrepreneurial team is necessary to address both ecological and economic goals of environmental entrepreneurship.
Uy et al. (2021)	How do within-team experiences of progress and setback shape passion convergence? What is the impact of passion convergence on team performance?	Passion convergence	Multilevel theory	Experiencing team progress facilitated passion convergence, whereas experiencing team setbacks did not have a significant impact on passion convergence. Teams with members converging on a high level of passion positively predicted team performance.

(continued)

Table 22.1 (continued)

Article	Research question	Key concept	Theoretical perspectives	Main contributions
Drnovsek et al. (2009)	What is the impact of entrepreneurial passion when the entrepreneur experiencing it is part of a founding team, rather than operating as a solo entrepreneur?	Collective passion	Affective and interindividual perspective	Diversity of entrepreneurial passions may influence emergence of a collective passion within the team and affects team-related processes as well as the venture's performance. In a focused team, team cohesion and cognitive conflict will be high and relationship conflict will be low because all team members feel passion for the same role identity. In a balanced entrepreneurial passion team, team cohesion, cognitive conflict, and relationship conflict will all be moderate. Finally, it seems that a mixed passion team is likely to face low team cohesion, moderate cognitive conflict, and high relationship conflict.
Cardon et al. (2017)	Through which mechanisms do the components of passion emerge at the team level of analysis as shared affect and collective identity, influenced by the diversity of individual passions within the team and how does TEP, in turn, influence individual passions within the team, as well as team member entries and exits from the team and team outcomes?	Team entrepreneurial passion (TEP)	Identity-based approach Similarity-attraction theory	The paper proposes an identity-based approach to an affective construct – passion – and shows how a team's diversity along two identity-based affective dimensions (focus and intensity) may combine to influence the emergence of team-level affect.

	Question	Concept	Perspective/Approach	Findings
West (2007)	What are the important structural characteristics of collective cognition in entrepreneurial teams and how does it influence new ventures decisions, actions, and performance?	Collective cognition	Sociocognitive approach	Two structural characteristics of collective cognition (differentiation and integration) are strongly related to firm performance
Kollmann et al. (2017)	How is team performance affected when members of entrepreneurial teams differ regarding the three individual entrepreneurial orientation dimensions of proactiveness, risk taking, and innovativeness?	Diversity (differences in personality and opinions, positions, beliefs, values, and attitudes)	Psychological perspective	The three IEO diversity dimensions – proactiveness, risk taking, and innovativeness diversity – affect team outcomes in different ways, although they belong to the same diversity type and even belong to a common superordinate construct.
Healey et al. (2021)	How do teams evaluate opportunities rather than individuals? How does the social cognitive mechanisms of team formation affect the ability of entrepreneurial teams to choose good opportunities and forgo bad ones?	Opportunity evaluation (as a collective process) Social cognitive mechanisms of team formation	Evolutionary approach	Opportunity evaluation decisions depend on the cognitive status of the lead entrepreneurs who found the team and the team formation strategy they use, i.e., whether they select team members based on interpersonal similarity (i.e., cognitive homophily) or complementary knowledge (i.e., cognitive heterophily). Learning moderates the effects of team formation on opportunity evaluation.
Boss et al. (2021)	Is allowing or disallowing autonomy of choice in team members or ideas improving team performance?	Autonomy	Organizational design perspective	Teams with autonomy over choosing either ideas or team members outperform teams in the baseline treatment as measured by pitch deck performance. The effect of choosing ideas is significantly stronger than the effect of choosing teams. However, the performance gains vanish for teams that are granted full autonomy over choosing both ideas and teams.

(continued)

Table 22.1 (continued)

Article	Research question	Key concept	Theoretical perspectives	Main contributions
Yang et al. (2020)	What are the paradoxical tensions between an entrepreneurial team's reliance on collective efforts for achieving success and individual members' tendencies to withhold their personal resources?	Resource provision paradox	The paradox perspective	The precarious nature of the early founding stage and the difficulty of redeploying some resources for other uses amplify the risk of early-stage resource contributions and may lead to team members withholding resources or even free riding. Two conditions may help overcome such collective action problems: adopting a formal contract to specify rewards and sanctions and encouraging reciprocal exchange among team members through the lead entrepreneur's voluntary contributions. Early-stage team members are reluctant to provide resources tailored to the business, even though such resources are critical to venture survival. We find that presigned formal contracts and founding entrepreneurs' initial contributions make members' contributions of such resources much more likely. Lead entrepreneurs' voluntary contributions to their businesses, signified by their provision of resources that impose high risks on themselves but increase the viability of the business, help mitigate collective action problems within entrepreneurial teams.

Jin et al. (2017)	How do the characteristics of entrepreneurial team composition (i.e., aggregated, heterogeneity, team size) affect new venture performance?	ET composition characteristics	Meta-analysis perspective	Entrepreneurial team characteristics affect new ventures.
Forbes et al. (2006)	How may new member identification and selection processes unfold as new ventures are formed?	ET formation process (team member addition)	A dynamic perspective	Paper identifies resource-seeking and interpersonal attraction as primary alternative motivators for new teammate addition; however, it illustrates how these motivations may be complementary in practice.
Hsu (2007)	What is the role of prior founding experience, academic training, and social capital in Venture Capital funding?	Founding experience	Social capital perspective	Prior founding experience (especially financially successful experience) increases both the likelihood of VC funding via a direct tie and venture valuation. Founders' ability to recruit executives via their own social network (as opposed to the VC's network) is positively associated with venture valuation. In the emerging Internet industry, founding teams with a doctoral degree holder are more likely to be funded via a direct VC tie and receive higher valuations, suggesting a signaling effect.
Knight et al. (2020)	Why are some startup teams more effective than others?	Startup team	Multidimensional Perspective	Startup teams: a multidimensional conceptualization, integrative review of past research, and future research agenda
Patzelt et al. (2021)	What are the stages that characterize the entrepreneurial team life cycle within each development phase of a venture?	Entrepreneurial team life cycle	Dynamic Perspective	This research develops a "double life cycle framework" covering entrepreneurial teams' formation, collaboration, and dissolution phases. It offers research suggestions on ET formation, collaboration, and dissolution in each venture phase, highlighting the role of entrepreneurial teams in advancing their ventures.

(continued)

Table 22.1 (continued)

Article	Research question	Key concept	Theoretical perspectives	Main contributions
Ma et al. (2022)	How can the presence of multiple teams in entrepreneurial firms create unexpected fault lines?	Team fault lines	Information, decision-making, and social classification perspectives	Modeling entrepreneurial team fault lines: collectivism, knowledge hiding, and team stability
Honoré & Ganco (2020)	What is the role of prior industry experience in the startup's next stage–its hiring of new employees?	Founding experience	Two-sided approach	Even firms founded by entrepreneurs without industry experience can attract new employees with such experience if the founders start with a large entrepreneurial team. Startups provide new hires with an earnings premium for their industry experience.
Zolin et al. (2011)	What is the impact of previously well-known people (strong ties) as entrepreneurial team members on the human resource flexibility of new ventures?	Resource flexibility (strong ties)	Social network	Choosing a well-known individual to join the entrepreneurial team increases the founder's ability to modify the team member's work role, but complicates asking the team member to leave the team if required. Hence, strong ties both increase and reduce human resource flexibility. However, the effect of strong ties on role modifiability is statistically significant only with novice entrepreneurs.

Entrepreneurial Team Dynamics: The Systemic Lens

Our ambition through this contribution is to (re)define the entrepreneurial team (and probably more generally collective entrepreneurship for instance in the context of inter-organizational networks or collaborative platforms) as a system. Hence, "a system is definable only by its cohesion in a broad sense, that is, the interactions of the component elements. In this sense an ecosystem or social system is just as "real" as an individual plant, animal, or human being, and indeed problems like pollution as a disturbance of the ecosystem, or social problems strikingly demonstrate their "reality." Interactions (or, more generally, interrelations), however, are never directly seen or perceived; they are conceptual constructs" (Von Bertalanffy, 1972, p. 422). Accordingly, general systems theory, then, consists of the scientific exploration of "wholes" and "wholeness" which, not so long ago, were considered to be metaphysical notions transcending the boundaries of science.

This point of view argued that the team as a whole differs from the sum of its members individually (Shepherd & Krueger, 2002). Collectively, entrepreneurial teams may simultaneously realize the full benefits of both brokerage and cohesive ties without incurring the trade-off faced by an individual entrepreneur who attempts both roles (Aven & Hillmann, 2018). Perceptions of collective efficacy are likely to also be important. Collective efficacy refers to "a team's belief in their conjoint capabilities to organize and execute the courses of action required to produce given levels of attainments" (Bandura, 1997, p. 477). Indeed, as the group efficacy results from the group interaction and the process of collective cognition, it seems like group efficacy is distinct from the individual beliefs group members hold about themselves or their group. As argued by Gibson (1999, p. 138), "a group efficacy forms as group members collectively acquire, store, manipulate and exchange information about each other and about their task, context, process and prior performance. Through processes of interaction, this information is combined, weighted, and integrated to form group efficacy. These same collective processes do not occur during self-efficacy formation or when members form individual beliefs about their group."

Moreover, opportunity evaluation as a dynamic social process is contingent upon entrepreneurs' networks and team founders' characteristics and their choices of who to turn to for judgments of an opportunity's potential (Healey et al., 2021). Indeed, the principle of small world networks reveals the tension hidden in calls for nascent entrepreneurs to "use networking" to build entrepreneurial teams and seek opportunities. Being embedded in dense clusters of social relations that have emerged through homophily and propinquity creates a highly circumscribed world for entrepreneurs (Aldrich & Kim, 2007). Accordingly, Aldrich & Kim (2007) claimed that local clusters of family, friends, work, and neighborhoods will serve as the pool of people available for recruitment into entrepreneurial teams, if nascent entrepreneurs follow the principle of interpersonal relations in team building. Additionally, they assumed that a great majority of entrepreneurial teams emerge out of the local clusters described by small world networks but without the bridging ties necessary to reduce the social distance to strangers qualified for team membership.

Systems, as Waltz nicely observed, "shape and shove" actors. He only addressed "shaping," though, through the interactional (rather than relational) mechanisms of "selection" and "emulation." We cannot, however, fully comprehend actors or their actions if we ignore systemic/relational "shaping" (Donnelly, 2019). Our vision through this contribution is to conceptualize the entrepreneurial team's dynamics especially in terms of actors' interdependencies and relations thereby referring to the systemic lens. This conceptualization could better reflect the dynamics of interactions between actors from the same team and from different firms. More importantly, it can describe actors' dynamics within and between platforms and ecosystems where network effects become the structuring element.

The Constructive Model

We seek to define the entrepreneurial team as a system that combines three dimensions: the ontological one, the functional one, and the genetic one (Von Bertalanffy, 2017). The ontology of entrepreneurial teams refers to what the team is, its structure, its identity (who are the members at the observed period), and is well documented by the literature as shown in the previous sections. The functional dimension evokes how it works and which are the rules and the practices of the team-members altogether. Last, the genetic dimension describes team evolution over time. This is naturally a more difficult object to manage because it requires generally a longitudinal research approach. As focused previously, literature usually focuses on functional dimensions. To suggest extensions of research in this important field, we will focus on a possible modeling of entrepreneurial teams dealing with functional and genetic dimensions. Moreover, the simultaneous combination of these three dimensions to describe entrepreneurial collective dynamics can be based on the identification of four components which interact to define a given entrepreneurial team (ontological aspect), how it moves (functional aspect) and how it evolves (genetics). These four elements are: a. *Affectio Societatis* (as meaning that all members wish to collaborate at the same level); b. *Synergy* (following Luecke, 2004; Amason et Sapienza, 1997; Ucbasaran et al., 2003, p. 110); c. *Commitment* (Vohora et al., 2004); and, d. *Shared vision* (Carland & Carland, 2012). The objective of relevant interaction was conceived through Candida Brush's model for describing women-entrepreneurship articulating five inseparables elements: money, management, market, meso-economy, and maternity (Brush, 1992). In the same way, our model (summarized in Figure 22.1) includes four dimensions that could be combined and articulated. In addition, in the case where one of these dimensions is missing or irrelevant to the others, then the entrepreneurial team functioning becomes critical and the issue can be the dislocation of the team.

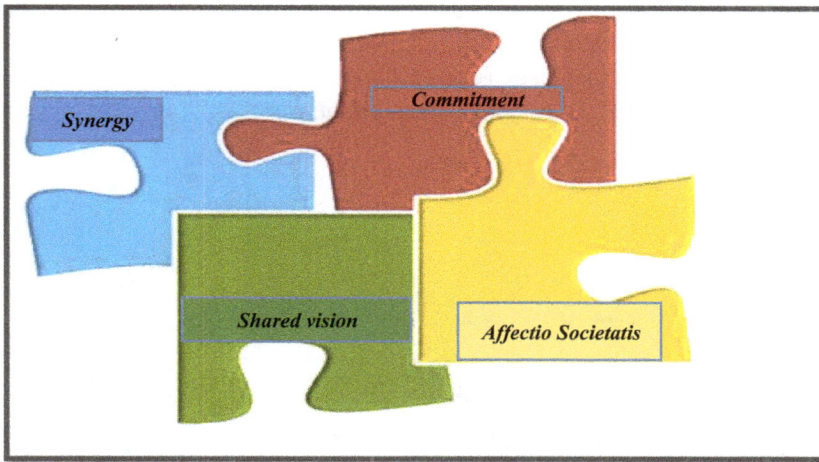

Figure 22.1: The four combined dynamic dimensions.

At the first level, the two first ones describe the interindividual relations. More precisely, Affectio Societatis means that all members wish to collaborate at the same level. Synergy (following Luecke, 2004; Amason & Sapienza, 1997; Ucbasaran et al., 2003, p. 110) means the members of the team share efficient resources with loyalty to promote their collective project. At the second level, Commitment is a key aspect which reveals the commitment of each member to the project and a collective sharing for acceding to shared objectives. Obviously, individual commitments are correlated to the efficacity of team-leading by the main entrepreneur. According to Vohora and colleagues (2004), commitment is one of the critical foundations for success. Through commitment, the co-entrepreneurs must demonstrate their commitment to the project, but also their willingness to participate personally in the common effort, to jointly develop a common vision, and to assume the risks arising from the common action. In the context of business venturing, one could think of the philosophical theory of Mickael Bratman for describing what is "joint-intention" (Bratman, 1993). Obviously, the collective commitment should appear in the speech and individual commitment to the collective project is also materialized by financial participation as suggested by Kamm and his colleagues (1990). Relatedly, despite possible differences of point of view, each member of an entrepreneurial team must feel jointly responsible with his teammates for decisions taken jointly (Katzenbach & Smith, 1994). Last, Shared Vision refers to the capacity of members to share projects for developing business (Carland & Carland, 2012).

Naturally, for the success of entrepreneurial team, the four elements should appear but they are affirmed sequentially during the entrepreneurial team process as shown in Figure 22.2. Following the well-known work of Vohora et al. (2004), it is possible to identify four different stages of business-venturing. At the two first ones (opportunity identification and entrepreneurial commitment), synergy and *affectio societatis* are necessary and sufficient to allow the birth of the collective enterprise. The collective commitment is only required for the firm to get credibility (stage 3). Shareholders may ask to be convinced by the team members. Finally, shared vision is fully required for the ultimate stage which occurs in the sustainability of business (stage 4).

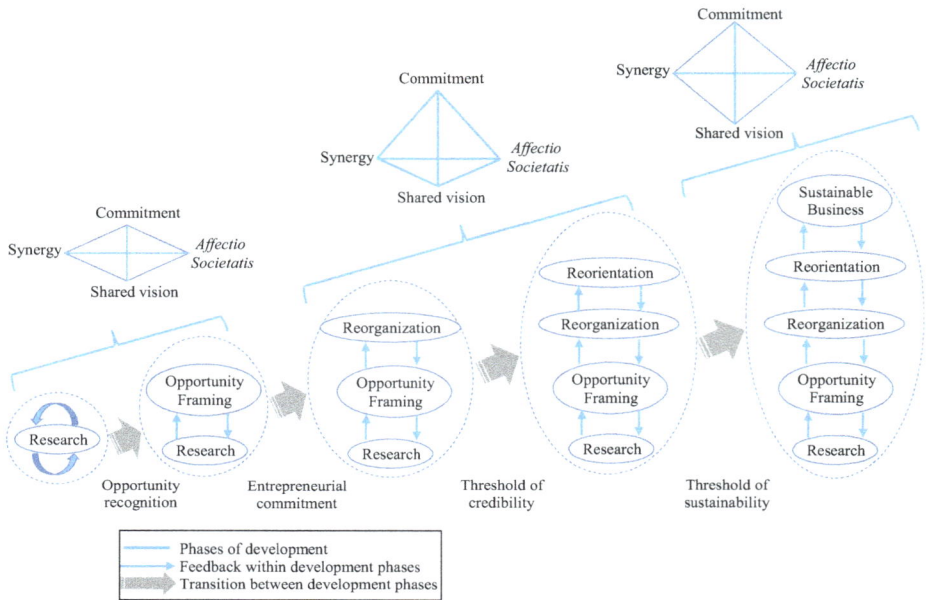

Figure 22.2: Towards a dynamic team-business venturing.

Platforms and Ecosystems as an Extension of the Entrepreneurial Team

Like all other disciplinary fields, International Entrepreneurship (IE) is embracing the digitalization challenges driven by the current fourth industrial revolution (Eden, 2018). In fact, Multinationals (MNEs) are unavoidably facing two emergent phenomena, namely innovation openness and business "platformization" that are jointly transforming the way MNEs pursue entrepreneurship opportunities (Nambisan et al., 2018) and build competitive advantage (Parker et al., 2016) across industries and countries in the digital age (Van Tulder et al., 2018). Recent scientific efforts have broadly extended International Business (IB) theories to incorporate digital artifacts (Ojala et al., 2018) which increasingly shape the global business economy (Chen et al., 2019). This emerging stream of research attempts to make more explicit the way digitalization and platformization are transforming the internationalization processes of MNEs

(Hennart, 2019; Nambisan et al., 2019), SMEs (Bell & Loane, 2010; Eduardsen, 2018; Glavas et al., 2019), and new ventures, namely born-globals (Kim & Cavusgil, 2020). Current research underlines a shift in the way multinationals are going abroad, thereby giving rise to critical questions regarding the applicability of traditional IB theories (Chen et al., 2019).

Recent literature deals extensively with the venue of platforms and digital tools in both entrepreneurship and international business fields. However, this literature is less documented and at its embryonic stage of evolution. Thus, with few exceptions (Ojala et al., 2018; Nambisan et al., 2019), the extent to which digital platforms extend IB theories remains less studied. The issue dealing with the role of platforms in scaling globally and rapidly transcending the national borders is still less explored. More precisely, extant literature has addressed the issue of the rapid internationalization driven by digital platforms. Scholars who deal with this issue have shown the immediate impact of the platforms on the MNEs' speed of internationalization (Kromidha & Robson, 2021; Deng et al., 2022). This recent work advances the current IB scholarship by highlighting the emergence of digital platforms and ecosystems (DPE) as affording new ways of internationalization, as facilitating new ways of building knowledge and relationships, and as enabling new ways of creating and delivering value to global customers (Nambisan et al., 2019). It is now widely accepted that the Internet and allied information communication technologies have facilitated small and medium enterprises' internationalization and provided new tools that enable such firms to internationalize more rapidly and engage more effectively with customers in a wider range of more complex business activities (Bell & Loane, 2010).

As a consequence, the radical metamorphosis of the business environment led to the emergence of a newly pervasive feature of globalization thus referring to global digitalized networks (Banalieva & Dhanaraj, 2019) or global platform and ecosystems (Nambisan et al., 2019). In fact, given the proliferation of digital tools, organizations and societies currently take another look at business and scholars unanimously stress the need for revisiting extant theory and urgently call for the development of new theories. More specifically, the magic and surprising proliferation of Internet architecture has unavoidably led to shrinking competition boundaries (Afuah, 2003). This requires modifying the way firms perceive competitive advantage in the global arena by hopefully shifting from firm-specific advantages to ecosystem-specific advantages (Kotha et al., 2001; Li et al., 2019). Effectively, globalization waves have fostered the emergence of digitally networked actors' dynamics which has rapidly become the dominant pattern of interaction by involving different actors from different sectors. As previously argued by Healey et al. (2021), opportunity evaluation as a dynamic social process is contingent upon entrepreneurs' networks and team founders' characteristics and their choices of who to turn to for judgments of an opportunity's potential. Similarly, brokerage as a specific case of structural role complementarity will enhance entrepreneurial teams' functioning (Aven & Hillmann, 2018).

Conclusion

The global world we live in is radically metamorphosing due to the fastest growing of digital technologies that have brutally changed our daily lives and disrupted established patterns thus marking the end of an era (Tasselli, 2019) and ushering in a new era in which the traditional cross-border ways of seeking global competitive advantage are increasingly questioned and refashioned. Specifically, information and communication technologies, especially the Internet, have transformed the local-global dichotomy leading to defining new industries and modifying existing industries (Hannibal & Knight, 2018).

The world has currently been changing dramatically, leading multinational enterprises (MNEs) to adapt to such dramatic changes and increasing complexity in the global competitive landscape (Hitt et al., 2016). For instance, international entrepreneurship, like most other domains, is inexorably jostled by the ubiquitous "digital revolution" that refers either to new technologies that eliminate the divide between the physical and the digital (Rindfleisch et al., 2017) or to the power of big data that transforms traditional businesses thereby bringing multinationals (called born digitals) into a new era, henceforth, digitalized (McAfee et al., 2012).

Further research on the entrepreneurial team could also embrace these new challenges. Relatedly, it will be important to encourage more research about the accompanying devices that are relevant for collective dynamics. Linking our model based on *Affectio Societatis* with the debates about entrepreneurial resilience could also be an extension. Are entrepreneurial teams more resilient than solo entrepreneurs and which factors explain such resilience following the invitation of Chen and Zhang (2021)? Finally, a specific focus could be interestingly attributed to the ethnical and gender diversities of entrepreneurial teams in relation to questioning the intercultural management of commitment, shared vision, and *affection societatis*.

References

Afuah, A. (2003). Redefining firm boundaries in the face of the internet: Are firms really shrinking? *Academy of Management Review*, *28*(1), 34–53.

Aldrich, H.E., & Kim, P.H. (2007). Small worlds, infinite possibilities? How social networks affect entrepreneurial team formation and search. *Strategic Entrepreneurship Journal*, *1*(1-2), 147–165.

Amason, A.C., & Sapienza H.J. (1997). The effects of top management team size and interaction norms on cognitive and affective conflict. *Journal of Management*, *23*(4), 495.

Aven, B., & Hillmann, H. (2018). Structural role complementarity in entrepreneurial teams. *Management Science*, *64*(12), 5688–5704.

Banalieva, E.R., & Dhanaraj, C. (2019). Internalization theory for the digital economy. *Journal of International Business Studies*, *50*(8), 1372–1387.

Bandura, A. (1997). The anatomy of stages of change. *American journal of health promotion*: *AJHP*, *12*(1), 8–10.

Beckman, C.M. (2006). The influence of founding team company affiliations on firm behavior. *Academy of Management Journal*, *49*(4), 741–758.

Bell, J., & Loane, S. (2010). 'New-wave' global firms: Web 2.0 and SME internationalisation. *Journal of Marketing Management*, *26*(3–4), 213–229.

Ben-Hafaïedh, C. (2017). Entrepreneurial teams research in movement. In C. Ben-Hafaïedh & T.M. Cooney (Eds.), *Research handbook on entrepreneurial teams: Theory and practice*. Edward Elgar Publishing.

Boss, V., Dahlander, L., Ihl, C., & Jayaraman, R. (2021). Organizing entrepreneurial teams: A field experiment on autonomy over choosing teams and ideas. *Organization Science*.

Bratman, M.E. (1993). Shared intention. *Ethics*, *104*(1), 97–113.

Brush, C.G. (1992). Research on women business owners: Past trends, a new perspective and future directions. *Entrepreneurship Theory and Practice*, *16*(1), 5–30.

Cardon, M.S., Post, C., & Forster, W.R. (2017). Team entrepreneurial passion: Its emergence and influence in new venture teams. *Academy of Management Review*, *42*(2), 283–305.

Carland, J.C., & Carland, Jr, J.W. (2012). A model of shared entrepreneurial leadership. *Academy of Entrepreneurship Journal*, *18*(2), 71.

Chandler G.N., Honig B., Wiklund J. (2005). Antecedents, moderators, and performance consequences of membership change in new venture teams. *Journal of Business Venturing*, 20 (5), 705–725.

Chen, L., Shaheer, N., Yi, J., & Li, S. (2019). The international penetration of ibusiness firms: Network effects, liabilities of outsidership and country clout. *Journal of International Business Studies*, *50*(2), 172–192.

Chen, M.H., & Wang, M.C. (2008). Social networks and a new venture's innovative capability: The role of trust within entrepreneurial teams. *R&d Management*, *38*(3), 253–264.

Chen, M.H., & Zhang, Y. (2021). Fostering resilience in new venture teams: The role of behavioral and affective integration. *Group and Organization Management*, July.

Chua, R., & Mengzi, J. (2020). Across the great divides: Gender dynamics influence how intercultural conflict helps or hurts creative collaboration. *Academy of Management Journal*, *63*(3).

Deng, Z., Zhu, Z., Johanson, M., & Hilmersson, M. (2022). Rapid internationalization and exit of exporters: The role of digital platforms. *International Business Review*, *31*(1), 101896.

Donnelly, J. (2019). Systems, levels, and structural theory: Waltz's theory is not a systemic theory (and why that matters for International Relations today). *European Journal of International Relations*, *25*(3), 904–930.

Drnovsek, M., Cardon, M.S., & Murnieks, C.Y. (2009). Collective passion in entrepreneurial teams. In *Understanding the entrepreneurial mind* (pp. 191–215). Springer.

Eden, L. (2018). The fourth industrial revolution: Seven lessons from the past. In *International business in the information and digital age*. Emerald Publishing Limited.

Eduardsen, J. (2018). Internationalisation through digitalisation: The impact of E-commerce usage on internationalisation in small-and medium-sized firms. In *International business in the information and digital age*. Emerald Publishing Limited.

Ferguson, A.J., Cohen, L.E., Burton, M.D., & Beckman, C.M. (2016). Misfit and milestones: Structural elaboration and capability reinforcement in the evolution of entrepreneurial top management teams. *Academy of Management Journal*, *59*(4), 1430–1450.

Forbes, D.P., Borchert, P.S., Zellmer-Bruhn, M.E., & Sapienza, H.J. (2006). Entrepreneurial team formation: An exploration of new member addition. *Entrepreneurship Theory and Practice*, *30*(2), 225–248.

Francis, D.H., & Sandberg, W.R. (2000). Friendship within entrepreneurial teams and its association with team and venture performance. *Entrepreneurship Theory and Practice*, *25*(2), 5–26.

Franke, N., Gruber, M., Harhoff, D., & Henkel, J. (2008). Venture capitalists' evaluations of start-up teams: Trade-offs, knock-out criteria, and the impact of VC experience. *Entrepreneurship Theory and Practice*, *32*(3), 459–483.

Gibson, C.B. (1999). Do they do what they believe they can? Group efficacy and group effectiveness across tasks and cultures. *Academy of Management Journal*, *42*(2), 138–152.

Glavas, C., Mathews, S., & Russell-Bennett, R. (2019). Knowledge acquisition via internet-enabled platforms: Examining incrementally and non-incrementally internationalizing SMEs. *International Marketing Review*.

Gregori, P., & Parastuty, Z. (2021). Investigating the process of entrepreneurial team member exits: A systematic review and future research directions. *Review of Managerial Science*.

Hannibal, M., & Knight, G. (2018). Additive manufacturing and the global factory: Disruptive technologies and the location of international business. *International Business Review*, *27*(6), 1116–1127.

Healey, M.P., Bleda, M., & Querbes, A. (2021). Opportunity evaluation in teams: A social cognitive model. *Journal of Business Venturing*, *36*(4), 106128.

Hennart, J.F. (2019). Digitalized service multinationals and international business theory. *Journal of International Business Studies*, *50*(8), 1388–1400.

Hitt, M.A., Li, D., & Xu, K. (2016). International strategy: From local to global and beyond. *Journal of World Business*, *51*(1), 58–73.

Honoré, F., & Ganco, M. (2020). Entrepreneurial teams' acquisition of talent: Evidence from technology manufacturing industries using a two-sided approach. *Strategic Management Journal*.

Hsu, D.H. (2007). Experienced entrepreneurial founders, organizational capital, and venture capital funding. *Research Policy*, *36*(5), 722–741.

Jin, L., Madison, K., Kraiczy, N.D., Kellermanns, F.W., Crook, T.R., & Xi, J. (2017). Entrepreneurial team composition characteristics and new venture performance: A meta-analysis. *Entrepreneurship Theory and Practice*, *41*(5), 743–771.

Kamm, J.B., Shuman, J.C., Seeger, J.A., & Nurick, A.J. (1990), Entrepreneurial teams in new venture creation: A research agenda. *Entrepreneurship: Theory & Practice*, *14*(4), 7–17.

Katzenbach, J.R., & Smith, D.K. (1994). Teams at the top. *The McKinsey Quarterly* (1), 71–80.

Khanagha, S., Volberda, H.W., Alexiou, A., & Annosi, M.C. (2021). Mitigating the dark side of agile teams: Peer pressure, leaders' control, and the innovative output of agile teams. *Journal of Product Innovation Management*.

Kim, D., & Cavusgil, E. (2020). Antecedents and outcomes of digital platform risk for international new ventures' internationalization. *Journal of World Business*, *55*(1), 101021.

Klotz, A.C., Hmieleski, K.M., Bradley, B.H., & Busenitz, L.W. (2014). New venture teams: A review of the literature and roadmap for future research. *Journal of Management*, *40*(1), 226–255.

Knight, A.P., Greer, L.L., & De Jong, B. (2020). Start-up teams: A multidimensional conceptualization, integrative review of past research, and future research agenda. *Academy of Management Annals*, *14*(1), 231–266.

Kollmann, T., Stöckmann, C., Meves, Y., & Kensbock, J.M. (2017). When members of entrepreneurial teams differ: Linking diversity in individual-level entrepreneurial orientation to team performance. *Small Business Economics*, *48*(4), 843–859.

Kotha, S., Rindova, V.P., & Rothaermel, F.T. (2001). Assets and actions: Firm-specific factors in the internationalization of US Internet firms. *Journal of International Business Studies*, *32*(4), 769–791.

Kromidha, E., & Robson, P.J. (2021). The role of digital presence and investment network signals on the internationalisation of small firms. *International Small Business Journal*, *39*(2), 109–129.

Lazar, M., Miron-Spektor, E., Agarwal, R., Erez, M., Goldfarb, B., & Chen, G. (2020). Entrepreneurial team formation. *Academy of Management Annals*, *14*(1), 29–59.

Lazar, M., Miron-Spektor, E., Chen, G., Goldfarb, B., Erez, M., & Agarwal, R. (2021). Forming entrepreneurial teams: Mixing business and friendship to create transactive memory systems for enhanced success. *Academy of Management Journal*, *65*(4), 1110–1138.

Li, J., Chen, L., Yi, J., Mao, J., & Liao, J. (2019). Ecosystem-specific advantages in international digital commerce. *Journal of International Business Studies*, *50*(9), 1448–1463.

Luecke, R. (2004). *Creating teams with an edge: The complete skill set to build powerful and influential teams*. Rutgers University Press.

Ma, H., Xiao, B., Guo, H., Tang, S., & Singh, D. (2022). Modeling entrepreneurial team faultlines: Collectivism, knowledge hiding, and team stability. *Journal of Business Research, 141*, 726–736.

McAfee, A., Brynjolfsson, E., Davenport, T.H., Patil, D.J., & Barton, D. (2012). Big data: the management revolution. *Harvard Business Review, 90*(10), 60–68.

Milliani-Mosbah, N. (2015). *Structure, fonctionnement et évolution des équipes entrepreneuriales: une modélisation systémique dans une perspective d'accompagnement à la création d'entreprises*. PhD Dissertation, supervised by T. Levy, University of Brest, France.

Nambisan, S., Siegel, D., & Kenney, M. (2018). On open innovation, platforms, and entrepreneurship. *Strategic Entrepreneurship Journal, 12*(3), 354–368.

Nambisan, S., Zahra, S.A., & Luo, Y. (2019). Global platforms and ecosystems: Implications for international business theories. *Journal of International Business Studies, 50*(9), 1464–1486.

Ojala, A., Evers, N., & Rialp, A. (2018). Extending the international new venture phenomenon to digital platform providers: A longitudinal case study. *Journal of World Business, 53*(5), 725–739.

Parker, G., Van Alstyne, M.W., & Jiang, X. (2016). Platform ecosystems: How developers invert the firm. *Boston University Questrom School of Business Research Paper* (2861574).

Patzelt, H., Preller, R., & Breugst, N. (2021). Understanding the life cycles of entrepreneurial teams and their ventures: An agenda for future research. *Entrepreneurship Theory and Practice, 45*(5), 1119–1153.

Pinzón, N., Montero, J., & González-Pernía, J.L. (2021). The influence of individual characteristics on getting involved in an entrepreneurial team: The contingent role of individualism. *International Entrepreneurship and Management Journal*, 1–38.

Rindfleisch, A., O'Hern, M., & Sachdev, V. (2017). The digital revolution, 3D printing, and innovation as data. *Journal of Product Innovation Management, 34*(5), 681–690.

Ruef, M., Aldrich, H., & Carter, N. (2003). "The structure of founding teams: Homophily, strong ties and isolation among US entrepreneurs." *American Sociological Review, 68*(2), 195–222.

Schjoedt, L., & Kraus, S. (2009). Entrepreneurial teams: Definition and performance factors. *Management Research News, 32*(6), 513–524.

Shepherd, D.A., & Krueger, N.F. (2002). An intentions-based model of entrepreneurial teams' social cognition. *Entrepreneurship Theory and Practice, 27*(2), 167–185.

Tasselli, S. (2019). At the end of an era: A model and three tales of memory, perception, and reality. *Academy of Management Review*.

Tenner, I., & Hörisch, J. (2021). Diversity matters: The influence of gender diversity on the environmental orientation of entrepreneurial ventures. *Journal of Business Economics*, 1–19.

Ucbasaran, D., Lockett, A., Wright, M., & Westhead P. (2003). Entrepreneurial founder teams: Factors associated with member entry and exit. *Entrepreneurship: Theory & Practice, 28*(2), 107–127.

Uy, M.A., Jacob, G.H., Gielnik, M.M., Frese, M., Antonio, T., & Wonohadidjojo, D.M. (2021). When passions collide: Passion convergence in entrepreneurial teams. *Journal of Applied Psychology, 106*(6), 902.

Van Tulder, R., Verbeke, A., & Piscitello, L. (Eds.). (2018). *International business in the information and digital age*. Emerald Group Publishing.

Vohora, A., Wright, M., & Lockett, A. (2004). Critical junctures in the development of university high-tech spinout companies. *Research Policy, 33*(1), 147–175.

Von Bertalanffy, L. (1972). The history and status of general systems theory. Academy of management journal, 15(4), 407–426.

Von Bertalanffy, L. (2017). The history and status of general systems theory. *Academy of Management Journal, 15*(4), 407–426.

West III, G.P. (2007). Collective cognition: When entrepreneurial teams, not individuals, make decisions. *Entrepreneurship Theory and Practice*, *31*(1), 77–102.

Yang, T., Bao, J., & Aldrich, H. (2020). The paradox of resource provision in entrepreneurial teams: Between self-interest and the collective enterprise. *Organization Science*, *31*(6), 1336–1358.

Yang, T., & Aldrich, H.E. (2014). Who's the boss? Explaining gender inequality in entrepreneurial teams. *American Sociological Review*, *79*(2), 303–327.

Zolin, R., Kuckertz, A., & Kautonen, T. (2011). Human resource flexibility and strong ties in entrepreneurial teams. *Journal of Business Research*, *64*(10), 1097–1103.

Ramchandra Bhusal

23 The Impact of Entrepreneurial Capital on Preferences for External Financing: An Empirical Study of Ethnic Minority Business Owners in the UK

Abstract: This chapter examines the impact of entrepreneurial capital (a pool of social, cultural and human capital) on preferences for external financing among ethnic minority business owners in the UK. The findings show that entrepreneurial capital has an impact on ethnic entrepreneurs' finance seeking behaviours. More specifically, entrepreneurs who choose to embrace extended social networks prefer bank financing and ethnic entrepreneurs who embrace multiculturalism and have a propensity for acculturation prefer alternative sources of financing. Similarly, business owners with postgraduate education have aa positive preference for alternative financing and a high level of education has a positive impact on shaping preferences for asset financing. The empirical study is based on 114 responses obtained through three different survey approaches. Multiple regression models are used to analyze data. This study provides a number of recommendations for policymakers, finance providers and practitioners.

Keywords: external financing, entrepreneurial capital, social capital, cultural capital, human capital, ethnic minority businesses

Introduction

A business owner's intention, ability, and resourcefulness determine the firm's fortune. Entrepreneurs can acquire a range of supplementary intangible resources that enable easier access to finance (Nofsinger & Wang, 2011; Heilbrunn & Kushnirrovich, 2008; Kim et al., 2006; Parker & van Praag, 2006; Uzzi, 1999; Sanders & Nee, 1996; Waldinger et al., 1990). Entrepreneurs' social capital (SC), cultural capital (CC), and human capital (HC) (as entrepreneurial capital – EC) play a vital role in enabling entrepreneurial activities (Marvel et al., 2016; Jayawarna et al., 2014). These intangibles are at the forefront of the ethnic entrepreneurial ecosystem (Gomez et al., 2015; Deakins et al., 2007; Basu & Altinay, 2002). Whilst the benefits of these vital resources in business formation have been widely discussed in ethnic minority entrepreneurship liter-

Ramchandra Bhusal, Queen Margaret University, Edinburgh

https://doi.org/10.1515/9783110747652-024

ature (Zhu et al., 2019; Morgan et al., 2018), the interplay of different forms of capital is seldom examined (Pret et al., 2016; Deakins et al., 2007).

Access to adequate finance is key to achieving entrepreneurial aspirations (Berger & Udell, 1998). However, a common theme in SME financing literature is that access to finance is one of the major obstacles in realizing full entrepreneurial potential among ethnic minority business (EMB) owners as they face additional barriers in acquiring suitable finance around the world (Howell, 2019; Samllbone et al., 2003). Firms with limited access to adequate financial capital are considered to be more likely to close and less likely to hire employees and make a profit (Howell, 2019). In the UK, there are huge variations in accessing external finance amongst EMB owners. EMBs such as owned by Black African, African Caribbean, and Bangladeshi groups are amongst the most deprived EMB owners when it comes to accessing adequate finance (Fraser, 2009; Smallbone et al., 2003; Storey, 2004).

Adequate access to external finance is related to both supply and demand of finance (Masiak et al., 2019). To an extent, limited use of formal sources of external finance by EMBs is related to their behavioural characteristics such as financing preferences (Smallbone et al., 2007; Desidero, 2014). The owner/ manager's preferences for certain types of financing play a crucial role in promoting access to finance (Baker et al., 2007; Baker & Wurgler, 2013). When it comes to demand-side issues, access to finance is rooted in entrepreneurs' willingness to consider different types of financing options. Hence, to better understand small business financing patterns, it is vital to understand business owners' preferences for a certain type of financing (Barker et al., 2007). Individual preferences may be a more prevailing constraint than the supply of finance, although conditions of supply in turn affect the demand for type and volume of finance (Daskalakis et al., 2013; Howorth, 2001). To that end, this chapter provides insights into the relationship that exists between entrepreneurs' holding of non-financial capital and their preferences for external sources of financial capital. The key research question is as follows: what is the relationship between types of social, cultural, and human capital and preferences for external financing amongst small business entrepreneurs?

The remainder of this chapter is structured as follows. The next section provides a literature review and hypotheses. Then the proceeding section outlines the data collection process and model of specification which is followed by empirical findings and discussions. This chapter concludes with policy implications and recommendations for future research.

Literature Review and Hypothesis Development

The extent of the holding of entrepreneurial resources has an invariable impact on the entrepreneurial ecosystem (Pret et al., 2016). The disparity in the possession of non-financial resources informs individual choices and identities (Attwell et al., 2018). The proprietorship of SC, CC, and HC works as a pool of information that has the potential to reduce information opaqueness for both lenders and borrowers. Social contacts and relationships are significant sources of competitive advantage that improve entrepreneurs' "ability to access, deploy, exchange, and combine valuable resources" (Chisholm & Nielsen, 2009, p. 12). The richness in HC portrays borrowers as "good borrowers" in the eyes of lenders (Coleman & Cohn, 2000). Furthermore, EC is substitutable (Light, 2004). Therefore, an optimal combination of such capital can have a compounding effect in entrepreneurial success.

Entrepreneurs and entrepreneurship are socially situated (Gedajlovic et al., 2013). The essence of SC theories in the entrepreneurial context relates to advantages and disadvantages derived from social relationships and ties (Chisholm & Nielsen, 2009). The social network is a valuable relational asset that acts as a substantial pool of information (Ferri et al., 2009) which yields both monetary and semi-monetary benefits (Bourdieu, 1986). SC is considered as a multidimensional concept and a number of dimensions are considered in defining it. The most commonly used dimensions include: trust, rules, and norms governing social action. Chisholm and Nielsen (2009) considered SC as internal and external to the firm: internal as embedded in the relationship between the firm's members, while external spreads beyond the boundaries of the firm.

Uzzi (1999, p. 500) proposed two approaches, "the weak tie approach" and "strong tie approach," in which weak ties are large non-redundant networks within arm's length and strong ties are closed tightly knit networks yielding benefits to holders. According to Danes et al. (2008), SC has both bonding and bridging attributes. Bonding SC is formed by people who like each other and is crucial for "getting by," while bridging SC is formed by people who do not like each other and is crucial for "getting ahead" (Hutchinson et al., 2004). Danes et al. (2008) indicated that EMB owners use bonding SC more often. Whilst SC is considered a great source of competitive advantages (Gedajlovic et al., 2013), it has the potential to subdue entrepreneurship when external information is restricted (Light & Dana, 2013). Figure 23.1 links the dimensions of social capital with the underlying notion.

This study uses EMB owners' propensity to engage in formal and informal networks within both ethnic and non-ethnic social networks as a proxy for SC. The manifestation of the weak SC is EME's involvement in both ethnic and non-ethnic network ties. It is believed that SC embedded in wider social networks can benefit EMB owners by developing a new array of relationships with wider entrepreneurial communities including finance providers, customers, suppliers, and public authorities. The following hypothesis is proposed to examine the relationship between EMB owners' extended social ties and preferences for external sources of financing:

H1a: EMB owners' weak SC embedded beyond immediate ethnic ties significantly influences their preferences for external financing.

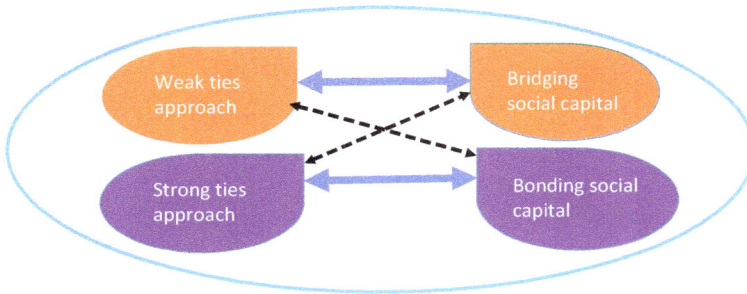

Figure 23.1: Social capital continuum.
Source: authors' creation.

Furthermore, EMB owners make the most of their ethnic networks as this has been identified as a pathway for entrepreneurial endeavors (Volery, 2007). Ethnic ties and networks provide invaluable resources in pursuing the entrepreneurial journey (Heilbrunn & Kushnirrovich, 2008). According to Masurel et al. (2004, p. 79), close kinship is beneficial in two ways: "1) presence of critical mass of potential customers of the same ethnic origin leading to viable market niches, and 2) rise of informal networks of a sufficient size which facilitate the recruitment of cheap personnel, up to date information or low-cost financing capital." Massey (1988, p. 396) defines ethnic networks as "sets of interpersonal ties that links [sic] migrants, former migrants and non-migrants in the origin or destination areas through the bond of kinship, friendship and shared community origin."

However, immigrants' offspring perceive their community networks more negatively, like a "restriction for their development" (Deakins et al., 2007). Emphasizing the downsides of ethnic-only networks, Oc et al. (1997) postulate that "networking of ethnic minority businesses may encourage solidarity but may also result in further isolation and marginalization." High reliance on an ethnic only network limits the ability to acquire relevant information and can lead towards social liability rather than SC (Chisholm & Nielsen, 2009). This can potentially lock EMB owners into a "constrained information continuum" (authors' emphasis). Immigrant entrepreneurs make minimal use of mainstream support services and hugely rely on and trust co-ethnic networks and advice (for example see Ram et al., 2002). Hence, ethnic-only networks provide limited competitive advantage compared to wider social networks (Siegler, 2014). Furthermore, close ties with ethnic-only networks and only exploiting ethnic-only resources such as cheap ethnic labor can diminish the SC of the locality, generating conflicts and increasing the chance of disintegration (Canello, 2016). Furthermore, a limited number of strong ties jeopardize EMB owners' ability to reap an extensive resource base (Kreiser et al., 2013). Reflecting upon this discussion, the following hypothesis is proposed to examine the relationship of EMB owners' strong SC and preferences for external financing:

H1b: EMB owners' strong SC confined in ethnic only ties significantly influences their preferences for external financing.

The extant literature on CC has a multitude of definitions and theoretical basis largely based on the context of a study (Pret et al., 2016). According to Bourdieu (1986), CC is high cultural knowledge that can be turned into economic profit for its owner. The particular culture and socio-economic class of every individual shape the way they think, speak, and represent themselves in a wider social context (Attwell et al., 2018). Culture is the value that individuals embrace, their informed approaches and histories and rituals that characterize their origin. Thus, some cultures produce more entrepreneurs than others (Busenitz & Lau, 1996), and immigrant entrepreneurs are inclined to become cultural entrepreneurs by making maximum use of their ethno-cultural heritages. Entrepreneurial studies focused on culture have utilized a number of theoretical notions to characterize the influence of cultural aspects in a variety of contexts. Attwell and Smith (2017) used social identity theory to understand the influence of shared identity and mutually reinforced behaviors. Pret et al. (2016) used Bourdieu's theory of practice to understand the multifaceted nature of different forms of capital and their interplay. This study builds onto Bourdieu's (1986) conceptualization of CC, specifically based on the notion of CC underpinned by high cultural knowledge and the individual's socio-economic route embedded in family business tradition. According to Hofstede (1980, p. 11), individuals "carry mental programs, which are developed in the family in early childhood and . . . these mental programs contain a component of national culture." Hofstede's characterization of CC provides cues to understand the ethnic variation in entrepreneurial activities as the origin of immigrant ethnic minorities extensively varies and so does the deployment of CC (Ballard, 1996). Furthermore, the offspring of entrepreneurial parents benefit from "informal training" and "pre-market experience" for which Kim et al. (2006) denote as CC.

Ethnic involvement in entrepreneurial activities is significantly larger in the UK and entrepreneurial culture is regarded as source of competitive advantages for nascent entrepreneurs. Hence, businesses owned by such entrepreneurs can be lucrative investment propositions for private investors. Extensive involvement in the business environment can provide innovative ways to manage resources such as bootstrapping. Having said that, a closely held entrepreneurial culture within the remit of family members can increase the information opacity and make it harder for lenders to assess the creditworthiness of such businesses. Based on this discussion the following hypothesis is proposed to examine the relationship between EMB owners' family business background and preferences for external sources of financing:

H2a: EMB owners' family business background significantly influences their preferences for external financing.

Moreover, CC has many different dimensions and such variation can have diverse impacts on entrepreneurial decision-making. Seeing culture as knowledge, Light (2004, pp. 1–2) suggests examples of cultural knowledge as "knowing how to dress for success, and arty chit-chat." According to Van Auken (2002, p. 293), CC includes "art and community amenities." Cultural gatherings, associations, and groups are conducive in developing several cognitive skills such as communication skills and improving language ability among immigrant entrepreneurs. Immigrants willing to adopt language, norms, values and behaviors of the host country get competitive advantages in pursing entrepreneurship (McPherson, 2010). These cultural trajectories have potential to mitigate information asymmetries in accessing adequate finance. Van Auken (2002) argues that communities with strong CC have a better chance of raising finance to fund highly informationally opaque and risky business.

Culture influences human thinking (Hofstede, 1980) and "cultural style" influences individual actions (Attwell & Smith, 2017). The way individuals process information has considerable implications in shaping their behavior (Attwell & Smith, 2017), such as acquiring resources. Thus, the cultural route of an individual can have a vital role in entrepreneurial activities such as choosing financing options. In this context, the following hypothesis is proposed to examine the relationship between EMB owners' propensity for acculturation in the host country and preferences for external sources of financing:

H2b: EMB owners' propensity for acculturation significantly influences their preferences for external financing.

HC is widely regarded as a strategic source for competitive advantages (Iversen et al., 2008). HC consists of knowledge and skills that can be classified as general or specific (Becker, 1964). According to Piazza-Georgi (2002, p. 463), HC is "a stock of personal skills that economic agents have at their disposal." As the human part of the business is becoming a very valuable asset, entrepreneurs' HC is one of the resources that offers competitive advantages such as by easing the entrepreneurship journey and enhancing entrepreneurial performance (Kim et al., 2006). Entrepreneurs with high quality HC have access to wider financial resources (Gimmon & Levie, 2010) and are better at perceiving profitable opportunities (Davidsson & Hoing, 2003). Entrepreneurs' previous knowledge which can be defined as tacit and explicit (Davidsson & Honig, 2003) has considerable implication in enhancing entrepreneurial performance (EI Shoubaki et al., 2019). According to Davidsson and Honig (2003), tacit knowledge is "know-how" and explicit knowledge is "know-what." Furthermore, Davidsson and Honig clarify that formal education assists entrepreneurs in accumulating explicit knowledge, whilst experience is tacit knowledge.

A number of extant studies manifest HC as a positive predictor of access to finance (Coleman & Cohan, 2000; Parker & van Praag, 2006). The offspring of EMB owners, predominantly of immigrant background, are regarded as opportunity entrepreneurs (Jones et al., 2012) with a high level of education (Basu, 2006). The conventional belief is that immigrant minorities start business as "necessity entrepreneur[s]" (Jones et al., 2012) but the offspring generation rich in country HC and other soft cognitive skills has the potential for opportunity entrepreneurship and such endeavors may appear as lucrative opportunities for a range of investors. The following hypothesis is developed to test the association between EMB owners' level of education and preferences for external financing:

H3a: EMB owners' level of education as a proxy for HC significantly influences their preferences for external financing.

Business owners' experience is regarded as an important asset in building entrepreneurial capabilities and deriving success (Hallak et al., 2018). Finance providers assign less probable uncertainty for the entrepreneur with a considerable length of business experience (Coleman & Cohn, 2000). Thus, HC accumulated through business experience strengthens entrepreneurs to negotiate good credit terms with finance providers. The majority of EMBs are family owned businesses and HC in a family business is complex due to the existence of the dual relationship of family and business (Sirmon & Hitt, 2003). Growing up in the family-focused business provides business-specific tacit knowledge and descendants of self-employed parents tend to be successful entrepreneurs (Henley, 2005). The offspring of immigrant entrepreneurs are marked as "free enterprise heroes" (Dhaliwal & Kangis, 2006). Moreover, entrepreneurs with richer HC are good at managing bootstrapping resources (Irwin & Scott, 2010), therefore reducing the need and preferences for external finance. In this context, the following hypothesis is proposed to investigate the association between EMB owners' experience and their preferences for external financing:

H3b: EMB owners' experience as a proxy for HC significantly influences their preferences for external financing.

Data Collection Process and Variables

The data in this study were collected by conducting surveys from February to July 2017 amongst the five largest ethnic groups in England. Target respondents' details were gathered from EMBs' directories (published and online), social media, personal and professional contacts, and from the Companies House database. A snowballing technique was used to add to the database and gain access to potential respondents. A total of 2,428 businesses' (believed to be owned by targeted ethnic minority groups) web address, social media page, e-mail address, contact phone number and owners' (contact) name were gathered. After that, businesses' existence was verified either by checking the Companies House database or the relevant business website, social media updates or by calling on the provided phone number. By doing so, the owner of the businesses and their

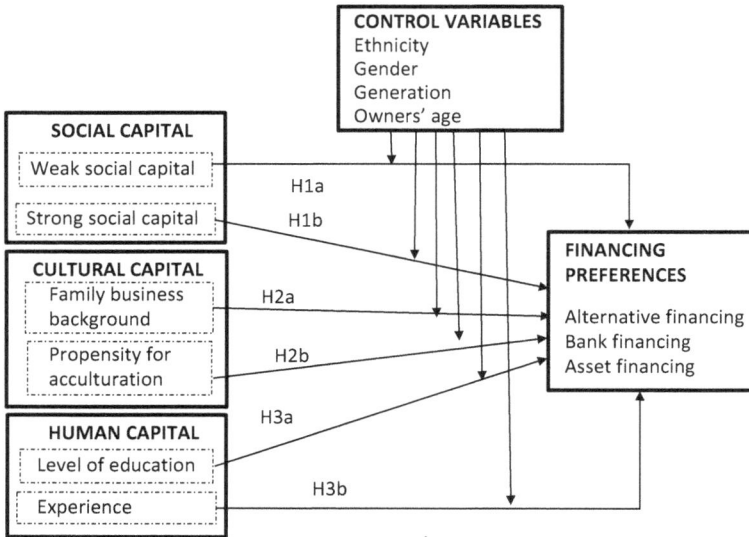

Figure 23.2: Conceptual framework of hypotheses.

ethnicity were identified, in most cases. Finally, for the online survey, a total of 473 businesses were identified as suitable participants and a survey link was e-mailed.

For the postal survey, a total of 700 businesses' contact details were obtained from Companies House. Owners' nationality was chosen as a basis for the sample selection. Participants were selected based on the nationalities that represent the ethnic groups studied, including Indian, Pakistani, Bangladeshi, Ghanaian, Nigerian, Zimbabwean, Somalian, South African, and any of the above plus British. Thus, in the postal survey mostly immigrant businesses must have been contacted as the probability of selecting ethnic minorities with British-only nationality was zero. From the list of 700, 300 businesses were strategically randomly selected to ensure proportional representation of the ethnic groups studied in this research and the survey was posted to a registered address with a prepaid return envelope. Furthermore, a face-to-face survey was conducted during the same period and a total of 80 businesses were approached in different locations of England. The response rate was 15%, 6%, and 38% for online, postal, and face-to-face surveys respectively. A total of 118 responses were received. However, four responses were excluded from the study due to substantially incomplete responses. Before executing the main survey, the survey was piloted to ensure reliability and validity.

As part of the dependent variables, a list of 14 external financing options commonly attributed to SME finance was developed. Respondents' preferences to each financing option was measured on a five-point Likert scale ranging from 1 = very low preference to 5 = very high preference. The expected structure of the composition of the financing options was tested and corroborated with principal component analysis.[1] The PCA corroborated the expected structure of the data. PCA grouped the number of financing options in the essence of preferences for alternative financing, bank financing, and asset financing. Options like crowdfunding, venture capital, and business angels are grouped in alternative financing, bank loans (short and long-term) and overdrafts are a constituent part of the preferences for bank financing, and preferences for asset financing comprise the composition of preferences for hire purchase and leasing.

EMB owners' SC was measured by employing 10 independent statements in which respondents rated their level of agreement on a 5-point Likert scale. The constructs were designed to capture entrepreneurs' propensity to seek financial advice, social engagement, family business heritage, and cultural and professional attributes. SC considered in this study is concerned with SC external to EMEs such as networks and ties and their related norms and values. Measuring the extent of SC in any given community is complex. Reflecting on this complexity, Grootaert and Van Bastelaer (2001, p. 10) suggested that "due to the strong contextual nature of social capital, it is unlikely that it will ever be possible to identify a few "best" indicators that can be used everywhere." As recommended by Ferri et al. (2009), the measures of SC are rooted in the study context to capture the micro level relationship. This study follows Williams' (2006) recommendations to develop dimensions and measures for SC. Furthermore, when designing measures, every attempt was made to make constructs as comprehensive as possible (Healy & Cote, 2001) to capture all dimensions such as network (Ferri et al., 2009), participation in the wider community (Putnam et al., 1994), and strong ties and weak ties networks (Uzzi, 19996).

The CC of respondents was measured by deploying seven independent statements in which respondents indicated their level of agreement. Measures include family business culture, cultural openness, and professionalism. CC was gauged in two ways: family business heritage and entrepreneurs' propensity for cultural adaptation. Business owners' level of education and previous experience represent HC. Six categories reflecting different levels of education and three categories of experience (general, specific, and no experience) were used to represent possession of HC. The expected structure of the measures of SC and CC was corroborated by PCA.

The reliability of measurement constructs was tested using Cronbach's alpha and all the concepts had an alpha value above 0.6 (financing preference 0.822, SC 0.672, and CC 0.727). The following formula was used to calculate the score of the latent variables as identified by PCA, which were then used in the multiple regression analysis. After calculating the variable score, the underlying assumptions such as multicollinearity, residual normality, and heteroscedasticity to perform multivariate analysis

---

1 The outcome of PCA is not presented in this chapter due to space consideration but can be made available upon request.

were tested. The robust standard errors are reported to further eliminate undictated heteroscedasticity.

$$\text{Variable Score} = \sum (R_i \times F_i) \div N$$

Where,
    R = Respondents' rating score to individual measure
    F = Factor loading score for relevant measure
    N = Number of measures in the component composition

Regression Models

To answer the research question and test stipulated hypotheses the following three multiple regression models were developed and tested.

$$\text{Preferences for External Financing}_i = \beta_0 + \beta_1(SC)_i + \beta_2(\text{control variables})_i + \varepsilon_i \quad (1)$$
$$\text{Preferences for External Financing}_i = \beta_0 + \beta_1(CC)_i + \beta_2(\text{control variables})_i + \varepsilon_i \quad (2)$$
$$\text{Preferences for External Financing}_i = \beta_0 + \beta_1(HC)_i + \beta_2(\text{control variables})_i + \varepsilon_i \quad (3)$$

Where,
    Preferences for external financing is represented by preferences for alternative, bank, and asset financing
    β = parameters to be estimated.
    i = variation in the data across firm
    ε = error term
    SC is represented by weak social capital and strong social capital
    CC is represented by family business background and propensity for acculturation
    HC is represented by level of education and previous experience
    Control variables includes EMEs' ethnicity, gender, generation, and age

The regression analysis was controlled for the effects of entrepreneurs' personal characteristics. The robustness of the main results was tested by respecifying the dependent variables with logistic regression. The dependent variables were dichotomously coded to run binary logistic regression models. This further corroborated the impact identified in the multivariate regression analysis. As an additional robustness check, multiple regression was rerun on preferences for alternative financing by excluding respondents' preferences for government grants in the composition of the variable and the results were identical. Therefore, findings of this study are robust to changes on specification and controlled for underlying characteristics. The generation variable was tested in the study but none of the results were significant, therefore it is not reported in the regression output tables and the result is not discussed for the sake of parsimony.

Main Results

The regression results about the relationship between types of SC and preferences for external sources of financing are shown in Table 23.1. The weak SC has a positive relationship with preference for external financing. The weak SC has a significant relationship with preferences for alternative financing when the effect of entrepreneurs' personal attributes is not considered. However, when considered, this relationship is weakened. The relationship between weak SC and preferences for bank financing is consistently significant. Although weak SC and preferences for asset financing are positively related, the regression analysis did not reach statistical significance. The results indicated that weak SC clearly influences entrepreneurs' preferences for external financing, particularly preferences for bank financing. Hence, H1a is supported. The impact of strong SC is not statistically significant to any type of external financing. Therefore, regression results did not support H1b.

Table 23.1: Regression Results – SC.

	Alternative financing		Bank financing		Asset financing	
	1	**2**	**3**	**4**	**5**	**6**
Key Independent variables						
Weak SC	.219**(.107)	.114(.115)	.344***(.106)	.281**(.112)	.204(.132)	.128(.137)
Strong SC	−.058(.074)	.050(.074)	.041(.077)	.049(.074)	.044(.091)	.062(.088)
Control variables						
Ethnicity						
Indian		.174(.177)		.321(.215)		.364(.244)
Bangladeshi		.211(.189)		.658**(.315)		.185(.341)
Black African		.563**(.213)		.138(.222)		.041(.244)
Black Caribbean		.729***(.222)		.097(.235)		.022(.263)
Pakistani		–		–		–
Gender (Male =1, female = 0)		−.070(.140)		.201(.147)		.035(.164)
Entrepreneurs' Age						
Below 30 years		–		–		–
30 to 40 years		−.021(.166)		.272(.182)		.241(.210)
40 to 50 years		−.210(.195)		−.126(.172)		−.382*(.215)
50 years above		−.062(.215)		−.071(.231)		.033(.268)

Table 23.1 (continued)

	Alternative financing		Bank financing		Asset financing	
	1	2	3	4	5	6
Constant	1.001**(.398)	.780**(.400)	.462(344)	.284 (.405)	.838 (.493)	.873(.543)
N	114	114	114	114	114	114
R^2	.03	0.21	.06	.18	.02	.10
F stat	2.38*	3.89***	6.26***	2.45**	1.33	1.58
Root MSE	.693	.65	.753	.729	.862	.855

[– indicates reference group, *** = 1%, ** = 5% and * = 10% significance level, figures in the parentheses are robust SE]

The regression results about the relationship between types of CC and preferences for external financing are presented in Table 23.2. The family business background has a marginally significant negative relationship with preferences for alternative financing. However, it is weakened when entrepreneurs' personal attributes are considered. Additionally, the resluts indicate no impact of family business background on preferences for bank and asset financing. Although there is an indication that family business background negatively influences preferences for alternative financing, the evidence is not robust enough to support hypothesis 2a. EMB owners' propensity for acculturation has a significant positive relationship with preferences for alternative financing. Although results show that acculturation has no influence in preferences for bank and asset financing, the impact on preference for alternative financing is robust. Hence, the results support hypothesis 2b.

Table 23.2: Regression Results – CC.

	Alternative financing		Bank financing		Asset financing	
	1	2	3	4	5	6
Key Independent variables						
Family business background	−.110*(.065)	−.046(.069)	.093(.074)	.090(.079)	.023(.084)	.012(.091)
Propensity for acculturation	.327***(.127)	.255**(.124)	.005(.156)	−.063(.167)	.242(.161)	.151(.168)
Control variables						
Ethnicity						
Indian		.116(.165)		.380*(.207)		.336(.241)
Bangladeshi		.171(.185)		.731**(.317)		.175(.339)
Black African		.466**(.210)		.187(.226)		−.010(.257)

Table 23.2 (continued)

	Alternative financing		Bank financing		Asset financing	
	1	2	3	4	5	6
Black Caribbean		.687***(.227)		.217(.234)		.020(.279)
Pakistani		–		–		–
Gender (male = 1, female = 0)		-.034(.146)		.209(.153)		.063(.172)
Entrepreneurs' Age						
Below 30 years		–		–		–
30 to 40 years		-.043(.171)		.309(.191)		.230(.214)
40 to 50 years		-.174(.191)		-.157(.201)		-.364*(.214)
50 years above		-.072(.220)		-.066(.231)		.028(.270)
Constant	.592(.467)	.494(.479)	1.473***(.573)	1.305**(.668)	.694(.573)	.915(.722)
N	114	114	114	114	114	114
R^2	.07	0.23	.01	.15	.02	.10
F stat	4.39***	4.60***	.081	2.03**	1.26	1.53
Root MSE	.677	.645	.771	.742	.860	.857

[– indicates reference group, *** = 1%, ** = 5% and * = 10% significance level, figures in the parentheses are robust SE]

The results about the relationship between the attributes of HC on preferences for external financing are presented in Table 23.3. EMB owners educated to postgraduate level have more positive preferences for alternative financing than their counterparts with no formal education and results revealed that entrepreneurs with any form of formal education have a positive preference for asset financing. Results indicated no statistically significant difference in preferences for bank financing based on entrepreneurs' level of education. The clear evidence of the impact on preferences for alternative and asset financing provide support to the hypothesis 3a. In relation to previous experience, entrepreneurs with specific experience such as managerial or start-up experience have a marginally ($p < 0.1$) higher significant positive preference for alternative financing. The impact is robust to the effect of other personal attributes. The results indicate no difference on preferences for bank and asset financing. Hence, the results partially support hypothesis 3b.

A number of control variables also show a significant effect on preferences for external financing. Entrepreneurs with Black Caribbean and Black African heritage have consistently significant positive preference for alternative financing in all the models. Similarly, entrepreneurs who have Bangladeshi heritage have a consistently significant positive preference for bank financing. Entrepreneurs with Indian heritage have a marginally ($p < 0.1$) significant positive preference for bank financing only

Table 23.3: Regression results – HC.

	Alternative financing			Bank financing			Asset financing		
	1	2	3	4	5	6	7	8	9
Independent variables									
Level of education									
GCSE or low	.064(.218)	-.024(.210)	-.015(.265)	-.289(.437)	-.266(.438)	-.107(.412)	.753*(.419)	.821*(.430)	1.175***(.376)
A Level	.668**(.289)	.662**(.272)	.524(.325)	-.367(.393)	-.372(.398)	-.137(.406)	.532(.338)	.533*(.324)	.787**(.354)
University (UG)	.531***(.210)	.544***(.197)	.383(.242)	-.265(.361)	-.328(.360)	-.129(.366)	.331(.337)	.295(.235)	.551**(.261)
University (PG)	.698***(.226)	.668***(.217)	.526**(.262)	-.204(.369)	-.269(.370)	-.198(.386)	.500*(.268)	.492*(.265)	.666***(.274)
Vocational	.626(.429)	.567(.433)	.454(.390)	-.364(.459)	-.451(.460)	-.292(.533)	.559(.392)	.559(.402)	.830*(.487)
No formal education –	–	–		–	–		–	–	
Work experience									
General		.105(.161)	.087(.169)		.187(.186)	.166(.193)		.012(.206)	-.007(.200)
Specific		.309*(.161)	.300*(.158)		-.071(.194)	-.001(.190)		-.231(.203)	-.174(.198)
No experience		–			–			–	
Control variables									
Ethnicity									
Indian			.198(.182)			.283(.236)			.460*(.254)
Bangladeshi			.148(.212)			.683**(.319)			.187(.338)
Black African			.472**(.222)			.106(.236)			.099(.263)
Black Caribbean			.710***(.208)			.133(.246)			.056(.290)
Pakistani			–			–			–

	(1)	(2)	(3)	(4)	(5)	(6)	(7)	(8)	(9)
Gender (male =1, female = 0)			.001(.143)			.195(.159)			.049(.172)
Entrepreneurs' Age									
Below 30 years			–			–			–
30–40 years			-.005(.168)			.331(.207)			.319(.227)
40–50 years			-.224(.208)			-.118(.221)			-.383*(.232)
Above 50 years			-.125(.218)			-.012(.258)			.140(.254)
Constant	1.033(.186)	.904(.166)	.776**(.335)	1.936***(.343)	1.939***(.365)	1.402***(.456)	1.205***(.207)	1.290***(.209)	.794**(.309)
N	114	114	114	114	114	114	114	114	114
R²	.10	.13	.28	.01	.03	.15	.04	.05	.17
F stat	4.52***	4.53***	5.0***	0.23	0.56	1.46	1.14	1.12	2.0**
Root MSE	.678	.673	.636	.783	.782	.761	.865	.866	.844

[– indicates reference group, *** = 1%, ** = 5% and * = 10% significance level, figures in the parentheses are robust SE]

when aspects of CC are considered, and a marginally significant positive preference for asset financing when modelled with attributes of HC. Additionally, matured entrepreneurs have a marginally (p < 0.1) more significant negative preference for asset financing than their younger counterparts. Table 23.4 provides a summary of the hypothesis test.

Discussion and Conclusion

The aim of this study was to investigate the relationship between entrepreneurial capital and preferences for external financing. The findings of this study, in line with that of extant studies such as Talavera et al. (2012) and Du et al. (2015), suggest that extensive social engagement influences small business owners' financing behaviours. Consistent with the empirical evidence, one of the respondents indicated, "I was legal in the country and could not open a business bank account without the help of my boss. Tried for months to get 10% loan of my startup cost. I had to have a Caucasian speak to the loan adviser/department to agree the loan. I had no bad credit history." This further corroborated the implication of a wider social network and relationship

Table 23.4: Summary of hypothesis test.

Hypothesis	Supported	Sig	Interpretation
SC 1a: wider social networks	Yes	5%	EMB owners with extended social networks beyond their immediate ethnic ties prefer bank financing
SC 1b: close ethnic ties	No	–	
CC 2a: family business background	No	–	
CC 2b: propensity for acculturation	Yes	5%	EMB owners that have propensity for acculturation prefer alternative and asset financing
HC 3a: level of education	Yes	5%	Highly educated EMB owners prefer external financing more than their less educated counterparts
HC 3b: experience	Partially	10%	EMB owners with business or working experience specific to their venture prefer alternative financing
Control: ethnicity – Black and Bangladeshi	Yes	1% and 5%	EMB owners with Black African and Caribbean heritage have a very strong preference for alternative sources of financing (1%) and EMB owners with Bangladeshi heritage have positive preferences for bank financing (5%)

building to secure a bank loan. The well-embedded social network with frequent contacts and interactions between borrowers and lenders is conducive to reducing information asymmetry (Davidsson & Hoing, 2003). Businesses with reduced information opaqueness due to embedded social ties are more likely to get loans with better terms (Le & Nguyen, 2009), and this study finds that such positive experience in accessing a bank loan influences business owners' preferences for bank financing.

Moreover, results indicated that cultural openness and inclination for professional conduct in dealing with business-related matters have a significant positive implication in shaping financing preferences. EMB owners pursuing professional conduct in business affairs and openness to different cultures might be more open to getting independent expert advice in acquiring financing sources. These practices can lead to a greater knowledge on the availability of financing options and entrepreneurs can have a more positive and optimistic outlook about the various sources of business financing. Research evidence in equity financing suggests a link between obtaining expert advice and accessing angel financing (Hustedde & Pulver, 1992). Supporting the importance of business communication and understanding of the wider business context, one of the respondents indicated, "it's all about how you represent yourself to the lenders. Running only business is not important, also you have to be updated about your business sector, growth, your plans, communication with lenders, etc." The empirical evidence from this study is consistent with previous studies such as that of Boubarkri and Saffar (2016) that have shown cultural dimensions affect business owners' ability to navigate sources of financing to overcome financial constraints. In particular, the findings further corroborated that cultural preferences impact business owners' preferences for the type of financing which was also found by Bedendo et al. (2019).

The positive association between entrepreneurs' HC and preferences for external financing, particularly alternative financing, suggests that a higher level of education is conducive in shaping entrepreneurs' alternative financing preferences perhaps due to greater confidence (Storey, 1994) in dealing with finance providers and due to better knowledge of financing alternatives (Seghers et al., 2012). The finding relating to positive association of a high level of education and preference for alternative financing is in line with the findings in the wider SME financing context (Baker et al., 2020). Finance providers consider experienced entrepreneurs as better performers than their less experienced counterparts (Abdulsaleh & Worthington, 2013) and owners with experience in the industry are likely to use external financing in the business financing mix (Nofsinger & Wang, 2011).

Borgia and Newman (2012) and Coleman (2007) suggested a positive association between SME owner/managers' level of education and use of financing leverage in the firm. By contrast, Baker et al. (2020) showed no influence between the level of education and financing leverage used among SMEs. Although research evidence suggests that entrepreneurs' level of education is one of the determinant factors in the bank deciding the loan amount and increasing entrepreneurs' confidence in dealing with bankers (Abdulsaleh & Worthington, 2013), findings of this study did not reveal that the level of entrepreneurs' education influences their preference for bank financing.

This study adds to the SME financing literature such as Lawless et al. (2015) and Moritz et al. (2016) by exploring the implications of demand-side issues in shaping financing behaviors of small businesses, which are not well understood (Rostamkalaei et al., 2018). In particular, this study adds to the extant body of knowledge in EMBs financing, by providing additional understanding on types of financing options sought and associated EC. This study is unique in its remit because it not only provides insights into EMB owners' preferences for external financing but also documents non-financial capital that drive such preferences. This new knowledge will provide a new idea for policymakers and finance providers aimed at developing suitable policies and financial products that are conducive to fostering EMBs' access to finance. Thus, these findings yield new insights into its field – access to finance – with respect to marginalized groups of entrepreneurs.

Additionally, this study contributes to the entrepreneurship and SC literature by providing fresh insights into the relationship that exists between specific aspects of SC and entrepreneurs' pursuit of financial capital. Similarly, the findings contribute to the literature on relationship lending potentially due to reduced information asymmetry. Furthermore, entrepreneurs' propensity for acculturation, a form of CC (Bourdieu, 1986), has a positive relationship with preferences for alternative financing, suggesting that embracing multiculturalism and acceptance of the host country culture do have an impact on EMBs' financing behavior. Further studies can investigate whether these propensities result in enhancing access to finance.

EMBs have a competitive advantage to embrace multicultural talents to support business growth and innovation. Given the increasing diversity in the marketplace and ever-growing diverse population in the UK, the greater propensity of integrating multicultural talents can yield substantial benefits in opening up new avenues for innovative financing for EMBs. Similarly, as indicated in the association between SC and preferences for bank financing, EMB owners should reap the benefit by embedding social ties with local entrepreneurs, finance providers, and wider communities.

This study further provides insights into designing business support products and services relevant to EMBs operating in the UK. Financial institutions such as British Business Bank looking into providing customized policies and services to meet the diverse needs of diverse business owners could design financial instruments that could help to minimize the reliance on inappropriate and often costly forms of finance such as equity financing which seems to be a preferred alternative in the finance search amongst EMBs.

This study has a number of limitations. Like many other research techniques, self-completion questionnaires have their own demerits. The sample was carried out based on what is available online and to some extent; the survey was sent to unsolicited emails and businesses. Thus, responses received might not always be from individuals involved in significant financial decision-making or the business owner.

However, instructions were clearly labelled on the survey to minimize this potential nonconformity. Furthermore, in the online survey, two screening questions were included to ensure the intended participants completed the survey.

The financing preferences are measured using qualitative perceptions rather than financial facts. However, challenges in obtaining financial and accounting data from SMEs are widely acknowledged, and more so for EMBs as often they operate in an informal manner. Therefore, the subjective approach was used. Thus, the findings of this study are based on the subjective judgement of entrepreneurs rather than objective data from business financial statements. Moreover, despite the best possible efforts to make the sample more representative in terms of both demographic composition and size, sector and location of the business operation, this study is conducted with a sample of 114 mostly micro businesses, and therefore wider generalization of the findings might be unwise.

This study solely focuses on demand-side issues but does not provide insights into supply-side factors such as availability of finance. Therefore, further investigation of demand-side issues of EMBs' financing in conjunction with supply-side factors would provide better insights. Future studies could conduct research that integrates the EMBs' existing financing mix to better understand whether their financing preferences are actually replicated in their capital structure or these preferences further constrain access to finance.

References

Abdulsaleh, M.A., & Worthington, A.C. (2013). Small and medium-sized enterprises financing: A review of literature. *International Journal of Business and Management*, *8*(14), 36–54.

Attwell, K., & Smith, D. (2017). Parenting as politics: Social identity theory and vaccine hesitant communities. *International Journal of Health Governance*, *22*(3), 183–198.

Attwell, K., Meyer, S.B., and Ward, P.R., 2018. The social basis of vaccine questioning and refusal: A qualitative study employing Bourdieu's concepts of 'capitals' and 'habitus'. *International Journal of Environmental Research and Public Health*, *15*(2018), 1044–1061.

Baker, K.H., Kumar, S., & Rao, P. (2020). Financing preferences and practices of Indian SMEs. *Global finance journal*, *43*, 1–16.

Baker, M., Ruback, R.S., & Wurgler, J. (2007). Behavioral corporate finance. In B.E. Eckbo (Ed.), *Handbook of empirical corporate finance* (pp. 145–186). Elsevier.

Baker, M., & Wurgler, J. (2013). Behavioral corporate finance: An updated survey. In *Handbook of the economics of finance* (pp. 351–417). Elsevier.

Ballard, R., 1996. Negotiating race and ethnicity: Exploring the implications of the 1991 census 1. *Patterns of Prejudice*, *30*(3), 3–33.

Basu, A. (2006). Ethnic minority entrepreneurship. In M. Casson, B. Yeung, A. Basu, & N. Waderson (Eds.), *The Oxford handbook of entrepreneurship*.

Basu, A., & Altinay, E. (2002). The interaction between culture and entrepreneurship in London's immigrant businesses. *International small business journal*, *20*(4), 371–393.

Becker, G., 1964. *Human Capital*. New York: Columbia University Press.

Bedendo, M., Garcia-Appendini, E., & Siming, L. (2019). Cultural preferences and firm financing choices. *Journal of financial and quantitative analysis*, 1–75 DOI: https://doi.org/10.1017/S0022109019000103.

Berger, A.N., & Udell, G.F. (1998). The economics of small business finance: The roles of private equity and debt markets in the financial growth cycle. *Journal of Banking and Finance*, *22*(1998), 613–673.

Borgia, D., & Newman, A. (2012). The influence of managerial factors on the capital structure of small and medium-sized enterprises in emerging economies: Evidence from China. *Journal of Chinese Entrepreneurship*, *4*(3), 180–205.

Boubarkri, N., & Saffar, W. (2016). Culture and externally financed firm growth. *Journal of corporate finance*, *41*(2016), 502–520.

Bourdieu, P. (1986). The forms of capital. In J. Richardson (Ed.), *Handbook of theory and research for the sociology of education*.

Busenitz, L.W., and Lau, C. (1996). A cross– cultural cognitive model of new venture creation. *Entrepreneurship: Theory and Practice*, *20*(4), 25.

Canello, J. (2016). Migrant entrepreneurs and local networks in industrial districts. *Research Policy*, *45*, 1953–1964.

Chisholm, A.M., & Nielsen, K. (2009). Social capital and the resource-based view of the firm. *International Studies of Management and Organization*, *39*(2), 7–32.

Coleman, S. (2007). The role of human and financial capital in the profitability and growth of women-owned small firms. *Journal of Small Business Management*, *45*(3), 303–319.

Coleman, S., & Cohn, R. (2000). Small firms' use of financial leverage: Evidence from the 1993 national survey of small business finances. *Journal of Business and Entrepreneurship*, *12*(3), 81–98.

Daskalakis, N., Jarvis, R. & Schizas, E. (2013). Financing practices and preferences for micro and small firms. *Journal of Small Business and Enterprise Development*, *20*(1), 80–101.

Danes, S.M., Lee, J., Stafford, K., & Heck, R.K.Z. (2008). The effects of ethnicity, families and culture on entrepreneurial experience: An extension of sustainable family business theory. *Journal of Developmental Entrepreneurship*, *13*(3), 229–268.

Davidsson,P., & Honig, B. (2003). The role of social and human capital among nascent entrepreneurs. *Journal of Business Venturing*, *18*(3), 301–331.

Deakins, D., Ishaq, M., Smallbone, D., Whittam, G., & Wyper, J. (2007). Ethnic minority businesses in Scotland and the role of social capital. *International Small Business Journal*, *25*(3), 307–326.

Desiderio, M.V. (2014). Policies to support immigrant entrepreneurship. Migration Policy Institute.

Dhaliwal, S., & Kangis, P. (2006). Asian in the UK: Gender, generation and enterprise. *Equal opportunities international*, *25*(2), 92–108.

Du, J., Guariglia, A., & Newman, A. (2015). Do social capital building strategies influence the financing behaviour of Chinese private small and medium-sized enterprises? *Entrepreneurship theory and practice*, *39*(3), 601–631.

El Shoubaki, A., Laguir, I., & den Besten, M. (2019). Human capital and SME growth: the mediating role of reasons to start a business. *Small Business Economics*. https://doi.org/10.1007/s11187-018-0129-y, pp. 1–15.

Ferri, P., Deakins, D., & Whittam, G. (2009). The measurement of social capital in the entrepreneurial context. *Journal of Enterprising Communities: People and Places in the Global Economy*, *3*(2), 138–151.

Fraser, S. (2009). Is there ethnic discrimination in the UK market for small business credit? *International Small Business Journal*, *27*(5), 583–607.

Gedajlovic, E., Honig, B., Moore, C.B., Payne, G.T., & Wright, M. (2013). Social capital and entrepreneurship: A schema and research agenda. *Entrepreneurship Theory and Practice*, *37*(3), 455–478.

Gimmon, E., & Levie, J. (2010). Founder's human capital, external investment, and the survival of new high-technology ventures. *Research Policy*, *39*(9), 1214–1226.

Gomez, C., Perera, B.Y., Weisinger, J.Y., Tobey, D.H., & Zinsmeister-Teeters, T. (2015). The impact of immigrant entrepreneurs' social capital related motivations. *New England Journal of Entrepreneurship*, *18*(2), 19–30.

Grootaert, C., & Van Bastelaer, T. (2001). *Understanding and measuring social capital: A synthesis of findings and recommendations from the social capital initiative*. World Bank, Social Development Family, Environmentally and Socially Sustainable Development Network.

Hallak, R., Assaker, G., O'Connor, P., & Lee, C. (2018). Firm performance in the upscale restaurant sector: The effects of resilience, creative self-efficacy, innovation and industry experience. *Journal of Retailing and Consumer Services*, *40*, 229–240.

Heilbrunn, S., & Kushnirovich, N. (2008). Impact of ethnicity on financing of immigrant businesses. *International Journal of Business and Globalisation*, *2*(2), 146–159.

Healy, T., and Côté, S. (2001). *The Well-Being of Nations: The Role of Human and Social Capital. Education and Skills*. ERIC.

Henley, A. (2005). Job creation by the self-employed: The roles of entrepreneurial and financial capital. *Small Business Economics*, *25*(2), 175–196.

Hofstede, G. (1980). *Culture's consequences: International differences in work-related values*. Sage.

Howell, A. (2019). Ethnic entrepreneurship, initial financing, and business performance in China. *Small business economics*, *52*(3), 697–712.

Howorth, C. (2001). Small firms' demand for finance: A research note. *International Small Business Journal*, *19*(4), 78–86.

Hustedde, R.J., & Pulver, G.C. (1992). Factors affecting equity capital acquisition: The demand side. *Journal of Business Venturing*, *7*(1992), 363–374.

Hutchinson, J., Vidal, A.C., Putnam, R., Light, I., Briggs, X., Rohe, W.M., et al. (2004). Using social capital to help integrate planning theory, research, and practice. *Journal of the American Planning Association*, *70*(2), 142–192.

Irwin, D., & Scott, J.M. (2010). Barriers faced by SMEs in raising bank finance. *International Journal of Entrepreneurial Behavior and Research*, *16*(3), 245–259.

Iversen, J., Jørgensen, R., & Malchow-Møller, N. (2008). *Defining and measuring entrepreneurship*.

Jayawarna, D., Jones, O., & Macpherson, A. (2014). Entrepreneurial potential: The role of human and cultural capitals. *International Small Business Journal*, *32*(8), 918–943.

Jones, T., Mascarenhas-Keyes, S., & Ram, M. (2012). The ethnic entrepreneurial transition: Recent trends in British Indian self-employment. *Journal of Ethnic and Migration Studies*, *38*(1), 93–109.

Kim, P.H., Aldrich, H.E., & Keister, L.A. (2006). Access (not) denied: The impact of financial, human, and cultural capital on entrepreneurial entry in the United States. *Small Business Economics*, *27*(1), 5–22.

Kreiser, P.M., Patel, P.C., & Fiet, J.O. (2013). The influence of changes in social capital on firm-founding activities. *Entrepreneurship Theory and Practice*, *37*(3), 539–567.

Lawless, M., O'Connell, B., & O'Toole, C. (2015). Financial structure and diversification of European firms. *Applied Economics*, *47*(23), 2379–2398.

Le, N.T., & Nguyen,T.V. (2009). The impact of networking on bank financing: The case of small and medium-sized enterprises in Vietnam. *Entrepreneurship Theory and Practice*, *33*(4), 867–887.

Light, I. (2004). Social capital's unique accessibility. *Journal of the American planning Association*, *70*(2), 145–151.

Light, I., & Dana, L. (2013). Boundaries' social capital in entrepreneurship. *Entrepreneurship Theory and Practice*, *37*(3), 603–624.

Marvel,M.R., Davis, J.L., & Sproul, C.R. (2016). Human capital and entrepreneurship research: A critical review and future directions. *Entrepreneurship Theory and Practice*, *40*(3), 599–626.

Masiak, C., Block, J.H., Moritz, A., Lang, F., & Kraemer-Eis, H. (2019). How do micro firms differ in their financing patterns from larger SMEs? *Venture Capital*, *21*(4), 301–325.

Massey, D.S. (1988). Economic development and international migration in comparative perspective. *The Population and Development Review, 14*(3), 383–413.

Masurel, E., Nijkamp, P., & Vindigni, G. (2004). Breeding places for ethnic entrepreneurs: A comparative marketing approach. *Entrepreneurship and Regional Development, 16*(1), 77–86.

McPherson, M. (2010). Business practices within South Asian family and non-family firms: A comparative study. *International Journal of Entrepreneurial Behaviour and Research,16*(5), 389–413.

Morgan, H.M., Sui, S., & Baum, M. (2018). Are SMEs with immigrant owner's exceptional exporters? *Journal of business venturing, 33*(2018), 241–260.

Moritz, A., Block, J.H., & Heinz, A. (2016). Financing patterns of European SMEs – an Empirical Taxonomy. *Venture Capital, 18*(2), 115–148.

Nofsinger, J.R., & Wang, W. (2011). Determinants of start-up firm external financing worldwide. *Journal of Banking and Finance, 35*(9), 2282–2294.

Oc, T., Tiesdell, S., & Moynihan, D., 1997. *Urban Regeneration and Ethnic Minority Groups: Training and Business Support in City Challenge Areas*. Policy Press.

Parker, S.C., & Van Praag, C.M. (2006). Schooling, capital constraints, and entrepreneurial performance: The endogenous triangle. *Journal of Business and Economic Statistics, 24*(4), 416–431.

Piazza-Georgi, B. (2002). The role of human and social capital in growth: Extending our understanding. *Cambridge Journal of Economics, 26*, 461–479.

Pret, T., Shaw, E., & Dodd, S.D. (2016). Painting the full picture: The conversion of economic, cultural, social and symbolic capital. *International Small Business Journal, 34*(8), 1004–1027.

Putnam, R.D., Leonardi, R., & Nanetti, R.Y. (1994). *Making democracy work: Civic traditions in modern Italy*. Princeton University Press.

Ram, M., Smallbone, D., Deakins, D., & Jones, T. (2003). Banking on 'break-out': Finance and the development of ethnic minority businesses. *Journal of Ethnic and Migration Studies, 29*(4), 663–681.

Ram, M., Jones, T., Abbas, T., & Sanghera, B. (2002). Ethnic minority enterprise in its urban context: South Asian restaurants in Birmingham. *International Journal of Urban and Regional Research, 26*(1), 24–40.

Rostamkalaei, A., Nitani, M., & Riding, A. (2018). Borrower's discouragement: The role of informal turndown. *Small Business Economics*, 1–16. https://doi.org/10.1007/s11187-018-0086-5

Sanders, J.M., & Nee, V. (1996). Immigrant self-employment: The family as social capital and the value of human capital. *American Sociological Review, 61*(2), 231–249.

Seghers, A., Manigart, S., & Vanacker, T. (2012). The Impact of human and social capital on entrepreneurs' knowledge of finance alternatives. *Journal of Small Business Management, 50*(1), 63–86.

Siegler, V. (2014). *Measuring Social Capital*. ONS.

Sirmon, D.G., & Hitt, M.A. (2003). Managing resources: Linking unique resources, management, and wealth creation in family firms. *Entrepreneurship theory and practice, 27*(4), 339–358.

Smallbone, D., Ram, M., & Deakins, D. (2007). *Access to finance by ethnic minority entrepreneurs in the UK*. In L. Dana (Ed.), *Handbook for research in ethnic minority businesses: A co-evolutionary View on Resource Management*. Edward Elgar.

Smallbone, D., Ram, M., Deakins, D., & Baldock, R. (2003) Access to finance by ethnic minority businesses in the UK. *International Small Business Journal, 21*(3), 291–314.

Storey, D.J. (2004). Racial and gender discrimination in the micro firms credit market?: Evidence from Trinidad and Tobago. *Small Business Economics, 23*(5), 401–422.

Storey, D.J. (1994). Understanding the small business sector. Thomson Learning Emea.

Talavera, O., Xiong, L., and Xiong, X. (2012). Social capital and access to bank financing: The case of Chinese entrepreneurs. *Emerging Markets Finance and Trade, 48*(1), 55–69.

Uzzi, B. (1999). Embeddedness in the making of financial capital: How social relations and networks benefit firms seeking financing. *American Sociological Review, 64*(4), 481–505.

Van Auken, H. (2002). A model of community-based venture capital formation to fund early-stage technology-based firms. *Journal of Small Business Management, 40*(4), 287–301.

Volery, T. (2007). Ethnic entrepreneurship: A theoretical framework. In L.P. Dana (Ed.), *Handbook of research on ethnic minority entrepreneurship* (pp. 30–41). Edward Elgar.

Waldinger, R., Aldrich, H., Ward, R., & Blaschke, J. (1990). *Ethnic entrepreneurs: Immigrant business in industrial societies*. Sage.

Zhu, H., Feng, J., & Pan, F. (2019). Mixed embeddedness and entrepreneurial activities of rural migrants in the host region: The case of Yuhuan City, China. *Journal of Urban Affairs*, *41*(3), 390–404.

Valerie Nickel, Lena Leifeld, and Anita Zehrer

24 Internalizing Gender Equality: Narratives of Family Business Entrepreneurs

Abstract: Any kind of entrepreneurial activity is related to its specific organizational context. Organizational identity work aims to understand the interplay occurring in the organizational context, with identity being built, changed, adapted and reconstructed with social interactions in organizations. Gender identities are reconstructed through existing structures in both the family and business life. Family businesses are often portrayed as gender-neutral, neglecting that these businesses are also influenced by gender-specific assumptions, norms, and discourses. This work studies strategies of gendered identities among family business entrepreneurs and thus adds to a relatively under-researched body of knowledge on identity work in family firms. Our data is based on ten narrative interviews with entrepreneurs of family businesses in Germany and Austria. Our findings are congruent with the growing awareness that the construction and reconstruction of entrepreneurial identities depend on interaction with the organizational context, often influenced by gender dynamics.

Keywords: gender identity, gender equality, family firms, narrative research

Introduction – Topic of Research

Entrepreneurial activity is closely intertwined with the respective cultural and social context (Watson, 2009a). Identity can be seen as a critical component for a better understanding of the interplay between environment and actors as well as among the different actors. Identity is a fluid construct that changes, adapts, and reconstructs within social interactions (Alvesson & Billing, 2009). From interpretive approaches, identity is understood as evolving, multiple, and temporary (Alvesson & Billing, 2009; Aygören & Nordqvist, 2015; Caza et al., 2018a). Identity provides a frame of reference for interpreting social situations and one's thoughts, actions and behaviors (Martin et al., 2020). In the entrepreneurial context, identity is shaped by the organizational environment and, as identity constitutes the motivator for behavior, reciprocally shapes the context through actions (Hytti et al., 2017). The concept of identity work captures the dynamic nature of identities and the ability of individuals to agentically craft one's own identities (Brown, 2017). Thus, the identity work approach becomes increasingly prominent in entrepreneurship, providing a processual lens to gain a deeper understanding of entrepreneurs and their internalizing of organizational con-

Valerie Nickel, Lena Leifeld, Anita Zehrer, Family Business Center, MCI | The Entrepreneurial School

https://doi.org/10.1515/9783110747652-025

texts (Leitch & Harrison, 2016). Identity talk constitutes the primary form of identity work as individuals use narratives responding to experiences for updating their identities daily in interactions (Ibarra & Obodaru, 2016; Snow & Anderson, 1987).

Socially and culturally anchored values, norms, and stereotypes, which significantly influence identity development, are predominantly male dominated. This fact is prominent in many current political and social debates (Alvesson & Billing, 2009; Champenois et al., 2020). Although women make up about half of the workforce, they are still underrepresented in positions of decision-making power (European Comission, 2018). Gender inequalities are reconstructed through existing structures in family life, work organization, and other interactions (Acker, 1990; Stamarski & Son Hing, 2015; West & Zimmerman, 1987). Accordingly, horizontal and vertical segregation exists in organizations, and the dynamic adaptation of entrepreneurial identities is closely interrelated (Byrne et al., 2021; Sentuti et al., 2019). Entrepreneurship and leadership are implied in identity development and simultaneously constructed in gendered patterns (Lewis, 2015; Lewis et al., 2016). The process of "doing gender" is created and enacted in social relationships; thus, it has a strong context-dependence reproduced in narratives (Zheng et al., 2021).

As one of the oldest forms of organization, family businesses employ women more frequently in leadership positions than non-family businesses. Therefore, family businesses are often portrayed as gender-neutral, neglecting that these businesses are also influenced by gender-specific assumptions, norms, and discourses (Essers et al., 2013). Furthermore, due to the unique characteristics of family businesses resulting from the linkage of the family and business systems, the requirement for a credible identity for different stakeholders is a more complex phenomenon than in other companies (Hytti et al., 2017). Therefore, family businesses are considered critical economic drivers and provide the ideal conditions to study how identities develop, adapt, internalize, and repurpose gender relations (Acker, 1990; Aygören & Nordqvist, 2015; Champenois et al., 2020; West & Zimmerman, 1987).

Gender and entrepreneurship are intertwined social practices (Essers et al., 2013) explored in the family business context, particularly in the succession process. The focus of other research regarding this topic is on the succession process (Swail & Marlow, 2018), identity formation (Bjursell & Melin, 2011), and the legitimization of successors (Swail & Marlow, 2018). Events such as business succession or parenthood offer potential for conflict in identity development, especially in family businesses, but at the same time, they constitute an opportunity to break with existing structures and influence interactions (Bruni et al., 2004; Hytti et al., 2017; Watson, 2008).

Building on the existing literature, this chapter attempts to bring together these different aspects of other research and focuses on the strategies to establish a legitimate identity as a family business entrepreneur. This objective contributes to the argument of management and organizational scholars who agree on the process-oriented concept of identity work, which implies that identities are fluid and dynamic as individuals are able to actively manage and continuously shape identity constructions (Brown, 2021;

Caza et al., 2018b). This chapter aims to enrich research on identity work and the corresponding narrative strategies of family firms, as it has only recently gained attention in that field (Aygören & Nordqvist, 2015). This chapter follows the growing awareness that the construction and reconstruction of entrepreneurial identities depend on interaction with the organizational context, which is often influenced by gender dynamics (Aygören & Nordqvist, 2015; Swail & Marlow, 2018). Initial research on this topic confirms that family businesses are an ideal setting for studying identities, as they provide a unique set for examining the interplay between work and non-work identities (Aygören & Nordqvist, 2015). A better understanding of identity processes and the narratives that shape identities can contribute to the discussion of key theoretical and practical problems in the field of gender and organizational studies as well as in the context of family businesses (Aygören & Nordqvist, 2015). The book chapter sheds a light on the strategy of gendered identity work of entrepreneurs in family businesses and tries to answer the following research question: "What are the predominant influencing factors for gender identity talk among entrepreneurs and executives in family businesses?"

Theoretical Underpinning – Literature Review

Identities have been extensively addressed in the literature concerning organizations and professions. Identities are an important component affecting organizational aspects (Caza et al., 2018b) and are considered malleable rather than fixed. They are changeable constructs that emerge from various interactions in different roles (Alvesson & Billing, 2009). The development and adaptation of identities play an essential part in comprehending the interaction in organizations (Brown, 2017). However, these structures and discourses are influenced by the gendered discourses of masculinity (Watson, 2009b; Welter, 2020). Gender inequality can thus be constantly reconstructed through internalization, actions, and interactions (Sentuti et al., 2019; West & Zimmerman, 1987).

Identity work is defined as the activities "creating, presenting, sustaining, forming, repairing, maintaining, strengthening, or revising identities" (Caza et al., 2018a). Identity talk has emerged as one of the essential forms of data gathering in this context (Snow & Anderson, 1987). Identities encompass many different aspects and are considered multifaceted; therefore, narratives involve individual identities and form an interplay of internal self-identity and an external discursive identity (Watson, 2009b). In addition, dealing with historical and structural influences represents an essential component of identity conversations (Chreim et al., 2007; Killian & Johnson, 2006).

For many decades, the question of how identities are constructed, and how self-meaning emerges, have remained relevant. Identities include a person's self-concept; subjective interpretations of the inner and outer world are fundamental components (Watson, 2009b). In organizational scholars, identities are an important component because most aspects can be linked to identities (Brown, 2017). Scholars consider identities as fluid and dynamic, thus, they change continuously over time. Consequently, individuals can agentically work on their identity to adapt to their everchanging environment (Caza et al., 2018b). Snow and Anderson (1987) were the first to establish the concept of identity work; they studied the narrative strategies of homeless individuals to understand the relationship between identity, role, and self-concept. Their findings indicate that identity talk is the most widely used form of identity work to relate and navigate the various facets of one's identity (Snow & Anderson, 1987).

In their initial study, the authors identified three different identity talk types that help create a coherent self-image (Snow & Anderson, 1987). The strategies are distancing, embracing, and storytelling, and these strategies can be broken down into different subtypes; the activation depends on the personal situation. The results of the study make clear that there are many different narrative strategies for coping. For example, homeless people try to keep their self-worth and dignity even when they have few resources at their disposal and no home. Narrative strategies are used to focus on parts of their lives while distancing themselves from others. In addition, fictional narration can help deal with discrepancies and cope with one's situation (Snow & Anderson, 1987).

Overall, an important particularity of identity elaborated by Snow & Anderson (1987) is that identities incorporate multiple facets. Social identities are related to the external world and are mainly influenced by responsibilities and demands. Personal identity reflects the inner self of an individual. The self-concept as an overarching framework connects the different aspects. Multiple scholars support this notion highlighting that identities can be considered as two-sided and context-dependent, with the application of strategies varying according to the relationship between the other parts (Brown, 2015; Caza et al., 2018a; Watson, 2009b).

The concept finds increasing importance in organizational studies, especially Alvesson and Willmott (2002) and Sveningsson and Alvesson (2003) who refer to the original concept, which they further developed in the organizational context. Identities are central connectors in organizations as external practices and discourses shape them, and on the other hand they are themselves shaped by constant reproduction. The focus of an identity conversation is the manner and the content of the communication. The narrative approach revolves around creating and constantly updating one's experiences, narratives, and available discourses. Engagement in identity conversations varies and is especially high in the face of change and uncertainty. An important goal is the achievement of coherence and plausibility (Caza et al., 2018a).

Self-narratives are an essential component in shaping and communicating one's identity, with reflection and interaction helping to understand the surrounding reality (Ibarra & Obodaru, 2016). At the same time, the present situation is always a product of the past. Self-narratives, therefore, always built upon and incorporate past experiences, as they are part of and have led to the current self-image (Zheng et al., 2021). Thus, creating coherence in and through narratives supports individuals' sensemaking of life events and leads to authenticity and external validation (Ibarra & Obodaru, 2016). For organizational scholars, self-narratives play a major role as positioning in the profession is a process of shaping influenced by identity talk (Caza et al., 2018a). Zheng et al. (2021) address origin stories that influence the development of leadership identities and the implementation of leadership emphasizing the close interplay of origin story and career path.

As identity narratives are embedded in a respective context, available discourses play an influential role with discourse significantly interacting with individual identity talk, as it portrays relevant views, established rules, and norms, being internalized and communicated by the individual (Kira & Balkin, 2014). There are different types of discourses: macro-level political or societal, or on a specific level like institutional discourses tied to a particular context or place. A discourse is embedded in a particular place or context and serves as an indicator of legitimacy or affiliation to a specific environment, and this applies to both professional and non-professional parts of society (Kira et al., 2012). For example, institutional discourses have an impact on certain professional positions and expectations, such as those associated with a leadership position (Cascón-Pereira et al., 2016). Thus, discourses are an essential resource for constructing, maintaining, and renegotiating identities. For this reason, discourse is anchored in a specific context and linked to identity talk, which connects between the social and internal worlds of individuals (Watson, 2009a).

Organizations are much more complex in today's world, whereas identities are less stable (Sveningsson & Alvesson, 2003). During a career, people face different changes, and simultaneously, the demands associated with different jobs are becoming more diverse. As a result, the available choice of discourses also increases (Sveningsson & Alvesson, 2003). Identity conversations are understood as situated activities. Since identities interplay with internal self-identities and external social identities, identity work processes manage different identities of a person. A significant aspect of identity work is managing structural and historical circumstances (Watson, 2008) and societal and organizational influences (Chreim et al., 2007; Killian & Johnson, 2006).

In family businesses, the complexity is even higher due to the combination of the two systems, family, and business. The entrepreneurial family is the linchpin of the family business. The focus of previous research on identity work was mainly on economic aspects, although the entrepreneurial family is the most influencing factor in social and economic areas. Accordingly, it is crucial to focus on the family aspects and relate them to economic aspects (Danes & Olson, 2003; Nordqvist & Melin, 2010). The two systems of family businesses influence each other, but the demands of the systems on the actors often differ (Memili et al., 2015). Role models in family businesses are often gendered; if one does not adhere to these norms, this can cause tension. This often results in an unclear role for women and a questioning of their authority over men, or it can even harm the success of the family business (Danes & Olson, 2003).

Family businesses employ more women in leadership positions, therefore they are better able to meet the demand for equality (Ahrens et al., 2015; Schlömer-Laufen & Kay, 2013, 2015). Especially for leaders, the compatibility of work and family is a great challenge. The developments result in uncertainties for men and women due to a lack of role models (Otten-Pappas & Jäkel-Wurzer, 2017). Role models are of particular importance in the corporate context as they can be an inspiration for behavior. Role models can shape perceptions of success and thus influence roles and career paths (Gretzel & Bowser, 2013). Along with this, it is so far unclear whether female role models can be considered full-fledged, as there is a shortage of female leaders who can be potential role models (Alvesson & Billing, 2009). Women in leadership positions do not have to be perceived as the exception to become role models. Female leaders are often associated with characteristics considered "masculine," such as competitiveness and aggressiveness. Usually, female leaders are childless, fostering perceptions of negative stereotypes (Gretzel & Bowser, 2013).

In family businesses, narratives are important for passing on values and beliefs to the next generation, which feeds into the self-concepts and identities of family members. Discourse is an essential link between different generations in family businesses (Wielsma & Brunninge, 2019). The concept of identity work is considered a relatively new approach in family business research, which extends the common understanding of stable identities (Aygören & Nordqvist, 2015). Bjursell and Melin (2011) have followed the process of business entry of women family business owners; the narratives reflected either proactive or reactive actions. Increasingly, the discourse also refers to gender, gendered images, and assumptions (Hatmaker, 2012). Several authors address the power of gendered discourse, particularly for women concerning their career development and parenting. Entrepreneurship is understood as a gendered construction part of identity development (Lewis, 2015).

Research Method – A Narrative Approach

Methodology

The research draws on a narrative approach to gain in-depth understanding through detailed narratives which can act as strategies to develop a legitime leadership identity (Caza et al., 2018b). Based on the assumption that identity conversations are the primary form of identity work (Snow & Anderson, 1987), they represent an appropriate inquiry tool. Individuals can derive meaning from narrative accounts and are considered a sense-making element (Zheng et al., 2021). Narrative studies as studies of life have been considered important methodological approaches in qualitative research since the 2000s (Czarniawska, 2004; Mussolino et al., 2019). The narrative method focuses on people's narratives and stories resulting from this approach consider their reality as socially constructed (Dawson & Hjorth, 2012). Czarniawska's (1997) work laid an important milestone for the narrative paradigm to become a component of organizational research.

The data basis is ten narrative interviews with executives in family businesses in Germany and Austria, lasting 50 minutes each. Table 24.1 displays the composition of the sample. The interviews were conducted one after the other with two leaders in each company. Two businesses were run by a pair of junior and senior; three companies by a combination of brother and sister. The comparison between siblings provides an all-encompassing picture of the possible inequalities between men and women. The different perspectives of the junior and senior generations can provide a differentiated view on the subject. The companies range from long-established family businesses in the tenth and seventh generation to businesses only run in the second or third generation. They operate in different industries, as the gender equality phenomenon concerns all sectors. The interviews cover three thematic blocks of different sizes: the history of the family business, the interviewee's own biography, and gender-specific experiences. Through a stimulus, the interviewees are asked to develop their own personal identity and to narrate their life story. The interviewer followed up at interesting points and asked questions of understanding, but the focus of the interviews was on the interviewees' stories about the company and their own history.

Table 24.1: Sample overview.

Company	Industry	Generation	Foundation	Interview partner
Company 1	Tourism	Tenth generation	1609	Sister (I1) & Brother (I2)
Company 2	Tourism	Second generation	1976	Sister (I3) & Brother (I4)
Company 3	Producing industry	Seventh generation	1790	Sister (I5) & Brother (I6)
Company 4	Producing industry	Second and third generation	1971	Junior (I7) & Senior (I8)
Company 5	Trade and craft	Third and fourth generation	1894	Junior (I9) & Senior (I10)

The interviews were transcribed and subsequently analyzed inductively. For data analysis, the methodology of Gioia et al. (2013) is used. The study aimed to answer the research questions "What are the predominant influencing factors for gendered identity talk among entrepreneurs and executives in family businesses?" and "What narrative strategies are used?" by examining the stories in essence (McAdams, 1996).

The analysis is based on an inductive approach, so new concepts and relationships between concepts can be developed based on the interview data. However, the interview and the analysis were not conducted separately, but proceeded simultaneously. Some concepts and codes appeared repeatedly in the initial interviews. The data structuring is divided into three different steps: first order concepts, second order themes, and aggregated dimensions. In the first order analysis, the codes are not broken down, but are strongly based on the statements of the interviewees. This can lead to up to 100 categories in the first step. To reduce this number to a manageable dimension, similarities and differences were sought. The newly created categories have been given new, paraphrased names based on the statements of the interview partners. In the second step of the analysis, the themes and concepts found are related to already existing theories. The focus is on the one hand on existing concepts, which can help to explain the found concepts, and on the other hand on results, which have no reference points in the existing literature. When enough concepts were found, the themes were further combined into aggregated second order dimensions. The first two steps provide the basis for the final step, where the data are grouped into larger related blocks of themes. The results are not a static concept, but an inductive, dynamic model based on the results of the interviews. As the findings shed light on the influencing factors for gendered identity talk in family businesses, they depict the contemporary gender equality and relevant aspects in family firms through the identity work lens (Gehman et al., 2018; Gioia et al., 2013).

Findings

The interviews reveal different narratives of family business entrepreneurs over their lifespan to navigate their identity construction and involvement with the family business calibrated by the status quo of contemporary gender equality. Interestingly, each narrative frame was used by all interviewees in a personalized manner. As none of the narratives are gender-specific per se but carry various gender specific meanings and implications, the narratives highlight the strong-context dependence of gender dimensions and mechanisms which can accelerate gender equality. All stories told about career paths, family businesses and entrepreneurial identities are success stories highlighting a fundamental amount of internalized gender equality. Due to the beneficial contexts, the narratives serve as best practice examples reflecting the holism of identity work strategies in family business entrepreneurship and supporting influences.

Different narratives were identified in the interviews, which came up again and again. The two narratives "filling the void" and "growing into the family business" highlight the prerequisites which are necessary to establish successfully in a family business and within society. These two aspects are barely influenced by gender narratives, even though it emerges from the interviews that women are somewhat more encouraged to take the helm. Other narratives influenced by a gender dimension could be identified in the interviews: "anchoring in the past," "proving oneself and gaining legitimacy" and "co-creation of work and family life."

The first narrative frame which all interviewees use is "filling the void" for describing their path, especially with respect to their involvement in the business side of the family firm and working on their entrepreneurial identity. For the sibling-constellations this narrative frame is closely connected to the frame "growing into the family business." The siblings of company 1, who lead and work together with their father, use these narratives to describe their paths which led them both separately first working abroad and then entering the family business, responding to the wish of their father to fill a position for employees leaving. The process of professional identity development in the family business is reflected by both interviewees as gradual, building on their personal contribution to the business. Company 2 is also operating in the tourism sector. The sibling used the same narratives to describe their entry into the business when their father was ill and asked them to step in. Similarly, their professional identity development within the business is also characterized by "serving and growing into the family business" as the brother puts it:

> Actually, we never really had the idea of joining the company (. . .) We were actually completely newcomers to tourism. (I4).

The siblings of company 3 rely on the same narratives although their path was different. At a young age their father introduced the option to join the family business at a later stage. Independently, both decided to take up on their father's offer and got an appropriate education in the relevant field. When entering the business, both filled in for employees leaving positions which were not completely in their field of expertise. From this point onwards, they "served and grew into the family business" (I5).

Both narratives of "filling the void" and "growing into the family business" were also found for the interviewees of the father-son constellations. Both fathers and sons decided early to follow their fathers into the family business; thus, both got the respective education and training and upon consultation then slowly joined the business, taking on available tasks at the beginning. Both constellations still work together harmoniously, and each son has at least half of the decision-making power whereby the son of company 5 did not establish his place thoroughly. Overall, these frames were used in an individualized manner by all interviewees and created coherence over their lifespan and crafted their identities as family business successors. Thus, the overarching-lifespan narratives and the construction of family business entrepreneurial identities support the notion that at the heart of a family business the opportunity for entrepreneurs should be to serve and develop along with the circumstances. This core aspect is found equally for all interviewees.

The following narrative frames which are important building bricks for the lifespan narratives "filling the void" and "growing into the family business" highlight the preconditions for successful entrepreneurial identity work, which is unrestricted from discriminatory gender narratives. The narratives "anchored in the past," "proving oneself and gaining legitimacy" as well as "co-creation of work and family life" were told by all interviewees, displaying a strong gender dimension and gender-specific meanings attached.

> So my own perception was that we all had the same opportunities to do what we want and if I had said now I want to do business and human resources like my sister did, it would have worked the same way as the other way around, if she had said I would like to study electrical engineering now, then there would not have been anyone who would have said this is not for a

> girl. Where the notion would have come for sure would have been with my grandparents. That is clear, so I think the generation is still very much shaped by different topics. (I7)

As expected for the development of family businesses and the evolvement of successors within the special environment, all interviewees connected their identity at various points of time to their ancestors using the narrative "anchored in the past." The anchors in the past are characterized very specific focussing on qualification, abilities, and milestones in the father and son constellation interviewees. Those interviewees used the narratives to create coherence by internalizing, following up their anchors and extending qualifications, abilities, and milestones. A similar usage of the narrative frame was found for the siblings of company 1 and 3. The siblings of company 2 used "anchored in the past" to create identities that opposed the patriarchal identity of the predecessor. The opposition to the patriarchal identity and leader of both the sister and brother shows an equal disapproval and generational shift. Interviewee I4 further evolves this narrative for his children, highlighting the impact of socialization:

> If I do something with my son now, like riding a motorcycle or something similar, maybe not that typical for women, my daughter wants to do that and take part, too. So, I think they grow up totally different and I think we gave them a lot more of what is possible, and I think it will be much more normal for them. (I4)

Further, the sisters of company 1 and 3 as well as the brother of company 3 use the "anchored in the past" narrative, referring to a successful female predecessor which normalizes the gender of female successors and served as a role model for the leader identity construction. Thus, the "anchored in the past" narratives incorporate the range of options for successors and their identity development. The ability for all interviewees to develop an entrepreneurial identity is built upon the opportunity to join and take over the family business. As all interviewees the refer strongly to the ancestors, the influence of role models is highlighted for both male and female successors. As the daughter of company 4 never joined the family business, we can only speculate about the impact of a female role model for her professional identity construction. The generational shift highlighted by I4 and I7 emphasizes the impact of gender-equal socialization and opportunity granting of pivotal figures in the interviewees' lives. In particular, the latter aspect is underlined in the next narrative frame.

> Because my grandmother was a hostess like in the book and could just inspire people and only lived for the guests and run her restaurant. Unfortunately, I wasn't allowed to get to know her anymore, but I always have the feeling her spirit is represented in the whole house. (I1)

The narrative of "proving oneself and gaining legitimacy" was also told by all interviewees. This narrative reflects the identity work connected to creating a legitimate successor identity for oneself and the various stakeholders. Only the sister of company 3, which operates in a highly male dominated sector, explicitly discussed her gender as an aspect that needed extra validation. Interestingly and in connection to the importance of legitimacy granting by pivotal figures as the predecessor, she had to legitimize her gender towards external stakeholders.

> The customer didn't talk to me at all. As if I were the secretary who was only traveling along. Conversely, my brother had absolutely no idea and the customer always spoke to my brother, and I always answered because my brother just didn't know about any values. And of course, he noticed relatively quickly that my brother was there, but that I was mainly responsible for the area, but well, that's just the way it is if we had been out to sell the new eco-fashion, then they would not have spoken to my brother, but rather to me. It's just industry-specific, but this company has become one of my biggest customers, all good. (I5)

Thus, this mechanism relates to the importance of gender-equality in socialization and role models not only for the development of successors but also for the perception and approval of persons surrounding their path. The sisters working in the tourism sector, which has a high share of female employees and managers, did not recall gender-specific legitimization work, assuming that in this field the gender-equal socialization and legitimacy granting is further consolidated. Also the absence of female successors in company 4 and 5 or female management in those firms, which both operate in a highly masculine context, hints at the influence of a lack of respective role models and socialization.

> So we never preferred men or anything, we just looked at what task has to be done next. (I8)

"Co-creation of work and family life" is a narrative which the interviewees made use of several times. The shared leadership of siblings in company 1, 2 and 3 is characterized by mutual complementing and support. The narratives of co-working with their siblings revealed that the shared constellation emanated from the effectiveness to lead and work together as the companies have multiple departments. In particular, the sibling of company 2 and 3 highlighted the benefits of close ties, absolute reliability, and the profound understanding which they consider to be an advantage. Thus, all co-create their professional identities with their sibling.

Partnership is at the heart of all success stories of the family businesses and the personal careers. This becomes apparent not only for co-working and co-leading among siblings but is also for couple relationships. All interviewees narrate that the balanced life cannot be achieved on one's own. In family businesses, the generational succession is in the firm's DNA. The interviewees talk about the need for balancing the familial and professional aspects whereby the spouse plays an important role.

> In my opinion, the succession starts much earlier. It actually begins, if you take it exactly, already when you have the right wife. (I10)

The narratives highlight the successful attitude of serving the family business to navigate the professional development and entrepreneurial identity work. All interviewees have internalized this perspective serving as an overarching frame for working and evolving in the family business. The interviewees highlight that many aspects are equally important for all successors. In particular, socialization, role models, and legitimacy granting are influencing factors representing the building bricks of equal opportunities for a more gender equal involvement of potential entrepreneurs in family businesses. The narratives of the interviewees reveal that these aspects are involved in generational change processes which are not at an equal state across industries and companies today.

It is highlighted that gender equality is a process of co-creation that needs the support of all stakeholders. This tendency can be seen in all five narratives, as confidence and support are crucial pillars to develop a legitimate identity as a leader. In general, challenges and life issues always seem to have a gender-specific calibration, yet the leaders do not seem to be aware of this. Even though most of the interviewees emphasize that they have hardly had any negative experiences regarding their gender, women and men have a different self-perception regarding their position. Men also must fight for their status, but they are more in tune with their own position on an individual and societal level. Women in higher positions must adapt to the people who are already established and at the same time be in harmony with the social expectations for this position. If they fail to meet these, irritation and criticism will result. Qualities such as self-confidence do not explicitly refer to men, but for women they play a decisive role with regarding their acceptance and legitimacy.

Contribution of Research

The aim of this paper was to study strategies of gendered identity narratives among family business entrepreneurs. Given that identities are fluid and dynamic as individuals are able to actively manage and continuously shape identity constructions (Brown, 2021; Caza et al., 2018a), our study adds to the relatively under-researched body of knowledge on identity work in family firms by analyzing narrative strategies of family firm actors (Aygören & Nordqvist, 2015). Our findings are congruent with the growing awareness that the construction and reconstruction of entrepreneurial identities depend on interaction with the organizational context, which is often influenced by gender dynamics (Aygören & Nordqvist, 2015; Swail & Marlow, 2018).

We also confirm that family businesses are an ideal setting for studying identities, as they provide a unique set for examining the interplay between work and non-work identities and thus build on the work of Aygören and Nordqvist (2015). By shedding light on the dynamics of gendered identity work among family firm entrepreneurs, we show its relevance for business practice (Lewis, 2015; Bruni et al., 2004). By adding to a better understanding of identity processes and the narratives that shape identities, we contribute to the discussion of key theoretical and practical issues in the field of gender and organizational studies and in the context of family businesses (Aygören & Nordqvist, 2015).

Due to the qualitative research design and the heterogeneity of the sample, results are only partially generalizable, and it is striking that the executives report similar life themes and use the same narratives. The narratives of "filling the void" and "growing into the family business" appear to be umbrella themes for the development into the role of leader. To form an established, accepted, and legitimate identity as a leader, a high degree of personal initiative is required. The dynamic character of the identity work is reflected in the continuous adaptation to changing challenges, especially at the time when entrepreneurs grow into the company and face the challenge of filling the gap and meeting all expectations and demands on their role. Particularly, they face these challenges at the time when entrepreneurs grow into the company and face the challenge of filling the gap while meeting all the expectations and demands of their role. The narratives "anchoring in the past," "proving oneself and gaining legitimacy" and "co-creation of work and family life" reveal a gendered dimension. The life theme "proving oneself and gaining legitimacy" represents an objective that is internalized. It becomes clear that in family businesses this challenge of an identity as a leader is particularly complex, since a multitude of actors from the different systems of family and business interact and make demands. Here, entrepreneurs in family businesses must demonstrate a special versatility and the ability to bring and hold different parts together. "Anchoring in the past" represents a basic prerequisite for successfully slipping into the role of a leader, internalizing, and adapting it to individual requirements. This narrative is explicitly supported by growing up and socializing into the leadership role. "Co-creation of work and family life" connect the interaction of the different systems and define the experienced everyday life.

Despite the findings of this paper, there are several limitations that we need to point out. In our case, we used a narrative approach to gain in-depth understanding through detailed narratives and identity conversations (Caza et al., 2018b). Although narratives are an appropriate inquiry tool which help us understand identity issues, future research could for instance focus on a longitudinal study, where the researchers accompany a family firm entrepreneur for a longer period to see how the identity is formed and changes over time. Second, it might be interesting to undertake the interviews not one after the other, but for example to do a tandem interview with the siblings to capture also the integral involvement among the different identities. Third, we looked into different industries and a greater sample of each of the industries could help see how these results replicate and generalize in these contexts. This might also improve the external validity and generalizability of our findings.

This study is one of the few to explore the pertinent issues of gendered identity narratives among family business entrepreneurs and thus provides an initial picture of identities of ten entrepreneurs in five distinguished companies. By applying a qualitative narrative research approach, we could follow a highly flexible procedure that openly explored identity constructions of the interviewees. We add the current knowledge that entrepreneurial identities in their organizational context depend heavily on interaction that is impacted by gender dynamics.

References

Acker,J. (1990). Hierarchies, jobs, bodies: A theory of gendered organizations. *Gender & Society*, *4*(2), 139–158. https://doi.org/10.1177/089124390004002002

Ahrens, J.-P., Landmann,A., & Woywode,M. (2015). Gender preferences in the CEO successions of family firms: Family characteristics and human capital of the successor. *Journal of Family Business Strategy*, *6*(2), 86–103. https://doi.org/10.1016/j.jfbs.2015.02.002

Alvesson,M., & Billing,Y.D. (2009). *Understanding gender and organizations*. SAGE.

Alvesson,M., & Willmott,H. (2002). Identity Regulation as organizational control: Producing the appropriate individual. *Journal of Management Studies*, *39*(5), 619–644. https://doi.org/10.1111/1467-6486.00305

Aygören,H., & Nordqvist,M. (2015). Gender, ethnicity and identity work in the family business. *European Journal of International Management*, *9*(2), 160–178.

Bjursell,C., & Melin,L. (2011). Proactive and reactive plots: Narratives in entrepreneurial identity construction. *International Journal of Gender and Entrepreneurship*, *3*(3), 218–235. https://doi.org/10.1108/17566261111169313

Brown,A.D. (2015). Identities and identity work in organizations. *International Journal of Management Reviews*, *17*(1), 20–40. https://doi.org/10.1111/ijmr.12035

Brown,A.D. (2017). Identity work and organizational identification. *International Journal of Management Reviews*, *19*(3), 296–317. https://doi.org/10.1111/ijmr.12152

Brown,A.D. (2021). Identities in and around organizations: Towards an identity work perspective. *Human Relations*, 001872672199391. https://doi.org/10.1177/0018726721993910

Bruni,A., Gherardi,S., & Poggio,B. (2004). Doing gender, doing entrepreneurship: An ethnographic account of intertwined practices. *Gender, Work & Organization*, *11*(4), 406–429. https://doi.org/10.1111/j.1468-0432.2004.00240.x

Byrne,J., Radu-Lefebvre,M., Fattoum,S., & Balachandra,L. (2021). Gender gymnastics in CEO succession: Masculinities, femininities and legitimacy. *Organization Studies*, *42*(1), 129–159. https://doi.org/10.1177/0170840619879184

Cascón-Pereira,R., Chillas,S., & Hallier,J. (2016). Role-meanings as a critical factor in understanding doctor managers' identity work and different role identities. *Social science & medicine (1982)*, *170*, 18–25. https://doi.org/10.1016/j.socscimed.2016.09.043

Caza,B.B., Moss,S., & Vough,H. (2018a). From synchronizing to harmonizing: The process of authenticating multiple work identities. *Administrative Science Quarterly*, *63*(4), 703–745. https://doi.org/10.1177/0001839217733972

Caza,B.B., Vough,H., & Puranik,H. (2018b). Identity work in organizations and occupations: Definitions, theories, and pathways forward. *Journal of Organizational Behavior*, *39*(7), 889–910. https://doi.org/10.1002/job.2318

Champenois,C., Lefebvre,V., & Ronteau,S. (2020). Entrepreneurship as practice: systematic literature review of a nascent field. *Entrepreneurship & Regional Development*, *32*(3–4), 281–312. https://doi.org/10.1080/08985626.2019.1641975

Chreim,S., Williams,B.E., & Hinings,C.R. (2007). Interlevel influences on the reconstruction of professional role identity. *Academy of Management Journal*, *50*(6), 1515–1539. https://doi.org/10.5465/amj.2007.28226248

Czarniawska,B. (1997). *A narrative approach to organization studies*. Sage Publications.

Czarniawska,B. (2004). *Narratives in social science research. Introducing qualitative methods series*. Sage Publications.

Danes,S.M., & Olson,P.D. (2003). Women's role involvement in family businesses, business tensions, and business success. *Family Business Review*, *16*(1), 53–68. https://doi.org/10.1111/j.1741-6248.2003.00053.x

Dawson,A., & Hjorth,D. (2012). Advancing family business research through narrative analysis. *Family Business Review, 25*(3), 339–355. https://doi.org/10.1177/0894486511421487

Essers,C., Doorewaard,H., & Benschop,Y. (2013). Family ties: Migrant female business owners doing identity work on the public-private divide. *Human Relations, 66*(12), 1645–1665. https://doi.org/10.1177/0018726713486820

European Comission. (2018). *2018 report on equality between women and men in the EU.* http://ec.europa.eu/newsroom/juststt/item-detail.cfm?item_id=615287.

Gehman,J., Glaser,V.L., Eisenhardt,K.M., Gioia,D., Langley,A., & Corley,K.G. (2018). Finding Theory-method fit: A comparison of three qualitative approaches to theory building. *Journal of Management Inquiry, 27*(3), 284–300. https://doi.org/10.1177/1056492617706029

Giddens,A. (1997). *Modernity and self-identity: Self and society in the Late Modern Age* (1. publ. in the U.S.A). Stanford Univ. Press.

Gioia,D.A., Corley,K.G., & Hamilton,A.L. (2013). Seeking qualitative rigor in inductive research. *Organizational Research Methods, 16*(1), 15–31. https://doi.org/10.1177/1094428112452151

Gretzel,U., & Bowser,G. (2013). Real stories about real women: Communicating role models for female tourism students. *Journal of Teaching in Travel & Tourism, 13*(2), 170–183. https://doi.org/10.1080/15313220.2013.786466

Hatmaker,D.M. (2012). Practicing engineers: Professional identity construction through role configuration. *Engineering Studies, 4*(2), 121–144. https://doi.org/10.1080/19378629.2012.683793

Hytti,U., Alsos,G.A., Heinonen,J., & Ljunggren,E. (2017). Navigating the family business: A gendered analysis of identity construction of daughters. *International Small Business Journal, 35*(6), 665–686. https://doi.org/10.1177/0266242616675924

Ibarra,H., & Obodaru,O. (2016). Betwixt and between identities: Liminal experience in contemporary careers. *Research in Organizational Behavior, 36,* 47–64. https://doi.org/10.1016/j.riob.2016.11.003

Killian,C., & Johnson,C. (2006). "I'm Not an immigrant!": Resistance, redefinition, and the role of resources in identity work. *Social Psychology Quarterly, 69*(1), 60–80. https://doi.org/10.1177/019027250606900105

Kira,M., & Balkin,D.B. (2014). Interactions between work and identities: Thriving, withering, or redefining the self? *Human Resource Management Review, 24*(2), 131–143. https://doi.org/10.1016/j.hrmr.2013.10.001

Kira,M., Balkin,D.B., & San,E. (2012). Authentic work and organizational change: Longitudinal evidence from a merger. *Journal of Change Management, 12*(1), 31–51. https://doi.org/10.1080/14697017.2011.652374

Leitch,C.M., & Harrison,R.T. (2016). Identity, identity formation and identity work in entrepreneurship: Conceptual developments and empirical applications. *Entrepreneurship & Regional Development, 28* (3–4), 177–190. https://doi.org/10.1080/08985626.2016.1155740

Lewis,K.V. (2015). Enacting entrepreneurship and leadership: A longitudinal exploration of gendered identity work. *Journal of Small Business Management, 53*(3), 662–682. https://doi.org/10.1111/jsbm.12175

Lewis,K.V., Ho,M., Harris,C., & Morrison,R. (2016). Becoming an entrepreneur: opportunities and identity transitions. *International Journal of Gender and Entrepreneurship, 8*(2), 98–116. https://doi.org/10.1108/IJGE-02-2015-0006

Martin,L., Jerrard,B., & Wright,L. (2020). Identity work in female-led creative businesses. *Gender, Work & Organization, 27*(3), 310–326. https://doi.org/10.1111/gwao.12357

McAdams,D.P. (1996). Personality, modernity, and the storied self: A contemporary framework for studying persons. *Psychological Inquiry, 7*(4), 295–321. https://doi.org/10.1207/s15327965pli0704_1

Memili,E., Chang,E.P.C., Kellermanns,F.W., & Welsh,D.H.B. (2015). Role conflicts of family members in family firms. *European Journal of Work and Organizational Psychology, 24*(1), 143–151. https://doi.org/10.1080/1359432X.2013.839549

Mussolino,D., Cicellin,M., Pezzillo Iacono, M., Consiglio,S., & Martinez,M. (2019). Daughters' self-positioning in family business succession: A narrative inquiry. *Journal of Family Business Strategy, 10*(2), 72–86. https://doi.org/10.1016/j.jfbs.2019.01.003

Nordqvist,M., & Melin,L. (2010). Entrepreneurial families and family firms. *Entrepreneurship & Regional Development, 22*(3–4), 211–239. https://doi.org/10.1080/08985621003726119

Otten-Pappas,D., & Jäkel-Wurzer,D. (2017). *Weibliche Nachfolge-Ausnahme oder Regelfall: Eine Studie Zur Aktuellen Situation Im Generationswechsel Deutscher Familienunternehmen*. Wittener Institut Für Familienunternehmen.

Schlömer-Laufen,N., & Kay,R. (2013). *Zum Einfluss des Geschlechts des Übergebers auf die Wahl des familieninternen Nachfolgers: Eine theoretische und empirische Analyse in deutschen Familienunternehmen* (Working Paper 01/13). Institut für Mittelstandsforschung (IfM) Bonn. https://www.econstor.eu/han dle/10419/71287

Schlömer-Laufen,N., & Kay,R. (2015). Zum Einfluss des Geschlechts des Übergebenden auf die Wahl des familieninternen Nachfolgenden. *ZfKE – Zeitschrift für KMU und Entrepreneurship, 63*(1), 1–23. https://doi.org/10.3790/zfke.63.1.1

Sentuti,A., Cesaroni,F.M., & Pediconi,M.G. (2019). Daughter entrepreneurs between birth family and gender stereotypes. In *Gender Studies, Entrepreneurship and Human Capital*. Springer. https://doi.org/10.1007/978-3-030-46874-3_5

Snow,D.A., & Anderson,L. (1987). Identity work among the homeless: The verbal construction and avowal of personal identities. *American Journal of Sociology, 92*(6), 1336–1371. https://doi.org/10.1086/228668

Stamarski,C.S., & Son Hing, L.S. (2015). Gender inequalities in the workplace: The effects of organizational structures, processes, practices, and decision makers' sexism. *Frontiers in Psychology, 6*, 1400. https://doi.org/10.3389/fpsyg.2015.01400

Sveningsson,S., & Alvesson,M. (2003). Managing managerial identities: Organizational fragmentation, discourse and identity struggle. *Human Relations, 56*(10), 1163–1193. https://doi.org/10.1177/00187267035610001

Swail,J., & Marlow,S. (2018). 'Embrace the masculine; attenuate the feminine' – gender, identity work and entrepreneurial legitimation in the nascent context. *Entrepreneurship & Regional Development, 30*(1–2), 256–282. https://doi.org/10.1080/08985626.2017.1406539

Watson,T.J. (2008). Managing identity: Identity work, personal predicaments and structural circumstances. *Organization, 15*(1), 121–143. https://doi.org/10.1177/1350508407084488

Watson,T.J. (2009a). Entrepreneurial action, identity work and the use of multiple discursive resources. *International Small Business Journal, 27*(3), 251–274. https://doi.org/10.1177/0266242609102274

Watson,T.J. (2009b). Narrative, life story and manager identity: A case study in autobiographical identity work. *Human Relations, 62*(3), 425–452. https://doi.org/10.1177/0018726708101044

Welter,F. (2020). Contexts and gender – looking back and thinking forward. *International Journal of Gender and Entrepreneurship, 12*(1), 27–38. https://doi.org/10.1108/IJGE-04-2019-0082

West,C., & Zimmerman,D. (1987). Doing gender. *Gender & Society, 1*(2), 125–151. https://doi.org/10.1177/0891243287001002002

Wielsma,A.J., & Brunninge,O. (2019). "Who am I? Who are we?" Understanding the impact of family business identity on the development of individual and family identity in business families. *Journal of Family Business Strategy, 10*(1), 38–48. https://doi.org/10.1016/j.jfbs.2019.01.006

Zheng,W., Meister,A., & Caza,B.B. (2021). The stories that make us: Leaders' origin stories and temporal identity work. *Human Relations, 74*(8), 1178–1210. https://doi.org/10.1177/0018726720909864

Nina Schumacher
25 Success Factors of Digital Start-ups
A Qualitative Analysis of the Entrepreneurial Personality from the
Perspective of German Venture Investors

Abstract: This exploratory study examines the personality characteristics that influence the success of digital start-ups from the perspective of German venture investors. The original research takes a three-dimensional approach and integrates the micro-perspective on the entrepreneurial personality, the meso-perspective on the business model, and the macro-perspective on the entrepreneurial context. Based on qualitative content analysis of expert interviews with German VC investors, this study considers personality and behavioral characteristics of entrepreneurs, such as entrepreneurial motivation and energy and willingness to learn, as the most relevant characteristics for success. Particularly in the start-up phase of a digital company, the ability to question one's approach and convictions regularly, not only when mistakes are recognized but also to consider information and assessments from others, characterizes successful entrepreneurship. In addition, German VC investors consider the overall group of personality characteristics (perspective on entrepreneurial personality) to be most important for entrepreneurial success. Furthermore, the experts' assessment of success characteristics provides a valuable perspective that has received little attention in the current literature. Finally, this study provides practical added value for researchers and practitioners regarding considering focal points in German VC investors' implicit or explicit valuation model.

Keywords: start-up success, entrepreneurship, entrepreneurial personality, venture capital investors, entrepreneurial motivation and energy, willingness to learn, digital start-up

Introduction

Digitization and related technological innovations have opened new opportunities for companies to create value and necessitate the development of new business models (Bouwman et al., 2019; Cosenz & Bivona, 2021; Dabić et al., 2021b; Hock-Doepgen et al., 2021). In today's digital economy, companies generate customer value through physical activities and create value at the virtual level, e.g., through platform business models and other forms of digital infrastructure (Aloulou, 2019, pp. 190–195). Consequently, the importance of the business model, i.e., the value creation model, has increased, making

Nina Schumacher, Leuphana University, Lüneburg, Germany

https://doi.org/10.1515/9783110747652-026

digital entrepreneurship (e-entrepreneurship) different from traditional entrepreneurship in several respects (Arlott et al., 2019, pp. 4–8; Wirtz, 2019, pp. 35–49).

Nevertheless, at least in the German-speaking world, entrepreneurship research remains bound mainly to classical approaches, i.e., those that emphasize personality factors (Blum & Leibbrand, 2001, pp. 15–16). Dualism, which integrates two perspectives on entrepreneurial success, as opposed to monism, extends this approach. To move beyond this dualism, Shepherd et al. (2019) propose a meta-framework and challenge entrepreneurship researchers to offer a different, three-dimensional approach that considers the entrepreneurial personality (micro-level research), the entrepreneurial context (macro-level research), and the characteristics of the business model (meso-level research). This study contributes to this line of inquiry by examining the relevance of success characteristics at all three levels for digital start-ups from the perspective of German Venture Investors. The systematic literature reviews by Köhn (2017) and Granz et al. (2020) suggest that venture investors can be considered as well-informed experts. Both studies conclude that Venture Capital (VC) investors seem to base their investment practices on multidimensional decision models on entrepreneurial success.

This chapter draws on the original empirical research. It addresses two research questions (RQs): first, to what extent do single entrepreneurial characteristics (micro-level research) in terms of personality, human capital, and actions influence the economic success of a digital start-up from the perspective of German venture investors? Second, what conclusions can be drawn from expert interviews with German venture capitalists regarding the relevance of success characteristics at the micro-, macro-, and meso-levels for the economic success of digital start-ups? To answer these two questions, this chapter first provides an overview of the current debate on different research approaches to entrepreneurial characteristics and then presents the results of the original empirical research.

This empirical investigation shows that from the perspective of German VC investors, micro-level success characteristics of e-entrepreneurship, such as motivation and entrepreneurial energy and the willingness to learn, are the most relevant predictors of success. Especially in the start-up phase of a digital company, successful entrepreneurship is not characterized by "heroic adherence" (Schumpeter, 1942) to an idea, but by the ability to regularly question one's approach and convictions, not only when the founder identifies mistakes, but also to take into account information and assessments of others (Anand et al., 2021). In this respect, the entrepreneur is not a homo economicus but rather a homo robustus.

Moreover, German VC investors consider the entire group of entrepreneurial characteristics most important for entrepreneurial success rather than macro- or meso-level success characteristics. Specifically, VC investors assume that digital start-ups with strong entrepreneurial personalities and based on solid business models will find business opportunities, VC, appropriate employees, and markets even if an entrepreneurial ecosystem does not support them.

Theoretical Perspectives

Academic entrepreneurship research focusing on personality characteristics has a long tradition of empirical research (Eckardt, 2015, p. 12; Ferreira et al., 2019, pp. 183–185; Meyer, 2020, pp. 24–29; Obschonka & Stuetzer, 2017, p. 203). This research line was developed in business psychology at the instigation of American VC investors and was the first systematic attempt to explain start-up activities or differences between entrepreneurs and employees (Volkmann et al., 2010, p. 9). The purpose was to identify specific personality characteristics of entrepreneurs in terms of their prospects of success and thus to gain additional criteria for investment decisions. The personality approach to understanding entrepreneurship assumes that personality characteristics distinguish entrepreneurs from non-entrepreneurs (Altinay et al., 2021). In contrast, economic policy has guided traditional academic entrepreneurship research in Europe. This research intended to identify personality characteristics to provide a blueprint for economic policy to promote entrepreneurship (Volkmann et al., 2010, p. 10). Insofar, this traditional approach to entrepreneurship research is, at its core, research on psychological success factors, i.e., of individuals rather than, e.g., of companies or the entrepreneurial environment.

Following these traditional approaches, Fueglistaller et al. (2008, p. 1) define entrepreneurship as a process initiated and carried out by individuals identifying, evaluating, and generating benefits from business opportunities. The classic concept of the entrepreneur traces back to Schumpeter, who defined the entrepreneur as a natural person who runs a business alone or with others (Meyer, 2020, pp. 24–25) to regularly destroy the market equilibrium through the introduction of innovations understood as new combinations of already existing resources (Ferreira et al., 2019, p. 183). In contrast to the manager, a key characteristic of the entrepreneur is the willingness to take risks. Thus, there is a real risk of losing the invested equity. The three classic characteristics of the entrepreneur in this context are first, independent action; second, organizational leadership and planning authority; and third, willingness to take risks (Blum & Leibbrand, 2001, pp. 6–9).

In the case of small businesses, it is first and foremost the personality of the founding team or the entrepreneur that determines economic performance, which could explain the focus on personality characteristics when researching start-up success (Andersson, 2007, p. 129; Najmaei & Sadeghinejad, 2019, p. 103; Obschonka & Stuetzer, 2017, p. 203). Consequently, entrepreneurship research that focuses on the micro-level uses psychological concepts such as personality, a core concept in psychological research (Kraus et al., 2018; Obschonka & Stuetzer, 2017). However, according to Rauch and Frese (2008), a static personality approach falls short as the sole model to explain and promote entrepreneurial success. Instead, a theory of entrepreneurship should also consider the business environment (e.g., McMullen & Shepherd, 2006).

However, actor-centered research at the micro-level is by no means limited to the actor (Audretsch, 2012, pp. 761–762; Cunningham et al., 2019). Audretsch (2012) points out that there has been an increase in the number of empirical studies with a greater emphasis on context and that entrepreneurs do not see contextual factors as limiting, but rather as having configurable potential, i.e., certain factors may be beneficial in that they can be manipulated and exploited by the entrepreneur in one way or another. Thus, research on the entrepreneur's interaction with the environment is increasingly becoming the focus of entrepreneurship research (Unger et al., 2011). The literature, e.g., has recently become more diverse in terms of both methodology and perspective (Audretsch, 2012, p. 755; Ferreira et al., 2019, pp. 187–195; Zahra et al., 2014, pp. 487–495).

Most theoretical approaches and models assume that entrepreneurial success results from behavioral dispositions rather than personality characteristics, especially the continuous search for business opportunities. However, recent research has examined the success factors of entrepreneurial action only in one phase of the business life cycle – the start-up and growth phase – and not in other phases. Moreover, most studies have not examined different types of entrepreneurs, but only those considered innovative, so-called high-impact entrepreneurs (Acs, 2010, p. 165). A more recent model to explain entrepreneurial success as the primary purpose of entrepreneurship research is the *Giessen-Amsterdam model of entrepreneurial success* (Rauch & Frese, 2008). Personality characteristics and human capital are the basis for entrepreneurial behavior and activities, while the firm's environment also influences entrepreneurial behavior and activities.

Given the many opportunities new digital technologies present, entrepreneurs must have the appropriate skills to identify and exploit entrepreneurial opportunities in the digital economy. For example, while entrepreneurs must have specific skills based on their professional education and previous experience (Levie et al., 2009), soft skills are essential for entrepreneurial process and success, especially in an increasingly digital economy. In addition, entrepreneurs need to have some technological awareness to recognize the potential of new digital technologies for their business model. This awareness is also critical for developing new products and services and new ways to deliver them (Bogdanowicz, 2015; Ghezzi & Cavallo, 2020; Nambisan, 2017). Although Rauch and Frese (2008) do not explicitly mention awareness of technological change, one could argue that they emphasize the importance of entrepreneurial orientation and innovation, among other aspects in their Giessen-Amsterdam model, which, in turn, would include technology awareness in the digital economy.

According to Laar et al. (2017), digital knowledge, digital skills, digital literacy, general knowledge, motivation and entrepreneurial energy, self-efficacy, and willingness to learn are essential for entrepreneurs to succeed in the digital economy. Furthermore, given the rapid changes in the economy associated with digitalization, these skills determine potential competitiveness and the ability to drive innovation (Dabić et al., 2021a). This finding is also in line with the personality concept of the Giessen-Amsterdam model (Rauch & Frese, 2008). However, as the Internet makes information widely available to everyone and virtually ubiquitous, disseminating and using the available knowledge are critical success factors for entrepreneurial performance (Kumar & van Welsum, 2013).

Shepherd et al. (2019) conclude that the focus in the literature and related findings confirm that micro-level factors (characteristics of the entrepreneur or founding team) seem to have the most significant impact on start-up success. Schumacher (2022) notes that this happens despite the growing number of positive findings demonstrating the importance of single contextual factors. However, this consensus may also have methodological reasons. Both the ecosystem and traditional entrepreneurship approaches focus on a specific research focus. As a result, they isolate either the contextual factors for successful entrepreneurship or the micro-level factors. However, Shepherd et al. (2019) conceive the entrepreneurial process as a multiple-stage one characterized by the interaction of individual, organizational, and contextual factors.

Research Design

This chapter presents new insights from a larger research project that adopts a multi-perspective approach to investigate the three dimensions of entrepreneurship research from the perspective of German VC investment managers. Initial results on the macro perspective have been published by Schumacher (2022). First, the researcher identified experts using the German Digital Economy Association (BVDW) membership list, including start-up investors focused on digital companies. Then, based on this list of 725 potential experts and an initial mailing by email or message via the professional online business network LinkedIn, 77 experts were recruited and interviewed between August 2018 and February 2019, mainly in person, by telephone, or in video conferences.

This research investigates the importance of and interaction between groups of success characteristics (categories) and single success characteristics (subcategories) across the three aforementioned research dimensions for entrepreneurship. To this end, one reference model was operationalized for each research perspective and used as the basis for data collection through guided expert interviews. First, the Giessen-Amsterdam model as an actor-centered model (Rauch & Frese, 2000, 2008). Second, the Isenberg model (2011) is a reference model for the entrepreneurial context. Third, the Osterwalder-Pigneur business model approach is a reference model for business model components (Osterwalder & Pigneur, 2010). However, the focus of this chapter is specifically to present exploratory research at the micro-level.

This study uses the Giessen-Amsterdam model of entrepreneurial success developed by Rauch and Frese (2008), as it is the most comprehensive psychological model to date for explaining entrepreneurial success at the micro-level (Rövekamp, 2011). However, this model assumes that the entrepreneur's actions determine success. Therefore, neither personality characteristics, human capital, nor the environment are directly related to entrepreneurial success, but they influence entrepreneurial behavior and activities (entrepreneur's action characteristics) and thus indirectly impact entrepreneurial success.

In addition, their model assumes that an entrepreneur's personality influences the structures and actions within the company, the type of employees hired, the priorities, the implementation of visions and strategies, and the corporate culture in general. By linking an entrepreneur's personality characteristics and human capital to action characteristics, the model provides a way to examine the influence of these two categories on success. According to Rövekamp (2011), the model contains action-relevant characteristics, including cognitive processes and learning processes such as learning from mistakes or learning by doing.

Table 25.1 lists the characteristics that may influence the economic success of a digital start-up derived from the Giessen-Amsterdam model. The present research does not consider attributes that relate to the company's environment, as the research on the macro perspective covers this aspect in the original study (Schumacher, 2022). The selection of the listed characteristics takes the best possible consideration of possible dependencies on personality, human capital, and action characteristics.

Table 25.1: Characteristics of the entrepreneur.

Dimension	Characteristics
Characteristics of the Entrepreneur (Micro-level)	Education
	Professional and Industry Experience
	Motivation and Entrepreneurial Energy
	Product-Specific Know-How
	Organizational Skills
	Team Leadership Skills
	Strategic Thinking
	Willingness to Learn
	Other Characteristics (mentioned by the expert)

Before the interview, the researcher asked a related filter question to ensure that the interviewee is an active professional investment manager making decisions about funding digital start-ups. Then, to answer the first RQ, the researcher first asked the experts about the relevance of single characteristics of the entrepreneurs' personality to success. To this end, the researcher provided the interviewees with a list of characteristics (cf. Table 25.1) and additional explanations on a handout. In a second step, the researcher asked the experts to select a maximum of three characteristics they thought had the most significant influence on a digital start-up's success. In the final step of the first part, the experts explained their decision in greater detail.

RQ2 asks about the conclusions regarding the relevance of the entire groups of success characteristics at the micro-, macro-, and meso-levels for the economic success of digital start-ups. Therefore, the second part of the interview was devoted to data collection to answer RQ2. The basis here were the entire groups of characteristics per research perspective (actor, context, and business model) already known from the first part of the interview. Here, the researcher asked the experts to evaluate the success relevance of the entire group of characteristics and give reasons for the decision.

The analysis of the total of 731 collected statements follows the structuring qualitative content analysis according to Mayring (2010). The approach taken was deductive-inductive: the categories of the content-analytical category system were derived theoretically (deductive), and the subcategories were developed from the transcript (inductive). The analysis process followed three steps: first, the transcripts of the interviews were divided into coding units (segments). The segments were determined based on content. Second, trial coding was conducted. Third, primary coding was conducted.

Interviewees

The present study analyzes the responses of experts interviewed by Schumacher (2022). An initial filter question ensured that all 77 venture investors were responsible for investment decisions regarding digital start-ups. Moreover, 35 have worked in this capacity for more than five years (45.5%), and 24.7% even have 10 or more years of professional experience. In addition, 42 (54.5%) have been investment decision-makers for up to 5 years. In terms of professional experience, the mean value is seven years, with a median of five.

A total of 5.2% of the interviewees are analysts, 11.7% Chief Executive Officers (CEO) of a VC company, 11.7% department heads in a VC company, about 17% managing partners, 22.1% managing directors, and 27.3% angel investors. In addition, 5.2% indicated that they have other professional roles and responsibilities. In terms of assets under management on a three-year average, 58.2% of the interviewees were responsible for assets of up to EUR 10 million and 9% even for more than EUR 100 million. The volume of the assets under management, i.e., the sum of cash, deposits, and shareholdings' market value, range from EUR 40,000 to EUR 1bn.

These numbers indicate that the interviewees had considerable experience and success when investing in and financing digital start-ups. It is safe to assume that these experts also have sufficient empirical knowledge to assess the financial risks in this context. A total of 55% of the interviewees estimate that their investment decision success rate is close to 60%. Some 45% claim that it is more than 60%. Elsewhere, 11.3% estimate that their investment decision success rate is less than 20%. As suggested by location parameters, which suggest nearly a normal distribution of the self-assessments of investment decision success rates (mean = 56.1%, median = 60%), the experts interviewed do not seem to be characterized by excessive confidence regarding their investment capabilities.

Given their performance and experience of successfully investing larger amounts of fund capital and managing the associated risk, one can conclude that the interviewees are experts in their field. Although these experts likely consider the personality of the entrepreneurs and founding teams, the start-up business model, and the entrepreneurial ecosystem when assessing investment risk, this study examines only the personality characteristics of the founder(s) in the following sections.

Effects of Characteristics of the Entrepreneur on Start-up Performance

This study derives eight characteristics (see Table 25.1) from the Giessen-Amsterdam model. By question 2a, the interviewed experts selected a maximum of three characteristics that they believe have the most significant influence on the success of a digital start-up and identified motivation and entrepreneurial energy and willingness to learn as the most critical.

Motivation and entrepreneurial energy should be interpreted primarily as a personality characteristic. Mitchell and Daniels (2003) and Pinder (1998) see motivation and entrepreneurial energy as the basis for developing an entrepreneurial activity on one's initiative, organizing situations and processes oneself, and maintaining the necessary motivation. However, the present study focuses only on the intrinsic part of this definition of entrepreneurial energy. Like willingness to learn, also a personality characteristic, motivation and entrepreneurial energy directly influence self-initiative as an action characteristic (Rauch & Frese, 2008).

The experts considered other characteristics such as leadership, strategic thinking, product-specific know-how, and professional and industry experience as of average relevance to success, while they did not consider the educational background at all. Finally, in the group of other characteristics, the experts mentioned characteristics that could not be assigned to the listed ones.

Some experts (Ex) (cf., e.g., Ex1, Ex3, Ex4, Ex12, and Ex14 in Tab. 2) emphasize that motivation and entrepreneurial energy are critical prerequisites for starting a business, successfully launching the first products, and managing the operation. One of these experts (Ex14) describes an entrepreneur as "born to fail." Failure, large and small, is a constant possibility and part of the everyday experience of entrepreneurs, especially in the start-up phase (see Ex74 in Table 25.2). In this respect, the archetype of the entrepreneur would not be the optimistic, opportunity-seeking Schumpeterian destroyer (Ferreira et al., 2019, p. 183), but rather the resilient type who finds himself or herself in a constantly precarious situation, at least in the start-up phase. Instead of strategically superior thinking, he or she demonstrates product know-how, leadership, or team skills and is characterized by a specific mental resilience when experiencing failure.

Table 25.2: Selected statements on motivation and entrepreneurial energy.

ID	Statement
Ex1	"Founding is an enormous burden on the founder – mentally and physically."
Ex3	". . . because you also have to fight your way through the valleys."
Ex4	"Many low blows mark start-up life . . . falling, getting up, carrying on, and not getting discouraged."
Ex5	". . . compensate many weaknesses and deficits with motivation and energy."
Ex6	"Ability to suffer . . . perseverance . . . much energy is required on this path of trial and error."
Ex12	"There is a great desire to deal with problems . . . to make new decisions again and again."
Ex14	"Start-ups are born to fail. So, you need the entrepreneurial spirit to get through it."
Ex17	"Motivation and entrepreneurial energy go hand in hand with a willingness to learn."
Ex30	". . . not to be discouraged."
Ex31	"Since money can buy almost everything else, motivation is the point that covers everything else I can't buy."
Ex34	"Because of my experience, I don't care about education and professional skills. It's about the guys; they have to have energy and be willing to learn."
Ex53	". . . is needed for one financing round after another."
Ex55	"Motivation makes a big contribution. If someone has entrepreneurial energy, the founders are acquiring exactly the skills they lack."
Ex62"	"The constant getting up, falling, getting up and not getting frustrated."
Ex71	"Motivation and energy are the most important, as a soldier on [sic], stay the course."
Ex73	"Entrepreneurship is, at its core, about dealing with challenges. This can balance many other insufficiencies."
Ex74	"The probability of failure is much greater than the probability of success. And then to move on, that's a start-up entrepreneur."

This result would be a starting point for understanding entrepreneurship that emphasizes resilience, persistence, and learning. Such an understanding assumes that the entrepreneur is not the rational utility maximizer who weighs the considerable risks of starting up in his or her favor in the constant search for opportunities but can turn failure into profit in the long run. In this respect, the entrepreneur is not a homo economicus but a homo robustus. The findings of this study are thus more in line with recent research on resilience, which examines the impact of the ability to cope with crises and to overcome and exploit them by drawing on personal and social resources (e.g., Fischer et al., 2016; Hallak et al., 2018).

Table 25.3: Selected statements on willingness to learn.

ID	Statement
Ex1	"Willingness to learn is just as important because you have to learn fast, [. . .]. Most of the time, the founders have no leadership experience and little organizational skills when they startup." "Willingness to learn because you have to react quickly. To the feedback of potential customers, e.g., especially in the launch phase."
Ex5	"With existing willingness to learn, the investor sees that the founder means business."
Ex7	"The ability to take in currents and clues, i.e., the willingness to learn, and that is very, very important."
Ex10	"Willingness to learn is essential, as digitization, in particular, requires a constant rethinking of the model." "You have to be willing to try many new things."
Ex11	"Willingness to learn is crucial . . . especially given the dynamics with which markets develop."
Ex12	"The existing willingness to learn is an important decision criterion for the venture capitalist. Conversely, resistance to consulting is a reason not to invest." "If a founding team can draw the right conclusions from the suggestions, that is an essential component of success." "One must always be able to adjust and adapt to current market conditions." "The founder must first become more familiar with the mechanisms of the industry."
Ex17	"Approach: Basically, everything can be learned. It's just a matter of how much energy the founder wants to put into it."
Ex18	"People are no longer hired based on work experience, but on their willingness to learn and many other soft skills. So, it's always more important if people can learn."
Ex30	"You have to learn a lot in the beginning to understand your own business's basic idea and framework. This understanding is fundamental so that the business idea can become profitable." "Most start-ups fail because they develop a solution to a problem that doesn't exist."
Ex32	"Willingness to learn is important because this is a journey that requires constant adaptation." "Learning happens mostly in the market . . . Getting the right nuggets, that's the high art . . . Taking those nuggets and using them for development."
Ex33	"Willingness to learn is important because the start-up phase is very volatile. So even if the training is excellent, the founder must still adapt if the situation changes."
Ex46	"Willingness to learn is also super important. Consider, e.g., Rocket Internet. They are extremely willing to learn. For example, if they notice that a process is not running, they change over immediately."
Ex52	"Willingness to learn includes flexibility."
Ex56	"From my experience, there are good founders, but it fails because people don't want to be advised in many cases." "The sage use and implementation of advice, taking advantage of the learning curves of others, that is also an art."

Table 25.3 (continued)

ID	Statement
Ex63	"Team leadership skills and strategic thinking etc., can all be balanced by a willingness to learn."
Ex65	"A founder cannot be familiar with all topics, so the willingness to learn is essential. "
Ex67	"One always questions the project, learns from it, and grows from it."
Ex70	"Willingness to learn. Feedback from others is critical, and to be exempt from this."
Ex71	"Resistance to counseling is the worst, therefore willing to learn in any case."
Ex72	"Willingness to learn and strategic thinking are almost equally important. People always influence and talk down to the founder, especially in the beginning[. . .], but you should never lose sight of the strategic, overarching goal. What is the vision?" "Nevertheless, a start-up has to learn quickly, react and adapt to changing conditions."
Ex74	"Willingness to learn is crucial. If someone always knows everything better, success is doubtful."

However, additional characteristics are required for this high frustration tolerance to contribute to organizational success. For example, Ex17 (Tables 25.2 and 25.3) and Ex34 (Table 25.2) explicitly point out the connection between trying, failing, and learning as a cycle of entrepreneurship, thus establishing the link to the second most crucial micro-level success characteristic: willingness to learn. For example, experts Ex5 and Ex12 point out that a willingness to learn is a prerequisite for success in the VC market (see Table 25.3). Ex30 goes one step further and states that even a mediocre start-up idea or a mediocre business model does not necessarily lead to failure if there is an apparent willingness to learn.

Change may be necessary because entrepreneurs have made incorrect assumptions and because some assumptions may no longer be valid. However, as Ex52 points out, entrepreneurs who are willing to learn and could quickly acquire new skills can quickly correct mistakes and adapt to constantly changing conditions, precisely because the dynamics of the markets may also require an adjustment of the original business model or product concept (see Ex11, Ex46, and Ex72 in Table 25.3).

In this context, Ex12 and Ex56 emphasize that willingness to learn also means being able and willing to learn from others. This result also contradicts some basic assumptions of the traditional entrepreneurship literature, especially the heroic Schumpeterian entrepreneur (Schumpeter, 1942), and is thus another argument for an understanding of entrepreneurship that emphasizes resilience, perseverance, and learning: successful entrepreneurship is not the heroic adherence to an idea against odds by the genius inventor-entrepreneur (i.e., an optimistic, heroic notion of entrepreneurship along the lines of Schumpeter's disruptive pioneer entrepreneurs), but rather the ability to question one's actions and beliefs continually, not only in the face of recognized mistakes, but also in light of information, assessments, and evaluations by others. This understanding refers to the entrepreneur failing but learning from mistakes.

However, there is also a risk, as Ex72 points out: "There are always people who influence the founder, especially in the beginning . . . However, you should never lose sight of the strategic, overall goal. What is the vision?" Ex72's statement implies that there must always be a strategic perspective that limits the option space. Ex19 makes a similar statement about Strategic Thinking as a further success factor, while Ex20 even posits a causal relationship between willingness to learn and strategic thinking (cf. Table 25.4). Ex20 thus sees strategic thinking itself as a function of the ability or willingness to learn.

Table 25.4: Selected statements on other items referring to the top success items.

ID	Theoretical Code	Statement
Ex19	ST	"Without a holistic, long-term strategic vision, getting lost in small details is usually hazardous."
Ex20	ST	"Strategic thinking requires the willingness to learn."
Ex57	LS	"All individual team members must complement each other – that's beyond question."
Ex65	LS	"Team leadership skills are essential to managing and organizing a heterogeneous team."

Abbreviations: ST = Strategic thinking; LS = Leadership skills.

In connection with the willingness to learn or to seek advice from others, interviewees such as Ex57 and Ex65 describe another critical skill: the ability to assemble a heterogeneous team that complements the profile of the founder or the founding team. Leveraging this heterogeneity, i.e., accommodating competing perspectives and approaches, ideally aligns with the founder's strategic perspective. The founder's objective is to make the best use of the different skills and resources for the company's direction and development.

In the final part of the interview, the researcher asked the experts about the relevance to the success of the entire group of characteristics per research perspective (actor, context, and business model). The highest relevance to success is attributed to personality characteristics, followed by business model components. However, according to the experts interviewed, entrepreneurial context contributes least to entrepreneurial success.

Key Findings: The VC Perspective on Personality Characteristics

The qualitative content analysis (Mayring, 2010) results show two prominent personality characteristics: motivation and entrepreneurial energy and willingness to learn, and two supporting characteristics: strategic thinking and leadership skills. The first, motivation and entrepreneurial energy, is the core characteristic of the start-up. This resource is why individuals acquire the knowledge and management skills they lack but need for their business. It enables entrepreneurs to accept mistakes made in the start-up process. In addition, this core characteristic allows the necessary flexibility in the orientation of the start-up even to a dynamic environment. The second, willingness to learn, is the basis for transforming failures and mistakes into new solutions, and thus one of the essential means to draw on motivation and entrepreneurial energy. In addition, the resource willingness to learn creates the basis for the company to adapt to changing markets.

Regarding the supporting characteristics, strategic thinking enables entrepreneurs to have a strategic orientation and thus acts as a counterweight to excessive energy or aimless learning as an end in itself. It also enables entrepreneurs to choose strategically relevant approaches from many ideas and solutions, especially in a founding team. The second supporting characteristic, leadership skills, serves as a prerequisite for creating a culture of error, learning, and diversity in solution generation (learning organization) (Anand et al., 2021).

Investors thus regard motivation and entrepreneurial energy as a personality characteristic of the entrepreneur relevant to success. This result aligns with other recent empirical studies that show that intrinsic motivation is more relevant than extrinsic motivation. For example, Murnieks et al. (2016) and Granz et al. (2020) find that angel investors view founder motivation and energy as relevant to success. Cardon and Kirk (2015) also find that motivation and energy affect self-efficacy, positively affecting firm growth. However, motivation and energy can change over time so that after a particular time extrinsic motivation in the form of business success can complement intrinsic motivation (Westhead et al., 2005). For investors, the question becomes whether entrepreneurs remain focused and motivated, especially during difficult times.

Since motivation and entrepreneurial energy and willingness to learn are both personality characteristics, they cannot be learned or acquired. Unger et al.'s (2011) meta-analysis of the effects of human capital on success shows that knowledge and skills, such as leadership skills and strategic thinking, are the result of human capital investments such as experience and training. Investing in acquiring knowledge and skills, in turn, requires sufficient entrepreneurial motivation and energy and willingness to learn. Thus, the meta-analysis of Unger et al. (2011) also confirms that these two identified key characteristics can be considered essential original resources of the start-up company. Recent studies also show that knowledge, in particular, is the moderating variable between motivation and energy and success (Wood et al., 2014), as expertise and skills enable individuals to find solutions under challenging conditions, so that motivation and energy can be transformed into problem-solving activities (Dabić et al., 2021a).

This study suggests that resource-based theories of entrepreneurship for start-up companies are better suited than market-based theories to explain the success of start-up companies, as resource-based theories assume that endogenous resources (firm-specific resources) explain firm growth (Andersson, 2007, p. 129; Brockhoff, 2017, p. 74). Based on these findings, one could conclude that the entrepreneur is the most critical resource, to the extent that he or she embodies the company, and the resource willingness to learn is the modus operandi of this resource.

However, it is important to note that this by no means implies a classic heroic image of entrepreneurship in the sense of the Schumpeterian entrepreneur. Instead, an understanding of entrepreneurship has emerged that emphasizes resilience, perseverance, and learning. Seen in this light, successful entrepreneurship is characterized by certain robustness in the sense of resilience and the ability to keep motivating oneself and learning from mistakes despite the very real possibility of failure in the future (Faradjollahi, 2019; Fischer et al., 2016; Hallak et al., 2018). In addition, there is a high degree of self-reflection, especially when questioning one's ideas, strategy, or business model; the ability to provide feedback and evaluate various external and internal suggestions and ideas concerning the most important and strategically relevant points; or the ability to create and foster a corporate culture that values learning and ideational and conceptual heterogeneity in the founder or top management teams (Rauch & Frese, 2008). Thus, the paradigm gained from the expert interviews differs from the lonely, heroic entrepreneur.

This explorative, qualitative study further suggests that the overall group of personality characteristics has the most significant influence on the success of a digital start-up in the view of German VC investors compared to the groups of contextual or business model characteristics. The focus on e-entrepreneurship, which can break down the spatial dependence of companies in general and digital companies in particular (Arlott et al., 2019, pp. 6–7), could explain the comparatively low relevance of the entrepreneurial context.

Limitation and Outlook

This exploratory qualitative study provides an initiative suggestion for entrepreneurship research of entrepreneurial success at the micro-level that could have implications for future entrepreneurship and firm performance resources. It is also a contribution to the literature on the relationship between intellectual agility, entrepreneurial leadership, and innovation capability (Dabić et al., 2021a), on knowledge sharing and thus enhanced organizational learning in SMEs that can ultimately improve performance

(Anand et al., 2021), and on the positive effects of motivation and entrepreneurial energy on self-efficacy and thus on firm growth (Cardon & Kirk, 2015).

The main contribution of this study is to take a different perspective on digital start-ups and digital start-up entrepreneurs by choosing that of German VC investors. Experts' assessments of success characteristics instead of interviewing digital start-up entrepreneurs and their attitudes toward success resources provide a valuable perspective that has received little attention in the current literature. Moreover, since the experts interviewed are observers and practitioners who take financial risks and analyze the founders, their business models, and the entrepreneurial context, this perspective provides valuable new insights into each aspect.

Answering the two key research questions provides new findings regarding the model used by German VC investors to evaluate the future economic success of digital start-ups. In the context of the qualitative content analyses (Mayring, 2010) conducted, it can be concluded that motivation and entrepreneurial energy and willingness to learn are the essential resources determining success. These two personality characteristics can be seen as the basis of relevant action characteristics and expanding human capital. This finding is in line with those presented in Unger et al.'s (2011) meta-analysis. Furthermore, the entrepreneur can use his or her entrepreneurial energy to influence all other resources, including contextual and business model characteristics. Therefore, it is not surprising that the experts also rated the overall group of personality characteristics as most relevant for entrepreneurial success.

The research findings of the present study allow researchers and practitioners to consider the focal points in the implicit or explicit valuation model of German VC investors. Thus, start-up entrepreneurs can find empirical added value regarding developing a diversity of the top management or founding team. Furthermore, transferring the associated prerequisites of leadership skills and strategic thinking into a practical approach can be advantageous when seeking funding. However, it is important to keep in mind that a content analysis of qualitative data can only provide approximate results and that a follow-up study using quantitative data and larger sample size will need to be conducted to confirm the findings discussed here.

References

Acs, Z.J. (2010). High-impact entrepreneurship. In Z.J. Acs and D.B. Audretsch (Eds.), *Handbook of entrepreneurship research: An interdisciplinary survey* (pp. 165–182). Springer.

Aloulou, W. (2019). Entrepreneurship and innovation in the digitalization era. In K. Mezghani & W. Aloulou (Eds.), *Business transformations in the era of digitalization* (pp. 179–204). IGI Global.

Altinay, L., Kromidha, E., Nurmagambetova, A., Alrawadieh, Z., & Madanoglu, G.K. (2021). A social cognition perspective on entrepreneurial personality traits and intentions to start a business: Does creativity matter? *Management Decision*.

Anand, A., Muskat, B., Creed, A., Zutshi, A., & Csepregi, A. (2021). Knowledge sharing, knowledge transfer and SMEs: Evolution, antecedents, outcomes, and directions. *Personnel Review*.

Andersson, S. (2007). The entrepreneur's influence on firms' international behavior. In R.A. Ajami & M.M. Bear (Eds.), *The global enterprise: Entrepreneurship and value creation* (pp. 109–136). International Business Press.

Arlott, A., Henike, T., & Hölzle, K. (2019). Digital entrepreneurship and value beyond: Why to not purely play online. In R. Baierl, J. Behrens, & A. Brem (Eds.), *Digital entrepreneurship: Interfaces between digital technologies and entrepreneurship* (pp. 1–22). Springer.

Audretsch, D. (2012). *Entrepreneurship research. Management Decision, 50*(5), 755–764.

Blum, U., & Leibbrand, F. (2001). *Entrepreneurship und Unternehmertum: Denkstrukturen für eine neue Zeit*. Gabler.

Bogdanowicz, M. (2015). Digital entrepreneurship barriers and drivers: The need for a specific measurement framework. In *JRC Technical Report*. Publications Office of the European Union.

Bouwman, H., Nikou, S., & de Reuver, M. (2019). Digitalization, business models, and SMEs: How do business model innovation practices improve performance of digitalizing SMEs? *Telecommunications Policy, 43*(9).

Brockhoff, K. (2017). *Betriebswirtschaftslehre in Wissenschaft und Geschichte: Eine Skizze*. Gabler.

Cardon, M.S., & Kirk, C.P. (2015). Entrepreneurial passion as mediator of the self-efficacy to persistence relationship. *Entrepreneurship Theory & Practice, 39*, 1027–1050.

Cosenz, F., & Bivona, E. (2021). Fostering growth patterns of SMEs through business model innovation. A tailored dynamic business modeling approach. *Journal of Business Research, 130*, 658–669.

Cunningham, J.A., Menter, M., & Wirsching, K. (2019). Entrepreneurial ecosystem governance: A principal investigator-centered governance framework. *Small Business Economics, 52*(2), 545–562.

Dabić, M., Stojčić, N., Simić, M., Potocan, V., Slavković, M., & Nedelko, Z. (2021a). Intellectual agility and innovation in micro and small businesses: The mediating role of entrepreneurial leadership. *Journal of Business Research, 123*, 683–695.

Dabić, M., Vlačić, B., Kiessling, T., Caputo, A., & Pellegrini, M. (2021b). Serial entrepreneurs: A review of literature and guidance for future research. *Journal of Small Business Management*, 1–36.

Eckardt, S. (2015). *Messung des Innovations- und Intrapreneurship-Klimas: Eine Quantitativ-empirische Analyse*. Springer.

Faradjollahi, M. (2019). *Entrepreneurship und Scheitern aus psychologischer Sicht. Welche Rolle spielen Volition und Resilienz?* GRIN Verlag.

Ferreira, J.J., Fernandes, C.I., & Kraus, S. (2019). Entrepreneurship research: Mapping intellectual structures and research trends. *Review of Managerial Science, 13*(1), 181–205.

Fischer, R., Maritz, A., & Lobo, A. (2016). Does individual resilience influence entrepreneurial success? *Academy of Entrepreneurship Journal, 22*(2), 39–54.

Fueglistaller, U., Müller, C., & Volery, T. (2008). *Entrepreneurship Modelle, Umsetzung, Perspektiven (2nd ed.)*. Springer.

Ghezzi, A., & Cavallo, A. (2020). Agile business model innovation in digital entrepreneurship: Lean startup approaches. *Journal of Business Research, 110*, 519–537.

Granz, C., Henn, M., & Lutz, E. (2020). Research on venture capitalists' and business angels' investment criteria: A systematic literature review. In A. Moritz, J. Block, S. Golla, & A. Werner (Eds.), *Contemporary developments in entrepreneurial finance. FGF studies in small business and entrepreneurship* (pp. 105–136). Springer.

Hallak, R., Assaker, G., O'Connor, P., & Leed, C. (2018). Firm performance in the upscale restaurant sector: The effects of resilience, creative self-efficacy, innovation, and industry experience. *Journal of Retailing and Consumer Services, 40*(1), 229–240.

Hock-Doepgen, M., Clauss, T., Kraus, S., & Cheng, C.F. (2021). Knowledge management capabilities and organizational risk-taking for business model innovation in SMEs. *Journal of business research, 130,* 683–697.

Isenberg, D. (2011). The entrepreneurship ecosystem strategy as a new paradigm for economic policy: Principles for cultivating entrepreneurship. *Babson Entrepreneurship Project.*

Kraus, S., Berchtold, J., Palmer, C. & Filser, M. (2018). Entrepreneurial orientation: the dark triad of executive personality. *Journal of Promotion Management, 24*(5), 715–735.

Köhn, A. (2017). The determinants of startup valuation in the venture capital context: A systematic review and avenues for future research. *Management Review Quarterly, 68*(1), 3–36.

Kumar, K.B., & van Welsum, D.V. (2013). *Knowledge-based economies and basing economies on knowledge.* RAND Corporation.

Laar, E.V., Deursen, A.J.V., Dijk, J.A.V., & Haan, J.D. (2017). The relation between 21st-century skills and digital skills: A systematic literature review. *Computers in Human Behavior, 72,* 577–588.

Levie, J., Hart, M., & Anyadike-Danes, M. (2009). The effect of business or enterprise training on opportunity recognition and entrepreneurial skills of graduates and non-graduates in the UK. *Frontiers of Entrepreneurship Research, 29*(23), 1–12.

Mayring, P. (2010). *Qualitative Inhaltsanalyse. Grundlagen und Techniken.* Beltz Juventa.

McMullen, J.S., & Shepherd, D.A. (2006). Entrepreneurial action and the role of uncertainty in the theory of the entrepreneur. *Academy of Management Review, 3*1(1), 132–152.

Meyer, K. (2020). *Persönlichkeit, Selbststeuerung und Schlüsselkompetenzen erfolgreicher Unternehmerinnen.* Springer.

Mitchell, T.R., & Daniels, D. (2003). Motivation. In W.C. Borman, D.R. Ilgen, and R.J. Klimoski, (Eds.), *Handbook of psychology, volume twelve: Industrial and organizational psychology* (pp. 225–254). John Wiley.

Murnieks, C.Y., Cardon, M.S., Sudek, R., White, T.D., & Brooks, W.T. (2016). Drawn to the fire: The role of passion, tenacity, and inspirational leadership in angel investing. *Journal of Business Venturing, 31,* 468–484.

Najmaei, A., & Sadeghinejad, Z. (2019). Metacognition, entrepreneurial orientation, and firm performance. In A. Caputo & M.M. Pellegrini (Eds.), *The anatomy of entrepreneurial decisions: Past, present and future research directions* (pp. 79–115). Springer.

Nambisan, S. (2017). Digital entrepreneurship: Toward a digital technology perspective of entrepreneurship. *Entrepreneurship Theory and Practice, 41*(6), 1029–1055.

Obschonka, M., & Stuetzer, M. (2017). Integrating psychological approaches to entrepreneurship: The Entrepreneurial Personality System (EPS). *Small Business Economics, 49*(1), 203–231.

Osterwalder, A., & Pigneur, Y. (2010). *Business model generation: A handbook for visionaries, game changers, and challengers.* Wiley.

Pinder, C.C. (1998). *Work motivation in organizational behavior.* Prentice-Hall.

Rauch, A., & Frese, M. (2000). Psychological approaches to entrepreneurial success: A general model and an overview of findings. *International Review of Industrial and Organizational Psychology, 15,* 101–142.

Rauch, A., & Frese, M. (2008). A personality approach to entrepreneurship. In S. Cartwright and C. Cooper (Eds.), *The Oxford handbook of personnel psychology* (pp. 121–136). Oxford University Press.

Rövekamp, C. (2011). *Was unterscheidet erfolgreiche von weniger erfolgreichen Gründerinnen? Qualitaitve Längsschnittuntersuchung von Kleinstunternehmer/–innen. Dissertation.* Freie Universität Berlin.

Schumacher, N. (2022). The relevance of entrepreneurship ecosystems for start-up success: A venture capital perspective. In S. Baumann (Ed.), *Handbook on digital business ecosystems: Strategies, platforms, technologies, governance and societal challenges* (pp. 109–125). Edward Elgar.

Schumpeter, J.A. (1942). *Capitalism, socialism, and democracy.* Harper and Brothers.

Shepherd, D.A., Wennberg, K., Suddaby, R., & Wiklund, J. (2019). What are we explaining? A review and agenda on initiating, engaging, performing and contextualizing entrepreneurship. *Journal of Management, 45*(1), 159–196.

Unger, J.M., Rauch, A., Frese, M., & Rosenbusch, N. (2011). Human capital and entrepreneurial success: A meta-analytical review. *Journal of Business Venturing, 26*(3), 341–358.

Volkmann, C.K., Tokarski, K.O., & Grünhagen, M. (2010). *Entrepreneurship in a European perspective: Concepts for the creation and growth of new ventures*. Springer.

Welsh, J.A., & White, J.F. (1981). Small business ratio analysis: A cautionary note to consultants. *Journal of Small Business Management, 19*(4), 20–23.

Westhead, P., Ucbasaran, D., Wright, M., & Binks, M. (2005). Novice, serial, and portfolio entrepreneur behavior and contributions. *Small Business Economics, 25*, 109–132.

Wirtz, B.W. (2019). *Digital business models: Concepts, models, and the alphabet case study*. Springer.

Wood, M.S., McKelvie, A., & Haynie, J.M. (2014). Making it personal: Opportunity individuation and the shaping of opportunity beliefs. *Journal of Business Venturing, 29*, 252–272.

Zahra, S., Wright, M., & Abdelgawad, S. (2014). Contextualization and the advancement of entrepreneurship research. *International Small Business Journal, 32*(5), 479–500.

Part 5: **SMEs and their Stakeholders: The Role of Customers, Investors, Employees, Suppliers, Communities, Governments, Trade Associations, etc.**

Duane Windsor
26 The Multiple Responsibilities of SMEs and Entrepreneurs

Abstract: The goal of this chapter is to integrate multiple owner responsibilities into a new understanding of business applicable to practical implementation by small and medium-sized or mid-size enterprises (SMEs) and entrepreneurs. The chapter systematically investigates the theoretical and practical aspects of defining and implementing five key responsibilities: economic, environmental sustainability, ethical, social or community, and stakeholder. Economic responsibility embeds but is broader than profitability. This multiple-responsibility conceptualization differs markedly from the conventional agency theory for large and typically publicly traded corporations. Agency theory views profitability as the key management responsibility. In this chapter's proposed conception, profitability is an opportunity or incentive rather than a duty. The responsibilities form a five-bottom-line conception – separate from profitability. The SME owner(s) or entrepreneur(s) addresses a solution for a multiple-responsibility business by integrating personal values with external conditions in interacting with the multiple stakeholders of the business. The chapter concludes that a multiple-responsibility conception improves welfare and sustainability of firms, stakeholders, society, and the natural environment. Furthermore, embedding by owner intention at the outset is superior to retrofitting efforts.

Keywords: commercial entrepreneurs, ethics, responsibilities, SMEs, social entrepreneurs

Introduction

A better conception of medium-sized or mid-size enterprises (SMEs) and entrepreneurs is desirable. Understanding of SMEs and entrepreneurial new ventures has depended too heavily on the agency theory of the large or publicly traded business. This chapter proposes a multiple-responsibility alternative suitable for practical implementation by SMEs and entrepreneurs. A SME is an established business entity, even if comprised of only one person. An entrepreneur is an individual or sometimes a tiny partnership beginning a business. In either setting of established SME or entrepreneurial new ventures, issues of innovation, monopolization, and corporate social responsibility (CSR) or corporate social irresponsibility (CSIR) may occur. Ferreira et al. (2019) provide a bibliometric study of the scientific structure of entrepreneurship research and the organization of scholarship in the field. This chapter adds a

Duane Windsor, Jesse H. Jones Graduate School of Business, Rice University

https://doi.org/10.1515/9783110747652-027

topic to the six groups of underlying theories of entrepreneurship those authors identify.

The chapter argues that a better conception for SMEs and entrepreneurs involves the theoretical and practical aspects of defining and implementing five key responsibilities: economic, environmental sustainability, ethical, social or community, and stakeholder. The chapter integrates these multiple perspectives into a new understanding applicable to implementation by SMEs and entrepreneurs. This conceptualization differs markedly from the conventional agency theory for large and typically publicly traded corporations. Agency theory views profitability as the overriding management responsibility. The proposed conception views profitability as an outcome of effective integration of multiple responsibilities.

Profitability is embedded within the idea of economic responsibility. The responsibilities thus form a five-bottom-line conception – separate from profitability. The alternative to simultaneous fulfillment of multiple responsibilities is to formulate a weighting or prioritization solution reflecting the mission, strategy, and values of the SME or the entrepreneur. Mission, strategy, and values form the purpose of the SME for being or the entrepreneur's purpose for starting a business venture. The SME owner(s) or entrepreneur(s) addresses this solution by integrating personal values with external conditions in interacting with the multiple stakeholders of the business.

The remainder of the chapter proceeds as follows. The second section explains definitions and economic contributions of SMEs and entrepreneurs. The third section discusses the mindset for moral imagination. The fourth section explains the chapter's methodology. The subsequent section explains the conceptual framework for multiple responsibility. The concluding section includes a statement of limitations and directions for future research.

Definitions and Economic Contributions

To focus on the other four responsibilities, the analysis holds constant the economic contributions of business. The vital problem is not trade-off of responsibilities but integration and simultaneous achievement of all responsibilities to the extent feasible.

A SME is an established business entity, even if just an owner-operator or a business with a small number of employees, say under five or even ten, sometimes labeled a micro-enterprise. The set of SMEs comprises every firm that does not qualify on some criterion as a large business. There is no fixed criterion for distinguishing between large, medium, small, and micro-firms. Generally, but not necessarily, SMEs are privately owned and often family owned. Each country sets domestic standards for defining SMEs or micro-firms in statistical reporting, and country standards could vary between industries (Ward, 2020). The European Union (EU) uses an SME criterion of fewer than 250 employees; the US uses a higher measure, typically 500, but for some purposes up to 1,200 (Ward, 2020).

An entrepreneur, as distinct from an intrapreneur within an established firm, is an individual or small group of individuals engaged in starting a business entity, typically but not necessarily at a micro-scale. Even the sole owner-operator of an established single-person SME is in a different role from an individual entrepreneur. An entrepreneur bears the risk of a startup venture. An SME, at whatever scale, is an established venture, however temporarily.

A key step in this chapter's approach is to hold constant the economic contribution and thus profitability of the several types of business entities and actors to focus attention on the other four responsibilities.

SMEs comprise a vital component of the US economy. Entrepreneurs and intrapreneurs play a crucial role in innovation (Keilbach & Sanders, 2009). The functions of SMEs and entrepreneurs are underdeveloped in economic theory, focused on large and publicly traded corporations (Bianchi & Henrekson, 2005). Hitt et al.'s (2002) seminal work on strategic entrepreneurship contained no chapter explicitly addressing roles of ethics, responsibility, stakeholders, or sustainability. This observation is not a criticism. Lack of direct emphasis was understandable in a first effort to establish a new research direction emphasizing resources, innovation, alliances, networks, internationalism, leadership, and growth. The focus was on developing a "new mindset" about integrating entrepreneurship and strategy for wealth creation (Hitt et al., 2001). The idea of a new mindset remains highly relevant to understanding the multiple responsibilities of SMEs and entrepreneurs.

The most recently available census data on the US business report for 2017 stated that there were about 5,996,900 enterprises operating 7,860,674 establishments, with a total employment of 128,591,812 and a total annual payroll of a little over $6.73 trillion (US Census Bureau, 2021). The US approach categorizes enterprises with more than 500 employees as large. In the 2017 data, there were 20,139 such enterprises – only about one-third of one percent of total enterprises – operating 1,347,872 establishments or 17.1% of total establishments with just over 68 million employees or nearly 53% of employees and just over $4 trillion in annual payroll or almost 60% of payrolls.

Treating firms of less than 500 employees as SMEs, the category includes over 99% of US enterprises operating 82.9% of establishments and providing 47% of employment and 40% of annual payroll. Taking the smallest class reported – under five employees – as truly "micro," there were 3,698,086 firms or 61.7% of total firms operating 3,703,759 establishments or 47% of total establishments and providing just 4.6% of employment and 4.1% of annual payroll. Very few such "micro" firms operated more than one establishment.

Many SMEs are family-owned, and family enterprises can be quite large. The Conway Center for Family Business (n.d.) estimates from various sources that family businesses generate 64% of US gross domestic product, 62% of US employment, and 78% of new job creation. About one-third of the Fortune 500 companies are family-controlled.

Family businesses may be entrepreneurial in orientation and across generations (Zell-weger et al., 2012).

An entrepreneur opens a business and bears the risk of doing so. Initially, a startup is likely to be small, but entrepreneurial ventures may grow to become large enterprises – illustrated by Amazon, Facebook, and Google. Entrepreneurship may be productive, meaning privately and socially beneficial, unproductive meaning privately and socially wasteful, or destructive as illustrated by criminal enterprises or irresponsible businesses (Baumol, 1990; see Aeeni et al., 2019). Entrepreneurship may be essential in overcoming poverty (Bruton et al., 2013; Sutter et al., 2019). One explanation is that SMEs may tend to provide non-tradeable goods, meaning essentially local goods and services within a market area. Entrepreneurs may tend to offer tradeable goods to other market areas that generate incoming revenues. Lee and Rodrí-guez-Pose (2021) document this difference in a panel study of US cities from 2005 to 2015. They look at tradeable entrepreneurship versus non-tradeable entrepreneurship, this chapter making the possible association with localized SMEs. Tradeables generate income for non-entrepreneurs in the home area through a multiplier effect. In contrast, the economic benefits of localized non-tradeables are not significant enough empirically to reduce poverty.

The distinction between SMEs and large enterprises partly overlaps with the difference between privately owned and publicly traded businesses. There is no hard and fast rule; some quite large corporations may be privately owned. However, as a broad generalization, SMEs tend to be privately owned and large corporations tend to be publicly traded. The vital issue is that public ownership subjects the business to the agency theory of management: directors, executives, and employees are agents of the shareholders. The prevailing agency theorem is shareholder wealth maximization (Windsor, 2010). There is a continuing debate between adherents of shareholder capitalism and proponents of stakeholder capitalism. The shareholder theory emphasizes the primacy of the owners of a public corporation. The stakeholder theory, formulated in variants, emphasizes the importance of the multiple stakeholders of an enterprise.

The examination of responsibilities distinguishes most precisely between large, publicly traded corporations although such a business can be privately owned or closely held and smaller, privately owned companies although such a business can be publicly traded. For the purposes of this chapter, large public corporations and private SMEs are polar-opposite, ideal-types. The large public corporation strongly associates with the agency theory of shareholder wealth maximization; the SME more closely associates with its multiple stakeholders and particularly local communities of operation (Spence, 2016). The SME is more likely to be tied to place and community than the large public corporation. The entrepreneur, at the startup stage, positions in-between these two kinds of businesses. Whether an individual or small group, the entrepreneur may aim at a public offering and may be less concerned with a community than with key stakeholders essential to the business' success.

The Mindset for a Business

Moral imagination is limited for the agent but is the essential attribute of SMEs and entrepreneurs for long-term stakeholder support (Brown et al., 2023). Both the SME and the entrepreneur may more closely associate with ethics and social responsibility because of the more personal nature than most sizeable public corporations where business ethics become more impersonal and intertwined with legal considerations. The emphasis in this chapter is on the delineation of multiple responsibilities, which may be, in theory, applicable to all businesses – whether large or small, public or private, and on why SMEs and entrepreneurs may more closely associate with those responsibilities than large, publicly traded corporations. What may be most critical in this difference is the set of values and perceptions of the managers or owners.

A 2007 survey reported that 60% of family businesses think their ethical standards are more robust than competitors' standards. The same companies discuss ethical standards frequently with customers and employees and at board meetings (Conway Center for Family Business, n. d., citing MassMutual et al., 2007, p. 6). These firms are often embedded in their communities (MassMutual et al., 2007, p. 6).

The mindset for business, reinforced by the rising roles of social entrepreneurship and CSR, is changing with important implications for the conceptualization of SMEs and entrepreneurship. The definition of "wealth" is under reexamination in terms of reconceptualizing "organizational wealth" for all stakeholders (Post et al., 2002) and the relationship of economic wealth to social welfare. Addressing climate change is becoming an overriding consideration for all entrepreneurs and businesses. An essential feature of change since 2001 is the idea expressed by Dov Seidman, CEO of the ethics and compliance consulting firm LRN (LRN, 2019), that moral leadership is putting people first and sacrificing to do so. Seidman states that "moralware" is needed in addition to engineering and business model solutions (Friedman, 2018). The mindset for business is shifting from an economic conception of wealth toward a moral vision of welfare. The SME is the critical organizational form in this shift, rather than the publicly traded corporation. Entrepreneurs can significantly shape the founding values of the enterprise and choose among organizational forms.

The SME is often family-owned or closely held. The entrepreneur is most ideally suited for this change in mindset rather than the publicly traded and typically large corporation or the state-owned enterprise (SOE). Friedman (2007) exempted the private business, and, thus by extension, the entrepreneur from the constraints of the agency theory dominant in any CSR conception for the publicly traded corporation. Management agents are not strictly free to impose personal values on corporate decisions. A private business or entrepreneur is essentially as free as a household to make value choices. The B Corporation and hybrid organizations are not in bulk a substitute for how SMEs operate, as SMEs form the large count of businesses in the world. There is no agency problem in the SME; instead, there is a values choice. SMEs can lead the way rather than follow in values implementation. The conceptual/theoretical problem is to use the SME as a model for other organizational types such as publicly traded corporations, rather than vice versa. The chapter documents this view from the literature. Although SMEs may operate as multinational enterprises across national boundaries, the SME is typically a domestic and, often, a community-based business.

Methodology of the Chapter

The methodology draws on three sources: (1) logical development of the proposed conceptual/theoretical framing from the relevant literature; (2) an examination of the extant literature on SMEs and entrepreneurs, with particular attention on the relevant dimensions of ethics, social responsibility, stakeholder management, and sustainability; and (3) illustrations of what SMEs and entrepreneurs are doing. The theoretical focus is on the development of the conceptual framing for academics and practitioners. The practical focus is on assisting managers and owners in understanding values and implementation in economics, ethics, responsibility, sustainability, and citizenship. This chapter assembles the relevant literature into a conceptual and theoretical framework suitable for both researchers and practitioners. The chapter takes the perspective of SME owner(s) and entrepreneurs. The theoretical approach is what formal scholarship can recommend to the owner(s). The practical approach is about the values choices and implementation issues facing the owner(s). These two approaches are the contribution of the chapter (see Figure 26.1).

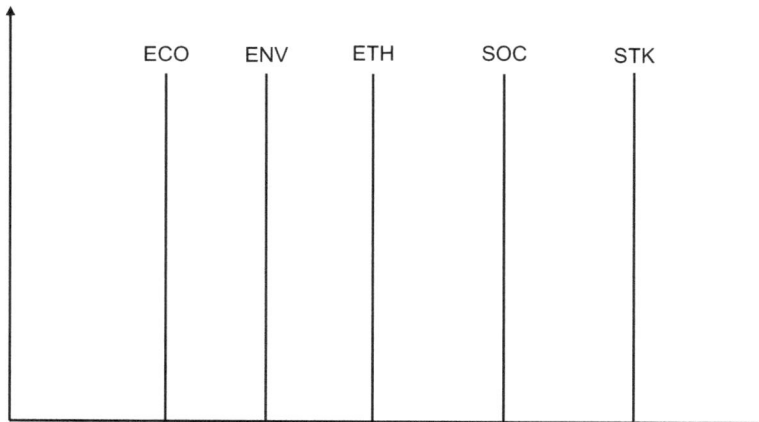

ECO = economic, ENV = environmental, ETH = ethical, SOC = society, STK = stakeholders

Figure 26.1: A depiction of the multiple bottom-line conception for SMEs and entrepreneurs.

Figure 26.1 displays five vertical lines. The vertical axis is the profitability, or wealth-generating outcome, of the business. The horizontal axis is flexible in its definition. For purposes of exposition, the chapter separates financial performance from economic responsibility. Each of the other vertical lines is one of the five responsibility bottom lines: economic, environmental, ethical, social, and stakeholder. The owner or manager has three decisions to make. The first is where to set profit or wealth on the vertical axis: high versus low. The second is to evaluate the relative importance of each additional bottom line: high versus low. The third is ordering the bottom lines from left to right across the horizontal axis: the initial arrangement shown in Figure 26.1 is alphabetical. Even at constant heights, one can emphasize relative ordering differently. The agency theory is straightforward: managers maximize the vertical axis, constrained by the power of the stakeholders, such as government enforcement of laws. SMEs and entrepreneurs have a mindset decision problem. They can choose to reduce profitability in favor of the other bottom lines, evaluate the relative importance of each bottom line, and order the sequence of their attention across the horizontal axis. Thus, one individual might regard sustainability as more important; another might regard the community as more important. For example, a social entrepreneur may increase the relative height of that bottom line by, in effect, reducing the relative size of the other bottom lines, as with profitability. An environmental activist may increase the relative height of that bottom line analogously, and so forth. In this formulation, economic – separated from profitability – means products and services for consumers, jobs, compensation for employees, and innovation for social welfare improvement. SMEs and entrepreneurs may elect to balance financial and non-financial considerations (Zellweger et al., 2013). On the other hand, entrepreneurs – and by extension SMEs – may be under pressure in corrupt contexts to practice bribery (Baron et al., 2018).

Business opportunities can be for profit or social benefit. There are new conceptions such as social entrepreneurship, new organizational forms such as benefit enterprises, and new ideas concerning entrepreneurial corporate social and environmental responsibilities (Alonso & Austin, 2018). Entrepreneurial ventures are initially private businesses – exempted from economic arguments against philanthropy but subject to, as public corporations, moral arguments against irresponsibility. The point of social entrepreneurship, as with government, is that markets cannot address everything necessary; there may be pervasive market failures calling for voluntary and governmental activities (Sandel, 2012; see also Figure 26.2).

A vital aspect of SMEs and entrepreneurship is combining personal benefits from commercial activities with a social purpose. Such combination or integration can occur along a spectrum, including hybrid organizational forms. Figure 26.2 explains a proposed spectrum of organizational types classified by internal purpose and external context. The depiction illustrates the key possibilities and is not an exhaustive logical or empirical typology. The polar-opposite endpoints of 100% pure private benefit and 100% pure social contribution are logical ideal-types. This spectrum – drawing on a

Continuum Defining Internal Purpose (Organizational Missions) (horizontal stub)

Continuum Defining External Context (vertical stub)	Private Benefit (100% Profit)	Hybrid Organizations ("Doing Well" and "Doing Good")		Social Purpose (100% Social Contribution)
	Commercial Entrepreneurship ("Doing Well")	From Business Enterprise toward Hybrid Organization	From Social Enterprise toward Hybrid Organization	Social Entrepreneurship ("Doing Good")
Market Context (Commercial Opportunities)	PRICES Public Corporation Private Business	CSR Orientation Community Supporter	Limited profit above cost of activity	USER CHARGES B-Corporation Social Enterprise State-Owned Enterprise
Non-Market Context (Market Failures)	[private benefit businesses cannot address market Failures]	[a social benefit orientation is required to address market failures]	Selling activity may be needed for financial sustainability	Nonprofit (voluntary) Organization (philanthropy) Government Agency (taxation)

Figure 26.2: A spectrum of organizational types classified by internal purpose and external context.

commonplace idea in the social entrepreneurship literature (Dees & Elias, 1998; Haigh et al., 2015) – combines two continuums for greater precision. The vertical continuum along the left stub of the figure distinguishes between market context meaning commercial opportunities for selling and non-market context reflecting market failures. The horizontal continuum along the top stub of the figure distinguishes among private benefit, hybrid organizations, and social purpose.

Market failure requires nonprofit organizations involving volunteerism dependent on philanthropy and government agencies drawing on tax revenues to provide goods and services that are not commercially feasible. Given market failure, commercial enterprises cannot operate unless subsidized as social agents. Enterprises – whether publicly traded, privately owned, or state-owned – sell to markets. There is a distinction between the "prices" and "user charges" used in Figure 26.2. Prices aim at rent extraction from demand; user charges aim at cost recovery. The former will dominate in commercial ventures (Strine, 2012). The latter may be necessary for social enterprises. A state enterprise is a government agency that sells to markets: it might operate on either a cost recovery or rent extraction principle.

A simple distinction between commercial and social entrepreneurship emphasizes purpose or mission (Kanter & Summers, 1987). Commercial entrepreneurship aims at profitable innovations for "doing well." Social entrepreneurship aims to improve social welfare, directly through stakeholders or indirectly through environmental improvement benefiting stakeholders by "doing good."

A hybrid organization pursues more than one purpose or mission simultaneously: "doing good" and "doing well." In a broad sense, a hybrid is an organization that does not pursue a strictly commercial or a purely social purpose. The horizontal continuum in Figure 26.2 may vary between 100% profit and 0% social contribution other than the wealth effects of the market economy or between 0% profit and 100% social contribution. There is a difference between the simultaneous pursuits of two or more purposes – "doing well" and "doing good" – and satisfaction of hierarchically ordered multiple purposes involving determining whether either "doing good" or "doing well" is more primary.

The relevant kinds of literature contrast two opposing conceptions of business. The economics and finance literature on the publicly traded corporation emphasizes profit-seeking and agency theories (Friedman, 2007; Jensen, 2010; Jensen & Meckling, 1976). A corporation's primary purpose is to generate profits for the shareholders (Jensen, 2010). The manager is a strictly fiduciary agent (Strine, 2012; Windsor, 2010). The ethics and CSR literature emphasize moral duties to avoid harming stakeholders and the natural environment, and practice corporate citizenship to improve stakeholder welfare and the natural environment (Carroll & Brown, 2018; Carroll & Shabana, 2010). In reality, CSR practices vary considerably across industries. A literature of 302 articles published from 1995 to 2014 in 99 academic journals establishes this wide variance (Dabic et al., 2016).

Privately owned ventures provide the opportunity to integrate these two conceptions. An entrepreneurial venture can be embedded at founding rather than retrofit ethics, social responsibility, stakeholder orientation, and environmental sustainability. The entrepreneurial team chooses a mission or purpose, from commercial to social entrepreneurship (Kay, 2018).

A Conceptual Framework for Integrating – Ethics, Social Responsibility, Stakeholders, and Sustainability

The conceptual framework explained in Figure 26.3 reformulates, adapts, and extends the work of Windsor (2013b). Generally, the figure structures as follows as the reader views the page. There is a vertical axis from top to bottom of the figure, across which, from left to right, there is a horizontal axis. On both left and right, the set of stakeholders appears above the horizontal axis, and environmental sustainability appears below the horizontal axis. As shown across the top, from left to right, the figure separates into zones or spheres for morality, legality, and good citizenship.

The vertical axis depicts an external environment at the top, a regulated market economy at the center, and a social welfare outcome at the bottom. The external environment and the regulated market economy comprise the institutional structure of a society. This society can be local, state or provincial, national, regional, or global in scope. The regulated market economy combines a market economy and a constitutional government, described in more detail as a set of regulatory laws and public pol-

MORALITY   LEGALITY   GOOD
(Business Ethics)   (Citizenship)   CITIZENSHIP

                    External Environment
                      of the Society

STAKEHOLDERS   STAKEHOLDERS
(people)   (people)
            social harm   social contribution
Negative Change ◄─────────┌──────────┐──────────► Positive Change
In Welfare   │ Regulated │   In Welfare
            environmental │ Market   │ environmental
              harm   │ Economy │ improvement
                          └──────────┘
SUSTAINABILITY   SUSTAINABILITY
(nature)   (nature)
                     Social Welfare
                       Outcomes
                     (instantaneous
                      equilibrium)

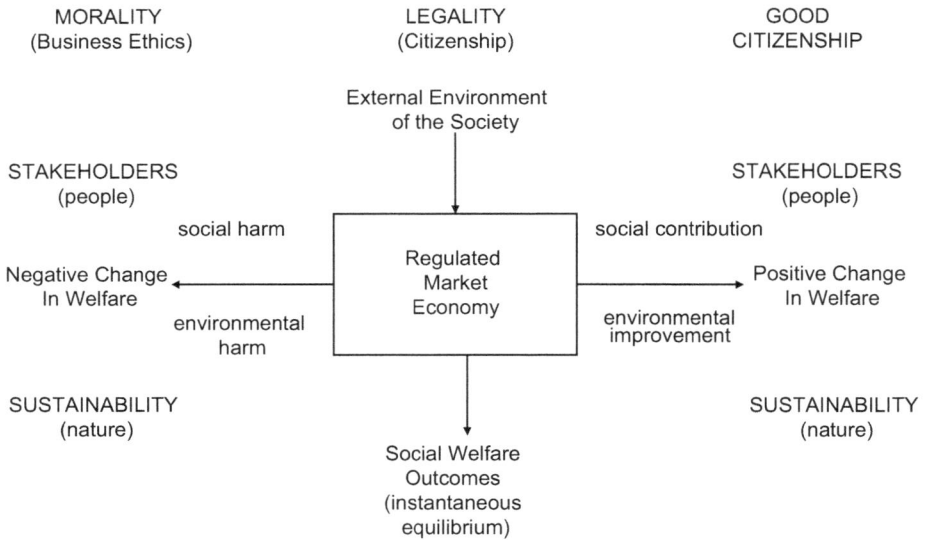

Figure 26.3: A conceptual framework for integrating multiple responsibilities of SMEs and entrepreneurs.

icies and a collection of public goods. Some governmental activities may reduce business profits, while other governmental activities may increase business profits. The
dynamic interaction of the dimensions of the institutional structure is a social welfare
outcome, defined as the aggregation of individuals' welfares, shown at the bottom of
the vertical axis. Technically, this outcome is an instantaneous or temporary equilibrium. Dynamically, as an element of the regulated market, the economy endogenously
changes or the society's environment exogenously changes, as does the social welfare
outcome. The vertical axis is dynamic over time, and a particular picture is a snapshot
of an instantaneous equilibrium.

Enterprises and entrepreneurs make decisions within the described setting. The
horizontal axis defines negative changes and positive changes to the social welfare outcome due to the separate actions of businesses. One could undertake a similar analysis
of the separate activities of individuals and organizations other than business or governmental and then aggregate all these separate actions into net effects. The focus of
this chapter is narrowly on companies, so attention restricts to this component. Left of
the regulated market economy is the set of negative impacts on social welfare; right of
the regulated market economy is the set of positive effects on social welfare.

The logic of Figure 26.3 facilitates the definition of the key concepts addressed in
this chapter. The figure divides executive judgment into three issues, each of which is
a different zone or sphere along the horizontal axis of negative and positive changes
to social welfare due to business decisions. The vertical axis is the zone of legality or
citizenship. To the left of the vertical axis is the zone of morality or business ethics. To
the right of the vertical axis is the area of good citizenship.

The zone of legality is restricted to or coincident with the vertical axis. A business should comply fully with the set of laws within the regulated market economy. The only exception to legal compliance is when the company has a moral objection to a particular law: such moral objection generates a problem in civil disobedience. One can think of laws in this context as prohibitions of misconduct.

To the left of the vertical axis, the zone of morality begins where the zone of legality ends. In effect, morality is voluntary self-regulation on a matter not addressed effectively by laws. The law, viewed as highly technical in details, may permit socially undesirable conduct. Friedman (2007) emphasized the moral foundations of business; while profit seeking, a business should engage in honest and non-fraudulent dealing. Economics and ethics do not disagree on the essential requirement for business ethics or morality, so defined. "Necessity" – for instance, business survival under intense competition – is not a justification of unethical business conduct such as lying, cheating, and stealing.

To the right of the vertical axis, the zone of good citizenship begins where the area of legality ends. Public policy provides guidance and seeks to influence behavior: it signals standards for good citizenship. Public policy commands positive behavior as distinct from legal prohibitions of misconduct. Whereas there is no "necessity" escape from business ethics, there is a significant question of reasonable limits to good citizenship. Society cannot properly command a business to destroy itself to provide goods and services for the general welfare.

In Figure 26.3, business ethics means not harming stakeholders or causing environmental damage. In general, business ethics also means legal compliance, except in instances of morally justifiable civil disobedience. Good citizenship (Matten & Crane, 2005) means figuring out how to make a social contribution for stakeholders or make environmental improvements – as distinct from avoiding causing harm. Adam Smith, in *The Theory of Moral Sentiments*, distinguished citizenship from good citizenship as follows: "He is not a citizen who is not disposed to respect the laws and obey the civil magistrate; and he is certainly not a good citizen who does not wish to promote, by every means in his power, the welfare of the whole society of his fellow-citizens" (Smith, 1759/1790, VI.ii.2, Paragraph 11).

This conceptual framework is compatible with the idea of the conventional four-step pyramid of CSR as redesigned by Kang and Wood (1995). Their foundation is ethics – corresponding to the zone of morality of Figure 26.3. The second step is legal compliance – corresponding to the zone of legality. The third step is economic performance – which in Figure 26.3 bundles with the regulated market economy. The fourth step, or apex, is discretionary philanthropy or altruism – expanded in Figure 26.3 to a broader conception of good citizenship. The redesign inverts the original four-step CSR pyramid formulated by Carroll (1991, p. 50). Carroll regarded economic responsibility as the foundation, followed by legal responsibility and ethical responsibility, with philanthropy at the apex. In Carroll's formulation, society requires economic and legal responsibilities, expects ethics, and desires philanthropy. Carroll (1991, pp. 51–55) distinguishes among immoral management, amoral management, and moral management. Immoral managers regard ethics and laws as barriers (Carroll, 1991, p. 52). Amoral managers lack awareness of ethics and are insensitive to harmful effects on others (Carroll, 1991, p. 54). Moral managers behave ethically, obey the laws, and act as good citizens (Carroll, 1991, p. 53). Each zone or sphere of Figure 26.3 has some moral aspect infused (Carroll, 1991, p. 49).

The shift in Figure 26.3 from the CSR pyramid formulations is to broaden the traditional idea of voluntary philanthropy to good citizenship, defined as promoting the general welfare. While desirable, philanthropy or altruism is not the defining characteristic.

Commercial entrepreneurship emphasizes profit seeking, subject to the constraint of doing no harm (Strine, 2012). Social entrepreneurship, reducing the importance of profit seeking, adds social contribution to doing no harm. The difference lies in motivation or purpose. Entrepreneurs, both commercial and social, help create the future (Waddock, 2008).

Ethics

Ethics here means doing no harm to stakeholders or the natural environment. Theranos, a private health technology firm, allegedly issued false claims concerning blood testing. These false claims harmed stakeholders. The reason is to draw a distinction with responsibility, which takes the meaning of good citizenship to improve stakeholder welfare and the natural environment. The combination takes the form of minimizing harm and maximizing benefit. Ethics and profit are not necessarily incompatible. The relationship between financial and social performance may be that an irresponsible business can be profitable, and a responsible business can be profitable.

Ethics is about personal values. "In response to stakeholder expectations of corporate social responsibility it is the chief executive officer's values and ethics, moderated by managerial discretion, that frame the firm's actions and ethics" (Sirsly, 2009, p. 78). The essential requirement at the founding of an entrepreneurial venture whether commercial or social in purpose is to define and implement moral integrity (Gintis & Khurana, 2007).

The absence of integrity underlies recent scandals at corporations (Treviño et al. 2014) such as DuPont polluting for decades, Siemens operating a global bribery scheme, Volkswagen defeating diesel emissions tests, and Wells Fargo manipulating customers' accounts. SMEs and entrepreneurs can select and prepare personnel and organizational climates in ways that are much more difficult for public corporations having to retrofit. There are many moral exemplars in business (Windsor, 2013a).

Social Responsibility

"Responsibility" can broadly mean ethics, defined here as doing no harm, legal compliance defined here as obeying all laws, and good citizenship. "Responsibility" stands in distinction to "irresponsibility" and means good citizenship beyond ethics and legal compliance. CSR is an argument concerning public corporations and not privately owned ventures. For this chapter, responsibility concerns society and community – in separation from ethics.

The agency theory leads to the restriction of CSR (Bosch-Badia et al., 2013) to voluntary activity that can be profitable, in the form of creating shared value (CSV) in which there is both profit and social benefit (Porter & Kramer, 2011). A widely cited definition of CSR is: ". . . actions that appear to further some social good, beyond the interests of the firm and what is required by law" (McWilliams & Siegel, 2001, p. 117). This definition, however, applies to a public corporation focused on profit seeking. Considerable scholarship has focused on why public corporations should practice CSR as distinct from ethics and legal compliance (Campbell, 2007). The definition does not apply to any private business, whether commercial or social, in orientation. The essential feature of this definition is a purely voluntary social contribution, at no profit and possibly at cost to the business. McWilliams and Siegel (2001) point out that a profitable CSR activity is simply a variety of a business project. They formulate a model of the firm in which CSR means costly activities that some stakeholder group is willing to support such that business profit remains constant. The approach excludes any relatively high-cost CSR initiative but not a low-cost reputational strategy or employee performance motivator.

Stakeholders

In August 2019, the Business Roundtable (2019) issued an updated "Statement on the Purpose of a Corporation" signed by 181 CEOs arguing against traditional shareholder wealth primacy. The Business Roundtable recommends five objectives: customer value delivery, employee investment, fair and ethical dealing with suppliers, community support, and long-term shareholder value generation. This multiple-objective framework draws on stakeholder theory, emphasizing five primary stakeholders: customers, employees, suppliers, communities, and shareholders.

Any business is dependent on the support and satisfaction of its stakeholders. Sound strategy creates value for all the stakeholders (Freeman & Elms, 2018) – a position endorsed by the Business Roundtable. In the stakeholder approach, responsible capitalism is the entrepreneurial creation of multiple values that obviate conflicts of interest among the stakeholders (Freeman, 2017). Relationships among stakeholders are dynamically evolving with changes in the business environment and entrepreneurial innovations.

An empirical study in Greece studied SMEs participating in CSR activities (Magrizos et al., 2021). The setting was the economic crisis in the Eurozone beginning in 2009 concerning the risk of sovereign debt. Several countries, including Greece, were unable to repay or refinance government debt. The study finding is that stakeholder considerations – specifically salience and proximity to the SME – moderated between

CSR and financial performance. The problem in such a crisis is how each SME prioritizes its stakeholders.

Sustainability

One of the crucial influences on the environmental commitment of entrepreneurs and executives is their perceptions of stakeholders (Henriques & Sadorsky, 1999). Sustainability is a broad term that includes three specific ideas. One idea is sustainable development. A second idea is planetary or environmental sustainability. A third idea is a sustainable business. These three ideas combine in the triple bottom line (TBL) framework. Social entrepreneurs may focus on social welfare or environmental sustainability. Commercial entrepreneurs emphasize sustainable business. Sustainable development requires the combination of the two foci – and the combination may prove very difficult to attain. The future for sustainable development may prove grim given world population growth and accelerating climate change. Entrepreneurship plays a crucial role in sustainable innovation.

Some airlines offer their passengers voluntary carbon offset contribution options. The net cost of the contribution to an individual or organization depends on tax deduction status. By an estimate (Geiling, 2014, drawing on 2009 data provided by Bofinger and Strand, 2013), the aviation industry contributes 2% of global carbon emissions, a New York City to San Francisco round-trip coach ticket accounts for two metric tons of carbon dioxide; and the transcontinental offset might be $5 to $6. The annual environmental impact and cost per person increases with frequent flying and first-class seating. Eco-activists urge air travelers to pay to offset their carbon emissions through these options. The carbon emission of an air trip is an unpriced negative externality.

Both the airline and the employer of a business traveler are shifting the negative externality of carbon emission to the individual traveler. The employer of a business traveler typically will not reimburse for the voluntary contribution. Eco-activists may pay the carbon offset or, in the extreme, not travel by air. However, most travelers will not personally agree to bear the carbon-offset cost. The problem is worse if a voluntary carbon emission offset is not tax-deductible. Under conditions in which an employer will not reimburse, and the contribution is not tax-deductible, the entire burden falls on the individual traveler as a moral choice.

Kraus et al. (2020) examine how environmental strategy and green innovation mediate between CSR and the environmental performance of the firm. They report that CSR does not influence environmental performance of large manufacturing firms: there is no direct relationship. However, CSR does have a positive relationship with environmental strategy and green innovation, which are the mediators between CSR and environmental performance. The mediators do have a significant positive effect on environmental performance. The findings come from a study of 297 large manufacturing firms in Malaysia.

Conclusion

This chapter commends embedding ethics, responsibility, stakeholder orientation, and environmental sustainability in SMEs and new entrepreneurial ventures to improve stakeholder welfare and sustainability of both firms and the natural environment. Embedding by intention at the outset is superior to retrofitting efforts.

Ethics means avoiding harm to stakeholders and the natural environment. Responsibility means improving stakeholder welfare and the natural environment. A commercial entrepreneur extends from business ethics toward corporate citizenship through CSR activities. A social entrepreneur has as a purpose such citizenship activities focused on stakeholders and sustainability.

All private businesses, including commercial entrepreneurs, are relieved from the fiduciary responsibility of agency theory commonly applied to public corporations (Friedman, 2007). Even if definable in practice, profit maximization is not a binding ethical or legal duty of directors and executives of a public corporation (Elhauge, 2005; Stout, 2012). Friedman (2007) states public corporations must comply with ethical and legal norms while permitting lobbying of governments and non-altruistic community investments supporting strategic advantage.

The Business Roundtable (2019) has adopted a multiple-objective purpose statement emphasizing welfares of primary stakeholders and shifting to a long-term view of shareholder value creation (Guerrera, 2009, citing Jack Welch, former CEO of General Electric).

Limitations of the Research

The approach in this chapter has some specific limitations. First, the methodology emphasizes logical or conceptual development in combination with a selected literature and certain illustrations supporting the multiple-responsibility framework. There is no formal empirical testing of the proposed approach. Second, there is no cross-country consideration. So, for instance, there is no inquiry into how family-owned businesses may vary across countries in which such businesses are very important. The methodology is effectively logical rather than empirical. Third, the reader must choose between the agency theory of the publicly traded business and the proposed multiple-responsibility approach for SMEs and entrepreneurs. The two conceptions may not translate very easily across different types of businesses.

Recommendations for Future Research

The chapter focuses on two specific targets. One target is to draw on extant formal scholarship to develop the multiple-responsibility conception for SMEs and entrepreneurs. A second target is to make that conception compatible with the value choices and implementation for owners. The chapter's argument is that multiple-responsibility choices are easier for owners of SMEs to make, and particularly at the formation of the business. The approach developed in this chapter suggests several directions for future research efforts.

One research direction, empirical in character, should address the motives and intentions of SME owners and entrepreneurs. Since these individuals, or small groups of individuals, make the choice, it is important to study motives for choosing between profit seeking and multiple responsibilities. Another research direction, also empirical in character, should address cross-country, cross-industry, and cross-business-type variations. We do not know enough about these differences.

A third research direction is theoretical in orientation. Important scholarship remains to be undertaken into the theory of the firm. The agency theory of the publicly traded business, emphasizing profit seeking for owners, tends to dominate scholarly understanding of whether owners of SMEs and entrepreneurs also seek profit primarily or understand multiple responsibilities. The argument of the chapter is that a multiple-responsibility conception is more readily compatible with SMEs and entrepreneurial ventures.

A fourth research direction is partly empirical and partly theoretical. The chapter's conception is simultaneous fulfilment of multiple responsibilities. However, research should be undertaken into whether empirical reality causes at the early stage of SME or entrepreneurial venture formation focus on profitability for survival, and that it is profitability that facilitates subsequent addressing of additional responsibilities. The chapter's argument is that it would be easier to imprint multiple responsibilities at the outset rather than attempting to retrofit, but empirical reality could compel profit orientation followed by retrofitting, depending on specific conditions for each business.

References

Aeeni, Z., Motavaseli, M., Sakhdari, K., & Dehkordi, A.M. (2019). Baumol's theory of entrepreneurial allocation: A systematic review and research agenda. *European Research on Management and Business Economics*, *25*(1), 30–37. https://doi.org/10.1016/j.iedeen.2018.09.001

Alonso, A.D., & Austin, I.P. (2018). Entrepreneurial CSR, managerial role and firm resources: A case study approach. *Competitiveness Review: An International Business Journal*, *28*(4), 368–385. https://doi.org/10.1108/CR-10-2016-0064

Baron, R.A., Tang, J., Tang, Z., & Zhang, Y. (2018). Bribes as entrepreneurial actions: Why underdog entrepreneurs feel compelled to use them. *Journal of Business Venturing*, *33*(6), 679–690. https://doi.org/10.1016/j.jbusvent.2018.04.011

Baumol, W.J. (1990). Entrepreneurship: Productive, unproductive, and destructive. *Journal of Political Economy*, *98*(5, Part 1), 893–921. https://doi.org/10.1086/261712

Bianchi, M., & Henrekson, M. (2005). Is neoclassical economics still entrepreneurless? *Kyklos, 58*(3), 353–377. https://doi.org/10.1111/j.0023-5962.2005.00292.x

Bofinger, H., & Strand, J. (2013, May). Calculating the carbon footprint from different classes of air travel. *World Bank Policy Research Working Paper* (6471). http://documents.worldbank.org/curated/en/1411851468168853188/pdf/WPS6471.pdf

Bosch-Badia, M.T., Montllor-Serrats, J., & Tarrazon, M.A. (2013). Corporate social responsibility from Friedman to Porter and Kramer. *Theoretical Economics Letters, 3*(3A), 11–15. http://dx.doi.org/10.4236/tel.2013.33A003

Brown, J.A., Forster, W.R., & Wicks, A.C. (2023). The fork in the road for social enterprises: Leveraging moral imagination for long-term stakeholder support. *Entrepreneurship Theory and Practice, 47*(1), 91–112 https://doi.org/10.1177/10422587211041485

Bruton, G.D., Ketchen Jr, D.J., & Ireland, R.D. (2013). Entrepreneurship as a solution to poverty. *Journal of Business Venturing, 28*(6), 683–689. https://doi.org/10.1016/j.jbusvent.2013.05.002

Business Roundtable. (2019). *Business roundtable redefines the purpose of a corporation to promote 'an economy that serves all Americans'. Business Roundtable.* https://www.businessroundtable.org/business-roundtable-redefines-the-purpose-of-a-corporation-to-promote-an-economy-that-serves-all-americans

Campbell, J.L. (2007). Why would corporations behave in socially responsible ways? An institutional theory of corporate social responsibility. *Academy of Management Review, 32*(3), 946–967. https://doi.org/10.2307/20159343

Carroll, A.B. (1991). Stakeholder thinking in three models of management morality: A perspective with strategic implications. In J. Näsi (Ed.), *Understanding stakeholder thinking* (pp. 47–74). LSR-Julkaisut Oy.

Carroll, A.B., & Brown, J.A. (2018). Corporate social responsibility: A review of current concepts, research, and issues. In *Corporate social responsibility (Business and Society 360, Vol. 2)* (pp. 39–69). Emerald Publishing Limited. https://doi.org/10.1108/S2514-175920180000002002

Carroll, A.B., & Shabana, K.M. (2010). The business case for corporate social responsibility: A review of concepts, research and practice. *International Journal of Management Reviews, 12*(1), 85–105. https://doi.org/10.1111/j.1468-2370.2009.00275.x

Conway Center for Family Business. (n. d.). Family Business Facts. Retrieved April 19, 2023 from https://www.familybusinesscenter.com/resources/family-business-facts/

Dees, J.G., & Elias, J. (1998). Review: The challenges of combining social and commercial enterprise. Book review of *University-business partnerships: An assessment,* by Norman E. Bowie, Lanham, MD: Rowman & Littlefield Publishers, Inc.,1994. *Business Ethics Quarterly, 8*(1), 165–178. www.jstor.org/stable/3857527

Dabic, M., Colovic, A., Lamotte, O., Painter-Morland, M., & Brozovic, S. (2016). Industry-specific CSR: Analysis of 20 years of research. *European Business Review, 28*(3), 250–273. https://doi.org/10.1108/EBR-06-2015-0058

Elhauge, E. (2005). Sacrificing corporate profits in the public interest. *New York University Law Review, 80*(3), 733–869. https://www.nyulawreview.org/wp-content/uploads/2018/08/NYULawReview-80-3-Elhauge.pdf

Ferreira, J.J., Fernandes, C.,I., & Kraus, S. (2019). Entrepreneurship research: Mapping intellectual structures and research trends. *Review of Managerial Science, 13*(1), 191–205. https://doi.org/10.1007/s11846-017-0242-3

Freeman, R.E. (2017). The new story of business: Towards a more responsible capitalism. *Business and Society Review, 122*(3), 449–465. https://doi.org/10.1111/basr.12123

Freeman, R.E., & Elms, H. (2018). The social responsibility of business is to create value for stakeholders. *MIT Sloan Management Review, 4.* https://sloanreview.mit.edu/article/the-social-responsibility-of-business-is-to-create-value-for-stakeholders/

Friedman, M. (2007). The social responsibility of business is to increase its profits. In *Corporate ethics and corporate governance* (pp. 173–178). Springer. Reprinted from *New York Times Magazine* (September 13, 1970).

Friedman, T. (2018, April 2). How Mark Zuckerberg can save Facebook – and us. *The New York Times.* https://content.lrn.com/blog/dov-seidman-quoted-in-nyt-opinion-by-thomas-friedman-how-mark-zuckerberg-can-save-facebook-and-us#

Geiling, N. (2014). *Can eco-conscious travelers do anything to fly green?* Smithsonian.com, August 11. https://www.smithsonianmag.com/travel/if-you-travel-and-care-about-environment-you-should-buy-carbon-offsets-180952222/

Gintis, H., & Khurana, R. (2007). Corporate honesty and business education: A behavior model. In P.J. Zak (Ed.), *Moral markets: The critical role of values in the economy* (pp. 300–327). Princeton University Press.

Guerrera, F. (2009, March 12). Welch condemns share price focus. *Financial Times 12.* https://www.ft.com/content/294ff1f2-0f27-11de-ba10-0000779fd2ac

Haigh, N., Walker, J., Bacq, S., & Kickul, J. (2015). Hybrid organizations: Origins, strategies, impacts, and implications. *California Management Review, 57*(3), 5–12. https://doi.org/10.1525/cmr.2015.57.3.5

Henriques, I., & Sadorsky, P. (1999). The relationship between environmental commitment and managerial perceptions of stakeholder importance. *Academy of Management Journal, 42*(1), 87–99. https://doi.org/10.5465/256876

Hitt, M.A., Ireland, R.D., Camp, S.M., & Sexton, D.L. (2001). Strategic entrepreneurship: Entrepreneurial strategies for wealth creation. *Strategic Management Journal, 22*(6–7), 479–491. https://doi.org/10.1002/smj.196

Hitt, M.A., Ireland, R.D., Camp, S.M., & Sexton, D.L. (Eds.). (2002). *Strategic entrepreneurship: Creating a new mindset.* Wiley-Blackwell.

Jensen, M.C. (2010). Value maximization, stakeholder theory, and the corporate objective function. *Journal of Applied Corporate Finance, 22*(1), 32–42. https://doi.org/10.1111/j.1745-6622.2010.00259.x

Jensen, M.C., & Meckling, W.H. (1976). Theory of the firm: Managerial behavior, agency costs and ownership structure. *Journal of Financial Economics, 3*(4), 305–360. https://doi.org/10.1016/0304-405X(76)90026-X

Kang, Y.C., & Wood, D.J. (1995). Before-profit corporate social responsibility: Turning the economic paradigm upside-down. In *Proceedings of the International Association for Business and Society* (Vol. 6, pp. 809–829). DOI: 10.5840/iabsproc1995672

Kanter, R.M., & Summers, D.V. (1987). Doing well while doing good: Dilemmas of performance measurement in nonprofit organizations and the need for a multiple-constituency approach. In W.W. Powell (Ed.), *The nonprofit sector: A research handbook* (pp. 154–166). Yale University Press.

Kay, J. (2018, May 3). *Theories of the firm.* https://www.johnkay.com/2018/05/03/theories-of-the-firm/

Keilbach M., & Sanders M. (2009). The contribution of entrepreneurship to economic growth. In M. Keilbach, J.P. Tamvada, & D.B. Audretsch (Eds.), *Sustaining entrepreneurship and economic growth* (pp. 7–25). Springer. DOI: 10.1007/978-0-387-78695-7_1

Kraus, S., Rehman, S.U., & García, F.J.S. (2020). Corporate social responsibility and environmental performance: The mediating role of environmental strategy and green innovation. *Technological Forecasting and Social Change, 160*, 120262. https://doi.org/10.1016/j.techfore.2020.120262

Lee, N., & Rodríguez-Pose, A. (2021). Entrepreneurship and the fight against poverty in US cities. *Environment and Planning A: Economy and Space, 53*(1), 31–52. https://doi.org/10.1177/0308518X20924422

LRN. (2019). *The state of moral leadership in business: HOW Metrics®: New metrics for a reshaped world – Rethinking the source of resiliency, innovation, and growth.* https://content.lrn.com/research-insights/moral-leadership-report-2019

Magrizos, S., Apospori, E., Carrigan, M., & Jones, R. (2021). Is CSR the panacea for SMEs? A study of socially responsible SMEs during economic crisis. *European Management Journal 39*(1), 291–303 https://doi.org/10.1016/j.emj.2020.06.002

MassMutual Financial Group, Kennesaw State University, and Family Firm Institute. (2007). American Family Business Survey. Retrieved April 19, 2023 from https://www.uvm.edu/sites/default/files/2007MassMutualAmericanFamilyBusinessSurvey.pdf

Matten, D., & Crane, A. (2005). Corporate citizenship: Towards an extended theoretical conceptualization. *Academy of Management Review, 30*(1), 166–179. https://doi.org/10.2307/20159101

McWilliams, A., & Siegel, D. 2001. Corporate social responsibility: A theory of the firm perspective. *Academy of Management Review, 26*(1), 117–127. https://doi.org/10.2307/259398

Porter, M.E., & Kramer, M.R. (2011). Creating shared value: Redefining capitalism and the role of the corporation in society. *Harvard Business Review, 89*(1/2), 62–77. https://hbr.org/2011/01/the-big-idea-creating-shared-value

Post, J.E., Preston, L.E., & Sauter-Sachs, S. (2002). *Redefining the corporation: Stakeholder management and organizational wealth*. Stanford University Press.

Sandel, M.J. (2012). *What money can't buy: The moral limits of markets*. Farrar, Straus and Giroux.

Sirsly, C.A.T. (2009). 75 years of lessons learned: Chief executive officer values and corporate social responsibility. *Journal of Management History, 15*(1), 78–94. https://doi.org/10.1108/17511340910921808

Smith, A. (1759/1790). *The theory of moral sentiments*, sixth edition, 1790, London: Printed for A. Strahan; and T Cadell in the Strand; T. Creech, and J. Bell & Co. in Edinburgh *(originally published in 1759)*.

Spence, L.J. (2016). Small business social responsibility: Expanding core CSR theory. *Business & Society, 55*(1), 23–55. https://doi.org/10.1177/0007650314523256

Stout, L.A. (2012). *The shareholder value myth: How putting shareholders first harms investors, corporations, and the public*. Berrett-Koehler Publishers.

Strine Jr, L.E. (2012). Our continuing struggle with the idea that for-profit corporations seek profit. *Wake Forest Law Review, 47*, 135–172. http://www.wakeforestlawreview.com/wp-content/uploads/2014/10/Strine_LawReview_4.12.pdf

Sutter, C., Bruton, G.D., & Chen, J. (2019). Entrepreneurship as a solution to extreme poverty: A review and future research directions. *Journal of Business Venturing, 34*(1), 197–214. https://doi.org/10.1016/j.jbusvent.2018.06.003

Treviño, L.K., den Nieuwenboer, N.A., & Kish-Gephart, J.J. (2014). (Un)ethical behavior in organizations. *Annual Review of Psychology, 65*, 635–660.

US Census Bureau, Statistics of US Businesses (2021, May). Number of firms, number of establishments, employment, and annual payroll by small enterprise employment sizes for the United States and states, NAICS sectors: 2017. https://www.census.gov/data/tables/2017/econ/susb/2017-susb-annual.html

Waddock, S. (2008). *The difference makers: How social and institutional entrepreneurs created the corporate social responsibility movement*. Routledge.

Ward, S. (2020, June 29). What Are SMEs? Definitions and examples of SMEs. https://www.thebalancesmb.com/sme-small-to-medium-enterprise-definition-2947962

Windsor, D. (2010). Shareholder wealth maximization. In J.R. Boatright (Ed.), *Finance ethics: Critical issues in theory and practice* (pp. 437–455). Wiley.

Windsor, D. (2013a). A typology of moral exemplars in business. In *Moral saints and moral exemplars* (pp. 63–95). Emerald Group Publishing. https://doi.org/10.1108/S1529-2096(2013)0000010008

Windsor, D. (2013b). Corporate social responsibility and irresponsibility: A positive theory approach. *Journal of Business Research, 66*(10), 1937–1944. https://doi.org/10.1016/j.jbusres.2013.02.016

Zellweger, T.M., Nason, R.S., & Nordqvist, M. (2012). From longevity of firms to transgenerational entrepreneurship of families: Introducing family entrepreneurial orientation. *Family Business Review, 25*(2), 136–155. https://doi.org/10.1177/0894486511423531

Zellweger, T.M., Nason, R.S., Nordqvist, M., & Brush, C.G. (2013). Why do family firms strive for nonfinancial goals? An organizational identity perspective. *Entrepreneurship Theory and Practice, 37*(2), 229–248. https://doi.org/10.1111/j.1540-6520.2011.00466.x

Lise Aaboen, Elsebeth Holmen, and Ann-Charlott Pedersen

27 Exploring Early Customer Portfolios of Start-ups: Capturing Patterns of Relationship Development States

Abstract: This chapter explores patterns of relationship development states in the early customer portfolios of start-ups. Our theoretical framework combines literature on customer portfolios and relationship development states. We use this framework to analyze data on customer relationship development captured through interviews with 20 start-ups. Our main contribution is that we identify four patterns in the portfolios of customer relationship development states: Paradise lost, Pearls on a string, Picture perfect, and Persuasion. Start-up managers can use these patterns to map their current customer portfolio, to assess the degree of fit between their current customer portfolio and their strategy, and to provide input on how to strategize in a resource-efficient manner to achieve such a fit. To our knowledge, this is the first study to combine the literature on relationship development states with that on customer portfolios.

Keywords: start-up, portfolio, customer, relationship, development, state, pattern

Introduction

Start-ups are important for national economies because they create employment and enable technology transfer (Storey & Tether, 1998). These companies have been studied from several different perspectives, such as the resource-based view, the business model perspective, and the institutional perspective (Mustar et al., 2006). Some studies have concentrated on the importance of single resources, particularly venture capital (e.g., Bertoni et al., 2011), or genetic characteristics, such as whether the origin is academic or non-academic (e.g., Colombo & Piva, 2012), that can determine the future development of a start-up. Common to many studies on start-ups is the goal of identifying success factors and understanding why some start-ups grow and others do not.

When the research field of entrepreneurship and start-ups shifted from internal factors toward an increased emphasis on external factors and development processes as explanatory factors for growth, the field became more closely connected to research from the Industrial Marketing and Purchasing (IMP) perspective (Snehota, 2011), which underscores the value of buyer-supplier relationships (see, e.g., Axelsson

Lise Aaboen, Elsebeth Holmen, Ann-Charlott Pedersen, Department of Industrial Economics and Technology Management, Norwegian University of Science and Technology, Trondheim, Norway

https://doi.org/10.1515/9783110747652-028

& Easton, 1992; Ford et al., 2003; Gadde & Håkansson, 2001; Håkansson, 1982; Håkansson et al., 2009; Håkansson & Snehota, 1995). In the IMP perspective, these relationships are often defined as "mutually oriented interaction[s] between two reciprocally committed partners" (Håkansson & Snehota, 1995, p. 25). Each relationship can be viewed as a set of connected exchange episodes, and each episode is limited in time and may concern, for instance, the production of deliveries, joint development projects, product tests, or negotiations of long-term contracts (Håkansson, 1982). In addition, each episode is assumed to be affected by the relationship of which it forms a part, and each episode, in turn, affects the relationship itself. In complex relationships between buying and supplying organizations, what is exchanged is created in the interaction between the parties and, hence, is variable (Håkansson, 1982).

Consequently, a start-up forms its network and develops its products and services, as well as its strategic direction and position, in interaction with its early customers (cf. Aaboen et al., 2011). Within the IMP perspective, relationships differ in part due to divergent relationship dynamics, being either at different predetermined stages of development (Ford, 1980) or in undetermined states of development (Batonda & Perry, 2003). To explore relationship development patterns in early customer portfolios, we pose the following research question: how can customer relationship development states create patterns in the early customer portfolios of start-ups?

The early customers of a start-up constitute its "early customer portfolio." Since this portfolio is what enables the start-up to attain its position in the network, develop products and services, and devise its strategy, it seems likely that part of the explanation for how the start-up develops can be found in the early customer portfolio. In the early customer portfolio concept, we include a small set of early customer relationships. For a relationship to be a customer relationship, the start-up must intend to develop it such that the other actor becomes a buying customer.

To answer our research question, we present in Section 2 the theoretical framework consisting of customer portfolio literature and literature on relationship development states and then combine the two in an analytical framework for studying patterns of customer relationship development states in the early customer portfolio. To our knowledge, the customer portfolio literature and relationship development state literature have not been combined and explored in this context before. When applying the framework to empirical data on 20 start-ups, four different patterns of the customer relationship development states in the portfolio emerge: Paradise lost, Pearls on a string, Picture perfect, and Persuasion. Thereby, the present chapter contributes to previous start-up studies applying the IMP perspective (e.g., Aaboen et al., 2011; Baraldi et al., 2019; Bjørgum et al., 2021; Ciabuschi et al., 2012; Ingemansson & Waluszewski, 2009; La Rocca et al., 2013; La Rocca et al., 2019; Santos & Mota, 2020; Snehota, 2011) by exploring early customer relationships as a portfolio with a focus on relationship development states, connecting relationship dynamics to a start-up's early strategizing.

Theoretical Framework

A few previous studies examined the early customer portfolios of start-ups. Grossman et al. (2012) studied portfolios with individuals as the level of analysis, focusing on whom the entrepreneurs want to include in their network. Phillips et al. (2013) studied the customer relationship portfolio of one entrepreneur and found that this entrepreneur tended to initiate relationships characterized by similarities, making it easier to develop the relationships further. In other words, the portfolio became heterogeneous even though it consisted of homophilous relationships. Ozcan and Eisenhardt (2009) focused on high-performing customer portfolios. They argued that these portfolios can be created by initiating several relationships simultaneously and visualized the context of the start-up. Sigfusson and Harris (2013) studied relationship portfolio development over time along the dimensions of strength of the relationship and degree of embeddedness of the parties in foreign markets. They concluded that start-ups with no domestic market move toward developing stronger relationships over time. Kapoor and Lee (2013) connected the choice of coordination (arm's-length vs. alliances) to the start-up's strategy and found linkages between the two in their statistical analysis. Despite the previous interest in early customer portfolios in the literature, there were no suitable frameworks for our research purpose. In this section, we therefore combine portfolio models with customer relationship states into a framework for analyzing the portfolios of customer relationship states in start-ups.

Portfolio Models

Portfolio analysis entails identifying several dimensions along which a set of items (whether businesses, projects, or customers) can be arranged. By dividing the dimensions into sub-dimensions, different categories emerge. Hence, portfolio analysis provides an overview of the distribution of this set of items among different categories. For some portfolios, a balanced distribution is preferable; for others, some categories are to be avoided. In addition to serving the purpose of classifying and overviewing the distribution of the set, portfolio analysis is often used as a point of departure for choosing which strategies to apply for the items in each category, for allocating resources among items in the different categories, or for formulating ideas for moving items from one category to another.

 Among the most widely known portfolio models is the BCG business portfolio (Hedley, 1977). Based on the two dimensions of business growth rate and relative competitive position, the BCG matrix allows for identifying differences in the financial characteristics and strategic options for further development among businesses in a corporation. Having identified how businesses are scattered across the different quadrants in the matrix, corporate managers can assess whether the business portfolio is presently sound or unbalanced and consider how to best manage and develop the portfolio. Portfolio analysis has also entered other management disciplines. For example, companies can analyze their product portfolio (Day, 1977), service portfolio (Rosemann, 2010), brand portfolio (Aaker, 2009), project portfolio (Archer & Ghasemzadeh, 1999), product innovation portfolio (Cooper et al., 1999), customer portfolio (Woodside, 1996), supplier and supplier relationship portfolio (Bensaou, 1999; Olsen & Ellram, 1997), account portfolio (Fiocca, 1982), customer relationship portfolio (Johnson & Selnes, 2004), R&D partnership portfolio (Frankort et al., 2012), or alliance portfolio (Greve et al., 2014; Lavie, 2007; Mohr et al., 2014).

Acknowledging the importance of relationships to a company's profitability and strategic development, some research has paid attention to relationship portfolios. According to Ritter et al. (2004), a firm's relationship portfolio consists of the direct relationships in which it is simultaneously engaged. While portfolio analysis models may focus on relationships of any type, most relationship portfolio models concentrate on one particular counterpart – either the supplier relationship or customer relationship portfolio. Several models for analyzing customer relationship portfolios have been suggested. For reviews of these models and the suggested dimensions and categories see, for example, Zolkiewski and Turnbull (2002) and Sanchez and Sanchez (2005). While the suggested dimensions differ, many models seem to incorporate some elements related to the strategic importance of the relationship for the company and aspects of attractiveness and profitability related to costs to serve customers, benefits, profit contribution, or volume.

Relationship Development States

Characteristics of business relationships and how such relationships may develop over time have been studied for decades (cf. Håkansson, 1982). In the literature on relationship development and initiation processes, different models for describing the evolution of a business relationship have been suggested – in particular, stage models or states models – where initiation is captured by the first and/or second phase of the development process (see, e.g., Aarikka-Stenroos, 2008; Batonda & Perry, 2003; Dwyer et al., 1987; Edvardsson et al., 2008; Ford, 1980; Holmen et al., 2005; Wilson, 1995). The most well-known and cited stage model was proposed by Ford in 1980. The model is based on the IMP perspective and takes its point of departure in exchange episodes between buying and selling firms. The model has five stages: (1) the pre-relationship stage; (2) the early stage; (3) the development stage; (4) the long-term stage; and (5) the final stage. Each stage is characterized by five important dimensions: experience, uncertainty, distance, commitment, and adaptation. Similar stage models have been developed, for example, by Dwyer et al. (1987) and Wilson (1995). For a review, see Batonda and Perry (2003). However, stage models have been criticized for emphasizing deterministic paths: "The principal focus has been that relationship development in inter-firm networks occurs in sequential/incremental and irreversible stages" (Batonda & Perry, 2003, p. 1459). Other critical issues concern difficulties in defining the boundaries between stages and stage models not taking into account the complexity of the network in which the relationship develops.

In contrast to stage models, states models assume that the relationship development process is not predetermined and does not necessarily progress in an orderly manner over time. Rather, relationships can move from one state to another in a random fashion, including jumping from the start to the end (Ford & Rosson, 1982). Batonda and Perry's (2003) frequently cited states model contains five states resembling the classical stages: (1) searching process; (2) starting process; (3) development process; (4) ongoing maintenance process; and (5) termination process (this last state is lacking in many stage models but is called the dissolution stage in Dwyer et al., 1987). However, Batonda and Perry (2003) introduced a novel sixth state, dormant process, which occurs when a relationship becomes inactive for a shorter or longer period. This can happen due to a change in business, project completion, or failure to meet specific requirements (Batonda & Perry, 2003). A relationship may jump to the dormant state from either state (2), (3), or (4) and may exit the dormant state by moving to any other state, except state (1). The path through states is undetermined, and some states can be left out or the sequence may be reversed. Our analytical framework is based on Batonda and Perry's (2003) model comprising six states.

Framework for Analyzing Portfolios of Customer Relationship States in Start-ups

Based on the assumption that the longer the customer relationship exists the more profitable the relationship will be for the company, some element of relationship longevity is often used as a proxy for the importance and profitability of the relationship. A relationship investment logic implies that costs can be assumed to exceed revenue in the initiating states of the relationship, and it may take several years before revenue will start to exceed costs, implying that it is possible to break even only in relationships that exist over an extended period. Such investment logic has led companies to focus on "increasing efficiency and effectiveness in maintaining current customers rather than prospecting new customers" (Sanchez & Sanchez, 2005, p. 309).

In their review of customer portfolio analysis models, Ang and Taylor (2005) identified Storbacka et al. (1994) as the first to inject a dynamic aspect into their model by including a relationship longevity dimension to accompany their customer relationship profitability dimension. Building on their work, Ang and Taylor (2005) proposed a model containing a length of tenure dimension ranging from low to high tenure. Hence, both models seem to be based on the assumption that older and more long-term relationships can be expected to be more profitable, and hence more valuable, than recently established or more short-term relationships. More explicitly inspired by relationship life cycle models, Johnson and Selnes (2004) distinguished among relationships to customers who are strangers, acquaintances, friends, and partners and suggested that a company's ability to transform strangers into acquaintances, acquaintances into friends, and friends into partners is central to the company's strategic development and profitability. While the model by Johnson and Selnes (2004) quite explicitly incorporates aspects of customer relationship dynamics, other portfolio models also rely on some kind of life cycle classification of customer relationships. For example, Campbell and Cunningham (1983) discerned tomorrow's customers, today's special customers, today's regular customers, and yesterday's customers. In a similar vein, Ford et al. (2011) identified eight categories of customer relationships: today's profits, cash cows, yesterday's profits, old men, tomorrow's profits, new technical requirements, new commercial requirements, and minor relationships.

While the investment logic may be dominant, it is not necessarily accurate that all relationships follow this pattern. As Gadde and Håkansson (2001) pointed out, costs and benefits in relationships may vary considerably over time; while some follow the expected pattern of an investment with costs preceding benefits, others follow alternative patterns, for example, where benefits are most prominent in the early stages/initiating states and costs are relatively stable or are characterized by several investment cycles over time. While some elements of customer relationship longevity and life cycle logic seem to underpin many of the portfolio models, none of them explicitly use the more recent relationship states models to classify the relationships. Furthermore, while it is assumed, more or less explicitly, in the customer portfolio models that the importance and profitability of a customer relationship vary over time, it is not universally to be assumed that the importance and profitability increase with time (Ang & Taylor, 2005; Johnson & Selnes, 2004; Zolkiewski & Turnbull, 2002). Rather, it may depend on whether the relationship is presently in a state focused more on developing rather than maintaining the exchange.

Most customer portfolio models appear as a matrix with different customer relationships plotted into different sections of the matrix to provide an overview for making strategic decisions. We combine customer portfolio literature with literature on relationship development states and propose the model depicted in Table 27.1 as a starting point for the analysis. The model of relationship development suggested by Batonda and Perry (2003) includes six different relation development states; these

Table 27.1: The starting point for exploring patterns in portfolios of customer relationship states.

Relationship intensity	High					
	Medium					
	Low					
	Search	Start	Development	Maintenance	Dormant	Termination
	States of relationship development					

form our x-axis, while the y-axis captures relationship intensity, and thus the start-up's extent of interaction and involvement in the customer relationship. By plotting the customer relationships in the portfolio into the model, managers in start-ups can analyze the present status and dynamics of a single relationship, present the status of the set of customer relationships, and scrutinize connections across customer relationships. We use the model for uncovering, examining, and explaining patterns of customer portfolio development and strategic development of start-up companies.

As Snehota (2011) noted, a start-up is not outside the network at the point of origin but is always a part of it. In other words, there will always be a number of relationships in the different states regardless of how many customer relationships the start-up has at a point in time. These relationships may or may not transform into customer relationships (Aarikka-Stenroos, 2008; Jack et al., 2010). Furthermore, as soon as the start-up has started to initiate customer relationships at least once, there will always be relationships in the termination and/or dormant state. Having such relationships can be positive for start-ups because it means they have more relationships to possibly reactivate or use as third actors for initiating other customer relationships. The start-ups will also have learned about how to develop their product and how to interact with customers from the interaction and will be able to use this knowledge in future interactions (Aaboen et al., 2011). Such relationships may be part of all start-ups' portfolios of customer relationship states regardless of the pattern, and while interesting per se, we shall not attend to them in this paper (and therefore the columns are blocked out in the portfolio tables presented in the following sections). Rather, we focus on the relationship states that discriminate between the specific patterns described.

Method

The initiation of this research resembled what Dubois and Gadde (2002) referred to as systematic combining. During several years of doing interviews with representatives of start-ups, an idea emerged and the interviewer often found herself thinking while conducting the interviews, "Aha, it is one of those types of start-ups!" In discussions with the co-authors, it became clear that the emerging taxonomy must have something to do with portfolios and relationship development states. This led us to the relationship state literature and the customer portfolio literature. Our attempts to conceptually combine these two streams of literature then enabled us to develop a tentative framework that we could apply to the empirical data, refine in interaction with theory and the empirical data, and apply again to identify four different patterns.

For capturing the sets of relationships in which the start-ups were engaged and sorting them into different categories, we employed a qualitative inquiry, since we needed to understand the interviewees' viewpoints (Graebner et al., 2012). This was particularly important for gaining insight into customer relationships in the search and start states of development as well as in the dormant state. In these states, there is little evidence to be found of relationships except from interviews. We used transcripts around 20 recently conducted interviews with representatives of start-ups in Norway and Sweden, which were part of a longitudinal study on network development in start-ups. Some of the start-ups in the data set have also been discussed in depth in other papers. All start-ups are technology-based and one of the criteria was that they should have found at least one paying customer. The interviews focused on how the first customers were found, how the start-ups interacted with them, the intended future relationship, and how the start-up developed over time. For many of the start-ups, interviews were conducted at more than one point in time. We are aware of the potential problem of using interviews to gather data for this type of analysis. As Hoholm and Araujo (2011) pointed out, when interviewees give retrospective accounts, they tend to post-hoc rationalize past events and forget that things could have turned out differently. Further, there are no guarantees that interviewees will correctly report the present and intended future. For example, in one of the start-ups, the pattern that emerged after the first interview showed several customers in different relationship development states. However, during the second interview, the interviewee acknowledged that the start-up at that point had already been in negotiations to be acquired by one of the customers, but since it was unofficial at that point in time, it had not been mentioned during the first interview. Moreover, there could be a bias toward wanting to give the impression of having several customers and being a robust start-up in relation to stakeholders.

We analyzed the transcripts in two steps. First, we scanned the transcripts to see which relationships the start-ups had developed so far, and we divided the start-ups into four groups that showed similarities according to the descriptions of their portfolios of customer relationship development states. Second, we analyzed the transcripts in more detail to crystallize the characteristics of the four groups. In this step, some start-ups were moved to another group, and movements between patterns over time became clearer.

Four Patterns of Relationship States in the Start-ups' Customer Portfolios

Of the around 20 start-ups in our data set, we found four displaying the first pattern, nine displaying the second pattern, three displaying the third pattern, and four displaying the fourth pattern.

Start-ups Displaying the First Pattern: Paradise Lost

None of the firms displaying the Paradise lost pattern are "up and running" in the sense of having a steady stream of deliveries (see Table 27.2). This may seem like a contradiction to the selection criteria of having found a first paying customer. The three start-ups that developed their products in interaction with a multinational company received funding from the multinational company. In addition, the founders sold consulting hours on issues related to the product they were developing. The Materials start-up had made small deliveries, first, to one customer in one industry, before this relationship was ended, and then to a customer in another industry, before this relationship was ended.

Table 27.2: Start-ups displaying the Paradise lost pattern.

Industry/ business	Energy	Software	Offshore	Materials
Product	Equipment for offshore windpower	Software for equipment for subsea mapping	Equipment for temporary oil drilling facilities	Light-weight metal
Development so far	Developed the product idea at a university; first major relationship with a multinational corporation	Idea developed at a university; important relationship with multinational company and with a governmental organization	Developed the idea at a research institute; first major relationship with a multinational corporation	Has tried to apply the material for products used for defense, aircraft, automobiles, and boats
Characteristics displaying the Paradise lost pattern	Unable to develop the relationship with the multinational corporation further and could not form other relationships	Has developed the product further in interaction with the multinational company, but it has not resulted in a finished product	Has developed the product further in interaction with the international company, but it has yet to result in sales of the finished product	All customer relationships and all relationships with potential customers have ended

A typical characteristic of start-ups displaying the Paradise lost pattern is having one relationship that is rather well developed and few or no other relationships (see Table 27.3). If this relationship is terminated or becomes dormant, the start-up finds itself with no customers until a new "first" customer is found and developed. Hence, the pattern is illustrated by an intense customer relationship in the development state in Table 27.3. However, in reality, it may be that a start-up displaying this pattern also has relationships in the dormant or termination states if it has tried to develop customer relationships before or it has moved to this pattern from another pattern by losing customers. Table 27.3 only illustrates the one relationship as being the typical characteristic of the Paradise lost pattern. It is important for such start-ups to either develop additional relationships or develop the one relationship further – otherwise, its efforts will have been wasted. The example of the Energy firm shows this very clearly. A multinational corporation provided seed funding that generated additional funding from the Norwegian governmental instrument for enterprise development. The multinational corporation also joined the advisory board of the start-up and financed the prototype as well as its testing. The start-up developed few other relationships besides the relationship with the multinational corporation and some with a couple of private investors. The multinational corporation therefore had several roles that other stakeholders otherwise could have had. Currently, the start-up has developed the product to a rather advanced level but does not see a market for it and has, therefore, decided to put the start-up on hold until the market catches up. This pattern also covers start-ups with an explicit exit strategy of being acquired by a particular company – the first and possibly only customer.

Table 27.3: The portfolio of customer relationship states displayed in Paradise lost.

Relationship intensity	High		●			
	Medium					
	Low					
	Search	Start	Development	Maintenance	Dormant	Termination
			States of relationship development			

Start-ups Displaying the Second Pattern: Pearls on a String

There is some variation in the manner in which the nine start-ups displaying the Pearls on a string pattern created their customer relationship states portfolios (see Table 27.4). For example, the start-up designing software for safety solutions originated at a research institute after a train accident. A researcher believed that the train company could have handled the accident in a better way and, therefore, developed a safety solution. The train company then became the first major customer. After drawing this first customer, the start-up was able to initiate and develop additional customer relationships with transportation infrastructure companies, ferry companies, and aviation companies. After a while, the start-up realized that the safety solution was generic and decided to initiate customer relationships with companies in the offshore sector, since this sector has larger margins, higher profits, and allocates more money to safety solutions compared to the transportation sector. Currently, the start-up is also initiating customer relationships within the energy and university sectors. However, the first major customer relationships within these two sectors are less developed compared to the first major customers within transportation and offshore operations.

Table 27.4: Start-ups displaying the Pearls on a string pattern.

Industry/ business	Offshore and vehicles	Offshore and construction	Offshore and transportation	Offshore and windpower
Product	Systems controlled remotely or through autopilot	Material for improved acoustics	Software for safety solutions	Software for construction
Development so far	Has developed different applications of the product in interaction with customers	Has delivered the product to several different customers	Adds customers one by one, started in transportation, continued to offshore, and is now exploring additional industries	Started from scratch one time but then added projects and customers continuously; mainly offshore
Characteristics displaying the Pearls on a string pattern	The degree of interaction with each customer and the number of customers and product applications	The degree of interaction with each customer and the number of customers and product applications	The degree of interaction with each customer and the number of customers and product applications	The degree of interaction with each customer and the number of customers and product applications

Industry/ business	Biotech	Surveillance	Offshore	E-marketing	Materials
Product	Production processes for the pharmaceutical industry	Software for monitoring and alarms systems	Software for finding oil	Software for websites	Chemical formulas for changing the properties of materials
Development so far	Adding customers but not yet for the intended product	Customer relationships with chain owners and owners of many buildings	Initiated relationships with large corporations and then added small firms to the portfolio	Many small firms locally and nationally are subscribing to the product	Several development projects in parallel to learn between projects; has added customers and business areas
Characteristics displaying the Pearls on a string pattern	The degree of interaction with each customer and the number of customers and product applications	The degree of interaction with each customer and the number of customers and product applications	The degree of interaction with each customer and the number of customers and product applications	The degree of interaction with each customer and the number of customers and product applications	The degree of interaction with each customer and the number of customers and product applications

A typical characteristic among the start-ups displaying the Pearls on a string pattern is that they interact with one customer and then initiate relationships with similar customers that are interested in a similar product and/or that complement the portfolio with customers within a new sector that are interested in the same or a similar product. This is illustrated in Table 27.5.

Table 27.5: The portfolio of customer relationship states in Pearls on a string.

Relationship intensity	High						
	Medium	●●●	●●	●●●		●●	
	Low		●●				
		Search	Start	Development	Maintenance	Dormant	Termination
				States of relationship development			

Start-ups Displaying the Third Pattern: Picture Perfect

A typical characteristic of start-ups displaying the Picture perfect pattern is a focus on many relationships with users or customers as illustrated in Table 27.6. These relationships are usually in one of the early development states and are nicely distributed to cover a wide range of geographical areas, industrial sectors, or parts of the value chain. The portfolio of customer relationships in the Picture perfect pattern demonstrates the potential of both the product idea and the firm. However, this strategy also provides varied input for further product development.

Table 27.6: Start-ups displaying the Picture perfect pattern.

Industry/ business	Software	Boat equipment	Packaging	Packaging
Product	Software for time management	Device for measuring the contents of containers	Part of packaging	Barrier for packaging material
Development so far	After having found 4–5 potential customers, the focus shifted to recruiting users	Sold the device to private boat owners and found potential customers that tried the device in factories	Found customers, mediates between customers; focus on key customers in each country	Sold development projects to actors representing several of the steps in the chain between content and finished package in the store

Table 27.6 (continued)

Industry/ business	Software	Boat equipment	Packaging	Packaging
Characteristics displaying the Picture perfect pattern	The start-up has little information about the 70 users except their industrial sector, country of origin, and the feedback they provide	Has little information about the consumers but knows that they are many, from different countries, and with different boats; also focusing on potential customers in different countries and industry sectors	Current focus on finding key partners in each country that can find additional customers	Has not brought any of the development projects to a finished product and focuses on development projects in several of the steps in the chain simultaneously

Table 27.7: The portfolio of customer relationship states in Picture perfect.

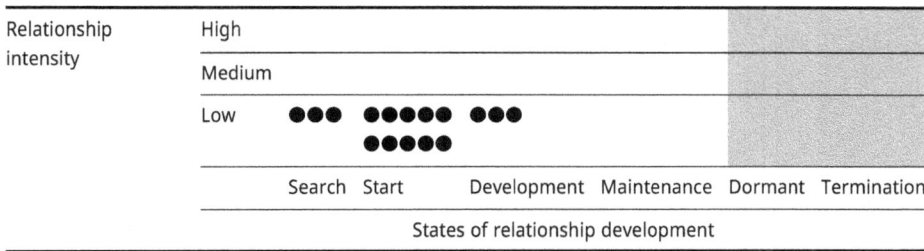

Relationship intensity						
High						
Medium						
Low	●●●	●●●●● ●●● ●●●●●				
	Search	Start	Development	Maintenance	Dormant	Termination

States of relationship development

The software start-up most clearly exhibits Picture perfect characteristics (Table 27.7). Initially, the start-up called potential customers and visited them to persuade them to try out the software as a complement to their company's current accounting software. After having found four or five customers in this manner, the start-up began posting advertisements on Google inviting parties interested in trying out the software to sign up by e-mail to receive a link to download the software. Seventy new users were quickly recruited this way. The start-up does not know who these users are, having no other information about them other than what the users have divulged themselves. The start-up tries to make note of which industrial sector they belong to and which country they are from. The start-up's focus is on developing the functionality of the software for all users.

Start-ups Displaying the Fourth Pattern: Persuasion

A typical characteristic of start-ups displaying the Persuasion pattern is having one customer relationship that is much more developed, and where the interaction is much more
intense, compared to the other relationships illustrated in Table 27.8 and Table 27.9. None
of the start-ups we studied started out by displaying the Persuasion pattern; instead, it
arose when they identified a potentially important relationship among their relationships.

Table 27.8: Start-ups displaying the Persuasion pattern.

Industry/ business	Software	Software	Clean Tech
Product	Software for detecting forbidden internet content	Software for predicting behavioral patterns	Mediation and recycling of industry waste
Development so far	Developed four different products for four different types of customers; currently has three of the products for five different types of customers	Developed a new product in interaction with each customer with the goal of finding additional customers for thedeveloped products; was acquired by its first major customer	Collected, processed, and reused industry waste through mediation; expanded to new types of waste and increased geographical area; was acquired by its main competitor
Characteristics displaying the Picture perfect pattern	When an important potential partner was identified, the portfolio of products and types of customers were redesigned to fit the potential partner	When the first major customer started showing interest, all other products were dropped and only the first major customer's products were developed further	Customer and waste portfolio adapted to complement the main competitor when the main deliverers of industrial waste were shut down

The software start-up focused on detecting forbidden internet content knew early on that
it would not be able to sell its software solution to all computer owners in the world on
its own. Initially, therefore, the start-up displayed the Picture perfect pattern. To attract
the attention of major software companies, the start-up developed one software solution
for each of the four major customer segments of the major software companies. As soon
as one of the major software companies started interacting with the start-up through the
network, the start-up directed all its efforts toward that relationship. The products that
were less interesting for that particular software company were cancelled and the other
products were adjusted to fit the major software company's portfolio.

Table 27.9: The portfolio of customer relationship states in Persuasion.

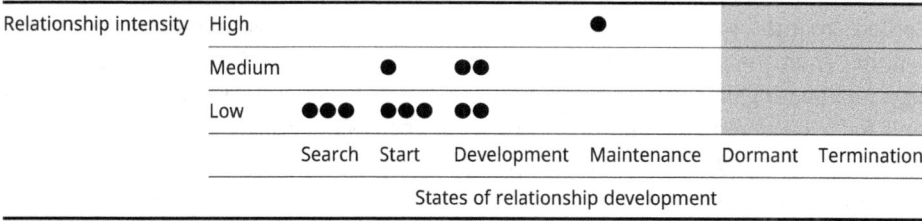

Relationship intensity							
High				●			
Medium		●	●●				
Low	●●●	●●●	●●				
	Search	Start	Development	Maintenance	Dormant	Termination	

States of relationship development

Differences Among Customer Relationship State Portfolio Patterns

To grasp the similarities and differences among the four patterns, we may position them along two dimensions. One dimension is captured by asking which states the customer relationships are mainly in. Here, we discern portfolio patterns consisting of relationships that are only in the searching, starting, and early development states from portfolio patterns consisting of relationships that are (also) in the late development and maintenance states. The second dimension is captured by asking how many relationships are intense and characterized by heavy interaction. Here, we discern portfolio patterns consisting of mainly one intense relationship characterized by heavy interaction from portfolio patterns consisting of several intense relationships characterized by heavy interaction. By positioning the four customer relationship state portfolios within these two dimensions, we obtain the following matrix in Table 27.10.

Table 27.10: Similarities and differences among the four customer relationship state patterns.

		How many relationships are intense and characterized by heavy interaction?		
		Mainly one	Several	
Which state(s) of development the customer relationships are mainly in	Only searching, starting, and development (early)	Paradise lost	Picture perfect	Enticement
	Also development (late) and maintenance	Persuasion	Pearls on a string	Engineering
		Narrow	Broad	

In Table 27.10, we have added the labels "Enticement" and "Engineering." Enticement refers to the process of trying to attract potential customers without fully having settled what the value offering will include and who the most important customers will be. Thus, the start-up tries to demonstrate the potential of its team and technology. Engineering, in contrast, refers to the start-up's belief in its proven value offering and focus on organizing and orchestrating its portfolio accordingly. Engineering includes both finding new customers and maintaining current customer relationships. Start-ups characterized as Paradise lost or Persuasion engage in heavy interaction within one intense relationship and thus represent a narrow relationship strategy. However, while a start-up characterized as Paradise lost is continually working to entice its first customer with its value offering in a single customer relationship in the early states, a start-up characterized as Persuasion has entered the maintenance state in a single relationship and is oriented toward engineering the rest of the customer relationship state portfolio to this important relationship. Start-ups characterized as Picture perfect or Pearls on a string are involved in several customer relationships and thus represent a broader relationship strategy. However, while a start-up characterized as Picture perfect is continually working to entice its network with its value offering through many relationships in earlier states and learning across many different relationships, a start-up characterized as Pearls on a string has (also) entered the maintenance state in one or several relationships and is (also) oriented toward engineering with a focus on the value proven in (this) these relationship(s) by developing new product applications and finding additional customers and markets for the already developed applications. Hence, the customer relationship state portfolio of a start-up may be characterized by whether the start-up is pursuing a narrow or broader customer relationship portfolio strategy, and whether it mostly utilizes its value offering potential for enticement or engineering in its relationship portfolio.

Implications and Future Research

While the use of portfolio analysis for analyzing business relationships is not new, its use for analyzing relationship states is. In addition, the four patterns and the strategizing connected to handling a pattern or moving (or not) between patterns may be useful for all companies, irrespective of the age and state of development of their customer relationships. Nevertheless, we argue that our model is particularly relevant for start-up companies for understanding, explaining, and influencing their development. Previous research has shown that early relationships play a significant role for start-up companies and heavily influence their development (e.g., Aaboen et al., 2011). Furthermore, building relationships often requires considerable effort and resources, and given the often emphasized scarcity of resources available to a start-up company, it is of particular importance to consider start-up companies' portfolios of relationship states at different points in time. For actors specializing in evaluating the potential of start-ups, the suggested patterns may also shift some of the focus from the founding team and the product when determining the potential future of the start-up.

Future research should address the strategies start-ups use to move relationships from one pattern to another. In addition, the patterns could be investigated in relation to the survival, growth, profitability, and exit strategies of start-ups.

Conclusion

We initially asked how relationship development states create patterns in the early customer portfolios of start-ups. We combined customer portfolio literature with literature on relationship development states and identified four different patterns: Paradise lost, Pearls on a string, Picture perfect, and Persuasion. In Paradise lost, the start-up has found its first customer. In Pearls on a string, the start-up develops several customer relationships in the maintenance state as well as several other customer relationships in the other states. In Picture perfect, the start-up mainly fosters customer relationships in the early development state and focuses on having many customer relationships in many geographical areas and industrial sectors to demonstrate its value to potential customers and to companies that might acquire the start-up. In Persuasion, all the start-up's efforts are directed at adjusting to one, or very few, customers, potential acquiring companies, or collaboration partners. All other customer relationships are overshadowed by the efforts to adjust in interaction with the potential acquiring company or collaboration partner that may or may not also be a customer of the start-up's product.

References

Aaboen, L., Dubois, A., & Lind, F. (2011). Start-ups starting up – Firms looking for a network. *The IMP Journal, 5*(1), 42–58.

Aaker, D.A. (2009). *Brand portfolio strategy: Creating relevance, differentiation, energy, leverage, and clarity.* Simon and Schuster.

Aarikka-Stenroos, L. (2008). What really happens in initiation? – Investigating the subprocesses and features of emerging buyer-seller relationships. *Proceedings from the 24th IMP Conference*, Uppsala, Sweden.

Ang, L., & Taylor, B. (2005). Managing customer profitability using portfolio matrices. *Journal of Database Marketing & Customer Strategy Management, 12*(4), 298–304.

Archer, N.P., & Ghasemzadeh, F. (1999). An integrated framework for project portfolio selection. *International Journal of Project Management, 17*(4), 207–216.

Axelsson, B., & Easton, G. (1992). *Industrial networks: A new view of reality.* Routledge.

Baraldi, E., Ingemansson Havenvid, M., Linné, Å., & Öberg, C. (2019). Start-ups and networks: Interactive perspectives and a research agenda. *Industrial Marketing Management, 80*, 58–67.

Batonda, G., & Perry, C. (2003). Approaches to relationship development processes in inter-firm networks. *European Journal of Marketing, 37*(10), 1457–1484.

Bensaou, M. (1999, Summer). Portfolios of buyer-supplier relationships. *Sloan Management Review*, 35–44.

Bertoni, F., Colombo, M.G., & Grilli, L. (2011). Venture capital financing and the growth of high-tech start-ups: Disentangling treatment from selection effects. *Research Policy, 40*, 1028–1043.

Bjørgum, Ø., Aaboen, L., & Fredriksson, A. (2021). Low power, high ambitions: New ventures developing their first supply chains. *Journal of Purchasing and Supply Management, 27*, 100670.

Campbell, N.C.G., & Cunningham, M.T. (1983). Customer analysis for strategy development in industrial markets. *Strategic Management Journal, 4*, 369–380.

Ciabuschi, F., Perna, A., & Snehota, I. (2012). Assembling resources in the formation of a new business. *Journal of Business Research, 65*(2), 220–229.

Colombo, M.G., & Piva, E. (2012). Firms' genetic characteristics and competence-enlarging strategies: A comparison between academic and non-academic high-tech start-ups. *Research Policy, 41*, 79–92.

Cooper, R.G., Edgett, S.J., & Kleinschmidt, E.J. (1999). New product portfolio management: Practices and performance. *Journal of Product Innovation Management, 16*, 333–351.

Day, G.S. (1977, April). Diagnosing the product portfolio. *Journal of Marketing*, 29–38.

Dubois, A., & Gadde, L.-E. (2002). Systematic combining – An abductive approach to case research. *Journal of Business Research, 55*(7), 553–560.

Dwyer, F.R., Schurr, P.H., & Oh, S. (1987). Developing buyer-seller relationships. *Journal of Marketing, 55*(2), 11–27.

Edvardsson, B., Holmlund, M., & Strandvik, T. (2008). Initiation of business relationships in service-dominant settings. *Industrial Marketing Management, 37*, 339–350.

Fiocca, R. (1982). Account portfolio analysis for strategy development. *Industrial Marketing Management, 11*(1), 53–62.

Ford, D. (1980). The development of buyer-seller relationships in industrial markets. *European Journal of Marketing, 14*(5/6), 339–354.

Ford, D., Gadde, L.-E., Håkansson, H., & Snehota, I. (2003). *Managing business relationships*. John Wiley & Sons Publishers.

Ford, D., Gadde, L.-E., Håkansson, H., & Snehota, I. (2011). *Managing business relationships* (3rded.). John Wiley & Sons Publishers.

Ford, D., & Rosson, P.J. (1982). The relationships between export manufacturers and their overseas distributors. In M. Czinkota & G. Tesar (Eds.), *Export management* (pp. 257–275). Praeger.

Frankort, H.T.W., Hagedoorn, J., & Letterie, W. (2012). R&D partnership portfolios and the inflow of technological knowledge. *Industrial and Corporate Change, 21*(2), 507–537.

Gadde, L.E., & Håkansson, H. (2001). *Supply network strategies*. Wiley.

Graebner, M.E., Martin, J.A., & Roundy, P.T. (2012). Qualitative data: Cooking without a recipe. *Strategic Organization, 10*(3), 276–284.

Greve, H.R., Rowley, T.J., & Shipilov, A.V. (2014). *Network advantage: How to unlock value from your alliances and partnerships*. Jossey-Bass.

Grossman, E.B., Yli-Renko, H., & Janakiraman, R. (2012). Resource search, interpersonal similarity, and network tie valuation in nascent entrepreneurs' emerging networks. *Journal of Management, 38*(6), 1760–1787.

Håkansson, H. (Ed.). (1982). *International marketing and purchasing of industrial goods: An interaction approach*. John Wiley & Sons Publishers.

Håkansson, H., Ford, I.D., Gadde, L.-E., Snehota, I., & Waluszewski, A. (2009). *Business in networks*. John Wiley & Sons.

Håkansson, H., & Snehota, I. (1995). *Developing relationships in business networks*. Routledge.

Hedley, B. (1977). Strategy and the "business portfolio." *Long Range Planning, 10*, 9–15.

Hoholm, T., & Araujo, L. (2011). Studying innovation processes in real-time: The promises and challenges of ethnography. *Industrial Marketing Management, 40*(6), 933–939.

Holmen, E., Roos, K., Kallevåg, M., von Raesfeld, A., de Boer, L., & Pedersen, A.-C. (2005). How do relationships begin? *Proceedings from the 21ˢᵗ IMP Conference*, Rotterdam, the Netherlands.

Ingemansson, M., & Waluszewski, A. (2009). Success in science and burden in business. On the difficult relationship between science as a developing setting and business as a producer-user setting. *The IMP Journal*, 3(2), 20–56.

Jack, S., Moult, S., Anderson, A., & Dodd, S. (2010). An entrepreneurial network evolving: Patterns of change. *International Small Business Journal*, 28(4), 315–337.

Johnson, M.D., & Selnes, F. (2004). Customer portfolio management: Toward a dynamic theory of exchange relationships. *Journal of Marketing*, 68(2), 1–17.

Kapoor, R., & Lee, J.M. (2013). Coordinating and competing in ecosystems: How organizational forms shape new technology investments. *Strategic Management Journal*, 34, 274–296.

La Rocca, A., Ford, D., & Snehota, I. (2013). Initial relationship development in new business ventures. *Industrial Marketing Management*, 42, 1025–1032.

La Rocca, A., Perna, A., Sabatini, A., & Baraldi, E. (2019). The emergence of the customer relationship portfolio of a new venture: A networking process. *Journal of Business & Industrial Marketing*, 34(5), 1066–1078.

Lavie, D. (2007). Alliance portfolios and firm performance: A study of value creation and appropriation in the U.S. software industry. *Strategic Management Journal*, 28, 1187–1212.

Mohr, V., Garnsey, E., & Theyel, G. (2014). The role of alliances in the early development of high-growth firms. *Industrial and Corporate Change*, 23, 233–259.

Mustar, P., Renault, M., Colombo, M.G., Piva, E., Fontes, M., Lockett, A., Wright, M., Clarysse, B., & Moray, N. (2006). Conceptualising the heterogeneity of research-based spin-offs: A multi-dimensional taxonomy. *Research Policy*, 35, 289–308.

Olsen, R.F., & Ellram, L.M. (1997). A portfolio approach to supplier relationships. *Industrial Marketing Management*, 26(2), 101–113.

Ozcan, P., & Eisenhardt, K.M. (2009). Origin of alliance portfolios: Entrepreneurs, network strategies, and firm performance. *Academy of Management Journal*, 52(2), 246–279.

Phillips, N., Tracey, P., & Karra, N. (2013). Building entrepreneurial tie portfolios through strategic homophily: The role of narrative identity work in venture creation and early growth. *Journal of Business Venturing*, 28, 134–150.

Ritter, T., Wilkinson, I.F., & Johnston, W. (2004). Managing in complex business networks. *Industrial Marketing Management*, 33(3), 175–183.

Rosemann, M. (2010). The service portfolio of a BPM center of excellence. In J. vom Brocke & M. Rosemann (Eds.), *Handbook on business process management 2*. Springer.

Sanchez, R., & Sanchez, R. (2005). Analysis of customer portfolio and relationship management models: Bridging managerial dimensions. *Journal of Business & Industrial Marketing*, 20(6), 307–316.

Santos, J.N., & Mota, J. (2020). The value of initial relationships in new business start-ups. *Journal of Business & Industrial Marketing*, 36(9), 1585–1599.

Sigfusson, T., & Harris, S. (2013). Domestic market context and international entrepreneurs' relationship portfolios. *International Business Review*, 22, 243–258.

Snehota, I. (2011). New business formation in business networks. *The IMP Journal*, 5(1), 1–9.

Storbacka, K., Strandvik, T., & Grönroos, C. (1994). Managing customer relationships for profit: The dynamics of relationship quality. *International Journal of Service Industry Management*, 5(5), 21–38.

Storey, D.J., & Tether, B.S. (1998). New technology-based firms in the European union: An introduction. *Research Policy*, 26, 933–946.

Wilson, D.T. (1995). An integrated model of buyer-seller relationships. *Journal of the Academy of Marketing Science*, 23(4), 335–345.

Woodside, A.G. (1996). Customer portfolio analysis among competing retail stores. *Journal of Business Research*, 35(3), 189–200.

Zolkiewski, J., & Turnbull, P. (2002). Do relationship portfolios and networks provide the key to successful relationship management? *Journal of Business & Industrial Marketing*, 17(7), 575–597.

Nazha Gali and Susanna L.M. Chui

28 The Role of Research Universities in Catalyzing Value Creation

Abstract: Through this chapter we focus on the impact of research universities' publicly funded research projects on the economy in terms of knowledge creation, knowledge transfer, and business ethics promotion. We aim to answer the research question of how universities and science can provide tools that have a positive effect on the economy, including small and medium enterprises (SMEs). This chapter sheds light on how universities provide tools, evidence, and new knowledge that catalyze value creation. With the illustrations of two university contexts, one in the US and the other in Hong Kong, we offer insights on how scientific research projects do not only serve the sole purpose of publication. Scientific research projects serve to connect the academic and practice fields in knowledge creation and exchange; to create an experiential learning ground for students; and to provide examination and curation of market trends for sectoral growth. Through the first part of the book chapter, we present past research on the impact of universities on the economy, SMEs, and their communities. The second part of the chapter explains the data curation efforts led at the Institute for Research on Innovation and Science (IRIS), which is a consortium of US research universities adopting large administrative data, to investigate and provide the evidence of the effect of higher education universities on the economy, SMEs, the career pathways of students, and on national prosperity. We examine cases in which federally funded projects have led to a positive impact on the economy, including SMEs. The third part of the chapter examines the engagement of business school students in the examination of entrepreneurial ethics in a research university in Hong Kong, a rising economy. Students were engaged in an active knowledge creation process. The experience of students' research contribution to a business ethics index which was published annually for ten years is discussed. Students at a business school who collected data for a Junzi Corporation Survey every year in Hong Kong embarked on a learning journey that stimulated their business ethics learning. The outcomes of the research serve to inform the business sectors in terms of the values that shape responsible management towards the important customer stakeholder group.

Keywords: research universities, small and medium enterprises (SMEs), Institute for Research on Innovation and Science (IRIS), responsible management

Nazha Gali, Odette School of Business, University of Windsor, Institute for Research on Innovation & Science, University of Michigan

Susanna L. M. Chui, School of Business of the Hang Seng University, Hong Kong

https://doi.org/10.1515/9783110747652-029

Chapter Purpose and Structure

We present the impact of university research in two geographical contexts: the US and Hong Kong in China. The former is the Institute for Research on Innovation and Science (IRIS) at the University of Michigan, and the latter is The Hang Seng University of Hong Kong. They present two different societal roles of which universities can play in social value creation. One focuses on science and innovation, and the other focuses on community engagement and ethics. Through the research efforts of IRIS, reports and de-identified datasets for research are produced to reveal the economic impact of research spending, the career pathways and academic outcomes of research-funded employees and faculty, and the industries that are involved in providing the research-associated services and goods. Similarly, through the research efforts at the Hang Seng University of Hong Kong, the university has been measuring and publicly releasing the business ethical level of Hong Kong corporations and identifying those that are distinguished through the perceptions of the Hong Kong citizens. The subsequent findings help promote a concept of "Five Virtues" in the business context. Our chapter presents the impact of research universities on the economy including small and medium enterprises (SMEs), confirming that universities in both the developed and the rising economy contexts embrace social value creation through research that is relevant for the society (Marginson, 2011). Nevertheless, universities in rising economies are structurally different from US universities, in which in the US the university system is decentralized. In rising economies such as China the university system is centralized, and universities are tightly regulated by the Central Ministry of Education and funded nearly completely by the government. Due to their close connections to the national governments and their reliance on national funding, universities in rising economies are responsive to their nation's needs (Sine & Shen, 2020). Previous work has focused on research universities within the US context (Owen-Smith, 2018), whereas we uncover the impact of universities within a rising economy as well.

Through the first part of the chapter, we present a literature review of previous research conducted on the effect of research universities on the economy including SMEs. The second part describes the data curation efforts led at IRIS which reveal the initial inputs to publicly funded research projects conducted at US universities including a heterogenous mix of skills (students, staff, postdocs), and showcase the extent of student involvement in research projects that led to value creation in the US. The third part depicts a research index project that had been conducted annually over the last 10 years by a business school in Hong Kong on business ethics and responsible management using measurement scales inspired by the Confucius values.

Part I: Research and Innovation at Universities: The Power to Discover New Knowledge

Research universities are not only engaged in providing scientific education but are also unique constituents of the global and national system of innovation in which they have certain distinct characteristics as sources, hubs, and anchors which allow them to consistently innovate in response to emerging and pressing challenges and opportunities (Owen-Smith, 2018). Modern universities may potentially bring about economic development effects through the generation of knowledge and human capital; the transfer of know-how and knowledge; the catalyzing of innovation and capital investment; and the exercising of regional leadership or influence in the regional context (Drucker & Goldstein, 2007).

Research universities are unique entities that need to balance the trade-offs between being the providers of legacy knowledge which serving the industrial needs of the present and in being the creators of novel knowledge and the entrepreneurs who lead the progress of the future. Previous researchers have advocated the key role that higher education universities play in producing economic and social value through university research incubators (Phan et al., 2005), university-based entrepreneurship curriculum (Perkmann et al., 2013), and value generation from research (Mindruta, 2013). Research universities contribute to the creation of novel knowledge and leading to new venture formation that drive local economic growth. Researchers have noted that 69 percent of new ventures generated from universities to commercialize the university technology remain in the universities' local communities (Sine & Shen, 2020). While some scholars have delved into the question of how academic research outputs lead to economic and social returns, there is little accurate research evidence to corroborate the public value of research conducted at universities, leading to the problem of possible inaccurate misconceptions about the practical implications of research (Owen-Smith, 2018).

Universities are sources of new knowledge and discoveries and creators of entrepreneurial organizations. They are anchors for their communities ensuring the stability of local communities which is required for their sustainability. They are also hubs of activity, whose connections cover all main parts of society, that address known and unknown challenges, essentially driving society forwards (Owen-Smith, 2018). The diverse networks of researchers comprising the scientific teams are sources for new skills development and discoveries, in which such individuals carry their skills into the knowledge economy. Research universities are unique machines which are able to address complex challenges of an uncertain future.

Research universities play a vital role in generating novel and new knowledge which is pivotal towards sustainable development and the generation of social and economic value (Waas et al., 2010) and it is of utmost importance to maintain funding and provide basic investment to such an invaluable resource (Owen-Smith, 2018). Socio-economic research that is conducted at universities does not only impact academic audiences, but also has an impact on non-academic audiences in which the conducted research has societal and policy implications and has a significant impact on current policy, social, and management practices (Molas-Gallart et al., 2000). To evaluate the research activities at universities, it is important to understand the ways in which the research teams leading such projects have certain sets of characteristics and skills and lead to the generation of new and at times breakthrough knowledge which can transform societies and disrupt the technology landscape of current industries.

The Non-Academic Impact of Grant Funding

The non-academic effect of grant funding at universities is realized when the research data is used in non-academic activities. Non-academic impact of universities could be direct when the research results are directly adopted in particular applications or policy implementation, for example when companies use the research results on the effective creation and management of design teams in their management of design operations (Molas-Gallart et al., 2000). However, the research results may not have such straightforward utilization and the non-academic impact of universities may be indirect through the students' cognitive and research skill development and diffusion into the high skills sectors of our economy (Weinberg et al., 2014).

Scientific work is collaborative in nature and involves a team-oriented endeavor in which research is mostly conducted by teams of two or more individuals. Complex scientific and societal challenges require the collaboration of diverse individuals at different stages of their career (e.g. staff, postdocs, graduate students) who may come from different disciplines and fields. Teams may use similar inputs but organize work differently depending on their team characteristics and this would shape their team outputs and their impact. There are short-term effects to research investments in which economic activity occurs instantly through the employment of a skilled workforce via the funded grants and there are long-term benefits that are generated from the outputs of research.

More specifically, there are public investments, federally and non-federally funded grants, in university knowledge which lead to short-term and long-term economic returns. There are short-term benefits given that the funds allow principal investigators (PIs) on the grant to hire workforce and buy material from vendors needed to conduct their research. However, these grants also foster collaborations among students, faculty, staff and such collaborative networks or research teams may conjoin on multiple research projects. Such an interdisciplinary network of various individuals with different set of skills and research expertise may span multiple fields and underpin a unique social system which creates a skilled workforce and generates new knowledge. The long-term social and economic benefits of research projects are revealed when the skills developed by the workforce are utilized for nonacademic pursuits or the integral research findings and new knowledge are transmitted from the academic to the public realm (Owen-Smith, 2018).

SME Support and Growth

In today's turbulent fast-paced environment, SMEs are challenged to improve their performance in the face of the growing pace of innovation. In this light, universities play a fundamental role to support SMEs through their education programs (for e.g. entrepreneurship) by developing the SMEs' entrepreneurial capacity which leads to regional economic development (Etzkowitz, 2016). Moreover, universities also play a role in nurturing entrepreneurial competencies amongst students who will support and drive entrepreneurial pursuits in local contexts.

Previous research has reported that universities develop SME's entrepreneurial orientation (EO) or their potential for being proactive, innovative, and risk taking. That is, universities that embrace an entrepreneurship perspective and aim to establish a knowledge-based economy to improve their region's entrepreneurial culture should pay their attention on the EO of students, academic staff, and companies (Alvarez-Torres et al., 2019). Universities are key in sparking the entrepreneurial orientation of SMEs. Entrepreneurship education programs result in a variety of benefits for SMEs and for their region as well. Through the engagement in entrepreneurship education programs small business owners or managers extend their network and this supports their business growth and development. Engagement in entrepreneurship education programs does not only positively enhance the way that small business owners perceive their role, but also the way that small business owners manage their business (Gordon et al., 2012).

SMEs may be driven by getting their products rapidly to the market which may require quick decision making whereas universities are driven by other imperatives and their technology transfer offices must follow certain institutional procedures. Yet, the technology transfer offices are just one mode of interaction between universities and SMEs, in which SMEs may prefer to engage with individual researchers. It is necessary for universities to promote frequent interactions and opportunities for small business owners and faculty members to personally collaborate (Collier et al., 2011).

Universities act as knowledge agents, entrepreneurial hubs, and catalysts for innovation by connecting a variety of stakeholders such as students, faculty, and start-ups to SMEs (Fayolle & Redford, 2014), which eventually improves the entrepreneurial potential of SMEs (Alvarez-Torres et al., 2019). Universities may act as entrepreneurs supporting the notion that entrepreneurship is not restricted to businesses. Entrepreneurial universities have a key role in the support and growth of SMEs through incubating start-ups, technology transfer, and leading the regional development and renewal efforts. Promoting a continuous process of new venture creation and firm rejuvenation by adopting advanced technologies which are often university-originated, is important for the implementation of an innovation strategy (Etzkowitz & Zhou, 2017).

The first wave of the rise of entrepreneurial universities occurred in pioneering universities in the US such as MIT and Stanford which have pioneered the definition of a university-wide patent policy, the establishment of a technology transfer policy, in addition to the creation of ventures (Rasmussen & Wright, 2015).

The outcomes of research universities include knowledge creation and technological innovations that can pave the way for future entrepreneurial pursuit such as product commercialization, spin-offs, and nurturing of future entrepreneurs. Universities are informed about the challenges in their local environment and translate the knowledge obtained from the academic institutions into economic activities. Universities provide support for their region's development with their ability to produce spin-offs and many of the region's start-ups may have originated as university spin-offs. Faculty members who are principal investigators on the grant may encourage their students or graduates who are working with them to spin-off their funded technology and may even hold dual roles in high-tech firms (Etzkowitz & Zhou, 2017).

Universities are hubs of different forms of knowledge, and they have the right facilitating environment for fueling innovations and new discoveries. Scientific discoveries may be serendipitous and may originate from the most unexpected mix of people and ideas within the interdisciplinary research teams. Universities construct a network of scientists in different disciplinary frontiers, locations, and occupations initiating the environment in which serendipitous discoveries take place (Sine & Shen, 2020). For example, Stanford University played a major role in being the source of regional innovation whereby a postdoctoral student, Sergio Bren, who is a Google cofounder, was working on a NSF grant for assisting research in library science during the period of the founding of Google. This led to the emergence of the page rank technology which underlies the search engine of Google. The core technology that Google's search engine is built on is a result of a cross-disciplinary collaboration ranging from the fields of library science to mathematical sociology. Similarly, research universities played a vital role in combating the Zika virus outbreak in 2016 that impacted more than 40,000 people in over 50 countries. Scientific research teams responded to the emergency of such a novel disease and generate the knowledge that was required to cure patients within a short timeframe. Essentially, advanced technologies, which are often university-originated, foster the process of new venture formation and are the future engines of economic growth and of fostering technological advancements at the local and regional level (Guerrero et al., 2015).

A Call for a Shift Towards Boxed-out Approach to the Impact of Universities on the Economy

Past research has argued that a majority of researchers in the social sciences, including management and organization studies, have been mostly focused on narrow and specific issues within specialized intellectual terrains whose investigations would provide incremental theoretical contributions, but less focus has been given on the practical implications or managerial relevance of their work (Alvesson & Sandberg, 2014). There is a disconnect between the academic arena and the real-world realm, in which managers may rarely use academic advice as they might be at a discord with academic theory and most academics could be out of sympathy with practical relevance (Berry et al., 2006). This is an issue to date as recent scholarly conversations have been on important topics such as doing meaningful research by Professor Mats Alvesson,[1] scholarly impact: finding the holy grail by Professor Herman Aguinis,[2] and research universities and the public good by Professor Jason Owen-Smith,[3] and these scholarly discussions center around the significance of conducting interesting and influential relevant research that is of public value and the impact it can have beyond the scholarly arena. There is a need to shift focus from an in-boxed approach of what research universities spend or how they impact their faculty and staff towards a box-breaking approach of how universities impact their economy through their research spending and findings.

Part II: US Context: Background on Impact of Universities on the Economy Including SMEs

Showcasing the impact of research universities is divided into two parts: one part displays the knowledge production function and the other reveals the knowledge transfer role, in which both constitute the fundamental purpose of research universities. Knowledge creation is the outcome of the research and scholarly activities, and knowledge transfer is the impact of the university's scientific work beyond the boundaries of the university in the form of spin-offs and other types of technology transfer. An evaluation of the university's research activities requires an understanding of the ways that the research teams leading to scientific discoveries are organized or have certain characteristics. To address the vital question on the origins of scientific discov-

---

1 Responsible Research for Business and Management (RRBM) Webinar, Doing Meaningful Research: Traps and Tricks on October 22, 2020.
2 Responsible Research for Business and Management (RRBM) Webinar, Scholarly Impact: Finding the Holy Grail on November 18, 2020.
3 Research Universities and the Public Good in the Time of COVID-19 Webinar on December 2, 2020.

eries and in unravelling the practical implications of research universities, IRIS and its data are integral to filling this gap.

First, we describe and outline the data curation effort led at IRIS and lay out the framework of the first tranche of rich data that documents the short-term as well as the long-term effects of scientific activities at US research universities. We introduce IRIS which is integral for better understanding the value of science by collecting, improving, and using big data to reveal the dynamics of science and the economy. Second, we outline the research investigations and findings using IRIS data. Third, we examine cases from the IRIS data and reports in which federally funded projects have led to a positive impact on the economy including SMEs in the US.

The Institute for Research on Innovation and Science (IRIS)

IRIS[4] is an IRB-approved data repository housed at the University of Michigan's Institute for Social Research. IRIS reveals detailed data from US member universities and represents more than 41% of US total R&D spending at universities. To provide clarity to how IRIS works we include Figure 28.1.

IRIS was founded in 2015 with the support of the Ewing Marion Kauffman and Alfred P. Sloan foundations ("Creating Trusted Independent Data About the Impact of Research," 2021) since science funding agencies such as the National Science Foundation (NSF), National Institutes for Health (NIH), and U.S. Department of Agriculture (USDA) were interested in the process of how discoveries were made, and ideas were created, transmitted, and adopted by researchers. The infrastructure for research and reporting represented by IRIS is a unique resource for scholarly communities in the social sciences, network science, the science of science policy, and information science.

IRIS houses the UMETRICS (Universities Measuring the Effects of Research on Innovation, Competitiveness, and Science) data infrastructure which falls within the realm of "big data"[5] (Einav & Levin, 2014; Lane et al., 2015). To provide some context, UMETRICS evolved from the STAR METRICS project which started by US universities and federal agencies with the engagement of the Federal Demonstration Partnership (FDP) in 2009. The project aimed to develop an open source data platform that keeps evolving and that was intended to inform policymakers about the process of research and inform researchers about research funding and its related outcomes. Given that

---

4 IRIS is a consortium of US research universities using big administrative data to explain the impact of higher education universities on the economy, SMEs, the career pathways of students, and national prosperity.
5 "Big data" is often described as a rich and complicated set of characteristics, techniques, practices, and outcomes related with data and deals with data sets that may be complex and large that when analyzed can reveal patterns and associations related to researcher characteristics and research productivity and outcomes.

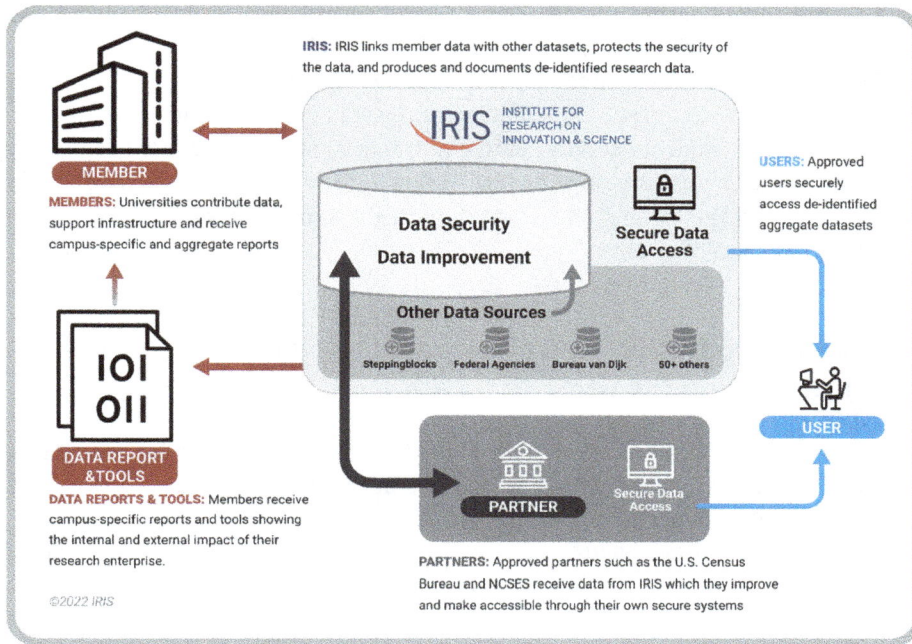

Figure 28.1: How IRIS works.
Source: https://iris.isr.umich.edu/about/

it was impossible to gather data from all scientific researchers whose research is supported from different federal agencies, the STAR METRICS project collected info from the research universities' administrative grant records that have record-level data on wage payments that the university researchers received from the federal grants (Lane et al., 2015).

The UMETRICS data has been considered the first large scale big data social infrastructure (Lane, 2018, p. 245). The data provide project-level info about the occupations of the workforce paid through the funded grants and about the purchases made from the vendors who supply the scientists (Weinberg et al., 2014). Such data lays the foundation for capturing the impact of research that is conducted at universities. The core UMETRICS data infrastructure was laid out in the work of Lane et al. (2015) which has outlined the linkages that are being done by utilizing the identified employer and vendor data.

Fundamentally, the UMETRICS data contains transaction-level information of over 450,000 sponsored projects that employ more than 720,000 individuals with coverage from 2001 till 2023. UMETRICS centers on university personnel administrative and financial data that pertain to funded project expenses submitted by IRIS member universities. Each IRIS member university provides information from its funded projects, procurement, and human resources systems. IRIS removes the personal identities from the individual campus files, clean, and then assemble them to generate the annual data release (which can be acesssed through the IRIS Virtual Data Enclave).

The UMETRICS data contains information on all individuals on federally funded research projects. These grant-level data are aggregated to the team level by integrating all employees (students, faculty, staff, and trainees) paid by any grant associated with the same principal investigator (PI). The result is complete teams that closely mimic the labs and research groups that established PIs fund and staff by drawing on multiple related project grants.

Knowledge Production Role of Research Universities: Research Evidence of Using the UMETRICS Data

The value of the UMETRICS data in showcasing the knowledge generation function of universities has been validated in use and has been used by previous researchers (Chang et al., 2019; Coupet & Ba, 2021; Lane et al., 2015; Tham, 2020).

Usually, researchers who are in the field of team science consider the team of researchers as the set of individuals who have co-authored a paper (Liu et al., 2020). Yet, by using the UMETRICS data one would be able to identify a more expansive definition of teams which accounts for all the individuals who worked on the grant and contributed to the subsequent set of scientific publications. Without the UMETRICS data it would be difficult to identify all team members who contributed to a research project.

The UMETRICS data allows researchers to conduct a longitudinal analysis on the team associated with the PI and team-level outcomes (e.g. publications, career outcomes). The UMETRICS data covers the observations over time for each of the team of researchers and would allow researchers to construct time-varying measures of team-level characteristics (e.g. gender distribution of the team, team size) and test their impact on the team's outputs (e.g. scholarly publications). Further, the UMETRICS data provides information on the amount, sources (e.g. NSF, NIH), and duration of funding for each of the team of researchers. Teams may have similar funding but have different members on the team (one team may be dominated with postdocs and another may be predominantly staff members) and this would lead to different team outputs. Through using the UMETRICS data, one would be able to uncover the impact of team characteristics on the team's outputs.

Not only do research investments generate new discoveries, but they also train individuals who are paid on research grants and create new collaboration networks that may sustain for the long-term and become sources for new innovations. Such individuals who gain new research ideas and skills from their research endeavor may move on to non-academic sectors. The application of new research ideas in different non-academic settings would drive social and economic impact. If researchers use the

UMETRICS data, then they would be able to track such movements and influences beyond scholarly boundaries.

The UMETRICS data contains information on the researchers that would enable linkages to outside sources of data such as to Census data, ProQuest dissertations, and Survey of Earned Doctorates (SED). For instance, previous researchers have outlined the possibilities of linking the UMETRICS data to the Survey of Earned Doctorates, which is a vital US survey dataset that has information on the doctoral workforce (Chang et al., 2019). By linking data from UMETRICS on research funding to SED on the doctoral qualified workforce, one would be able to track the number of individuals who are supported by different research funding agencies and in which disciplines. One would be able to link the UMETRICS data to other information about the researchers such as their networks and scientific outputs (publications) through linkages to PubMed or Web of Science, and patents through linkages to US patents. Researchers can also link information from the UMETRICS data to economic output measures such as job placements, earnings, and career trajectories of the researchers on the team (Lane et al., 2015). Through using the UMETRICS data, one can trace how many researchers who worked on different research projects end up driving policy changes or how many of them would be in industrial sectors.

Previous research has used the UMETRICS data to examine funding interruptions and their impact on research outcomes (Tham, 2020). The U.S. federal budget has been a major source of uncertainty in recent years leading federal agencies to delay spending. This may negatively impact economic activity, for example research. Tham (2020) found that researchers responded to such delays in funding or funding interruptions by spending less in the months leading up to the expiration of the funding, and even after funding resumed in the first month spending was still substantially lower. Funding interruptions have a disruptive effect on research even if funding becomes available to the researchers. By using the UMETRICS data, one would be able to show how integral it is for funding agencies to consider the continuity of funding when they award research projects.

Other researchers have adopted the UMETRICS data to investigate the degree to which federal funding from different sources affects the university's technology transfer performance (Coupet & Ba, 2021). Previous researchers were unable to conduct such an investigation due to the limited nuanced data on external research funding and investments. Coupet and Ba (2021) used the UMETRICS data and linked it to data on technology transfer known as AUTM (Association of University Technology Managers). Their study has implication for policymakers and university administrators and revealed that universities may utilize external funding to obtain various technology outcomes. Yet, performance in one dimension might not imply performance in other dimensions (e.g. high performance from licensing and patent activity did not correspond with performance in producing revenue from entrepreneurial activities or launching start-ups). The study also found that NSF funding improved the commercialization performance of universities whereas NIH or USDA funding did not have a significant impact on technology transfer production.

The UMETRICS data can provide researchers with the opportunity to address research questions that would not only advance the fields of science and social science, but also by analyzing the social and economic effects of research investments it would have implications for policy makers, funding agencies, and the member universities on how research investments impact the economy including SMEs.

Knowledge Transfer Function of Research Universities: Case Examples Using the IRIS Data and Reports

Students as the beneficiaries are not only the sole recipients of the services received by the university but are also part of the value-creating process that occurs at universities. Their active involvement in research projects at universities may lead to innovative outputs and to a positive impact on their economy including SMEs.

IRIS data is integral in revealing the impact of universities on SMEs and women- or minority- owned businesses. Case examples of how IRIS member universities impact SMEs are: (1) a small female owned business located in Michigan has obtained more than $500,000 in research related contracts since 2017 for supplying research teams across the university of Michigan with laboratory supplies and equipment; (2) a construction company based in Michigan obtained a $1 million contract to develop artificial spawning reef units; and (3) overall Michigan based firms have obtained more than $517 million since 2017 to supply goods and services to assist the University of Michigan's research activities (Keeves, 2022). One prominent case example, Carlin's creations, is a business that received a research contract from a Professor from the University of Michigan Kinesiology department and the company produces treadmills used by infants with Down Syndrome which Professor Ulrich discovered and helps such children develop more quickly. The discovery of the importance of treadmills for children with Down Syndrome led to a partnership with Sam Carlins, owner of Carlin's Creations in Michigan, to produce treadmills for children with Down Syndrome. The Carlin's Creations is now one of many vendors based in Michigan which supply their products and services to support IRIS. Such a small medium enterprise has produced more than 400 treadmills for patients across the country and it has had to expand to meet demand (Use Cases, 2021).

IRIS reports have indicated the economic impact that research funding has made possible. One case example is Kansas University, which supported the salaries of more than 3,000 individuals in the university in 2020 and accounted for $38.7 million spending with Kansas businesses on goods and services used for research. About 34% of research-funded employees were students (at the graduate and undergraduate level) and 19% were faculty members. Having a higher proportion of students on the team has been positively related to a more novel output (Zhang et al., 2017).

The IRIS institute has also provided evidence on how Northwestern University led an economic boost of almost $800 million on the US economy between 2009 and 2017, and their report showed how small businesses and minority-owned vendors were among the beneficiaries. Specifically, the IRIS reports show that spending from federal research funding flowed to 10,415 vendors and subcontractors over that period and of those almost 1,500 were small businesses. About 730 vendors were minority- or women-owned businesses that attracted almost $17 million in federal research spending from Northwestern university.

IRIS has revealed how Boston University had a powerful economic impact in which its research projects generated $395 million in new businesses nationally between the fiscal years 2015 and 2018. Not only did Boston University fuel business growth, but it also employed an average of 5,700 people per year between 2014 and 2017. Of those research-funded employees, nearly 55% were students (graduates and undergraduates) and only 9% were faculty members. Such reports exhibit evidence of how students have constituted the majority of contributors steering the sponsored research projects that have had a positive impact on the economy.

Additionally, IRIS displays evidence through its reports portal of the number and job titles of the individuals (faculty, staff, students) who are paid on research grants in all the IRIS member universities ("Reports & Products," 2021). In the fiscal year 2017, their report revealed that a majority of the people paid through grants in all member universities were students (whether graduate or undergraduate students) followed by staff and then faculty members.

Not only have IRIS reports shown the involvement of students on research grants but also IRIS has revealed through its vendor reports that a large portion of IRIS member universities' vendors were small business and minority or woman-owned businesses. Specifically, their reports show that between 2015 and 2019, 8,939 of the member universities' vendors were small businesses and 5,519 were minority- or woman- owned businesses ("Reports & Products," 2022). Their vendor report reveals that IRIS member universities spending in 2019 was $54.64 million on 2,654 small businesses, of which 45% of that spending was on woman-owned businesses and 47% of the spending was on minority-owned businesses.

Research universities play a vital role in supporting micro-level student-faculty interactions in which students are heavily involved in sponsored research projects that are led by a research professor as the PI. By having more students on the research team and more students engaging in research, and not only faculty members, brings more diversity to the group (Dolan & Johnson, 2010) and results in innovative research outputs (Zhang et al., 2017). Studies have shown that dyads involving students are the most likely to involve a new collaboration (or initiation of work with scientists whom they did not collaborate with before) (Colatat, 2015). Through the longitudinal analysis of the UMETRICS data one is able to trace the influence that research investments have on those employed on the grant.

Part III: China Context: Junzi Index Research and Business Ethics Education at The Hang Seng University of Hong Kong (HSUHK)

This part of the chapter carries the same structure as Part II by providing the background of the HSU business school in Hong Kong, the knowledge creation of the 10-year old Junzi Index that is essentially an ethical pulse check of business operations in Hong Kong, and the knowledge transfer efforts involved. Confucius-based education and research activities are attracting more research interests (Marginson, 2011). It was considered that the hybrid values of the East and the West were creating a new perspective of harmony that could shape modernization in the knowledge economy. Furthermore, sustainable economic growth requires moral business leaders who are conscious in handling stakeholders and sustainable practices with minimum negative externalities (Svensson et al., 2010). With the rising trend of sustainability reporting, SME growth and economic development are not only about financial growth but the mitigation of negative impacts on the natural environment and stakeholder wellbeing. The moral and ethical practices rooted in good values that shape a cognitive route of thinking therefore can create social value. The Junzi Index is promoting the conscious practice of Confucius values that can impact the decision-making process in business operation and address environmental and social concerns.

The Hang Seng University of Hong Kong and its Pursuit in Knowledge Creation and Transfer

HSUHK adopts a liberal art and professional education model that puts particular emphasis on research and partnership with industry players. It has five schools (Business, Communication, Decision Sciences, Humanities & Social Science, and Translation), with around 6,000 full-time students and 200 full-time faculty members. Under the promotion of a collaborative research culture, the Junzi Index research has been steered and conducted over the last ten years through the collaboration of the School of Business and School of Communication.

Knowledge Creation Rationale in Driving an Inquiry-based Learning Approach for the Junzi Index Research Project

In view of the importance of sustainability and corporate social responsibility practices, virtue ethics, which is value and character-based, has become a topical discussion for practitioners and academics. Virtue ethics, that is applied by businesses, involve the drive of moral excellence in stakeholder management, decision-making, and general right conduct in managing businesses. Entrepreneurs or business decision-makers with perceived and trusted moral character are able to help organizations gain customers' trust and loyalty because of the perceived integrity (Cheung & King, 2004). As the brand personality of an organization becomes an important area of consumer research, the moral character traits are an important attribute to business performance if consumers consider a brand ethical and hence trustworthy (Keller & Richey, 2006; Tian, 2010). Hence, customer loyalty can be attained. The stronger business case of practicing virtue ethics is particularly valid in a Chinese context that upholds the values of benevolence and collectivism. Therefore, the understanding of the moral character of organizations within a Chinese context is an important area of knowledge creation. The study of the customer-organization perception fit can advance the knowledge in entrepreneurial marketing, particularly related to customer loyalty (Kwong et al., 2015).

The Junzi concept has been considered as an exemplar in Confucianism, an area of Chinese philosophy, which promoted an ethical and responsible orientation for individuals and organizations (Tian et al., 2021; Lee, 2020). Adopting the core virtues in the Junzi concept (including the benevolence of "Ren"; the appropriateness of "Yi"; the propriety of "Li'; the wisdom of "Zhi'; and the integrity of "Xin"), the research involved understanding consumer perception towards 30 organizations (Junzi enterprises) in different sectors using survey questionnaires. The consumer rating of the organizational culture of each organization was based on Junzi orientation scale along the five virtues. The sectors examined included "retailing," "hotel and catering," "financial and insurance," "postal and transport operation," "tourism," 'information system and mobile services," and "real estate." The final findings contributed to the exposition of which three sectors were rated above the other sectors. Moreover, under each virtue aspect, the organizations rated the highest were also identified.

In terms of the tasks, student research assistants in teams of two to three went to the 17 Hong Kong districts according to the geographic delineation of the District Councils in Hong Kong to collect opinions from district residents. This round of face-to-face interviews helped select 30 organizations for the seven sectors. Then research assistants conducted a survey in seven districts on the respondent perceptions towards the 30 organizations. These two rounds of data collection as tasks contributing to the research outcomes impacted students on their moral development, other than helping out with the data collection. Their curiosity and motivation were stirred because they were part of a scientific research process that could reveal the reality of customer perception directed towards ethical organizational leadership. In the process of data collection, the student research assistants saw for themselves how the virtuous aspects could be rated by consumers, validating that consumer perception, which could be abstract but captured through a systemic research process. It is part of the project design that student researchers could establish a connection between customer perception and an organizational culture. Moreover, in the process of data collection, these student researchers also witnessed for themselves directly how one organization was rated above another. Hence, the differentiation of consumer perception could possibly affect their purchase, investment or even career decision-making depending on how the public engaged with different organizations in different capacities.

In terms of resources, students were given training to pick up the research and analytical skills after the data were collected. This served as a form of empowerment as they took up a research role. Moreover, when performing the related tasks, students were exposed to a research process and environment that could trigger their sense of discovery related to ethical organization culture. This helped to widen student exposure and cognitive awareness as a form of inquiry-based learning. Finally, in terms of guidance, the close working relationship with teacher experts who could provide guidance, in-depth research perspective, and insights as collaborators instantly elevated students' roles as research collaborators. This new role could sharpen students' cognitive ability in understanding responsible enterprise practices that uphold ethical values.

Participated students expressed their "spirit to serve" as the dominant reason for joining the Junzi research. Moreover, they also felt proud of being part of an important research effort which could promote the virtuous values of Junzi and facilitate the sustainable development of the responsible practices within Hong Kong. Therefore, using the inquiry-based learning produces the positive outcome in enhancing students' awareness and learning of business ethics.

Junzi Research Methodology and Results

By integrating the virtuous values of the Junzi concept, the Junzi Index research aimed at setting the five virtuous aspects as the standard of ethical enterprise practices. This Junzi Index research was initiated in 2011 at HSU. The five virtues include the benevolence of "Ren"; the appropriateness of "Yi"; the propriety of "Li"; the wisdom of "Zhi"; and the integrity of "Xin." By conducting a systematic research approach in evaluating the public perception, with a sample size of around 2000, towards the prominent organizations in different sectors, the Junzi Index research had established a consistent, valid, and committed research effort that informed different sectors in Hong Kong on consumers' perceived values upheld by organizations in different business sectors. Every year, the research results contributed to the selection of ten organizations that attained the highest scores. These organizations, to some extent, served as the role models for ethical enterprise practices in their own sectors. Over time, the Junzi Index has offered a standard of responsible management practices that could be measured by consumer perception.

Data Collection and Methodology

To empower students to pursue inquiry-based learning, the data collection of the Junzi index research was conducted predominantly by students, from the marketing and communication majors. After the student applicants had been selected, they were given the necessary training on conducting data collection and data analysis. Students were trained to conduct qualitative interviews as well as conduct face to face surveys.

Two stages were involved in conducting the index research. In the first stage of research, a standardized interview protocol and a survey questionnaire were used. The first stage involved identifying 30 organizations to be included for the next stage of survey research. With technology advancement, internet nominations of organizations by the public started to be made available from 2019. The nominated organizations totaled 210. Students then followed up to explain the definition of Junzi values and invited the nominators to rate the nominated organizations. At the end of the first stage of research, a total of 2,346 respondents participated in the simple survey rating to select the top 30 organizations that covered the seven sectors for the second round of survey research.

In the second stage of data collection, random sampling, around a sample size of 500, was adopted to conduct a survey with the public in Hong Kong. The survey ratings, towards the seven sectors including retailing, hotel and catering, financial and insurance services, postal and transport, tourism, information and mobile services, and real estate, were collected and analyzed.

Data Analysis and Results

The total score of the Junzi Index is 100. Over the years, the Junzi Index had volatility in terms of the total score. This indicated that the perception of the public changed, subject to economic, organizational, and individual factors. This justified the persistent efforts in conducting the Junzi Index research to monitor the pulse of the public in rating the ethical performance of different sectors. Figure 28.2 provides the score trends of the Junzi Index between 2011 and 2019. Figure 28.3 shows the comparison of the score differential between sectors over the period of 2011 to 2019.

When looking at the comparison of the Junzi Index amongst different sectors, there were some interesting findings. The sectors that had stayed consistently in the top three or four rankings included retailing, postal and transport, hotel and catering, and tourism. The real estate sector had consistently had low scores over the years. This indicated that the public's perception of different sectors differentiated, possibly based on their subjective view towards the ethical organizational culture. The financial and insurance sector dropped drastically in 2018 and 2019.

Every year, the breakdown of the scores in the different Junzi Index dimensions were published to allow the public rating of different sectors. These different Junzi Index dimensions included benevolence (Ren), appropriateness (Yi), propriety (Li), wisdom (Zhi), and integrity (Xin). The Junzi scores of each sector were generated from the average score. These five dimensions were also interpreted as the five virtues of the Junzi orientation. Table 28.1 provides the breakdown of the 2019 score data.

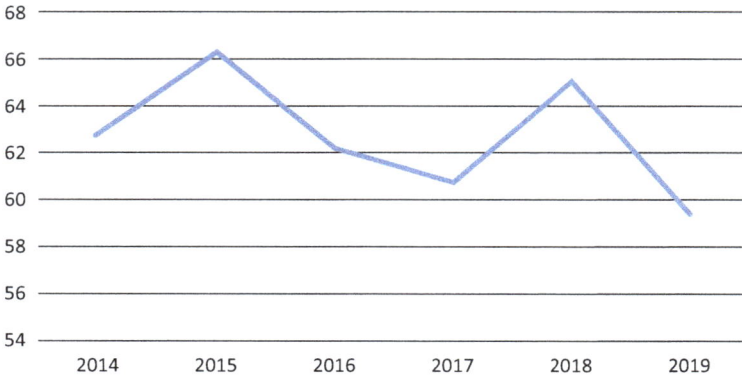

Figure 28.2: Score trends of the Junzi Index between 2011 and 2019.

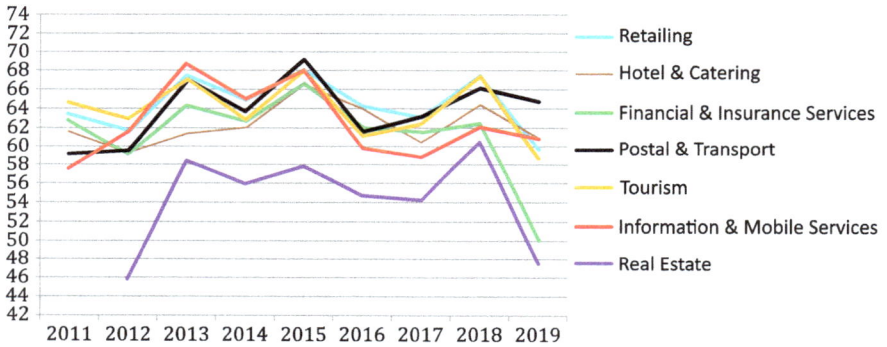

Figure 28.3: Score trends of different sectors between 2011 and 2019.

Moreover, the Junzi Index research also published the score trends of each sector. Figure 28.4 showed the score trends of the postal and transport sector from 2011 to 2019. Furthermore, the score trends of each Junzi Index dimension for each sector were also published every year.

The Junzi Index served as a barometer for Hong Kong business practices in terms of the public perception towards the most vibrant sectors in operation. The longitudinal index analysis indicated that there was a statistically significant asymmetric, contemporaneous differentiation amongst sectors. Business practices within the different sectors could be better informed of the public perception towards their practices as a form of knowledge. Moreover, the Junzi Index could also serve as a form of intelligence in providing a comparative analysis of the cross-sectoral performance perceived by the general public.

Table 28.1: Junzi Index research – sectoral scores in 2019.

Sectors	Five Virtues of the Junzi Orientation					
	Benevolence (Ren)	Appropriate-Ness (Yi)	Propriety (Li)	Wisdom (Zhi)	Integrity (Xin)	Junzi Score
Postal & Transport	64.0	65.8	63.8	64.1	65.7	64.8
Hotel & Catering	60.9	63.80	61.3	62.0	61.7	61.0
Information & Mobile Systems	60.3	63.2	59.9	62.2	60.8	60.8
Tourism	58.3	60.4	61.0	61.5	59.1	58.7
Retailing	60.3	62.0	61.5	61.0	59.9	59.8
Financial and Insurance Services	49.1	50.5	53.2	57.5	49.4	50.2
Real Estate	46.3	48.1	58.9	54.4	46.6	47.6

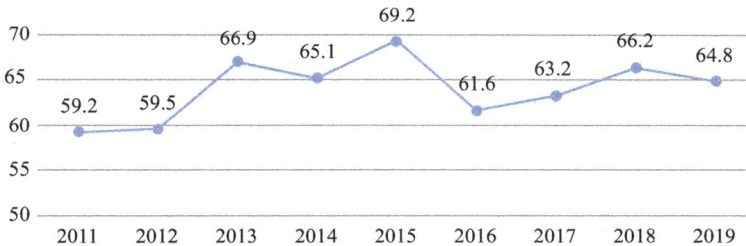

Figure 28.4: Score trends of the postal and transport sector from 2011 to 2019.

Findings and Knowledge Transfer of the Junzi Index Research

Engaging Multiple Stakeholder Groups

The Junzi Index research had engaged the participation of multiple stakeholder groups throughout the years and raised the joined effort opportunities in promoting responsible business practices and ethical organizational culture.

At the data collection stage, students were engaged in inquiry-based learning as student researchers. This action learning opportunity enhanced their knowledge and skill set in not only conducting research but the knowledge and understanding of responsible management practices and the Junzi orientation. Moreover, student-teacher collaboration offered an important learning environment in sustaining a purposeful research effort that informs the business sectors and general public.

After the research analysis was completed every year, the organizations attaining the highest Junzi Index scores would attend an award presentation ceremony jointly organized with a local chamber of commerce. The university took the opportunity to turn the award presentation ceremony into a learning environment with awardees sharing their responsible practices. As a result, the event attracted over 200 participants, including not only awardee organizations but also other business executives, every year in supporting and learning about responsible management.

Facilitating Social Awareness of Ethical Enterprise Practices through Media Coverage

Journalists were also an important stakeholder group that attended the award ceremony every year. Moreover, press releases were sent to all media organizations and published on the university website to facilitate the dissemination of the research results. Further, media coverage of the awardee organizations provided more in-depth understanding of the responsible practices through the direct narratives from the related business executives. Through the media coverage, a wider audience could be informed about the Junzi Index, Junzi orientation, and the five virtues being measured as a perspective of responsible management in practice. As repeated coverage over the years reached different readers, this served as a sustained effort in developing responsible management within the society.

Knowledge Creation Published in Academic Journals and at Conferences

The Junzi Index research had contributed to knowledge creation with participating scholar-teachers publishing their conference and academic journals. Research that examined the relationship between customer loyalty and the perceived virtuous character of employees (Kwong et al., 2015); the measurement of the Junzi values (Kwong et al., 2016); and corporate culture and business performance from a Confucian perspective (Tian et al., 2021) was advanced and provided a unique perspective for business practices particularly situated in the Chinese context.

Created Ripple Effects in Promoting Inquiry-based Learning

As the institution successfully established the Junzi Index research that had informed the business sectors on responsible management, a ripple effect of extending inquiry-based learning and knowledge creation to influence organizational practices has resulted. Other non-profit organizations find it attractive to partner with the institution in fostering positive organization culture. Another new research collaboration based on the "Chief Happiness Officer" social movement that aims at examining workplace happiness beyond COVID-19 is expected to become another research effort that will impact and inform business practices.

Conclusions

We reveal the seminal role of research universities in being the future engines of value creation in a knowledge-based economy. At the sole of advanced technologies and start-ups is university-based sponsored research in which most scientific work depends on a mix of individuals with various skills and different occupations who steer the research projects. To understand the origins of scientific advancement one needs to examine the scientific teams that are leading the research work. We have uncovered the contribution of research universities to societal advancement through fulfilling their essential role in producing and transferring new and novel knowledge in the US context but also in underpinning value-based business ethics in the Chinese context. These are two different ways in which research is being conducted that makes the university and its impact the subject of study in an effort to comprehend, elucidate, and enhance the public value of research and higher education and to have a data-informed understanding of how the research impacts its communities with regards to business ethics and the fulfillment of social responsibility. At one end, we provide case examples from IRIS which produces reports and data to illuminate the positive impact of US universities' scholarly activities on the economy including SMEs. At another end, the moral character of businesses operating in the Hong Kong economy have been examined in a sustained manner to validate the importance of customers' perception towards responsible organizations, with research conducted by The Hang Seng University of Hong Kong (HSU). The Junzi Index findings can be applied in further research such as drawing possible relations between the perception of moral character and customer perceived quality and value of goods (Kwong et al., 2015).

Future research can build upon the IRIS work and the UMETRICS initiative as we have revealed the contributions of the institute's empirical work in uncovering the positive impact of research universities on their economy including SMEs. The foundations of such empirical work can be utilized not only in the US but also possibly in other countries worldwide. Further, the value of nurturing inquisitive and morally responsible future generations has so easily been overlooked as an unintended outcome of research pursuit. In reality, many of the future responsible entrepreneurs and academic researchers have benefitted from the knowledge creation experience through the engagement in research projects and the insights gained from the in-depth understanding of business theories and operations. The outcome is part of the human capital investment for an economy that requires entrepreneurial, inquisitive, and moral responsible players to create future economic and social development.

References

Adams, J.S., Harris, C., & Carley, S. (1998). Challenges in teaching business ethics: Using role set analysis of early career dilemmas. *Journal of Business Ethics*, *17*(12), 1325–1335.

Alvarez-Torres, F.J., Lopez-Torres, G.C., & Schiuma, G. (2019). Linking entrepreneurial orientation to SMEs' performance: Implications for entrepreneurship universities. *Management Decision*, *57*(12), 3364–3386.

Alvesson, M., & Sandberg, J. (2014). Habitat and habitus: Boxed-in versus box-breaking research. *Organization Studies*, *35*(7), 967–987.

Arlow, P., & Ulrich, T.A. (1988). A longitudinal survey of business school graduates' assessments of business ethics. *Journal of Business Ethics*, *7*, 295–302.

Berry, A.J., Sweeting, R., & Goto, J. (2006). The effect of business advisers on the performance of SMEs. *Journal of Small Business and Enterprise Development*, *13*(1), 33–47.

Chang, W.Y., Cheng, W., Lane, J., & Weinberg, B. (2019). Federal funding of doctoral recipients: What can be learned from linked data. *Research Policy*, *48*(6), 1487–1492.

Cheung, T.S., & King, A.Y.-C. (2004). Righteousness and profitableness: The moral choice of contemporary Confucian entrepreneurs. *Journal of Business Ethics*, *54*(3), 245–260.

Colatat, P. (2015). An organizational perspective to funding science: Collaborator novelty at DARPA. *Research Policy*, *44*(4), 874–887.

Collier, A., Gray, B.J., & Ahn, M.J. (2011). Enablers and barriers to university and high technology SME partnerships. *Small Enterprise Research*, *18*(1), 2–18.

Coupet, J., & Ba, Y. (2021). Benchmarking university technology transfer performance with external research funding: A stochastic frontier analysis. *The Journal of Technology Transfer*, 1–16. https://doi.org/10.1007/s10961-021-09856-3

Creating Trusted Independent Data About the Impact of Research. (2021, October 25). https://iris.isr.umich.edu/about/

Dolan, E.L., & Johnson, D. (2010). The undergraduate-postgraduate-faculty triad: Unique functions and tensions associated with undergraduate research experiences at research universities. *CBE – Life Sciences Education*, *9*(4), 543–553.

Drucker, J., & Goldstein, H. (2007). Assessing the regional economic development impacts of universities: A review of current approaches. *International Regional Science Review*, *30*(1), 20–46.

Einav, L., & Levin, J. (2014). The data revolution and economic analysis. *Innovation Policy and the Economy*, *14*(1), 1–24.

Etzkowitz, H. (2016). The entrepreneurial university: Vision and metrics, *Industry and Higher Education*, *30* (2), 83–97.

Etzkowitz, H., & Zhou, C. (2017). *The triple helix: University-industry-government innovation and entrepreneurship*. Routledge.

Fayolle, A., & Redford, D.T. (2014). *Handbook on the entrepreneurial university*. Edward Elgar Publishing.

Giacalone, R.A., & Promislo, M.D. (2013). Broken when entering: The stigmatization of goodness and business ethics education. *Academy of Management Learning & Education*, *12*(1), 86–101.

Gordon, I., Hamilton, E., & Jack, S. (2012). A study of a university-led entrepreneurship education programme for small business owner/managers. *Entrepreneurship & Regional Development*, *24*(9–10), 767–805.

Guerrero, M., Cunningham, J.A., & Urbanos, D. (2015). Economic impact of entrepreneurial universities' activities: An exploratory study of the United Kingdom. *Research Policy*, *44*(3), 748–764.

Keeves, K. U-M research contributed nearly $100M to state's economy in '21. (2022, March 7). https://record.umich.edu/articles/u-m-research-contributed-nearly-100m-to-states-economy-in-21/

Keller, L.K., & Richey, K. (2006). The importance of corporate brand personality traits to a successful 21st century business. *Brand Management*, *14*(1/2), 74–81.

Kwong, K.K., Tang, F., & Xie, T. (2016). Is the concept of Junzi measurable? A consumer perspective of virtue ethics in China. *6th World Business Ethics Forum*.

Kwong, K.K., Tang, F., Tian, V., & Fung, A.L.K. (2015). Can customer loyalty be explained by virtue ethics? The Chinese way. *Asian Journal of Business Ethics*, *4*(1), 101–115.

Lane, J. (2018). Building an infrastructure to support the use of government administrative data for program performance and social science research. *The ANNALS of the American Academy of Political and Social Science*, *675*(1), 240–252.

Lane, J., Owen-Smith, J., Rosen, R.F., & Weinberg, B.A. (2015). New linked data on research investments: Scientific workforce, productivity, and public value. *Research Policy*, *44*(9), 1659–1671.

Laurillard, D. (2012). *Teaching as a design science. Building pedagogical patterns for learning and technology*. Routledge.

Lee, Y. (2020). The narrative of the Junzi as an exemplar in classical Confucianism and its implications for moral and character education. *Education Philosophy and Theory*, *53*(6), 634–643.

Liu, Y., Wu, Y., Rousseau, S., & Rousseau, R. (2020). Reflections on and a short review of the science of team science. *Scientometrics*, 1–14.

Man, T.W.Y., & Lau, T. (2005). The context of entrepreneurship in Hong Kong. *Journal of Small Business and Enterprise Development*, *12*(4), 464–481.

Marginson, S. (2011). Higher education in East Asia and Singapore: Rise of the Confucian Model. *Higher Education*, *61*(5), 587–611.

Mindruta, D. (2013). Value creation in university-firm research collaborations: A matching approach. *Strategic Management Journal*, *34*(6), 644–665.

Molas-Gallart, J., Tang, P., & Morrow, S. (2000). Assessing the non-academic impact of grant-funded socio-economic research: Results from a pilot study. *Research Evaluation*, *9*(3), 171–182.

Oliver, R. (2008). Engaging first year students using a web-supported inquiry-based learning setting. *Higher Education*, *55*(3), 285–301.

Owen-Smith, J. (2018). *Research universities and the public good: Discovery for an uncertain future*. Stanford University Press.

Perkmann, M., Tartari, V., McKelvey, M., Autio, E., Broström, A., D'este, P., & Sobrero, M. (2013). Academic engagement and commercialisation: A review of the literature on university-industry relations. *Research Policy*, *42*(2), 423–442.

Phan, P.H., Siegel, D.S., & Wright, M. (2005). Science parks and incubators: Observations, synthesis, and future research. *Journal of Business Venturing*, *20*(2), 165–182.

Rasmussen, E., & Wright, M. (2015). How can universities facilitate academic spin-offs? An entrepreneurial competency perspective. *The Journal of Technology Transfer*, *40*(5), 782–799.

Reports & Products (2021, October 25). https://iris.isr.umich.edu/membership/reports-and-products/

Reports & Products (2022, March 7). https://iris.isr.umich.edu/membership/reports-and-products/

Sine, W.D., & Shen, X. (2020). Jason Owen-Smith: Research universities and the public good: Discovery for an uncertain future. *Administrative Science Quarterly*, *65*(3), NP30–NP32.

Svensson, G., Wood, G., & Callaghan, M. (2010). A corporate model of sustainable business practices: An ethical perspective. *Journal of World Business*, *45*, 336–345.

Tian, V. (2010). Junzi orientation and business performance. Unpublished Doctoral Dissertation. The Chinese University of Hong Kong.

Tian, V., Tang, F., & Tse, A.C.B. (2021). Understanding corporate culture and business performance from a Confucian perspective. *Asia Pacific Journal of Marketing and Logistics*. https://doi.org/10.1108/APJML-08-2020-0555

Tham, W.Y. (2020). Science, interrupted: Funding delays reduce research activity but having more grants helps.

Use Cases. (2021, October 25). https://iris.isr.umich.edu/use-cases/

Waas, T., Verbruggen, A., & Wright, T. (2010). University research for sustainable development: Definition and characteristics explored. *Journal of Cleaner Production*, *18*(7), 629–636.

Weinberg, B.A., Owen-Smith, J., Rosen, R.F., Schwarz, L., Allen, B.M., Weiss, R.E., & Lane, J. (2014). Science funding and short-term economic activity. *Science*, *344*(6179), 41–43.

Zhang, H., Easterday, M.W., Gerber, E.M., Rees Lewis, D., & Maliakal, L. (2017, February). Agile research studios: Orchestrating communities of practice to advance research training. In *Proceedings of the 2017 ACM Conference on Computer Supported Cooperative Work and Social Computing* (pp. 220–232).

Reija A. Häkkinen and Juha Kansikas

29 Entrepreneurial Culture Creation through Employee Effectuation

Abstract: In tourism services, the value creation for the consumer is not just transaction-focused transfer of financial capital and services and products sold, but also transactional experience: socially constructed interaction between tourism employees and customers. The challenge in tourism services is that consumers have versatile expectations, which creates demand for unique value-creation in each transaction. Thus, employees often need to respond to customer expectations without prior detailed planning. This paper aims to increase understanding on how entrepreneurial endeavors, aimed towards high performance and good service for customers, are initiated by employees.

This study investigates theoretically enabling and preventing idea-generation, behavior, and actions in customer service through the lens of effectuation logics. Focus groups were conducted with the aim to understand the perspectives and reasoning of the participants also empirically. The purpose was to analyze the research data at two levels: among the groups and between the groups. Four focus group discussions were held for three hierarchy groups: the management team, middle-managers, and employees, consisting of six to eight members. Practically, this study creates perspectives on how employee effectuation can be a way to model entrepreneurialism in a SME, as a positive and enabling asset in value-creative mechanisms.

The results increase understanding of employee effectuation, suggesting that only a positive attitude of management is not enough in fostering and supporting entrepreneurial and service-related behaviors among employees. A more concrete HR support and acknowledgement of skills and capabilities of employees is needed, in order for the organization to benefit from the entrepreneurial and service-related behaviors. This study also enlightens the process of employee effectuation. Thus, employee effectuation can be cultivated in entrepreneurial organization culture in which employees can use their full potential and become independent entrepreneurial actors, and role models for new employees.

Keywords: entrepreneurial behavior, effectuation, organization, employee, service behavior

Reija A. Häkkinen, University of Jyväskylä
Juha Kansikas, School of Business and Economics, University of Jyväskylä, Finland

https://doi.org/10.1515/9783110747652-030

Introduction

Future customer needs and risks related to demand are difficult to predict and manage in small and medium-sized organizations (SMEs). Service organizations in the tourism and hospitality industries not only face challenges in planning services for new seasons but are also struggling for survival during the COVID-19 pandemic, which first emerged worldwide in 2020 (e.g., Fotiadis et al. 2021; Sigala, 2020). Under uncertain conditions, employee flexibility, service willingness, and service capability, together with the financial and nonfinancial rewarding mechanisms from an employer, can effectively manage future uncertainties. However, Ettlie and Rosenthal (2011) think service processes have been understudied by researchers because of the peculiar nature of service innovations and their processes. Effectual employees, units, and organizations take the initiative to find innovative solutions and new opportunities in the programs they launch in service markets (Nguyen et al., 2018). Designing a new service is an uncertain process with unpredictable results. Thus, effectuation fits into the service industry, as it provides a logical framework for managing uncertain entrepreneurial processes in organizations (Jiang & Rüling, 2019). Entrepreneurial culture is intertwined with everyday practices and processes, and for that reason, studying it through managers and employees in a service-oriented organization is meaningful. Therefore, in this paper, we study how effectuation logic may help to understand the microlevel structures of employee effectuation and the creation of entrepreneurial culture.

Neessen et al. (2019) mention that employees are currently asked to be more innovative and intrapreneurial and have an impact on organizational performance. Internal corporate venturing creates opportunities for effectual culture in service-oriented organizations. Internal corporate venturing, as a form of intrapreneurship, contributes to a firm's strategic evolution and to its capability development processes. As one study puts it, "Organizational performance, growth and development may depend considerably on entrepreneurship in existing organizations (intrapreneurship) and intrapreneurship-employee-related antecedents" (Antoncic & Antoncic 2011, p. 589).

Through entrepreneurial behavior, employees can influence other employees, teams, and even whole organizations. As organizations are systems that have common rules and behavioral patterns that may affect both service and the possibilities to act effectually, this study set out to investigate employee effectuation and the creation of entrepreneurial culture. The following research questions are answered through focus group discussions and their qualitative analysis:

1. What kinds of opportunities for employee effectuation are there in service design and development-related discussions of employees?
2. What kinds of opportunities are there for the creation of entrepreneurial culture through employee effectuation in a service-oriented organization?

In this paper, we suggest that effectual employees, units, and organizations are required to find innovative solutions and new opportunities to meet the changing needs of service markets.

This paper is organized as follows. The first section introduces the topic, while the second presents a literature review where the focus is on creating a conceptual pre-understanding of employee effectuation. The third section presents the study method, describing data collection in focus group discussions and the approach to data analysis. Fourth, the findings of the study focus on understanding employee effectuation and the creation of entrepreneurial culture, and fifth, discussion and conclusions reflect on conceptual understanding based on the empirical material gathered, while the study's contributions, limitations, and future research ideas on effectuation are also covered.

How does Effectuation Increase Employee Innovation?

Effectuation is a theory (e.g., Sarasvathy 2001, 2008) that explains how expert entrepreneurs start to seek partnerships, invest only what they can afford to lose, and leverage contingencies starting from the factors that are in their control. It must be noted that effectuation logic was originally developed based on the approaches of expert entrepreneurs, but this should not be held as a restriction against using it to understand other contexts (Welter et al., 2016). Deligianni et al. (2016) encourage researchers to study effectuation in fields of entrepreneurship other than new venture creation. Thus, in this paper, we study how effectuation logic may help in understanding the microlevel structures of employee effectuation and the creation of entrepreneurial culture.

Causation and effectuation are methods used in decision-making simultaneously by entrepreneurial employees, but studies have shown that they can be analyzed separately in empirical research (e.g., Perry et al., 2011; Read et al., 2009). Causation is a goal-driven logic where the market is defined, or the goal is otherwise predetermined. In causation, knowledge is used to build a competitive advantage over competitors. In effectuation, on the other hand, the creation process is open, and knowledge is shared between stakeholders (Reymen et al., 2015). Competitors can occasionally be cocreators in effectuation.

Contextually, effectuation denotes different types of normative behavioral forms. It describes expert entrepreneur behavior in relation to their cocreators. Thus, when accounting for the context of an organization, researchers need to consider effectuation according to the working styles of the specific unique organization. The work-related behavior of individuals differs: some employees work with each other, others are possibly forced to do so, and some cocreate new solutions innovatively. With this heterogeneity of organizations in mind, we respond to the call by Smolka et al. (2018)

to study effectuation at the level of the organization – how does it occur as employee effectuation, and how can it be used in entrepreneurial culture creation.

Emergence of Entrepreneurial Activities in an Organization

When we want to study effectuation inside an organization, we need to consider in our research that all employees are possible effectuators. Additionally, all employees are also possible noneffectuators. An effectuator is an active agent who considers his or her means, invites the stakeholders into cooperation and starts building a future where stakeholders participate in shaping the outcome. Thus, effectuation reflects internally motivated action.

Active agency requires reciprocity. Sarasvathy and Dew (2008) debate with Goel and Karri (2006) about overtrust in effectuation. According to Goel and Karri (2006), effectuation assumes overtrust, which means trusting others without objectively understanding the situation. However, in effectuation, stakeholders are assumed not to trust more than they can afford to lose (Sarasvathy & Dew, 2008). Here, we introduce the concept of reciprocity, which may be more functional in the context of the organization. Armstrong-Stassen and Schlosser (2008) found that because of the normative nature of reciprocity, employees who perceive their organization to be committed to them are more likely to give resources and effort back to their organization. According to them, one sign of this kind of commitment by an organization is an organizational culture that supports developmental activities by employees. Lack of support and dysfunctional corporate strategy, as well as bureaucratization, may hinder intrapreneurship (Neessen et al., 2019). Basically, in the organization, reciprocity does not only occur between persons but is also experienced in the relation between the person and the organization.

Furthermore, in order for employee effectuation to occur, organizational culture needs to support intrapreneurial efforts and, for example, creativity of action. Creativity of action is further explained by Sarasvathy (2008) with the help of, for example, Joas (2005). In an organization, using creativity is not merely the decision of the employee but is also affected by the circumstances. Antoncic and Antoncic (2011) point out that many researchers have shown that organizational culture, management support, and organizational values have an effect on employee intrapreneurship. Atienza (2015) mentions that an organizational culture supporting intrapreneurship gives employees the feeling that they have a freedom to share their ideas and that their active initiatives are encouraged, supported, and rewarded. According to Amabile (2012, 3), ". . . creativity should be highest when an intrinsically motivated person with high domain expertise and high skill in creative thinking works in an environment high in supports for creativity." When surprises occur, creativity is needed to overcome them

(Sarasvathy 2003, 2008). Thus, employee effectuation in an organization requires management to understand the conditions enabling and encouraging creative, active and innovative behavior.

Finally, management in effectual organizations needs to tolerate unpredictability. As Duening et al. (2012, p. 209) mention, "Managers seeking to make their enterprise entrepreneurial will be forced to resort to exhortations to be more 'flexible', 'adaptable', or 'innovative' like entrepreneurs appear to be, without knowing how these virtues are operationalized." Effectuation has the potential to be a tool with the help of which an enterprise might be able to systematically adopt entrepreneurial action and behavior in the organization.

As Kerr and Coviello (2020) remind us, effectuation strategies go in line with the opportunity-creation school of thought as it defines actions toward controlling an unpredictable future. Building unknown futures together with other stakeholders requires dialogue between parties. Sarasvathy et al. (2014) consider an effectuator to be an active agent with access to resources. Effectuation requires agency, which is a prime driver for opportunity creation (Sarasvathy, 2008). Therefore, to be considered an effectuator, employees need to identify themselves as active agents who participate in creating opportunities. In relation to understanding oneself as an active agent, being an effectuator also requires determination and a mutual vision toward a common goal. Cocreating the outcome requires a willingness to consider the perspectives of others, new information, and change. In effectuation, all these aspects may be assembled together as a patchwork quilt in cooperation with the other interested parties (e.g., Sarasvathy, 2001). In addition to striving toward a common goal, these active agents need to feel a sense of responsibility for actions that influence the outcome. An effectuator needs to consider resources available – whether they are tangible or intangible, or whether they are knowledge- or person-related – as potential, and he or she needs skills to affect the outcome (Sarasvathy et al., 2014).

Methodological Choices in this Study: Focus Group Discussions and Data Analysis

Peurunka is an organization located in Central Finland that is seeking organizational renewal and ways to foster service innovations. The case organization is an SME with approximately 150 employees. This organization was chosen for empirical study because it provided opportunities to understand employee effectuation within an organization where (a) the services are multiple, (b) there is often a need for customization, (c) there is a need to cooperate with experts from different fields, and (d) there is a strong customer service focus in its strategies. The case provides opportunities for a qualitative study of service supply, a heterogeneous employee base, and an ownership that is divided into a foundation and a corporation. Although this change from a rehabilitation center into a service provider happened in 2014, it has provided opportunities to adopt more flexible strategies to survive the COVID-19 pandemic, and thus it reflects the long-term development of an effectual culture in a service-oriented organization.

Focus group discussions were chosen as a research method to gain in-depth information on the interaction among the participants and to obtain an idea of the collective nature of the main themes in organizational development (Eriksson & Kovalainen, 2008). Focus groups aim to understand the perspectives and reasoning of the participants (Hennink, 2007). In this study, the purpose was to analyze the research data at two levels: among the groups and between the groups.

Four focus group discussions were held for three hierarchical groups: the management team, the middle managers, and the employees, consisting of six to eight members (the recommendation being between four and 12; Litosseliti, 2003, 3; Eriksson & Kovalainen 2008). Twenty-two individuals participated in the discussions. Six of them represented the management team, eight were middle managers, and eight were employees. The discussions were held from the end of November 2014 to mid-January 2015. Discussions were recorded with two voice recorders and a video recorder. The discussions lasted approximately 60 to 90 minutes and were transcribed into files 21 to 33 pages long. All of the focus groups discussed the following themes:

– Own job and the use of one's own strengths at work;
– Other respondents' jobs and how the others see their strengths;
– Changes at work and how they affect one's own work;
– How the participants receive and give feedback, and what customer interactions were like; and
– How their jobs developed from the beginning until the present

The analysis adopted procedures similar to the Gioia method, utilizing first-order codes, sub-theoretical categories, theoretical categories, and aggregate theoretical dimensions within the data (e.g., Gioia et al., 2012; Shepherd & Williams, 2014; Patzelt et al., 2014). The analysis is not entirely emergent in nature but was conducted using effectuation characteristics. This approach was chosen in the process of analysis because the findings were considered to provide a deeper understanding of the effectuation dynamics within an organization. As Gioia et al. (2012) state, new tools and concepts are needed to gain a better understanding of reality. However, our view is that another means to gain a better understanding of reality is to trust previous research results, which here regard effectuation, and to seek a deeper understanding of emergent employee actions with their help. We have applied the Gioia method to more deeply understand the different dimensions of employee effectuation. We seek to further explore effectuation dimensions and explain them more carefully within the context of an organization. Effectuation as a background theory gives us a frame to study the process of employee effectuation, but the result is "a static picture of a dynamic phenomenon" (Gioia et al., 2012, p. 22) grounded in both effectuation theory and our empirical data.

The analysis was conducted as follows. First, the transcriptions were read to obtain general impressions. Then, theoretically driven content analysis (Stemler, 2015) was used to study effectuation in the context of an organization. The idea behind this choice was twofold: to deepen our understanding of emergent entrepreneurial employee behavior and to seek additional avenues to support the use of emergent behavior in an organization when appropriate. As theorized in Häkkinen (2015), effectuation might help us understand how employees can actively affect an organization. Effectuation principles were held as aggregate dimensions, and the written data were analyzed under effectuation principles. The first author read the material several times and placed direct quotations of text into effectuation categories. Direct quotations were considered first-order concepts. After this phase, second-order themes emerged from the first-order concepts and those were linked with aggregate dimensions.

How Does Effectuation Appear in the Organizational Context?

This part of the study reports the results of the focus group discussions. The features of effectuation dimensions are considered in the organizational context with the help of the theoretical background of effectuation in Table 29.1. The original effectuation principle is mentioned shortly at the top of each table, and the contents are considered with the help of several extant theories explaining the phenomenon in a deeper fashion as employee features.

Table 29.1: Features of effectuation dimensions from the theoretical background.

Means; bird-in-hand principle – who I am, what I know, whom I know (Sarasvathy, 2001)	
Employee feature	**References**
Awareness of one's own capabilities and those of others, open conversations, and not trying to seek specific expertise Limited and specialized abilities that are fit for exchange with others	Brettel et al., 2012; Read & Sarasvathy, 2005
Making an effort in a collectively defined direction and supporting cooperation among cocreators	Read & Sarasvathy, 2012
In the organization, having an effect means enactment, cooperation, and negotiation, e.g., the employees can control their situation and how they do their assigned job	Read & Sarasvathy, 2012

Table 29.1 (continued)

Because the outcome gets created during the process, the actors are going to encounter failure, success, change responsiveness, and learning from experiences	Read et al., 2011
Trying without knowing the consequences requires action, courage, and persistence, and it might as well include getting rejected	Read & Sarasvathy, 2005

Affordable loss; nonpredictive control (Sarasvathy, 2001)

Employee feature	Reference
Paying attention to the cheapest alternatives and coming up with creative ways to do things more efficiently with no additional costs requires intellectual ability and participation, and deciding bravely what not to do	Read et al., 2011; Read & Sarasvathy, 2005
Risking less and making small changes along the way can be interpreted as investing only extra time and extra wealth, putting your reputation and emotions into the game.	Read et al., 2011; Sarasvathy, 2008

Partnerships, patchwork quilt principle (Sarasvathy, 2001)

Employee feature	Reference
Dynamic interactions between various stakeholders require interaction, disclosing new worlds and ways of worldmaking, taking something away, and adding something	Spinosa et al. 1997
The cocreation of markets needs transformation, change, cocreation, and the crafting and relating of compelling stories	Read & Sarasvathy, 2005
In order to reduce uncertainty and entry barriers, alliances and precommitments are realized through teamwork, communication, idea sharing, and delegating responsibilities	Read & Sarasvathy, 2005
Cocreation is inherent in effectuation	Read & Sarasvathy, 2012

Leveraging contingencies, lemonade principle (Sarasvathy, 2001)

Employee feature	Reference
Creativity is needed in finding ways to benefit from surprises	Sarasvathy, 2003, 2008
Surprises can be used as building blocks Resources may be re-bundled in order to better respond to changes in environments	Sarasvathy, 2008 Sarasvathy, 2008

Next, we will consider aspects that emerged from focus group discussions on the effectuation dimensions.

Means: Reflecting a Strong Sense of Identity

Means are limited and specialized abilities that are fit for exchange with others. The comments that characterized abilities considered the awareness of one's own and others' capabilities, open conversations, and interaction between interested parties. Expertise development and other learning-related processes are slow, and quality formation requires time. The skills of individual employees will increase and develop while they work and obtain more experience. Long-term employee relations and deep expertise may be especially beneficial when employees are aware of how to use their knowledge and experience for the benefit of others. Table 29.2 explains how the first-order codes were categorized into subcategories, and representative quotes are presented related to the effectual means.

Table 29.2: Means characteristics in focus group discussions of the case organization.

Aggregate Theoretical Dimension	Sub-Category	Representative quotes
MEANS		
	Abilities	"Ability to simplify and concentrate on the essential. Ability to keep the message short. Pick up the right things in the right scale and scope." (Management 1) "I have been able to use my capabilities according to my interests and learn as well as being able to use new systems." (Prmm14)"Everyone has their own capabilities but also general interest in each other's work; everyone brings their own vision, participates in conversations and helps solving problems." (Management 1) "Employees are encouraged to develop versatile capabilities." (Middle managers)
	Personality characteristics	"Using one's personality as means to make difficult topics interesting and easily understandable by others. Making them humane." (Prdm12)
	Experience	Strong expertise in one's own field, and ability to listen and understand others. (Management 1, interpretation by the authors)

Table 29.2 (continued)

Aggregate Theoretical Dimension	Sub-Category	Representative quotes
		"Professional capabilities are up to you, they are never up to your employer. If you don't like to develop yourself, try to be selfish – all the capabilities will follow you. They never follow your employer." (Pref18)"Long employee relations are beneficial when they know how to use their knowledge and experience for the benefit of others." (Middle Managers)
	Learning	"That's how you should think about it. Everything is experience and everything teaches you." (Pref12) "You have to acknowledge that you don't know. I have been thinking that human life is like a curve where in the beginning there are asking states. Now I have allowed myself to realize that I have again moved to this kind of asking state. I ask a lot of things, strange things, and it has been truly interesting. Really! People like to tell." (Pref18)

The *means* category was divided into personality characteristics, abilities, experience, and learning according to the empirical data. All of these are individual characteristics, and one's attitude among other control-related characteristics may affect all of them.

Affordable loss: Adopting New Opportunities through Shaping

Creating something new in service-oriented organizations might cause losses, changes, and an exit from old routines, services, and customer relationships. Organizations must therefore calculate how much they can afford to lose in innovative cocreation. The principle of affordable loss in effectuation aims to choose options that create more opportunities in the future by preferring long-term opportunities to short-term profits (Sarasvathy, 2001, 2008). The affordable loss principle is based on more than evaluating how much an organization can afford to lose in entrepreneurial processes. It also aims to develop service-oriented organizations and to recognize and eliminate behavior that restricts doing work efficiently. Finding new ways to bring one's own ideas into existence requires cooperation, changing plans, interaction, transformation, and creativity. Staff actions and motivation help control risks at service-oriented organizations, thus helping management recognize affordable losses (Read et al., 2011). Table 29.3 shows how the first-order codes were broken down into subcategories. In addition, representative quotes related to affordable loss are presented.

Table 29.3: Characteristics of affordable loss in focus group discussions of the case organization.

Aggregate Theoretical Dimension	Sub-category	Representative quotes
AFFORDABLE LOSS		
	Choosing	"What to hold onto and what to get rid of? How to decide what to offer the customers?" (Management 1) "The firm is starting to get rid of that "for war veterans only" stamp . . ." (Prmm12) "Now we also have a polyclinic, laboratory, and spa. Many think that it is not even possible." (Prmm12)
	Combining	"Awareness of the skills and competencies of oneself and others so that it is possible to combine them in order to improve the product, service, or the customer experience." (Management 2)
	Awareness	"Awareness of the whole so that you do not stick in the wrong things." (Prdm15) "Maybe the most essential place to be is not participating in the highest possible meeting in the hierarchy level, sometimes you have to prioritize by looking at things from the holistic perspective." (Prdm14) "To understand how strategy affects one's own job." (Management 1) "Strategy aims toward informing the focus on the essential, not on the superficial matters. To have the big picture in shape." (Prdm11)

Partnerships: The future Emerges in Cocreation

Interactions between customers, employees, and other stakeholders may create a process of discussion, sharing, and understanding of what services and products mean to others (Read et al., 2011; Read & Sarasvathy, 2005). By re-bundling resources in negotiations, cooperation means putting available but unused resources into use (Bradley et al., 2011). This increases the value for customers, organizations, and other stakeholders. However, the process requires awareness of the capabilities of others as well as discussion. This outcome in the effectuation literature is called the patchwork quilt (Sarasvathy, 2008). In the context of an organization, this means working with others, noticing their strengths, virtues, and tastes. Cooperation with others using available means allows individual capabilities to affect and develop the cocreational process of employees, business partners, and customers (Ordanini & Parasuraman, 2010). Table 29.4 presents the first-order codes by partnerships and their subcategories.

What we found from the discussions, presented in the form of quotes, is that partnerships in organizations consist of management, collective efforts, outcome creation, reflective development, and opportunities to fail and to try again. Partnerships are

Table 29.4: Partnerships in focus group discussions of the case organization.

Aggregate Theoretical Dimension	Sub-category	Representative quotes
PARTNERSHIPS		
	Management	"There is a bunch of professional people around me which makes it so much easier to understand the whole. You don't have to ask for an opinion, everyone will give it." (Prdm13) "This feels like a really mature way to function. It requires responsibility, knowledge sharing, and follow-through." (Management 1) "I'm spreading out the responsibility further, so that the middle managers are aware of their business responsibilities to do actions that increase revenue or decrease the costs." (Prdm14)
	Collective effort	"We have a really good 'esprit de corps,' cooperative vision, and follow-through here. And we also support each other." (Prdm11) "We collectively plan with marketing and sales how to schedule the bigger events." (Prmm11) "Holistic success is important, because it is not enough if one unit succeeds really well." (Prdm24)
	Reflective development	"The cooperation with different stakeholders has led into an understanding of well-being tourism in Finland." (Prdm14) "Customers want sometimes specified menus and we usually try to offer them. Of course, you have to look after the ingredient purchases, so that unnecessary products do not pile up." (Prmm16)"It gives a positive lift to employees, really, when after some big events or big groups they get feedback that it went really well." (Prmm15)
	Interaction	"How can we know about customer expectations if we do not interact with them?" (Prdm22) "We are at the tables where changes are planned and we try to have an influence. We don't always succeed in the best way possible but at least we are aware of what happens." (Prdm14) "Awareness of the industries and awareness of others." (Management 2) "She can make the matters more down-to-earth, more human, and they do not feel so dry . . ." (Prdm12)

built through interactions, and altruism helps in finding outcomes that are not necessarily dependent on the opinion of key managers but that emerge in open discussion.

Leveraging Contingencies: Creating new Opportunities from Contingencies

Uncertainty can be perceived as both a resource and as a process. It is continuous, leaves traces, and demands a reaction from service-oriented organizations. Leveraging unexpected contingencies requires creativity in finding ways to benefit from the current and future surprises in the markets (Sarasvathy, 2003, 2008). Both positive and negative surprises can be used as inputs when creating something new. The unexpected future and the contingencies it contains create resources and opportunities for resource combinations that may be valuable in making new business opportunities (Sarasvathy, 2008). Table 29.5 presents the first-order codes and subcategories of leveraging contingencies.

Table 29.5: Characteristics of leveraging contingencies in focus group discussions of the case organization.

Aggregate Theoretical Dimension	Sub-category	Representative quotes
LEVERAGING CONTINGENCIES		
	Flexibility	"Versatile services bring along the needs for flexibility, and there are a lot more surprises during the work day." (Prmm12) "All the employees are not so flexible for this because they have never had to be. It is enough that they do their jobs as they are used to and when a customer group challenges him or her, well . . ." (Prmm15) [Referring to the internal change process] "From a rehabilitation center into a spa center with laboratories, multiple professional and well-being services." (Middle managers)
	Proactive Change	"The webstore was opened at a great time as the Ukrainian crisis and disturbances in Russia disabled all the travel agencies." (Prdm13) "Integrating the expertise of the crowd from different sectors and units." (Employees) "You just have to stay with the change and preferably create models." (Prdm14)
	Unpredictability	"The behavior of the funding agencies in the social and health industry has changed. It has not been possible to count on them." (Prdm14) "This is a strange time and economists can't predict what's going to happen. That is why it's important that we have all networked in our own special areas." (Prdm13)

Table 29.5 (continued)

Aggregate Theoretical Dimension	Sub-category	Representative quotes
	Surprise	"We have been able to bring something extra to the customers because they still have continued coming here despite the higher prices." (Prdm13) "To surprise the customers by greeting and serving them well." (Prdm23) "Offering coffee to the customer who has been waiting too long." (Management 1)

As shown in the quotes, principles of effectuation were found in focus group discussion interactions in a slightly different form than they appear in the original Sarasvathy (2001, 2003, 2008) papers explaining effectuation as found among expert entrepreneurs. In sum, we can describe employee effectuation with the following characteristics:

- Means-principle in employees is explained by abilities, personality characteristics, experience, and learning
- Affordable loss in employees can be characterized by choosing, combining, and awareness
- Partnerships appear as management, collective effort, reflective development, and interaction
- Leveraging contingencies is described through flexibility, proactive change, unpredictability, and surprise.

Control Principle Among Effectual Employees

The overarching principle in effectuation is control, whether it is control for resources in hand or control over performance (e.g., Sarasvathy 2001, 2008). The empirical findings of this study suggest that there were three overarching themes in the empirical data, which further explain the control principle of effectuation. The three themes are (1) entrepreneurial culture creation, (2) enablers or facilitators in the organization, and (3) employee attitudes. We propose that these all need to be considered on several organizational levels to encourage effectuation and its characteristics in the context of an organization.

Entrepreneurial Culture Creation

An organizational culture that supports the developmental activities of employees is one sign of reciprocity (Armstrong-Stassen & Schlosser, 2008). The decision to act is internal and depends on how the actor perceives the situation (Joas, 2005). Thus, although the actor might perceive the situation differently depending on earlier personal experiences, organizational culture can provoke trust and encourage action. An enabling factor may also be fluency in information flow. In our empirical data, one of the informants suggested listening to both employees and managers and picking up the best and the most functional practices. Employees need to feel that they have the freedom to share their ideas and that their active initiatives are encouraged, supported, and rewarded in effectuation-based organizations (Atienza, 2015).

Johansson and McKelvie (2012) found that individual decision-making style is affected by organizational context. The organizational context may be restrictive, and it has been suggested that individuals might feel that their action is constrained by an "iron cage" (e.g., DiMaggio & Powell, 1983) of institutionalized practices in an organization. As Lusch and Vargo (2014, 6) explain, "Humans create organizations and structures that in turn influence and control them." Rising against these practices, as an employee, may look and feel like a rebellious act against the employer, causing uncertainty.

Enabler(s) of Facilitator(s) in the Organization

Tolerating unpredictability and uncertain circumstances enables entrepreneurial behavior (Duening et al., 2012). Sharing and discussing difficult experiences with others may help to solve work-related issues. For example, according to the employee discussion, cooperation between departments would lead to a better understanding of the customer as well as better abilities to serve the customer.

Based on the findings of this study, the starting point in effectual culture creation is not just idea generation but also organizational support. As we brought up earlier, Sarasvathy (2008) mentioned that effectuation requires agency, which is a prime driver for opportunity creation. Employees feel they have ideas about how to improve services, but at the same time they feel helpless. They do not recognize what the next step would be in putting ideas into action. It seems that there is a lack of enablers, facilitators, or other entrepreneurial decision-makers, and perhaps because of the underlying organizational culture, individuals are not yet sure how to be active and how to independently take the initiative. Using a multilevel reconceptualization of the dynamics of effectuation designed by Kerr and Coviello (2020), it could be assumed that the employees are in a loop between level 1 (individual dynamics) and level 2 (dyadic relationship dynamics), waiting for one or several collaborators on board to iterate the idea to achieve level 3 (entrepreneurial network dynamics). These enablers can be middle managers or other organizational members who know how to create strong ties between specialists and help individual dynamics evolve further into dyadic relationship dynamics.

Employee Attitude

Not only management but also employee attitude positively and negatively influences effectual culture creation. Perspectives by new employees can increase entrepreneurial behavior in a service-oriented organization. Perceived control over one's own choices also has an impact on it. According to the first management discussion, service-oriented businesses need to prioritize tasks. Control can also be at least partially conditional according to the middle managers, when the supervisor enables, directs, and delegates responsibilities and power. According to the findings of the study, work development should belong to everyone: not only to those planning how the work is done but also to the employees who perform their duties. Intrinsic motivation and high domain expertise entail possibilities for creativity (Amabile, 2012). The employees saw that spontaneity also leads to insights, where one's own intuition and creativity may blossom. It also requires the freedom to make one's own decisions. Autonomy is therefore one of the signs of effectual culture creation.

Not only individual skills, but also one's own attitude affects the development opportunities offered by an employer; it may also have an effect on how customers are actually served and how they feel about the service provided by employees. The responsibilities of one's own job may also reflect employee attitudes, as well as how employees perceive the possibilities around them, as seen in the following discussion:

> a lot could be given if there were some possibilities. Somehow it feels that there are quite strict limitations on what you can do within a product, but somehow it just feels like a train. (Pref13)
>
> It feels that the possibilities to impact narrow all the time as the years go past. (Pref13)
>
> Nowadays the funding agencies (payers) determine what the products contain. They clearly determine what there can be and that probably really affects your work. (Pref12)
>
> You might have really good ideas, but if you tell them to your supervisor, they may say that yes, it is a good idea, but nothing happens. That is quite frustrating. (Pref17)
>
> You can develop your job under the big themes but you cannot be too innovative because nobody pays for it. (Prmm17)

Table 29.6 shows factors that hinder development and employee possibilities for effectual behavior.

Table 29.7 illustrates through quotes how different factors were perceived to encourage development and add motivation toward entrepreneurial enactment, learning, and creativity.

Table 29.6: Development hindering factors.

Hindering factors	Representative Quotes
Blocks in the information flow	"There should be enough information available in order to independently develop one's job." (Survey)
	"We always go through the negative feedback but the positive may go unnoticed." (Prmm11)
Own attitude	"I think we perceive each other's job descriptions as narrower than what they really are." (Prmm17)
	"One needs to be pro-active and willing to be aware of the products and services, so that you can sell something extra and tell the customer how he or she could spend his or her free time." (Prmm12)
Paying attention to well-being	"In customer service, employee well-being should be followed." (Prmm13)
	"One precondition for managing one's own work is positive feedback" (Prmm12)
	"Many are on sick leave, because of foot, shoulder or back problems. Perhaps it could be better if our well-being was more central than the numbers." (Pref17)
	"And we could perhaps have more strength to keep smiling if we did not feel so much pressure." (Pref17)
	"The numbers could also be improved by well-being." (Pref12)
Unawareness of each other's jobs	"If there is a change in eating hours, at a minimum, we have all processes mixed up!" (Prmm11)
Solitude	"Then, there is not that much support, the group is not standing behind you, there is no alliance, and it is challenging to assimilate oneself with a certain professional group. It is quite negative to notice that it would be really nice to develop and share things with someone . . ." (Pref13)

Table 29.7: Development-enabling factors.

Enabling factors	Representative Quotes
Own attitude	"When someone is especially good at holistic thinking, it is an advantage because they may perceive things differently and communicate it so that it is understandable also by others. Perhaps closer to as it really is." (Prdm14)
	"Everyone can take as much responsibility in their own roles as they dare." (Prdm13)

Table 29.7 (continued)

Enabling factors	Representative Quotes
	"Self-directedness and self-active role in bringing matters forward so that they can be processed. Own active employee role. That is the point that gives added value; taking new ideas forward, fostering them and picking up the best, not just the basic formal tasks." (Prdm15)
Control over one's own choices	"When you understand why things are done like this, why we want to go there, and when you see that you can do it, you just go forward." (Prdm12)
	"It is important to be able to influence the various decisions and one needs versatile networks among the management group." (Prdm14)
Freedom	"Freedom to use one's own thinking, so there's not someone all the time telling us how to do things." (Prmm11)
	"Freedom to do as we please, a possibility to succeed through our own choices." (Prmm16)
Networking	"We are all cooperating in our own networks with different stakeholders and background organizations. We bring that knowledge to the management meetings." (Prdm13)
	"We are at the tables where it is planned. We do not always succeed as we would like but at least we know what changes are coming." (Prdm14)
Awareness of each other's jobs	"It is really good that we get to know each other's jobs; you can always decide whether to value or evaluate . . . at least to get some actual knowledge before evaluating." (Prmm12)
	"I still think that although I have been here for a long time, a lot of individuals working here have something to give me. I would not have to go far to learn something valuable." (Pref16)

Discussion

In the studied organization, the realities of managers and employees differ. Management viewed themselves as entrepreneurial and collaborative, and they were puzzled why employees did not promote more entrepreneurial behavior in their daily work. In line with the findings of Kerr and Coviello (2020), the organization and its members seemed to be stuck between individual (level 1) and dyadic relationship dynamics (level 2). This loop could be broken by a facilitator or enabler or by changing practices to include more interactional mechanisms.

Focus group discussions demonstrated that creative resources and autonomy, together with the support of leadership and control, are needed to have an effectual culture. In addition, reward systems reinforce desired behavior (Yost & Plunkett, 2010). In a theoretical framework, we introduced conditions that may enable entrepreneurial behavior and act as starting points for effectual culture creation: reciprocity (Armstrong-Stassen & Schlosser, 2008), creativity (Amabile, 2012), intrapreneurship (Atienza, 2015), and how management tolerates unpredictability (Duening et al., 2012) and failures by employees (ul Haq et al., 2018).

This study set out to answer two research questions: "What kinds of opportunities for employee effectuation are there in service design and development-related discussions of employees?" and "What kinds of opportunities are there for entrepreneurial culture creation through employee effectuation in a service-oriented organization?"

Drawing from the observation made by Courpasson et al. (2014) that entrepreneurial behavior, such as corporate entrepreneurship, has mainly been researched as a managerial effort, in this study on effectuation, the focus on employees revealed behavioral microlevel structures. The study responds to the call by Nair et al. (2013) to consider the microlevel core competence strategies influencing business models. In line with Nair et al. (2013), one way to encourage effectual actions in organizations would be to benefit from creative outputs as a form of cocreative customer service improvement. This study also addresses the question posed in Read and Sarasvathy (2012, p. 227): "Under what circumstances can cocreation shape competitive advantage?" We suggest that the circumstances should support creativity and entrepreneurial behavior that seeks to improve organizational circumstances or develop products and services cocreatively either with customers or with other employees based on customer feedback.

We need to find more ways to promote and encourage employee ideas that challenge the persistent beliefs of dysfunctional structures to make those actions easier to notice and be leveraged. This is especially valuable for management because leveraging this kind of behavior may require a change in managerial perceptions. This study echoes the statement by Courpasson et al. (2014) that although management may first view free interaction among the employees as rebellious and chaotic, it may also lead to revival and renewal outcomes, which can be fostered by giving more space for free interaction between organizational members.

Sarasvathy et al. (2008, p. 336) have asked "How can we understand the micro-foundations, i.e., the decisions and actions at the entrepreneurial level that drive the processes of organizational design?" Similarly, Venkataraman and Sarasvathy (2000, p. 4) stated, "Strategy essentially focuses on existing firms and the activities of existing firms. Entrepreneurship, on the other hand, has been focusing attention on the creative process, particularly that of new firms. Where they overlap is at the nexus of the creative process of existing firms." In line with these ideas, we found the following outcomes of this study. In understanding the creative process of existing firms and the decisions and actions that are used in building it, researchers need to study the interaction between the organizational members and understand their realities in their unique organizational context through a range of qualitative methods. This interaction may contain multiple types of communication, including tension, contradiction, and paradoxes between the parties, as suggested by Langley et al. (2013, p. 9) in their change process studies. Langley et al. (2013, p. 10) believe that an individual level of analysis could illuminate management and organizational concerns, which is what this study aims to accomplish.

As noted at the beginning of this chapter, human action has a central role in effectuation (Sarasvathy, 2008). The goals may change (Sarasvathy 2003; Welter et al., 2016), and commitment is re-evaluated during the process of change. This chapter has set out to identify the opportunities for effectuation in an organization as an interactional development of outcomes. In the future, it might be interesting to study partnerships in effectuation and their formation more closely in an organization. This might increase the understanding of social mechanisms and relationships between stakeholders and their commitment to new outcomes.

Effectuation might be of use for management when they are willing to encourage entrepreneurial behavior in the organization. When the organization is the context, employees might need assistance and encouragement to become active agents and realize their means, partnerships, affordable loss, unpredictability, and control. Means need to be identified for them to be beneficial to the employee. Sometimes it only requires someone to pay attention to another's strengths and to offer them positive feedback. Encouraging self-development and self-reflection helps individuals become more aware of their daily work.

Partnerships need space to evolve informally and formally. The formation and comparison of different professional perspectives and dealing with possible contradictions could help in solving problems. Affordable loss becomes visible when employees dare to say what doesn't work and how processes or services could be improved. When employees are aware of their own work but also that of others, they are more prone to make more informed choices when prioritizing tasks. Unpredictability, changes, challenges, and opportunities to discuss them are the first signals of creating an effectual culture together. When different professionals from various fields look at the same challenge from different angles, it becomes less unpredictable. Planning strategies to overcome these challenges is a way to control the unpredictable future and its contingencies.

Conclusion and Limitations of the Study

In addition to its functionality in explaining the behavior of expert entrepreneurs, effectuation logics help us to understand emergent entrepreneurial behavior among the organizational members who can be considered experts in their own field. The results of this study suggest that the entrepreneurial attitude of management is not enough to foster and support creative and innovative service-related behaviors among task-performing employees. A more concrete acknowledgment of the skills and capabilities of the employees is needed to benefit from entrepreneurial and service-related behaviors at the organizational level.

Langley et al. (2013, p. 4) suggest that although we have many types of process research studies, they are usually based on controlled lab experiments or large quantitative samples. The focus group discussions conducted in this study were a functional technique for capturing a community view and the methods of interaction within the different groups and levels of the organization. The in-depth nature of the discussions enabled tentative suggestions to increase the understanding of effectuation possibilities between the different hierarchical levels and groups in the organization. Understanding organizations and their mechanisms can produce future research on effectual social mechanisms and interactions.

Our study reveals that when studying effectuation in the organization, several hierarchical, interactional and power-based factors need to be considered relative to expert entrepreneur-type effectuation. We suggest that the positive attitude of management is not enough to foster and support entrepreneurial and service-related behaviors. Direct acknowledgment of the skills and capabilities of the employees is needed for the organization to benefit from entrepreneurial and service-related cocreational behaviors in the organization.

Managerially, employee effectuation creates many opportunities for flourishing organizations. Employee effectuation benefits from an organizational culture in which autonomy and creativity are appreciated and in which full individual potential can be used. Typically, effectuation is useful in sales and marketing professions in which decisions need to be made immediately and directly with customers. Sales performance can thus be increased by having entrepreneurial employees and by nurturing effectual culture in an organization. Agility in decision-making can increase performance in service sales and decrease some of the costs that arise from communicational, organizational, and individual errors. Entrepreneurship, in the forms of thinking, new idea generation, and agile decision-making, enables an organizational culture in which employee effectuation can flourish. This requires resource access and the capabilities to combine resources in new ways. Individually, employee effectuation is captive to organizational culture, management, and profession. However, enabling a working culture that is friendly to entrepreneurial behavior leads to employee effectuation and decision-making tailored for customer problem solving. In an organization, the talent, skills, knowledge, and knowhow of each employee influence how effectuation takes place and how the possibilities of organizational renewal occur.

Educationally, employee effectuation is born and cultivated over the long term, meaning entrepreneurship education should take place throughout the school system and through the interaction of theory and practice. Experience-based projects, work experience, summer jobs, traineeships, and career development offer opportunities for the birth of employee effectuation processes. Entrepreneurial learning can reflect effectual culture creation. Enabling creativity, innovativeness, and the proactive behavior of employees leads to understanding what opportunities effectuation can bring. In addition to encouraging entrepreneurial behavior, employees and employers together set the limits and the organizational rules for the opportunities for the continuous development of professions. Entrepreneurial behavior and effectuation are not appropriate for every task. Controlled routines and repeated working tasks are also needed in the workplace. Additionally, the performance stemming from customers and from effectuation influences how the organization and work will be developed as well as how it will change.

A limitation of the study is that the results cannot be generalized. They reflect an understanding of a single organization and its members. In addition, the data collected reflect the past five years of the organization and its development but not the post-COVID-19 era and future strategies. Group dynamics (Hennink, 2007) typical of focus group limitations also need to be considered. There is a likelihood that some of the employees and the managers might answer based on group dynamics. The moderator was aware of this and accounted for it by discussing it with different personnel.

This paper examined the possibilities of employee effectuation from the interaction and discussions of employees. In the future, employee effectuation could also be studied by understanding resource accumulation and the resource access employees need when consciously creating an effectual culture in the workplace. Many of the earlier studies have shown that entrepreneurs use both effectuation and causation styles in daily decision-making. A greater understanding of the relationships between employee effectuation and causation would increase our understanding of how employees benefit from different decision-making styles in different tasks in the service industry. In relation to causation and effectuation, it would be interesting to study the decision-making styles and reasoning used by employees who do not want to or who cannot apply effectuation in their work. As effectuation is dependent on the employer up to a point, cross–cultural studies can also increase the value of understanding the cultural differences of entrepreneurial behavior across continents.

Acknowledgements: We want to thank professors Tarja Niemelä and Tanja Leppäaho from the University of Jyväskylä for their comments and assistance during the writing process of this article. This article has been discussed in the third effectuation conference in Enschede, The Netherlands 8th –9th December 2014 under the label: "An Effectual organization, a possibilism or an idealism?" and in Taloustutkijoiden XXXII kesäseminaari, Jyväskylä, Finland 10th –11th June 2015 and in the doctoral conference the Academy of Management Conference, Vancouver, Canada 7th –11th August2015 under the label "Organizational effectuation – effectuation among employees." We also want to thank professor Helle Neergaard from the University of Aarhus with tutoring this manuscript in the ECSB PDWW Postdoctoral Writing Workshop in RENT XXIX Conference under the name "Effectuation in employees." Funding for working with this paper has been enabled by the University of Jyväskylä, Peurunka, Foundation of Economic Education (No: 8-4096), Foundation for Private Entrepreneurs.

References

Amabile, T.E. (2012). Componential theory of creativity. Working paper. In E.H. Kessler (Ed.), *Encyclopedia of management theory*. Sage Publications. http://www.hbs.edu/faculty/Publication%20Files/12-096.pdf

Antoncic, J.A., & Antoncic, B. (2011). Employee satisfaction, intrapreneurship and firm growth: A model. *Industrial Management & Data Systems, 111*(4), 589–607. https://doi.org/10.1108/02635571111133560

Armstrong-Stassen, M., & Schlosser, F. (2008). Benefits of a supportive development climate for older workers. *Journal of Managerial Psychology, 23*(4), 419–437.https://doi.org/10.1108/02683940810869033

Atienza, C. M.R. (2015). Organizational culture as a key enabler of intrapreneurship: A critical review of literature. *Journal of Asia Entrepreneurship and Sustainability, 11*(3), 85–128. https://www.proquest.com/scholarly-journals/organizational-culture-as-key-enabler/docview/1773198490/se-2?accountid=11774

Bradley, S.W., Wiklund, J., & Shepherd, D.A. (2011). Swinging a double-edged sword: The effect of slack on entrepreneurial management and growth. *Journal of Business Venturing, 26*(5), 537–554. https://doi.org/10.1016/j.jbusvent.2010.03.002

Brettel, M., Engelen, A., & Küpper, D. (2012). Corporate effectuation: Entrepreneurial action and its impact on R&D project performance. *Journal of Business Venturing, 27*(2), 167–184. https://doi.org/10.1016/j.jbusvent.2011.01.001

Courpasson, D., Dany, F., & Martí, I. (2014). Organizational entrepreneurship as active resistance: A struggle against outsourcing. *Entrepreneurship Theory and Practice, 40*(1), 131–160. https://doi.org/10.1111/etap.12109

Crevani, L., Palm, K., & Schilling, A. (2011). Innovation management in service firms: A research agenda. *Service Business, 5*(2), 177–193. https://doi.org/10.1007/s11628-011-0109-7

Deligianni, I., Voudouris, I., & Lioukas, S. (2016). Do effectuation processes shape the relationship between product diversification and performance in new ventures? *Entrepreneurship Theory and Practice, 41*(3), 349–377. https://doi.org/10.1111/etap.12210

DiMaggio, P. J., & Powell, W. W. (1983). The Iron Cage Revisited: Institutional Isomorphism and Collective Rationality in Organizational Fields. *American Sociological Review, 48*(2), 147–160. https://doi.org/10.2307/2095101

Duening, T.N., Shepherd, M.M., & Czaplewski, A.J. (2012). How entrepreneurs think: Why effectuation and effectual logic may be the key to successful enterprise entrepreneurship. *International Journal of Innovation Science, 4*(4), 205–216. https://doi.org/10.1260/1757-2223.4.4.205

Eriksson, P., & Kovalainen, A. (2008). *Qualitative methods in business research*. Sage Publications Ltd.

Ettlie, J.E., & Rosenthal, S.R. (2011). Service versus manufacturing innovation. *Journal of Product Innovation Management, 28*(2), 285–299. https://doi.org/10.1111/j.1540-5885.2011.00797.x

Fotiadis, A., Polyzos, S., Huan, T.C. (2021). The good, the bad and the ugly on COVID-19 tourism recovery. *Annals of Tourism Research, 87*, 1–14. https://doi.org/10.1016/j.annals.2020.103117

Gioia, D.A., Corley, K.G., & Hamilton, A.L. (2012). Seeking qualitative rigor in inductive research: Notes on the Gioia methodology. *Organizational Research Methods, 16*(1), 15–31. https://doi.org/10.1177/1094428112452151

Goel, S., & Karri, R. (2006). Entrepreneurs, effectual logic, and over-trust. *Entrepreneurship Theory and Practice, 30*(4), 477–493.

Häkkinen, R.A. (2015). Effectuating person–organization fit – Effectuation in organizations. *Journal of Entrepreneurial and Organizational Diversity, 4*(2), 1–26. https://doi.org/10.5947/jeod.2015.009

Hennink, M.M. (2007). *International focus group research: A handbook for the health and social sciences*. Cambridge University Press.

Jiang, Y., & Rüling, C.-C. (2019). Opening the black box of effectuation processes: Characteristics and dominant types. *Entrepreneurship Theory and Practice, 43*(1), 171–202. https://doi.org/10.1177/1042258717744204

Joas, H. 2005. *The Creativity of Action*. Polity Press.

Johansson, A. & McKelvie, A. 2012. Unpacking the Antecedents of Effectuation and Causation in a Corporate Context, *Frontiers of Entrepreneurship Research*, 32(17) Article 1, 1–14. Available at: http://digitalknowledge.babson.edu/fer/vol32/iss17/1

Kerr, J., & Coviello, N. (2020). Weaving network theory into effectuation: A multi-level reconceptualization of effectual dynamics. *Journal of Business Venturing*, *35*(2), 1–20. https://doi.org/10.1016/j.jbusvent.2019.05.001

Langley, A., Smallman, C., Tsoukas, H., & Van de Ven, A.H. (2013). Process studies of change in organization and management: Unveiling temporality, activity, and flow. *Academy of Management Journal*, *56*(1), 1–13. https://doi.org/10.5465/amj.2013.4001

Litosseliti, L. (2003). *Using focus groups in research. Continuum research methods*. MPG Books Ltd.

Lusch, R.F. and Vargo, S.L. (2014) *Service-Dominant Logic: Premises, Perspectives, Possibilities*, Cambridge University Press, CPI Group Ltd, UK.

Nair, S., Paulose, H., Palacios, M., & Tafur, J. (2013). Service orientation: Effectuating business model innovation. *The Service Industries Journal*, *33*(9–10), 958–975. https://doi.org/10.1080/02642069.2013.746670

Neessen, P.C.M., Caniëls, M.C.J., Vos, B., & de Jong, J.P. (2019). The intrapreneurial employee: Toward an integrated model of intrapreneurship and research agenda. *International Entrepreneurship and Management Journal*, *15*(2), 545–571. https://doi.org/10.1007/s11365-018-0552-1

Nguyen, N.M., Killen, C.P., Kock, A., & Gemünden, H.G. (2018). The use of effectuation in projects: The influence of business case control, portfolio monitoring intensity and project innovativeness. *International Journal of Project Management*, *36*(8), 1054–1067. https://doi.org/10.1016/j.ijproman.2018.08.005

Ordanini, A., & Parasuraman, A. (2010). Service innovation viewed through a service-dominant logic lens: A conceptual framework and empirical analysis. *Journal of Service Research*, *14*(1), 3–23. https://doi.org/10.1177/1094670510385332

Patzelt, H., Williams, T.A., & Shepherd, D.A. (2014). Overcoming the walls that constrain us: The role of entrepreneurship education programs in prison. *Academy of Management Learning & Education*, *13*(4), 587–620. https://doi.org/10.5465/amle.2013.0094

Perry, J.T., Chandler, G.N., & Markova, G. (2011). Entrepreneurial effectuation: A review and suggestions for future research. *Entrepreneurship Theory and Practice*, *36*(4), 837–861. https://doi.org/10.1111/j.1540-6520.2010.00435.x

Read, S., & Sarasvathy, S.D. (2005). Knowing what to do and doing what you know: Effectuation as a form of entrepreneurial expertise. *The Journal of Private Equity*, *9*(1), 45–62. https://doi.org/10.3905/jpe.2005.605370

Read, S., & Sarasvathy, S.D. (2012). Co-creating a course ahead from the intersection of service–dominant logic and effectuation. *Marketing Theory*, *12*(2), 225–229. https://doi.org/10.1177/1470593112444381

Read, S., Sarasvathy, S.D., Dew, N., Wiltbank, R., & Ohlsson, A-V. (2011). *Effectual entrepreneurship*. Routledge.

Read, S., Song, M., & Smit, W. (2009). A meta-analytic review of effectuation and venture performance. *Journal of Business Venturing*, *24*(6), 573–587. https://doi.org/10.1016/j.jbusvent.2008.02.005

Reymen, I.M.M.J., Andries, P., Berends, H., Mauer, R., Stephan, U., & van Burg, E. (2015). Understanding dynamics of strategic decision making in venture creation: A process study of effectuation and causation. *Strategic Entrepreneurship Journal*, *9*(4), 351–379. https://doi.org/10.1002/sej.1201

Roach, D.C., Ryman, J.A., & Makani, J. (2016). Effectuation, innovation and performance in SMEs: an empirical study. *European Journal of Innovation Management*, *19*(2), 214–238. https://doi.org/10.1108/EJIM-12-2014-0119

Sarasvathy, S.D. (2001). Causation and effectuation: Toward a theoretical shift from economic inevitability to entrepreneurial contingency. *Academy of Management Review, 26*(2) 243–263. https://doi.org/10.5465/amr.2001.4378020

Sarasvathy, S. (2003). Entrepreneurship as a science of the artificial. *Journal of Economic Psychology, 24*(2), 203–220. https://doi.org/10.1016/S0167-4870(02)00203-9

Sarasvathy, S.D. (2008). *Effectuation: Elements of entrepreneurial expertise. New horizons of entrepreneurship.* Edward Elgar Publishing.

Sarasvathy, S., & Dew, N. (2008). Effectuation and over-trust: Debating Goel and Karri. *Entrepreneurship Theory and Practice, 32*(4), 727–737.

Sarasvathy, S.D., Dew, N., Read, S., & Wiltbank, R. (2008). Designing organizations that design environments: Lessons from entrepreneurial expertise. *Organization Studies, 29*(3), 331–350. https://doi.org/10.1177/0170840607088017

Sarasvathy, S.D., Kumar, K., York, J.G., & Bhagavatula, S. (2014). An effectual approach to inter-national entrepreneurship: Overlaps, challenges, and provocative possibilities. *Entrepre-neurship Theory and Practice, 38*(1), 71–93. https://doi.org/10.1111/etap.12088

Sigala, M. (2020). Tourism and COVID-19: Impacts and implications for advancing and resetting industry and research. *Journal of Business Research, 117*, 312–321. https://doi.org/10.1016/j.jbusres.2020.06.015

Shepherd, D.A., & Williams, T.A. (2014). Local venturing as compassion organizing in the aftermath of a natural disaster: The role of localness and community in reducing suffering. *Journal of Management Studies, 51*(6), 952–994. https://doi.org/10.1111/joms.12084

Smolka, K.M., Verheul, I., Burmeister-Lamp, K., & Heugens, P.M.A.R. (2018). Get it together! Synergistic effects of causal and effectual decision-making logics on venture performance. *Entrepreneurship Theory and Practice, 42*(4), 571–604. https://doi.org/10.1177/1042258718783429

Stemler, S.E. (2015). Content Analysis. In R. Scott & S. Kosslyn (Eds.), *Emerging Trends in the Social and Behavioral Sciences.* John Wiley & Sons.

ul Haq, M.A., Jingdong, Y., Usman, M., & Khalid, S. (2018). Factors affecting entrepreneurial behavior among employees in organizations: Mediating role of affective commitment. *Journal of Enterprising Culture, 26*(4), 349–378. https://doi.org/10.1142/S0218495818500139

Venkataraman, S., & Sarasvathy, S. (2000). *Strategy and entrepreneurship: Outlines of an untold story.* Darden Graduate School of Business Administration University of Virginia. Working Paper No. 01–06.

Welter, C., Mauer, R., & Wuebker, R. (2016). Bridging behavioral models and theoretical concepts: Effectuation and bricolage in the opportunity creation framework. *Strategic Entrepreneurship Journal, 10*(1), 5–20. https://doi.org/10.1002/sej.1215

Yost, P.R., & Plunkett, M.M. (2010). Ten catalysts to spark on-the-job development in your organization (Commentary). *Industrial and Organizational Psychology - Perspectives on Science and Practice, 3*(1), 20–23. https://doi.org/10.1111/j.1754-9434.2009.01190.x

List of Figures

https://doi.org/10.1515/9783110747652-031

List of Tables

https://doi.org/10.1515/9783110747652-032

Index

https://doi.org/10.1515/9783110747652-033

www.ingramcontent.com/pod-product-compliance
Lightning Source LLC
Chambersburg PA
CBHW081209220326
41598CB00037B/6724